## About the Author

Born in Germany, Edgar Rothermich studied music prestigious Tonmeister program at the Berlin Instit University of Arts (UdK) in Berlin where he graduated in 1989 with a Master's Degree. He worked as a composer and music producer in Berlin, and moved to Los Angeles in 1991 where he continued his work on numerous projects in the music and film industry ("The Celestine Prophecy", "Outer Limits", "Babylon 5", "What the Bleep Do We Know", "Fuel", "Big Money Rustlas").

For the past 20 years Edgar has had a successful musical partnership with electronic music pioneer and founding Tangerine Dream member Christopher Franke. Recently in addition to his collaboration with Christopher, Edgar has been working with other artists, as well as on his own projects.

In 2010 he started to release his solo records in the "Why Not ..." series with different styles and genres. The current releases are "Why Not Solo Piano", "Why Not Electronica", "Why Not Electronica Again", and "Why Not 90s Electronica". This previously unreleased album was produced in 1991/1992 by Christopher Franke. All albums are available on Amazon and iTunes, including the 2012 release, the re-recording of the Blade Runner Soundtrack.

In addition to composing music, Edgar Rothermich is writing technical manuals with a unique style, focusing on rich graphics and diagrams to explain concepts and functionality of software applications under his popular GEM series (Graphically Enhanced Manuals). His bestselling titles are available as printed books on Amazon, as Multi-Touch eBooks on the iBooks Store and as pdf downloads from his website.

(some manuals are also available in Deutsch, Español, 简体中文)

www.DingDingMusic.com                    GEM@DingDingMusic.com

## About the Editor

Many thanks to Tressa Janik for editing and proofreading this manual.

## Special Thanks

Special thanks to my beautiful wife, Li, for her love, support, and understanding during those long hours of working on the books. And not to forget my son, Winston. Waiting for him during soccer practice or Chinese class always gives me extra time to work on a few chapters.

The manual is based on Logic Pro X v10.2
Manual: Print Version 2015-0913
ISBN-13: 978-1503182752
ISBN-10: 1503182754

**About the GEM (Graphically Enhanced Manuals)**

### UNDERSTAND, not just LEARN

What are Graphically Enhanced Manuals? They're a new type of manual with a visual approach that helps you UNDERSTAND a program, not just LEARN it. No need to read through 500 pages of dry text explanations. Rich graphics and diagrams help you to get that "aha" effect and make it easy to comprehend difficult concepts. The Graphically Enhanced Manuals help you master a program much faster with a much deeper understanding of concepts, features, and workflows in a very intuitive way that is easy to understand.

All titles are available in three different formats:

........... pdf downloads from my website www.DingDingMusic.com/Manuals

............ multi-touch iBooks on Apple's iBooks Store

.... printed books on Amazon.com

(some manuals are also available in Deutsch, Español, 简体中文)

For a list of all the available titles and bundles: www.DingDingMusic.com/Manuals

To be notified about new releases and updates, subscribe to subscribe@DingDingMusic.com

**About the Formatting**

I use a specific color code in my books:

*Green colored text* indicates keyboard shortcuts or mouse actions. I use the following abbreviations: **sh** (shift key), **ctr** (control key), **opt** (option key), **cmd** (command key). A plus (+) between the keys means that you have to press all those keys at the same time.

*sh+opt+K* means: Hold the shift and the option key while pressing the K key.

*(light green text in parenthesis indicates the name of the Key Command)*

*Brown colored text* indicates Menu Commands with a greater sign (➤) indicating submenus.

*Edit ➤ Source Media ➤ All* means "Click on the Edit Menu, scroll down to Source Media, and select the submenu All.

Blue arrows indicate what happens if you click on an item or popup menu ●———➤

# Table of Contents

## The GEM Advantage

If you've never read any of my other books and you aren't familiar with my Graphically Enhanced Manuals (GEM) series, let me explain my approach. As I mentioned at the beginning, my motto is:

### "UNDERSTAND, not just LEARN"

Other manuals (original User Guide or third party books) often provide just a quick way to: "press here and then click there, then that will happen ... now click over there and something else will happen". This will go on for the next couple hundred pages and all you'll do is memorize lots of steps without understanding the reason for doing them in the first place. Even more problematic is that you are stuck when you try to perform a procedure and the promised outcome doesn't happen. You will have no understanding why it didn't happen and, most importantly, what to do in order to make it happen.

Don't get me wrong, I'll also explain all the necessary procedures, but beyond that, the understanding of the underlying concept so you'll know the reason why you have to click here or there. Teaching you "why" develops a much deeper understanding of the application that later enables you to react to "unexpected" situations based on your knowledge. In the end, you will master the application.

And how do I provide that understanding? The key element is the visual approach, presenting easy to understand diagrams that describe an underlying concept better than five pages of descriptions.

**The Visual Approach**

Here is a summary of the advantages of my Graphically Enhanced Manuals that set them apart from other books:

 **Better Learning**

 **Better Value**

### ☑ Graphics, Graphics, Graphics

Every feature and concept is explained with rich graphics and illustrations that are not found in any other book or User Guide. These are not just a few screenshots with arrows in it. I take the time to create unique diagrams to illustrate the concepts and workflows.

### ☑ Knowledge and Understanding

The purpose of my manuals is to provide the reader with the knowledge and understanding of an app that is much more valuable than just listing and explaining a set of features.

### ☑ Comprehensive

For any given feature, I list every available command so you can decide which one to use in your workflow. Some of the information is not even found in the app's User Guide.

### ☑ For Beginners and Advanced Users

The graphical approach makes my manuals easy to understand for beginners, but still, the wealth of information and details provide plenty of material, even for the most advanced user.

### ☑ Three formats

No other manual is available in all three formats: PDF (from my website), interactive multi-touch iBooks (on Apple's iBooks Store), and printed book (on Amazon).

### ☑ Interactive iBooks

No other manual is available in the enhanced iBook format. I include an extensive glossary, also with additional graphics. Every term throughout the content of the iBook is linked to the glossary term that lets you popup a window with the explanations without leaving the page you are currently reading. Every term lists all the entries in the book where it is used and links to other related terms.

### ☑ Up-to-date

No other manual stays up to date with the current version of the app. Due to the rapid update cycles of applications nowadays, most books by major publishers are already outdated by the time they are released. I constantly update my books to stay current with the latest version of an app.

### ☑ Free Updates (pdf, iBook only)

No other manual provides free updates, I do. Whenever I update a book, I email a free download link of the pdf file to current customers. iBooks customers will receive an automatic update notification and 24h after a new update, the printed book will be available on Amazon. They are print-on-demand books, which means, whenever you order a book on Amazon, you get the most recent version and not an outdated one sitting in a publisher's warehouse.

## Self-published

As a self-published author, I can release my books without any restrictions imposed by a publisher. Rich, full-color graphics and interactive books are usually too expensive to produce for such a limited audience. However, I have read mountains of manuals throughout the 35 years of my professional career as a musician, composer, sound engineer, and teacher, and I am developing these Graphically Enhanced Manuals (GEM) based on that experience, the way I think a manual should be written. This is, as you can imagine, very time consuming and requires a lot of dedication.

However, not having a big publisher also means not having a big advertising budget and the connections to get my books in the available channels of libraries, book stores, and schools. Instead, as a self-published author, I rely on reviews, blogs, referrals, and word of mouth to continue this series.

If you like my "Graphically Enhanced Manuals", you can help me promote these books by referring them to others and maybe taking a minute and write a review on Amazon or the iBooks Store.

Thanks, I appreciate it:

 http://amzn.to/1sP8jvl    http://bit.ly/1oJ7ftQ

**Disclaimer**: As a non-native English speaker, I try my best to write my manuals with proper grammar and spelling. However, not having a major publisher also means that I don't have a big staff of editors and proofreaders at my disposal. So, if something slips through and it really bothers you, email me at <GrammarPolice@DingDingMusic.com> and I will fix it in the next update. Thanks!

# Logic Pro X - the second book

This book "**Logic Pro X - The Details**" is the follow-up book to my first Logic book "**Logic Pro X - How it Works**", which was the first manual on the market after the new *Logic Pro X* was released in the summer of 2013. A year later, the long awaited follow-up book was ready. As a sneak preview, I pre-released the Automation chapter in October 2014 as a free pdf file and iBook. This chapter is now included in the final release of this book.

### For Advanced and soon-to-be Advanced alike

This book dives into the more advanced topics of Logic Pro X, and for the first time it enables the intermediate and even the beginner to learn those powerful and amazing features with the easy to understand graphics and diagrams. This is where my graphically enhanced style has the advantage over traditional text-only based books. I even provide the necessary background information to explain those more challenging features in Logic.

Get ready for that "aha, now I get it" effect with features you were always struggling with or were afraid to use in the first place.

### Pick your Pace

While the first book was structured so it introduced the new Logic Pro X step-by-step through the chapters, this book can be studied in random order depending on the readers interest and curiosity about the various topics. I refer to specific chapters if necessary for the understanding of some of the features.

### Printed Version: Part 1+2

Due to the size limitation for print-on-demand books on Amazon, I had to split the printed book version into two parts: Chapter 1-11 and Chapter 12-20.

Preferences ➤ Advanced

enable

### Advanced Preferences

Logic has an Advanced Pane in its Preferences Window that lets you disable some of the advanced features. Needless to say, make sure to have all those checkboxes enabled.

**No more training wheels, you are ready to play in the big league now.**

# What you will Learn

**1 - Introduction**: This is the chapter you are reading right now.

➡ *Part 1* (the book you are reading right now, ISBN-13: 978-1503182752)

**2 - Workflow**: The most important and most underrated topic when using Logic is how to use it efficiently. That's why I start the book with that chapter.

**3 - Advanced Editing**: To really become a Logic "Pro-user", you need all the available editing tools on your Logic tool belt.

**4 - Flex Introduction**: Finally, Audio Regions have the same freedom when it comes to editing as their MIDI Region counterparts.

**5 - Flex Time**: No time restrictions for Audio Regions anymore. No matter what tempo an audio file was recorded in, you can change it and even quantize it.

**6 - Flex Pitch**: If you ever wanted to change the pitch information in Audio Regions but couldn't afford the Melodyne app or couldn't (under-)stand it, then Logic has the most easy to use tool for you.

**7 - Browsers**: The three Browsers in Logic don't get the same respect from their users. Either they frown upon Apple Loops or don't know what to do with the Media Browser in the first - now you will.

**8 - Audio File Management**: The problem with having a lot of stuff is how to manage that stuff. This is also true for all the Logic related files. You better learn how to manage them before you start to lose them.

**9 - Advanced Audio**: There is much more to Audio in Logic that meets the eyes. I dive into all those pro features Logic has to offer to show you what is going on under the hood.

**10 - Advanced MIDI**: You can also advance your knowledge about the MIDI features in Logic, in addition to its audio features.

**11 - Automation**: Automation is such big topic, I had to split it into two chapters. The first part covers Track Automation, the main automation mode that gets you started.

**12 - Automation (advanced)**: There is Track Automation, Region Automation, MIDI Draw, Trim Mode, Absolute Mode, Relative Mode, to name just a few. Ready to become an expert on all of that?

➡ *Part 2* (ISBN-13: 978-1506122175)

**13 - Music Notation**: There are applications just for music notation. With Logic, that is included. No matter if you want to print out a single melody or an entire orchestral score - you can do it.

**14 - Tempo & Time**: Tempo and Time seems to be easy topics on the outside. But be warned, this chapter goes deep, where no other manual has gone before.

**15 - Working to Picture**: Logic is the best and most popular DAW when it comes to scoring to picture. Learn all the stuff you need to know - to do exactly that.

**16 - Synchronization**: If you made it through the Tempo & Time chapter, then this one is the right chapter for you with lots of information beyond Logic.

**17 - The Environment**: The scariest place in Logic, sending shivers down the spine of most Logic users - unless you know your way around … then all of a sudden it becomes the most powerful place in Logic.

**18 - Surround Sound**: If two speakers are not enough to do your Project good, then it's time to move up to the world of Surround Sound.

**19 - Control Surfaces**: Logic will also surrender to outside powers. Learn how to use and setup those devices, no matter if it is just a single Mod Wheel, or a fully equipped Control Surface.

**20 - Gobbler and Connect**: This is not a new cop show on CBS. Starting with version 10.2, Logic has integrated support for Gobbler and Apple Music Connect, two services that let you collaborate with other Logic users and share your work to others.

# 2 - Workflow

I want to start this book with the Workflow chapter for a specific reason. In addition to mastering all the various features in Logic, from the easy to the most advanced topics, an efficient and often highly customized workflow is what sets a casual Logic user apart from the true power user. In this chapter, you will learn some of those important and essential tools that help you to *make your work in Logic - flow*.

> **Being in charge - Being efficient - Being creative**

Don't we all know these situations?

- ☑ If you are struggling with many tasks in Logic, then there is no workFLOW. You are constantly interrupted, figuring out stuff, and it seems that the computer is in charge instead of you.
- ☑ If you don't know all (or most) the options that Logic provides for the task you are performing, then you don't know that there might be a better, maybe easier, and more efficient way to do your tasks.
- ☑ All those annoying things will have a negative impact on your creativity. You want to achieve a smooth workflow when working in Logic, so this amazing app helps you with your creativity and not hinder it.

## Windows

No matter if you use Logic on a laptop with a small screen or have a big setup with multiple computer displays, the first step in your workflow is the window management. Before you can do anything in Logic, you have to open the right window so you can see what you are doing.

If you spend too much time opening, closing, and rearranging windows on your screen, then you already have the first problem with your workflow.

All these buzzwords on the right play a role when it comes to window managements. So let's have a look at them.

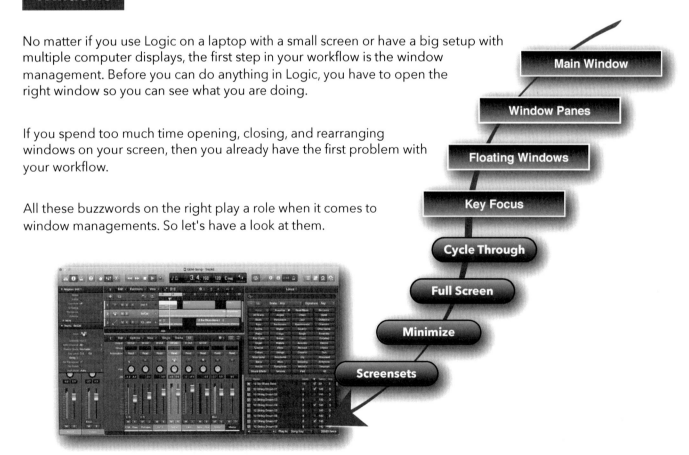

- Main Window
- Window Panes
- Floating Windows
- Key Focus
- Cycle Through
- Full Screen
- Minimize
- Screensets

# Windows Management

I already discussed a lot of details about Window Management in my first Logic book. Here are some of those elements in the context of the workflow:

## ➡ *Window Types*

Whenever you are working in a specific Logic window or move windows around, you have to be aware of what type of window that is. This is very critical because those windows behave quite differently as we will see (or you already know). Be aware of their special powers, but also their limitations.

### ◉ Main Window (Window Panes)

This is the "main window" in Logic. It can show/hide other windows, so-called "Window Panes" inside.

### ◉ Standalone Windows

These are all the other standard windows that you can open in Logic. Some of those windows can also have smaller Window Panes that you can show/hide. They are more hidden and you have to know that they are there, and know where they are (hint: always check the local View Menu).

### ◉ Floating Windows

These are also standalone windows that have the special function: They stay on top of other standard windows. The potential problem is that if you have too many Floating Windows open, then they cover each other, defeating the purpose of Floating Windows. So, use them in moderation or place them well.

## ➡ *Key Focus*

The Key Focus is one of the most important concepts when it comes to working and editing in a multi-window application like Logic. When you use the mouse, you make a change right there on an object on a specific window, so you know what the target is.

However, if you use your keyboard to send a Key Command or type any text and enter number values, you have to make sure which window is the target, the recipient of those keys you are typing. The answer is, the window that has "key focus", also referred to as the **"Key Window"**. So before you type anything in Logic, you need that "visual feedback" to recognize the current Key Window.

- ▸ A Standard Window with Key Focus has its Title Bar Buttons colored ❶ instead of grayed out ❷.
- ▸ The Plugin Window has a white window frame ❸ instead of gray ❹.
- ▸ A Window Pane that has Key Focus has a blue frame ❺ around it.
- ▸ Any Text entry field with Key Focus also has a blue frame ❻ around it.

## ➡ Cycle *Windows* - Cycle *Window Panes*

The easiest step to speed up your workflow is using Key Commands whenever possible. It often takes too much time to "travel around" with the mouse to find and click on the right menu item. The same is true for selecting windows to bring a specific window to the foreground and make it the Key Window. Also, you could click on a window to select it, but not if it is hidden behind other windows.

There are two commands that let you cycle through open windows:

### 💀 Cycle through **Windows**

*Cmd+`* (the tilde key above the tab key). This command lets you cycle through all the currently open windows in Logic, bringing them to the front with key focus. Please be aware that a window could be in the foreground but still not visible if it is covered (sometimes fully covered) by a Floating Window. Some Logic windows are excluded from that cycle, for example, the Key Commands Window or the Musical Typing Window.

All the currently open windows are also listed at the bottom of the Logic's Window Menu (with a dot), even if you have multiple Projects open. The active window (key focus) has a check mark and windows not belonging to a Project have none.

**Window**
Show Step Input Keyboard
Show All Plug-in Windows
● GEM-Song - Environment
● GEM-Song - Mixer: All
● GEM-Song - Tracks
✓ HitSong - Environment
● HitSong - Signature List
● HitSong - Tracks
Musical Typing - SoCal

### 💀 Cycle through **Window Panes**

Here is a problem with the "Cycle through Window" command. For example, if you have the Main Window ❶, a standalone Mixer Window ❷, and a Plugin Window ❸ open, then the command will cycle between the three windows. However, if you have three Window Panes open in the Main Window (Tracks Window ❹, Library Window ❺, Editor Window ❻), then the Cycle through Windows command selects the Main Window with whatever Window Pane has Key Focus and then goes to the next window.

In order to cycle through the different Window Panes inside the Main Window you need a different command: *Cycle through Window Panes sh+tab*.

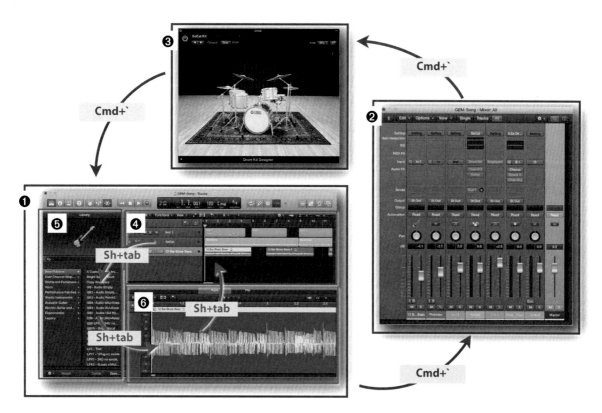

## ➡ *Title Bar Buttons*

The Title Bar Buttons, these three buttons in the upper left corner of a window, already exist since the beginning of OSX and even in OS9 (as square buttons). Usually, users don't pay much attention to them. However, Yosemite (OSX version 10.10) just changed their functionality a bit, which also affects Logic. Before showing the new functionality, here are two modes you have to be aware of:

▶ **Window Zoom**: Usually, you manually resize a window by dragging its borders with the Cursor Tool. Using this Zoom command then resizes the current size of the window automatically to the maximum size possible for the available computer screen. This uses, in most cases, the entire screen. Using the command again resizes the window back to the size you had before. You can toggle back and forth.

▶ **Full Screen Mode**: The Full Screen Mode is slightly different , and it is now more and more implemented in many apps. The main difference compared to Zoom is that the content of a window takes over the entire screen, hiding its Window Title and the Main Menu Bar on top. You still can access them by moving the mouse to the top to slide them out, making them temporarily accessible.

You enter Full Screen Mode with the Menu Command *View ➤ Enter Full Screen* and exit it with the menu item that has changed to *View ➤ Exit Full Screen*

And here is how you can use these two window modes with the Title Bar Buttons:

**Close Button**: The solid red button (on any Logic window) indicates that the Project has been saved. If the button has a dot ● inside, then it indicates that you made changes to the Logic Project since you saved it manually. When you move the mouse over the button, it changes to:

**✗** *Click* to close the window. This is the same as the Key Command *cmd+W* or the Menu Command *File ➤ Close Window*. If this is the only open window in your Project, then the command will close the Project with a Warning Dialog if you have unsaved changes. In that case, its function is the same as the Key Command *opt+cmd+W* or the Menu Command *File➤ Close Project*. Be careful when you have multiple Projects open at a time.

**Minimize Button**: When you move the mouse over this button, it changes to:

**⊖** *Click* to move the window to the Dock. This is the same as the Key Command *cmd+M* or the Menu Command *Window ➤ Minimize* ❶.

**Zoom Button**. When you move the mouse over this button, it could change to three different states:

**+** Zoom: This indicates a standard window. *Click* to toggle between the maximum size and the current size. This is the same as the Menu Command *Window ➤ Zoom* ❷ or Key Command *ctr+cmd+M*.

**◐** Enter Full Screen: This button is only visible on Logic's Main Window, which indicates that it is capable of Full Screen Mode. *Click* to switch to Full Screen Mode (the Window Title and the Main Menu disappear). When you move the mouse to the top to make them appear again, then it shows a different Button:

**◓** Exit Full Screen: *Click* to exit Full Screen Mode.

Please note that you can still use the regular Zoom feature on the Main Window with the Menu Command *Window ➤ Zoom* ❷, or holding the *opt* key (switches to the Zoom button **⊕**), or *double-click* the Window Title Bar.

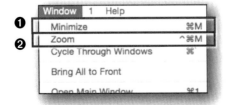

| Window | 1 | Help | |
|--------|---|------|---|
| ❶ Minimize | | | ⌘M |
| ❷ Zoom | | | ^⌘M |
| Cycle Through Windows | | | ⌘ |
| Bring All to Front | | | |
| Open Main Window | | | ⌘1 |

➡️ *Screensets vs. Mission Control*

### 💀 Screensets

Of course, the secret weapon in the constant struggle over screen real estate, are Screensets. This is one of Logic's unique signature feature that let's you store the current size and placement of the open windows into Presets, even remembering the selected Cursor Tool in those window. Later, you can recall the Screensets (any of 81) with the click of a button to have everything ready the way you like it.

This is the ultimate time saver with the highest priority on your workflow tool belt. It lets you manage the small screen size on a laptop as well as a setup with multiple computer displays, remembering every window placement and size on each screen.

### 💀 Mission Control

OSX also has a window management tool, "Mission Control". This is what was formerly known as "Spaces" and "Exposé". You can create multiple Desktops, place different apps in different Spaces, and switch between those Spaces similar to switching Screensets in Logic.

If you already use Mission Control in your general workflow, then you can try it with Logic too. Place different Logic windows in different Spaces and switch between them. One problem, however, are the floating windows. They will show up in all of Logic's Spaces regardless of where you put them. This might not necessarily be a bad thing, because Logic uses a similar preference for the Movie window to be independent from the Screenset. However, the major downside of Mission Control is that the placements cannot be stored (like Screensets) and if you actually switch Screensets, all your Spaces are gone!

## Settings & Preferences

Another step in optimizing your workflow is the proper setup, to make yourself comfortable in your work.

That means, configuring various aspects of Logic that suits your personal preference. There is no need to squint your eyes to see that thin Playhead line if you have the option to make it appear wider.

One of the most often used quotes when Logic users talk about Logic is *"Oh, I didn't know that you can do that"*. This is also true for the settings. You have to know what is available, what you can optimize before you actually do optimize it. And by the way, don't hesitate to change your setting if needed, when it doesn't fit your current workflow anymore.

I will now go through a selection of settings that you might consider for your setup.

## ➡ *Preferences vs. Project Settings*

Logic has two "places" where you configure your preferences and settings:

### 💀 Logic Settings (Preferences)

Open the Preferences window with the Menu Command *Logic Pro X ➤ Preferences ➤* or with the standard Key Commands *cmd+,*

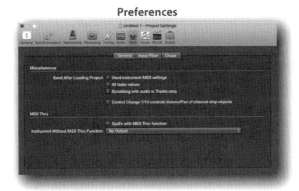

Preferences

These settings are Logic settings and apply to every Project you are opening. The settings are stored in a separate file stored in your user Library *~/Library/Preferences/ com.apple.logic10.plist*

One common cause of Logic starting to act strange is a corrupted Preferences file. In that case, you have to trash it. So always make sure you have a backup strategy in place where you can retrieve an earlier Preferences File. One reason of a workflow killer is being forced to stop your work and to re-configure you settings for the next hour or two.

Also, keep in mind that settings related to Control Surfaces are stored in a separate Preferences file. *~/Library/Preferences/com.apple.logic.pro.cs*

### 💀 Project Settings

Open the Project Settings window with the Menu Command *File ➤ Project Settings ➤* or with the Key Commands *opt+P*

Project Settings

Settings you make in this window apply only to the current Project, they are stored with the Project File.

Some features like Score, MIDI, and Audio have settings available in the Preferences window and the Project Settings, depending on if they apply to the current Project or all Projects.

Although the Project Settings are stored with the Project File, you have the option to import the settings from any Project to your currently open Project. This saves you time of re-configuring settings you haven't saved to a Template yet.

Import Project Settings

### *Templates*

Project Chooser (with Templates)

Whenever you change/optimize the Preferences settings for your workflow, they will be available for any Project you open in Logic from then on. However, as I just mentioned, the Project Settings that you change apply only to that Project. That is the reason to create your own Templates that have your personal workflow-optimized settings right there when you open a new Template Project. Also, make sure to regularly update your Templates when your settings have changed.

## ➡ Main Window Configuration

Here are a few configurations you can do without going into the Preferences or Project Settings:

### 🔘 Control Bar

*Ctr+click* on the Control Bar background ❶ or use the Menu Command *View ➤ Customize Control Bar and Display...* to open its settings window ❷.

- Enable all the Buttons and Controls you need and remove the ones you don't need to save space.
- *Click* on the "Save As Default" button ❸ to save the configuration as Logic Preferences, so it will be there when you open Logic from now on.
- You can toggle the visibility of the Control Bar from Logic's Main Window:
  - 🔘 Menu Command *View ➤ Show/Hide Control Bar*
  - 🔘 Key Command *(Show/Hide Control Bar)* **unassigned**.
- You can open the Control Bar as additional Floating Windows configuring them independently. This is especially useful when you have multiple computer displays:
  - 🔘 Menu Command *View ➤ Open Transport Float*
  - 🔘 Key Command *(Open Control Bar)* **unassigned**

### 🔘 Control Bar Display

*Ctr+click* on the Display Mode Button ❹ to select which Display Mode for the Control Bar Display suits your Project best.

- Selecting the Custom Display Mode lets you customize the elements on the display.
- *Double-click* on the Load Meters to open them as a separate floating window ❺.
- If you want to use two or more Control Bar Displays, just open a new Control Bar and disable everything except the Control Bar Display ❻.
- You can open the (multiple) "Giant Beats Display" and "Giant Time Display" ❼ that can be resized big enough so the assistant across the room can take proper notes during a spotting session.

### 🔘 Toolbar

*Ctr+click* on the Toolbar background ❽ or use the Menu Command *View ➤ Customize Toolbar* to open its settings window ❾.

- Enable all the Buttons and Controls you need and remove the ones you don't need to save space.
- *Click* on the "Save As Default" button ❿ to save the configuration as Logic Preferences so it will be there when you open Logic from now on.
- You can toggle the visibility of the Toolbar from Logic's Main Window:
  - 🔘 Menu Command *View ➤ Show/Hide Toolbar*
  - 🔘 Key Command *(Show/Hide Toolbar)* **ctr+opt+cmd+T**.

## ➡ Scroll Bars

Here is a configuration that is set in the *System Preferences ➤ General* ❶, and therefore, affects all apps including Logic.

System Preferences ➤ General

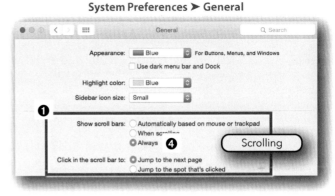

**Scroll Bars**

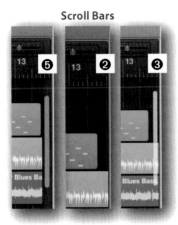

It is about the behavior of the Scroll Bars in a window. As a default, the scroll bars are now hidden ❷. You don't see them unless you move the mouse over that area or start to scroll with the trackpad, then they are transparent ❸. If that is all too much "if-then", just select the option "Show scroll bar: always" ❹ in the System Preferences and the behavior is back "old school style". Not only do you see if there is something to scroll ❺ in a window, the length of the scroll bars indicate how much there is to scroll. This visual feedback might be an important information when working in Logic, more valuable than the new fancy user interface behavior.

## ➡ Appearance

Most of the Preferences and Project Settings affect the configuration on how Logic behaves. They are important to learn when operating Logic. However, there are quite a few settings that just affect the appearance how Logic looks. Although this might be less important because it seems it is just about your personal taste for aesthetics, I would argue that they are equally important because they affect your workflow. Remember, the more comfortable, the more efficient, the more fun, the more productive.

Let me introduce a few:

**Preferences ➤ General**

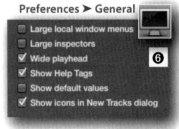

### 🔵 Preferences ➤ Display ➤ General ❻

▸ **Large local window menus**: This increases the size of all the local menus. Select the size that is more comfortable to read for you.

▸ **Large inspectors**: This is again about your eyesight and the resolution of your computer screen.

▸ **Wide playhead**: This affects the vertical Playhead ❼ and also the horizontal Playhead in the Event List.

▸ **Show Help Tags**: Please note that this does not affect the always enabled yellow Tooltips that provide a short info about an object or area when you move the mouse over it (in Yosemite, OSX 10.10, they are now gray). The Help Tag checkbox affects the black Help Tags that show information when you click or drag objects around. They should definitely be enabled.

▸ **Show default values**: This affects the Parameter values in the Inspector. Here is why I prefer to have them off. If you have too much information (all the default values), it is harder to spot a value that is important to see (the one you changed ❽).

**Yes - Default values - No**

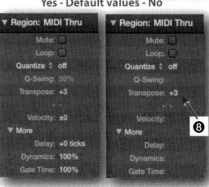

▸ **Show icons in New Tracks dialog** ❾: This is definitely a personal preference. I like visual feedback with the icons.

**New Tracks Dialog**

## ➡ *Bar/Time Displays*

Another often overlooked area is the time display. Logic can display it in Musical Time (bars, beats) and Absolute Time (min, sec). This is a typical example for TMI, "too much information". If you don't do precise editing in the ticks or sample range, then maybe you should turn off those extra digits.

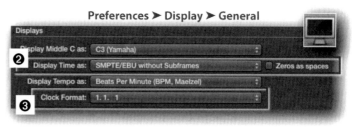

Preferences ➤ Display ➤ General

Event List

Less digits provide a much cleaner readout when you just see the bars and beats or minutes and seconds without the extra information.

You can set the display format (that also effects any numerical display in the Event List ❶ or Event Float) in the *Preferences ➤ Display ➤ General*. Select a format for Absolute Time in the "*Display Time as*" popup menu ❷ and for the Musical Time in the "*Clock Format*" popup menu ❸.

Here are a few examples of display formats with more digits ❹ and less ❺ digits:

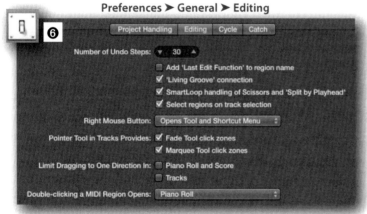

## ➡ *Editing*

The *Preferences ➤ General ➤ Editing* ❻ contains quite a few settings you should make yourself familiar with.

Preferences ➤ General ➤ Editing

They are pretty much self explanatory. You can play around with different settings to see which one fits your personal workflow best.

Snap & Drag

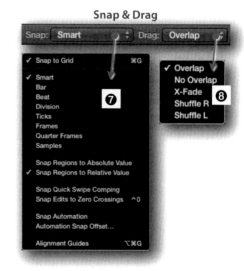

## ➡ *Snap & Drag*

The Snap settings ❼ and the Drag settings ❽ are two important Menu Buttons that set the preferences, not how Logic looks, but how it behaves - during editing.

They are a big cause for confusion and mistakes during editing. Spending the time and trying to understand (once and for all) what these settings mean will definitely improve your workflow.

I will discuss that in the "Advanced Editing" chapter.

# Help & Notifications

In this last section about workflow and windows I want to talk about various Help Windows.

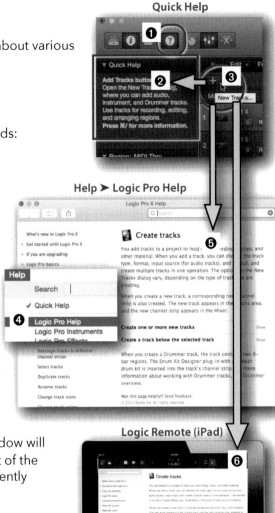

Quick Help

## ➡ Quick Help

You can toggle Logic's Quick Help feature with these commands:

- *Click* the Quick Help Button in the Control Bar ❶
- Menu Command *Help* ➤ *Quick Help*
- Key Command (*Show/Hide Quick Help*) *unassigned*

This will add a little window ❷ on top of the Inspector (*drag* the Header to tear it off as a separate floating window). It will now show a short description of any object or section you move the mouse over ❸.

## ➡ Logic Pro X Help (online)

OSX has a system-wide Help mechanism that can be accessed from the Help Menu in most of the apps, including Logic (Main Menu *Help* ➤ *Logic Pro Help* ❹). It is an online User Guide that opens in its own floating window.

But it gets better. Whenever you have Quick Help activated in Logic ❷ and you point your mouse ❸ over an object or window element, you press *com+/* and the Logic Pro Help window will automatically open and update its page to display the content of the Logic User Guide ❺ explaining the object/feature you are currently moving the mouse over.

Help ➤ Logic Pro Help

Logic Remote (iPad)

## ➡ Smart Help

You can "outsource" this online help feature to the iPad running the free Logic Remote app using "Smart Help". This frees up the space on your screen because the iPad now always displays ❻ and updates the page of the online Logic User Guide that explains the object/section you are moving your mouse over.

## ➡ Notifications

And here is a little tip regarding assistance.

You can activate the Logic Notifications in the *System Preferences* ➤ *Notification* window ❼. Now, if Logic want's to tell you something (you have a new MIDI port, you lost your MIDI connection, there are new sounds available, etc.), you will get a notification ❽ depending on how you set it up in the System Preferences. You can also view the notes on the Notification Menu ❾ by clicking in the right upper corner of your screen.

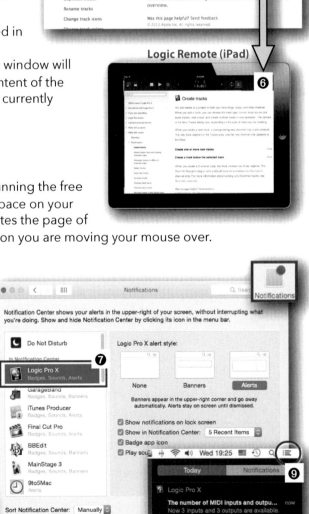

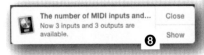

Managing the Zoom feature is another important element that determines an efficient workflow. If you spend too much time zooming in and out, and scrolling, and more zooming, etc., then your workflow will definitely be interrupted. You have to use the available zoom features to your advantage so you can quickly get to a specific spot with the right zoom level to do the best possible edit.

## Overview

The Zoom feature is only available in windows that display a Workspace, the ones with a timeline. These are the Tracks Window, Piano Roll, Score, Step Input, Audio Track Editor, and Audio File Editor.

Of course, Logic wouldn't be Logic if it would only provide one Zoom Button. You have a wide variety of zoom features to choose from. Some of them have so many options that they could get a little bit confusing. Same as with other features, you have to take the time and try them first in order to pick the ones that fit your workflow.

I will introduce them individually with all the details, but first a quick overview what we've got:

▶ **Quick & Easy Zoom**

One simple Key Command "Z" that toggles between your current zoom level and the maximum zoom level of the selected object(s) or all objects (if nothing is selected).

▶ **Zoom Slider**

Zoom in and out vertically or horizontally with the Zoom Sliders or the equivalent mouse and key commands.

▶ **Zoom Tool**

Drag a selection with the Zoom Tool at the area that you want to zoom in and click again to quickly zoom back out.

▶ **Zoom Presets**

Use the three Zoom Presets to store and recall your most used zoom levels.

▶ **Zoom Selection**

Zoom in based on various selections or the Cycle Range and store their zoom level and scroll position as Navigation Snapshots, that you can recall.

▶ **Track Zoom**

Configure the zoom behavior for the Tracks you select in the Tracks Window.

▶ **Vertical Auto Zoom**

Logic automatically zooms the Track to display all Tracks in your Project

▶ **Vertical Waveform Zoom**

Adjust the vertical zoom levels for the waveform that are displayed in the Tracks Window and Audio Track Editor.

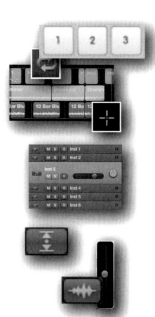

# Zoom Features

### ➡ *Quick & Easy Zoom*

Main Window

I call this feature Quick & Easy Zoom, although it is only a single Key Command *(Toggle Zoom to fit Selection or All Contents)* assigned to the (easy to remember) letter **Z**. On the Toolbar, you can also *click* the

Zoom Button .

Unlike other zoom features in Logic, this one is just plain and simple. It serves two common scenarios:

▸ **Zoom Selection**: Imagine you look at your Project with tons of Tracks and Regions, and you need to check or edit a specific Region or a group of Regions:

☑ Select the Region(s)

☑ Hit the Key Command **Z**. This will zoom all the way in to use the entire window to display the selected Region(s)

☑ Do your necessary edit

☑ Hit the Key Command **Z** again to return to the original zoom level and scroll position you had before

▸ **Zoom All**: You can use the same Key Commands for a different purpose. Sometimes you are caught up in the middle of your project and just need a quick look at your entire Project, especially if you work on long and complex film cues.

☑ Make sure nothing is selected. Key Command *(Deselect All)* **sh+opt+D**

☑ Hit the Key Command **Z**. This will zoom all the way in to use the entire window to display your whole Project. This is not from beginning to the end of your Project Timeline. It displays the area from the first to the last Region (left to right, top to bottom). Unfortunately, any looped Regions at the last Region are not included in the zoom.

### ➡ *Zoom Slider*

This is the standard Zoom feature. You have one control to zoom in-out vertically and one control to zoom in-out horizontally. The sliders are placed at the upper right corner of the Tracks Window and the Editor Windows. If a slider is missing, then you know that you cannot zoom in that direction. For example, no vertical zoom in the Score and Audio Track Editor. No zoom at all in the Drummer Editor.

Although the Zoom Sliders are the main tool to gradually zoom in and out, they are not really good in precisely setting the zoom level. The Key Commands are more precise, or even better, use the gestures on a trackpad. Here are all the options:

**Vertical Zoom:**

- Use the Vertical Zoom Slider
- Key Command *(Zoom Vertical IN / Out)* **cmd +ArrowUp** and **cmd+ArrowDown**
- **Opt+scroll** up/down

**Horizontal Zoom:**

- Use the Horizontal Zoom Slider
- Key Command *(Zoom Horizontal IN / Out)* **cmd+ArrowLeft** and **cmd+ArrowRight**
- **Opt+scroll** left/right
- Pinch in/out on a trackpad
- *Click-hold* on the Playhead Thumb ❶ on the Ruler (the Pointer changes to a double arrow ) and then hold down the *option* key. Now you can drag up/down to zoom

## ⚫ Zoom and Scroll

Zooming in and out horizontally has one major problem, which might be the number one nuisance when it comes to zooming.

> Here is a typical day at the studio: You positioned the song to the spot in the Audio Region where you want to make an edit. To perform that edit more precisely, you zoom in ... but while you are looking now at a better zoom level, that spot you wanted to edit scrolled "out of sight". Now you scroll left and right to find the spot, which you can't, because the waveform looks different in a higher zoom level, so you zoom out to find the spot again (hopefully), and then zoom in, %#^& .. It scrolled again. You get the idea.

The good news is, it doesn't have to be that way. You can exactly predict or control where the window will scroll to or better, not scroll to.

## Lock the Scroll

Here are the different scenarios that determine which part is locked, that means, stays fixed, doesn't scroll.

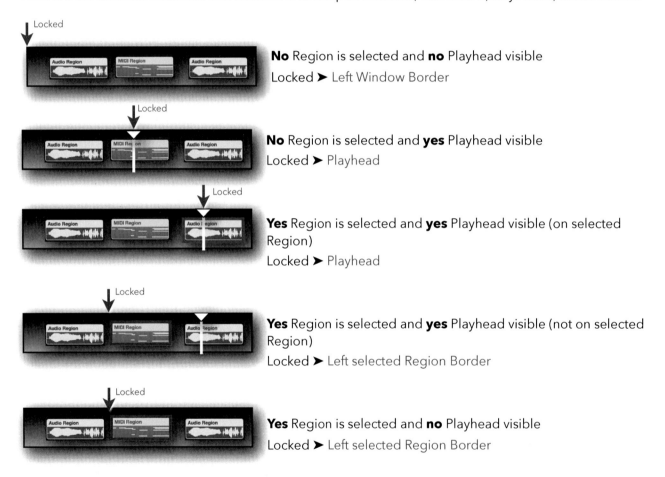

**No** Region is selected and **no** Playhead visible
Locked ➤ Left Window Border

**No** Region is selected and **yes** Playhead visible
Locked ➤ Playhead

**Yes** Region is selected and **yes** Playhead visible (on selected Region)
Locked ➤ Playhead

**Yes** Region is selected and **yes** Playhead visible (not on selected Region)
Locked ➤ Left selected Region Border

**Yes** Region is selected and **no** Playhead visible
Locked ➤ Left selected Region Border

## Place the Playhead where you want to lock the Scroll Position (nothing selected)

That is pretty much the easiest solution if you don't want to remember the five different scenarios. Just make sure that no Region is selected (*sh+op+D*) and then place the Playhead at the position of the Timeline that you want to lock no matter how much you zoom in or out.

## ➡️ *Zoom Tool*

**Tool Menu**

This is another easy way to zoom in and out. Instead of increasing or decreasing the zoom level, you draw an area in the window with the Zoom Tool 🔍 and that area will be zoomed so it fills the entire window. To switch back to the previous zoom level, just click in the background with the Zoom Tool. Here is the procedure:

▸ **Select the Tool**: You have three options to choose the Zoom Tool:

- Switch the Cursor to the Zoom Tool by selecting it from the Tool Menu.
- Holding down the *option* key will automatically switch to the Zoom Tool as long as you don't move over a Region.
- Holding down the *control* and *option* key will also switch to the Zoom Tool, but this time, you can move the tool over any area inside the Workspace. This makes it the preferred choice.

**Ctr+opt+drag** 🔍

▸ **Procedure**: It won't get easier than that:

- ☑️ *Ctr+opt+drag* 🔍 an area to zoom into that area
- ☑️ *Ctr+opt+drag* 🔍 another area to zoom in even more
- ☑️ … repeat as much as you want (up to the maximum zoom level)
- ☑️ *Ctr+opt+click* 🔍 on the background of the window (not on a Region or Event) to zoom out to the previous zoom level
- ☑️ … repeat that step to zoom out step-by-step if you have zoomed in multiple steps

- This works in the Piano Roll or Step Editor to zoom in on MIDI Events
- In the Score Editor to zoom in on a section of the score
- It works in the Audio Track Editor and Audio File Editor to zoom in on the waveform (only horizontally)

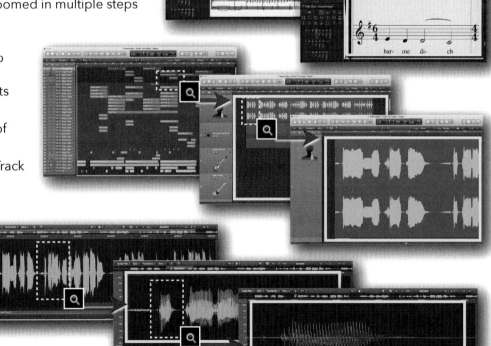

### 🌐 Navigation Snapshots

Logic stores each step with a different zoom level in so-called "Navigation Snapshots" that let you step back and forth the most recent zoom levels (plus their scroll position). More on that in a minute.
Use the Key Command (*Navigation Back*) **opt+Z** and (*Navigation Forward*) **sh+opt+Z**

## ➡ *Zoom Presets*

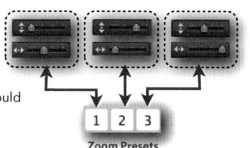

**Zoom Presets**

Logic can save a specific zoom level (horizontal and vertical zoom value) to a Preset that you can recall at any time. It provides three of those Presets (per window type) and they are so easy to use that you should definitely incorporate them into your workflow.

▶ **Procedure**

☑ Whenever you have a specific zoom level that you might need more often, use the Key Command (*Save as Zoom 1*) **sh+ctr+opt+cmd+1** to save it as Preset 1.

☑ Save other zoom levels to Preset 2 and Preset 3 as needed.

☑ Saving a zoom level to a Preset will overwrite its previously stored values.

☑ Whenever you want to set the zoom level of a window to the zoom level you stored in Presets 1 just use the Key Command (Recall Zoom 1) **ctr+opt+cmd+1** to apply it. Same procedure for Preset 2 and 3.

**Key Commands**

| | |
|---|---|
| •Recall Zoom 1 | ^⌥⌘1 |
| •Recall Zoom 2 | ^⌥⌘2 |
| •Recall Zoom 3 | ^⌥⌘3 |
| •Save as Zoom 1 | ^⌥⇧⌘1 |
| •Save as Zoom 2 | ^⌥⇧⌘2 |
| •Save as Zoom 3 | ^⌥⇧⌘3 |

*Things to be aware of:*

- All three Zoom Presets already have a default value.
- The Zoom Presets you save are stored to the Preferences file and are available in any Project.
- Each type of window in Logic that has Zoom Sliders (Tracks Window, Piano Roll, Audio Track Editor, etc.) has its own three independent Zoom Presets.
- The Presets only store the zoom level, not the scroll position. That means, the same rules apply regarding the scrolling, as if you would zoom with the Zoom Sliders: Remember, deselect all objects and position the Playhead to lock the scroll position to the Playhead Position.

## ➡ *Zoom Selection*

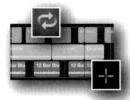

While the Zoom Tool lets you zoom into a selection that you draw with the Zoom Tool 🔍, Logic lets you define a selection also in other ways:

**Key Commands**

Zoom to fit Selection vertically and horizontally, store Navigation Snapshot
Zoom to fit Selection horizontally, store Navigation Snapshot
Zoom to fit Selection vertically, store Navigation Snapshot
Zoom to fit Locators, store Navigation Snapshot
Zoom to fit All Contents, store Navigation Snapshot

Every type of selection has its special Key Command:

▶ **All Objects**: This command zooms to display all objects in your current Project. This is similar to the Key Command "*Toggle Zoom to fit Selection or All Contents*". Here it is called *Zoom to fit All Contents, store Navigation Snapshot.*

▶ **Cycle Range**: The Cycle Range doesn't have to be enabled for that. *Zoom to fit Locators, store Navigation Snapshot*

▶ **Any Objects Selection or Marquee Selection**: There are three variations of that command that lets you choose to zoom in vertically, horizontally or both.

- Vertically and horizontally: *Zoom to fit Selection vertically and horizontally, store Navigation Snapshot*

- Horizontally only: *Zoom to fit Selection horizontally, store Navigation Snapshot*

- Vertically only: *Zoom to fit Selection vertically, store Navigation Snapshot*

## 🕹 Navigation Snapshot

You may have noticed in those long names for Key Commands that they have the addition "store Navigation Snapshot". Here is the very useful concept behind it:

▶ **30 Snapshots**: Logic has 30 Presets that can store Navigation Snapshots in the Tracks Window. It works in some of the Editor Windows, but it is a little bit of a hit and miss in my experience.

▶ **Content**: A Navigation Snapshot can include the zoom level plus the scroll position.

▶ **Automatic Save**: Logic stores the zoom level and scroll position for most Zoom commands, especially if they have the "store Navigation Snapshot" in their name.

▶ **Manual Save**: You can manually store the current zoom level and scroll position as a Snapshot with the Key Command (*Store Navigation Snapshot*) **sh+Z**.

▶ **Recall**: You can't recall a specific Snapshot by number like you can with the three Zoom Presets. You can only step through the Navigation History sequentially between #1 and the highest number that has been saved.
The Key Commands are (*Navigation: Back*) **opt+Z** and (*Navigation: Forward*) **sh+opt+Z**.

▶ **Storage**: Navigation Snapshots are stored temporarily with Logic and apply to all open Projects until you close Logic. Launching a new Project will maintain the Snapshots, but re-launching Logic will reset all the Snapshots.

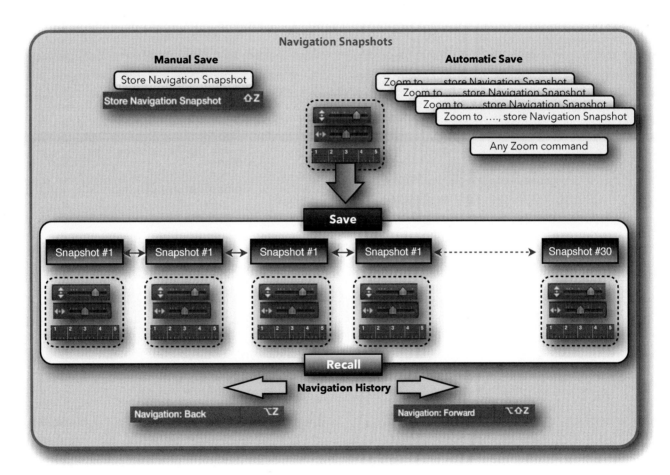

### Use in your Workflow

Because the Navigation Snapshots are not stored with the Projects and are reset when you close Logic, their use is mainly for temporarily going back and forth between zoom settings. Whenever you applied a zoom level, either with a command or manually with the Zoom Slider or Zoom Tool, you can use the Navigation commands to quickly go back and forth or step through the history, like a quick toggle zoom settings.

## ➡ *Track Zoom*

When you work on a Project with a lot of Tracks, then you have to zoom-in the Tracks Window vertically in order to see all (or most ) of the Tracks. When zoomed in too much, you might see less controls on the Track Header, but more problematic, the height of the Regions is also getting lower. Although you can edit Regions in the separate Editor Windows, sometimes, you can do edits more quickly in the Workspace of the Tracks Window, while maintaining the perspective of the entire Project.

There is a common feature called "Track Zoom" that solves that problem. Here is the basic concept:

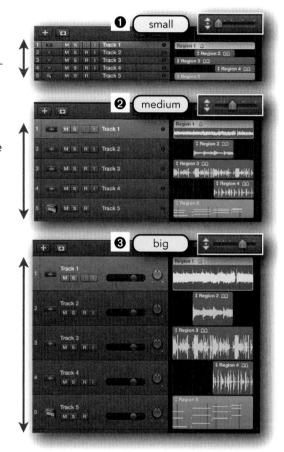

▶ **"All" Zoom Level**: When you use the vertical zoom controls in the Tracks Window (*cmd+ArrowUp* and *cmd+ArrowDown*), then all the Tracks are affected equally. You can see the trade-off. Zooming out will let you display a lot of Tracks, but there is no space on the Regions to display any waveform or MIDI Events ❶. Zooming in a little will reveal those informations ❷, but the Track Header might not be high enough to show all the controls. Only at a certain zoom level can you see Volume Sliders ❸. But now, all the Tracks are so high that you have to scroll up and down to see a specific Track.

▶ **"Individual" Zoom Level**: Instead of zooming in on all Tracks, you can set an individual zoom level ❹ that is more zoomed-in.

- Manual Toggle: When you want to edit on a particular Track, you just select the Track and manually toggle between the "All" Zoom Level (like all the other Tracks ❷) and the zoomed-in "Individual" Zoom Level ❹.

- Auto Track: When you enable "*Zoom Focused Track*", Logic automatically toggles the currently selected Track to the zoomed-in "Individual" Zoom level.

▶ **"Individual-separate" Zoom Level**: In addition to these two zoom levels, you can adjust each Track to its own zoom level ❺. I call this the "Individual-separate" Zoom Level (in a lack for a better term). For that, you have to have "*Zoom Focused Track*" disabled.

Track Zoom can also be enabled for Groups (Main Menu *Mix ➤ Show Groups*) so all Tracks belonging to a specific Group adapt to the same Track Zoom level.

### 💀 Track Zoom - Detailed Explanation

Here is a more detailed explanation on how Track Zoom works. For an easier summary skip to the next page.

▶ **Two Zoom Levels**: As a default, each Track can switch between two different zoom levels. I call them *All Zoom Level* and *Individual Zoom Level* .

  - *All Zoom Level* : This is the zoom level set with the standard zoom controls (i.e. Zoom Slider).

  - *Individual Zoom Level* : This is actually a zoom level offset and not a fixed zoom level. It increases the height of the Track by a percentage based on the *All Zoom Level* . If you change the *All Zoom Level* with any of the controls, the *Individual Zoom Level* changes proportionally.

▶ **Switch Between Them**: You can switch a Track between those two zoom levels with two different commands:

  - *Switch Manually*: You can toggle individual Tracks between *All Zoom Level* and *Individual Zoom Level* with the Key Command (*Toggle Individual Track Zoom*) **ctr+opt+cmd+Z**.

  - *Switch Automatically*: The *Zoom Focused Track* mode switches all Tracks to *All Zoom Level* and only one Track (the currently selected Track) switches to the *Individual Zoom Level*. Enable this mode with any of the two Key Commands:
      - 💀 Tracks Window Local Menu *View* ➤ *Zoom Focused Track*
      - 💀 Key Command (*Toggle Zoom Focused Track*) **ctr+Z**

▶ **Change Individual Zoom Level**: A new Project has a default value for the *Individual Zoom Level*. Here is how you adjust it:

  - Select a Track and enable *Zoom Focused Track*, which switches to the *Individual Zoom Level* for that Track. Adjust its height by dragging the divider line 🔀 at the bottom of the Track Header. This becomes now the new *Individual Zoom Level*.

  - Select a Track and enable the *Toggle Individual Track Zoom* command, which switches to *Individual Zoom Level* for that Track. After adjusting its height, you have to toggle back, which stores the height as the new *Individual Zoom Level*.

▶ **Overwrite Individual Zoom Level**: You can overwrite the *Individual Zoom Level* for each Track individually to set a Track's height to the separate *Individual-Separate Zoom Level*. Just drag the divider line 🔀 at the bottom of the Track Header. A few things to keep in mind:

  - Using the *Toggle Individual Track Zoom* command will now switch that Track between *All Zoom Level* and its own *Individual-Separate Zoom Level*.

  - Be careful, when you toggle a Track after you adjusted its height, it will store that zoom level as the new *Individual Zoom Level*.

  - Enabling the *Zoom Focused Track* and selecting any Track will reset the *Individual-Separate Zoom Level* on all Tracks to the *Individual Zoom Level*.

▶ **Reset**: There are two Reset commands (you can undo those Reset commands!)

  - *Individual Track Zoom Reset*: This will switch the currently selected Track to *All Zoom Level* and restores its *Individual Zoom Level*, resetting any *Individual-Separate Zoom Level*.

  - *Individual Track Zoom Reset for All Tracks*: This will switch all Tracks to *All Zoom Level* and restores their *Individual Zoom Level*, overwriting any *Individual-Separate Zoom Level*.

▶ **Multiple Tracks Windows**: What if you have multiple Main Windows open?

  - Each Main Window can be set to its independent *All Zoom Level* .

  - The *Individual Zoom Level* and any *Individual-Separate Zoom Level* remains the same in every window, but because it is a percentage value, it affects the height based on the *All Zoom Level* of each window.

  - Enabling *Zoom Focused Track* or *Toggle Individual Track Zoom* will switch those Tracks in all open Main Windows.

## 🎧 Track Zoom - Simple Explanation

Here is a more simple and graphical explanation:

▸ **Set the Default Track Height**: Set the overall zoom level for the Tracks Window with the vertical Zoom Slider (or *cmd+ArrowUp/Down*)

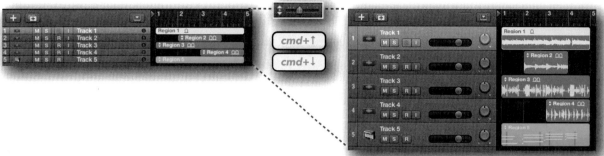

▸ **Increase individual Track Height bigger**: Adjust the height of Tracks individually with those commands:

   🎧 *Drag* the divider line ✥ at the bottom of the Track Header up/down.

   🎧 Select the Track and use the Key Commands (*Individual Track Zoom In*) *ctr+opt+cmd+ArrowDown* and (*Individual Track Zoom Out*) *ctr+opt+cmd+ArrowUp*

▸ **Manually Toggle Track Height**: To toggle a selected Track between the default Track Height and the individual (bigger) Track Height, use the Key Command (*Toggle Individual Track Zoom*) *ctr+opt+cmd+Z*

▸ **Automatically Toggle Track Height**: Use any of the following commands:

   🎧 Tracks Window Local Menu *View ➤ Zoom Focused Track*

   🎧 Key Command (*Toggle Zoom Focused Track*) *ctr+Z* or on the Toolbar *click* the Track Zoom Button

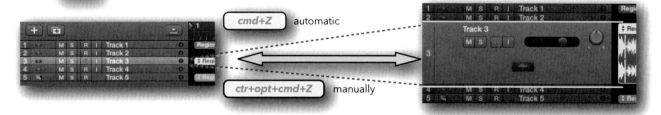

▸ **Reset Track Height**: You can either reset the selected Track or all Tracks to the default Track Height you set with the vertical Zoom setting:

   🎧 Key Command (*Individual Track Zoom Reset*) *ctr+opt+cmd+delete*

   🎧 Key Command (*Individual Track Zoom Reset for All Tracks*) *sh+ctr+opt+cmd+delete*

## ➡ *Vertical Auto Zoom*

LPX v10.1 introduced "Vertical Auto Zoom". This is not only a cool new feature, but also an extremely useful (and simple to use) new feature.

You toggle the Vertical Auto Zoom Mode in two ways:

- 🎚 In the Menu Bar of the Tracks Window next to the Zoom Slider, *click* on the Vertical Auto Zoom Button to toggle the Vertical Auto Zoom Mode on and off .
- 🎚 You can also toggle the mode with the new Key Command *Toggle Vertical Auto Zoom*, which is unassigned by default.

**Main Window**

### 💀 What does it do?

The Track Zoom feature that we discussed on the previous pages is good for focusing on the currently used Track that you record on or edit. However, sometimes you just want to see all the Tracks, which requires to vertically zoom your Project until all the Tracks are displays in the current Tracks Window. Now with Vertical Auto Zoom, you can accomplish that with just one command.

- Turn Vertical Auto Zoom on, and all the Tracks are zoomed vertically so they fit the current size of the Tracks Window.
- Turn Vertical Auto Zoom off and the previous zoom Level is restored.
- Any relative zoom Zoom Level between Tracks (using Zoom Focused Track) remain intact.
- If you have only a few Tracks that don't fill the Tracks Window vertically, then you can use Vertical Auto Zoom to zoom in and fill the Tracks Window vertically with those Track.
- **Dynamic Adjustment**: When Vertical Auto Zoom is enabled and you resize the Tracks Window, then the vertical Zoom adjusts automatically while you resize the window, to always fill the window vertically with all Tracks. Try it out, you have to see it to believe it.

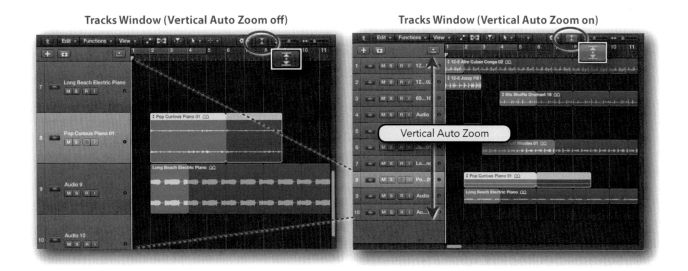

### ➡ Waveform Vertical Zoom

There is a problem when trying to edit Audio Regions that have a very low signal level ❶. If you try to zoom in ❷ with the vertical Zoom Slider, you just blow up the Region, but the actual waveform stays proportionally low ❸, still difficult to edit.

To help with that issue, there is a special Zoom feature.

### 😎 Audio Track Editor / Tracks Window

The Tracks Window and the Audio Track Editor have a special Waveform Zoom Button next to the Zoom Slider, which functions independently in both windows.

▸ When you *click-hold* the Waveform Zoom Button next to the Zoom Slider, a vertical slider will appear. This is the Waveform Zoom Slider ❹.

▸ The Waveform Zoom Button is disabled and gray 🔳 when the slider is at its lowest position. That means, all the waveforms are displayed in their original form on the Region.

▸ You can move the slider up to zoom-in vertically on the waveform all the way to the top, which represents a x8 zoom factor. ❺

▸ The Track height is not affected and the zoom level for the Region itself did not change ❻. Only the waveform looks like you increased the gain of the audio signal (which you didn't).

▸ The zoom level affects all Audio Regions in the Tracks Window.

▸ **Change Zoom Level**: You can change the Waveform Zoom in three ways:

  😎 *Click-hold* the Waveform Zoom Button and *drag* the slider up/down

  😎 Key Command (*Waveform Vertical Zoom In/Out*) *cmd+equal* and *cmd+minus* (14 steps) ❼

  😎 Use the Key Command to apply a fixed zoom level (*Waveform Vertical Zoom X1, x2, x4, x8*) ❽

**Key Commands**

| |
|---|
| Waveform Vertical Zoom x 1 (Normal) |
| Waveform Vertical Zoom x 2 |
| Waveform Vertical Zoom x 4 ❽ |
| Waveform Vertical Zoom x 8 |
| Waveform Vertical Zoom Out ⌘- |
| Waveform Vertical Zoom In ⌘= |
| Toggle Waveform Vertical Zoom |

▸ **Toggle Zoom Level**: You can toggle between the current Waveform Zoom level and the original waveform without any Zoom value (x1).

  😎 *Click* the Waveform Zoom Button to toggle between zoomed 🔳 and not zoomed 🔳

  😎 Key Command (*Toggle Waveform Vertical Zoom*) *unassigned*

### ⚉ Audio File Editor:

The Audio File Editor does not have a Waveform Zoom Button. The displayed waveform in this window(s) can be zoomed with the standard Zoom Tools (Zoom Slider ❶ and equivalent commands ❷).

Please note the changing y-axis ❸ while you zoom-in that indicates the signal level and the scroll bar that lets you scroll vertically ❹.

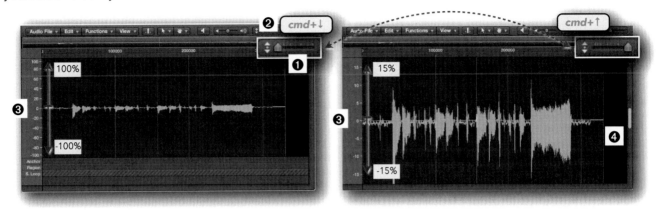

# Zoom Summary

Here is a quick summary with the important Key Commands that you might adapt in your workflow:

▶ **Quick Zoom**

Select Object(s) and toggle to zoom in and out with `z`

▶ **Zoom gradually**

`cmd+ArrowKeys` Keep the arrow keys pressed to continue zooming in or out

▶ **Zoom drag a selection**

`ctr+opt 🔍` Drag to zoom into that selection and click to zoom back out

▶ **Navigation Snapshot**

Use for quickly toggling back and forth the last and current zoom setting (zoom level and scroll position)

Previous Snapshot: `opt+Z` Next Snapshot: `sh+opt+Z`

▶ **Zoom Preset**

Store three often used zoom levels (high, medium, low)

`sh+ctr+opt+cmd+1`  `sh+ctr+opt+cmd+2`  `sh+ctr+opt+cmd+3`

`ctr+opt+cmd+1`  `ctr+opt+cmd+2`  `ctr+opt+cmd+3`

▶ **Zoom Waveform**

Increase or decrease the vertical zoom of the audio waveform `cmd+=`  `cmd+-`

Maybe the action you are doing the most during recording and editing is scrolling. If you think about it, there are two types of scrolling. There is the one you are doing intentionally to go to a specific position in your song to do a specific task (*the good scrolling*), and there is the other kind of scrolling that happens unintentionally (<u>the bad scrolling</u>) because you did something and all of a sudden Logic jumped to some other location in your song. Now you have to interrupt whatever you were doing and have to do more scrolling instead to find your way back. Looks like your workflow was interrupted.

So let's have a closer look at scrolling and see how to maintain the control over it.

## Basics

Here is the very basic concept about scrolling in the Tracks Window:

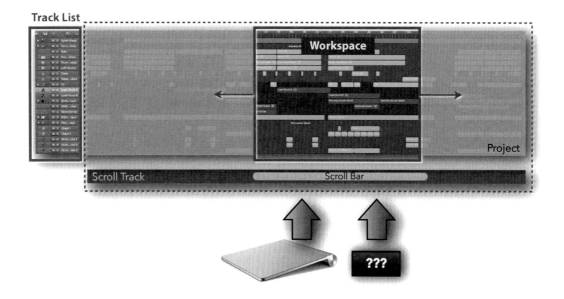

▶ **Track List**: On the left of the Tracks Window, you have the Track List with the Track Headers, each one representing a single Track (or Track Stack). Horizontally, a Track can only be resized but not scrolled. Of course you can scroll the Track List vertically.

▶ **Workspace**: Each Track Header extends into its Track Lane where you place the content in the form of Regions and Automation Curves for that specific Track. All the Track Lanes of the existing Tracks are linked together to a Ruler on top that represents the Timeline so you know at which bar or which time you place the Regions or Events on those Track Lanes.

▶ **Scroll Bar/Scroll Track**: If the Project is too long and exceeds the width of your Workspace window, then what you actually see in the Workspace is only a portion of the Song. In that case, you have to move the Workspace window left or right to display a specific portion of your Song you want to see or work on. It is like a "window" into your Song. The horizontal Scroll Bar ("Scroller") at the bottom indicates the width of the displayed portion in reference to the Scroll Track, which represents the entire length of your Song. You can either drag the scroll bar or use the two-finger scroll gesture on the trackpad. The horizontal zoom level, as we have seen in the previous Zoom section, determines how much content you see "inside" that workspace window.

**???**     Now the big question is: Besides you, what actions or what circumstances in Logic will move the Scroll Bar.

# Who is Scrolling

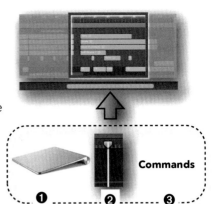

## ➡ *Active Window*

First, we look at all those scrolling circumstances when working on a single window. This is the window that shows the three Window Title Buttons in color or has a blue frame around if it is a window pane. This is the so-called Active Window, or the Key Window, the window that has "key focus". The reason I emphasize on that is because the scrolling behavior is different on an Inactive Window, which I'll get to in a moment.

On an Active Window, there are three "forces" that can change the scrolling: You (doing the manual scrolling), the Playhead, and various commands.

## Manual ❶

There are two actions to move the Scroll Bar manually, and therefore, move the visual portion of your Song, the Workspace.

> **Scroll Bar**: *Drag* the horizontal scroll bar at the bottom left or right. The visibility of the Scroll Bars depends on the settings in the *System Preferences ➤ General ➤ Show scroll bars*.

> **Gestures**: The two-finger gesture on a trackpad is much more efficient in your workflow, because you don't have to click exactly on the scroll bar, just have your mouse over the Workspace and drag the two fingers left or right. This has to be enabled in the *System Preferences ➤ Trackpad ➤ Scroll & Zoom*.

## Playhead ❷

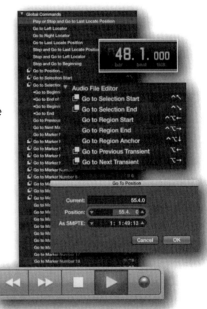

The Playhead is the boss, the "main commander", when it comes to scrolling your Project horizontally. There are three initiators for the movement (with a closer look at them in a moment):

> **Playhead is moved manually**: You just grab the Playhead and slide it left or right (or slide the Control Bar Display). The Workspace will scroll if you move against the left or right edge of the window.

> **Playhead moves during Play**: When you use your transport controls, the Playhead moves automatically. However, if it will affect the scrolling depends on a few settings.

> **Playhead is moved by a "Go to Command"**: Logic offers a wide variety of "Go To" commands that lets you move the Playhead to a specific time position based on references in your song. For example, the beginning, the end, Region beginning, Locator position, Marker position, etc.

## Others ❸

There are also a few commands that can move the Scroll Position without being linked to the Playhead Position.

- Scroll to Selection
  - Main Menu *Navigate ➤ Scroll To Selection*. This does not move the Playhead!
  - Key Command (*Scroll to Selection*) **sh+`**
- Navigation Snapshot: I discussed that in the previous Zoom section (Navigation: Back, Navigation: Forward)

## ➡ *The Playhead*

Let's have a closer look at the Playhead and how it affects the scrolling:

### 🔵 Playhead - Timeline

The Tracks Window, the Editor Windows, and the List Windows, all have one thing in common, a Timeline.

All those windows display the actual content of your song (in the form of Regions and other Events) along a time-axis represented by the Timeline. No matter if the Timeline runs horizontally ❶ (in the Tracks Window and Editor Windows) or vertically ❷ (in the List Editors), there is always a Playhead indicating the current position in your song, when your song is playing or paused. The Control Bar Display ❸ shows that current Playhead Position.

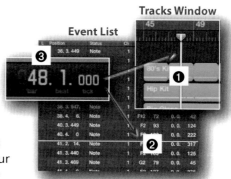

> Two exceptions: The Drummer Editor is the only Editor Window without a Timeline and the Audio File Editor displays the Timeline of the audio file it is currently displaying.

### 🔵 Catch Mode

Each window that has a Timeline, also has a special button in their Menu Bar, the *Catch Playhead Button*. It turns the Catch Mode on or off. The important thing to be aware of is that the Catch Playhead Button can be enabled or disabled independently in each window.

**Off**: The Playhead Position will not scroll the Workspace area. The only exception is when you click on the Playhead and drag it around.

**On**: Logic always scrolls the Workspace area to display the section of your song the Playhead is positioned at. It constantly follows it, updates the Workspace, to "catch up" with the Playhead Position.

There are three ways to turn the Catch Mode on:

▶ **When Logic Starts**: When this checkbox is enabled ❹ in the *Preferences ➤ General ➤ Catch ➤ Catch When Logic starts*, then the Catch Mode will be enabled on the currently Active Window (if it was off) at the moment the Project starts playing. It stays on when you stop.

▶ **When the Playhead Moves**: When this checkbox is enabled ❹, then moving the Playhead on the Timeline manually will enable Catch Mode (if it was off).

▶ **Manually**: You can toggle Catch Mode manually by clicking on the Catch Playhead Button or use the Key Command (*Catch Playhead Position*) ` . This is the key above the tab key.

Personally, I only use the Key Command to switch the Catch Mode manually instead of the two Preferences. This way, I'm the only one in charge when to turn Catch Mode on or off. No "surprises" that can interrupt my workflow.

## ⚫ When Playing

Now if Catch Mode is enabled , you can have two different behaviors when playing your Song.

- ▶ **Scroll forward**: Whenever Logic is playing and the Playhead reaches the right edge of the window, it automatically scrolls the Workspace one page forward.
- ▶ **Continuous Scroll**: "Scroll in Play" is an alternate mode. When enabled, the Playhead moves forward until it reaches the center of the Workspace Window. Now it locks the Playhead at that position and the content of the window, your song, starts to move underneath from right to left. You can enable this mode from the Local Menu *View ➤ Scroll in Play* or with the Key Command (*Scroll in Play*) **ctr+`** in the Tracks Window and the Editor Windows separately.

From a workflow perspective, which one to use is more of a personal preference. *Scroll in Play* keeps you focused on one spot without that sudden jump when the page scrolls. However, depending on the size of your screen, it might be a bit more taxing on your computer by constantly redrawing your screen.

"Go to" Key Commands

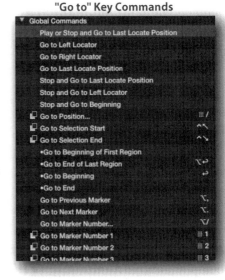

## ⚫ Go to Commands

Navigation Menu

The following commands, when Catch Mode is enabled, have the potential of dramatically improving your workflow and the speed you are working on your Project. It all depends on your "navigation skills". Find out which Key Commands you might use the most and then incorporate them into your workflow so they become second nature to you. Many of those Key Commands are also available in the Main Navigation Menu.

*Attention*: Those navigation commands are even more important when they serve a double duty as a reference to quickly move objects to the Playhead Position. I will get to that later.

Go To Position Window

Here are your options:

- ▶ **Go to Position...** : This Key Command (forward slash /) is very handy to quickly position the Playhead at a precise location. It opens a little window where you can enter the position (as Bar or SMPTE). Hit *return* and the Playhead jumps there.
- ▶ **Go to Selection Start / End**: This command should definitely be on your Logic tool belt. It lets you position the Playhead to the beginning or end of a selected Region.
- ▶ **Last Locate Position**: This places the Playhead at the position you started playback the last time.
- ▶ **Go to Beginning / End**: These commands refer to the *Start of Project Marker* and *End of Project Marker*.
- ▶ **Go to Beginning of First Region / End of Last Region**: These two commands refer to the first and last Region in your Project.
- ▶ **Go to Left / Right Locator**: Another handy command.
- ▶ **Marker Position:** You have a wide variety of commands to place the Playhead at a specific Marker:
  - Marker Number: This opens a window to type in the Marker number.
  - Marker Number 1...20: You have dedicated Key Commands to go to Marker 1 ... 20.
  - Previous, Next, Marker: Step through the Markers with the Playhead.
  - You can also select a Marker (position the Playhead) by *opt+clicking* on it in the Marker Track or Marker List.

Go to Marker Window

**"Go to" Commands (Audio Files Editor)**

The "Go to" Key Commands for the Audio File Editor are special. Their Playhead refers to the timeline of the Audio File and not the Project Timeline. These commands are extremely important for editing audio files.

**Audio Files Key Commands**

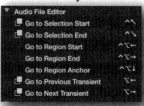

 **Navigation Commands**

You can move the Playhead (and therefore, scroll to that position when Catch Playhead is enabled) with the various Forward and Rewind navigation controls.

Here is a list of what is available to you:

| Increment | Command | Key | Command | Key | Remarks |
|---|---|---|---|---|---|
| **8 bars** | Fast Rewind | *sh+,* | Fast Forward | *sh+.* | |
| **4 bars** | Rewind Button | *cmd+click* | Forward Button | *cmd+click* | |
| **1 bar** | Rewind | , | Forward | . | Same as transport control buttons |
| **1 beat** | | | | | Create with a utility app |
| **1 Division** | Rewind by Division Value | | Forward by Division Value | | |
| **1 Frame** | Rewind one Frame | | Forward one Frame | | |
| **30 Ticks** | Scrub Rewind | | Scrub Forward | | |
| **(dynamic)** | Shuttle Rewind | | Shuttle Forward | | |

- **Keep Pressing**: You can keep pressing the keys to continuously move the Playhead forward or backward by that increment.
- **Transport Control**: The Forward Button and Rewind Button on the transport controls move the Playhead by one bar. *Cmd+clicking* on those buttons moves the Playhead by four bars (and plays a 4 bar Cycle Range at that position).
- **No Beat increments**: Unfortunately there is no "1 beat" increment. However, if you use a third party automation app (i.e. QuicKeys), then you can configure a Key Command that repeats the Division Key Command four times (if the Division is set to /16).
- **Scrub**: The Scrub command is mainly used for audio editing, but you can use it as a navigation command to move the Playhead just by 30 Ticks.

- **Shuttle**: The Shuttle command is a special playback feature found on video tape machines in the form of a Shuttle Wheel. The more you move the wheel to the right, the faster will be the playback speed. Moving it to the left from its center position will increase the playback speed backwards. Every time you click the Shuttle Forward command, you "dial the wheel to the next notch on the right". Clicking the Shuttle Rewind command "dials the wheel one notch back", which slows down the playback speed until you reach the virtual center position, where it starts to increase the playback speed backwards. You have to play with it to get the idea.
  Some external control surfaces (i.e. Avid Artist Control) have a Shuttle Wheel that can be used for that Shuttle control in Logic.

### *Advanced Navigation Tip*

Here is one of the shortcomings in Logic when it comes to placing the Playhead on your Workspace: You can't just click on the Workspace to place the Playhead at that click position. You have to move the mouse up to the Ruler and click on the Ruler position.

However, here is a little (advanced) workaround that lets you move the Playhead to wherever you click on the Workspace even directly on a Region (not the Region Header).

You need a third party automation utility app like QuicKeys to create a macro (a sequence of commands that is triggered by a single key combination) and the BetterTouchTool app to assign that key combination to a gesture on your trackpad. Here is what you do:

### Create the Macro (QuicKeys)

QuicKeys

I create the following sequence of commands in the QuicKeys, which then can be triggered by a key combination, a key combination that I am not using in Logic (i.e. *sh+ctr+opt+cmd+F19*). This will be the key combination to trigger the macro:

Here are the steps:

- ▶ **Step 1**: Create a *Type Stroke* step. Enter the key combination that you assigned in Logic to the Key Command "*Set Marquee Tool*". This will switch the Cursor in Logic to the Marquee Tool.

  •Set Marquee Tool

- ▶ **Step 2**: Create a *Mouse Clicks* step. This will be the click that is performed later in Logic. Because you will click with the Marquee Tool, it will create a Marquee Selection with a single line. This will be the position to move the Playhead to.

- ▶ **Step 3**: Create a *Type Stroke* step. Enter the key combination that you assigned in Logic to the Key Command "*Go to Selection Start*". This will move the Playhead to the Marquee line you created in Step 2.

  Go to Selection Start

The first three steps would just place the Playhead at the click position. If you want to automatically play when you click, you have to add Step 4 to your sequence.

- ▶ **Step 4**: Create another *Type Stroke* step. Enter the key combination that you assigned in Logic to the Key Command "*Play from Selection*". This will move the Playhead to the Marquee line you created in Step 2 and starts to play.

  •Play from Selection

The next two steps are optional if you want to remove the Marquee Selection and return to the Pointer Tool (eliminating all the traces of that little workaround).

- ▶ **Step 5**: Create a *Type Stroke* step. Enter the key combination that you assigned in Logic to the Key Command "*Set Pointer Tool*". This will change the Cursor Tool back to the Pointer Tool. Remember, we had to switch it to the Marquee Tool in Step 1.

  •Set Pointer Tool

- ▶ **Step 6**: Create a *Mouse Clicks* step with a few pixels offset. This creates a click with the Pointer Tool to deselect the Marquee Selection we created in Step 1.

### Assign a Gesture (BTT)

BetterTouchTool

Now I use the BetterTouchTool app and assign a gesture to the key combination *sh+ctr+opt+cmd+F19*. I use the "Two Finger TipTap Middle".

**The Action**: I move the index finger to place the mouse on the Workspace where I want to click.
Once there, I place the ring finger without lifting the index finger and tap with the middle finger. This triggers the key combination in QuicKeys, which runs through the six Steps.

## ➡ *Inactive Window*

On the last few pages, we saw all the elements that can scroll the Workspace. However, there is one more level of complexity to the whole thing. When determining who scrolls the Workspace of a window, you have to differentiate between two types of windows in Logic.

- 💡 **Active Window**: This is the window that has Key Focus, also referred to as the Key Window. All the rules we discussed regarding the scrolling are for the Active Window. There are slightly different rules when it comes to Inactive Windows.

- 💡 **Inactive Window**: All the open windows, other than the Active Window, are the Inactive Windows. In Logic, Inactive Windows that have a Timeline with a Workspace can be "linked" to the Active Window, so they always display the same content. This is Logic's infamous "*Link Mode*" with the different Display Levels. I covered that topic already in my first Logic book. As we will see, scrolling in Inactive Windows is controlled not only by the Catch Mode, but also by the Link Mode.

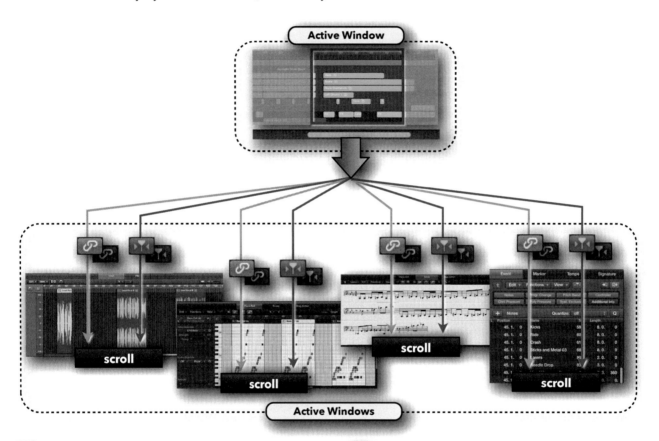

**Catch Off**: An Inactive Window with Catch Mode off will still have its Playhead Position linked to the Active Window (if the Playhead moves in the Active Window, it moves in all others). Please note that this has nothing to do with the Link Mode. The Timelines are always linked. However, the window will not scroll to follow the Playhead Position.

**Catch On**: Only when an Inactive Window has Catch enabled, will it automatically scroll to follow the Playhead Position in the Workspace.

**Link Off**: An Inactive Window with Link Mode off will still select an object (Region or Event) when it is selected in the Active Window, but only if it happens to be on the same Display Level.

**Link On**: When Link Mode is enabled (Content Link to be specific), then the Inactive Window will switch to that Display Level, and here is the important part, it also scrolls the window to show the selected object (Region or Event) in the Workspace.

So always keep Catch Mode and Link Mode enabled in Inactive Windows, unless you want them to be unlinked and independent.

## 🕱 Workflow

So, having Catch Mode and Link Mode enabled in an Inactive Window guarantees that it always follows whatever you do in the Active Window.

When you scroll on the Active Window with any of the commands we just discussed, the Inactive Window will scroll to the same position so you always see the same section of Timeline in those Workspaces. Only if you want to focus on a specific section, for example, in an Editor Window, you might want to disable Catch, so the window does not scroll.

When having one or multiple Editor Windows open (as Inactive Windows), you might want them to display the Region or Events that you select in the Active Window. The Main Window is most likely the Tracks Window, but even when you edit in an Editor Window (now it is the Main Window), you want other Editor Windows (i.e. The Event List) to be linked, follow whatever you currently select. The enabled Link Mode guarantees that all the open windows are all "on the same page", so to speak, by scrolling the Inactive Window to the selected object (Region or Event). This guarantees a quick and efficient workflow.

The Score Editor is one exception where you specifically might want to disable Link Mode and Catch Mode based on how the Display Levels are used. I cover that in the *Notation* chapter.

## 🕱 Catch Content

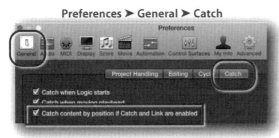
Preferences ➤ General ➤ Catch

There is one additional Preferences setting that is part of that whole Active Window - Inactive Window configuration and that is "Catch Content" *Preferences ➤ General ➤ Catch ➤ Catch content by position if Catch and Link are enabled*.

Here is the problem that it fixes.

When you select a Region ❶ in the Tracks Window (Main Window), then any open Editor Window (Inactive Window) that has Content Link Mode enabled will scroll their Timeline to that position and displays the content of that Region ❷ (the waveform or the MIDI Events). If an Editor Window can only show one Region at a time, then that window is stuck when the Playhead moves to a new position ❸.

The Link Mode has priority and continues to only display that selected Region ❹ until you select another Region in the Tracks Window. The "Catch Content" ❺ setting "breaks" that priority and allows the Editor Window to display the content of another (unselected) Region ❻ when the Playhead moves over it ❼, but only on the same Track that has the Region selected on the Tracks Window.

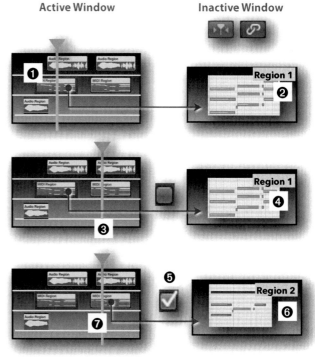

**Affected**: The Step Editor can only display the content of a single Region and is affected by this setting. The Score Editor and Event List can display their content on different Display Levels, so this settings is useful when displaying the Region content.

**Not Affected**: The Audio Track Editor and the Piano Roll Editor displays an entire Track with all the Regions on it, so the settings have no purpose for them. Please note that the Piano Roll can switch its view to display only the one selected Region (Local Menu *View ➤ Selected Region*) or all Regions on that Track (Local Menu *View ➤ One Track*). The Audio File Editor only shows one selected Region at a time and has no Link Mode settings anyway.

# Markers

Markers are definitely a great tool to help you when working on your Project and speed up your workflow. I introduced them briefly in my first Logic book. Here is a closer look.

## Overview

First of all, when talking about the Markers in Logic, you have to be aware that there are three different areas where you can view and work with Markers:

- ▶ **Marker Track ❶**: The Marker Track is part of the Global Tracks
- ▶ **Marker List ❷**: The Marker List is part of the List Editors
- ▶ **Marker Text ❸**: The Marker Text is the least known of all three

### ⚙ Commands

When it comes to accessing all the Marker-related commands, you have to keep the following places in mind:

- ☑ **Track Menu ❹**: The *Track ➤ Global Tracks* contains the command to toggle the Marker Track.
- ☑ **Navigation Menu ❺**: The Navigate menu contains most of the Marker-related commands.
- ☑ **Key Commands ❻**: When it comes to speeding up your workflow, the Key Commands, again, are the way to go.
- ☑ **Toolbar**: Don't forget the Toolbar Buttons "Previous/Next Marker ❼

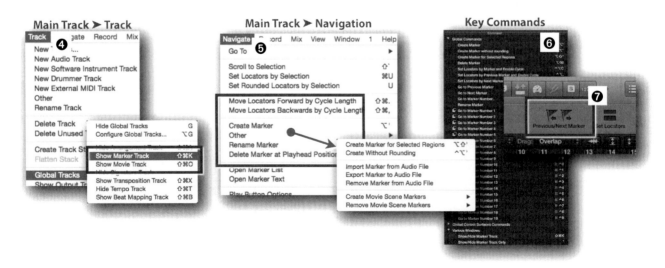

# Marker Track

Logic Pro X versions prior to v10.1 had a Marker Track Button [icon] [icon] next to the Global Tracks Button that let you toggle the Marker Track independent from the other Global Tracks. This button has been removed in v10.1, but the functionality is still there when using the Key Command *(Show/Hide Marker Track Only)* ' (the apostrophe key).

### ☻ Show/Hide UI Elements

One of the steps when it comes to a speedy workflow is to quickly show/hide UI (User Interface) elements. Here are the commands that let you quickly work with those user interface elements:

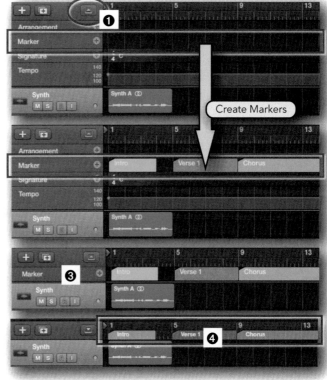

Create Markers

▶ **Show Hide Global Track** [icon] [icon]: The Marker Track is one of the seven Global Tracks. So one option to show the Marker Track is to show the Global Tracks by *clicking* on the Global Tracks Button ❶, use the Key Command *G*, or use the Menu Command *Track ➤ Global Tracks ➤ Show/ Hide Global Tracks*.

▶ **Configure Global Tracks**: The Marker Track is shown by default when you open the Global Tracks. Keep in mind that each Global Track can be shown/hidden by using the *Configure Global Track* Popover Window ❷ *(opt+G)*. If the Marker Track is hidden, enable it with the following command:

▶ **Show/Hide Marker Track**: The Key Command *sh+cmd+K* or Menu Command *Track ➤ Global Tracks ➤ Show/Hide Marker Track* lets you show/ hide the Marker Track in the Global Tracks area. This command also works when the Global Tracks are hidden. In that case, it will open the Global Tracks with the Marker Tracks.

▶ **Show/Hide Marker Track Only**: This command (previously available as a separate Master Track Button [icon]) is slightly different. It opens the Global Tracks area with only the Marker Track visible ❸ regardless of the Global Tracks Configuration ❷. Use the Key Command *(Show/Hide Marker Track Only)* ' (the apostrophe key).

▶ **Marker Track on Timeline**: Any Markers on the Marker Track will be displayed on the Timeline once you close the Marker Track ❹. This is a read-only display and you have to open the Marker Track if you want to edit the Markers.

▶ Marker Tracks as the rest of the Global Tracks can be displayed in the Tracks Window, Piano Roll, Score, Step Editor, and Audio Track Editor.

### ☻ Marker Commands

The advantage of the Marker Track is that you can manage Markers visually:

Create [icon] - Rename [icon] - Move [icon] - Resize [icon][icon] - Delete ⌫

Marker: GEM Markers ↕

### ☻ Marker Sets

You can also create and manage up to nine Marker Sets by clicking on the Marker label.

# Marker List

The Marker List displays all the Markers as a list view and provides more precise control of the placement of the Markers, plus additional commands.

## ➡ *Windows*

Like with many windows in Logic, the Marker List can be displayed as a Window Pane, part of Logic's Main Window, or as a standalone floating window. When it comes to quickly show/hide the window, you have to keep their differences in mind.

### 🌑 **Window Pane:**

- *Click* the List Editors Button ▦ in the Control Bar and *click* on the Marker tab
- Menu Command *View* ➤ *Show/Hide List Editors* and *click* on the Marker tab
- Key Command (*Show/Hide List Editors*) *D* and *click* on the Marker tab

### 🌑 **Standalone Floating Window**

- Menu Command *Navigate* ➤ *Open Marker List*
- Key Command (*Open Marker List*) *unassigned*
- *Drag* the blue Marker tab in the Marker List to "tear off" a separate Marker List window.

## ➡ *Naming*

You can name a Marker in the Marker Track (*double-click* on a Marker and enter text), but only the "first line". The Marker List, however, lets you enter complete sentences and paragraphs with all the text formatting tools, which turns each Marker into a text document.

You can toggle the Text Area with the Edit Button ▦ ❶ in the right upper corner. *Click* the Edit Button
[ Edit ] ❷ to switch to "Text Entry Mode" to edit the text in the Text Area. *Double-clicking* on a Marker will also open the Text Area (if not open yet) and enters the "Text Entry Mode" right away.

The Edit Button turns into a *Done* Button [ Done ] when in Text Edit Mode. *Click* on it to exit "Text Edit Mode".

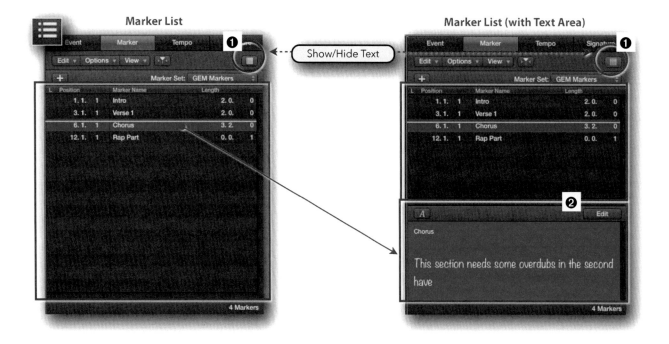

# Marker Text

Here is the concept of the Marker Text:

- ▶ Each Marker can contain a complete section of text
- ▶ That text can be made visible in all three windows:

  - **Marker Track ❶**: *Drag* the divider line on the Global Track to extend the height of the Marker Track. The Marker Name stays centered, but if the Marker includes text, it will be displayed (without text formatting).

  - **Marker List ❷**: *Click* on the Edit Button 🔲 to show the Text Area in the lower portion of the window.

  - **Marker Text ❸**: The text of a Marker can be displayed in a separate Floating Window.

Marker Track

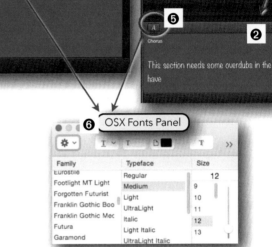

Marker Text

Marker List

## 💀 Standalone Window

You open the Marker Text window with the following commands (the window header names it "Marker List")

- 💀 Menu Command *Navigate ➤ Open Marker Text*
- 💀 Key Command (*Open Marker Text*) **unassigned**
- 💀 *Opt+click* on a Marker in the Marker Track

OSX Fonts Panel

## 💀 Edit Text

You can enter, edit, and format text:

- ▶ **Enter Text**: Although the Marker Track can display the entire text, when *double-clicking* on the Marker, it lets you only edit the name of the Marker (the first line). You can fully edit the text in the Marker Text Area of the Marker List and the Marker Text Window by switching to *Text Edit Mode*. *Click* the Edit Button [ Edit ] ❹ (or *double-click* in the Text Area), which turns the button into the Done Button [ Done ] that lets you exit *Text Edit Mode*.

- ▶ **Format Text**: You can format the text by clicking the Fonts Button [ A ] ❺, which opens the OSX Fonts Panel ❻. You can choose any color for the text, however, the background color is determined by Logic's Color Picker. The background color is also the color of the Marker displayed on the Marker Track. If you paste text (mostly black color), you have to change the font color or background color.

## 💀 Functionality

Here are two examples as to what you can use the Marker Text in your workflow.

- ▶ **Lyrics**: The most obvious use for the Marker Text is for Lyrics. You can enter the lyrics of your song into the markers (Verse 1, Verse 2, Chorus, etc.) and drag the window wide open (with a big font, so you can read it while you are singing). When the Catch Playhead Button [ ▶▼◀ ] is activated, then the window updates when the Playhead moves across the Markers, functions like a teleprompter.

- ▶ **Notes**: Another way to incorporate the Marker Text into your workflow is production notes. You have the two Note Pads Window (Open from the Control Bar 📝 ) that lets you enter separate notes for your Project and each individual Tracks. With the Marker Text, you can enter notes specific for your song's Timeline. For example, on the Chorus with "add another synth pad", or at the end "fade out into reverb during mix". You can create those Marker/Notes in different Marker Sets. For example, notes for Mixing, notes for the recording session with the vocalist, etc. Remember, it is Logic ... you have many options.

# Managing Markers

## ➡ Create Markers

There are a wide range of different commands to create Markers. You don't have to memorize all of them. Just try them to see which one fits into your workflow.

### ▶ Not Rounded

- On the Marker Track, *click* the Plus icon
- Main Menu *Navigate ➤ Other ➤ Create Without Rounding*
- Marker List Local Menu *Options ➤ Create Without Rounding*
- Key Command (*Crete Marker without rounding*) **ctr+opt+'**
- **Ctr+opt+cmd+click** on the Marker Track, which opens a name field for entering a Marker Name

### ▶ Rounded to closest Quarter Note

- In the Marker List, *click* the Plus Button

### ▶ Rounded to closest Bar

- Main Menu *Navigate ➤ Create Marker*
- Marker List Local Menu *Options ➤ Create*
- Key Command (*Crete Marker without rounding*) **opt+'**

### ▶ Create Markers for Selected Regions

This will create Markers for each of the selected Regions inheriting their name and color.

- Main Menu *Navigate ➤ Other ➤ Create Marker for Selected Regions*
- *Click* on the Marker Label in the Marker Track Header and select "*Create Markers from Regions*"
- Key Command (*Crete Markers for Selected Regions*) **sh+opt+'**

### ▶ Create Marker from Cycle Range

*Drag* a Cycle Range to the Marker Track

## ➡ Marker Length

Logic handles the Length of the Markers in a strange way.

- When you create a Marker, it stretches all the way to the end of the Project (or to the beginning of the next Marker).
- However, the length is listed as "0.0.1". That means, it has no specific length.
- If you create a second Marker after that first Marker, the first Marker now ends at the beginning of the second Marker ❶ still listing it length as "0.0.1"❷.
- Only if you resize a Marker, it becomes a Marker with a specific length ❸.
- Marker cannot overlap. If you drag the beginning of a Marker B to the left over an existing Marker A, then Marker A will automatically be shortened.
- You can use the "Junction Tool" 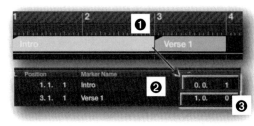 ❹ that appears when you move the Cursor between two adjacent Markers. This lets you resize the ending and beginning together.
- The Local View Menu in the Marker List has two options to display the Position and Length as Absolute Time ❺ and display the Length value ❻ as an absolute position (where it ends) instead of its length (its duration).

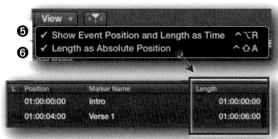

## ➡ Marker Name

Please note that the Markers are automatically named sequentially "Marker 1", "Marker 2", etc. They will display the placeholder name "Marker ##" ❶ when you switch to "Text Edit Mode".

<u>Attention</u>: Pay attention to the automatic naming of Markers. Here are two screenshots (before - after).

- <u>Before</u> ❷: I have one Marker named "Vers 1 and three Markers that I haven't named, They have the generic name Marker 1, Marker 3, and Marker 4. Logic just counts the Markers from left to right and applies the sequential number.

- <u>After</u>: Now I created a new Marker ❸ and named it "Vers 2". Logic recognizes the new amount of Markers and updates the numbers, resulting in new names for the Markers. Marker 3 becomes Marker 4 ❹ and Marker 4 becomes Marker 5 ❺.

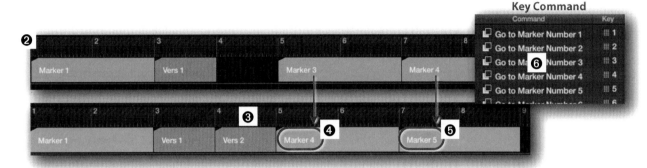

You have Key Commands that let you jump directly to a specific Marker Number ❻. The problem is that these are not specific Markers, just their sequential position, which could change if you create any new Marker in between. I still wish Logic would have dedicated Memory Locators like on a tape machine!

## ➡ Special Markers

There are two special types of Markers that are flagged with an icon in the first L ("locked") column ❼ of the Marker List:

🔒 **SMPTE-Locked Marker**: The command "Lock SMPTE Position" links the Marker to the Absolute Time instead of the default Musical Time. I discuss that feature in great detail in the *Tempo & Time* chapter.

**Scene Marker**: Logic can automatically generate Scene Markers by analyzing an imported movie. These Markers are also SMPTE-locked. You can also manually convert Markers between Standard Markers to Scene Markers with the available commands in the Local Options Menu ❽ of the Marker List. I discuss that feature in the *Working to Picture* chapter.

### Protected

The status of a Marker, if it is locked/protected, depends on where you try to change it.

- SMPTE-locked Marker or Scene Markers cannot be changed in the Marker List. On the Maker Track you also cannot move them, but you can resize them.

- If the Marker Track is protected ❾ (the padlock 🔒 is only visible if it is visible for the Track Header, "Configure Track Header" *opt+T*), then you cannot change it (Error Message ❿), but you could in the Marker List.

## ➡ *Move Markers*

You can move Markers by changing their position in the Marker List or by dragging them around on the Marker Track. However, because Markers cannot overlap, there could be weird interactions, sometimes.

## ➡ *Import/Export Markers*

This is one little known feature in Logic. It can embed the Tempo and Marker information as metadata in an audio file (uncompressed AIFF, WAV, CAF only). I will discuss the Tempo feature in the *Tempo & Time* chapter. Here is how it works with the Markers.

- **Embed Marker**: Any Audio File you record in your Project or bounce from your Project automatically adds the information about the Markers as metadata at the end of the file. That includes all the Markers along the Timeline of the duration of the audio file. You can see the names of the Markers when you open the audio file in a text editor ❶. Only the names and locations of the Markers are stored, not any additional text or color.

- **Export Marker**: If you created the Markers after you recorded your Audio Regions in your Project, then you can select the Audio Region and use the Menu Command ❷ *Navigate ➤ Others ➤ Export Marker to Audio File*. This will write the metadata to the Audio File referenced to the currently selected Audio Region.

- **Import File**: When you import an Audio File to your Project that has embedded Markers, then you will get a Dialog Window ❸ that lets you choose to import those Markers. The Markers will be created at the position relative to the position of the Project Timeline you place the Audio File to. This will overwrite any existing Markers, so you might want to switch to a different Marker Set first.

- **Import Marker**: You can import the embedded Markers of an Audio File later by selecting the Audio Region in your Project and use the Menu Command ❷ *Navigate ➤ Others ➤ Import Marker from Audio File*. A Dialog Window ❹ tells you if there where no Marker info embedded in the file.

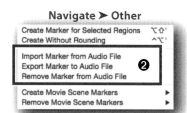

- **Convert**: *Click* on the Marker Label in the Global Track Header to open a Shortcut Menu ❺. It contains three commands to create Markers from selected Regions or Arrangement Markers, and also to convert selected Markers to Arrangement Markers.

- **Remove Marker**: The Menu Command ❷ *Navigate ➤ Others ➤ Remove Marker from Audio File* will delete the metadata for the Marker info in the Audio File referenced to the currently selected Audio Region.

## ➡ *Delete Marker*

You can delete any Marker, even the SMPTE-locked and Scene Marker in the Marker Track or Marker List. Only the Track Protect Button 🔒 on the Track List prohibits that.

- ▶ **Delete Selected Marker**: Although there is a separate command "Delete Marker" in the Shortcut Menu and as Key Command *opt+delete*, you could use any standard delete command.

- ▶ **Delete Marker at Playhead Position**: Use the Menu Command *Navigate ➤ Delete Marker at Playhead Position*.

Logic is famous for its huge arsenal of Key Commands (over 1,200). They play a significant role when it comes to speeding up your workflow. It is so much faster to hit a key or a key combination on your keyboard instead of grabbing the mouse, moving around to find the cursor on your multi-display setup, travel to the button or menu and submenu to finally select the command. Especially if you use a command more often.

## Concept

The Key Command concept is fairly simple:

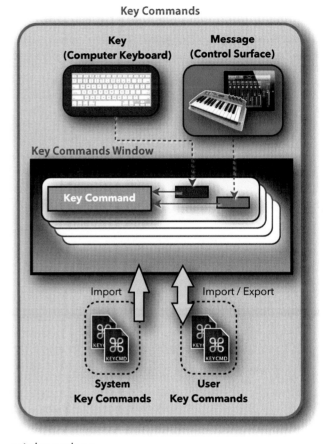

Key Commands

- **Window**: You manage the Key Commands in one window, the Key Command Window.
- **Commands**: It lists the 1,200 Logic commands. These are mostly commands that are available in various Logic menus or through buttons. In addition, a wide variety of commands on this list are only available as Key Commands, sometimes marked with a dot in front of the name.
- **Trigger**: For each Command you can assign two types of trigger:
  - ▶ **Key**: You can assign one key or key combination on your computer keyboard to trigger a specific command.
  - ▶ **Assignment**: You can assign one or multiple messages sent from an external Control Surface to trigger a command.
- **Presets**: A whole set of configured (assigned) Key Commands is called a Preset. Logic comes with a set of preconfigured Key Commands (based on specific languages) that you can import to your Project. You can also create your own customized Key Command configurations as your own Key Command Presets to export and import them on other Logic computers you might work on.

_Advice_: The default set of Key Commands is a good start. However, unless you are teaching Logic and need to be familiar with that default set, I highly recommend you develop your own personalized set of Key Commands. There is no good or bad set of Key Commands, only the one that makes sense to you and are easy for you to remember. Some users have used specific Key Commands that they are developed over the years or were costumed to from Pro Tools or Cubase. Also, there is no need to have specific keys assigned to commands that you never use in your workflow. Just learn the commands that are part of your daily routine, even delete the ones you don't use to avoid triggering some actions by accident.

_Tip:_
There is a cool website dedicated to the Logic Key Commands. You can browse through, search for all the key commands based on different keyboard layouts and language (US, UK). Is nicely done in an interactive way.

http://www.logicprokeycommands.com/logic-pro-x-key-commands/

# Interface

There are three ways to open the Key Command Window (a floating window):

 Main Menu *Logic Pro X* ➤ *Key Commands* ➤ *Edit...*

 Key Command (*Open Key Commands*) **opt+K**

 *Ctr+click* on any command in a Logic menu or submenu, and the Key Command Window opens with that specific command selected.

The Key Commands Window has four sections:

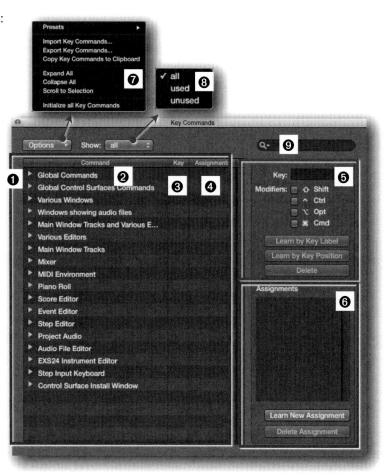

##  Key Commands

This section on the left lists all the available Commands that you can assign a key combination to. The commands are grouped in 18 Key Command Groups that you can show/hide with the disclosure triangle ❶.

The list has three columns, displaying the name of the *Command* ❷, the assigned key combination in the *Key* ❸ column and in the *Assignment* ❹ column a number indicating how many Control Surface assignments have been configured for a specific Command.

##  Key Assignment ❺

This section provides the controls to assign a key combination from your computer keyboard to a specific Command.

##  Controller Assignment ❻

This section provides the controls to assign a message from a button of an external Control Surface to a specific Command.

## ⬤ Header

The Header lists two Menu Buttons and a Search Field:

▶ **Options ❼**: The Options Menu provides the commands to manage the Presets, plus three commands to navigate the (long) list of Key Commands below. Open (Expand) or close (Collapse) all disclosure triangles of the Key Command Groups. The "*Scroll to Selection*" scrolls the window up or down to show the currently selected Command.

▶ **Show ❽**: The Show Menu lets you restrict the displayed commands to "*all*" the Commands, the ones that have a Key assignment ("*used*") or no Key Assignment ("*unused*").

▶ **Search ❾**: Enter any text in the Search Field to list only those commands that match that text string. *Click* on the magnifying glass 🔍 to open up a menu with your most recent search terms.

  • **Alternate Search**: This is an alternate search function. Instead of searching for the name of a command, you can also search for a Key Combination you have already assigned: *Click* on any command in the Key Commands list (so the search field doesn't have key focus) and type the key combination, for example, *op+cmd+K*. The window scrolls to that command and selects it. Hit the key combination again to scroll to the next Key Command if a key combination is assigned to multiple Key Commands.

# Assignment

### ➡ *Key Assignment*

Here is a list of the symbols for the various keys. Please note that the delete key ⌫ on the Standard Keyboard cannot be assigned to any Key Command. The delete key ⌦ on the Extended Keyboard can.

> **Standard Keyboard:** ↺ esc, ⇥ Tab, ⌫ delete, ↵ Return, Space ␣ , ⇧ shift, ^ control, ⌥ option (alt), ⌘ command
>
> **Extended Keyboard**: ⌧ clear, ⌦ delete, ↖ home, ↘ end, ⇞ ⇟ Page up and down. ← → ↑ ↓ Arrow Keys, ⌤ Enter

When using any kind of Key Commands, you have to keep a few rules in mind:

▸ **Reserved Key Combination**: There are a few OSX key combinations that you cannot use. If you try, you will get an error message ➊.

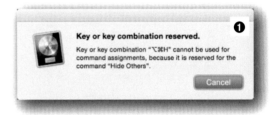

▸ **System Key Commands**: There are some Key Commands that are also used by the OSX System but they can be configured in the *System Preferences ➤ Keyboard ➤ Shortcut*. You can disable them there if you really need them in Logic. For example, *cmd+space* will open the Spotlight window.

▸ **3rd Party Utilities**: Make sure you don't have any Key Command utilities like QuicKeys programmed that interfere with the Logic Key Commands.

▸ **Logic Defaults**: There are a few Key Commands that cannot be re-assigned (for example, *cmd+C*, *cmd+V*, etc.). Those commands are grayed out ➋.

▸ **Priority** ▣ : You can assign the same key combination to multiple Key Commands as long as they have different "Priorities" in Logic. For example, using a key for a command that is only used in the Score Editor and a command that is only used when the Step Input Keyboard is open. Move the mouse over it to read the Tooltip ➌ for its other assignment.

▸ **Key Focus**: Selecting a text entry field in Logic will move the key focus to that field. Now, typing the key "R" will not start recording. Opening the Musical Keyboard will shift the Key Focus only for the keys needed for playing the notes. The key "A" will not switch Automation but the key "R" still starts recording, because it is not used in the Musical Typing Window.

▸ **Conflict** ⓘ : If you have two Key Commands assigned to the same key combination in the same Group, then they will be marked with an exclamation point and a Dialog Window opens that lets you resolve the conflict. ⓘ Rewind

▸ **In Use**: If you try to assign a key combination that is already used with another Key Command, then you can get two different Dialog windows:

  • **Either - Or ➍**: If this key combination can only be used for one of the Key Commands, then you have the option to *Replace* it, using the new assignment.

  • **Both ➎**: In that case, you could use both assignments because the Key Commands operate on different Priority levels.

▸ **Key Command Only**: If the name of the Key Command starts with a dot, then this is a command that is only available as a Key Command. •Show Tool Menu

## 🟣 Assign Key

Assigning a key combination to a Key Command is straight forward:

- ☑ **Step 1**: Enable the *Learn* Button ❶
- ☑ **Step 2**: Select the Key Command from the List ❷
- ☑ **Step 3**: Whatever key (plus modifier key) you hit next will be assigned to the selected Key Command ❸
- ☑ … repeat Step 2 and 3 to make more key assignments
- ☑ **Step 4**: Disable the Learn Button ❶

**Key Commands Window**

However, there are two Learn Buttons. Here is the difference:

▶ **Learn by Key Label ❹**:

When you hit a key, Logic records only the label of that key, what's printed on it. For example, you can hit the number "1" key on the numeric keypad ❺ of an extended keyboard or the number "1" key above the tab key ❻. This has the advantage that you can use a Key Command programmed with the key "1" regardless if you have an extended keyboard or a standard keyboard.

▶ **Learn by Key Position ❼**:

When you use this learn option, Logic records the actual position of the key. That means, when you hit the number "1" key on the numeric keypad ❺, then that Key Command would not respond when you hit the number "1" key above the tab key ❻. This has the advantage that you have more programmable keys available on an extended keyboard, but the Key Commands for the numeric keypad would not work on a Laptop keyboard or any Standard Keyboard. Those keys programmed with the "Learn by Key Position" option have the additional keypad symbol ▦ .

### *There are a few things to be aware of:*

- Although the icon ▦ next to a Key Combination looks like a numeric keypad, it does not mean that this Command was assigned to a key on the numeric keypad. It only indicates that the key was programmed with the "Learn by Key Position" button ❼.

- In this screenshot ❽ I assigned one Command to the key "1" on the numeric keypad ❺ and one Command to the key "1" above the tab key ❻. Both were assigned with the "Learn by Key Position", so both have the special icon ▦ without knowing which Command is assigned to what key. One will work on the Laptop keyboard, the other one will not.

- Please note that some of the keys on the right of the extended keyboard have equivalent keys on the standard keyboard (red) while other keys (blue) are unique to the extended keyboard.

**Extended Keyboard**

When using the "Learn by Key Position", then the Key Commands using any keys that are unique to the extended keyboard (blue), or any of the red-marked keys will not be available in Logic when on a Standard Keyboard (laptop).

For keyboards without numeric keypad: **home** = *fn* + ←, **end** = *fn* + →, **page up** = *fn* + ↑, **page down** = *fn* + ↓

### Modify Keys

Key assignments cannot be modified. You have to delete them or just overwrite them with a new assignment. The Key and Modifier areas are read-only to display the Key Combination of the selected Command ❶.

### Delete Key

There are two ways to delete a Key assignment:

- Select the Key Command and click on the Delete Button ❷
- Select the Key Command, enabled "*Learn by Key Label*" ❸ or "Learn by Key Position" and hit on your keyboard the delete key ⌫. Remember, this key can't be assigned to any command.

## ➡ *Controller Assignment*

Instead of a key on your computer keyboard, you can use any message sent from your external Control Surface to trigger a Key Command.

- ▶ Program the Assignment:
  - ☑ Select the Key Command ❹
  - ☑ Click on the "Learn New Assignment" button ❺
  - ☑ Click a button on your Control Surface and the assignment is done.
- ▶ The Assignment area ❻ displays the incoming message that will now also trigger the Key Command.
- ▶ The area displays one line per Assignment with details about the message.
- ▶ The Assignment column ❼ in the Key Command List only displays how many Controller Assignments exist for the Key Command.
- ▶ *Double-clicking* on a line will open the Controller Assignments Window ❽ displaying that command.
- ▶ If you are in the Controller Assignments Window displaying a Key Command Assignment, you can *click* on the "*Show*" button ❾ to open the Key Commands Window displaying this assignment ❻.
- ▶ Delete an Assignment by selecting the line and hit the "Delete Assignment" button, or delete it from the Controller Assignments Window.

| **Key Commands Window** | **Controller Assignments Window** |
|---|---|

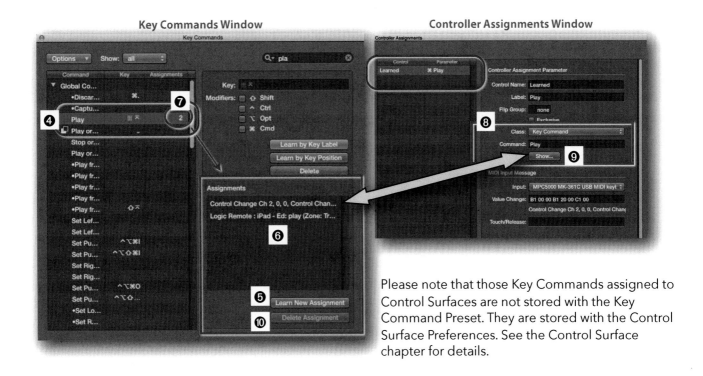

Please note that those Key Commands assigned to Control Surfaces are not stored with the Key Command Preset. They are stored with the Control Surface Preferences. See the Control Surface chapter for details.

# Presets

GEM KeyCom.logikcs

The Key assignments in the Key Command Window can be saved as a Key Command Preset file. You can access the available Presets directly from two locations:

- Main Menu *Logic Pro X* ➤ *Key Commands* ➤ *Presets* ➤ ❶
- Key Commands Window *Options* ➤ *Presets* ➤ ❷
- Use the command *Options* ➤ *Import Key Commands...* ❸

- The menu lists the six System Presets ❹ on top based on the available localization for Logic.
- Select a different Preset to load it. This will overwrite any changes you made without any warning. The Preset menu changes from a checkmark to a hyphen ❺ to indicate that you made changes to the currently loaded Preset.
- The command "*Initialize all Key Commands*" ❻ will reload the "US" Preset.

**Main Menu**

## ⚫ Custom Preset

- To save your custom Preset, use the command from the local menu *Options* ➤ *Presets* ➤ *Export Key Commands...*
- The default location will be *~/Music/Audio Music Apps/ Key Commands/*
- Those Preset files with the extension .logikcs can be freely exchanged between computers. If you have to work on a different Logic machine, just bring that file with you and import it, so you have all your custom Key Commands available.
- To import your custom Preset (and overwriting any existing Key Command assignments, use the command from the local menu *Options* ➤ *Presets* ➤ *Import Key Commands...* ❸ and navigate to the file in the Open Dialog.
- Any Presets located in the *~/Music/Audio Music Apps/ Key Commands/* will be listed in the Presets menu below the System Presets ❼.
- Use the command *Copy Key Commands to Clipboard* and then paste it into a text document or spreadsheet to "study and memorize" your Key Commands. The Show button ❽ (*all*, *used*, *unused*), plus any search criteria applies to what is copied to the clipboard.
- Of course, any assigned Key Command will be displayed in Logic's menus next to the item ❾, which is a great way to keep you reminded.

**Key Command Window**

## ➡ *External Control*

**Logic Remote (iPad)**

You can use many Control Surfaces to trigger Key Commands, some of them, like Avid's Artist Series, with built in support for the Key Commands. Also, using automation and macro utility apps like *QuicKeys* or *Keyboard Maestro* allows you to build highly customized sequences of Key Commands.

Best of all, the Logic Remote app. This is a free app that lets you use your iPad as a Touch Pad, which lets you freely customize Logic's Key Commands. Check out my manual "**Logic Remote - How it Works**" for details.

## Move / Nudge

Moving or nudging objects (Region or Events) in your Project is not really considered advanced editing, but it is so essential that I want to go over it. Speeding up those tasks will tremendously increase your workflow and editing skills.

As I mentioned in the Workflow chapter, you have to first review what commands and actions are available in Logic and then pick the ones that you could use the most.

When it comes to moving objects, you have to ask yourself two fundamental questions:
-  **Moving What?**
-  **Moving How?**

## Moving What?

###  Move the Object

This action moves the entire object without changing its length. Although this seems to be an easy "no brainer" task, there are a few important things you always have to keep in mind:

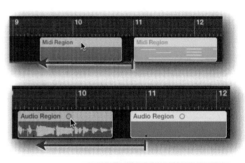

- When moving an object along the Timeline, you assign a new "start address" for that object, telling Logic where along the Timeline it should start playing back the Region or Event.

- This start address is linked to the grid of the Musical Time (bar, beat) per default.

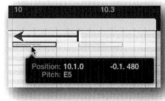

- The finest time resolution an object can be placed on is 1 Tick. This is the equivalent of 0.5ms at a Tempo of 120bmp.

- Enabling "SMPTE Lock" for any object (Region, Event, Control Points) will assign the start address to the grid of the Absolute Time. This has some major implications that I discuss in the *Tempo & Time* chapter.

- The start address is referenced to the left border of the object.

- The start address of an Audio Region, however, is referenced to its "*Anchor*." That Anchor position is also at the left border of an Audio Region by default, but can be moved anywhere along the Audio Region. When moving Audio Regions, any sync, snap, or quantize command applies to that Anchor position.

- Most rules for moving objects also apply to copying objects.

###  Move the Object Borders

This action moves the left or the right border of an object, which is technically a resize command.

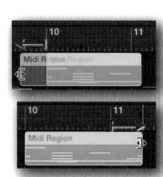

- Moving the right border only changes its length.
- Moving the left border changes its length, but also the start position of the object without changing its relative position on the Timeline.
- While MIDI Regions (or MIDI Events) can be freely resized, Audio Regions are limited by the length of the Audio File it is referenced to.

# Moving How?

You can move an object or its borders with different procedures. Being a true editing ninja means that you are familiar with all of them and quickly choose the one that is the fastest one, the more precise one, or the most efficient one. Some of the commands are available in the Main Menu or the Local Menu under *Edit* ➤ *Move*, or in their Shortcut Menu.

## ➡ Drag It

This is the most intuitive method. You use the Pointer Tool to drag the object. The Pointer Tool automatically changes to the Resize Tool 🔲 🔲 when you move it over the left or right border of the object.

## ➡ Enter Numerically

You can also enter position values numerically if you know exactly the bar and beat or the timecode address. There are two windows where you can do that:

### 🔘 Event List

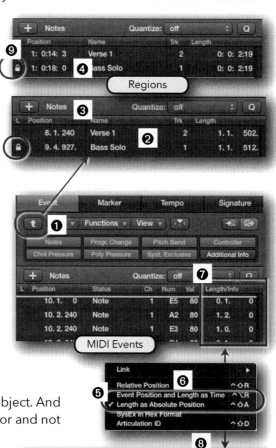

The Event List shows every object as a single entry with all its parameters. You just *double-click* a number, enter a new value and hit return. But first, you have to know what numbers you are looking at before changing them.

- ▸ **Display Level**: By default, the Link Mode of the Event List is set to "Content Link" (*Local Menu View* ➤ *Link* ➤ *Content*). That means, selecting a MIDI Region in the Tracks Window will display its content, the MIDI Events. Click on the Display Level Up Button 🔼 ❶ to display all the Regions ❷ in your Project. In this view (highest Display Level), you can enter a precise start position for a Region.

- ▸ **Time Display**: The numbers in the Event List are displayed in Musial Time ❸ or Absolute Time ❹ depending on your Project Type (*Project Settings* ➤ *General*). You can toggle the display in the Local Menu ❺ *View* ➤ *Event Position and Length as Time/Bar* (Key Command *ctr+opt+R*).

- ▸ **Position**: This column displays the start position of the object. And again, for Audio Regions, this is the position of the Anchor and not necessarily the left border of the Audio Region. For MIDI Events, you can enable from the Local Menu *View* ➤ *Relative Position* ❻ to display the position of MIDI Events in relation to the start of their MIDI Region.

- ▸ **Length / Off Position**: The Last column displays the Length ❼ of the object (duration). You can change that in the Local Menu *View* ➤ *Length as Absolute Position* to display the end position ❽.

- ▸ SMPTE Lock: If an object is SMPTE-Locked 🔒 ❾ (*cmd+Page up/down*), then you cannot change its position, but you can change its length.

- ▸ Please note that changing the value in the first column (Position) will move the object, changing the value in the last column (Length/Off Position) will resize the right border of the object. You cannot resize the left border of an object in the Event List.

## 💀 Event Float

Although you might want to use the option to enter positions numerically, it requires that you have the Event List open, either as a window pane in the Main Window or as a standalone window. An alternative, that I highly recommend, is the Event Float. It is a little Floating Window that acts like a "Single Line Event List".

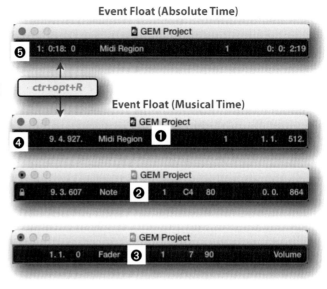

Toggle it from the Main Menu **Window ➤ Show/Hide Event Float**, or use the Key Command (*Show/Hide Event Float*) **opt+E**. Here is how it works:

▶ The Event Float displays the currently selected (last selected) object. This can be a Region ❶, a MIDI Event ❷, and even the Control Point ❸ of an Automation Curve (a Fader Event).

▶ The displayed parameters for an object are displayed the same way as in the Event List.

▶ You can also toggle the time display between Musical Time ❹ and Absolute Time ❺ with the Key Command **ctr+opt+R**. The format for both follows the settings in the **Preferences ➤ Display ➤ General ➤ Displays**.

## ➡ *Slide it*

In the Event List or the Event Float you can also drag the numbers up/down to change their value. This lets you slide an object to a new position. Please keep in mind that you can use this method to move objects very precisely. Like with any other numbers, you can slide the individual number values. For example, slide the bar value, the beat value, or the Tick value. Having the Event Float open (part of your Screenset), you always have a quick access to adjust objects on the timeline.

## ➡ *Move to Reference Point*

This method of moving an object to a reference point is extremely powerful and fast, especially when combined with all the options where to position the Playhead, as I pointed out in the Workflow chapter.

### 💀 Move to Playhead

You use the Playhead as a "proxy tool" because you can place it to so many positions, for example, the beginning, end, beginning selecting, Markers, Locators, etc. (make sure to memorize those Key Commands). Now, when you want to place an object ❻ to one of those positions, you position the Playhead there first and then use one command to place the object to the Playhead ❼. A quick Two step process.

You can use the Key Command (*Move Region/Event to Playhead Position*) ; (the semicolon) or click the Move to Playhead Button in the Main Window's Toolbar.

You can also move the left border ❽ and right border ❾ of an object to the Playhead Position with the Key Command (*Set Region/Event/Marquee Start to Playhead Position*) **cmd+[** or **cmd+]** for the end position.

### 💀 Move to left/right Object

Another reference you can move an object to is the end of the previous object or the beginning of the next object. This procedure is called "Shuffle".

The command ("Shuffle Left" or "Shuffle Right") is available from the **Shortcut Menu ➤ Move** when you **ctr+click** on an object, as Key Command **opt+[** and **opt+]**, and as the Shuffle Button in the Main Window's Toolbar (looks like a magnet, one pulling to the left and one to the right).

## ➡ *Move by Increments (Nudge)*

This type of command ("Nudge") lets you move an object by a specific increment. Here is how it is implemented in Logic:

- ▸ You can nudge the Position and the Length of an object
- ▸ You can nudge it to the left or to the right
- ▸ You can use dedicated commands to nudge by any of the 26 value
- ▸ You can use a separate "Nudge Value" command, a variable, that you can set to one of the 26 nudge values

How to use Nudge in your Workflow:

### 💀 Key Commands

There is an easier way than assigning all of the 75 "Nudge" Key Commands and memorize them.

☑ You use only four Key Commands. Two for nudging the Position and two for nudging the Length. These commands use the variable "Nudge Value"

- • Nudge Position Left: *opt+ArrowLeft*
- • Nudge Position Right: *opt+ArrowRight*
- • Nudge Length Left: *sh+opt+ArrowLeft*
- • Nudge Length Right: *sh+opt+ArrowRight*

☑ You use the individual "Nudge Value to …" Key Command to set the Nudge Value to whatever value you need at a time. You can see below ❶ that the default Key Commands are really easy to remember, even if you choose only a few values that you use regularly.

Nudge Value to … ❶

| | Nudge Value | Key Command |
|---|---|---|
| **Musical Time** | Bar (Measure) | *ctr+opt+M* |
| | Beat | *ctr+opt+B* |
| | Division | *ctr+opt+D* |
| | Tick | *ctr+opt+T* |
| | 1/2 … 1/64 Notes | |
| **Absolute Time (SMPTE)** | 5Frames | |
| | Frame | *ctr+opt+F* |
| | 1/2 Frame | *ctr+opt+H* |
| | Bit (1/80frame) | |
| **Absolute Time (Clock)** | 10ms | *ctr+opt+0* |
| | 1ms | *ctr+opt+1* |
| | Sample | *ctr+opt+S* |

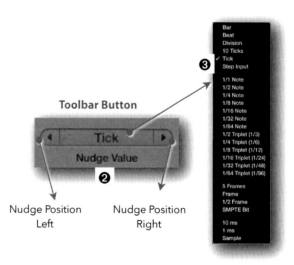

**Toolbar Button**

❸

❷

Nudge Position Left          Nudge Position Right

### 💀 Toolbar Button

If you have the Toolbar visible in Logic's Main Window (*View ➤ Show/Hide Toolbar cmd+opt+ctr+T*), then you can use the Nudge Value Button ❷. The left and right arrow nudges the position of the selected object left or right and clicking on the center button ❸ opens a popup menu that lets you set the value to any of the 26 time values.

### 💀 Menu Commands

These basic Nudge commands are also available in the Main Menu, Local Menu, or in their Shortcut menu under *Edit ➤ Move*

Edit Menu ❹

## Snap Mode

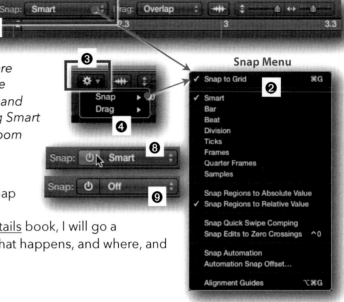

Here is an often used (and inaccurate) explanation of Snap Mode: "*Select a snap grid from the Snap Menu and the object you are moving or resizing snaps to that grid. Hold down the control key to disable snap and hold down the shift and control key to get an even finer resolution. Selecting Smart Snap will adapt the snap grid depending on your zoom level*".

Although these statements are partially true, the Snap Mode is a little bit more complex the way it is implemented in Logic. Because this is my Logic <u>Details</u> book, I will go a little more into those details so you know exactly what happens, and where, and when, when using Snap Mode.

### ➡ *Snap Menu*

You can see the dedicated Snap Menu Button in the Menu Bar of the Tracks Window ❶ and the Piano Roll Editor to open the Snap Menu ❷. This menu changes to the Action Button ❸ 🔧▾ when the window is not wide enough to display all the menus. *Click* on it to open a menu with the Snap and Drag submenus ❹. Moving the Cursor Tool over the Snap Button will reveal a Power Button ❽ that lets you toggle Snap on and off. This is the same function as toggling the "*Snap to Grid*" command in the menu or the Key Command *cmd +G*. The Power Off Button 🔌 stays visible if Snap is disabled ❾.

However, before you make any selections, read on to understand what these items really mean or not mean.

### ➡ *Snap Mode Implementation*

For a better understanding on how the Snap Mode works, I will answer the following eight questions:

### 🔘 1 - What is "Snap to Grid"?

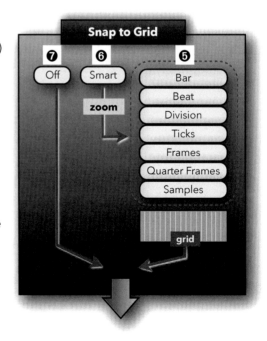

Snap to Grid defines a vertical time grid (similar to a Quantize Grid) that is used to align (snap) objects to that grid when you move them manually on the Timeline. There are three main settings that determine the main behavior of the Snap to Grid:

- **Specific Grid ❺**: Similar to the quantize feature, Logic provides various time units to choose from (Bar, Beat, Ticks, Frames, etc.). Selecting one of those units defines the grid that is used to snap (align) an object to.
- **Smart Grid ❻**: This is a special Snap Mode that sets the grid dynamically. The more you zoom in, the finer the grid will be (i.e. Frame, Ticks), and the more you zoom out, the higher the time grid units will be (i.e. bar, beat).
- **No Grid ❼**: When Snap to Grid is off, no grid will be applied. You can move the objects horizontally without restrictions.

**2 - Where is Snap Mode available?**

The Snap feature is only available in Logic's time-based windows. These are the windows with a Timeline, where Logic assigns objects (Regions, Events, Control Points) a time reference along the horizontal time axis, based on their placement on the vertical time grid in the workspace.

There is no Snap Mode available in the various List Editors and the Drummer Editor.

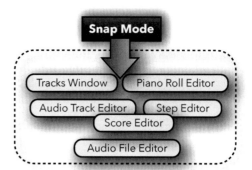

 **3 - What Objects are affected by the Snap Mode?**

There are two types of objects, the ones that have only a single address (i.e. a Control Point) and the other ones that have a duration, and therefore, have two addresses (beginning and end).

- **Single Address ❶**: Start Project Marker, End Project Marker, Tempo Control Points, Automation Control Points, Playhead
- **Beginning-End Address ❷**: Regions, Note Events, Cycle, Marquee, Markers

 **4 - What Actions are affected by the Snap Mode?**

The actions that are affected by the Snap Mode are the ones that you perform manually by clicking or click-dragging with any of the Cursor Tools.

- **Move an Object** 🖐: This is the basic action where you grab an object and move it to a new position without affecting its duration (if it is an object with a duration like a Region or a Note Event).
- **Resize an Object** ◀❚ ❚▶ : The resize action is technically also a moving action. You move the individual borders of an object, the beginning or the end. Of course, this applies only to objects that have a duration.
- **Create an Object** ✏ : This action is often overlooked in the context of the Snap Mode. When creating a new object (Region, Event, Control Point) by clicking on the Workspace with the Pencil Tool, the position of that object can be affected by the currently selected Snap to Grid setting.

 **5 - How to select the Snap Mode?**

There is no single switch that turns Snap Mode on or off in Logic. There are four areas that can have different Snap Modes:

- **Tracks Window ❸**: The Snap Mode for all objects in the Tracks Window (with the exception of the Playhead) is configured in its own Snap Menu.
- **Piano Roll Editor ❹**: The Snap Mode for all objects in the Piano Roll Editor (with the exception of the Playhead) is configured in its own Snap Menu, which is independent from the Snap Menu of the Tracks Window.
- **Other Windows**: The objects in every other window don't have a Snap Menu. They are set to Snap Mode "Smart" by default.
- **Playhead**: The Playhead is always in Snap Mode "Smart", regardless which window and what Snap Mode is set in that window.

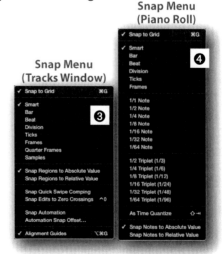

### 🕹 6 - What about Modifier Keys?

You can change/overwrite the current Snap Mode by holding down modifier keys when moving an object or the boundaries of an object. Please note that there is a difference between a Specific Snap Mode (Bar, Beat, etc.) or the Smart Snap Mode regarding the use of the modifier keys:

- *Drag* 🖱: The objects will align to the selected (or default) snap grid when dragging the objects horizontally.
  - *Specific Mode*: The movement snaps to whatever grid is selected
  - *Smart Mode*: The snap grid changes automatically, depending on the zoom level. The more you are zoomed-in, the finer (smaller) the grid value, the more you zoomed out, the higher the grid values.

- *Ctr+drag* [^] 🖱: Holding down the control key while dragging an object changes the Snap Mode:
  - *Specific Mode*: If you have selected a specific Snap value (other than Smart), then the snap grid changes to the Division value when holding down the ctr key while dragging. If the selected unit is already set to Division, then this modifier key changes the grid to "40 Ticks".
  Please note that the control key doesn't switch to a finer grid resolution, it switches to the Division grid. If you have your Snap value set to a smaller grid than Divisions (Tick, Frames, etc.), then the control key will actually increase the grid value.
  - *Smart Mode*: When Smart is selected, then the ctr+drag movement does not snap to a grid, it turns Snap temporarily off. Please note, that you have to move the object a little before holding down the control key, to avoid that the Shortcut Menu pops up.

- *Sh+ctr+drag* [⇧] [^] 🖱: Holding down the shift and control key while dragging an object changes the Snap Mode only in the Tracks Window and Piano Roll Editor.
  - *Specific Mode*: The snap grid changes to Ticks value. In addition, there is another important "side effect", the **trackpad speed**. The actual distance you move the mouse will now result in a much smaller distance the object is actually moved on the screen. Great for precise positioning.
  - *Smart Mode*: Same effect as *ctr+drag*.

### 🕹 8 - Are there additional settings?

Yes, the Snap Menu ❶ has a few additional settings. They are also available as Key Commands.

- **Automation**: Snap Mode can be enabled separately for Automation Control Points. There is even an additional Preferences Settings that lets you set a Snap Offset in the *Preferences ➤ Automation ➤ Snap Offset* ❷. This places the Control Points a few Ticks before or after the actual grid lines.
- **Quick Swipe Mode**: Snap Mode can also be enabled/disabled separately for Quick Swipe Comping.
- **Zero Crossing**: *Snap Edits to Zero Crossing* is for Audio Regions to avoid clicks by moving an edit to the position where the amplitude of an audio waveform crosses the zero line.

Snap Menu

Preferences ➤ Automation

### 🕹 One more thing ... Alignment Guides

*Alignment Guides* ❸ is an additional Snap feature that is independent from *Snap to Grid*. It can be enabled even if Snap to Grid is off.

When moving a Region while this mode is enabled, a yellow vertical Alignment Guide ❹ will appear across the Workspace at the beginning ❺ and end ❻ of any Region on another Track when you are close to that position. The Region you are moving will snap to that yellow Alignment Guide regardless what the current Snap Grid is.

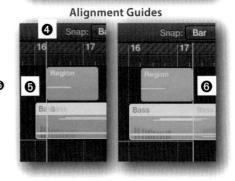

Alignment Guides

## ➡ Enable Snap Mode

There are different steps and actions how to turn Snap on/off:

### 🔮 Tracks Window

The Tracks Window has its own Snap Menu that only affects the settings on that window (Playhead is not affected and is always in Smart Snap Mode).

▸ **Toggle** Snap to Grid on/off with the following commands. It remembers the Snap Mode when it was last turned off:

- Select *Snap to Grid* from the Snap popup menu ❶
- Use the Key Command (*Snap to Grid on/off*) ***cmd+G***

▸ **Select/Switch** to a specific Snap Mode:

- Select the unit (Bar, Bear, Division, etc.) from the popup menu ❷.
- Every Snap Mode has a dedicated Key Command (*unassigned*).

Snap Menu
(Tracks Window)

#### A few things to be aware of:

- Disabling Snap Mode will also disable Snap Mode for all the additional features: Automation, Zero Crossing, Quick Swipe. They are grayed out ❹ but still keeping their check mark.
- If Snap Mode is disabled, then the Power Off Button 🔘 is visible ❸.
- The Alignment Guide ❺ feature is not affected by the status of the "*Snap to Grid*". It is independent.

### 🔮 Piano Roll Window

The Piano Roll Editor has its own Snap Menu that works independently from the Snap Menu in the Tracks Window.

#### A few things to be aware of:

- The functionality for enabling and disabling Snap Mode is the same. The Key Commands ***cmd+G*** will be aware that the Piano Roll Window has key focus to direct the commands to it.
- The menu doesn't include the items "Quarter Frames" and "Samples", but lists 13 musical values ❻ and the "As Time Quantize" ❾ command, which uses the quantize value from the Piano Roll Local Inspector.
- If Snap Mode is disabled, then the Power Off Button 🔘 is visible ❼.
- The settings "Snap Regions to Absolute/Relative Value", are listed in the menu ❽, but it seems they are controlled by the Snap Menu from the Tracks Window.

Snap Menu
(Piano Roll)

### 🔮 All other Windows

As I already mentioned, Snap Mode (Smart) is always enabled for the Playhead and the following windows that don't have a Snap Menu: Score Editor, Step Editor, Audio Track Editor.

## ➡ *Absolute - Relative*

There are two ways in which the grid value is applied. Choose between those two modes in the Snap Menu that only affect Regions, Note Events, and Markers (despite the command "Snap <u>Region</u> to..."):

**Absolute Value**: Wherever you move your object, it will snap to the closest grid. In the example below, I move Region ❶ to the right, so it is now at a position ❷ close to bar 5. The Absolute Snap Mode will move the Region ❸ onto bar 5.

**Relative Value**: Now I move Region ❶ to the same position ❷. In Relative Snap Mode, however, the Grid is applied to the "distance". The Region ❹ snaps to an underlying grid (dotted blue line) that starts relative to the original position of the moved Region.

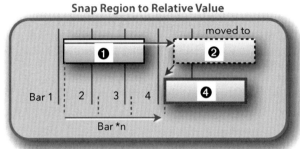

## ➡ *Summary*

Here is a summary of the Snap implementation in Logic:

☑ **Tracks Window** and **Piano Roll Editor**:
  - You can set the Snap Mode individually in their Snap Menu
  - *Ctr+drag* will snap to a Division grid
  - *Sh+ctr+drag* will snap to a Tick grid
  - *Sh+ctr+drag* will also change the tracking speed of your cursor when moving a Regions or Region border
  - Automation, Quick Swipe Mode, and Zero Crossing can be enabled individually
  - You can snap Regions and Events to the absolute grid or to their relative grid distance

☑ **Score Editor, Step Editor** and **Audio Track Editor**
  - The Snap Mode is automatically set to Smart
  - *Ctr+drag* will move an object with Snap Mode off

☑ **Audio File Editor**
  - No Snap Mode, only the optional "Snap to Zero Crossing"

☑ **Playhead**
  - The Snap Mode is automatically set to Smart
  - *Ctr+drag* will move the Playhead with Snap Mode off

☑ **Automation Control Points**
  - Control Points don't allow any Snap modifier key

☑ **Alignment Guides**
  - This is a separate Snap feature independent from the *Snap To Grid* functionality

# Drag

The Drag Menu Button is only available in the Tracks Window. If the window is too narrow, then the Action Button ⚙▾ will contain the Drag menu.

All five Drag Modes have their own Key Command.

**Tracks Window**

**Drag Menu**

✓ Overlap
No Overlap
X-Fade
Shuffle R
Shuffle L

▸ **Overlap**: This mode behaves differently for MIDI, Audio, and Drummer Regions.
- MIDI: When you drag one Region partially over another Region, then both Regions are preserved, they just overlap. The MIDI Events of both overlapping MIDI Regions are playing. This is a situation that should be avoided. Either move the Regions to different Tracks (assigned to the same Channel Strip), or join the Regions (*cmd+J*).
- Audio Region: On Audio Tracks, only one Audio Region can play at a time. If two Audio Regions are overlapping, then the right most Region has priority regardless of which Region is visible on top of the other one.
- Drummer Region: The moving Region will shorten the Region you are moving into, from the left or from the right.

▸ **No Overlap**: The moving Region will shorten the Region you are moving into, from the left or from the right. Be careful when moving all the way and completely covering an existing Region.
- MIDI Region: The "fully covered" Region will be deleted.
- Audio Region: The fully covered Audio Region will also be deleted, but it is still available in the Project Browser.
- Drummer Region: The "fully covered" Region will be deleted.

▸ **X-Fade**: The overlapping area of two Audio Regions are crossfaded.
- MIDI Region: Overlapping MIDI Regions default to Overlap Mode.
- Audio Region: Overlapping Audio Regions will crossfade.
- Drummer Region: Overlapping Drummer Regions defaults to No Overlap Mode.

▸ **Shuffle L**: Regions to the left of the moving Region stay fixed:
- Moving: Dragging a Region towards any adjacent Region will snap it to the Region you are moving towards regardless if left or right. Other Regions stay untouched.
- Deleting: Deleting a Region will move all the Regions on its right towards the left by the length of the deleted Region.
- Resize: Resizing the right border of a Region will move all the Regions on its right by the same amount. Resizing the left border of a Region will snap back to its position and instead move all the Regions on its right by the amount you moved the left border.

▸ **Shuffle R**: Regions to the right of the moving Region stay fixed:
- Moving: Dragging a Region towards any adjacent Region will snap it to the Region you are moving towards regardless if left or right. Other Regions stay untouched.
- Deleting: Deleting a Region will move all the Regions on its left towards the right by the length of the deleted Region.
- Resize: Resizing the left border of a Region will move all Regions on its left by the same amount. Resizing the right border of a Region will snap back to its position, instead moving all the Regions on its left by the amount you moved the left border.

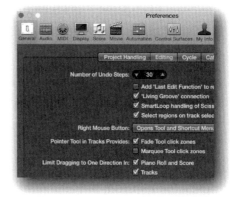

Don't forget the settings in the *Preferences* ➤ *General* ➤ *Limit Dragging to One Direction* ➤ Piano Roll and Score, Tracks.

When editing your Project, you usually have three options, three different actions to perform an edit:

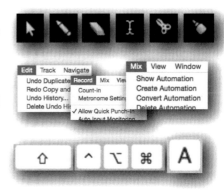

- ▶ **Cursor Tool**: Use a mouse action by clicking or dragging directly on the object with a specific cursor tool in a specific way with optional modifier keys.
- ▶ **Menu Command**: Select a command from the Main Menu or one of the Local Menus and apply that command to the selected object(s).
- ▶ **Key Command**: Type a key combination to apply a specific command to the selected object(s).

## Overview

In this section, we will look at the various Menu Commands, plus their equivalent Key Commands if available. The problem is, there are soooo many commands, it could be overwhelming and impossible to remember them all. So you have to come up with a strategy.

Here are a few tips:

☑ Take your time and go through the Edit Menu (in the various windows) and look through all the submenus. Just browse through to make yourself familiar with what is available, even if the commands don't make sense (yet).

☑ Recognize the different types of edits, the different categories. These are all the commands with an arrow ➤ (Split, Join, Move, etc.) that indicates a submenu with all the commands related to that type of edit.

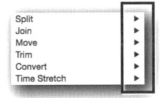

☑ Instead of trying to memorize as many commands as possible, prioritize the commands. Maybe it's time to start a spreadsheet, your personal cheat sheet, with a list of only the Key Commands you are using in your personal workflow. When you explore the Edit Menu, add only the Key Commands based on the following priority.

- Priority 1: These are all the Commands you already know and know how to use. For example, copy, paste, select all, split, etc. Add them to your list.

- Priority 2: These are all the commands you don't use yet, but they might be useful for the type of work you are doing. Add them to your list and try to use them more often so you memorize them.

- Priority 3: These are all the commands that are not relevant for your type of work, or too specific. It is also very important to ignore stuff, so you can concentrate on the important stuff.

☑ Revisit the Edit Menu once in a while to see if you might add a command to your personal list because your workflow has changed, or you are getting better and ready for more advanced (efficient) editing techniques.

☑ The menus always list their Key Commands next to a command. Use this as a little reminder technique for memorizing the Key Commands every time you open a menu.

# ➡ *Main Edit Menu - dynamic*

A few things you have to be aware of before we start exploring the various commands:

## 💀 Dynamic Menus

Please note that the Main Edit Menu is highly dynamic:
The content of the Main Edit Menu changes, depending upon what window or window pane has key focus or what object is selected (MIDI Region, Audio Region, etc.).

## 💀 Multiple Locations same Command

▶ **Main Menu ❶ - Local Menu ❷**

If the current window (the one with the key focus) has a Local Edit Menu, then the Main Edit Window will display that same content as that Local Edit Menu.

▶ **Shortcut Menu ❸**

*Ctr+clicking* on an object (Event, Region) will open its Shortcut Menu. Those Shortcut Menus are also highly dynamic, only displaying the commands relevant for the object or area you are clicking on. The Shortcut Menu, when clicking on a Region, also lists the most recent commands ❹ you used. In case you want to reuse them again, there are right there on top.

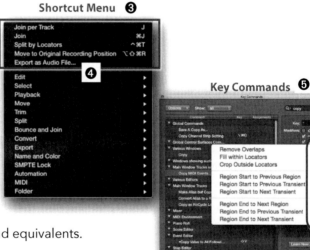

▶ **Key Commands ❺**

Most Edit Commands have Key Command equivalents.

▶ **Toolbar Buttons ❻**

The Toolbar that can be displayed on top of Logic's Main Window by clicking on the Toolbar Button 🔲 in the Control Bar, has a couple of dedicated buttons for some of the often used Edit commands.

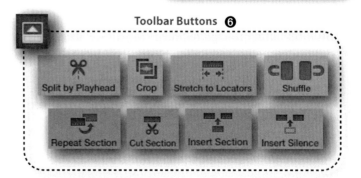

# Regions and Events

I discuss the commands in the following groups: Commands that can be used for Regions and Events, commands used only for Regions or Events, and some special commands for Audio Files.

Here are the commands that apply to Regions and Events.

## ➡ *Select*

When you use a Cursor Tool, you just click on the object you want to edit. With a Menu Command or Key Command, however, you have to select the object(s) first, to let Logic know to which object(s) you want to apply the command to. This sounds trivial, but a Select command is as important as the actual command you want to apply. Having a command applied to the wrong objects is definitely something you want to avoid, especially if you don't notice it right away.

> ### Select - The most important Command

Of course, you can select Regions and Events with the Cursor Tool by clicking on them or lasso around. The Select commands give you the option to select objects by specific conditions.

Here are two screenshots that show the Select submenu for windows that display Regions or MIDI Events. Please note that there are other windows with different purposes that have other select options (Environment Window, Project Audio, Audio File Editor:

▸ **Regions ❶**: This menu is displayed when you have a window selected that shows Region: Tracks Window or the Audio Track Window.

▸ **Event ❷**: This menu is displayed when you have a window selected that shows MIDI Events: Piano Roll Editor, Score, Step Editor, Event List.

Most of the commands are the same for Regions and Events, only the section that I marked, are select commands that are specific for Regions ❸ and Events ❹.

| ❶ Regions | |
|---|---|
| All | ❺ ⌘A |
| All Following | ⇧F |
| All Following of Same Track | ^⇧F |
| All Inside Locators | ⇧L |
| Muted Regions | ⇧M |
| Overlapped Regions | ⇧O |
| Equal Colored Regions | ⇧C |
| Empty Regions | |
| Similar Regions | ❸ |
| Equal Regions | |
| Next Region | ❼ → |
| Previous Region | ← |
| Deselect All | ❻ ⌥⇧D |
| Deselect Global Tracks | |
| Deselect Outside Locators | |
| Invert Selection | ⇧I |

| ❷ Events | |
|---|---|
| All | ❺ ⌘A |
| All Following | ⇧F |
| All Following of Same Pitch | ^⇧F |
| All Inside Locators | ⇧L |
| Muted Events | ⇧M |
| Overlapped Events | ⇧O |
| Equal Colored Events | ⇧C |
| Similar Events | ⇧S |
| Equal Events ❹ | ⇧E |
| Same MIDI Channel | ⇧H |
| Same Subposition | ⇧P |
| Same Articulation ID | ⇧D |
| Highest Notes | ⇧↑ |
| Lowest Notes | ⇧↓ |
| Next Event | ❼ → |
| Previous Event | ← |
| Deselect All | ❻ ⌥⇧D |
| Deselect Outside Locators | |
| Invert Selection | ⇧I |

Here are just four Select commands and their Key Commands that you should definitely have memorized:

- ☑ **Select All** *cmd+A* ❺
- ☑ **Deselect All** *sh+opt+D* ❻
- ☑ **Next Region/Event** ❼ *ArrowRight* (*sh+ArrowRight* will add/remove the next Region/Event to the selection)
- ☑ **Previous Region/Event** *ArrowLeft* (*sh+ArrowRight* will add/remove the previous Region/Event to the selection)

Look through the other commands and see which one you are using (or could use) more often in your workflow. For example, *All Inside Locators sh+L* or *Overlapped Regions/Events sh+O*.

## ➡ *Move*

Let's start with the easiest command, Move.

I already spent a whole section earlier on this important command, especially how to use the Playhead as a reference to move objects to or use the Nudge commands to move objects by specific increments. The Move submenu lists some of those commands.

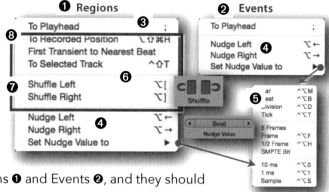

The following commands are available for both Regions ❶ and Events ❷, and they should definitely be on your favorites list.

- ☑ **To Playhead** *;* (semicolon) ❸
- ☑ **Nudge Left/Right** ❹ *opt+ArrowLeft* or *opt+ArrowRight*. The Nudge Value can be set in the *Set Nudge Value to* submenu ❺ or with their easy to remember Key Commands.

When the Tracks Window or the Audio Track Editor is selected, then you have a few more commands ❻ available. I want to point out two of those:

- ☑ **Shuffle Left/Right** ❼ *opt+[* and *opt+]*. This will move the beginning of the selected Region to the end of the previous Region on the left, or moves the end of the selected Region to the beginning of the next Region on the right. You can also use the Toolbar Button ◁▯▯▷ "*Shuffle*".
- ☑ **To Recorded Position** ❽ *sh+opt+cmd+R*. This is an important feature that, once you know about it, can be really helpful. It is called Timestamp. Here is a little more detail about it.

## 🎚 Timestamp

Audio File (viewed in Text Editor)

Tempo: 120.0    ± Marker 1 ❾    Timestamp: 158936400  .GWV

Every Audio File that you record in Logic or bounce out of Logic (as uncompressed audio file) will have metadata embedded in the Audio File in addition to the data of the actual audio signal. These metadata are Tempo information, Markers, and also a Timestamp ❾. The Timestamp contains the following information:

▸ **Audio File Recorded in Logic**: When you record an audio file in your Project, the time position (Absolute Time) where you started the recording will be stored as a Timestamp with the audio file.

- Using Musical Time (bar/beat) reference: When you move the Audio Regions around in your Project, you can always put them back at their original position where they were recorded using the "*To Recorded Position*" command. As long as you use the Audio Region in the original Project, or copy-paste them to another Project that is open (or drag them over), Logic seems to use the Musical Time (bar, beats) as the recorded position.

- Using Absolute Time (SMPTE) reference: When you copy the Audio File(s) out of the Project File to import it in a different Project, you could still use the "To Recorded Position" to place them all to their original position. This time it uses the Absolute Time (SMPTE) stored in the Timestamp as a reference.

▸ **Audio File Bounced in Logic**: When you bounce your mix, stems, or portions of your mix, the audio file will also store the Timestamp of the start time of the bounce. You can bring all those individual audio files into a new Logic Project, select the "To Recorded Position" command and all the files will move magically to their exact position. This is especially useful when working to picture with a common SMPTE timecode where you can exchange audio files for music, dialog, and SFX with any Project.

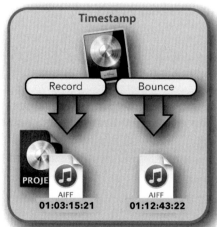

## ➡ *Split - Join - Trim*

The next three commands will change the size of a Region or Note Event:

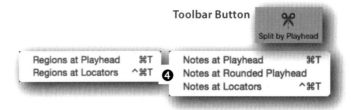

Toolbar Button

### 💀 Split

You can split a Region ❶ or a Note Event at the current Playhead Position (one cut ❷) or at the current Cycle Range (two cuts ❸). The Cycle doesn't have to be enabled for the action.

Of course, the Playhead or the left and right locator must cover the area of the Region or Event to have an effect.

☑ **Split Regions/Notes at Playhead** *cmd+T*: This command is also available as a "rounded" command, which moves the split point to the closest bar. The command is available as Key Command for Notes and Regions, even if it is not listed in the Menu Command for Regions ❹. You can also use the Toolbar Button ✂ "*Split by Playhead*".

☑ **Split Regions/Notes at Locators** *sh+cmd+T*:

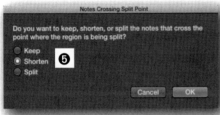

**Overlapping Notes**: If any cut falls over a long note in a Region, then you will get a Dialog Window ❺, asking what to do: *Keep* the length of the note, *Shorten* the note to the split point, or *Split* the note into two notes.

### 💀 Join

The Join command merges all selected objects.
Different types of objects have different rules you have to pay attention to:

☑ **Join Notes** ❻ *cmd+J*: When selecting multiple Notes in a Region, all the notes with the same pitch are joined together as a single long note. You can also use the Toolbar Button 🎨 *Join*. Be careful when there are unselected notes between two selected notes. This will create overlapping notes!

☑ **Join Regions** ❼ *cmd+J*: This will merge all selected Regions together into one Region. Be careful, if the selected Regions are on different Tracks, then all the Regions on all Tracks will be merged to one single Region on the first Track. You can also use the Toolbar Button 🎨 *Join*.

☑ **Join Regions per Track** *J*: This command merges all the selected Regions and if they are on separate Tracks, then they will only merge and stay on their own Track.

**Attention** **Audio Regions**: The Join command only works on Audio Regions if they have been split before (and even resized) without being moved. This makes sense if you remember that Audio Regions are just play instructions for their referenced audio files.

If the Audio Regions have been moved or they are referenced to different audio files and you try to use the Join command, then a Dialog Window pops up ❽. When you click *Create*, Logic will perform a "bounce in place" of the selected Audio Regions and puts the new Audio Region on the Track. The newly created Audio File is listed in the Project Browser ❾ with the word "merged" added to its name.

## 💀 Trim

Trim is just another word for resizing, and as we have seen in an earlier section, resizing means, moving the boundaries of an object. And again, you can resize Audio Objects only inside the boundaries of the audio file it is referenced to.

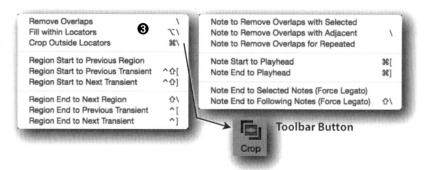

Trimming an object with a command instead of manually dragging its borders, has the advantage that you can move the borders precisely to the position of a reference point. Here are the available commands grouped by those reference points:

▸ Adjacent Regions

   ☑️ **Trim Region Start to Previous Region** *unassigned*: Extends the start position to the Region on the left ❶.

   ☑️ **Trim Region End to next Region** *sh+\\*: Extends the end position to the Region on the right ❷.

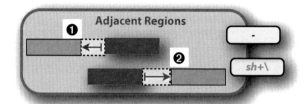

▸ Playhead

   ☑️ **Set Region/Event/Marquee Start to Playhead Position ❹** *cmd+[*: This is the most versatile command, because you can position the Playhead using so many commands. Strange that this command is not listed in the Edit Menu ❸. However, this is the same Key Command as moving Events or even the Marquee selection.

   ☑️ **Set Region/Event/Marquee End to Playhead Position ❺** *cmd+]*: Same procedure, now extending the Region/Event to the Playhead Position on the right.

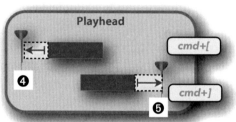

▸ Cycle

   ☑️ Extend ❻ **Fill within Locators** *opt+\\*: The "Fill" command will extend the Region borders to the borders of the Cycle Range (if they are positioned more to the left or right).

   ☑️ Shorten ❼ **Crop Outside Locators** *cmd+\\*: The "Crop" command shortens the Region borders to the borders of the Cycle Range. Be careful, any selected Region outside the Cycle Range will be deleted. You can also use the Toolbar Button 🗖 "*Crop*".

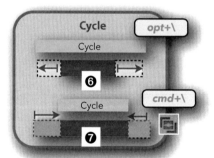

▸ Overlap

   ☑️ **Remove Overlaps** \\: If you have partially or fully overlapping Regions ❽, then this command shortens the right border of a Region to the position of the left border of the following (overlapping) Region. The following Region on the right always has priority.

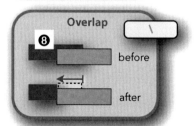

▸ Transients

   ☑️ **Start to Previous/Next Transient** *sh+ctr+[* or *sh+ctr+]* : This command only applies to Audio Regions. It uses transients ❾ in the audio signal (sudden changes in the amplitude) to trim the left border.

   ☑️ **End to Previous/Next Transient** *ctr+[* or *ctr+]* : This command trims the right border to the transients in the audio signal.

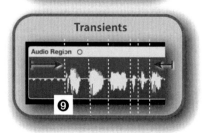

Some of the Trim commands also apply to Note Events, but there are a few additional commands that could be confusing if you don't know the meaning of "Selected", "Adjacent", Following", and "Repeated".

I will group the commands differently than they appear in the Edit Menu to better explain how they work:

Playhead

☑ **Note Start to Playhead** *cmd+[* : This is the same command used for Regions to adjust the left border ❶ of a Note Event to the Playhead.

☑ **Note End to Playhead** *cmd+]* : This is the same command used for Regions to adjust the right border ❷ of a Note Event to the Playhead.

Unselected Notes

☑ **Note End to <u>Following</u> Notes (Force Legato)** *sh+\* : The length of each selected Note will be lengthened (fix gap ❸) or shortened (fix overlap ❹) to end exactly at the beginning of the following note ❺.

☑ **Note to Remove Overlaps with <u>Adjacent</u>** \ : This command fixes only notes that overlap the following (adjacent) notes. Technically you could also use the "Note to Following Notes" command.

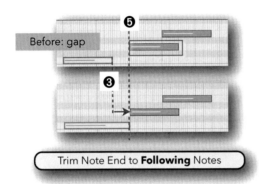

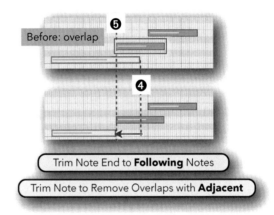

Selected Notes

☑ **Note End to <u>Selected</u> Notes (Force Legato)**: This command functions the same as the "Following" command with the difference that it only lengthens or shortens to the next selected note ❻, not necessarily the note right next it ❼.

☑ **Note to Remove Overlaps with <u>Selected</u>**: Same thing here, a selected note will only be shortened if it overlaps another selected note.

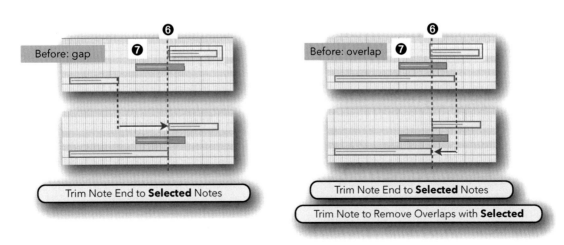

## Overlapping Notes - Same Pitch

☑️ **Note to Remove Overlaps with _Repeated_**: This is the situation where two overlapping notes have the same pitch (hence the term "repeating"). In this example, you can't see that the two notes at the bottom are overlapping. When you apply the command, the first note will be shortened ❶ so it ends at the beginning of the next note ❷ (of the same pitch).

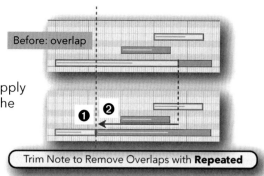

### _Attention Chords:_

This "Force Legato" trimming procedure works well with monophonic notes (one note after another). However, if you have two or more notes with the same start time ❸ (like a chord), then Logic doesn't know which note comes first. In that case, a Dialog Window ❹ pops up. _Delete_ will delete any note but the lowest note ❺ while the other two options extend all notes of the chord to the next note ❻.

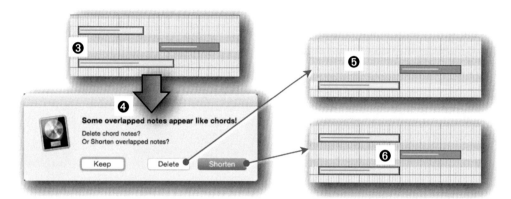

## ➡️ _Copy - Paste - Delete_

| Cut | ⌘X |
|---|---|
| Copy | ⌘C |
| Paste | ⌘V |
| Paste Replace | ⇧⌘V |
| Paste at Original Position | |
| Delete | |
| Delete and Move | |

The standard cut-copy-past-delete commands work as expected. However, Logic has a few variations that are extremely helpful in your daily editing workflow.

☑️ **Copy** _cmd+C_: You can select multiple objects (Region, Events. Control Points) to copy them to the clipboard, even multiple Regions across different Tracks.

☑️ **Paste** _cmd+V_: Before pasting the content of the clipboard, make sure to select the two (!) elements. First of all, the Playhead to determine the time position where you want to paste, but also the destination Track, if you are pasting Regions.

- **Drag: Overlap** : The default behavior for pasting Regions is "Overlap". That means, that any existing Region will not be altered. Although you might have to "clean up" the overlapped situation afterwards.

- **Drag: No Overlap** : If you have "_No Overlap_" selected in the Drag Menu, then any paste procedure over existing Regions will shorten them to avoid overlaps.

☑️ **Paste Replace** _sh+cmd+V_: This is basically "Paste+No Overlap". Any paste procedure over existing Regions will shorten them to avoid overlaps.

☑️ **Paste at Original Position** (_unassigned_): This command ignores the current Playhead Position and pastes the content of the clipboard at its original position you copied it from. This is extremely useful when copying Regions or Notes to different Tracks but maintain their original Position (play in unison).

☑️ **Paste Multiple** (at original Position) _sh+opt+cmd+V_: This is a special command in the Score Editor.

☑️ **Delete and Move** _unassigned_: This special Delete Command removes any selected Region and moves any Region on the right towards the left by the same amount of the deleted Region(s). This is basically a delete procedure with Drag Mode "Shuffle L" enabled.   **Drag: Shuffle L**

## ➡ *Repeat*

You can use the Paste command multiple times if you want to copy Region(s) or Event(s) more than once. However, this might be easier by using the special Repeat command. You can use the feature also when multiple objects are selected, even multiple Regions across multiple Tracks.

☑ **Repeat**: Use the Menu Command *Edit ➤ Repeat* or the Key Command *cmd+R* to repeat a Region or Event. The selected Region(s) are repeated so that the beginning of the (first) Region/Event is copied at the end of the (last) Region/Event every time you use the command. If a Note Event is shorter than a beat, then the repeated Note is copied with one beat distance.

☑ **Repeat Multiple...**: Use the Menu Command *Edit ➤ Repeat Multiples...* or the Key Command *Repeat Regions/Events Multiple Times...* (**unassigned**) to open the *Repeat Regions/Events* window where you can set specific parameters:

   ▸ **Number of Copies**: Enter a number, how many times you want to copy the object.

   ▸ **Adjustment**: Select from the popup menu the time interval between repetitions.

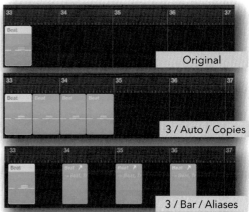

   - *Auto*: Every new repetition of a new Region/Event starts at the end of the previous Region/Event without any gaps. Selecting "None" seems to have the same effect.
   - *Discrete Time Value*: Selecting any value between Bar and Quarter Frame determines the distance between each start time of the next repetition. If the original object is longer than the selected value, then you will end up having overlapped objects.

   ▸ **As**: This setting is only relevant for Regions. If set to "Aliases or Clones" then repeating MIDI Regions and Drummer Regions will be Alias Regions and repeating Audio Regions will be Clones Regions (similar to Alias, just a different name).

# Regions only

Now let's look at the Edit commands that only apply to Regions.

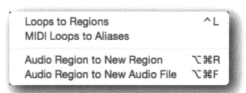

## ➡ *Convert* (Region)

The Convert commands lets you convert Regions to different states. Based on the different nature of Audio and MIDI Regions, some commands are specific to a Region Type.

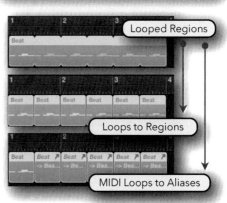

☑ **Loops to Regions** *ctr+L*: Any Regions that you looped 🔁 will be converted to standard Regions. This works for Audio, Drummer, and Audio Regions.

☑ **MIDI Loops to Aliases**: The looped Regions will be converted into Alias Regions. This works for MIDI and Drummer Regions. Looped Audio Regions will be converted to standard Audio Regions.

- ☑️ **Audio Region to New Region** *opt+cmd+R*: This command will create a new copy of the Audio Region (listed in the Project Browser) and replaces it on the Track Lane. This is a quick safety procedure, if you want to make changes to an Audio Region but don't want to affect other clones of that same Audio Region that you might have in your Project.

- ☑️ **Audio Region to New Audio File** *opt+cmd+F*: This command will open a Save Dialog ❶ first. Enter the name and location ❷, plus the file format ❸ for the new Audio File. Click Save to create a new Audio File from the selected Region (you can select multiple Regions to create multiple files at once). The current Audio Region on the Track Lane will be replaced with the new Audio Region linked to the new Audio File.
This command is also available in the File Menu *File ➤ Export ➤ Region as File...*

- ☑️ **Convert to New Sampler Track** *ctr+E*: This command is not listed in the Edit Menu, only in the Shortcut Menu when you click on a Region. It is a hidden little secret with tremendous powers. You can create a new EXS24 Instrument ❹ out of Audio Regions in your Project, just with the click of a button. You can have Logic automatically assign each selected Audio Region ❺ a separate Zone or use one Audio Region and have Logic automatically chop up individual samples based on the transients ❻. A checkbox lets you set the samples to "1Shot" Zones ❽. Click OK and Logic creates a new Software Instrument Track and loads an EXS24 Instrument with the newly created EXS Instrument ❹. Wait that's not all. It also creates a MIDI Region with notes playing that new EXS Instrument to replicate the original Audio Region (which is now muted).

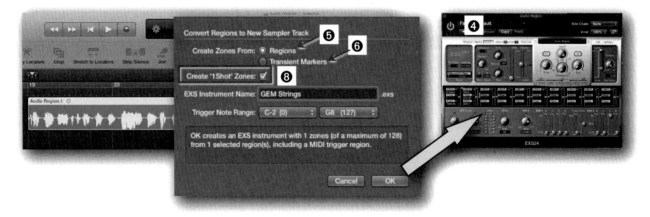

## ➡️ *Time Stretch*

You can Time Stretch a Region (compress or expand) either by using the Cycle Range as a length reference (doesn't have to be active) or the nearest bar. An additional submenu ❼ lets you select the used algorithm for that procedure (Audio Regions only).

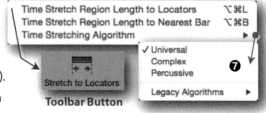

- ☑️ **Time Stretch Region Length to Locators** *opt+com+L* You can also use the Toolbar Button

- ☑️ **Time Stretch Region Length to Nearest Bar** *opt+cmd+B*

The Time Stretch command is the same procedure as *opt+dragging* the Region borders 🔲 🔳 (based on the "*Time and Pitch Machine*"). For Audio Region, it will create a new Audio File unless Flex is enabled 🔲 on that Track. In that case, it uses Flex Time to time stretch the Audio Region without creating a new Audio File.

## ➡ *Cut/Insert*

The Cut/Insert submenu contains four commands.

Before getting into the details of what these commands are doing, you have to understand first how they are implemented.

▶ The four commands are available in the Edit Menu ❶, as Toolbar Buttons ❷, and as Key Commands ❸.

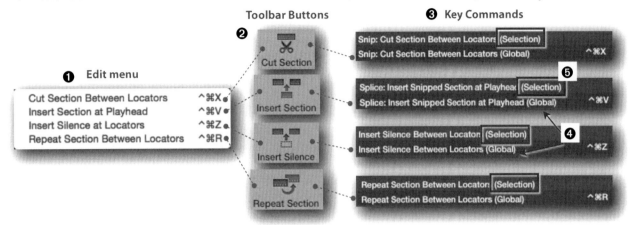

▶ The commands affect your entire Workspace: All the Regions, all the Automation, and all the Global Tracks.

▶ The name of those Key Commands have the additional word "Global" in parenthesis ❹, because they affect your Workspace globally.

▶ Each of those four Key Commands are also available as a variation with the additional word "Selection" in parenthesis ❺.

▶ The four commands labeled with "Selection" will affect only the selected Regions in the Workspace. When you use any of those "Selection" commands, an additional Dialog Window ❻ lets you choose if you want to apply the command to the Global Tracks or not.

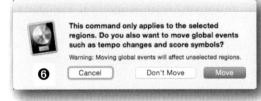

### 💀 Insert Silence

*Drag* a Cycle Range at that area you want to insert silence.

- Every Region that is located on ❼ or after ❽ the Left Locator is moved to the right. The amount of the movement is determined by the length of the Cycle Range.
- Regions that span over the Left Locator ❾ are split at the Left Locator Position. The part left of the split stays unaltered, the part starting at the Left Locator is moved to the right by the length of the Cycle Range.
- Regions that that are positioned before ❿ the left Locator are not affected.
- Automation and Global Tracks are treated the same.

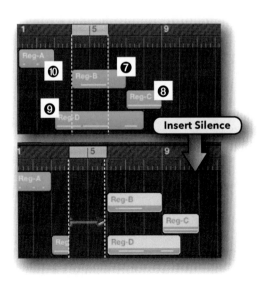

## 🎱 Cut Section

*Drag* a Cycle Range at that area you want to cut out.

- Every Region that falls under the Cycle Range is cut ❶.
- If a portion of a Region falls under the Cycle Range, then the Region will be split and only the portion along the Cycle Range gets cut.
- Every Region to the right of the Right Locator ❷ is moved to the left by the amount of the Cycle Range.
- Regions that are positioned before the left Locator are not affected.
- Any Region that was cut is actually copied to the clipboard, so you can paste that content at any other location of your song.

## 🎱 Insert Section

Place the Playhead ❸ at the position you want to insert a section.

- The current content of your clipboard is inserted at the Playhead Position.
- If you just want to move a section, then you can use the Cut Section procedure first (this moves the content to the clipboard), and then use this Insert Section procedure.
- If you want to copy a section, also use the Cut Section first to move that content to the clipboard ❹, but use the Undo command right away to put the Regions back on the Tracks. The content stays on the clipboard.
- Now, when you use the Insert Section command, Logic uses the Insert Silence procedure to move all the Regions at the Playhead Position to the right ❺ (the length depends on the length of the content that is currently on the clipboard) and copies the content of the clipboard ❻ at that free space.

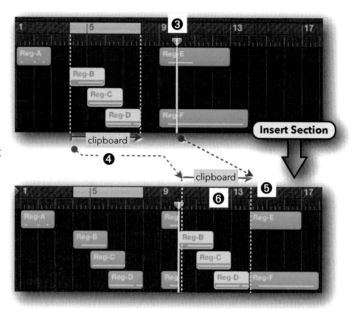

## 🎱 Repeat Section

*Drag* a Cycle Range at that area ❼ you want to repeat.

- First, if a portion of a Region falls under the Cycle Range, then the Region will be split at the Left Locator and Right Locator ❽.
- Every Region to the right of the Right Locator will be moved to the right ❾ by the amount of the Cycle Range.
- Any Region between the Left Locator and Right Locator are copied (repeated) to the Right Locator Position ❿.
- Regions that are positioned before the Left Locator are not affected.

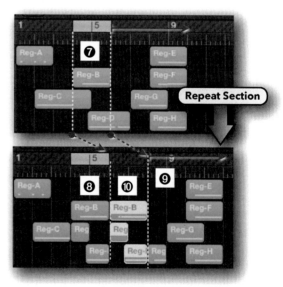

Please note that you can also use the Arrangement Marker in the Global Tracks to re-arrange sections of your Song.

# MIDI Events only

The following edit commands are only relevant for MIDI Events.

| | |
|---|---|
| +1 Semitone | ⌥↑ |
| -1 Semitone | ⌥↓ |
| +12 Semitones | ⌥⇧↑ |
| -12 Semitones | ⌥⇧↓ |

## ➡ *Transpose*

The Transpose commands are indispensable when you are working with MIDI in your Project. The default key commands are so easy to remember that you don't even have to go to any Edit Menu. Just select one or multiple MIDI Notes and quickly transpose them up or down by 1 semitone or 12 semitones (octave).

- ☑ **Transpose Event +1 Semitone / -1 Semitone** *opt+ArrowUp* / *opt+ArrowDown*
- ☑ **Transpose Event +12 Semitone / -12 Semitone** *sh+opt+ArrowUp* / *sh+opt+ArrowDown*

## ➡ *Copy MIDI Events ...*

The *Copy MIDI Events...* command opens a configuration window ❶. The Source Area (Cycle Range) ❷ defines what Events to copy and the Destination ❸ (Playhead Position) where to copy to. The different Modes ❹ defines the specific action.

Please note that this affects all MIDI Events, that means, notes and controllers. Have your MIDI Draw Area visible to check the results. The command applies to all selected MIDI Regions.

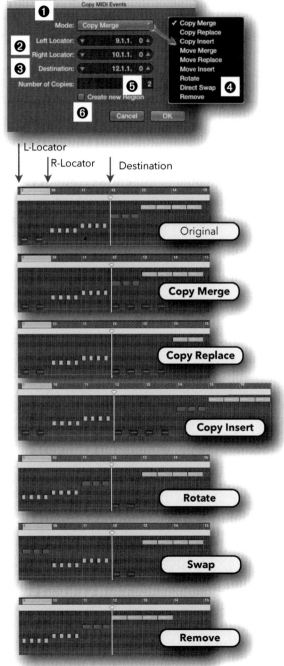

- ▸ **Copy Merge**: The copied Events are added to the current MIDI Region at the Playhead Position.
- ▸ **Copy Replace**: The copied Events will replace any existing Events at that position.
- ▸ **Copy Insert**: The copied Events will move any existing Events to the right, by the length of the Cycle Range.
- ▸ **Move Merge, Move Replace, Move Insert**: With this mode, the selected Events are moved instead of copied with the same Mode behavior.
- ▸ **Rotate**: The source Events are moved to the destination position. Every Event between the Right Locator and the Playhead Position are moved towards the Left Locator.
- ▸ **Direct Swap**: This swaps the source data with the data at the destination position. Use for quick bar swaps.
- ▸ **Remove**: Removes the source Events and moves other Events on the right towards the left by the amount of the Cycle Range.
- ▸ **Left Locator and Right Locator ❷**: Displays the current Cycle Range. You can change it.
- ▸ **Destination ❸**: Displays the current Playhead Position. You can change it.
- ▸ **Number of Copies ❺**: Define the number of copies. This value is ignored for Rotate, Swap, and Remove.
- ▸ **Create new Region ❻**: Creates a new MIDI Region for the moved/copied MIDI Events.

# Basics

"Comping" or "to create a comp track" is a common procedure in audio production. The term "comp" is just an abbreviation of the word "composite". You create a Comp, a "composite track".

Another term in the context of comping, and audio recording in general, is a "Take".

> **A "Take" is one piece of recording from start-to-stop,**
> **one pass, represented by one Region**

Let's look at four different scenarios when recording audio, for example, a guitar solo:

1- **Single Track - Single Take**: You create one new track, hit record, and the guitarist performs the perfect solo in one take ❶. Done.

2 - **Single Track - Overdubs**: After you recorded the first Take, which was almost perfect, you need to fix two sections on it. That means, you stay on the same Track and punch in-out on bar 3 so the guitar player can hit that high note ❷ again on bar 3. You do the same "overdub" procedure on the first two beats of bar 5 to fix a timing issue ❸. In this scenario, overdubbing means that you are "recording over" (replace) a section of the exciting recording on the same Track. On an

actual Tape Machine, this was sometimes difficult, not to record over a good part. Now with disk-based DAWs, not a problem anymore. Everything is non-destructive and just one undo step away.

3 - **Multiple Tracks - Single Take** (and/or overdubs): With this approach, you leave the first (almost perfect) Take alone ❹. You mute it and create a second Track ❺ to record the second Take of the guitar player and maybe a third Track ❻ for a third Take. This has two advantages. Musically it is better to have a performer do an entire section instead of let him sing or perform just a single note or phrase. In addition, you might end up having more options to choose from later in the mix. Maybe the third Take was even better than the already great first Take.

The downside is, you need extra time later to listen through the Takes again and choose the right one, or create a combination of all three Takes, a "Composite Track".

4 - **Single Track - Take Folder**: This procedure gives you the best of option 2 and 3. You don't clutter your Tracks Window with a lot of Guitar Tracks. You are still using only one single Guitar Track ❼. The different Takes are now recorded as separate "*Take Regions*"❽, enclosed in a single "*Take Folder*"❾. Not only does this provide a great user interface to deal with a high number of Takes, but it also allows you to do the comping in a much more elegant and faster (= efficient) way.

So let's look at the Take Folder next.

# Take Folder

The Take Folder is the foundation that provides the various tools for Logic's special Quick Swipe Comping.

> ## Take Folder + Comping => Quick Swipe Comping

Before you can use all those cool Quick Swipe Comping tricks that Logic provides, you have to create a Take Folder first. Although you can create them manually ("Pack Take Folder"), you want Logic to create those Take Folders automatically during recording. For Logic to do that, you have to choose the proper Recording Mode.

## ➡ Recording Mode: "Create Take Folder"

I discuss all the different Recording Modes in my first Logic book Logic Pro X - How it Works. Here is just the summary regarding the Take Folder:

**Project Settings ➤ Recording**

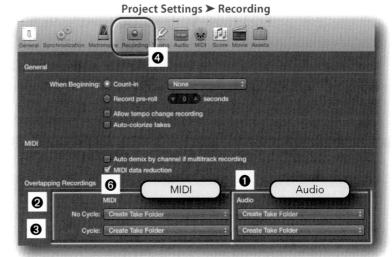

### 💀 Audio Recording ❶

There are three different Recording Modes for recording audio signals. You can set them independently for Cycle Mode off ❷ and Cycle Mode on ❸ in the *Project Settings ➤ Recording ➤ Overlapping Recordings* ❹. Please note that the Record Mode Button 🗵 ❺ overwrites "Create Take Folder" when Cycle Mode is off 🔁.

### 💀 MIDI Recording ❻

There are eight different Recording Modes for recording MIDI signals. You can also set them independently for Cycle Mode off ❷ and Cycle Mode on ❸ in the *Project Settings ➤ Recording ➤ Overlapping Recordings*. One of them is *"Create Take Folder"*. The Record Mode Button 🗵 ❺ can also overwrite the settings, but it is inconsistent and hard to remember when. My advice, ignore the button and only set the Recording Modes in the Project Settings ❹, which also has a "Replace" option.

**Replace Mode Button**

🔁 **Cycle Mode**: The Recording Mode *Take Folder* only kicks in when you have overlapping Regions (record over existing Regions). Although you can record over any existing Region to evoke the creation of a Take Folder, this technique is especially useful in Cycle Mode. You let Logic record in Cycle Mode one pass after another (creating one Take Region after another) while the performer (vocalist, soloist, etc.) repeats that section over and over again. Logic fills the Take Folder with multiple Takes that you can edit later.

You can have the individual Takes automatically colored with the *Project Settings ➤ Recording ➤ General ➤ Auto-colorize takes*.

## ➡ *Interface*

Here are the various interface elements of a Take Folder for Audio Regions:

### 💀 Interface Elements (Audio Regions)

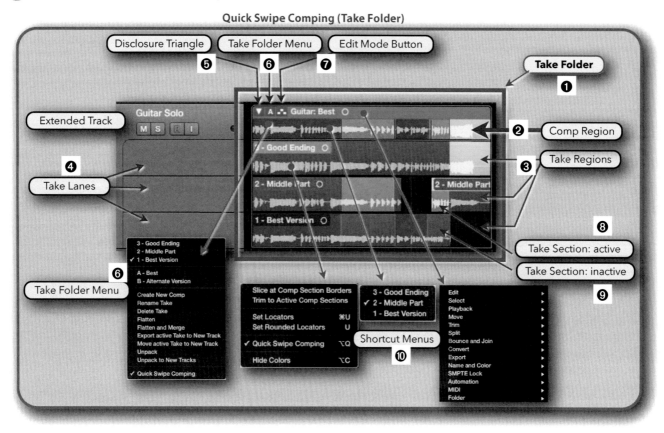

- ▶ **Take Folder ❶**: A Take Folder consists of the Comp Region and the enclosed Take Regions.
- ▶ **Comp Region ❷**: This is the Region on the Track Lane "the Composite Region" that displays the combined sections of the individual Take Regions, a Comp.
- ▶ **Take Regions ❸**: The Take Regions are the individual Regions that were recorded during each pass (Takes). They are placed on separate Take Lanes, part of the Extended Track the Take Folder is placed on.
- ▶ **Take Lanes ❹**: The Take Lanes belong to the extended Track. The more Take Regions a Take Folder has, the more Take Lanes are displayed. The maximum number depends on the Take Folder with the highest number of Take Regions on that Track. You can show/hide the Take Lanes by *double-clicking* on the Comp Region or *clicking* its disclosure triangle.

- ▶ Three Buttons: The header of the Comp Region has three buttons:
  - • **Disclosure Triangle ❺**: *Click* to show/hide the Take Lanes with the Take Regions.
  - • **Take Folder Menu ❻**: *Click* to open/close the Take Folder Menu with commands for managing Takes and Comps.
  - • **Edit Mode Button ❼**: *Click* to toggle between the two Edit Modes: Take Sections Editing (Quick Swipe Comping) 🔲, Take Regions Editing 🔲.
- ▶ **Take Sections**: The sections you mark on the Take Region to be used in the Comp are the Take Sections. The colored ones are active Take Sections ❽ (used in the Comp) and the gray ones are the inactive Take Sections ❾ (not used in the Comp).
- ▶ **Shortcut Menus ❿**: The Take Folder has three different Shortcut Menus depending on where you *ctr+click*. On the Comp Region Header, on the Comp Region, or on a Take Region.

### 💀 Take Lane vs Take Regions

Any Track that has a Take Folder on it (either you record the Take Folder on it or you move a Take Folder on that Track) has the ability to extend vertically to show addition lanes, the Take Lanes.

The main Track Lane displays the Comp Region ❶ of the Take Folder and the additional Take Lanes display the Take Regions ❷. The Track extends to as many Track Lanes as needed (depending on the Take Folder).

Here is a screenshot of an Audio Track with two Take Folders, one with three and one with five Takes inside.

- The Take Folder uses the required Take Lanes from top to bottom without any empty lanes in between.
- If you delete a Take Region, then the Take Lane becomes empty and all the Take Lanes (below the deleted Take Lane) for that Take Folder move up, to close the gap.
- The Take Folder always has a frame around it ❸ (in its Region color) to mark the left and right border of the Take Folder.
- As a default, each Take Lane has one Take Region ❹ when you record a Take Folder in Cycle Mode. However, with the various editing tools (that we explore in a minute) you can split Take Regions, so a Take Lane can have multiple Take Regions. They can be adjacent ❺ or have gaps in between ❻.
- A Take Lane doesn't have to be "filled" with a Take Region. It can have empty sections ❼ with no Regions on it.

### 💀 Comp vs. Comp Region

Please note the difference between a "Comp" and the "Comp Region".

▶ A **Comp** is a specific combination of the Take Sections that you create with the Quick Swipe Comping tools. You can create different Comps that are listed in the Take Folder Menu ❽ where you can switch between them (different mixes, or just leave your options open).

▶ The **Comp Region**, is the Region on the Track's Track Lane ❾ that displays the Comp that is currently selected in the Take Folder Menu. In this menu ❽ you can select a specific Comp (A, B, C, D,…), but also a single Take (1, 2, 3, …), a specific Take Lane.

### 💀 Take Folder (MIDI)

Logic will also create a Take Folder when you record on a MIDI Track in Take Folder mode. Although many interface elements are the same, the main feature, the Quick Swipe Comping, is missing ❿ (no third button on the Comp Region 🔲 ✂ ).

You can only use the Take Folder to store multiple Takes. No real comping capabilities, only select one Take.

## ➡ *The Default Take Folder*

Here is what a basic Take Folder looks like after recording three Takes in Cycle Mode. Although the Take Folder is automatically "open" when you stop recording, let's start with the first command you need in Quick Swipe Comping: Open/close the Take Folder.

### ⚫ Open/Close Take Folder(s)

To open/close a Take Folder means, displaying only the Comp Region (closed ❶), or expanding the Track vertically to show the Comp Region plus all the enclosed Take Regions on their separate Take Lanes (open ❷).

If you have more than one Take Folder on a Track Lane, then opening the first Take Folder will extend the Track. Only if all other Take Folders are collapsed (hiding their Take Regions), then hiding the Take Regions on the last Take Folder will also hide the Take Lanes again.

These are the various commands to show/hide the content of the Take Folder:

-  *Double-click* the Comp Region
-  *Click* the disclosure triangle ❸ on the header of the Comp Region
-  *Opt+click* the disclosure triangle to open/close all the selected Take Folders on a Track
-  Key Command (*Un/disclose Take Folder*) *ctr+F*

### ⚫ Default Take Folder

This is the status of a new Take Folder:

- The Take Regions are listed from bottom (first) to top (last) ❹.
- The last recorded Take ❺ (on top) is displayed as the Comp Region ❻. In this example, the Take Folder Button on the Comp Region displays the Take number "3" ❼.
- There is no Comp create yet. The Take Folder lists all the Take Regions ❽ but no Comps, only the command "Create New Comp" ❾, which is only listed if a Take is selected.
- Quick Swipe Comping is selected ❿ ▦ so you can start comping right away.

### ⚫ On-the-fly Comp

There is one special, and actually really handy Key Command: "*Select Previous Section for Realtime Comping*". It is *unassigned* by default.

Here is how it works:

On-the-fly Comp

- Record your Take Folder in Cycle Mode and when you note a pretty good take, hit that Key Command. You still can continue recording.
- Once you press stop, the Take Folder is created. In addition, a Comp named "on-the-fly comp" is automatically created (listed in the Take Folder Menu ❶).
- The Comp includes the Take during which you hit the Key Command (in this example Take 3). It has two Take Sections (see the separation line ❷): One from the beginning of Take 3 to the position you hit the Key Command ❸, and the second Take Section from that mark to the end of Take Region 3 ❹.

# Quick Swipe Comping

Now let's explore how to use Quick Swipe Comping. This is the basic concept:

☑ The Comp Region (the top Region of a Take Folder) is the Region that is played on your Track. Like a folder, It functions as a container. Here, you add aliases of specific Regions or sections of a Region to it by marking them on the Take Lanes.

☑ All the Take Regions represent the available material that you can mark to be played on the Comp Region, to put its alias into that container.

☑ You can choose a specific Take Region to put on the Comp Region container, or define specific sections of a Take Region, the so-called "Take Sections" to be put on the Comp Region.

☑ The Quick Swipe Comp feature provides the various tools and techniques to make those markings, select and edit the Take Sections.

☑ You can create multiple Comps (different versions) in a single Take Folder and select which Comp to use on the Comp Region.

☑ There are two Edit Modes: "Take Section Edit" (Quick Swipe Comping)  lets you create the actual composite of all the available material, and "Take Region Edit"  let's you edit the individual Regions as if they would be placed on a regular Audio Track.

☑ There are additional commands to further manage Comps and Takes in a Take Folder.

## Two Edit Modes

These are the two Edit Modes:

- 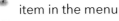 **Edit Take Sections** (Quick Swipe Comping): This is the Quick Swipe Comping mode that lets you edit the Take Sections on each Take Region to create a combination, the actual Comp.

- **Edit Take Regions**: This lets you edit the Take Regions, the Regions themselves, as if they would be just single Audio Regions on an Audio Track. Depending on the edit, this might also affect the Comp.

You can toggle between the two Edit Modes with the following commands:

- *Click* on the Quick Swipe Comping Button on the Comp Region ▦ - ✄
- *Click* on the Take Folder Button and select/deselect the Quick Swipe Comping item in the menu
- *Ctr+click* on a Take Region to open its Shortcut Menu and select/deselect the Quick Swipe Comping item in the menu
- Use the Key Command (*Toggle Take Folder Quick Swipe Comping Mode*) **opt+Q**

## Flex Mode

There is one limitation for Quick Swipe Comping when using Flex Mode:

You still can use Flex Mode on individual Take Regions, however, when Flex Mode is enabled  on a Track ❶, the Quick Swipe Comping Button disappears on the Take Folder ❷ and you can't edit the Comp until you disable ▦ Flex Mode on that Track again.

More on Flex Mode in the next chapter.

**Take Folder (Flex Mode)**

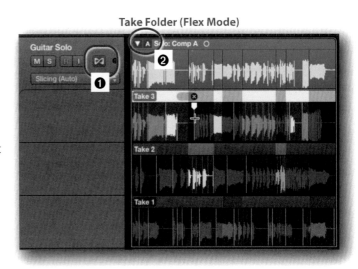

## Default Take Folder vs. Edited Take Folder

One more thing before introducing all the editing tools.

I want to point out some subtle details and changes that you need to be aware of when using Quick Swipe Comping.

Here are two examples: On the left is the new Take Folder we have seen earlier without any Quick Swipe Comping. On the right is the same Take Folder with my first Quick Swipe edits. I selected the first half of Take Region 2 and the second half of Take Region 1. Now let's compare those two examples:

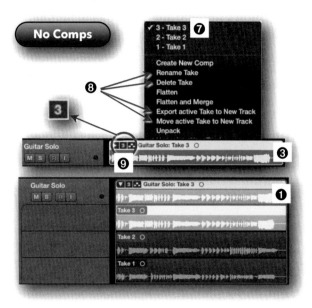

- ▶ **Comp Region (open)**: On the left, the Comp Region displays the entire Take (Take 3) in its Take own color ❶. On the right, the Comp Region displays the two Take Sections I selected, displayed by their colors ❷, which helps to visualize the cuts. Please note that the header of the Comp Region and the thin frame around the Take Folder is displayed in the color of the Take Folder (in this case, blue).

- ▶ **Comp Region (closed)**: If the Take Folder is closed, then only the Comp Region is displayed ❸, now entirely in the Take Folder color (blue). On the right, the waveform displays the composite waveform of your Comp and a thin vertical line ❹ indicating the cut from one Take Section to the other.

- ▶ **Take Folder Menu**: The Take Folder Menu is highly dynamic. Here are a few things to pay attention to:

  - On the right, the menu now displays "*Comp A*" ❺. It is checked, meaning, this is the active Comp that is used (displayed) on the Comp Region ❷.

  - The command "*Create New Comp*" (on the left) has changed now to "*Duplicate Comp*" ❻ (on the right), because a Comp is selected.

  - On the left, I have a Take selected ❼ ("3 - Take 3"), and on the right, I have a Comp selected ❺ ("A - Comp A"). Please note that these two areas on top of the menu let you select what is displayed (and played) in the Comp Region. Even if you have made a Comp already, you still can select a Take in the menu to play back only that single Take, the content of a single Take Lane.

  - Selecting a Take or a Comp will change four of the commands in the menu ❽: *Rename ...*, *Delete ...*, *Export active ... to New Track*", and "*Move active ... to New Track*".

- ▶ **Take Folder Button**: The Take Folder Button displays the Take Number ❾ (if a Take is selected) or the Comp Letter ❿ (if a Comp is selected).

## ➡ *Edit Take Sections (Quick Swipe Comping)*

Now let's finally look at the various Quick Swipe commands that are available to create the comp:

### 💀 Take Folder - Click Zone

When you are in Quick Swipe Editing Mode  and have the Take Folder open, then the area turns into an active Click Zone. That means, depending on where you move or click inside the Take Folder, the Pointer Tool 🔼 will change to different Tools so you can perform a specific action right away without switching Tools.

Many of the other standard Editing Tools are also working:

### 🌐 First Comp

A newly created Take Folder has no Comp yet. The Take Folder Button displays the number of the last Take and that's the one that is displayed in the Comp Region ❶. That's the one which is playing. Now you have two options to create a new Comp, which will be named "Comp A":

> ☑ *Click* on the Take Folder Button and select the "*Create New Comp*" item from the menu. This new Comp uses the current Take Region, so performance-wise, nothing has changed.

> ☑ *Drag* over a Take Region, which creates the first Take Section, and automatically the first Comp.

Let's have a closer look at that second option:

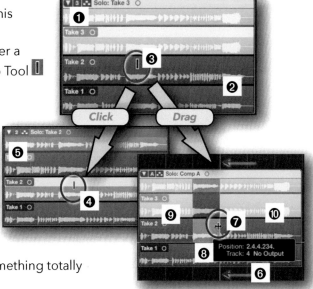

- As a default, the last Take Region is selected ❶. In this case, Take 3, Take 2, and Take 1 are grayed out ❷.
- When you move the Pointer Tool (or Pencil Tool) over a gray (inactive) Take Region, it changes to the Comp Tool 🗍 ❸.
- When you *click* on Take 2, for example, then that Take Region is selected ❹. The Comp Region changes its color to indicate which Take Region is playing and the Take Folder Button now displays the number, indicating that the entire Take 2 is selected ❺. Please note that still no Comp has been created. You just switched to a different Take Region.
- Now, instead of clicking on Take Region 2, if you *drag* on the gray Region with the Comp Tool 🗍, something totally different will happen:
- The black Help Tag displays the Position you've clicked and a vertical Alignment Guide moves along your drag position ❻. The Comp Tool 🗍 changes to the Comp Resize Tool ⊞ ❼. You are about to create a new Take Section on Region 2 over the area you drag. The currently active Take Section (in this case, the entire Take Region) resizes while you drag. The area you drag into becomes active on Region 2, while the same area on Region 3 now turns inactive (gray).
- Once you release the mouse, the new Take Section ❽ has been created on Region 2, plus two Take Sections on Region 3, one before ❾ and one after ❿ the the newly active Take Section on Region 2.
- Because this was your first creation of a Take Section on the Take Folder, a new Comp (with the default name "*Comp A*") has been automatically created with the edit you just made.

## 🕱 Editing Procedures ⠠⠂

Here are all the editing procedures you can perform while in Quick Swipe Comping mode:

▶ **Create Take Section** ⊓ *Drag* in an unselected area of the Take Region (gray) to draw a Take Section. The Comp Tool ⊓ turns into the Comp Resize Tool ✛ while dragging.

▶ **Crossfades**: The Crossfade defined in the *Preferences ➤ Audio ➤ Editing* will apply.

▶ **Resize Take Section (connected)**: Move the cursor over the border of a Take Section (it changes to the Resize Tool ✛ ), and *drag* the Take Section. The borders of the adjacent Take Sections are connected. Moving a border to the left will move the adjacent border to the right and vice versa ❶.

▶ **Resize Take Section (disconnected)**: *Sh+drag* the borders of a Take Section. The Tool changes to the standard Resize Tool ◧◨. Now only the Section you are resizing is moving ❷. The adjacent border stays fixed ❸ (if you move away from it), creating a blank (empty) section in the Comp Region ❹.

▶ **Slide Take Section**: Moving the Pointer Tool over the center of an active Take Section changes to the Slide Tool ◀▶. Moving the Take Section means, sliding the "window" (length of the Section stays the same) over a different part of the Take Region. **Alternate Take Section**: *Click* on any unselected Take Section with the Comp Tool ⊓ to move the range of the Take Section at that position to this Take Region. You can also *ctr+click* on a section in the Comp Region and select from the Shortcut Menu the Take Region for that Section.

▶ **Remove Take Section**: *Sh+click* on a Take Section and that Take Section turns gray (inactive). That section on the Comp Region will now be blank (silent).

▶ **Remove all Take Sections**: *Sh+click* on the header in the upper left corner of the Take Region will remove all Take Sections on the Take Region. Those sections on the Comp Region will be blank.

▶ **Auto-create Take Section**: When *Sh+clicking* on the header of a Take Region that has no Take Sections selected, then for all the "blank" areas on the Comp Region (if there are any) will be filled with new Take Sections from that Take Region.

▶ **Cut Out Section of a Region**: *Click* on a Take Section to select it and hit *delete* This will make two splits at the Take Section border to create a separate Take Region. This Region will be deleted, leaving a blank space on the Track Lane.

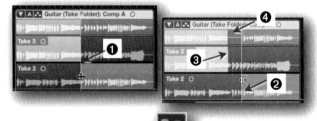

## ➡️ *Edit Take Regions* ✂️

While the Edit Take <u>Sections</u> Mode lets you create and modify the Take Sections, the Edit Take <u>Regions</u> Mode lets you edit the actual Regions on the Take Lane. This is mostly standard Audio Region editing with the same tools you use when editing Audio Regions on a single Audio Track.

## 🕱 Group Editing

If the Track that has the Take Folder on is part of a Group and the "*Editing*" ❺ is enabled in the Group Inspector ❻, then you have to be aware of the following functions before you start editing:

Group Inspector

- The Take Folder follows the edit commands of Region Edits on other Tracks within the same Group.
- Editing the Take Folder (the Comp Region) will also affect the Regions on the other Tracks in the same Group.
- Editing the Take Regions inside a Take Folder, however, does not affect any Region edits on other Tracks in the Groups.

## ☻ Editing Procedures ✂

▸ **Resize**: *Drag* the lower right or lower left border of the Region to resize the actual Audio Region. The two standard Resize Tools appear ⬛⬛ depending on where you click. *Dragging* over a Take Section will remove that Take Section and that area on the Comp Region will be blank.

▸ **Resize Adjacent**: You can resize two Take Regions that are adjacent on the same Take Lane. Position the Pointer Tool in the upper half of the Region border and the Junction Tool ⬛ appears. *Dragging* the border will move the borders of both Regions together. Please note that you cannot apply any crossfades on the Take Lanes, not between Take Regions and not between Take Sections. You have to flatten the Comp first.

▸ **Move/Copy**: *Drag* the Take Region left or right if you need to correct some timing issues or *opt +drag* to copy a phrase on the same Take Lane. Moving a Region beyond the borders of the Take Folder will extend the Take Folder. Moving a Region over another Region will shorten the existing Region. This is always "No Overlap" Mode, regardless of the Drag Setting in the Tracks Window.

▸ **Edit**: *Double-click* on a Take Region to open the Audio Track Editor or Audio File Editor (depending on what was selected before). You can still edit Take Regions in those Editors, even if they are part of a Take Folder.

▸ **Copy Take Region between Take Lane**s: *Drag* the Take Region up or down between Take Lanes. Any existing Take Region will be truncated based on the "No Overlap" rules.

## ➡ *Edit in both Edit Modes*  *or* 

Here are some editing procedures that work in either of the two Edit Modes:

▸ **Rename Take Region**: *Click* with the Text Tool ⬛ on the Region Header and enter a new name.

▸ **Color Region**: *Click* on the Take Region Header or the Comp Region to select it and choose a color from the Color Window (*opt+C*).

▸ **Delete entire Take Region**: *Click* on the header of the Take Region to select it and hit *delete* or click on the Take Region with the Eraser Tool ⬛. A Dialog Window pops up if sections of that Take Region are used in any other Comp.

▸ **Marquee Selection**: *Drag* a Marquee Selection (even across Take Lanes) and *click* on it to split at the selection borders or hit *delete* to delete that section. New Regions will be created for the remaining sections.

▸ **Split**: Use the *Split at Playhead* command (*cmd+T*) or the Scissors Tool ⬛. The standard Scissors techniques work: *Drag* before releasing to solo-scrub the Region. *Opt+click* to create multiple splits. Remember, the Snap value (set in the Snap popup menu on the Menu Bar) applies to any click position!

▸ **Split Region at Take Section**: *Ctr+click* on the Take Region to open the Shortcut Menu and choose *Slice at Comp Section Borders*. The Take Region will be split at the Take Section borders, creating new Take Regions on that Take Lane.

▸ **Split Region at every Take Sections and remove unused**: *Ctr+click* on the Take Region to open the Shortcut Menu and choose *Trim to Active Comp Section*. This will Split the Take Region at every Take Section and removes all the unused Take Regions.

**Take Region Shortcut Menu**

## ➡ Manage Comps

The Take Folder Menu contains a list of commands that let you manage its Takes and Comps. Most of those commands are also available as Key Commands.

Key Commands

| | |
|---|---|
| Pack Take Folder | ⌃⌘F |
| Unpack Take Folder to Existing Tracks | ⌃⌘U |
| Unpack Take Folder to New Tracks | ⌃⇧⌘U |
| Un/disclose Take Folder | ⌥F |
| Flatten Take Folder | ⌥⇧U |
| Flatten and Merge Take Folder | ⌥U |
| Toggle Take Folder Quick Swipe Comping Mode | ⌥Q |

### 🔘 Dynamic Menu

As I already mentioned, the Take Folder Menu is dynamic. Besides the amount of available Takes and Comps, five of the commands change ❶, depending on if a Take ❷ is selected or a Comp ❸.

### 🔘 Select Takes and Comps

The first two sections of the menu list all the available Takes (representing the individual Take Lanes) and the Comps. The Takes have sequential numbers assigned and the Comps have sequential letters assigned besides their names.

- ▶ **Select from List**: Select a Take or a Comp to be used (active) on the Comp Region.
- ▶ **Step through with Key Commands**: You can step through the list of Takes and Comps with the two Key Commands (Take Folder can be opened or closed for that):
  - 🔘 Key Command (*Select Previous Take or Comp*) **unassigned**
  - 🔘 Key Command (*Select Next Take or Comp*) **unassigned**
- ▶ **Select from Shortcut Menu**: *Ctr+click* on the Comp Region to open its Shortcut Menu ❹ with a list of all the available Takes. When an entire Take is used in the Comp Region, then this will select a different Take. However, if a Comp is selected, then this command swaps only that specific Take Sections (you clicked on) with the same Take Section from the selected Take.

Comp Region Shortcut

| | |
|---|---|
| 4 - Take 4 | ❹ |
| 3 - Take 3 | |
| ✓ 2 - Take 2 | |
| 1 - Take 1 | |

### 🔘 Basic Commands

Here are the basic "house keeping" commands in the menu:

- ▶ **Create New Comp**: This command is only visible when a Take is selected. It creates a new Comp with the currently selected Take and selects that Comp to be the active Comp Region.
- ▶ **Duplicate Comp**: This command is only visible when a Comp is selected. It creates a new Comp with the duplicate settings and selects it.
- ▶ **Rename Take/Comp**: This command lets you rename the currently selected Take or Comp. The initial Take number or Comp letter are still listed ❺.
- ▶ **Delete Take/Comp**: The currently selected Take or Comp is deleted. A Dialog Window ❻ pops up with a warning if you are about to delete a Take that is used in other Comps.
- ▶ **Delete all other Comps**: This deletes all the Comps except the currently selected one. This is useful if you decided on the final version of a Comp.

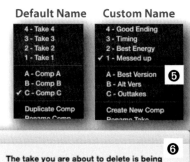

**Default Name**

| |
|---|
| 4 - Take 4 |
| 3 - Take 3 |
| 2 - Take 2 |
| 1 - Take 1 |
| A - Comp A |
| B - Comp B |
| ✓ C - Comp C |
| Duplicate Comp |
| Rename Comp |

**Custom Name**

| | |
|---|---|
| 4 - Good Ending | |
| 3 - Timing | |
| 2 - Best Energy | |
| ✓ 1 - Messed up | |
| A - Best Version | ❺ |
| B - Alt Vers | |
| C - Outtakes | |
| Create New Comp | |
| Rename Take | |

❻

The take you are about to delete is being used by at least one comp. Are you sure you want to delete it?

Cancel | OK

## 💀 Major Surgery

Next are the commands that you have to use with care. They let you manage Comps and Takes on a "bigger scale" and you have to make sure to understand their individual "consequences".

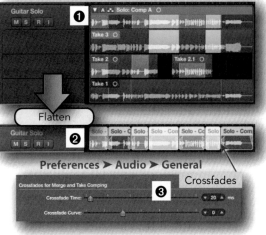

Preferences ➤ Audio ➤ General

- ▶ **Flatten**: This command replaces the Take Folder ❶ (and all its content) with individual Regions ❷, representing the Take Sections of the currently selected Comp. The new Audio Regions have a default crossfade (Time and Curve set in the Preferences ❸) and the name of the Comp added to the Region name.

- ▶ **Flatten and Merge**: This bounces the currently selected Comp to a new audio file and replaces the Take Folder with the Audio Region of that audio file. This is final, the individual Takes and all the other Comps are gone. No more adjustments.

- ▶ **Export active Take/Comp to New Track**: A new Audio Track is created below the currently selected Track with a flattened version of the currently selected Comp. That means, the Take Sections are converted to individual Audio Regions with crossfades. The original Take Folder stays untouched.

- ▶ **Move active Take/Comp to New Track**: This is the same procedure as the previous command with the only difference that the exported Comp is now removed from the original Take Folder.

- ▶ **Unpack**: Logic creates a separate Track for each Take and each Comp. All Tracks are assigned to the same Channel Strip as the original Audio Track that Take is on. All Comps are flattened with the currently selected Comp placed on the first Track, followed by all the Takes and the rest of the Comps. The original Take Folder is deleted.

- ▶ **Unpack to New Tracks**: This is the same procedure as the previous command with the difference that all Tracks, with exception of the selected Comp, are assigned to new Channel Strips with the same Channel Strip Settings as the original Track.

- ▶ **Quick Swipe Comping**: This is one of the many commands that toggles the Edit Modes: ⬛ - ✂.

## 💀 Pack Take Folder

You can select one or multiple Regions in your Project and "pack" (move) them into a Take Folder. *Ctr+click* on the selected Region (you want to pack) and choose from the *Shortcut Menu ➤ Folder ➤ Pack Take Folder* or use the Key Command (*Pack Take Folder*) *ctr+cmd+F*

- The command creates a new Take Folder on the topmost Track of all the selected Regions.
- All the selected Regions are moved into that Take Folder.
- Regions that were originally on different Tracks are placed on separate Take Lanes and Regions that were on the same Track are placed on the same Take Lane in that new Take Folder.
- You can even pack a single Region into a Take Folder.

## 💀 Add Regions to Take Folder

You can move any Audio Region into a Take Folder by selecting a Region (or multiple Regions on the same Track), use the copy command (*cmd+C*), select the Track the Take Folder is on, place the Playhead Position somewhere between the beginning and end of the Take Folder, and use the paste command (*cmd+V*). The Region(s) are placed on a new Take Lane on top of the Take Folder.

## 💀 Record into Take Folder

You can record on a Track over an existing Take Folder. The new recording will be added to that Take Folder as a new Take. Any recording that starts before the Take Folder will extend the left border of the Take Folder and any recording that ends after the Take Folder will extend the right border of the Take Folder. You can even use Cycle Mode over the range (or part of the range ) of the Take Folder. If you record over two Take Folders, then the new recording will be split at the beginning of a Take Folder to place the first and second part of the Region into the first and second Take Folder.

I already covered the basics of the Audio File Editor in my first book "Logic Pro X - How it Works". Now let's go deep and discover all the powerful features, everything you can do to an audio file.

> **Fixing stuff - Improving stuff - Creating stuff -  Messing with stuff**

Here are a few of the main features in the Audio File Editor:

- ☑ Accurately resizing, creating Audio Regions
- ☑ Adjusting the Audio Region's Anchor Point
- ☑ Fix technical issues in the audio file (Phase, DC Offset, clicks)
- ☑ Edit the audio file (length, level, time and pitch)
- ☑ Create Transient Markers (required for Flex Editing)
- ☑ Sample Loop Creation (to use in EXS24)
- ☑ Outsource audio file editing to a third party audio editor

**Warning** Most of the edits you perform in the Audio File Editor are **destructive**. Here is what you have to be aware of:

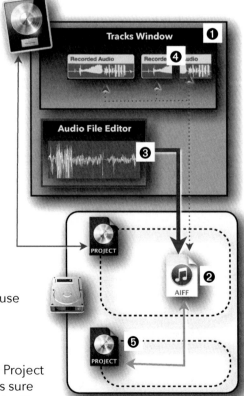

- When you edit Audio Regions in the Tracks Window ❶ or the Audio Track Editor, you are performing non-destructive edits. All the changes are applied in real-time when you play back the Audio Region. Cutting and splicing, tempo and pitch changes do not alter the actual audio file ❷ in any way.
- Performing edits in the Audio File Editor ❸, on the other hand, will apply most of the changes directly to the audio file. You overwrite the original audio file ❷.
- You still have a "safety net" with some of the Undo functionality.
- Altering audio files can have potential damaging consequences to other parts of your Project if you use other Audio Regions ❹ in your Project that refer to the same audio file ❷.
- Altering audio files can even have potential damaging consequences to other Logic Projects ❺ on your drive if they use those same audio files ❷ in their Project. This underlines the important topic of "File Management" that I discuss in a later chapter.
- Rule of thumb: Always keep audio files contained within your Project instead of referencing them to "outside locations". This makes sure that any changes to the audio files in your current Project don't affect other Project..

# Interface

➡ *Open Audio File Editor*

## 💀 Two Windows to choose from:

Before doing all that cool "damaging" editing in the Audio File Editor, you have to open the File Editor Window first. And right there, there are a few things that you have to be aware of to avoid any confusion:

The Audio File Editor can be displayed in two different windows:

▸ **Audio File Editor Pane ❶**: This Editor Pane is part of Logic's Main Window

▸ **Audio File Editor Window ❷**: This is a single Standalone Window

> Although you can have both windows open, displaying the same or a different audio file, changes the behavior of the Key Commands and also the procedure of what is automatically displayed when you select an object in a different window. Therefore, I recommend having only one of the windows open.

## 💀 Windows are closed

If the Audio File Editor is closed, then you can open them with any of the standard Menu Commands or Key Commands. You can also open the Audio File Editor directly by double-clicking on an Audio Region, which displays the audio file of that Audio Region right way. The click action depends on what window will open:

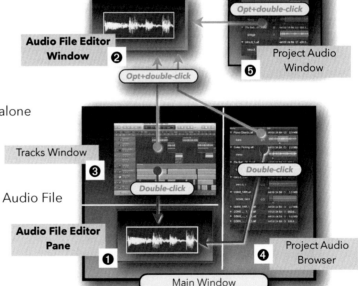

▸ **Tracks Window ❸**

> 🖱 *Double-click* on an Audio Region toggles the Editor Pane ❶ (Audio Track Editor or Audio File Editor, whatever was open before).

> 🖱 *Opt+double-click* toggles the standalone Audio File Editor Window ❷.

▸ **Project Audio Browser ❹**

> 🖱 *Double-click* on an Audio Region (the waveform display) to open the Audio File Editor ❶ in the Editor Pane.

> 🖱 *Opt+double-click* opens the standalone Audio File Editor Window ❷.

▸ **Project Audio Window ❺**

> 🖱 *Opt+double-click* (or double-click) on an Audio Region (the waveform display) always opens the standalone Audio File Editor Window ❷.

## 💀 Window is open

If any of the two Audio File Editors (window pane or standalone window) are open, then selecting any Audio Region in any of the three windows (Tracks Window, Project Audio Browser, Project Audio Window) will automatically display that audio file in the Audio File Editor. That means, the Audio File Editor is always in Link Mode.

## ➡️ *Window Elements*

Here are all the elements of the Audio File Editor that are only displayed if the window is open wide enough.

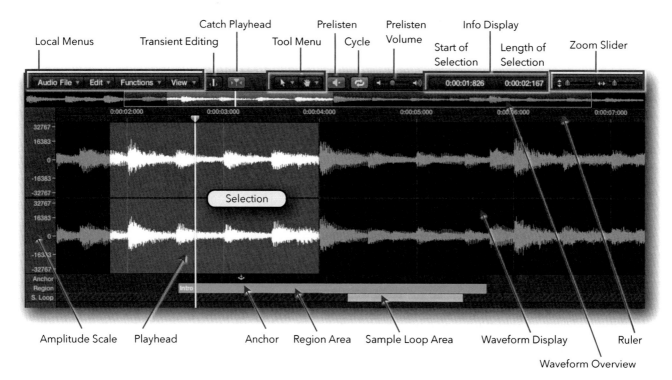

The Audio File Editor looks the same in the window pane and the standalone window. The standalone window has the additional file path shown in its Window Title ❶.

## 🔘 Terminology

Here are a few terms you have to get yourself familiar with:

▸ **Waveform Overview ❷**: The waveform of the entire Audio File ❸ is always displayed from the left to the right border of the window. The zoom is automatically adjusted whenever you resize the window.

▸ **Waveform Display ❹ / Visible Section ❺**: The Waveform Display is the main area where you perform most of the edits. If you are zoomed in and the window shows only a section of the entire waveform horizontally, then you have to scroll left/right. This is the Visible Section indicated by a rectangle frame ❺ on the Waveform Overview.

▸ **Selection Area ❻**: You can draw a Selection Area on the Waveform Display that becomes the target of any edit command (highlighted ❼ on the Waveform Overview and the Waveform Display). *Clicking* on the Waveform Display creates just a single Selection Line.

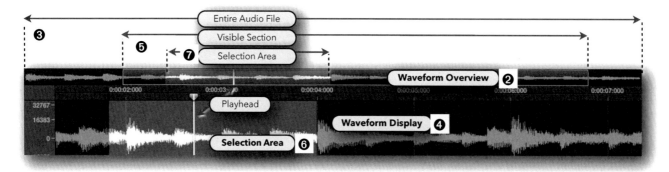

# Audio File vs. Audio Region

Before getting into the actual editing procedures in the Audio File Editor, I want to review the important relationship between Audio Regions and Audio Files. Not only does the Audio File Editor demonstrate that relationship very nicely, it is also crucial in understanding what is actually displayed in the Audio File Editor.

Here is the concept of Audio Files vs. Audio Regions and how it is implemented in Logic:

- Regardless whether you record a new audio signal in your Project or import an existing audio file to your Project, the audio file itself is stored on your drive ❶.
- Any audio file that you use in your Project is listed in the Project Audio Browser (same as Project Audio Window) ❷.
- At the moment an "audio file" is placed on your workspace, a Track Lane of an Audio Track to be specific, an Audio Region ❸ is created in the Project Audio Browser (every Audio Region in the Workspace has to have a counterpart in the Project Browser, but not the other way around).
- A copy of that Audio Region ❹ is what is placed on the Track Lane, not the audio file itself.
- An Audio Region is just a reference to its parent audio file. It only contains the following information:
  - Time position on the audio file where to start playing the file (left border of the Audio Region)
  - Time Position on the audio file where to stop playing the file (right border of the Audio Region)
  - Time Position on the audio file to use to sync to the Project Timeline (Anchor)
  - Additional Playback instructions (Flex, transpose, etc.)
- The Project Browser always displays each Audio Region as the entire length of the audio file ❺ with the actual Audio Region marked in its Region color ❻.
- The Tracks Window only displays the Audio Region, the segment ❼ of the audio region it defines. You have to imagine the underlying (full length ❽) audio file, which marks the limits how far you can resize an Audio Region on the left and right border.

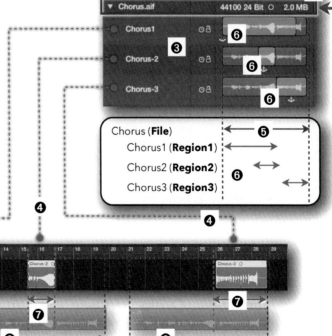

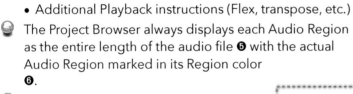

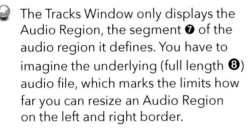

**Warning** All the three Audio Regions in this example are referenced to the same audio file. Changing this audio file in the Audio File Editor will affect all three Audio Regions. And that is the first concern you should have before using any edit command: Are there any other Regions affected by this edit and would that be ok?

## ➡ Timelines

Remember that you can display the Audio Region by selecting it in the Tracks Window or in the Project Audio Browser. This is not just an option. It has some significant differences.

Here are seven screenshots from the Audio File Editor displaying the same audio file when selecting a specific Audio Region, either in the Workspace or the Project Audio Browser.

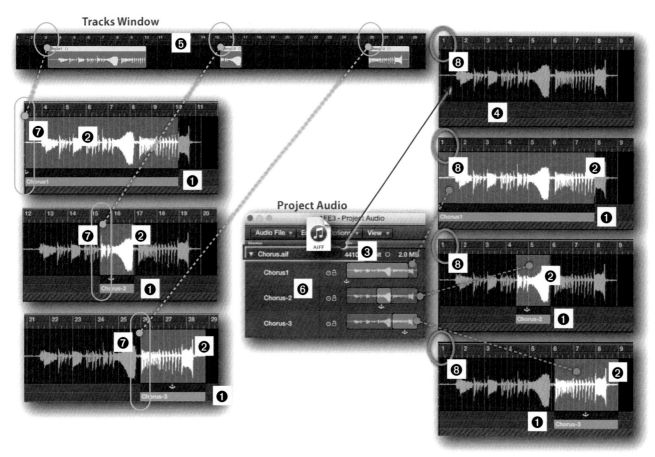

### Basic Observations

- A selected Audio Region is displayed in the Audio File Editor superimposed on the waveform of the entire audio file.
- Regardless where you click, the Audio File Editor will always display the waveform of the entire audio file it is referenced to.
- The beginning and end of a Region is indicated by a horizontal bar (which you can resize right there) in the Region Area ❶ below the Waveform Display.
- The section of the waveform representing the range of that Audio Region is highlighted (Selection Area ❷).
- One exception is when you click on the entry in the Project Audio Browser that represents the actual audio file ❸. In that case, nothing is selected in the Region Area of the Audio File Editor ❹, it is disabled.

### The Timeline !

Please look at the Timeline of the Audio File Editor's screenshots that display the Regions. It displays different times depending on if you selected the Audio Region on the Tracks Lane ❺ or in the Project Audio Browser ❻.

- **Project Timeline**: When you select an Audio Region from the Tracks Window, then the Audio File Editor displays the time of the Project Timeline ❼. You can see on the Timeline where in the Project the Region is playing.
- **Audio File Timeline**: When you select an Audio Region from the Project Audio Browser ❻, then the Audio File Editor displays the Timeline of the Audio File itself ❽, always starting at 0, or bar 1 ,depending on your selected time scale.

## ➡ *Summary*

Here is what is displayed in the Audio File Editor:

- ☑ The Audio File Editor displays the waveform ❶ of the parent audio file ❷ of the selected Region ❸.
- ☑ The Audio File Editor displays the beginning and end of the Region ❹, plus its Anchor ❺ along the audio file's waveform ❶.
- ☑ The Audio File Editor displays the audio file's waveform referenced to the Timeline ❻ of the Project ❼ or the audio file ❽.
- ☑ So basically, what you see and what you edit in the Audio File Editor is the currently selected Audio Region and its parent audio file.
- ☑ Any changes to the audio file will also affect any other Audio Region in your Project or even other Projects that use that same audio file.

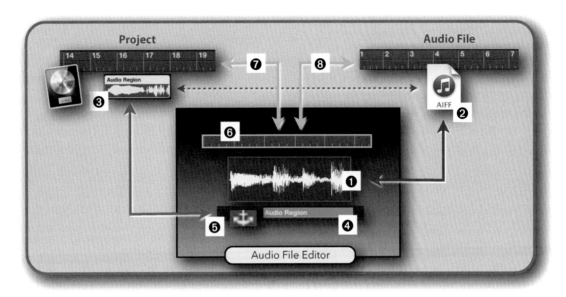

# Navigation

Now that we know what is displayed in the Audio File Editor, we have to know how to navigate around in that window so we can perform the necessary edits in the most efficient way.

### 🌑 Zoom

The Zoom feature is not only important to get a closer look at the waveform, you also have to make sure that you keep the Zoom center locked, or you will be doing more scrolling than zooming.

### 🌑 Playback

The Audio File Editor has its own playback features, something you really have to pay attention to. In addition, Scrubbing is one essential playback technique used when editing audio.

### 🌑 Selection

A Selection is the key element for doing destructive editing in the Audio File Editor. You have to define the target, to what Logic has to apply the edit command to. One key to success for "audio-click-free" editing is the concept of Zero Crossing.

Now lets have a closer look at those topics.

## ➡ *Zoom*

I already covered the "Zoom" topic in the Workflow chapter. Here are the commands that are available in the Audio File Editor.

▸ **Zoom Window**: This command is often overlooked, but it is especially useful when editing waveforms where you need to zoom in very closely to do precise editing, sometimes even on the sample level. You use that command with the standalone Audio File Editor Window where you toggle between the current size of the window and the maximum size to fill the entire screen (you can do that with any Logic window).

> 🔘 *Click* the Green Tittle Bar Button ➕ in the upper left corner of the window
> 🔘 Key Command (*Zoom Window*) **sh+opt+cmd+M**
> 🔘 *Double-click* the Window Title Bar

▸ **Zoom Tool** 🔍 : The Zoom Tool works the same as in other Logic windows. *Ctr+opt+drag* a selection on the Waveform Display to zoom in to that area and *ctr+op+click* with the Zoom Tool on the Waveform Display to zoom back out to the previous zoom level. You can repeat the procedure to zoom in multiple steps and then zoom back out through the same zoom levels.

▸ **Zoom Horizontal**: This is another way to quickly zoom in/out on the waveform.

> 🔘 Key Command (*Zoom Horizontal In/Out*) **cmd+ArrowRight** / **cmd+ArrowLeft**. Press once to zoom step-by-step or keep pressing to continuously zoom in or out
> 🔘 Touch Gesture on the Trackpad Pinch and Spread
> 🔘 *Drag* the Zoom Slider

▸ **Zoom Vertical**: You can also zoom vertically, although, not that important as horizontal zoom.

> 🔘 Key Command (*Zoom Vertical In/Out*) **cmd+ArrowUp** / **cmd+ArrowDown**
> 🔘 *Drag* the Zoom Slider

## 🔘 Zoom Center:

I also already discussed in the Workflow chapter the important connection between zooming and scrolling. Remember, you scrolled to the section where you want to edit, you zoom in, and boom, that section is scrolled to the left or right (out of sight). Unlike other Logic windows where the Zoom Center is defined by the Playhead Position and the selected Region, in the Audio File Editor, the Zoom Center is determined by the Selection. This applies to the horizontal zoom commands:

▸ **Selection Area**: When the Waveform Display shows an active Selection Area (highlighted section), then the left border of that Selection Area becomes the Zoom Center. Scroll to that section (or use the command Go To Section Start *cmd+home*) and when you zoom in and out, the waveform is locked to that Zoom Center.

▸ **Selection Line**: If you want to zoom in to any section that you display right now, just click on the Waveform Display with the Pointer Tool 🔺. This creates a single Selection Line (a Selection Area with the same address for the left and right border). That Selection Line now becomes the Zoom Center.

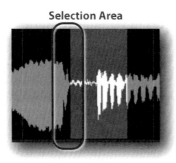
**Selection Area**

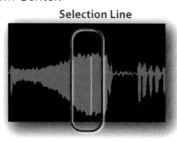
**Selection Line**

## ➡ *Playback*

The playback in the Audio File Editor needs some getting used to, because it has its independent playback mechanism. The Playhead is either controlled by the Project Playback or by its own Prelisten Playback.

### 💿 Project Playback vs. Prelisten Playback

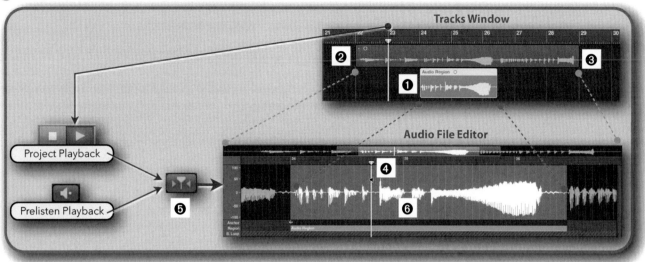

### ▶ Project Playback [▶]

- Every Audio Region in your Project has an absolute position on the Project Timeline (in this case, it starts at bar 24 ❶).
- In this example, the Audio Region starts two bars after the start of its parent audio file ❷.
- We already learned that the Audio File Editor displays the entire audio file the selected Audio Region is referenced to. This entire audio file is always displayed in the Waveform Overview of the Audio File Editor or when the Waveform Display is completely zoomed out.
- The theoretical start of the underlying audio file (I indicate that with the brown Audio Region) is bar 22 ❷ and the end is bar 29 ❸. Now, whenever the Project is playing back and the Playhead moves between bar 22 and 29, you will see a Playhead (a thin white vertical line) moving along the Waveform Overview ❹.
- What you will see on the Waveform Display depends on the status of the Catch Playhead Button ❺. If it is disabled [▶◀], then you will see the Playhead moving along only when the Project plays that section that is currently

displayed (in this example, bar 23-28 ❻). If the button is enabled [▶◀], then the Waveform Display automatically scrolls to the section where the Playhead is moving, between bar 22 ❷ and 29 ❸.
- If you play back any other section outside the range of that audio file, then the Waveform Display will not change its current display.
- Please note that the Audio File Editor does not "wait" for the Project Playhead to reach the selected Audio Region ❶ in the Tracks Window. It already starts to scroll when it reaches the "virtual" start time ❷ of the audio file the Audio Region is referenced to.

### ▶ Prelisten Playback [🔊]

- You can play back the currently displayed audio file in the Audio File Editor with its own playback commands, called the Prelisten Playback. These commands are independent from the Project Playback. The Prelisten Button [🔊] lights up in that mode.
- The Catch Playhead Mode also affects the Prelisten Playback. When enabled [▶◀], it automatically scrolls to the next page to show the current playback position.

You can toggle the optional *Scroll in Play* feature from the Local Menu *View ➤ Scroll in Play* or with the Key Command *ctr+`*. Catch Playhead [▶◀] must be enabled (toggle with Key Command ` ).

Here are the different Prelisten Playback commands:

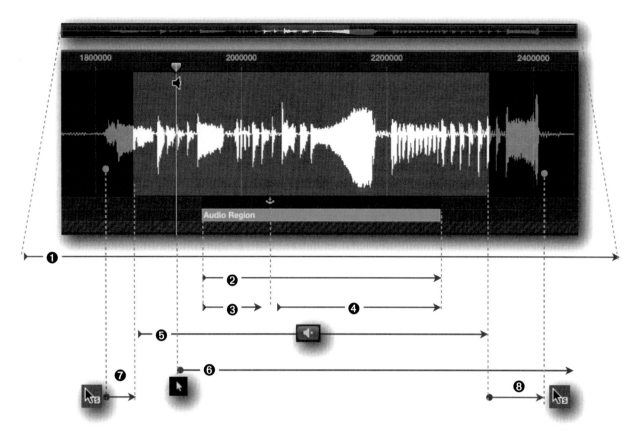

▶  ❶ **From Beginning to End**: Key Command (*Play/Stop All*) ***ctr+opt+cmd+spacebar***. Please note that this starts at the beginning of the audio file. You can see the Local Playhead on the Waveform Overview moving, but not necessarily on the Waveform Display if it is zoomed in at a different position.

**Key Commands**
| | |
|---|---|
| •Play/Stop All | ⌃⌥⌘_ |
| •Play/Stop Region | ⌃⌥⇧_ |
| •Play/Stop Region to Anchor | |
| •Play/Stop Region from Anchor | ⌃⌥_ |
| Play/Stop Selection | ⌃_ |

▶  ❷ **Region only**: Key Command (*Play/Stop Region*) ***sh+ctr+opt+spacebar***

▶  ❸ **Region Start to Anchor**: Key Command (*Play/Stop Region to Anchor*) ***unassigned***

▶  ❹ **Anchor to Region End**: Key Command (*Play/Stop Region from Anchor*) ***ctr+opt+spacebar***

▶  ❺ **Selection Only**: Click on the Prelisten Button to start 🔊 and stop 🔊 , or use the Key Command (*Start/Stop Selection*) ***ctr+spacebar***.

▶  ❻ **From Click Position**: *Double-click* on the Timeline or the Waveform Overview with the Pointer Tool ▸ to start from that click position and *double-click* again (on any position) to stop. Alternatively, you can *click-hold* on the Waveform Overview to play from that click position until you release the mouse.

▶  ❼ **From Click to Selection Start**: *Opt+click-hold* with the Solo Tool 🔲 to the left of the Selection Area to play from that position up to the left border of the Selection Area.

▶  ❽ **From Selection End to Click**: *Opt+click-hold* with the Solo Tool 🔲 to the right of the Selection Area to play from the End of Selection to the end of the audio file.

### In Addition

- Use the *Play/Stop All* Key Command ***ctr+opt+cmd+spacebar*** at any time to stop the Prelisten Playback.

- Click on the Cycle Button 🔁 to enable Cycle Mode, or use the Key Command (*Cycle Audition*) ***ctr+C*** This is independent from the Cycle Mode 🔁 in the Control Bar.

- If you press the space bar to stop the playback (out of reflex) but you were playing the Prelisten Mode, then you actually did start the Project at the current Playhead Position.

###  Scrubbing

"Scrubbing" is a special type of transport control used for editing when trying to locate a position in your audio signal. Usually, you drag the Playhead along the Timeline to reposition it. Now in Scrub Mode, the Playhead is "engaged", which means, the Playhead is in constant Play Mode even when moved only a tiny bit. The speed and direction of your mouse movement controls the playback. By "wiggling" the Playhead back and forth around a specific area on the Waveform Display, you are closing in on that spot. This is a special technique used in tape-based audio recording that requires a lot of experience and skills. Now with disk based audio, you can "see" the audio waveform while you are scrubbing, which makes scrubbing much more easier.

There are two ways to scrub in the Audio File Editor. You can scrub along the Timeline (Ruler) or directly on the Waveform Display.

#### ▶ Ruler Scrubbing

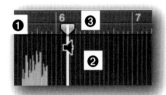

*Drag* along the Ruler ❶ above of the Waveform Display. Once you *click-hold* on the Ruler, the Cursor Tool changes to the speaker symbol ❷, plus the Playhead ❸ appears underneath that position (the mini Playhead also appears on the Waveform Overview). The Playhead now follows the mouse movement (speaker symbol) while playing back that section of the audio file in that speed.

#### ▶ Waveform Scrubbing

Scrubbing on the Waveform Display requires that you switch first to the Solo Tool . However, this method has the advantage that you can also set the borders of the Selection Area. When you click with the Solo Tool, it changes to the speaker symbol ❹ without the Playhead (the Playhead on the Waveform Overview is still visible).

Here is an example how to use Waveform Scrubbing to find the precise borders of a Selection Area:

- Nothing is selected, only one Selection Line.
- **Set Start**: *Drag* with the Solo Tool to scrub the audio to close in on the start point. When you release the mouse, the Selection Line moves to that position. You can repeat that step to move the Selection Line to a different position.
- **Set End**: *Drag* with the Solo Tool to the right of the Selection Line to scrub the audio and find the end position for the Selection Area. Here is the important part. When you find the right spot, hold down the *shift* key before releasing the mouse. That spot now becomes the right border of the Selection Area.
- **Reposition Start**: *Drag* with the Solo Tool to the left of the left border of the Selection Area to scrub the audio file in order to find the right spot. Now you do the same key combination. If you would release the mouse, nothing would happen, the Selection Area stays the same. However, if you press the *shift* key before releasing the mouse, then the left border of the Selection Area extends to that spot.
- **Reposition End**: *Drag* with the Solo Tool to the right of the right border of the Selection Area to scrub the audio file in order to find the right spot. Again, the same key combination. When you release the mouse, nothing happens, the Selection Area stays the same. If you press the *shift* key before releasing the mouse, then the right border of the Selection Area extends to that spot.

Preferences ➤ Audio ➤ Audio File Editor

- **Undo**: Use the Undo command (*cmd+Z*) if you made a selection or changed a selection and want to return to the previous Selection. For this you have to enable the setting
*Preferences ➤ Audio ➤ Audio File Editor ➤ Record selection changes in Undo History* ❺.

**Tip**

Set your second Tool Menu (Command Tool) to the Solo Tool. This lets you edit audio files super easy, super fast:

Use the Pointer Tool for the standard operations:

- *Click* to set the Selection Line
- *Drag* to draw a Selection Area
- *Sh+click* to extend the Selection Area
- *Ctr+opt+drag* to Zoom

Hold down the command key to switch to the Solo Tool for the scrub and scrub-selection procedures:

- When Selection Line is visible: *Cmd+drag* to scrub and set the Selection Line when releasing the mouse.
- When Selection Area is visible: *Cmd+drag* to scrub. Release the mouse without changing the Selection Area, or hold down the *shift* key before releasing the mouse to extend the Selection Area.

**Tool Menus**

## 🕱 Prelisten Routing

As a default, when using Prelisten Playback, the audio signal is routed to the Audio Channel Strip #256 (the same used by the Apple Loop Audition or Project Audio Prelisten). The Volume Slider acts as a remote control for the Fader on Audio Channel Strip 256.

*Ctr+click* on the Prelisten Button to bring up a Shortcut Menu where you can choose to play through the Channel Strip of its Audio Region (Auto-select Channel Strip).

## ➡ *Selection*

In general, you cannot use an edit command without making a selection first. Logic needs to know to what it should apply the edit to. The Audio File Editor is no different. You have to select an area on the Waveform Display, a so-called Selection Area. Any of the destructive edits will be applied to that area of the waveform or to everything outside that area.

## 🕱 Selection Line vs. Selection Area

There are two kinds of selections on the Waveform Display:

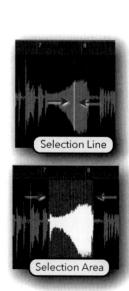

Selection Line

Selection Area

- ▸ **Selection Line**: When you just click on the Waveform Display, it creates a single Selection Line. This is basically a Selection Area where the left border and the right border have the same address.
  - *Click* anywhere to use that click position to start the Prelisten Playback by clicking on the Prelisten Button or by using the Key Command (*Start/Stop Selection*) *ctr+spacebar*.
  - *Click* anywhere to define the left border of a Selection Area (and then *sh+click* anywhere to set the right border).
- ▸ **Selection Area**: A Selection Area is what you use for most of the editing in the Audio File Editor. Creating, changing, and doing all kinds of things with the Selection Area should be your solid foundation when you work in the Audio File Editor.

Here are the various commands to create and change a Selection Area:

▶ **Select All**: You can select the entire Waveform Display with the standard Menu Command *Edit ➤ Select All* or the Key Command *cmd+A*

▶ **Create**: You can *drag* anywhere on the Display Area to create a Selection Area, drag left, drag right, and also, drag over an exciting Selection. A black Help Tag displays the start, stop, and the length (Count) in the amount of Sample Words ❶.

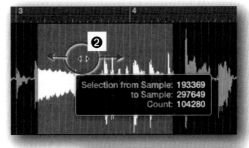

▶ **Extend**: These are a few commands that let you extend the borders of an existing Selection Area.

- *Sh+click* on the left or on the right of a Selection Area to define the new border. The border closest to the click position will be moved to the click position.

- *Sh+opt+click* on the left or on the right of a Selection. The border furthest away from the click position will be moved to the click position.

- You can extend the right border of a Selection all the way to the end of the waveform. Use the Menu Command *Edit ➤ Select All Following* or the Key Command *sh+ctr+opt+ArrowRight*.

- You can extend the left border of a Selection all the way to the beginning of the waveform. Use the Menu Command *Edit ➤ Select All Previous* or the Key Command *sh+ctr+opt+ArrowLeft*.

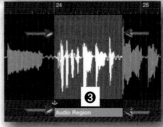

▶ **Move**: *Opt+drag* the Selection to move the entire Selection left or right. The Cursor Tool changes to the double Arrow Tool ⬌ ❷.

▶ **Delete**: *Click* the with the Eraser Tool ◣ anywhere on the Waveform Display to remove the current Selection Area and place a Selection Line at the click position.

▶ **Use Region**: You can set the Selection Area to the position and length of the Region Bar in the Region Area ❸. Use the Menu Command *Edit ➤ Region -> Selection* or the Key Command *PageUp*.

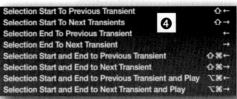

▶ **Use Sample Loop**: You can set the Selection Area to the position and length of the Loop Bar in the Loop Area. Use the Menu Command *Edit ➤ Sample Loop -> Selection* (Key Command is unassigned). More about Sample Loops a little bit later.

Edit ➤ Set... ➤

▶ **Set to Transients**: There are a couple of commands that let you adjust the left and/or right border of a Selection Area to the next/or previous Transient. They are listed in the *Edit ➤ Set... ➤* submenu ❹ and are also available as individual Key Commands.

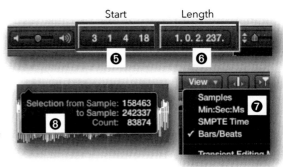

### 🍏 Info Display

- The Info Display in the Menu Bar between the Volume Slider and the Zoom Slider displays the start ❺ and the length ❻ of the current Selection Area. It updates while you are dragging. The units are displayed depending upon what you set in the View Menu ❼.

- Set the units for the Ruler and the Info Display in the Local View Menu ❼. (Samples, Min:Sec:Ms, SMPTE, Bars/Beats).

- *Opt+click-hold* on a Selection to show the black Help Tag. It always displays the start, stop, and the length (Count) in the amount of Sample Words ❽.

## 🕹 Zero Crossing

Whenever you make a cut in an audio signal, you have to make sure that the resulting waveform at the cut

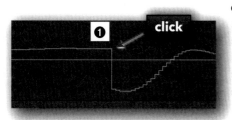

doesn't' have a big jump ❶ in its sample value (y-axis). This could add an audible click sound to your audio signal. Instead of finding the same sample value where you want to cut, you choose an easier solution. Just look where the waveform crosses the 0-line (Sample value = 0) on both sides of the cut. This ensures that the left side of the cut ❷ and the right side of the cut ❸ have the same

y-value. It is zero.

**Snap Edit to Zero Crossing**

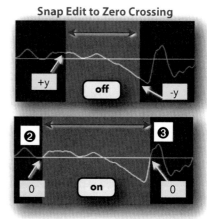

▶ **Snap Edits to Zero Crossing**: The good news is that you don't have to search for those Zero Crossings yourself. Just enable "*Snap Edits to Zero Crossing*" in the Edit Menu or use the Key Command *ctr+0* (the number on the main keyboard). Now every time you set a selection, Logic shifts the borders of that Selection Area to the closest Zero Crossing point.

It is a good idea to leave that mode on. Only if you have to make sure that the Selection Area is exactly at the point where you set it, then turn it off.

## 🕹 Show as Sample & Hold

Digitizing an analog signal involves two main steps. First, a sample is taken, for example, 48,000 time per second (Sample Rate = 48kHz), then each sample is on "hold" for a brief moment to measure its value (with a 16bit or 24bit resolution). The Audio File Editor displays the audio signal as a "smoothed out" continuous waveform ❹, even when you zoomed in all the way to the individual sample level (the x-axes displays the units of individual samples ❺).

**Show as Sample & Hold**

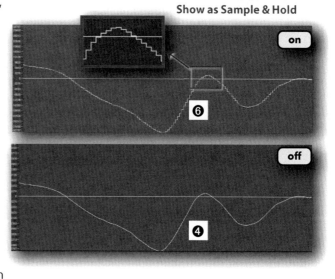

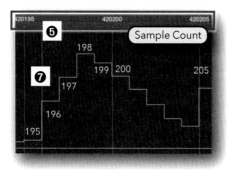

If you want to do really precise editing, you can enable "Show as Sample & Hold" in the Edit Menu and the waveform will then display the discrete sample steps ❻ that make up the waveform. You can even see each sample number (the steps) ❼ on the Ruler ❺, when it displays Samples and you are zoomed in all the way.

## 🕹 Go to (Scroll)

The Audio File Editor doesn't have markers to use as a navigation tool, but it provides seven commands that automatically scroll to those locations. They are available in the submenu *Edit ➤ Go To... ➤* and also as dedicated Key Commands:

- ☑ Selection Start/End
- ☑ Region Start/End
- ☑ Transient Previous/Next
- ☑ Anchor

# Audio Region Editing

The Audio File Editor always displays the selected Audio Region (unless you click on the audio file in the Project Audio Browser) in relation to its parent audio file. That parent audio file is shown in the full length Waveform Display where you apply the destructive audio file editing.

In addition to all the audio file editing, you can also perform the non-destructive Audio Region editing.

- ☑ Set the Region boundaries
- ☑ Set the Region Anchor

Let me repeat one of the most important parts you have to understand about the Audio File Editor. If you have, for example, three Audio Regions referenced to the same audio file in your Project, then:

- ▶ Selecting any of those three Audio Regions will always display the same parent audio file, its Waveform Display.

- ▶ Only the Audio Region related data (Region Bar and Anchor) is different.

- ▶ To perform any destructive edit on the audio file, you can select any of the three Regions. However, making an edit on the audio file could potentially affect the other (non-selected) Audio Regions that are referenced to that same audio file.

## ➡ *Region Boundaries*

Here is a screenshot of Logic's Main Window with its three window panes: Tracks Window, Project Audio Browser, and Audio File Editor. It has three Audio Regions referenced to the same audio file. The third Audio Region is selected:

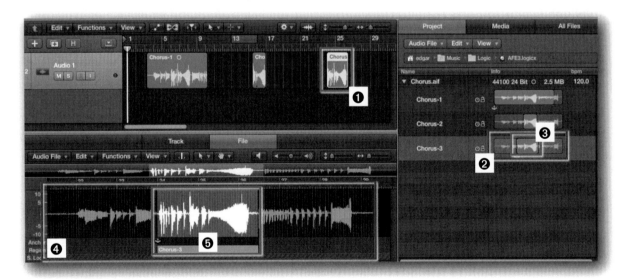

- 💡 **Tracks Window**: The Tracks Window shows only the Audio Region ❶, the section of its parent audio file defined by the left and right border of the Audio Region.
- 💡 **Project Audio Browser**: The Project Audio Browser always displays the full length of the audio file's waveform ❷ (in gray) with the Audio Region boundaries in the color of the Audio Region ❸.
- 💡 **Audio File Editor**: The Audio File Editor always displays the full length of the audio file's waveform ❹ with the boundaries of the Audio Region indicated by the Region Bar ❺ in the Region Area below. The Region bar is displayed in the Audio Region Color.

Please note that you can edit the Region boundaries in all three windows. Let's concentrate on the Audio File Editor.

Here are the commands and things you have to pay attention to when editing Regions in the Audio File Editor:

▶ **Resize Region**: You can resize the Audio Region in the Audio File Editor in two ways:

  ◉ Move the Cursor Tool over the beginning or end of the Region Bar. It changes to the standard Resize Tool ⬛⬛. *Drag* the edges left or right to reposition the start or the end. The Selection Area will adopt the length of the Region bar while you are dragging. This has the advantage that you can monitor the start and length of the Region in the Display Info while you are dragging. "*Snap Edits to Zero Crossing*" will also apply to the resizing.

  ◉ *Drag* any Section Area in the Waveform Display and make that the new Region with the command "*Selection -> Region*" from the Edit Menu , or use the Key Command *PageDown*.

▶ **Resize with Anchor**: Be aware what happens when you resize the left border of a Region. As a default, it is also the location of the Region's Anchor ⚓. I will discuss the implications in the next Anchor section.

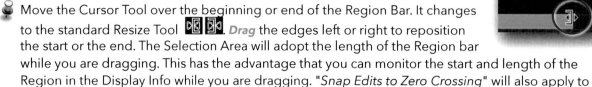
Anchor

▶ **Move Region**: You can't move the Region directly by dragging it left or right. Instead, use the "*Region -> Selection*" command (*PageUp*), move the Selection (*opt+drag*), and then move the Selection Area back as Region with the "*Selection -> Region*" command (*PageDown*).

▶ **Color Region**: As long as the Audio File Editor has key focus, open the Color Window (*opt+C*) and select a color from the Color Palette.

▶ **Shortcut Menu**: *Ctr+click* on the Region Bar to open the Shortcut Menu with the two commands.

▶ **Locked Region**: If you have the Region locked 🔒 in the Project Audio Browser, then you can't resize the Region Bar in the Audio File Editor. The Cursor Tool changes to the prohibit symbol 🚫. However, if the Track is locked in the Tracks Window, which prohibits a resizing of the Region on the Track Lane, then you can still resize the Region in the Audio File Editor.

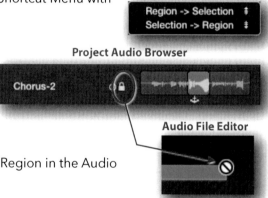
Region -> Selection
Selection -> Region

Project Audio Browser

Chorus-2

Audio File Editor

▶ **Undo**: The Undo commands do not work for resizing the Region in the Audio File Editor.

## ➡ *Anchor*

Despite the fact that many Logic users don't know about the existence of the Anchor, it is arguably the most important element of an Audio Region next to its left and right borders.

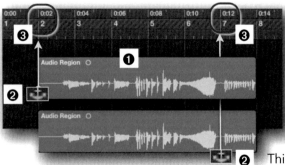

Although it looks like that the Audio Region is "placed along" the Track Lane ❶, the truth is that only one single time address of the audio file ❷ (the Audio Region is referenced to) is synced to a single address on your Projects Timeline ❸. This sync reference tells the audio file to start **WHEN** at **WHAT** position when you play your Project. Once the audio file is playing, it is playing independently determined by its own speed (Sample Rate). Flex Mode and Follow Tempo is a different story.

This single reference point on the audio file is defined by positioning the Anchor ❷ along the audio file's waveform. Any position information for that Region that you see in the Event List refers to where the Anchor is placed on the Project Timeline, not necessarily the beginning of the Audio Region.

### 🕱 Anchor - what for?

As a default, the Anchor Position is always placed at the left border of the Audio Region, the start of the Region. That means, you can position the Audio Region on the Project Timeline exactly where you want it to start. That works most of the time and is the reason why you don't have to bother about the Anchor in the first place.

However, there are situations, where you don't want to sync an Audio Region to its left border. Although you can move and nudge the Region to any position you want, having the ability to place the sync point anywhere along the audio file has its advantages. You can use the Snap feature to position the sync point exactly on a beat or use the Event List to enter a specific bar/beat or SMPTE time when working with SFX against picture.

Here are just three examples:

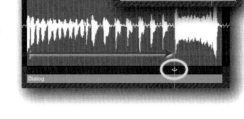

🕱 The first note of an instrument has a little attack. If you would place the Audio Region start time on the downbeat, then the note would sound late. In that case, you move the Anchor exactly on the transient and sync that to the downbeat. The Region actually starts a bit early, but the transient (the note) sounds exactly on the beat.

🕱 If you have a sting sound that ramps up over 1 or 2 seconds, then there is no point to position the start of the Region to the downbeat. The climax of the ramp should be on the downbeat and moving the Region manually to find that spot is tedious. Instead, you move the Anchor to the climax point. Now, you move the Region so the Anchor position snaps to the downbeat and you are done.

🕱 Any kind of SFX or dialog where you need to sync a specific position in the audio file to an address on the Timeline (bars or SMPTE) is as easy as positioning the Anchor to that spot on the waveform.

### 🕱 Lock Position in Track when moving Anchor

✓ Lock Position in Track when moving Anchor ⌃A

This is an important mode that can be toggled in the Edit Menu, or when *ctr+clicking* on the Anchor in the Audio File Editor, or with the Key Command *ctr+A*.

This mode determines what happens to the Region when you move the Anchor. Please note that the tiny Anchor symbol changes slightly depending on the mode. If it is disabled, the Anchor shows the little lines of a Timeline, indicating that it is now linked to the Timeline. Here is the behavior:

▶ **Enabled** (default): <u>Region</u> Position is locked to the Ruler - Region does not move
  - Moving the Anchor will not change the position of the Region
  - Moving the Anchor will only reposition the Anchor
  - Moving the Anchor defines a new sync point for the Region (see example for consequences)

▶ **Disabled**: <u>Anchor</u> Position is locked to the Ruler - Region will be moved
  - Moving the Anchor will not change its position on the Ruler
  - Moving the Anchor will move the Ruler with it against the Region
  - By sliding the Ruler against the Region, you effectively re-position (move) the Region on the Project Timeline

On the next page, I try to show the effect of this setting, which is a little bit tricky. You have to try it yourself to wrap your head around it.

## Here is an example

**1 -** This is original audio file with an Audio Region spanning for its entire length of 4 bars. The Region starts at bar2 on the Timeline. The Anchor is also at the same position, bar2, and therefore, the Event Float displays the Region start at bar2.

**2 -** Now I move the Region start in the Audio File Editor one bar to the right, from bar2 to bar3. The Anchor moves with it.

> **The result**: The Region did not move, only the Anchor together with the Region start. The Event Float displays the Region start as bar3.

**3a -** Now I move only the Anchor one bar to the right, from bar3 to bar4 with "*Lock Position in Track when moving Anchor*" enabled.

> **The result**: On the Tracks Window, the Region didn't move, it is locked to its position. However, the Anchor is now at bar4, and therefore, the Even Float displays the Region start as bar4 (the Anchor position) and not bar3 (the Region start).

**3b -** Now I undo that step, to repeat the procedure, this time with the "*Lock Position in Track when moving Anchor*" disabled.

> **The result**: By moving the Anchor 1 bar to the right, you would notice that the Timeline in the Audio Editor moves with it, linked to bar3. By moving the Anchor (and the Timeline) 1 bar to the right (against the fixed waveform), you effectively move the Region to the left, by the same amount, 1 bar.  On the Track Lane, you can see the Region moved from bar3 to bar2, while the Anchor stayed at bar 3. That's why the Event Float still displays the start time as bar 3 (the Anchor position).

**3c -** Now I undo that step again and move the Region start (and the Anchor with it) 1 bar to the right while still having the "*Lock Position in Track when moving Anchor*" disabled.

> **The result**: You have to pay attention to two things that happen. You shortened the Region by one bar (as you can see on the Track Lane) and you moved it 1 bar to left, because you moved the Anchor 1 bar to the right (!). As a result, the Region is one bar long, starts at bar 3, and is displayed with a Region start of bar 3 in the Event Float (the Anchor position).

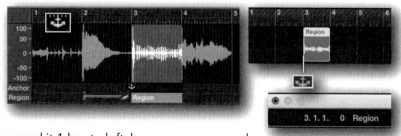

**Attention** There is one visual inconsistency in that Anchor moving procedure that you have to be aware of, so you're not getting confused about what happens (or what does not happen).

When the Anchor is positioned at the left border of the Region (default), then moving the left Region border will move the Anchor with it. But, here is the inconsistent and slightly confusing part:

> When the Anchor is set to "Lock Position in Track when moving Anchor", then moving the Anchor is not linked to the Ruler and should not move the Ruler (as we have just seen in Step 3a on the previous example). However, when moving the left Region border and with it the Anchor, the Ruler <u>does</u> move with Anchor. This is visually incorrect and as soon you release the mouse, the Ruler snaps back to its (locked) position.

**Audio File Editor**

### 🞧 Related Anchor Stuff

There are a few more Anchor related things to be aware of:

- You can move the Anchor to the previous or next transient with a separate command *Edit ➤ Set ➤ Region A to Previous/Next Transient* or assign a key combination to those Key Commands.

**Project Audio Browser**

- Please note that you can't Undo any movements of the Anchor.
- Besides the Audio File Editor ❶, the Anchor is also visible on the Region in the Project Audio Browser (as a tiny Anchor ❷) and the Track Lane (as an almost invisible black dot ❸). You can move the Anchor in the Project Browser, but unfortunately not in the Tracks Window.

**Track Lane**

### 🞧 Anchor and Tempo Change

Here are two Regions referenced to the same audio file. The Region on top ❹ has the Anchor positioned at bar2 and the Region at the bottom ❺ has its Anchor placed at bar7. It doesn't seem that it makes a difference. Both Regions are 10sec long, as you can see on the Ruler ( 2s … 12s).

However, look what happens in the second screenshot when you apply a tempo change between bar2 and bar7. As I mentioned before, the Audio Region only syncs to one position on the Timeline, that gives it the information where to start. From that on, it plays independently. The Region on top still starts at bar2 ❼ and plays for 10 seconds (2s … 12s). It just ends in bar 5 ❽ due to the tempo slow down. The interesting thing happens to the second Region. Its Region end is synced to bar7 ❾ (the Anchor position) and that didn't change. But now, bar7 represents the real-time absolute time position of 18s and Logic has to calculate that it needs to start the Region at time position 8s ❿ (10s before). It looks up the corresponding bar position for the 8s mark (which is after the second beat of bar4), and that is where the second Region now starts.

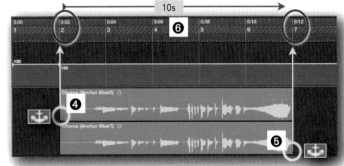

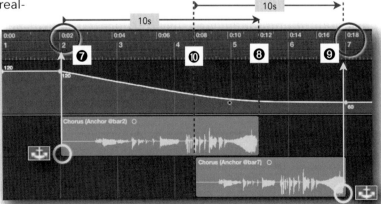

Once you throw in the "SMPTE lock" feature, then the real fun starts. More about those advanced topics in the *Tempo and Time* chapter.

# Audio File Editing

Now finally, let's get to the cool stuff, the destructive editing.

Make sure to have "Follow Tempo" disabled for the Region in the Region Inspector or you get a Dialog Window ❶ with a warning. Also, if you don't have write privileges to the audio file, then the editing commands are unavailable (dimmed) ❷.

## ➡ Safety Net

Before applying your destructive edits, consider the various safety nets that Logic has to offer.

### 🙂 Undo

Destructive audio edits are not endlessly available as with other edits you perform in Logic. For Logic to provide an undo step means, it has to save the audio file first. Depending on the size of the audio file and the number of audio edits you perform, that could require some serious storage capacity. That's why Logic let's you configure a few settings in the *Preferences ➤ Audio ➤ Audio File Editor* ❸:

Preferences ➤ Audio ➤ Audio File Editor

- ▸ **Number of Undo Steps**: Enter the number of undo steps Logic should store with your Project.
- ▸ **Record Normalize operation in Undo History**: Enable this checkbox to also undo Normalize operations.
- ▸ **Clear Undo History when closing project**: All the saved audio files in the Undo History are deleted when closing your Project. Maybe you want to enable this only if you are sure you don't need to revert to a previous step.
- ▸ **Warning before processing function by key command**: Key Commands let you speed up your workflow, but sometimes, in the heat of the moment, you hit the wrong key combination by accident. With this checkbox enabled, you always get a Warning Dialog ❹ before executing an edit operation triggered with a Key Command, plus it tells you how many Undo Steps are left.

### 🙂 Interrupt

You can interrupt any ongoing operation with the standard Key Command *Cmd+.*

### 🙂 Backup

Using the Undo steps to go back is a quick way to undo what you just did, but sometimes, it is part of the overall Undo History, so if you made other edits in your Project that you want to keep, then rolling back the last few edits on the audio file is a little bit more tricky. For that, Logic provides a simple mechanism:
*Create Backup - Revert to Backup*

Whenever you are about to make some serious destructive edits to the audio file, just use the "*Create Backup*" command.

 Local Menu *Audio File ➤ Create Backup*

 Key Command (*Create Backup*) **ctr+B**

A Dialog Window ❶ tells you that Logic is storing a copy of the current audio file with the file extension dup (in the same location as the original audio file). That's it, just one command. You might not even use it. It is there, just in case.

If it happens that the last few edits you did on that audio file were not so good after all, and you want to go back to the version when you saved the backup, you have to use only one command.

 Local Menu *Audio File ➤ Revert to Backup*

Key Command (*Revert to Backup*) **ctr+opt+cmd+B**

Now, Logic automatically swaps out the current audio file (with all the not so great edits) with the version you saved with the *Create Backup* command earlier. No need to manually copy-paste, remember where the original copy is, reestablish the links to the Audio Region, etc. Everything is automatically taken care of with just that one command. A Dialog Window ❷ even tells you the time stamp of the backup file, plus the warning that you cannot undo that step!

Because it is just a click away, you might get into the habit of always using that command, whenever you need to go back to a specific state. If there is already a backup file (.dup) for a specific audio file that you created previously, it will be overwritten with the new version.

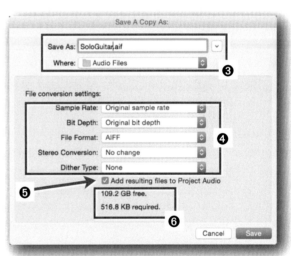

###  Save a Copy As...

This is another option to save a copy of the current audio file. It's purpose is less for backing up and safety, but for those situations, when you want to use a specific audio file twice in your Project and want to apply different destructive audio edits to it.

 Local Menu *Audio File ➤ Save A Copy As...*

The available Key Command with the same name is for saving the Project, not the audio file.

A Save Dialog provides the following settings:

▶ **Name and Location** ❸
▶ **Audio Format Settings** ❹: Sample Rate, Bit Depth, etc.
▶ **Add resulting files to Project Audio** ❺: Enable this checkbox to have the saved audio file available in your Project Audio Browser right away.
▶ **Storage Info** ❻: Logic calculates the size of the new audio file, plus how much storage is available on the selected drive.

###  Save Selection As...

This command opens the same Save Dialog ❼. The only difference is that instead of saving the entire audio file, you save only the current Selection Area as a new audio file.

## ➡️ *Cut - Copy - Paste - Delete*

Let's start with the most basic edit command. Although most of the destructive audio editing commands are listed under the Local Functions Menu, the Cut-Copy-Paste commands are standard editing operations that are listed under the Edit Menu.

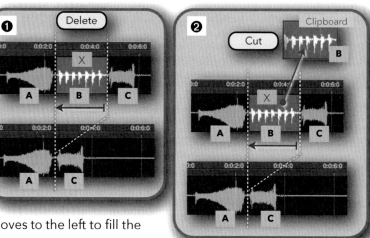

### 💀 **Delete ❶** *delete*

This command will remove the Selection Area and the section to its right moves to the left to fill the gap.

### 💀 **Cut ❷** *cmd+X*

This is a "delete and move" command. The Selection Area gets copied to the clipboard and deleted from the audio file. The section to the right moves to the left to fill the gap. To delete a section without moving anything on the waveform, use the *Silence* operation.

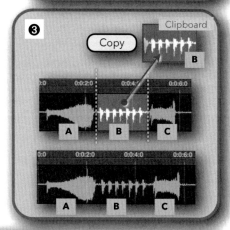

### 💀 **Copy ❸** *cmd+C*

This command just copies the Selection Area to the clipboard without doing anything to the audio file.

### 💀 **Paste** *cmd+V*:

Please note that there are two variations of the Paste commands:

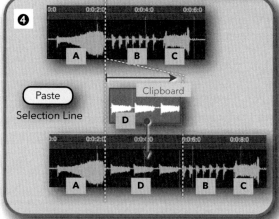

▸ Insert ❹: If you have only a Selection Line on your waveform, then the content of the clipboard gets inserted at that position. The part of the waveform to the right of the Selection Line gets moved to the right.

▸ Overwrite ❺ ❻: If you have a Selection Area on your waveform, then that section gets removed and the content of the clipboard gets inserted at the left border of the Selection Area. The part to the right of the Selection Area moves to the right border of the new audio content. This operation could shorten or lengthen the original audio file, depending on the length of the Selection Area and the content on the Clipboard.

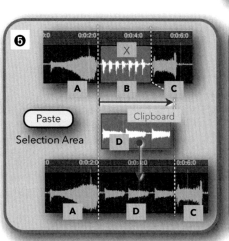

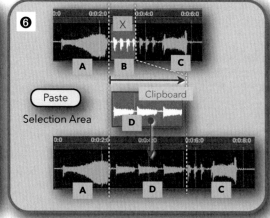

## ➡ Draw

This edit procedure is not listed in any edit menu, because it is not a command. It is a mouse action. This is the ultimate destructive edit of the audio file, because you are manually re-drawing the waveform. The purpose of this is not to draw a good sounding audio file waveform, it is for fixing clicks.

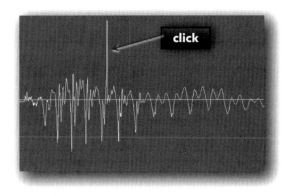

Whenever you hear a click in your audio recording, zoom into that area on the waveform and you will most likely see a sudden high amplitude spike. This is the perfect situation to use the zoom and scrubbing technique we discussed earlier. Once you located the click, you can go ahead and "draw it out".

- Switch to the Pencil Tool to draw on the waveform.
- You have to zoom in far enough on the waveform to do the drawing. If you are not zoomed in enough, then the Pencil Tool automatically switches to the Zoom Tool when you try to draw. Not only is this a hint that you have to zoom in more, you have the right Tool right at your fingertips to do the zooming.
- *Drag* (Mono Draw) to draw the waveform. The waveform edges are smoothed out. While drawing, move back to the left before lifting the mouse to undo the drawing.
- *Opt+drag* (Stereo Draw) to draw on one channel of a stereo waveform and have it apply to both channels of the audio signal.
- Optional, choose *View > Show as Sample & Hold* to show the individual Sample Bits as I discussed earlier.

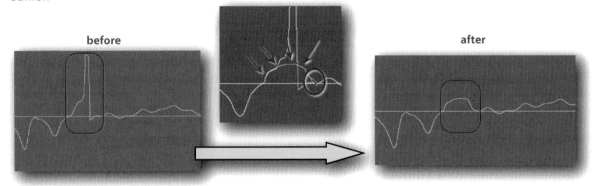

### Drawing Tips:
- When you draw the waveform, make sure to create a smooth line. Any sudden changes can create high frequencies (changes the sound) and in the worst case scenario, another click.
- You can fix technical clicks (a dropped sample word or two), but also acoustic imperfections (to some extend). Even if you can't eliminate those acoustic noises (smack, hits, etc.), sometimes you can reduce them.
- Listen to the result. Sometimes it looks worse than it sounds. If you can't hear it, don't sweat it.
- Make sure to listen to your subwoofer, because your new waveform drawing can create some unwanted low frequency pops.

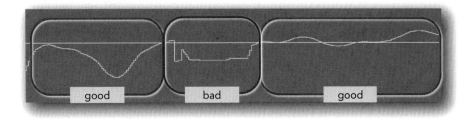

## ➡ Trim

This command is an easy one. To "Trim" means to delete the sections before and after the Selection Area, for example, any pauses before and after the actual signal.

Use any of the following commands:

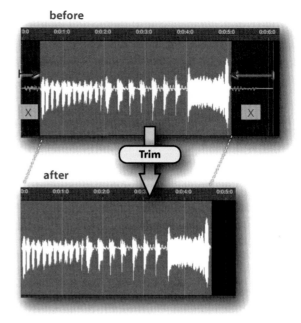

before

after

Trim

- Local Menu *Functions* ➤ *Trim*
- Key Command (*Trim*) *cmd+T*

You can use this command to "finalize" the Audio Regions in your Project to trim any unnecessary sections of its parent audio file (and save some disk space). Use the command *Region-> Selection* to select the area of the Region. But only use it if you are really sure and only on one Audio Region per audio file.

**Warning! The selected portion will be permanently deleted (the audio file stored on your hard drive will be overwritten).**

2 Regions in the Tracks area use this audio file. The length of these Regions will be adjusted automatically.

Cancel    Delete

Please note that this command deletes portions of the audio file, and therefore, changes its length. Any Audio Region that is referenced to that audio file could also change in length and even its position. That's why you get an extra Dialog Window where you have to confirm this "Delete" operation.

## ➡ Silence

The Silence operation lets you "delete" a section of the audio file without changing its length. Remember, the delete command or Cut command will fill the deleted gap, and therefore, shortens the audio file.

Use any of the following commands

before

after

Silence

- Local Menu *Functions* ➤ *Silence*
- Key Command (*Silence*) *ctr+delete*

## ➡ Change Gain

The Change Gain command opens an additional Dialog Window ❶ first:

    Local Menu *Functions ➤ Change Gain...*
    Key Command (*Change Gain...*) *ctr+G*

The Change Gain Dialog is a "modeless" Dialog, which means, you can leave the window open while making changes in another window. For example, make a different selection, select another file, and so on.

These are the settings:

▶ **Search Maximum ❷**: *Click* the "*Search Maximum*" button to let Logic look for the highest level in the current Selection Area.

▶ **Maximum**: These two numbers display the maximum level of the Selection in percentage (100% = 0dBFS) and dB.

▶ **Change Relative ❸**: These are the two fields that you can use to enter how much you want to change the level. *Click* on the number and enter a numeric value, *click* on the up/down arrow, or *slide* the values up/down.

▶ **Results in Absolute**: These two numbers display the resulting level in percentage and dB ("Maximum" + "Change Relative").

You can change the gain between -40dB ... +12dB. Make sure not to exceed 0dB as the resulting level to avoid any clipping. The Change Gain Dialog will indicate that with "(Clipped)" ❹.

*Example*: A solo recording might have some noise level during pauses. Cutting those sections out would sound unnatural. Using an expander might work, and using automation might be too "fragile" when moving stuff around. In such a case, lowering the level of just a couple dBs might sound more natural.

## ➡ Normalize

**Local Menu ➤ Functions ➤ Settings...**

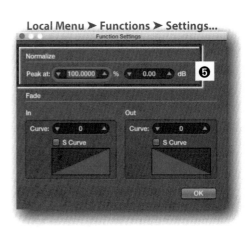

To normalize an audio file (or a section of it) means to raise the overall level (without changing its dynamics) to reach a specific value. Usually this is 0dBFS, the maximum level of a digital audio signal without any distortion (FS=Full Scale, all available bits).

With this Normalize command, you can set the level to any other value other than 0dB in the *Function Settings* window ❺ (*Functions ➤ Settings...*). These settings will be stored in the Logic Preferences file.

Use the Normalize commands with:

    Local Menu *Functions ➤ Normalize*
    Key Command (*Normalize*) *ctr+N*

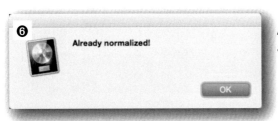

A Dialog Window ❻ reminds you if the section of the audio is already normalized at 0dB.

## ➡️ Fade In - Out

You can apply a Fade-in or a Fade-out to a Selection Area. This is useful when you have the beginning or ending of an audio file starting or ending with a noticeable level (i.e. background noise). With a short Fade-in or Fade-out you can avoid any sudden signal jumps. You can also use it to smoothen out a harsh attack ❶ of a signal (maybe it was cut improperly).

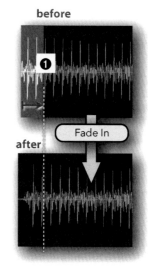
before
Fade In
after

Use any of the following commands:

- 🎚️ Local Menu *Functions ➤ Fade In / Fade Out*
- 🎚️ Key Command (*Fade In* or *Fade Out*) *ctr+I* or *ctr+O*

You can adjust the Fade Curves independently for the Fade In and Fade Out in the Functions Settings Window ❷. Set it between -99 to +99 (0 is linear curve). Enable the checkbox to use an S-Curve ❸.

**Local Menu ➤ Functions ➤ Settings...**

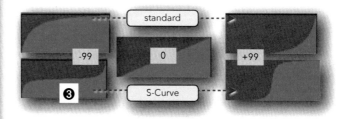
standard
-99    0    +99
❸    S-Curve

## ➡️ Reverse

This procedure is mainly used as an effect. For example, select the ring-out out of a reverb tail from a cymbal ❹ or any sting, copy it to the beginning of the cymbal and reverse it as a reverse attack to the actual signal. Or, you can take any audio segment and reverse it, to mix it creatively with the original signal.

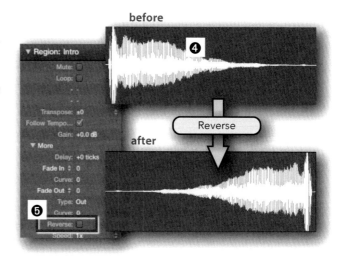
before
❹
Reverse
after

Use any of the following commands:

- 🎚️ Local Menu *Functions ➤ Reverse*
- 🎚️ Key Command (*Reverse*) *sh+ctr+R*

You can also reverse an Audio Region no-destructively in the Region Inspector ❺.

## ➡️ Invert

This procedure "flips the phase" by 180°. That means, all the positive values become negative and the negative values become positive. You don't hear any difference when listening to just a single signal (mono). It is mainly used to improve or fix phase issues between two channels dues to delays or latencies. For example, a signal recorded with two microphones or two identical signals running through different channel strips with individual (latency-inducing) plugins.

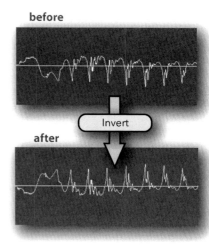
before
Invert
after

Use any of the following commands:

 Local Menu *Functions ➤ Invert*
 Key Command (*Invert*) *sh+ctr+I*

**Remove DC Offset**

DC stands for "Direct Current" (the other one is AC, Alternate Current).

A cheap or faulty audio interface can add such a low level DC voltage to your audio signal. It is visible when the waveform is centered a little bit above or below the center line. Although this DC signal might not be audible (except when the actual audio signal reaches a lower level), it definitely becomes audible when you edit such an audio signal by cutting it.

This command detects any DC offset level and eliminates it. You can see the before after effect.

 Local Menu *Functions ➤ Remove DC Offset*

Key Command (*Remove DC Offset*) *ctr+D*

 **Time and Pitch Machine**

The Time and Pitch Machine is the granddaddy of changing an audio file's time and pitch parameter in Logic. This procedure was available in Logic before the introduction of the more "hip" features like Apple Loops and Flex, which handle most procedures more efficiently. However, the gold-old Time and Pitch Machine still has some tricks up its sleeves that makes it worth using.

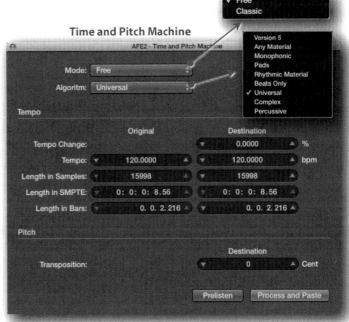

Time and Pitch Machine

Open the window with the menu command

*Functions ➤ Pitch and Time Machine...*

These are the parameters:

▶ **Mode**: Choose "*Free*" to change the Tempo without affecting the Pitch, and vice versa. For a traditional "varispeed" effect used on a tape machine, select "*Classic*".

▶ **Algorithm**: Choose from nine different algorithms optimized for specific types of audio material. This is only available in Free Mode.

▶ **Tempo Parameters**: You can either set a change of the tempo (as percentage or a specific tempo value) or a change of the length (in Samples, SMPTE, or Bars/Beats) of the selection in the audio file. The first column shows the original value (read only) and the second column lets you change any of the parameters (type, slide, click on arrows). Changing one unit will update the other fields accordingly.

▶ **Pitch Parameters**: Set the pitch change between -2400 … 2400 cents (two octaves).

▶ **Prelisten**: *Click* this button to toggle between start-stop for auditioning the audio selection with the Pitch value applied (not the Tempo).

▶ **Process and Paste**: This will execute the operation with the chosen parameters.

Please note that the Time and Pitch Machine Window is a modeless window, which means, you can leave it open to change the selection on the Audio File Editor, or select a different audio file.

When you time compress or time stretch an Audio Regions in the Tracks Window by *opt+dragging* its borders (Time Stretch Tools appear ), then those operations use the Time and Pitch Machine (only if Flex Mode or Apple Loops is disabled).

# Others

The Audio File Editor has a few more features:

## ➡ *Sample Loop (EXS24)*

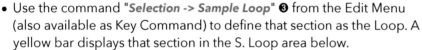

In previous Logic versions, the Audio File Editor was called the "*Sample Editor*". This was at a time when there weren't gazillion gigabytes of sample libraries available. Back then, you often created your own instruments with Logic's own Sampler, the EXS24. You can start to prepare the individual audio samples in the Audio File Editor that you want to use in your Sampler Instrument.

Here is the procedure:

- Let's assume you have an audio file in the Audio File Editor ❶ that you want to use as an audio sample in the EXS24, a piano note.
- You draw a Selection Area ❷ over the section you want to use as a Loop. You can use the Cycle Mode in the Audio File Editor to check how it sounds (without the crossfade you might add later in the EXS24).
- Use the command "*Selection -> Sample Loop*" ❸ from the Edit Menu (also available as Key Command) to define that section as the Loop. A yellow bar displays that section in the S. Loop area below.
- Use the command "Write Sample Loop to Audio File" ❹ from the Edit Menu (also available as Key Command) to write that Loop information as metadata to the actual audio file.
- Open an EXS24 Instrument ❺ and click the Edit Button ❻ to open the EXS24 Instrument Editor.
- Create a new Zone and load that audio file ❼.
- You can see the Loop Start and End values ❽ (in Samples) in the Instrument Editor match the Loop Start and End from the audio file in the Audio File Editor (*opt+click* on the Selection to display the Help Tag ❾).
- *Double+click* on any audio file ❿ in the EXS Instrument Editor to open that sample (audio file) in the Audio File Editor where you can edit it, independent from the audio files of our Project.

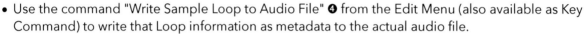

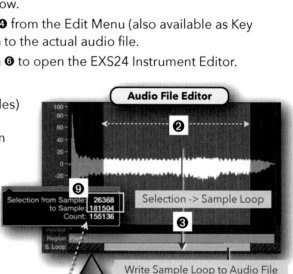
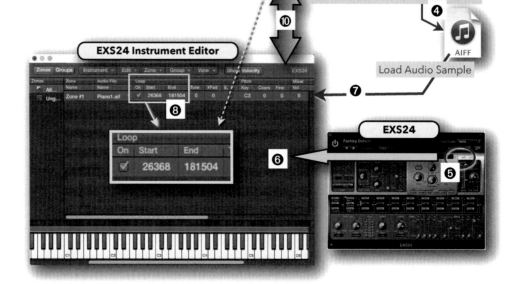

### Audio File Editor as a Sample Editor for the EXS 24

Let's discover a different side of the Audio File Editor:

▶ **Main Purpose**: The standard procedure for the Audio File Editor is to edit your audio files in your Project. In addition, on the previous page I showed you how to use the Audio File Editor to take one of those audio files in your Project (listed in the Project Audio Browser) and prepare it for an EXS24 Instrument, prepare the loop, and write that loop information to the actual audio file so the EXS Instrument Editor can use it.

▶ **Additional Purpose**: The Audio File Editor serves a second purpose. You can use it to edit audio samples directly from within the EXS24 Instrument Editor.

- Open an EXS24 Instrument ❶ and *click* on the Edit Button in the upper right corner to open the EXS24 Instrument Editor ❷.
- In the Instrument Editor, *double-click* on an audio sample ❸ to open that audio file directly in the Audio File Editor ❹ (standalone window).
- This audio file, displayed in the Audio File Editor, is not listed in the Project Audio Window, because it is not part of your Project, it is part of the EXS Instrument.
- The Title Bar ❺ of the Audio File Editor window displays the path to that audio file. Most likely to one of the folders for the EXS24 Samples directory ❻.
- Now you can edit that audio sample in the Audio File Editor with all the features we just learned, and it will be saved (overwritten!) to the original file ❼ in its original location.

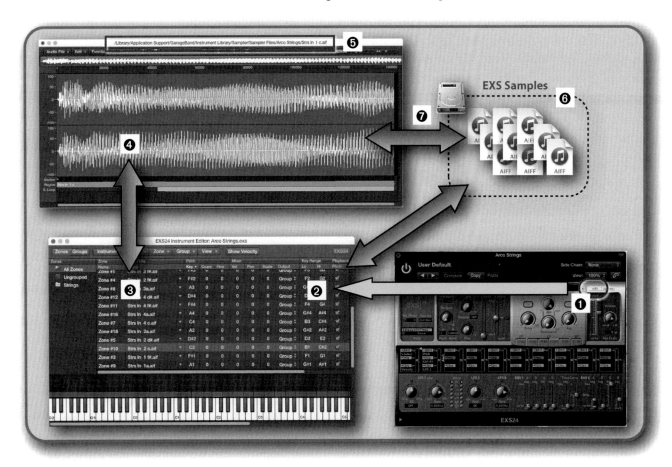

Remember when using the command "Write Sample Loop to Audio File". This will actually write the metadata at the end of the audio file. If you open that audio file with a text editor, you can see those additional entries *LpBeg* and *LpEnd* at the end of the file, after the data for the digital audio signal ❽.

## ➡ *External Sample Editor*

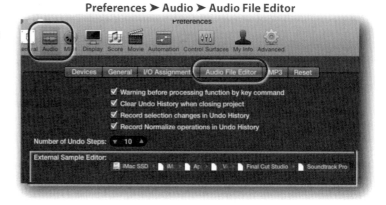

Logic also allows you to outsource the editing of audio files.

*Click* on the field next to the "External Sample Editor" in the *Preferences ➤ Audio ➤Audio File Editor*. This opens an Open Dialog that lets you navigate to a third party application that you want to use to edit audio files.

In my example, I selected the app "Soundtrack Pro", a now discontinued app from Apple that came bundled with previous versions of Logic Pro.

Now when you select an audio file in the Project Audio Browser, you can see in the Edit Menu the command "Open in Soundtrack Pro"

 Project Audio *Edit ➤ Open in "Name of Application"*
 Key Command (*Open in External Sample Editor*) *sh+W*

Here is the procedure:
- Select the audio file
- Choose the command *Open in Soundtrack Pro*
- The file will now open in the third party application
- Apply the edits and save
- The audio file will be saved in its original location and updated in Logic

Audio FIles Editor

Soundtrack Pro

## ➡ *Additional commands*

Here are the rest of the Local Menu Commands that I haven't covered so far:

### ⚙ Detect / Edit Transients

The Local Menus contain two commands regarding Transients. One lets you Detect Transients (*Audio File ➤ Detect Transients* ❶), and the second one lets you toggle the Transient Editing Mode (*View ➤ Transient Editing Mode* ❷). This is the same function as clicking on the Transient Editing Mode button  in the Menu Bar to edit the Transient Markers ❸.

I'll discuss that feature in the next *Flex* chapter.

### ⚙ Adjust Tempo by Selection and Locators

This is one of the tempo/time procedures that lets you adjust the Tempo of your Project. I discuss those features in great detail in the *Tempo and Time* chapter.

This command changes the tempo by matching the Cycle Range to the Selection Area.

⚙ *Local Menu ➤ Functions ➤ Adjust Tempo by Selection and Locators* ❹

### ⚙ Helpful Commands

Here are a few additional commands:

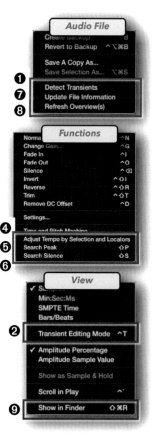

▸ **Search Peak** ❺: If there is no current Selection Area, then Logic will search between the current Selection Line and the end of the audio file. It moves the Selection line to that found peak (highest amplitude) and using the command again will create a Selection Area from that peak to the end of the audio file. You can create a Selection Area to search for the highest amplitude peak in that range.

⚙ *Local Menu ➤ Functions ➤ Search Peak*
⚙ Key Command (*Search Peak*) **sh+P**

▸ **Search Silence** ❻: When you use this command, Logic places the Selection Line at the first position it detects silence (flat line on the center of the waveform). This is either the first silence in the waveform or the first silence in the current Selection Area. Repeat the command to place the Selection Line to the next silence spot (if available).

⚙ *Local Menu ➤ Functions ➤ Search Silence*
⚙ Key Command (*Search Silence*) **sh+S**

▸ **Show in Finder** ❼: This is always a useful command that opens a Finder window with the folder location the audio file is stored in.

⚙ *Local Menu ➤ View ➤ Show in Finder*
⚙ Key Command (*Show in Finder*) **sh+cmd+R**

▸ **Update File Information** ❽: This command re-reads the file information stored in the audio file (format, Sample Rate, Bit Depth, metadata, etc.).

⚙ *Local Menu ➤ Audio File ➤ Update File Information*

▸ **Refresh Overview(s)** ❾: This command redraws the waveform of the audio file.

⚙ *Local Menu ➤ Audio File ➤ Refresh Overview(s)*

## The Concept

Flex is a feature in Logic that allows you to edit the timing and pitch of Audio Regions. Those edits are not just applied to the entire Audio Region, but to individual notes "inside" the audio recording.

This is a powerful tool that provides editing techniques that were previously only possible with MIDI Regions:

### MIDI Regions

When you record the MIDI signal of a hardware synthesizer as a MIDI Region in Logic, it records each individually played note as a discrete MIDI Event. The pitch and timing of each of those single MIDI Events can easily be edited in the Piano Roll Editor by changing the timing (horizontal position) and the pitch (vertical position) of those Events.

### Audio Regions

When you record the audio signal of that same hardware synthesizer as an Audio Region in Logic, it records a "sonic snapshot" of that audio signal. That "picture" is what you see as an "audio waveform" on the Audio Region.

Think of a photo that shows five people. Taking one person on that image and move him or her a little bit to the right, or make another person look 20 years younger, is only possible with digital images and powerful Photoshop tools. If you want to do similar "surgery" on an audio recording, you need the audio recording in digital form, plus a powerful tool that can manipulate the data, so you can alter the pitch and timing of discrete notes in an audio recording. That tool in Logic is called **Flex**.

### ➡ *Example of what you can do*

Although the magic of Flex can be applied in Logic to any Audio Region (not MIDI or Drummer Region), the best results (especially for editing pitch information) can be achieved on "monophonic" recordings, one instrument (or vocalist) performing a single melody or line. Here are a few examples:

- ☑ Move individual notes of a recording
- ☑ Apply a quantize grid to the entire Region of a live performance (drummer, bass, guitar, etc.)
- ☑ Make individual notes shorter or longer
- ☑ Correct the pitch of individual notes of a vocal or instrument performance
- ☑ Apply pitch correction to an entire Region of a vocalist
- ☑ Transpose individual notes to change the melody
- ☑ Make multiple copies of a vocal performance and change their notes to create harmony parts
- ☑ Change parameters of a human voice like vibrato and formants

# About Pitch and Time

If you record an audio signal, i.e. a strumming guitar, you can determine the two main parameters of that audio file:

- ☑ The **Key** the guitarist was playing: This is pitch information
- ☑ The **Tempo** the guitarist was playing: This is timing information

The problem with audio files is that these two parameters (pitch and time) are "connected" ❶.

- ☑ **Change the Pitch** (of an audio file): This would also change the timing. For example, raising the pitch of that guitar performance would play back the audio file faster, and lowering the pitch would play back the file slower.

- ☑ **Change the Timing** (of an audio file): This would also change the pitch. For example, slowing down the tempo would lower the pitch, and speeding up the playback would raise the pitch

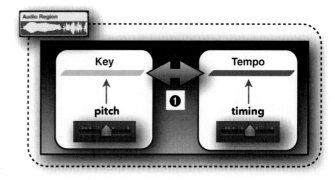

However, when you want to lower the key of your Logic Project because your singer can't hit the high note, then that strumming guitar you recorded earlier would play too slow if you changed the pitch of the Audio Region (and, therefore, the Audio File). Or, if you want to raise the Tempo of your Project by 5bpm and speed up your strumming guitar, it would play it back in a higher key. This is the main limitation when recording on tape or disk. Now that your recording is stored as digital audio files, you can take advantage of two techniques that break the connection ❷ between pitch and time.

- ☑ **Pitch Shifting**: This technology in digital audio allows you to change the pitch of an audio file without affecting its playback speed.

- ☑ **Time Stretching**: This technology in digital audio allows you to change the playback speed of an audio file without affecting its pitch.

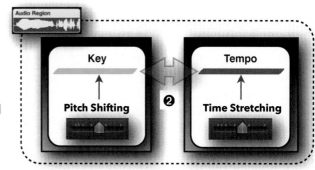

## ➡ *Sliced Audio*

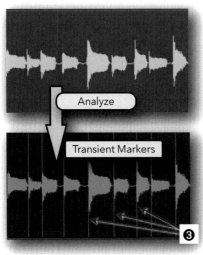

Pitch Shifting and Time Stretching use one special trick to make this work. Instead of treating an audio file as a whole, they cut it up into smaller slices and apply their digital audio processing to those individual slices in order to make the magic work. This requires the initial process of analyzing the audio file to look for significant peaks in the waveform, which are good locations to cut the waveform. Those peaks, sudden changes in the amplitude, are called Transients.

### Transient Markers

Instead of actually cutting the audio file at those Transients, Logic marks those peak positions in the audio file with so-called Transient Markers ❸.

## ➡ *How the Magic Works*

In the following screenshots, I demonstrate how Time Shifting of a single note in an Audio Region works by treating those smaller slices instead of the entire waveform.

### ❶ The Problem

We start with an audio file that has a note with bad timing. For example, this could be the recording of a strumming guitar where the player hits one chord a little before the downbeat.

### ❷ The Preparation

Now imagine that we split the audio file exactly on that note, make another split on a note before, and a split after that note. By making three splits on the audio file, we end up having created four files.

### ❸ The Operation

File 3 is the one that contains the note with the bad timing. Let's assume the note is 10ms too early. Here is the first trick. We would squeeze (compress) that audio file 3 so it is 10ms shorter. If we keep the right border of the file locked at its position, then the left border of the file will start 10ms later. The result, the guitar chord, which starts exactly at the left border of file 3, now plays 10ms later, exactly where we wanted it to be.

### ❹ The Clean-up

By making file 3 shorter, we left a gap of 10ms between file 2 and file 3. To fill that gap, we would take file 2 and stretch it by exactly the same amount of 10ms. This makes file 2 10ms longer. This time, we keep the left border of the file locked, which means it ends 10ms later. That right border of file 2 touches now exactly the left border of file 3 and the gap is closed.

### ❺ The Achievement

By closing up the gap, we end up with one continuous file when we merge the 4 individual files together again. The problem note is corrected by playing exactly on time and another important aspect: If we look at the area of the former file 1 and file 4, nothing has changed there. That means, the content in the audio file before and after the corrected note stayed untouched.

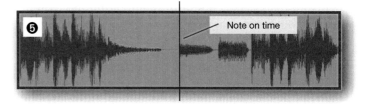

This was just a simplified example to demonstrate the procedure of the underlying Flex technology on how to do time correction inside an audio file. It uses time expansion and time compression, a common procedure in digital audio.

Please note that all that splitting, stretching, and squeezing is done in Logic in a non-destructive way. That means that the actual audio content in the file isn't altered at all. All the audio file manipulation is done as a playback procedure and you can modify it any time to get the best results.

# Transient Marker vs. Flex Marker

Now, when we begin to look at the Flex feature in Logic to learn how to perform such a time correction, we have to start with two important terms: Transient Markers (which I already mentioned) and Flex Markers. Working with Flex in Logic can get very confusing very quickly with all the various tools, procedures, and terminology, so let me point out the important difference between those two terms:

> A **Transient Marker** is only a <u>visual indicator</u> on the waveform
>
> A **Flex Marker** is "attached" to the waveform to <u>shift</u> the audio

### ☻ Transient Marker

The Transient Markers are only the visual indicators that are placed on top of the waveform to show where the peaks are, the sudden amplitude changes. There are two ways to generate Transient Markers:

▶ **Automatic**: You can let Logic analyze the audio file to automatically detect the transients in the audio waveform. It then displays Transient Markers on the waveform at those peak positions.

▶ **Manual**: You can modify the sensitivity for Logic, so it detects more or less transients, or you can directly move or delete existing Transient Markers and even create new Transient Markers anywhere on the waveform.

Here is a waveform displaying those Transient Markers as thin blue lines

Transient Markers

### ☻ Flex Marker

The Flex Markers are the actual tools that can shift a section of the audio waveform because they get "attached" to the waveform at that position. The existing Transient Markers function as possible "suggestions" where to place the Flex Markers. There are two ways to create Flex Markers:

▶ **Automatic**: Whenever you apply a quantize command to an Audio Region, Logic automatically creates Flex Markers first and then moves them to the selected Quantize Grid. Please note that Logic can place Flex Markers automatically only at a position of an existing Transient Marker. Logic can also create Flex Markers at a time position of a tempo change event from the Tempo Track.

▶ **Manual**: You can create Flex Markers anywhere on the waveform. You can even move or delete Flex Markers that Logic created automatically. Again, the Transient Markers only function as "suggestions", but you don't have to place the Flex Marker there.

Transient Markers and Flex Markers

Here is the same waveform with three added Flex Markers. They are the white lines that are a little thicker than the Transient Markers.

You still can see the thinner Transient Markers.

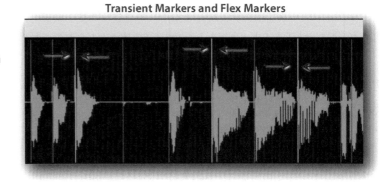

## ➡ *3 Flex Marker Needed*

You always need three Flex Markers for any operation where you want to shift a section of an audio waveform. Remember the three splits I demonstrated in the example earlier.

> **Any time-shift operation requires <u>THREE</u> Flex Markers**

That means a Flex Marker can have three different roles:

- ☑ **Flex Marker you are moving ❶**: This is the marker that you actually move left or right. Remember, a Flex Marker is "attached" to the waveform at that position. That means, moving the Flex Marker moves that section of the waveform with it. How big the section is that is shifted depends on the other two Flex Markers.

- ☑ **Flex Marker representing the left boundary ❷**: This is the Flex Marker that is located left of the Flex Marker you are moving. It marks the left boundary of the Flex process.
  - The section of the audio waveform ❹ between the Flex Marker you are moving and this left boundary Flex Marker will be the one that is affected when you move the center Flex Marker (time compressed or time expanded).
  - The section of the audio waveform left of this Flex Marker ❺ is not affected by the movement.
  - If there is no Flex Marker on the left, then the left Region border functions as the boundary.

- ☑ **Flex Marker representing the right boundary ❸**: This is the Flex Marker that is located to the right of the Flex Marker you are moving. It marks the right boundary of the Flex process.
  - The section of the audio waveform ❻ between the Flex Marker you are moving and this right boundary Flex Marker will be the one that is affected when you move the center Flex Marker (time compressed or time expanded).
  - The section of the audio waveform right of this Flex Marker ❼ is not affected by the movement.
  - If there is no Flex Marker on the right, then the right Region border functions as the boundary.

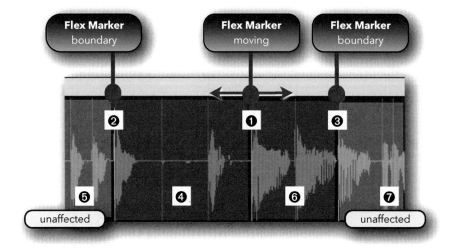

I hope this little demonstration makes it clear that you have to differentiate between the Flex Marker itself and its role it plays in a time shifting process.

- ▶ Are you placing a Flex Marker so you can move it (and the section of the waveform attached to it) to a new position in order to perform a time shifting?
- ▶ Are you placing a Flex Marker to set the boundaries for a specific time shifting process?
- ▶ Of course, a Flex Marker can have both roles, do the shifting and act as a boundary when you shift the Flex Marker next to it.

## ➡ *Location - Location - Location*

The placement of the Flex Markers is the key to a successful time shift process with the least amount of "side effects". The Transient Markers are often a good "suggestion" for a good location around a section that needs adjustment, but sometimes you need to place a Flex Marker where Logic didn't detect any peaks or it is not placed at the correct position. That's why you need the option to manually place the Flex Marker at any position or place the Transient Marker at any position to mark a location that you need later.

Here are two examples to show the importance of how to position the Flex Marker properly:

### 💀 Example 1

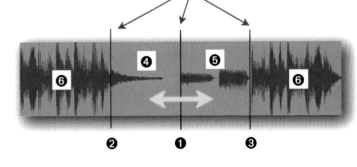

- ▶ The center Flex Marker ❶ is the one positioned at the note you want to move.
- ▶ The other two Flex Markers represent the left ❷ and right ❸ boundaries.
- ▶ The area of the waveform left ❹ of the center Flex Marker and right ❺ of the center Flex Marker are either extended or squeezed.
  Think of the center Flex Marker as a stick ❶ that is held in place by two rubber bands, which are tied to a pole on the left ❷ and a pole on the right ❸. If you pull the stick to the right, then the rubber band shortens on the right ❺ by the same amount the left ❹ rubber band extends. If you pull the stick to the left, then the rubber band shortens on the left by the same amount the right rubber band extends.
- ▶ The two areas outside that boundary ❻ are not affected by the squeezing and stretching and stay untouched.

In this example, the position of the right boundary marker ❸ is not a good choice. While we are moving the center Flex Marker ❶ to the right, the right section ❺ is squeezed. If you look closely at the waveform, you will notice that there is a second event (maybe a second guitar chord) that was played correctly in time. But now, by moving the chord at the center Flex Marker, we will move that second event too. Fixing one problem, but creating a new one.

### 💀 Example 2

Here is a better choice of how to set the Flex Marker in that case:

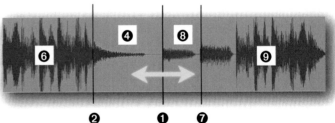

- ▶ We set the right boundary marker earlier, exactly at that chord ❼ that has the correct timing.
- ▶ Now the area to the right of the center Marker ❽ includes only the problematic chord. You affect only the note that needs to be shifted.
- ▶ The second chord (that shouldn't be shifted), which is at the position of the right Flex Marker ❼, lies outside the boundary ❾ and is, therefore, not affected wherever or how much you move the center Marker ❶.

Let's have a closer look at Transient Markers. Keep in mind that, in addition to Flex, Transient Markers can also be used for other tasks like slicing Audio Regions at Transient Markers or for various selections based on the position of Transient Markers.

## Where do Transient Markers Come From?

As we've already learned, Transient Markers can be created automatically by Logic during an analysis process that looks for transients in an Audio File. This automatic analysis is the first step of creating Transient Markers and can be triggered by various actions:

- Enabling Flex 🔀 on a Track ❶ (or selecting a Flex Mode) will analyze all the Audio Regions on that Track and any new Audio Region that is recorded on that Track or imported to that Track.
- Display an Audio Region in the Audio File Editor and select the command from the Local Menu *Audio File ➤ Detect Transient* or use the Key Command (*Detect Transients of Audio Files*) *unassigned*.
- Enable "Transient Editing Mode" by clicking on the Transient Editing Mode Button 📊 ❷ on the Menu Bar of the Audio File Editor.

Although all Flex procedures are non-destructive, and, therefore, don't alter the audio content of the Audio File, the information about the Transient Markers is written as metadata at the end of the Audio File. Any update of the Transient Markers will update the Audio File.

> **Transient Markers are written as metadata to the actual Audio File**

➡ *View Transient Markers*

The Transient Markers are visible in two places:

### ⚫ Audio File

When the Transient Editing Mode ❷ is enabled 📊, then the Transient Markers are displayed as thin orange lines ❸.

### ⚫ Audio Region

When Flex Mode ❶ is enabled 🔀, then the Transient Markers are displayed as thin white lines ❹ on the Audio Region in the Tracks Window or Audio Track Editor.

**Visible Transient Markers**

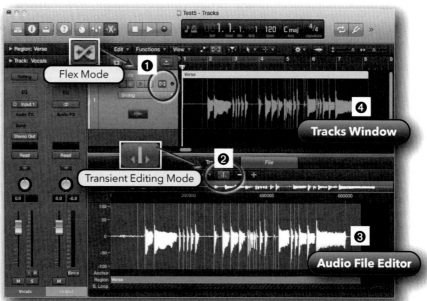

# Transient Editing Mode

The Transient Editing Mode has to be enabled to have the Transient Markers of an Audio File displayed in the Audio File Editor. And as the term indicates, this mode also has to be enabled in order to manually edit the Transient Markers.

### ➡ Enable Transient Editing Mode

Toggle the Transient Editing Mode with any of these commands:

- *Click* the Transient Editing Mode Button ▪️ ▪️ in the Menu Bar ❶
- Local Menu Command *View* ➤ *Transient Editing Mode* ❷
- Key Command (*Toggle Transient Editing Mode*) *ctr+T*
- Local Menu Command *Edit* ➤ *Detect Transients* ❸ (this will reset the Transient Markers if there were any manual edits)

Please keep in mind that when you enable the Transient Editing Mode for the first time on an Audio Region, the following things will happen (in a split second):

- ☑ Logic analyzes the Audio File and looks for peaks in the audio file.
- ☑ These detected peaks are displayed in the audio waveform with these thin orange vertical lines ❹, the Transient Markers.
- ☑ The information about those Transient Markers will be written to the Audio File as metadata.

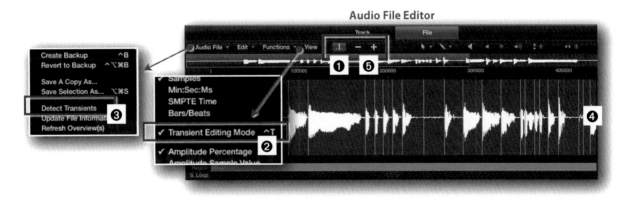

### 💀 Default Transient Detection

Logic uses some sort of threshold when it analyzes an Audio File where it decides if a peak is strong enough to be interpreted as a Transient, and, therefore, marked with a Transient Marker.

### 💀 Modify Transient Detection

- You can adjust that "detection sensitivity" so Logic creates more or less Transient Markers on the waveform. *Click* on the plus or minus button ❺ ▪️ ➕, the "Transient Detection Button", to increase or decrease the number of Transient Markers. These two buttons are only visible when Transient Editing Mode is enabled ▪️.
- Key Command (*Increase Number of Transients*) *ctr+=* (the equal key)
- Key Command (*Decrease Number of Transients*) *ctr+-* (the minus key)

The increase/decrease command can be applied to the entire waveform or just a selection of it by dragging a section across that area of the waveform (which will be highlighted).

## Manually Edit Transient Marker

You can manually add more Transient Markers at any position or remove any Transient Markers.

▸ **Create**: *Cmd+click* with the Pencil Tool on the waveform area to create a new Transient Marker. Please note that the Command-Click Tool automatically changes to the Pencil Tool when Edit Transient Mode is enabled. The new Transient Marker will only be placed at the click position if there is no peak in the waveform "nearby". If there is an amplitude peak, then the new Transient Marker snaps to that peak position.

▸ **Move**: When you place the Cursor Tool over a Transient Marker, it will change to a Reposition Marker Tool. With this tool you can *drag* any Transient Marker to a new position. You can restrict the positions to Zero Crossings:

- Local Menu *Edit* ➤ *Snap Edits to Zero Crossings*
- Key Command (*Snap Edits to Zero Crossings*) *ctr+NumberPad0*
- *Ctr+click* on the Waveform Display to open the Shortcut Menu *Snap Edits to Zero Crossings*

▸ **Delete**: *Click* on any Transient Marker with the Eraser Tool to delete a single one, or *drag* across the Transient Markers with the Eraser Tool to wipe out a whole section of Transient Markers. Don't drag across the Region Header or it will delete the Region instead of the Transient Markers. You can also *double-click* on a Transient Marker with the Pointer Tool to delete it or drag a selection on the Waveform Display and hit the *delete* key.

Please note that the Quantize commands ❶ in the Region Inspector create Flex Markers based on the Transient Markers to quantize the individual audio segments. If there are no Transient Markers ❷, then the Quantize command does not work.

## Restore Default Transient Marker

You can use any of the following two commands to re-analyze the Audio File and restore the default Transient Markers. This command enables Transient Edit Mode if it was off:

- Local Menu Command *Audio File* ➤ *Detect Transients*
- Key Command (*Detect Transients of Audio File*) *unassigned*

A Dialog Window pops up with a warning that this action will delete any manually edited Transient Markers.

## Architecture

Now, with the basic understanding of Transient Markers and Flex Markers, I want to take the time to introduce the architecture of Flex first and show how it is implemented in Logic before learning the actual editing procedures.

Before making all those cool edits, you have to be familiar with the underlying concept first so you know what you can do and what you cannot do. Most importantly, on which level do you change a parameter to achieve a specific effect. The Flex implementation can be quite confusing, so let me introduce a diagram that shows those important levels in Flex.

**Flex Architecture**

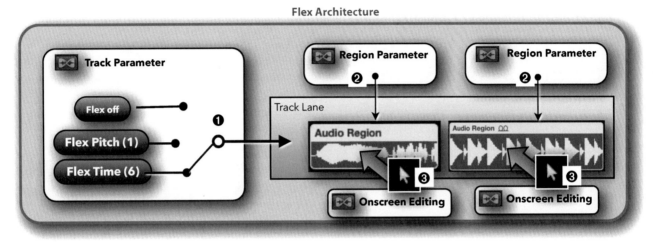

➡ *Three Levels*

Flex is not just one window in Logic where you set a few parameters. Flex operates on three levels (not counting the Audio File Editor). That means, all the necessary controls are spread all over the place on the Logic interface and whenever you are using Flex, you have to be aware of those places.

### Track Parameter ❶

This is the first and most important level: You turn on the Flex feature. Three important things:

- Flex is a track-based feature, which means each Track can be enabled and configured individually.
- There are two different Flex features: "Flex Pitch" that lets you manipulate the pitch and "Flex Time" that lets you manipulate the timing in an Audio Region.
- Flex Time provides six different algorithms (for specific types of audio material) and Flex Pitch only one. This makes a total of seven so-called "Flex Modes" to choose from.

### Region Parameter ❷

While the Flex Mode is determined on a track-based level, each single Region has its individual Flex Parameters that are stored as a part of the Region Parameters. You can even turn Flex off for an individual Region.

### Onscreen Editing ❸

While the Track Parameter affects the entire Track and the Region Parameter affects the individual Region, the actual power of the Flex feature is the editing of individual sections inside a Region. These edits are mostly done as Onscreen Edits by using various Cursor Tools directly on the Region. The Region will display Flex-specific interface elements that are superimposed on the Region's waveform, which makes Flex editing very intuitive as we will see in a moment.

## ➡ *Summary*

So here is a quick summary about the Flex feature:

☑ **Audio Regions only**: Flex applies only to Audio Regions on an Audio Track. It has nothing to do with MIDI Regions or Drummer Regions.

☑ **Track Based**: Flex Mode is a Track setting. That means that each Audio Track can be set individually to a specific Flex Mode. That also means that all Audio Regions on such a Track have the same Flex Mode applied to it (unless you turn it off for that Region).

☑ **Either - Or**: You can edit either Flex Pitch or Flex Time on an Audio Track (and all its Audio Regions on it), but not both at the same time. You can apply time and pitch edits one after the other, but there are some restriction that I will get into later.

☑ **Non-destructive**: Flex is a non-destructive editing technique. Whatever you do with it doesn't affect the Audio File itself (besides adding metadata), it is only a playback Parameter stored with the Audio Region.

# Interface

## *Show/Hide Flex*

The first button/command you encounter when using the Flex feature is the "Show/Hide Flex Button" ⬚. The concept is similar to Logic's Automation feature that also has a "Show/Hide Automation" Button ⬚. To use the Flex controls, you have to make them visible first (with one exception). It is the same concept as with the Automation feature. Once you are done with the editing, you can hide the controls again. Remember, this is only a visual command (you see it, you don't see it), it has no effect on the actual Flex functionality.

A few things to keep in mind:

▸ Similar to the Automation feature, the Flex feature also has two similar looking Flex Buttons. The more rectangular shaped button located on the Menu Bar is the "Show/Hide Flex Button" ⬚ ⬚ and the smaller square-shaped button located on each Track Header (when Flex is visible) is the "Enable Flex Button" ⬚ ⬚ .

▸ You can either show the Automation controls or the Flex controls in the Tracks Window. Turning on one will turn off the other ⬚ ⬚ and vice versa ⬚ ⬚ , or turn both off ⬚ ⬚ .

▸ In addition to the Show/Hide Flex Button, that is available in the Menu Bar of the Tracks Window, the Audio Track Editor has its own independent Show/Hide Flex Button on its Menu Bar to show/hide the Flex controls in the Audio Track Editor.

You can toggle the visibility of the Flex controls with the following commands:

🔘 *Click* the Show/Hide Flex Button ⬚ ⬚
The Tracks Window and the Audio Track Editor have that button, which toggles the display independently for each window. In addition, on the Audio Track Editor, the button also enables Flex Mode at the same time!

🔘 Main Menu *Edit ➤ Show/Hide Flex Pitch/Time*
(only if the Tracks Window has Key Focus)

🔘 Key Command (*Show/Hide Flex Pitch/Time*) **cmd+F**
Toggles the feature in the Tracks Window or Audio Track Editor depending on which one has Key Focus.

Here is a diagram that demonstrates the interface elements that are related to Flex. You can find them in three windows: The **Tracks Window ❶**, the **Main Inspector ❷**, and the **Audio Track Editor ❸**.

▶ **Show/Hide Flex Button ❹** (Global): This is a global button that only makes the Flex controls visible, but has no effect on the actual Flex feature. The button is available on two windows:

  • Tracks Window: When enabled, it increases the height of all Tracks, plus it displays the Flex Mode Menu and the Enable Flex Button on the Track Header of each Audio Track.

  • Audio Track Editor: This button on the Menu Bar toggles the visibility of the Flex Mode elements independent of the Tracks Window. It adds the Flex Mode Menu Button, the MIDI In Button, and the vertical zoom slider (only for Flex Pitch). Because this button also enables Flex Mode at the same time, it also changes the Waveform Display of the Audio Region for the onscreen Flex Editing.

▶ **Enable Flex Button ❺** (Track specific): This button, available on the Track Header of each Audio Track (when Show Flex Button is on), is an on/off button for the Flex Mode on that specific Track.

▶ **Flex Mode Menu Button ❻** (Track specific): This button opens the Flex Mode Menu, which lets you choose one of seven Flex Modes for the current Track. It is available on three Windows and you can choose the Flex Mode in either one, they are linked:

  • Tracks Window: The menu contains the seven Flex Modes. To turn Flex Mode off for that Track you have to turn off the Enable Flex Button next to it.

  • Track Inspector: The menu contains all the seven Flex Modes, plus the "Off" item. The "Off" selection has the same effect as deselecting the Enable Flex Button.

  • Audio Track Editor: The menu contains the seven Flex Modes, but you have no option to turn Flex off in the Audio Track Editor.

▶ **Flex Mode Parameters ❼** (Track specific): The Track Inspector is the only place that provides up to three additional Flex Mode Parameters (depending on the selected Flex Mode).

▶ **Flex Region Parameter ❽** (Region specific): The Region Inspector will display additional controls when Flex is enabled.

▶ **Flex Edit (Region specific) ❾**: The actual Flex Editing is done with the Cursor Tool on each individual Audio Region. The waveform area of the Region changes to show various onscreen controls when Flex is enabled. The onscreen Flex Editing can be done on the Tracks Window and Audio Track Editor.

▶ **Flex Pitch Controls ❿**: The Track Editor can display additional controls in its Local Inspector that is only available when Flex Mode is set to Flex Pitch.

## ➡ Tracks Window

And here is what these Flex elements look like on the actual Logic windows:

### Show/Hide Flex Button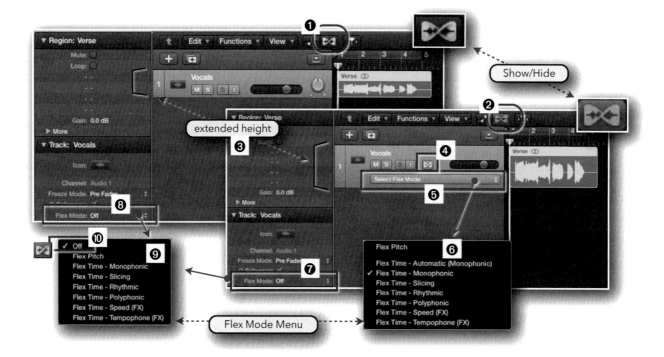

The two screenshots below show the Tracks Window with the Show/Hide Flex Button off ❶ and on ❷. This Project has just one Audio Track, but the visual changes apply to all Audio Tracks in the Tracks Window. Keep in mind that enabling the Show/Hide Automation Button will turn the Show/Hide Flex Button off, hiding all the Flex elements and displaying the Automation elements instead. You see three changes on a Track:

- ☑ **Track Height ❸**: The Track height increases to make room for the new Flex controls on the Track Header. Please note that all Tracks in your Tracks Window get higher, even MIDI Tracks, which don't have any Flex controls. Also, once you manually change the height of a Track, it will not be automatically resized anymore.

- ☑ **Enable Flex Button ❹**: This button is like an on/off switch for the Flex Mode on this Track. Any settings you made, the Flex Mode selection and the actual edits on the Audio Region are preserved, they are only bypassed when you turn the button off. The button is off by default.

- ☑ **Flex Mode Menu Button ❺**: This button displays the currently selected Flex Mode for this Track and when you *click* on it, it opens the Flex Mode Menu ❻ to choose a specific Flex Mode for this Track. The button displays "Select Flex Mode" if you haven't selected any Flex Mode yet on this Track.


## ➡ Track Inspector

The Track Inspector is part of the Main Inspector, the window pane to the left of the Tracks Window (toggle with Key Command *I*). It has one important, slightly different Flex control.

### Flex Mode Menu Button

The Flex Mode Menu Button ❽ is always displayed in the Track Inspector of an Audio Track regardless whether the Show/Hide Flex Button is on ❷ or off ❶. Although the Flex Mode Menu ❾ looks a bit different than the one on the Track Header ❻, it still lists the seven Flex Modes. In addition, it contains the "off" item ❿, which has the same function as turning off the Enable Flex Button on the Track Header. They are linked.

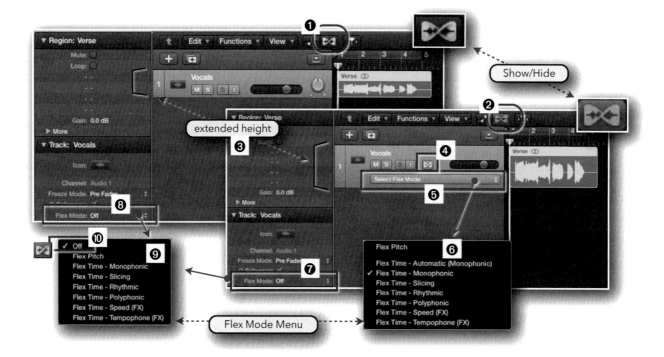

➡️ **Enable Flex Button**

Now let's look at the same Project and see what changes when you enable Flex for the first time:

☑️ **Turn on Flex:** You can do this in two ways (it is disabled when Track Protect Button is on 🔒):

    ◯ *Click* on the Enable Flex Button ❶ in the Track Header.

    ◯ Select a Flex Mode from the Flex Mode Menu ❷ (this automatically turns on Flex). Remember that the Flex Mode Menu Button is available in three locations (Track Header ❷, Track Inspector ❸, and Audio Track Editor). You can make the selection in any of those three menus.

☑️ **Confirm**: You will be prompted with a Dialog Window ❹ (only when you enable Flex for the first time on an Audio Track) to confirm that you really want to do this.

☑️ **Background Analyzes**: Logic will quickly analyze all the Audio Regions on that Track to prepare them for the Flex Editing. Importing an Audio File later on a Flex enabled Track will automatically analyze that file.

☑️ **Audio Region Appearance**: Please note that the Audio Region can have three different appearances:

- Flex Mode off ❺: Regular Audio Region appearance.

- Flex Mode on (Flex Pitch) ❻: The Audio Region is split with the Region Header on top for standard Region Editing and the Flex Edit Area underneath with the onscreen controls for the Flex Pitch superimposed over the waveform.

- Flex Mode on (Flex Time) ❼: The Audio Region is split with the Region Header on top for standard Region Editing and the Flex Edit Area underneath with the onscreen controls for the Flex Time on the waveform.

☑️ **Flex Mode Parameters ❽**: The Track Inspector displays the Flex Mode Menu Button, plus additional Flex Mode Parameters for the selected Track depending on the selected Flex Mode.

☑️ **Flex Mode Region Parameters ❾**: The Region Inspector displays additional Flex Parameters for the selected Region.

**Tracks Window**

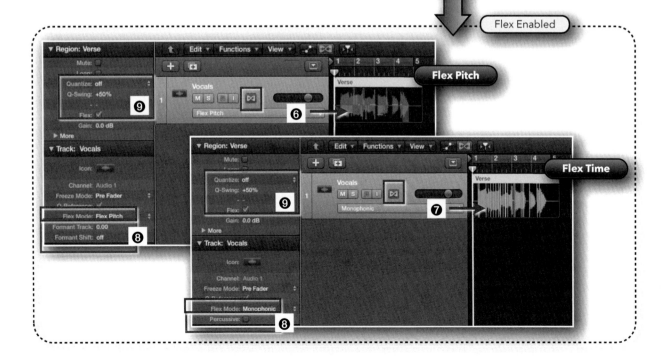

Flex Enabled

Flex Pitch

Flex Time

## ➡ *Audio Track Editor*

Here is a closer look at the interface changes in the Audio Track Editor when Flex is enabled.

### 💀 Flex Mode off

When Flex Mode is off 🔲, the Audio Region(s) are displayed as usual ❶ displaying the waveform.

### 💀 Flex Pitch

When Flex Pitch is selected from the Flex Mode Menu, the following things will change:

- The Show/Hide Flex Button is on ❷.
- The Flex Mode Button displays "Flex Pitch"❸.
- The MIDI In Button 🔸 ❹ is displayed.
- The vertical Zoom Slider is displayed 📊.
- The Audio Regions are displayed with the onscreen controls ❺ for Flex Pitch editing, plus a vertical keyboard on the side.
- The Local Menu *View ➤ Local Inspector* lets you display a Local Inspector ❻ with various controls for Flex Pitch.

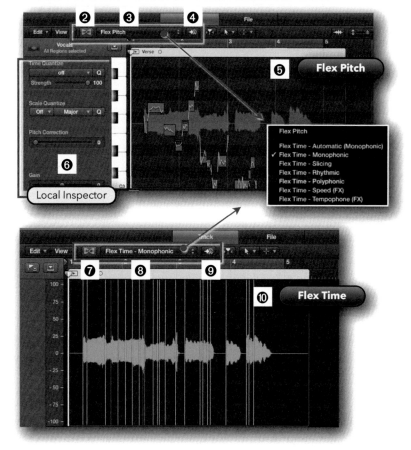

### 💀 Flex Time

When any of the six modes for Flex Time is selected, the following things will change:

- The Show/Hide Flex Button is on ❼.
- The Flex Mode Button ❽ displays any of the six selected modes for Flex Time.
- The MIDI In Button ❾ is displayed (but has no functionality).
- The Audio Regions are displayed with the Flex Time onscreen controls ❿.
- (There is no Local Inspector in this mode, the command in the Local View Menu is grayed out).

I think, by now, you have a good impression that the implementation of the Flex feature might be a little bit confusing with all the places to look out for. For example, what changes how and under what conditions, and we haven't even talked about the actual editing procedures yet.

So before entering that section, let me add another element that is highly dynamic, the Region Inspector with its displayed Parameters.

## ➡ *Region Inspector*

We just learned that one of the locations that changes when enabling Flex Mode is the Region Inspector.

Here is a closer look at what Parameters are changing. Please note that there are three types of Audio Regions: Audio Regions that you record in your Project, Audio Regions based on Apple Loops that you import into your Project, and Audio Regions based on standard Audio Files you import into your Project.

### 💀 Newly Recorded Audio and imported Apple Loops

Audio Regions that you are recording new in your Project or Audio Apple Loops that you are importing into your Projects have "special powers":

▸ You can enable "Follow Tempo & Pitch" ❶. Also available as Key Command (*Flex/Follow Tempo On/Off*) **ctr+F**.

  • The Audio Region follows any tempo changes.
  • The Audio Region can be transposed by the Transpose value you set with the Transpose Parameter above ❷.

▸ You can transpose the Audio Region in semitones. (max 1 octave up or down ❷).

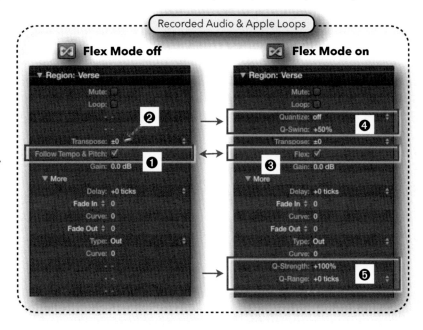

**Flex on** 🔀: When enabling Flex Mode, the following Parameters change:

▸ The "Follow Tempo & Pitch" checkbox changes to the "Flex" ❸ checkbox. Also available as Key Command (*Flex/Follow Tempo On/Off*) **ctr+F**. This allows you to disable Flex for an individual Region when Flex is enabled for the Track. Please note that when the Flex checkbox is checked, it will include the "Follow Tempo & Pitch" functionality.

▸ Four Quantize Parameters ❹ ❺ are added to the Region Inspector that let you quantize the Audio Region.

### 💀 Imported Audio

An Audio Region based on an imported Audio File has two Parameters missing ❻:

▸ No Transpose Parameter
▸ No "Follow Tempo & Pitch" checkbox

**Flex on** 🔀: When enabling Flex Mode, the following Parameters change:

▸ The Flex ❼ checkbox will be added. At least, this provides "Follow Tempo" functionality.

▸ The same four Quantize Parameters are added ❽ ❾ to the Region Inspector that lets you quantize the Audio File.

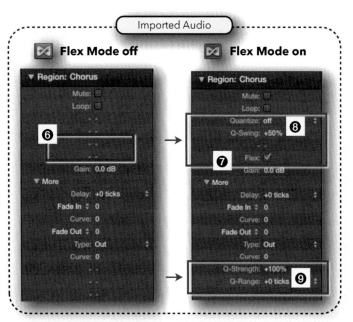

Equipped now with the basic understanding of the concept behind Flex and being familiar with the interface elements, let's finally learn how to use the Flex Time and Flex Pitch feature, starting with Flex Time.

## Getting Started

Wouldn't it be nice if there was just a button named "Flex Time" to enable the feature so we can start to edit the timing in Audio Regions. Unfortunately, it is not quite that simple. I already introduced many user interface elements that are related to Flex, but there are a few more things we have to discuss before performing the actual edit..

## Flex Time Algorithms

A big difference between Flex Time and Flex Pitch is that Flex Time offers six different Flex Modes not just one like with Flex Pitch. So before start using Flex Time, we have to decide which one of the six modes to choose. But the question is, what are these modes and how do I make the right choice?

> **The six Flex Time Modes (Algorithms) are optimized for**
>
> **six specific Audio Materials /Audio FXs**

Logic provides six different Flex Time Algorithms. Think of an algorithm as a set of rules and procedures that determine how to perform the time editing on an audio file. Each algorithm is optimized to produce the best results for specific types of audio material or an audio effect. For example, do you have a recording of a percussion instrument, a single monophonic melody instrument, or a more complex polyphonic recording.

So the decision which Flex Time Mode (which algorithm) to choose depends on the type of recording or what kind of timing effect you want to achieve. The good news is that you can switch between the different modes at any time to see if you get better results with one or the other.

**Six Flex Time Modes**

Flex Time - Monophonic
Flex Time - Slicing
Flex Time - Rhythmic
Flex Time - Polyphonic
Flex Time - Speed (FX)
Flex Time - Tempophone (FX)

I will explain the details of the different modes later in this chapter. Here is just a short description:

- **Monophonic**: Good for any solo vocals or solo monophonic instruments with more melodic content.
- **Slicing**: Good for percussive, non-tonal recording. Audio slices are only moved but not time compressed or time expanded.
- **Rhythmic**: Good for percussive, tonal recordings like rhythm guitars or rhythmical keyboard phrases.
- **Polyphonic**: Good for instruments performing chords or other complex audio material. This is the most accurate, but also most CPU-intensive algorithm.
- **Speed (FX)**: This changes the pitch together with the tempo.
- **Tempophone (FX)**: This also changes the pitch with any tempo changes, but in addition adds sonic artifacts similar to old tape machines.

Hold down the *shift* key while selecting a Flex Mode on an Audio Track to set all Audio Tracks in your Project to the same mode.

# Step One (5 different ways)

You have to understand that turning on Flex is the same as selecting a Flex Mode, that's why selecting a Flex Mode automatically turns on Flex (if it was disabled).

We already learned that the Flex Mode Menu is available in three places, so what is the proper way to start the Flex Time? In the typical Logic fashion, there is not one procedure, but actually six different ways to get Flex started, each one with their own "specialty":

### 💀 Tracks Window (#1)

- ☑ *Click* the Show/Hide Flex Button ▣ ❶ (it only makes the controls visible).
- ☑ Select a Flex Mode ❷ from the Flex Mode Menu.

### 💀 Tracks Window (#2)

- ☑ *Click* the Show/Hide Flex Button ▣ ❶.
- ☑ *Click* the Enable Flex Button ❸ ▣.
- ▶ Logic enables Flex and automatically selects the best suited Flex Time Mode based on the analysis.

### 💀 Track Inspector

- ☑ Select a Flex Mode from the Flex Mode Menu ❹.
- ▶ Logic enables Flex and automatically selects a Flex Time Mode based on the analysis and enables Flex Time.

### 💀 Audio Track Editor

- ☑ *Click* the Show/Hide Flex Button ▣ ❺. A Dialog Window pops up.
- ☑ Confirm the Dialog Window ❻ that you want to "Turn on Flex".
- ▶ Logic enables Flex and automatically selects the "Flex Time - Slicing" mode regardless of the analysis of the audio material.

### 💀 Flex Tool

I'll discuss that procedure a little bit later in detail.

- ☑ Select the Flex Tool ◀▶ from one of the Tool Menus ❾ in the Tracks Window.
- ☑ *Click* on the Audio Region with the Flex Tool (Flex View has to be hidden).
- ▶ Logic enables Flex and automatically selects a Flex Mode based on the analysis.

**Enabling Flex Time**

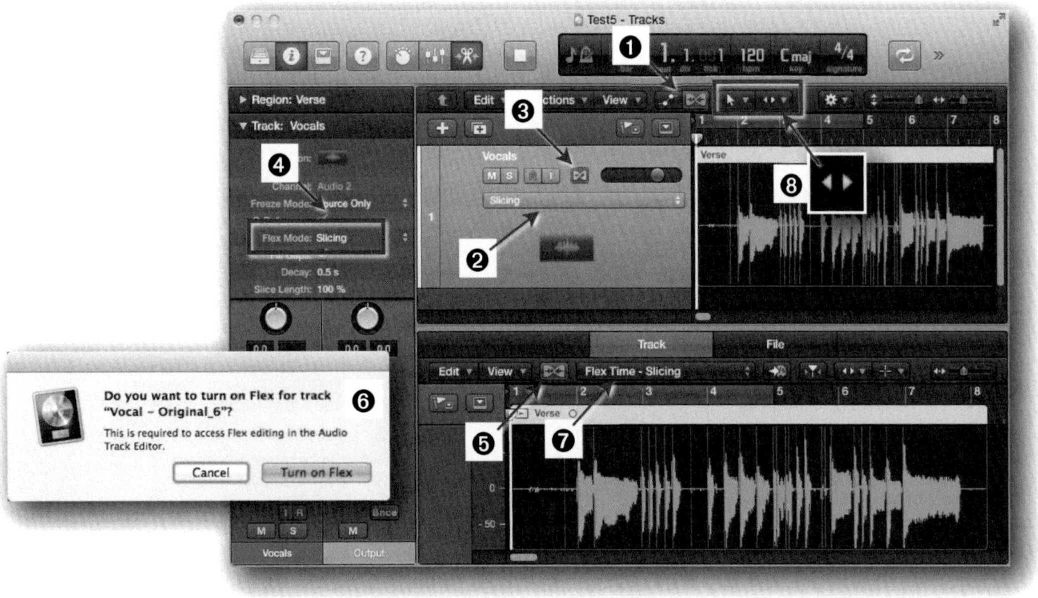

## ➡ *Flex Time - Automatic*

There is one little issue in the Flex Mode Menu that could lead to some confusion if you're not aware of it.

In addition to the six modes for Flex Time, the Flex Mode Menu lists on top a seventh Flex Time Mode named "Flex Time - Automatic" ❶. That is the mode (one of the six) that Logic chose when it analyzed the Audio File. When you select that item, then the button displays that mode, plus the word "(Auto)" ❷. This is an indication that the current Flex Mode is the one that Logic thinks gets the best results.

Now if you look at the first screenshot where I have selected Automatic, it adds the word "Slicing"❸ to the "Automatic" item in the menu. This makes sense because Slicing is the mode that Logic automatically chose in that case. However, if you select another mode (i.e. Monophonic ❹), then the name of that mode is added to the item Automatic ❺, which could be misleading if you think that the mode in parenthesis is the one Logic chose automatically.

Interestingly enough, if you manually chose the same mode that also was chosen by Logic (i.e. Slicing ❻), then the word "Slicing" is added to the Automatic item ❼ in the menu, but the word "Auto" is not added to the button ❽, even if Slicing was the mode that Logic chose automatically.

**Flex Mode Menu**

Slicing (Auto) ❷

❶ ✓ Flex Time - Automatic (Slicing) ❸
Flex Time - Monophonic
Flex Time - Slicing
Flex Time - Rhythmic
Flex Time - Polyphonic
Flex Time - Speed (FX)
Flex Time - Tempophone (FX)

Flex Pitch

Monophonic

Flex Pitch ❺
Flex Time - Automatic (Monophonic)
❹ ✓ Flex Time - Monophonic
Flex Time - Slicing
Flex Time - Rhythmic
Flex Time - Polyphonic
Flex Time - Speed (FX)
Flex Time - Tempophone (FX)

Slicing ❽

Flex Pitch ❼
Flex Time - Automatic (Slicing)
Flex Time - Monophonic
❻ ✓ Flex Time - Slicing
Flex Time - Rhythmic
Flex Time - Polyphonic
Flex Time - Speed (FX)
Flex Time - Tempophone (FX)

## *The next Step*

Selecting a Flex Time Mode from the menu (and, therefore, enabling Flex Time on that Track) prepares for the next step. It switches the appearance of the Region(s) on that Track, which enables the actual editing, the Onscreen Editing using all the various Flex Marker Tools.

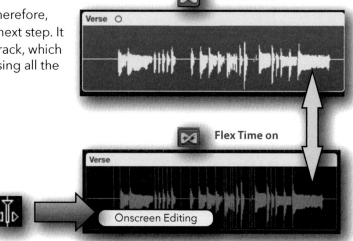

Flex Time off

Verse ○

Flex Time on

Verse

Onscreen Editing

**Flex Marker Tools**

## Interface

The single area of the Audio Region splits into two active areas when Flex Mode is enabled.

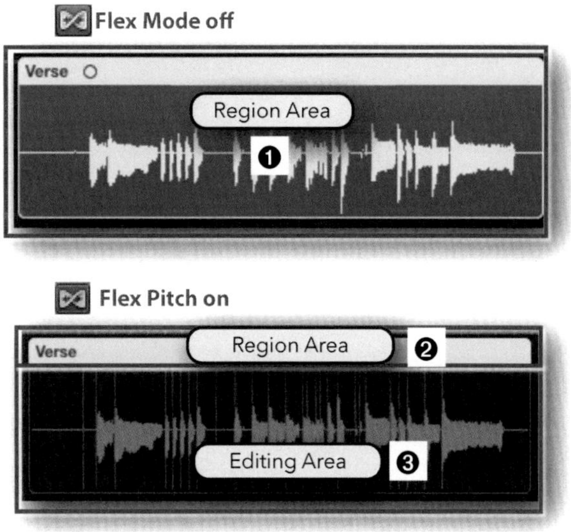
Flex Mode off
Verse
Region Area
❶
Flex Pitch on
Verse
Region Area
❷
Editing Area
❸

### Appearance

- **Region Area**: The click functionality of the regular Audio Region ❶ is now restricted to the small strip of the Track Header ❷:
  - *Click* to select the Region
  - Rename the Region
  - *Drag* the Region Header to move the Region
  - *Ctr+click* on the Region Header to open the Shortcut Menu for the Region
  - *Double-click* to toggle the Audio Track Editor (or Audio File Editor, whatever was open before)
- **Editing Area**: The area of the Region that displays the waveform ❸ now has a special function:
  - The waveform is dimmed and is overlaid with the onscreen controls that let you edit the timing
  - *Ctr+click* in this area is still possible and opens the Shortcut Menu for the Region (with additional Flex commands)

### Click Zones

Click Zones are the various "hot spots" on an object where the Cursor Tool changes to a different tool when moving the mouse over it or clicking on it.

The screenshots on the right show you the various Click Zones and what the Cursor Tools changes into when moving over that area.

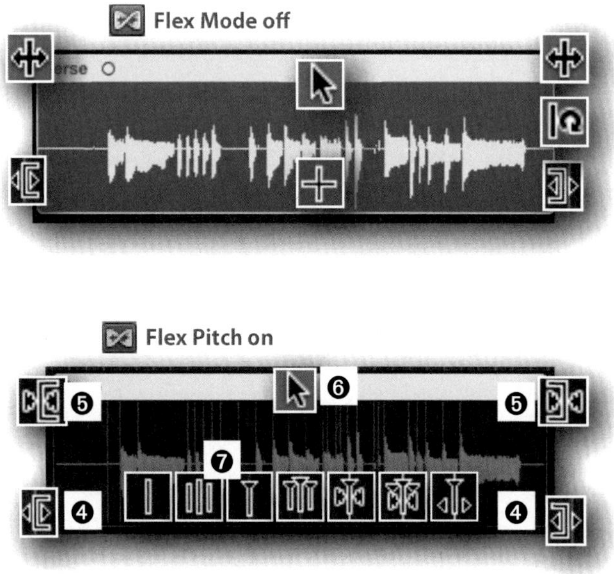
Flex Mode off
Flex Pitch on
❹
❺
❻
❼

Here are the Click Zones when Flex Time is enabled.
Please note that the Pointer Tool has to be the default tool in order for the Click Zones to have an effect!

- **Borders, lower half** ❹: Resize Region
- **Borders, upper half** ❺: Compress/Expand the entire Region (using Flex Time).
  Holding down the *option* key changes to the Fade Tool when "Fade Tool click zones" is activated in the ***Preferences ➤ General ➤ Editing ➤ Pointer Tools in Tracks Provides***
- **Region Area** ❻: The Pointer Tool only works in the Region Header.
- **Editing Area** ❼: The Editing Area where you perform most of the Flex Time editing changes to a different Cursor Tools depending on what section you move the Cursor Tool over.

# Types of Markers

You have to be absolutely clear about the differences between the various Markers, what they are, what they do, and what they look like. Otherwise, editing could be very confusing

There are four types of Markers with two different purposes:

⚫ **Transient Markers (for Orientation)**

▶ **❶ Transient Markers**: These are the Markers that Logic creates when analyzing the Audio File the first time. They function as a visual orientation where the peaks in your audio signal are. As we have seen in the previous section, you can edit those Transient Markers manually in the Audio FIle Editor.

- These markers are the thinnest lines of all of them.

⚫ **Flex Markers (for Time Correction)**

▶ **❷ Tempo Flex Markers**: Whenever you record an Audio Region over a section in your Project that has Tempo Events defined in the Tempo Track, then Logic automatically creates special Flex Markers at those positions, the Tempo Flex Markers.

- You can edit those Flex Markers and even delete them.
- You can restore the Tempo Flex Markers at any time with the "Reset all Flex Edits" command.
- The marker is a blue line (please note that the line changes into a white Manual Flex Marker when you apply a quantize value to the Region).

▶ **❸ Quantize Flex Markers**: These are the Flex Markers that Logic automatically creates when you apply a Quantize value to a Region.

- Logic moves these Flex Markers if you choose different Quantize values.
- You can edit the Quantize Flex Markers and even delete them.
- The marker is a thin white line (a little thinner than the Manual Flex Marker).

▶ **❹ Manual Flex Marker**s: These are the Flex Markers that you create manually at any position on the waveform.

- You can remove individual Flex Markers or all manually added Flex Markers in a Region.
- The line is a white line (thicker than the Quantize Marker).

Here is a screenshot where you can see the very subtle differences between the lines for those four Markers.

**Visual appearance of various Markers**

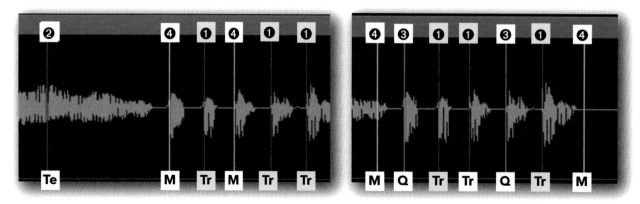

# Flex Tools

If you think the different looking Marker lines are a bit confusing, be prepared for the many different tools that create and edit those lines.

First of all, Flex Time Editing, like many other features, is done in two ways:

- **Apply Commands**: The commands are available from Menus, from the Inspector, or various Key Commands.
- **Perform Onscreen Edits**: This is the standard technique of clicking and dragging with various Cursor Tools directly on an object.

Commands

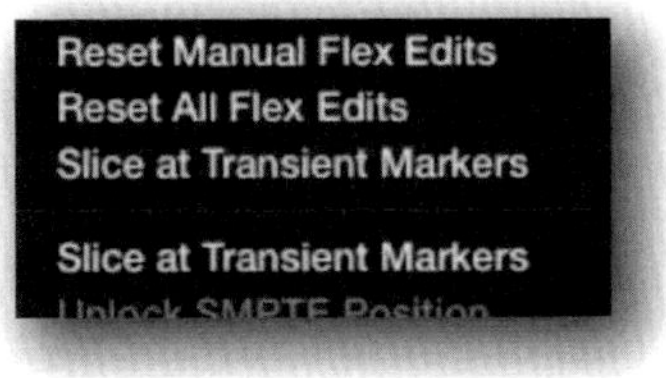


Cursor Tools

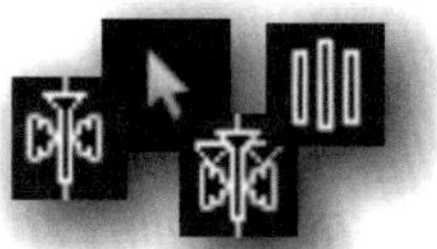

Let's start with the onscreen edits. There are two ways to get the right Cursor Tool for the job.

Tool Menu

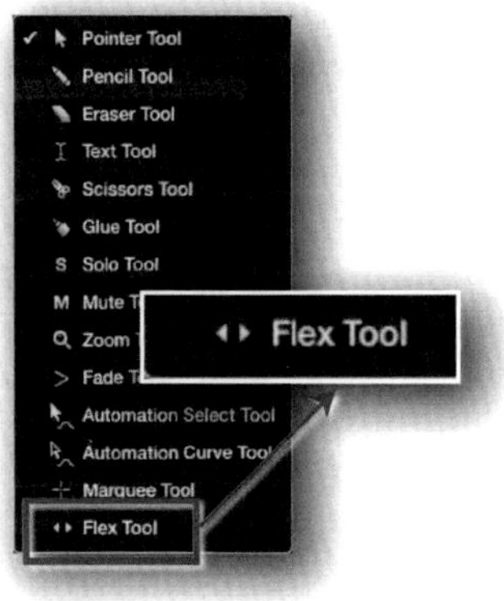


### Manually select a Tool (Tool Menu)

You can manually select a specific Tool from the Tool Menu whenever you need it and then switch back or switch to a different Tool.

- For Flex Time, there is only one Tool listed in the Tool Menu and that is the Flex Tool (mainly used when Flex Mode is hidden):

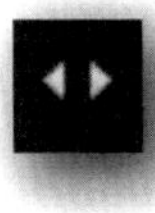

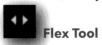

**Flex Tool**

### Automatically switched Tools (Click Zones)

Logic automatically switches to a different Tool when you move the Cursor Tool over a specific object or an area. These so-called Click Zones are very convenient because the required tool is right there where you need it and when you need it. However, you have to know about those Click Zones. Know when and what tool appears for what action.

Click Zones

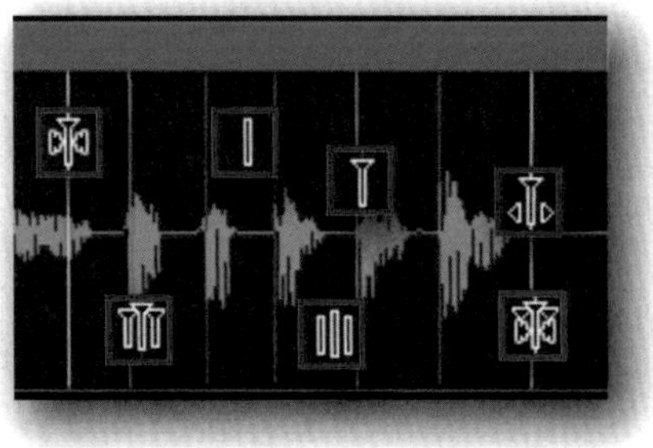

- For Flex Time, the Cursor Tool can switch to seven different tools depending on where you move the cursor in the Editing Area of an Audio Region.

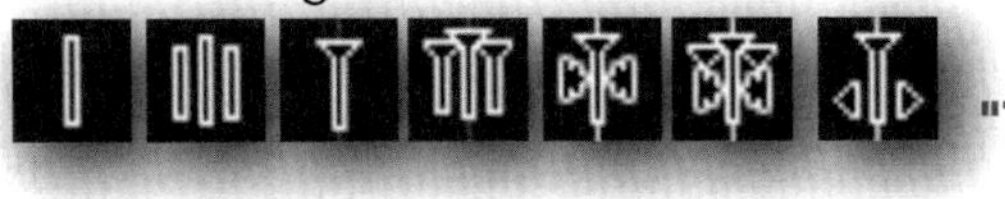

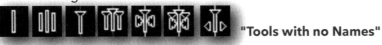

**"Tools with no Names"**

While most of the Cursor Tools have names, these seven tools used for Flex Time Editing have no specific names. The official Logic User Guide refers to them in general only as "*Pointer*" and when they change, it says: "*... note how the pointer changes!*"

These Click Zones are only in effect when you have the Pointer Tool selected. That means, you still can use the secondary or third tool assigned in the Command-click Tool Menu or Control+click Tool Menu.

# Click Zones

Here is a closer look at all the seven Click Zones with their specific tools. Again, the default tool has to be the Pointer Tool ![pointer] so the Click Zones can switch to the other tools. Which tool it switches to depends on three conditions:

## ⬤ 1st Condition: Area

The Click Zone divides the Editing Area into the upper and lower part:

▸ **Upper ❶**: Moving the Cursor Tool in the upper half of the Region switches to a tool with a single line. This indicates that when you click, you create one single Flex Marker.

▸ **Lower ❷**: Moving the Cursor Tool in the lower half of the Region switches to a tool with three lines. This indicates that when you click, you create three Flex Markers. Remember, we always need three Flex Markers for time shifting.

## ⬤ 2nd Condition: Marker

The second condition checks if you moved over a Marker. There are three options:

▸ **No Marker ❸**: If there is no Marker at your current cursor position, then you get a tool with just a line (1 or 3, depending on if you are in the upper or lower area).

▸ **Transient Marker ❹**: If there is a Transient Marker at the current cursor position, then you get a tool that has a line (1 or 3, depending on if you are in the upper or lower area) with a triangle on top.

▸ **Flex Marker ❺**: If there is a Flex Marker at the current cursor position (this can be a Manual Flex Marker, a Quantize Flex Marker, or a Tempo Flex Marker), then you get a tool that has a line (1 or 3, depending on if you are in the upper or lower area) with the triangle on top and the Flex symbol across.

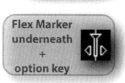

## ⬤ 3rd Condition: Modifier Key

The third condition is if you hold down a Modifier Key while moving over an object.

▸ **Flex Marker ❻**: Holding down the *option* key while moving over a Flex Marker will change the tool to a line with the triangle on top and two arrows, which indicate that you can reposition ("re-attach") that Flex Marker to the left or right without moving (shifting) the audio waveform.

Here are all the seven tools in an overview:

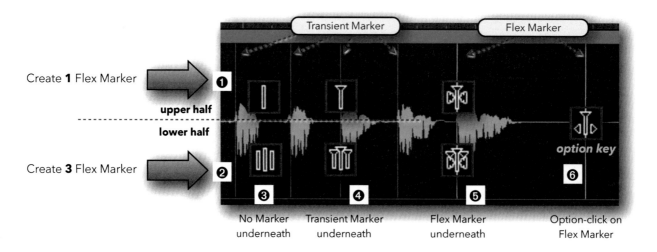

Now let's look at a few examples.

## ➡ *No Marker*

You move the Cursor Tool in the upper half of the Editing Area where there is no Marker ❶

  ▸ *Clicking* at that position will create a single Flex Marker ❷.

You move the Cursor Tool in the lower half of the Editing Area where there is no Marker ❸

  ▸ *Clicking* at that position creates a Flex Marker ❹. In addition, a second Flex Marker is created at the Transient Marker to the left ❺ and a third Flex Marker at the Transient Marker to the right ❻.

Please note: If the neighboring Marker is a Transient Marker, then a new Flex Marker will be created at that position. If the neighboring Marker is already a Flex Marker (a Manual Flex Marker, a Quantize Flex Marker, or a Tempo Flex Marker), then nothing will be added, because a Flex Marker is already there to function as the boundary for the time shifting.

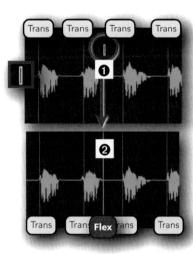 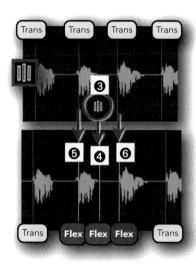

## ➡ *On Transient Markers*

You move the Cursor Tool in the upper half of the Editing Area over a Transient Marker ❶.

  ▸ *Clicking* at that position will create a single Flex Marker ❷ on that Transient Marker position.

You move the Cursor Tool in the lower half of the Editing Area over a Transient Marker ❸

  ▸ *Clicking* at that position creates a Flex Marker ❹ at that Transient Marker position. In addition, a second Flex Marker is created at the Transient Marker to the left ❺ and a third Flex Marker at the Transient Marker to the right ❻.

Again: If the neighboring Marker is a Transient Marker, then a new Flex Marker will be created at that position. If the neighboring Marker is already a Flex Marker (a Manual Flex Marker, a Quantize Flex Marker, or a Tempo Flex Marker), then nothing will be added, because a Flex Marker is already there to function as the boundary for the time shifting.

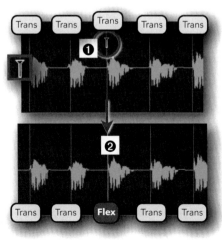 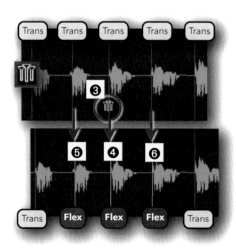

## ➡ On Flex Markers

You move the Cursor Tool in the upper half of the Editing Area over a Flex Marker ❶.

▶ *Clicking* at that position has no effect because a single Flex Marker ❷ already exists at that position.

You move the Cursor Tool in the lower half of the Editing Area over a Flex Marker ❸

▶ *Clicking* at that position does not create a Flex Marker ❹ because a Flex Marker already exists at that position. The second Flex Marker will only be created at the Marker to the left ❺ if it is a Transient Marker. The third Flex Marker will only be created at the Marker to the right ❻ if it is a Transient Marker.

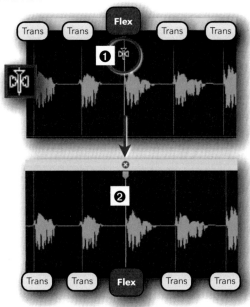 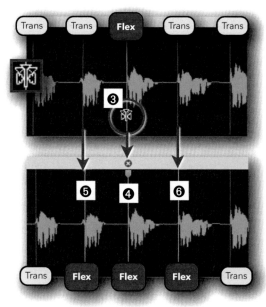

## ➡ On Marquee Selection

There are two special techniques to create Flex Markers using a Marquee Selection:

Switch the Cursor Tool to the Marquee Tool ⊞ ❶ and draw a Marquee Selection ❷, and then switch back to the Pointer Tool ▶

▶ *Clicking* in the lower area between Markers ▥ ❸ (or on an existing Marker ▥ ) will create a Flex Marker ❹ at that position, plus a Flex Marker at the left and right border ❺ of the Marquee Selection.

▶ *Clicking* in the upper half (note the Hand Tool ✋ ❻) will create four (!) Flex Markers. Two Flex Markers at the borders ❼ of the Marquee Selection, one at the Transient Marker before the left border ❽, and one at the Transient Marker after the right border ❾.

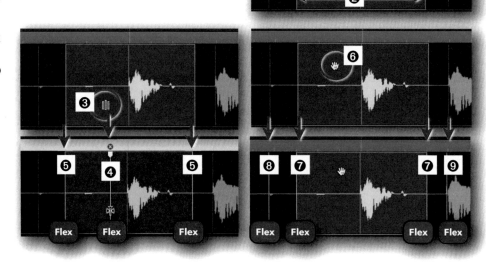

# Time Correction

I already explained a little bit about the underlying concept of Time Shifting or *Elastic Audio* as it is sometimes referred to. Here is a model that demonstrates how it works with the three Flex Markers:

### The Default:

The diagram represents a section of the Audio Region. Instead of the waveform, I display equally distant numbers 1-9. I created three Flex Markers on the waveform. Those Flex Markers, as we know by now, are "attached" to the waveform at those positions, here at numbers 2 , 5, and 8. This is the model:

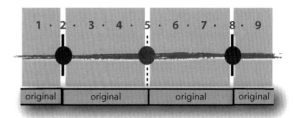

- The Audio Region is like a rubber band.
- You draw the numbers 1 to 9 in equal distance on that rubber band. Those numbers represent the waveform.
- You attach three sticks to that rubber band at the number position 2, 5, and 8. The three sticks represent the three Flex Markers attached to the waveform.
- You nail the sticks on the left (number 2) and the stick on the right (number 8) against the wall.
- Now we move the stick in the center at position 5 left or right: What will happen?

### Moving to the Right

When we move the center stick (at position 5) to the right, the following will happen:

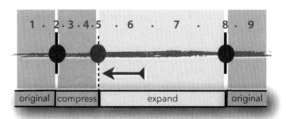

- ▶ The rubber band between the first and second stick gets extended (longer). That means, the audio waveform (2-3-4-5) gets time expanded.
- ▶ The rubber band between the second and third stick gets looser (shorter). That means, the audio waveform (5-6-7-8) gets time compressed.
- ▶ The rubber band before the first stick and after the third stick is not affected by the movement of the stick in the center. That means, the two neighboring Flex Marker before (position 2) and after (position 8) the Flex Marker you are moving (position 5) "protect" the rest of the waveform from being altered.

### Moving to the Left

When we move the center stick (at position 5) to the left, the following will happen:

- ▶ The rubber band between the first and second stick gets looser (shorter). That means, the audio waveform (2-3-4-5) gets time compressed.
- ▶ The rubber band between the second and third stick gets extended (longer). That means, the audio waveform (5-6-7-8) gets time expanded.
- ▶ And again, the rubber band (the audio waveform) before the first stick and after the third stick is not affected by the movement of the stick in the center.

### Please keep in mind:

- A Flex Marker, at any time, can be the "moving stick" (when you drag it) or the stick that is "nailed to the wall" (when it is next to a Flex Marker that you are moving).
- The "unaffected" area before and after the moving Flex Marker is just unaffected by the current movement. It could have been time stretched or time expanded already by another time correction you performed.

## ➡ *The Rules*

So here is the main rule for applying any type of time shifting using Flex Time:

> ### Any Flex Time Operation requires 3 Flex Markers

Although you actively move one Flex Marker, the result always depends on all three adjacent Flex Markers. The function of the center Flex Marker is to move that specific spot on the waveform and the function of the two neighboring Flex Markers is to "secure the borders" to make sure that only the waveform inside the borders is time shifted and the waveform outside the borders stay unaffected by the current movement.

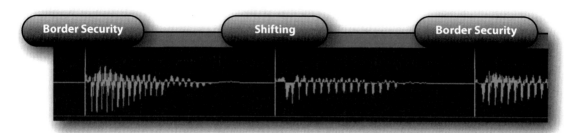

You can use two methods for the time shift:

### ☻ Two Steps Method

Create the Flex Markers first (as we discussed earlier) to determine the boundaries and the spot you are about to move, and then *drag* the Flex Marker.

### ☻ Single Step Method

You can create the required Flex Markers "on the fly". *Click-hold* at any position on the waveform and *drag* it without releasing the mouse first. There are a few conditions you have to consider:

▶ **About the click position**:
- If there is a Flex Marker at the click position, then you are using the existing one for the movement.
- If there is only a Transient Marker at the click position, then a new Flex Marker will be created at that position.
- If there is no Marker at the click position, then a new Flex Marker will be created "on the fly".

▶ **About the boundaries**:
- If the Marker to the left or right is a Flex Marker, then that will be used as the boundaries.
- If the Marker to the left or right is a Transient Marker, then a new Flex Marker will be created at that position and will be used as the boundaries.
- If there isn't any Marker to the left or right of the click position, then the Region border will be used as the boundaries.

## *Which Cursor Tool*

Two of the six Cursor Tools that are part of the Click Zones in Flex Time Editing for creating Flex Markers are also used for shifting a Flex Markers (performing the time shift):

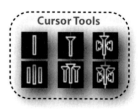

Remember, this tool didn't make much sense in creating a Flex Marker, because it appears when you move over an already existing Flex Marker. This is the main tool for shifting a Flex Marker (when moving over the upper half).

This tool can also be used to shift a Flex Marker, but you have to be aware that it also might create additional Flex Markers when the adjacent Markers are only Transient Markers.

## ➡ *Shifting a single Flex Markers*

Here is the final procedure when shifting a Flex Marker:

❶ When you move the Cursor Tool over the Flex Marker, three things will change:

- The Cursor Tool changes to one of the Flex Tools.
- A triangle marker sign appears on top of the line.
- An x sign appears on top of the line.

❷ When you *click-hold* on the Flex Marker, the triangle and x sign disappear and a vertical line extends across the Workspace (in the Tracks Window only, not the Audio Track Editor). The line is yellow to indicate the position where you clicked. When you move left and right, the line always turns yellow when you move back to that clicked position again.

❸ When you move the Flex Marker to the right, the waveform on the right gets time compressed (brighter color) and the waveform on the left gets expanded (lighter color). The movement follows the Snap to Grid settings. Only the Control Bar Display shows the current position when you move the Flex Marker, no separate Help Tag.

❹ When you release the mouse, the triangle and the X sign appear again as long as you have the cursor still parked over that Flex Marker. In addition, a horizontal bar appears on the Region Header that indicates how far you have moved the Flex Marker from its original ("neutral") position.

Original (neutral) Position

❺ Moving the Flex Marker very close to the adjacent Flex Marker on the right will result in a high time compression. This will prompt a Dialog Window, warning you about this extreme measure. If you are "OK" with that, then the waveform color turns red to remind you about that high compression.

**Do you really want to create a high speed section?**

The red section is time-compressed by factor 13 which may cause system overloads in a multi-track project. Click Cancel to undo this edit. Otherwise you may want to freeze this track at some point.

☐ Do not show this message again

Cancel | OK

Moving the Flex Marker to the left ❻ produces the same results, just in opposite directions.

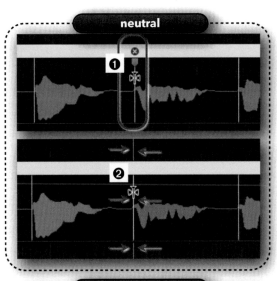

neutral

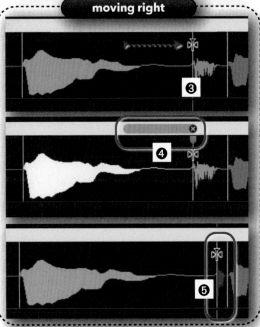

moving right

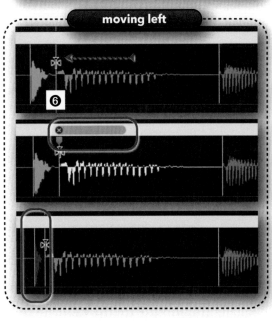

moving left

### ➡ *Shifting a Range (multiple Flex Markers)*

There is one advanced procedure by using a Marquee Selection to move an entire section of multiple Flex Markers instead of a single Flex Marker. This has to be done in the Audio Track Editor:

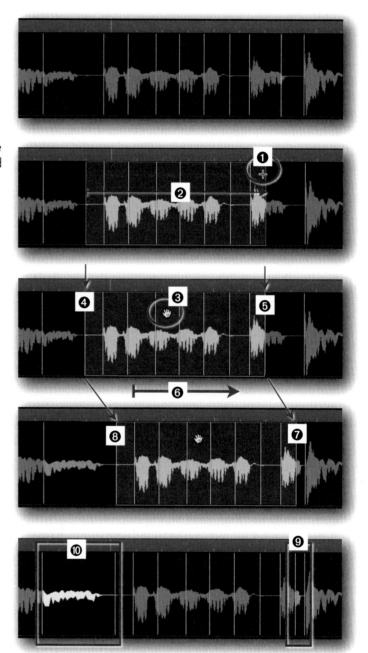

▶ Change the Cursor Tool to the Marquee Tool ➊ and drag a Marquee Selection ➋. The selection can even include existing Flex Markers.

▶ Switch the Cursor Tool back to the Pointer Tool and place it over the upper half of the Marquee Selection. The Cursor Tool changes to the Hand Tool ➌.

▶ When you *click-hold* on the selection, two Flex Markers are created, one of the left ➍ border and one at the right ➎ border of the Marquee Selection. These two Flex Markers, plus all the Flex Markers included in the selection, turn yellow indicating the original position when you clicked.

▶ When you *drag* ➏ the Marquee Selection (in this example to the right), then the following thing will happen:

- The entire waveform inside the Marquee selection (Range) will move as a whole.
- The waveform inside the selection will not be altered.
- The Flex Marker at the right border ➐ of the Marquee Selection squeezes the audio waveform towards the Flex Marker to its right.
- The Flex Marker at the left border ➑ of the Marquee Selection stretches the audio waveform away from the Flex Marker that is located to its left.
- When you disable the Marquee Selection, you see the time compressed section ➒ at the right and the time expanded section on the left ➓. The entire range of the waveform that was the Marquee Selection before just moved without changing its relative timing.

## ➡ *Alignment to other Tracks*

When you shift a Flex Marker on an Audio Track, you can use the Transient Markers or Flex Markers on another Audio Track as an Alignment Guide to snap to it. This is useful if you want to time correct some hits of a recording with bad timing to another Track with better timing.

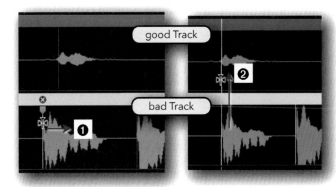

- ☑ *Drag* the Flex Marker left or right ❶ to move the Flex Marker on the "bad Track".
- ☑ While still holding down the mouse button, move the cursor up or down to the adjacent Track ❷ (the "good Track") close to its Transient Marker. The Flex Marker you are moving will snap to that Transient Marker.

## Overview

So far, we have already covered a lot of procedures for Flex Time and the wealth of information and possibilities can be a bit overwhelming. That's why I want to provide a little overview before continuing (yes, there is more to cover), so we don't get lost in the feature set.

Whatever you do with Flex Markers, always think of the four actions that are related to Flex Markers (we discussed only the first two so far):

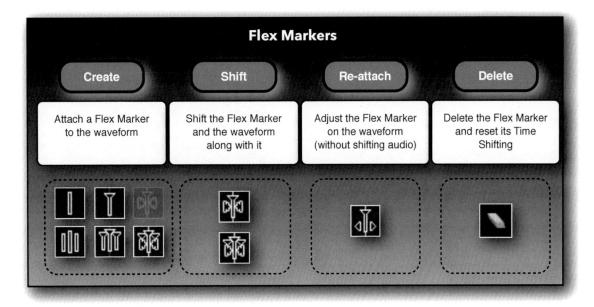

- ▶ **Create a Flex Marker**: This action attaches the Flex Marker to that spot on the audio waveform.
- ▶ **Shift a Flex Marker**: By shifting an existing Flex Marker to the left or right, you shift the portion of that audio waveform it is attached to (between the boundaries of the two neighboring Flex Markers).
- ▶ **Re-attach a Flex Marker**: This procedure lets you adjust the position of the spot the Flex Markers is attached to the waveform by sliding it left or right without time shifting the waveform.
- ▶ **Delete a Flex Marker**: This action not only deletes the Flex Marker, it also resets any time shifting it applied to the audio waveform.

# Flex Tool

The procedures I demonstrated for using Flex Time require that the Flex controls are visible by clicking on the "Show/Hide Flex Button" ⊠ . However, there is one way to perform time edits without displaying the Flex controls. This procedure, available only in the Tracks Window, actually requires that Flex is not visible.

In the Tracks Window, the "Show/Hide Flex Button" has to be off ⊠ ❶.

Switch the Cursor Tool to the Flex Tool ⬌ available from the Tool Menu ❷ or by using the Key Command *Set Flex Tool.*

The waveform of the Audio Region (standard view) now has three Click Zones:

You are moving over an area with no Transient Markers or Flex Markers

You drag a Flex Marker

You are moving over an area with a Transient Marker or Flex Marker

Here is the procedure:

▶ You position the Cursor Tool at the spot of the waveform that you want to move ❸.

▶ In my screenshot, I *click-hold* exactly at the beginning of that waveform blurb (i.e. a single kick drum) and *drag* it a little bit to the right ❹ so it aligns exactly with the downbeat of bar 3 ❺. During the dragging, the Cursor Tool changes to a different tool.

▶ A white Alignment Guide ❻ spans vertically across the Workspace for better adjustment. Having "Snap to Grid" enabled helps the positioning.

▶ This is what happened in the background during that procedure:

☑ Logic analyzed the audio file and assigned it a Flex Time Mode (if it hasn't done so before).

☑ The file now has Transient Markers applied to it.

☑ A Flex Marker has been created at the click position, plus two additional Flex Markers at the position of the adjacent Transient Markers.

☑ The audio segments around these three Flex Markers will be altered.

▶ Now, when you move with the Cursor Tool across the waveform you will see that it switches between the two cursors:

• No Marker exist at that position

• Marker exist at that position ❼

If you have the Audio Track Editor ❽ open with Flex visible, you can see what happens regarding the time shifting.

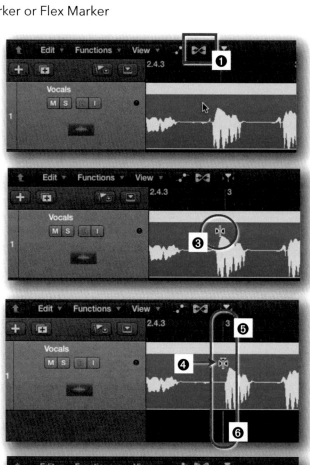

**Tool Menu**

Pointer Tool
Pencil Tool
Eraser Tool
Text Tool
Scissors Tool
Glue Tool
Solo Tool
Mute Tool
Zoom
Fade Tool
Automation Select Tool
Automation Curve Tool
Marquee Tool
Flex Tool ❷

⬌ Flex Tool

❽ **Audio Track Editor**

# Re-attach a Flex Marker

This Flex Marker action is very important and you have to make sure you understand its effect.

Once you created a Flex Marker on the waveform, it is attached to that spot. Moving that Flex Marker left or right will time shift the waveform underneath it (between the boundaries of the preceding and following Flex Marker). In case you didn't place the Flex Marker precisely at the correct spot, you can delete the Flex Marker and create a new one. Or, you can use the following procedure to re-attach the existing Flex Marker:

*Opt+click* **on the upper half of a Flex Marker**

This is one of the six unnamed Flex Tools that appears on the waveform depending on the various conditions for the Click Zones that I discussed earlier. It lets you re-attach a Flex Marker to a different spot on the waveform by moving it left or right (while holding down the option key) without shifting the waveform.

This is the procedure:

▸ When you move the Cursor Tool over the upper half of a Flex Marker, it changes to the following tool .

▸ Holding down the *option* key will change to the "Re-attach Tool" .

▸ Now you can *drag* the Flex Marker while the waveform underneath is not "affected". If you look closely, you can see the waveform adjusting 'in real time" while repositioning the Flex Marker.

▸ Release the mouse (and the option key) to attach the Flex Marker to that new position.

# Delete a Flex Marker

You can delete a Flex Marker in many different ways:

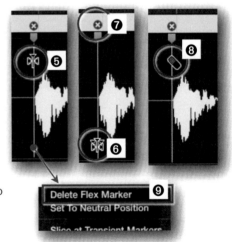

- *Double-click* on the Flex Marker with any of the tools in the upper half  ❺ or lower half  ❻.

- *Click* the X-icon  ❼ that appears when you move over a Flex Marker.

- *Click* on a single Flex Marker with the Eraser Tool  ❽ or drag across multiple Flex Markers to delete them.

- *Ctr+click* on a Flex Marker to select the command "Delete Flex Marker" ❾ from the Shortcut Menu.

- *Dragging* a Flex Marker over the adjacent Flex Marker(s) will also delete them.

**Three things to keep in mind:**

▸ The delete commands can be used for Manual Flex Markers, Tempo Flex Markers, and Quantize Flex Markers.

▸ This action not only deletes a Flex Marker, but it also resets any time shifting on the audio waveform that was caused by this Flex Marker.

▸ Any Transient Marker that existed at the position of a Flex Marker will "re-appear" on the waveform.

▸ Enabling the Track Protect Button  on the Track Header will also prohibit any Flex edits.

# Flex Commands

While you do most of the Flex Time Editing as onscreen editing using your Cursor Tool, some editing can be done by using commands.

## ➡ *Shortcut Menu*

The Shortcut Menu displays different commands depending on which two spots you *ctr+click*.

 **On Flex Marker**

Shortcut Menu ➤ Flex Marker

▸ **Delete Flex Marker**: This can delete a Manual Flex Marker or a Quantize Flex Marker, but not a Tempo Flex Marker.

▸ **Set to Neutral Position**: This moves that Flex Marker (that you shifted manually) back to its original position where you created it. It removes any time shifting on the waveform caused by the Flex Marker.

 **On the Background**

Shortcut Menu ➤ Background

The following command affects all the Flex Markers of all currently selected Regions (even on different Tracks):

▸ **Reset Manual Flex Edits**: This moves all the Flex Markers that you shifted manually to their original position where you created them. Any deleted Tempo Markers will be placed back.

▸ **Reset All Flex Edits**: This command resets all the Manual Flex Markers and the Quantize Flex Markers (it actually sets the Region Parameter to "Quantize: off"). Any deleted Tempo Markers will be placed back.

## ➡ *Quantize (Region Inspector)*

Once Logic has analyzed an audio file (by enabling Flex Mode on its Track) and added the Transient Markers based on its analysis, you can use the Quantize command to actually quantize an Audio Region similar to a MIDI Region.

Region Inspector

▸ Select a Region (or multiple Regions) and set the Quantize Parameters in the Region Inspector.

▸ The Quantize values are Region Parameters. That means, selecting a Region will display the values you have set for that Region before.

▸ You can use the Key Command (*Quantize Selected Events*) **Q**.

▸ The command creates Quantize Flex Marker at the position of any Transient Marker that is close to the selected Quantization Grid lines and shifts those Quantize Flex Markers to those grid lines.

▸ The result of the quantization depends on how accurate the Transient Markers are in the first place. You can edit the Transient Markers prior to that in the Audio File Editor using the Transient Editing Mode.

▸ You can edit any Quantize Flex Marker manually like any other Manual Flex Marker.

▸ The Command "*Reset All Flex Edits*" from the Shortcut Menu sets the Quantize value to off.

▸ If you look very closely, then you can see the subtle differences between the Markers.

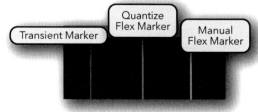

## Other Features

Here are a few areas in Logic that are affected by Flex Time:

### ➡ *Take Folder*

When you enable Flex Time on a Track with a Take Folder, you could see the Markers and the Time Shifting with their color-coded waveform on the individual Regions ❶ (Takes) but not on the Take Folder ❷ itself.

When you enable Flex, then the Quick Swipe Comping Button ❸ disappears and you cannot edit the comps.

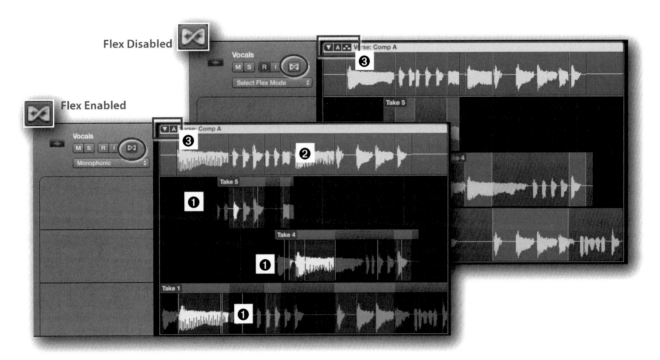

### ➡ *Freeze Mode*

When you enable Flex on a Track, then the Freeze Mode in the Track Inspector automatically switches from the default "Pre Fader" (freeze Regions with Plugin Effects) to "Source Only" (only Regions without Plugin Effects).

Track Inspector

### ➡ *Group Settings*

Group Settings Window

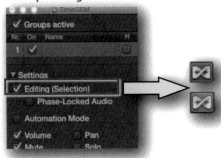

If you assign Channel Strips to a Group that has "Editing (Selection)" enabled in the Group Settings Window, then the Enable Flex Button on the Track Header will switch the Flex status of all Tracks that belong to the same Group.

## ➡ *Quantize: Flex Time - Flex Pitch*

Quantize is applied differently in Flex Pitch and Flex Time. That's why you'll get a warning from a Dialog Window when you switch to Flex Pitch.

## ➡ *Compress/Expand Region (with or without Flex)*

You can stretch or squeeze (expand/compress) an entire Audio Region by *opt+dragging* its left or right lower border. The Click Zone changes the Cursor Tool to the Compress/Expand Tool for this operation. This is especially useful when adjusting perfectly trimmed loops to the current tempo of your Project.

Please be aware that there are two completely different procedures:

**Without Flex Time**

When the Flex Time is off ❶ on the Track, then *opt+dragging* will automatically make a copy of that audio file and performs the edit as a destructive edit on the new audio file. You will only see a short progress bar window during the copy process. Otherwise, the procedure is transparent , happening in the background, and you wouldn't even notice it .

**With Flex Time**

When Flex Time is enabled ❷ on that Track, then *opt+dragging* will perform a time shift operation between all the Transient Markers that have been created during the analysis process that happened when you enabled Flex Time on that Track to compress or expand the Audio Region. Because it is a Flex Time operation, the edit will be performed as a non-destructive edit on the original audio file.

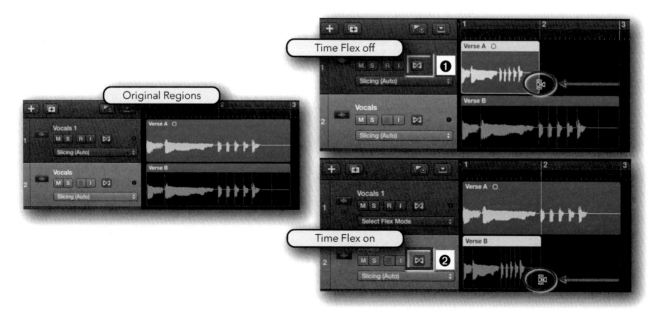

# Flex Time Algorithms

Earlier in this chapter, I briefly introduced the six algorithms that are available for Flex Time. These algorithms, also referred to as Flex Modes, are a set of rules and procedures that determine how Logic performs the time editing on an audio file based on the position of the Flex Markers. Each algorithm is optimized to produce the best results for specific types of audio material or an audio effect.

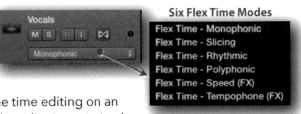

Here are a few things you have to keep in mind about those Flex Modes:

- 🌑 Each Auto Track can be set to its own Flex Mode.
- 🌑 All Regions on one Audio Track use that same Flex Mode. If you need a different one for a specific Region, then you have to create a new Audio Track with a different Flex Mode and place the Region there.
- 🌑 The Flex Modes don't affect the position of the Flex Markers they only determine how to process the time shifting of the audio waveform based on the position of the Flex Markers.
- 🌑 Copying an Audio Region with applied time shifting (moved Flex Markers) to an Audio Track with a different Flex Mode may result in a different outcome.
- 🌑 Each of the six Flex Modes has up to three Parameters in the Track Inspector that let you "fine tune" how the time shifting is performed.
- 🌑 Logic always determines a default (auto) Flex Mode for a Track based on the analysis of the first Audio Region on that track.

Now let's discuss the six Flex Modes in a little more detail:

## ➡️ *Monophonic*

- Recommended: The Monophonic Mode is good for any solo vocals or solo monophonic instruments with mainly melodic content (playing single notes). The recording should be dry without much reverb for best results.
- Technology: Using the Polyphonic Mode might produce better results but is more CPU-intensive.
- Parameters:
  - ▶ **Percussive**:

    🔲 unchecked (default): This is better for wind instruments or bowed instruments to prevent glitches on Transient Markers.

    ☑️ checked: This is better for percussive material where the area around the Transient Marker is preserved and not shifted to keep the impact of a percussive note like plucked instruments or any other percussive tonal instruments.

## ➡️ *Polyphonic*

- Recommended: The Polyphonic Mode is best for any complex polyphonic audio material. It can be used for any chord based material (i.e. guitar, piano, choirs, etc.) and even complex mixes.
- Technology: It uses a CPU-intensive process called "Phase Vocoding" ("*using phase information for time stretching audio signals without touching its pitch*").
- Parameters:
  - ▶ **Complex**:

    ☑️ checked: Enables more internal transients in the audio material.

## ➡ Rhythmic

- Recommended: The Rhythmic Mode is best for rhythmic guitars, keyboard parts, and Apple Loops.
- Technology: It stretches the audio material by looping the audio between slices in order to fill any gaps.
- Parameters:
  - ▶ **Loop Length** (0% ... 100%): This determines the percentage of the slice (how long the section at the end is) that is looped in order to achieve the time expansion.
  - ▶ **Decay** (0.1s ... infinite): The decay value defines the length of the crossfade between the looped areas.
  - ▶ **Loop Offset**: (-100ms ... 0ms):  This parameter can move the looped area up to 100 ms to the left, "*preventing pre-attack sounds from the following transient to appear in the looped and crossfaded area*".

## ➡ Slicing

- Recommended: The Slicing Mode is good for any drums and percussion instruments.
- Technology: The individual slices between Flex Markers are shifted without changing their speed and without applying any time compression or expansion. Any gaps can be filled with the decay function.
- Parameters:
  - ▶ **Fill Gaps**: If enabled (by default), it fills any gaps, caused by Flex, using the decay function.
  - ▶ **Decay** (0.1s ... infinite): This sets the decay time to fill the space that has no audio caused by the time shifting.
  - ▶ **Slice Length** (1% ... 100%): The percentage value determines how much a slice is shortened. This helps to avoid unwanted pre-attack from the following slice or to create a gated effect.

### Example:

Here is an example to demonstrate the Slicing Mode:

- 💬 The screenshot in the middle shows two original audio blurbs (❺ and ❶) surrounded by three Flex Markers.
- 💬 When you move the center Flex Marker to the left ❷, you would expect to extend the waveform on the right ❶. Instead, it moves to the new position with its original length ❸, leaving a gap ❹ behind. The slice to the left, however, will be compressed.
- 💬 Now let's move the Flex Marker in the center to the right ❻. Not only will the slice on the left ❺ not be expanded, it will stay at its position ❼ and you just open a gap ❽ by dragging the Flex Marker to the right ❻. This time, the slice on the right will be compressed.

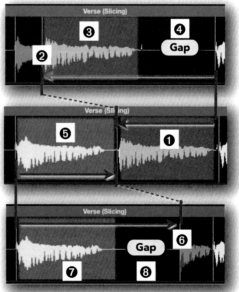

Flex Mode (Slicing)

This is an extreme example to demonstrate the Slicing Mode. Usually, when used on an Audio Region with percussive material, the slices would be moved by much smaller increments (i.e. by applying a quantize command). The result is that most of the slices would just be moved without any time compression or expansion.

**Comparison**

Here is the same example again. This time it shows the same Audio Region on two Tracks, where the upper Track is set to Slicing Mode ❶ and the bottom Track is set to Monophonic Mode ❷.

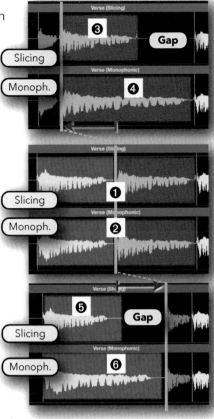

- 🔵 Moving the center Flex Marker to the left:
  While the Slicing Mode ❶ keeps the length ❸ of the right slice, the Monophonic Mode expands ❹ the slice.

- 🔵 Moving the center Flex Marker to the right:
  While the Slicing Mode keeps the length ❺ of the left slice, the Monophonic Mode expands ❻ the slice.

The last two Flex Modes for Flex Time are marked as effects (FX). That already indicates that, instead of time correction, you would use those modes more for getting creative with effects.

### ➡ *Speed (FX)*

- Recommended: The Speed (FX) Mode is useful for speeding up or slowing down percussive material. For other audio material it can be used as an effect.
- Technology: The time shifting changes the speed and the pitch of the audio material too.
- Parameters: none

### ➡ *Tempophone (FX)*

- Recommended: The Tempophone Mode is mainly used as an effect for emulating a tempophone, a historical tape-based time-stretching device. It produces time and pitch changes with more sonic artifacts.
- Technology: The effect is similar to those produced with granular synthesis techniques.
- Parameters:
  - ▶ **Grain Size**(0.1ms ... 500ms): This sets the size of the small elements (the grains) "*that are played or repeated in their original speed and crossfaded to create time compression or expansion*".
  - ▶ **Crossfade** (0% ... 100%): Varies the sound of the sonic artifacts by adjusting the crossfades between the slices from 0% (hard sound) to 100% (soft sound).

### ➡ *Flex Pitch*

I cover Flex Pitch in the next chapter, here are its two available Flex Mode Parameters:

- ▶ **Formant Track** (0.00 ... 2.00): "*Determines the interval at which formants are tracked along the signal*".
- ▶ **Formant Shift** (-24 ... off ... +24): "*Determines how formants adjust to pitch shifts. When set to 0, formants are adjusted together with pitch shifts*".

## Tracks Window

Now let's explore how to manipulate the pitch information of individual notes in an Audio Region using Flex Pitch.

# Interface

Once you Enable Flex ⊠ (with Flex Pitch selected), the appearance of the Audio Regions on the flex-enabled Tracks changes. The "single area" of the Region splits into two active areas:

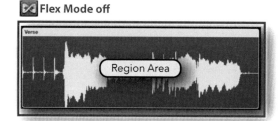

💀 **Appearance**

▸ **Region Area**: The click functionality of the regular Audio Region is now restricted to the small strip of the Track Header:

- *Click* to select the Region
- Rename the Region
- *Drag* the Region Header to move the Region
- *Ctr+click* on the Region Header to open the standard Shortcut Menu for the Region
- *Double-click* to toggle the Audio Editor

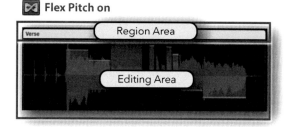

▸ **Editing Area**: The area of the Region that displays the waveform now has a special function:

- The waveform is dimmed and overlaid with the onscreen controls that let you edit the pitch.
- *Ctr+click* in this area to open a separate Flex Pitch Shortcut Menu. The menu items change depending on whether you click, on a "Note Bar" or on the background.

💀 **Click Zones**

Click Zones are the various "hot spots" on an object where the Cursor Tool changes to a different tool when moving the mouse over it or clicking on it.

The screenshots on the right show you the various Click Zones with the Cursor Tools they change to when moving over that area.

Here are the Click Zones when Flex Pitch is enabled:

▸ **Borders, lower half** 🔲 🔲: Resize Region

▸ **Borders, upper half** 🔲 🔲: Compress/Expand Region

▸ **Center, on "Note Bar"** ⬦: Edit the pitch of a Note Bar by dragging the pitch line up or down

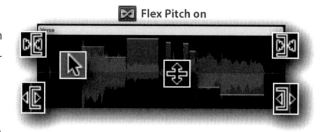

▸ **Center, outside "Note Bar"**: 🔖 *Drag* to select notes, *ctr+click* to open Shortcut Menu, or *double-click* to open the lower window pane in the Main Window with the Audio File Editor.

# Note Bars

Remember, when you first enable Flex Mode on a Track, Logic is performing an analysis of all the Audio Files on that Track to gather data that is needed to do all the magic with time and pitch alteration. For example, if you have a vocal performance, Logic tries to figure out the following things:

- ☑ Where are the individual notes of the melody?
- ☑ What is the "Course Pitch", the musical note (C, C#, D, D#, etc.) of each individual note?
- ☑ What is the "Fine Pitch", or the pitch deviation on each note? That means, did the singer hit the perfect pitch of each note or are some notes a little bit sharp or flat, and if so, how much?

## *About Cents*

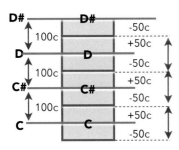

Without going too much into the physics territory, here are a few points you should know:

You can describe musical notes in absolute or relative units.

- **Absolute Unit**: Frequency is an absolute value and each musical note, i.e. C1, F#5, Bb4, etc., has a fix frequency measured in Hertz [Hz].

- **Relative Unit**: You can also describe the relationship between two notes. For example, G2 is two semitones higher than F2, or A5 is twelve semitones higher than A4 (twelve semitones is one octave). The scientific unit of one semitone is 100 cent. That gives you a finer measurement to describe the relationship between two notes. For example, if you raise the pitch of the note D2 by 100cents, you end up with D#2. However, if you raise D2 by 50cents, then it is just half a semitone higher, or +50cents out of tune.

With this knowledge, let's see what is displayed in the Audio Region:

- ☑ The actual waveform of the recording is still visible, slightly dimmed, as a reference.
- ☑ Each individual note that Logic detected during its analysis is marked as an individual segment, a **"Note Bar"**.
- ☑ The length of a Note Bar ❶ relates directly to the length of that note referenced against the Timeline (the x-axis).
- ☑ The y-axis ❷, however, does not indicate the absolute pitch of the note (i.e. C1, F#3, A6). The center line refers to the perfect pitch of this note (whatever note it is). If a detected note has a perfect pitch (without any intonation problems), then you would see only a highlighted line ❸ on the center line.

**Flex Pitch (Tracks Window)**

- ☑ Any note that the singer didn't hit on the right pitch is indicated by a positive bar (above the center line) or a negative bar (below the center line). The maximum positive value of the bar (hitting the Region Header) represents +50cents ❹ and the maximum negative value (bottom of the Region) represents -50cents ❺ pitch deviation from the perfect pitch.

- ☑ Any section on the Region that is not overlaid with a bar ❻ represents non-pitch audio or something that Logic couldn't identify as a pitch (percussive sound, noise, silence, etc.).
- ☑ Selected Note Bars are highlighted ❼.

# Editing

The editing procedure to change the pitch of those detected notes (Note Bars) is super easy. You use the Cursor Tool (it changes to the vertical Resize Tool ⬍) or use a command from the Shortcut Menu. There are two Shortcut Menus:

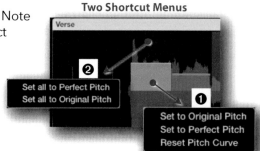

**Two Shortcut Menus**

- ❶ One pops up when you *ctr+click* on a single Note Bar or a Note Bar of a group of selected Note Bars. These commands affect only the selected one(s).
- ❷ One pops up when you *ctr+click* outside a Note Bar. These commands affect all notes of the Region.

▶ **Change to any Pitch**:
  - Single: *Drag* a Note Bar up or down ⬍ to adjust its pitch ❸.
  - Group: *Drag* around a group of Note Bars ↖ to select them first, and then *drag* any Note Bar up or down ⬍ to adjust the pitch of all selected Note Bars relatively ❹.

▶ **Set to Perfect Pitch**: This moves the bar(s) to the center line, which means, no pitch deviation.
  - Single: *Ctr+click* on a note to open the Shortcut Menu and choose *"Set to Perfect Pitch"*.

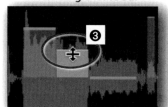

**Mode Single Note Bar**

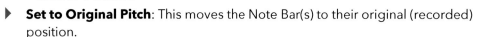

  - Group: *Drag* around a group of Note Bars ↖ to select them first and then *ctr+click* on a note to open the Shortcut Menu and choose *"Set to Perfect Pitch"*.
  - All: *Ctr+click* on the area outside a Note Bar to open the Shortcut Menu and choose *"Set all to Perfect Pitch"*. Your entire Region is in perfect pitch with the click of a button.

**Mode Multiple Note Bars**

▶ **Set to Original Pitch**: This moves the Note Bar(s) to their original (recorded) position.
  - Single: *Ctr+click* on a Note Bar to open the Shortcut Menu and choose *"Set to Original Pitch"*.
  - Group: *Drag* around a group of Note Bars ↖ to select them first and then *ctr+click* on a note to open the Shortcut Menu and choose *"Set to Original Pitch"*.
  - All: *Ctr+click* on the area outside a Note Bar to open the Shortcut Menu and choose *"Set all to Original Pitch"*.

▶ **Reset Pitch Curve**: This will undo any changes to the Pitch Curve of the selected Note Bar(s). You can display and edit the Pitch Curve only in the Audio Track Editor (which I explain in the next section).

## *Attention*

- When you *drag* a Note Bar, you will actually hear the result as a static sound.
- When you *drag* the Note Bar beyond the upper or lower border of the Audio Region, the bar flips over to the "other side" and you can keep on moving. What you cannot see is that Logic changed the note to the next semitone.
- Use the Waveform Zoom Control ❺ on the Tracks Window's Menu Bar to adjust the vertical display axis of the waveform.
- On a stereo file (with their two zero axis), the center line for the Perfect Pitch reference ❻ is still in the middle.

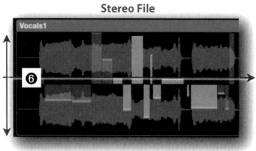

**Waveform Zoom**

**Stereo File**

**Audio Track Editor**

Although the pitch editing in the Tracks Window is super easy and quick, the Audio Track Editor provides much more control over how to manipulate the pitch of an Audio Region.

## Overview

Here is a comparison of an Audio Region how it looks like in the Tracks Window and the Audio Track Editor with their different onscreen controls.

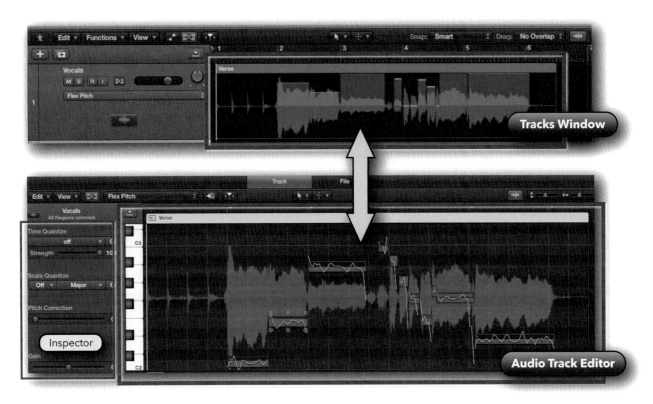

### 🔘 Onscreen Controls

As you can see, the onscreen controls that are overlaid on top of the waveform are completely different. Not only is the user interface different, the Audio Track Editor also lets you manipulate more pitch-related Parameters.

> ▶ **Piano Roll Grid**: In the Tracks Window, the Note Bars that were placed around the center line contain no information about the absolute pitch, only the pitch deviation. In the Audio Track Editor, the Note Bars are placed on a Piano Roll style grid like MIDI Notes in the Piano Roll Editor. That means, they now contain absolute pitch information (referenced against a musical keyboard as the y-axis), plus the pitch deviation and additional Pitch Curve are overlaid on top of the Note Bars.

### 🔘 Inspector Controls

The second noticeable difference in the Audio Track Editor is a separate Local Inspector on the left. You have to enable it from the Local Menu *View ➤ Show/Hide Local Inspector*. This Inspector is only available in the Audio Track Editor when you have Flex Pitch selected. Otherwise, the command is grayed out.

As with any other editor window, whatever edit you make in one window, will change accordingly in the other window.

## ➡ *Interface*

### 🙂 Show/Hide Flex Button

I already mentioned that the Show/Hide Flex Button, available on the Audio Track Editor, acts independently from the one on the Tracks Window. That means, you can display the regular view in the Tracks Window and only show the Flex controls in the Audio Track Editor.

Unfortunately, the functionality of the Show/Hide Flex Button is not consistent with the Tracks Window where it only switches the view on and off. Here, in the Audio Track Editor, when you turn the button on, it also enables the Flex Mode (if it wasn't enabled yet). Turning the button off, on the other hand, only turns the Flex View off, but does not disable the Flex Mode.

Also, there is no way in the Audio Track Editor to turn Flex off for the current Track. You have to do that in the Track Inspector or on the Track Header in the Tracks Window.

**Audio Track Editor**

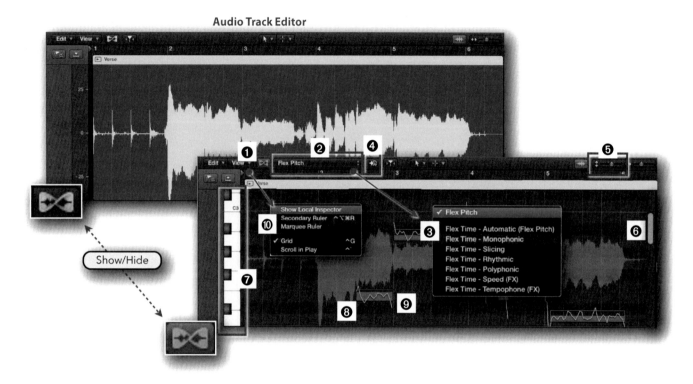

When the Show/Hide Flex Button is enabled ❶ 🔀 , the following elements will become visible:

▸ **Flex Mode Menu Button ❷**: The button opens the same popup menu ❸ as the one in the Track Header displaying all the seven Flex Modes.

▸ **MIDI In Button ❹** 🔀 🔀 🔀: This is the same MIDI In Button as in the Piano Roll Editor. I will describe its function a little bit later.

▸ **Vertical Zoom Slider ❺** 🔀 and **vertical Scroll Bar ❻**: Because the Workspace area now functions like in the Piano Roll Editor, you now also have a vertical Zoom Slider and a vertical Scroll Bar. Please note that the Waveform is not affected by the vertical scrolling and zooming of the overlaid onscreen controls.

▸ **Vertical Keyboard ❼**: The vertical keyboard is the reference for the absolute pitch of the Note Bars. Similar to the Piano Roll Editor, you can select one or multiple keys on the keyboard to select all Note Bars matching that note in the Edit Area.

▸ **Note Bars ❽** with **Pitch Curve ❾**: These are the elements that visually describe the parameters of each detected note.

▸ **Show Local Inspector ❿**: This menu item is only active in Flex Pitch mode to toggle the Local Inspector.

### ⇒ *Note Bars*

Now let's explore all the various editing techniques in the Audio Track Editor. A note of advice upfront. Although the interface is very easy to use, the whole topic of editing "inside an audio file" is still complex because you are doing serious "surgery" (everything is still non-destructive). These are advanced techniques and the more you know about the "anatomy" of a sound recording and the physics behind it, the better you will understand the procedure and the outcome of the applied edits.

In this section, I will go through each Parameter step-by-step.

### 👤 About Note Bars Pitch Curves

Same as in the Tracks Window, each detected note is visualized as a Note Bar. They can have three different appearances:

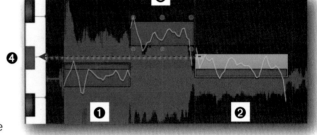

❶ **Unselected**: this is the default.

❷ **Selected**: Click on a Note Bar to select it. The corresponding note on the keyboard is also selected ❹ to indicate its absolute pitch. The standard procedure to select /deselect objects apply. *Click* for single selection, *sh +click* for multiple selection, and *drag* (lasso around) for a group selection.

❸ **Hotspots** (selected or unselected): Moving the Cursor Tool over a Note Bar will display six Hotspots. They represent six Parameters of a note that you can edit by sliding the spot up or down.

Here are the individual elements of a note that are displayed:

▶ **Position ❺**: The horizontal position of the left border of a Note Bar is the starting point of the note.

▶ **Duration ❻**: The length of the Note Bar is the actual duration of the note, same as in the Piano Roll Editor.

▶ **Pitch ❼**: The vertical position (referenced against the musical keyboard) indicates the absolute pitch of the note and the shaded area inside the Note Bar (above or below) indicates the average deviation from that absolute pitch.

▶ **Pitch Curve ❽**: The Pitch Curve, overlaid on top of the Note Bar, indicates the actual deviation from the absolute pitch over time (for the duration of the note). This lets you spot any out of tune problems.

▶ **Gain ❾**: The Gain of a note (how loud is it) is not displayed in the Note Bar but in the underlying waveform. You can actually change the Gain of the waveform only for that section that is detected as a note.

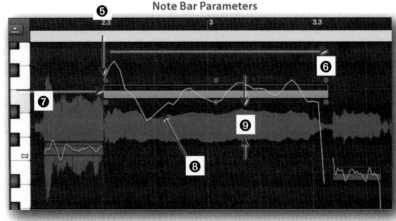

Note Bar Parameters

The more you work with Flex Pitch, the better you will get in "reading" the Audio Region. That means, you can "interpret" the characteristics of the performance and can spot the potential trouble notes.

Next, let's go through the details of each Parameter that you can change.

# Editing

## ➡ *What can be edited*

Before introducing all the procedures for editing the various parameters, let's have a quick look at all the parameters that are available for editing with Flex Pitch in the Audio Track Editor:

 **Level**

▶ **Gain**

You can change the level of each individual Note Bar form -30dB to +30dB

 **Pitch**

▶ **Course Pitch** (transpose)

You can transpose the Note Bar to any note.

▶ **Fine Pitch** (tune)

You can fine tune each Note Bar in cents: -50cent to +50 cents.

▶ **Vibrato**

You can adjust the amount of vibrato used in a note from -400% to +600%.

▶ **Drift**

You can adjust the Drift at the beginning and end of a note. This determines if a note starts on the right pitch or "slides" into it and out of it.

 **Sound**

▶ **Formant**

Formants are peaks in the frequency spectrum of an instrument or a voice that defines the specific character of an instrument or a voice. You can shift the formants of a Note Bar to change those sonic characteristic. For example, shifting up the formants of a vocal performance results in the typical "Mickey Mouse" effect.

 **Timing**

▶ **Length**

You can resize the length of a Note Bar, which means you time compress a note (make it shorter, squeeze it) or time expand it (make it longer, stretch it).

▶ **Position**

You can move the position of a Note Bar (within limitations) either individually or quantize the Note Bars to a Quantize Grid similar to quantizing MIDI Events.

 **Note Bars**

▶ **Split - Join - Delete**

Although the Note Bars are automatically created by Logic based on the analysis of the audio file, this note detection might not be perfect. Maybe there are two notes where Logic detected only one or there was only one note when Logic thought there were two. In that case you can split a Note Bar in two or join two adjacent Note Bars. You can even delete or create new Note Bars.

## ➡ *Gain*

I want to start with the Gain Parameter because it is very easy to apply. This feature has actually nothing to do with either the timing nor the pitch of an audio recording.

A Gain control is a level, or volume control. While a typical volume control is often available in the form of a fader or slider that lets you set the level to a fixed value or "ride" it dynamically, a Gain control is used to set a fixed level offset, either in the form of a knob (on a channel strip) or a numeric entry field.

Think about the big picture for a moment. You set the level of your mix with the Master Fader, you set the level of each Channel with the Channel Fader, and you can apply a level offset to each Region with the Gain Parameter in the Region Inspector. But now, with the Gain control in Flex Pitch, you can even apply a level offset for each individual Note Bar in an Audio Region detected by Flex Pitch.

Prior to Flex Pitch, if there was a note in an audio recording that was too loud or too soft, you had to use Automation to compensate that offset or cut the Region and apply a Gain offset for that separate Audio Region. Now, with Flex Pitch, you can simply drag a control up or down for each note to apply a Gain offset for that section inside an Audio Region to "level" an uneven performance.

Here is the procedure:

- ☑ Move the Pointer Tool over the Note Bar that you want to adjust (the six hotspots appear).
- ☑ Point at the Gain hotspot in the lower left corner ❶. A black Help Tag ❷ displays the current Gain Offset of the Note Bar.
- ☑ *Drag* the hotspot up or down to change the Gain offset (maximum +30dB, minimum -30dB).
- ☑ The dimmed waveform in the background adjusts while you are changing the offset ❸, so you see the effect on the waveform right away as a visual reference.

### *Local Inspector*

You can adjust only one Note Bar at a time when using the Gain Hotspot. However, with the Gain Slider ❹ in the Local Inspector, you can select multiple Note Bars first and then change the value on the slider to apply the Gain offset to all selected Not Bars equally.

You can also use the value display ❺ on the Gain Slider as a readout. It always displays the value of the last selected Note Bar.

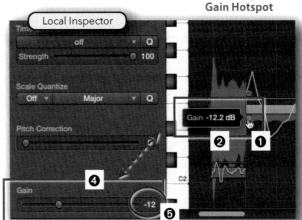

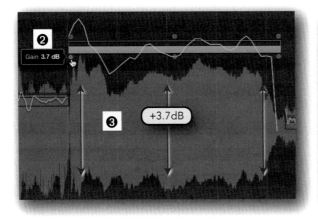

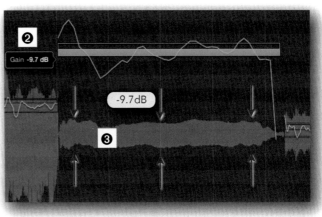

## ➡ *Fine Pitch*

Now let's look at the Fine Pitch Parameter. This is the one you can quickly adjust in the Tracks Window by dragging the Note Bar up and down ❶.

The interface in the Audio Track Editor, however, is different:

☑ All the Note Bars ❷, displayed as white frames, have the same height. The height represents 100cents.

☑ The vertical position of a Note Bar itself is referenced against the musical keyboard ❸ on the left.

☑ The keys extend into a horizontal grid across the Workspace. These rows, representing the black and white key, are also 100cents high ❹.

☑ The actual position of the Note Bar (the white frame) on that grid indicates its pitch.

☑ The Note Bar displays both pitch information.
  - **Course Pitch** (Perfect Pitch): This is the actual note, i.e. C3, C#3, D3, etc.
  - **Fine Pitch**: This is the deviation from the Perfect Pitch between -50cent and +50cent.

**Note Bars in Tracks Window**

**Note Bars in Audio Track Editor**

Here is how you read those two informations. Remember, when Logic analyzes an audio file and detects a note, it assigns it to a Course Pitch.

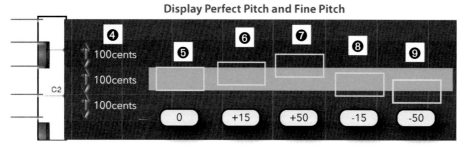

**Display Perfect Pitch and Fine Pitch**

▸ Let's assume that the detected note was a spot-on "C2", no intonation problems, not sharp and not flat. Now, think of a blue horizontal strip that represents the position of that perfect pitch C2. The Note Bar itself is represented by a white frame, which is placed vertically exactly on the blue strip. What you see is a blue bar ❺.

▸ Now, let's assume that note was not spot-on, it was a little sharp, for example, 15cents. This is how it is displayed ❻: The pitch of that note is a little higher, and therefore, the white frame of the Note Bar is now a little bit higher on the grid, +15cents higher. However, the blue strip, representing the note "C2" stays where it is. What you then see is the light blue color inside most of the white frame indicating the position of the perfect pitch and space in the upper portion of the white frame not covering the blue strip. This represents the positive pitch deviation (the note is sharp).

▸ The maximum positive pitch deviation ❼ is 50cent. Remember, the frame is "100cents high", so the frame being half of its height above blue" meaning 50cents sharp.

▸ If the note would be flat (negative pitch deviation), then the space inside the white frame (not covered by blue) is in the lower portion ❽ all the way to a maximum of -50cents pitch deviation ❾.

▸ So, think of the blue portion inside the frame of a Note Bar as the actual assigned note (the Course Pitch) that shines through the frame. The more the frame is filled with blue, the more the note is in tune with that Course Pitch.

▸ The more space is in the upper portion of the frame, the more the note is too sharp (positive pitch deviation).

▸ The more space is in the lower portion of the frame, the more the note is flat (negative pitch deviation).

Here is the procedure on how to change the Fine Pitch:

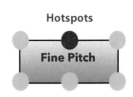

☑ Move the Pointer Tool over the Note Bar that you want to adjust (the six hotspots appear).

☑ Point at the Fine Pitch hotspot, the middle on top, ❶. A black Help Tag ❷ displays the current Fine Pitch value (pitch deviation) of the Note Bar.

☑ *Drag* the hotspot up or down to change the Fine Pitch. The white frame ❸ moves with the hotspot accordingly while the blue area ❹, indicating the Course Pitch (referenced to the musical keyboard ❺ to the left), stays fixed.

☑ When you move the hotspot higher or lower beyond the 50cent mark, then the blue area skips to the next (higher or lower) semitone, to indicate the new Course Pitch. You just transposed the note.

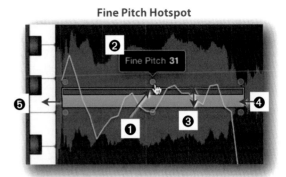

**Fine Pitch Hotspot**

### 🔲 Local Inspector

There is another way to correct the Fine Pitch.

The Local Inspector has a Pitch Correction Slider that also affects the Fine Pitch. Please pay attention to the difference between the two controls:

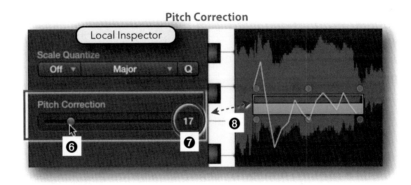

**Pitch Correction**

☑ While the Fine Pitch Hotspot ❶ moves the Note Bar up or down by applying a fixed Fine Pitch value to the note in cents (moving the note bar up or down), the Pitch Correction in the Local Inspector moves the Note Bar up or down by applying a percentage value (0 ... 100%) to the Fine Pitch, where 100% equals perfect pitch.

☑ Both methods (Hotspot and Pitch Correction) are just two different ways to move the Fine Pitch of a note.

☑ You have to select a Note Bar first before applying a Pitch Correction.

☑ You can select multiple Note Bars to apply a Pitch Correction to all of them at once. Remember, with the Fine Pitch Hotspot you can only adjust one Note Bar at a time.

☑ You can set the Pitch Correction by moving the Slider ❻. The number next to it indicates the numeric value field ❼.

☑ The Pitch Correction is an "active" Parameter, that means, selecting a Note Bar will move the slider, displaying the Pitch Correction value of that Note Bar ❽. If you have multiple Note Bars selected, then the Pitch Correction displays the value of the first Note Bar.

## ➡ *Transpose*

During the initial analysis process, Logic determines the Course Pitch of each detected note (i.e. C3, F#4, Gb1) and places the Note Bars in the Workspace referenced against the vertical keyboard. This enables you to transpose those notes the same way as MIDI Events in the Piano Roll Editor.

You can use this tool not only for fixing mistakes, but you can also get creative and "rewrite" a melody that you recorded with a singer or a solo instrument.

☑ Drag the Note Bar up or down to transpose it to a different note.

☑ Select multiple Note Bars and drag them as a group to transpose them together.

☑ While you transpose a Note Bar, the vertical note reference is displayed by a shaded horizontal area ❶ that indicates the note reference.

☑ The left and right border of the Note Bar is also indicated by two vertical Alignment Guides ❷.

**Transpose Notes**

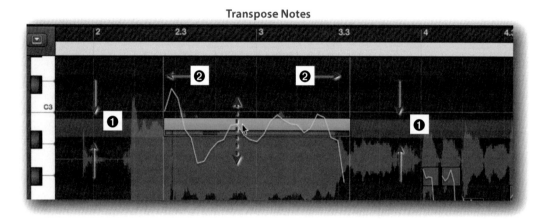

## 💀 Scale Quantize

The Local Inspector again has additional controls for transposing notes. The feature is called "Scale Quantize", and instead of time quantizing where you move a note left-right to a vertical grid, this type of quantization moves the note up-down on a horizontal grid, which means, the note will be transposed.

Applying the Quantize Command will transpose (only) the selected notes to the nearest note of the musical scale that you've chosen from the following popup menus:

▸ **Root Note ❸**: Select the Root Note for the Scale. The value "Off" will reset any transposition.

▸ **Scale ❹**: Select from a list of 19 Scales.

▸ **Quantize Button ❺**: Click the button to apply the selection to the selected notes.

There are two ways to apply a Scale Quantization:

- You can select the notes first. Now, selecting any value from the two popup menus will apply that value to the selected notes.

- You can select the Root Note and Scale first. Now, you can select the notes and *click* on the Q-Button 🄠 to apply the Scale to the selected notes.

**Scale Quantize**

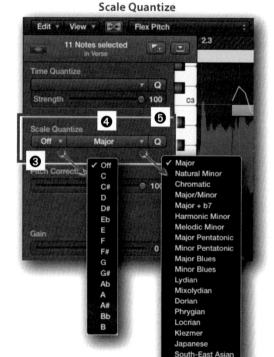

## ☺ MIDI In

Instead of transposing the Note Bars manually by dragging them with the Cursor Tool up or down, you can use your external MIDI Keyboard for that. This method could be faster, especially when you want to change multiple Note Bars, for example, "entering a new melody".

Remember, the MIDI In Button will only appear on the Menu Bar of the Audio Track Editor when Flex Pitch is enabled.

Audio Track Editor: Menu Bar

MIDI In Button

### ▶ MIDI Editor

The MIDI IN Button is also displayed on the Menu Bar of the Piano Roll Editor and the Score Editor. The functionality in Flex Pitch, however, is a little bit different.

First, a quick review of the original functionality in the MIDI Editor:

**Off**: the MIDI Input Button is disabled.

**Step Input Mode**: *Click* on the button to enable Step Input Mode. Playing a note (or a chord) will enter that note(s) at the Playhead position as, for example, a 1/16 note and the Playhead moves one sixteenth note ahead. Now, play the next key on your keyboard, which will be entered as the next new 1/16 note, and so on. Hitting the space bar on your computer keyboard moves the Playhead ahead by a 1/16th note without entering a note. The actual note value is determined by the Division value set in the Control Bar Display (in the Custom Display Mode). *Click* on the MIDI In Button again to disable it.

Control Bar Display (Custom)

Division

**Overwrite Mode**: *Double-click* on the button to enable Overwrite Mode. Please note the subtle difference of the icon. Select a note and then play any key on your external MIDI Keyboard to set the note to that key. Select the next note and play a key on your keyboard to set it to that key, and so on. *Click* on the MIDI In Button again to disable it.

### ▶ Audio Track Editor

Although you can set the MIDI In Button to Step Input and Overwrite, only the Step Input Mode is working in Flex Pitch. Also, the Step Input functionality is a little bit different:

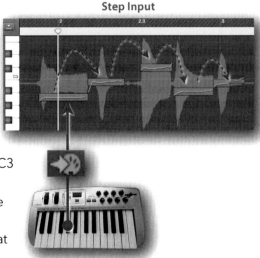

Step Input

☑ *Click* on the MIDI In Button ⟲ to enable Step Input Mode ⟳ .

☑ Place the Playhead at the position of the Note Bar you want to change.

☑ Hit the key on your external MIDI Keyboard, for example, C3 and the Note Bar moves to C3.

☑ The Playhead automatically moves to the beginning of the next Note Bar.

☑ Hit the key on your MIDI Keyboard that you want to set that Note Bar to, and so on.

☑ *Click* on the MIDI In Button to disable Step Input Mode ⟲ when you finished.

## ➡ *Vibrato*

If a vocalist sings a longer note or an instrumentalist plays a sustained note on his instrument, the Flex Pitch analyzes the frequency of that note (i.e. 440Hz) and assigns it a specific musical note (i.e. A3), displayed by the position of the Note Bar in the Audio Track Editor. If the note is a little higher (sharp) or lower (flat) than the target frequency, then the Note Bar indicates that too as we have just learned. However, those notes never have a constant frequency. This is one of the aspects that makes the human voice or an instrument sound "live", those little imperfections, the slight fluctuation in pitch during the duration of a note.

Being aware of that little fact, let's look again at what happens during the analysis procedure:

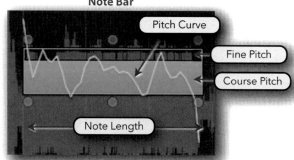

- ☑ **Note Length**: Flex Pitch has to detect first the boundaries of the individual notes out of an often continuous audio signal. That determines the length of a detected note.
- ☑ **Pitch Curve**: Once a note is isolated (i.e. a half note ♩ ), Flex Pitch has to analyze its pitch. Remember, a single "live" note always varies more or less in pitch over the duration of that note. That means, Flex Pitch has to follow that frequency over time. It displays that "frequency over time" as a graph on top of the Note Bar. This is the Pitch Curve. The x-axis represents the time (the duration of the note) and the y-axis its frequency.
- ☑ **Course Pitch**: From that segment of the Pitch Curve, Flex Pitch now calculates the average frequency and rounds it to the closest frequency of the Course Pitch, based on the system of the musical scale (C1, C#1 , D1, etc.). For example, the note A3.
- ☑ **Fine Pitch**: Any rounding error (how far off from the perfect pitch of the note, i.e. A3) is indicated as the Fine Pitch. For example, the actual detected note was 20cent higher from the perfect pitch of A3.

Let's compare that Pitch Curve to two parameters often used with MIDI Events:

### ▶ Modulation Wheel

When the pitch of a sustained note changes periodically up and down, then the musical term is Vibrato, and the technical term is Pitch Modulation. Many synth patches are programmed so you can use the Modulation Wheel on an external MIDI Keyboard to create those Pitch Modulations. The more you turn up the wheel, the higher the pitch alterations will be. Although this imitates the natural vibrato (Pitch Curve) of a live instrument, it still can sound static because the up-down frequency of the pitch alteration is often constant (controlled by an LFO). Please note that the Modulation value is not a pitch value, just the amount of how much the pitch is modulated.

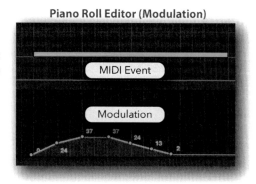

### ▶ Pitch Wheel

To better understand the displayed Pitch Curve on the Note Bar, I would compare it to the Pitch Bend controller. This wheel on an external MIDI Keyboard can increase (moving forward) or decrease (moving backward) the Fine Tune of the currently played note. Although it is harder to control than a Mod Wheel, it is more similar to the natural occurrence in live instruments or a vocal performance. You can control *when, how much,* and in *what direction* you alter the pitch.

### *Vibrato Hotspot*

There are three controls that can modify the Pitch Curve: Vibrato, Pitch Drift Left, and Pitch Drift Right. Let's look at the Vibrato first.

**Hotspots**

Move the Cursor Tool over the Note Bar to make the six Hotspots visible and point at the center spot below the Note Bar. This is the Vibrato Hotspot.

A black Help Tag pops up ❶ and shows: "**Vibrato 100%**".

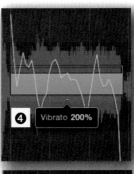

### 💀 Vibrato vs bad performance

A vibrato is usually a controlled pitch variation that is performed on purpose. The Pitch Curve looks like an up and down movement around a center (an invisible horizontal line in the middle of the Note Bar). The higher the peaks and dips of the curve, the more the pitch goes up or down. However, untrained singers who have problems with intonation often vary in their pitch "uncontrolled" that looks more like a random Pitch Curve. Although this is technically not considered a Vibrato, the Vibrato control can help with those performance issues too.

### 💀 Vibrato Control

You can drag the Hotspot up or down to increase or decrease the Vibrato value from -400% to +600%. What does that mean?

- The shape of the Pitch Curve stays the same.
- The values that make up the curve are changing proportionally.
- The "feel" of the actual performance is, therefore, maintained. For example, *when* does the vibrato start, *where* is more vibrato (peaks), *where* is less vibrato.
- The hotspot controls the "intensity" of the vibrato, reduces or increases the amount of vibrato (how far off the center).
- However, you cannot alter the shape itself (add vibrato where there is none).

### 💀 Change the Vibrato:

▶ **100%**: ❶ This is the default value, the original shape of the Pitch Curve, the original performance.

▶ **0% ... 100%**: ❷ Lowering the value will decrease the amount of vibrato, the peaks are getting lower.

▶ **0%**: ❸ There is no vibrato, no deviation of the current pitch, which results in an "unnatural", static sound.

▶ **100% ... 600%**: ❹ This increases the Vibrato to a maximum of 600%

▶ **-1% ... -400%**: ❺ The negative values increase the Vibrato up to -400%, but this time inverse. Positive peaks (higher pitch) are now negative peaks (lower pitch) and vice versa.

> You can select multiple Note Bars and drag one of their Vibrato Hotspots to change their Vibrato values proportionally.

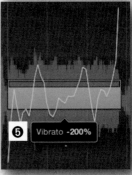

**Note Bar Shortcut Menu**

### 💀 Reset Pitch Curve(s)

To reset the Pitch Curve to its original shape (100%), *ctr+click* on the Note Bar and select "Reset Pitch Curve" from the Shortcut Menu.

## ➡ *Pitch Drift*

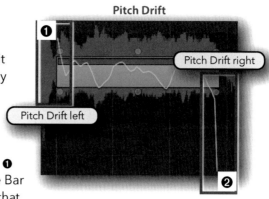

Pitch Drift

The Pitch Drift is the section at the beginning and end of a note. Especially when a singer performs a melody, he or she will not hit each note at the beginning spot-on with the perfect pitch. Usually the notes are connected, sliding into each other. This is not a big dramatic glissando-like slide, but more of a subtle effect that makes a performance sound natural (if not overdone).

During the analysis of the audio material, Flex Pitch will "detect" and display that off-pitch in the Pitch Curve as a line coming into ❶ the Note Bar (from above or below) and going out ❷ of the Note Bar (going up or down). With the Pitch Drift controls, you can adjust that portion of the Pitch Curve if that transition was a bit too much.

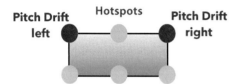

Move the Mouse over the Note Bar to make the six Hotspots visible and point at the upper-left spot (for adjusting the Pitch Drift at the beginning of the Note Bar) or point at the upper-right spot (for adjusting the Pitch Drift at the end of a Note Bar).

A black Help Tag pops up ❸ and shows: "**Pitch Drift 0.00**". You can set it between -100.00 and +100.00. You can also adjust the value for multiple selected Note Bars at the same time.

Look at the following screenshots where I increased ❹ and decreased ❺ the Pitch Drift on the left and increased ❻ and decreased ❼ the Pitch Drift on the right. As you can see, although the drift only affect the section at the left and right border, the more dramatic you change the value, the more the rest of the Pitch Curve is affected (maybe in a negative way). Like so many controls, the Pitch Drift cannot perform wonders and your milage may vary. At the end, trust your ears to determine what sounds right.

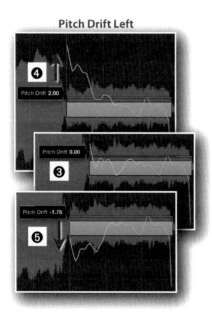

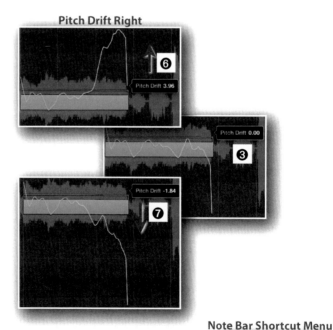

## 💀 Reset Pitch Curve(s)

*Ctr+click* on the Note Bar and select "Reset Pitch Curve" from the Shortcut Menu to set the Pitch Drift (and the Vibrato) back to their original shape.

Note Bar Shortcut Menu

Set to Original Pitch
Set to Perfect Pitch
Reset Pitch Curve

Once you understand what the Pitch Curve is displaying and get more practice, you will quickly learn to "read" an entire Audio Region.

### ➡ *Formant Shift*

Before explaining how to change the Formant, let me give you a quick introduction about the Formants:

- Formants determine the sonic characteristics of the human voice, but the concept can also be applied to acoustic instruments. Based on the physical shape and material of an instrument or the human vocal tract, there are acoustic resonances (peaks at a specific frequency in the spectrum), the Formants.

- The frequency of those Formants are constant for a specific instrument or voice (always at the same position of the frequency spectrum), independent of the frequency of the actual note you perform on an instrument or sing.

- When you transpose a note by changing the playback speed (changing the Sample Rate or change the speed of a tape machine), you are not only transposing the frequency of the note, but also the frequency of the Formants. That means, you change the sonic characteristic of the audio signal (the voice or the instrument).

- If you have a vocalist sing the note C3 and then C4, you would identify the same vocalist (same sonic characteristics) with both notes. If you have a vocalist sing the note C3, record it on a tape, and speed it up so the note is C4, you hear the vocalist sing the note C4, but his sonic characteristics have changed because you also transposed the Formant frequency. The result is, the vocalist sounds like if Mickey Mouse sings the note C4.

- In order to keep the integrity of the Formants, any pitch or timing alterations on an audio signal have to keep the Formants "in place". This is done by using Pitch Shifting and Time Shifting processes.

So, if a Formant is something that you shouldn't touch in order to maintain the sonic characteristics of a vocal performance, then why do you have a control that lets you shift the Formants?

- Maybe you have a younger singer that should sound a little bit older or vice versa.
- Maybe you record multiple parts of a vocal arrangements with the same singer. Changing their Formants slightly make it sound that you have different (sounding) singers.

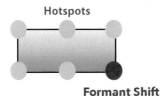

**Hotspots**

**Formant Shift**

Move the mouse over the Note Bar to make the six Hotspots visible and point at the lower-right spot. A black Help Tag ❶ pops up and shows: "**Formant Shift 0**". *Drag* it up or down to shift the Formants. You can also adjust the value for multiple selected Note Bars at the same time.

### Ghost Note Bars

When you drag the Hotspot up or down, a shaded ghost copy ❷ of the Note Bar moves up or down away from the Note Bar the higher you drag the value. This is barely visible. Once you applied a Formant Shift value and you *click* twice on the Formant Shift Hotspot that "Ghost Note Bar" will be better visible ❸.

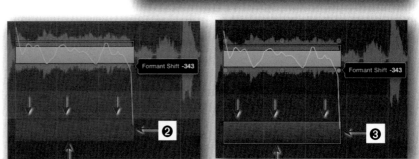

Formant Shift

## ➡ *Timing*

Before trying to move a Note Bar horizontally to change its timing position or resizing a Note Bar, you have to think for a moment about what you are trying to do (to the waveform).

The MIDI Events in the Piano Roll are independent objects that can be freely moved around. However, the Note Bars extracted by Flex Pitch in the Audio Track Editor look like independent objects, but they are not. The Note Bars are more like markers that are overlaid on the waveform (the "sonic snapshot"). The waveform itself is still a single object in itself. That means, you cannot move the Note Bars around freely like MIDI Events. First of all, the sequence of the Note Bars always stays the same, you can only move their boundaries around, affecting the Note Bar(s) next to it.

So, when moving anything horizontally, the question is:

- ☑ Which other Note Bars are affected?
- ☑ How are they affected?

Here are a few examples that demonstrate what happens when you resize the border of a Note Bar:

## *Example 1 (resize)*

### ▶ **Original ❸**

The screenshot in the middle is the original (unaltered) version ❸. There are five Note Bars and we will resize the right border of the second Note Bar. As I showed earlier, the Note Bar has various Click Zones.

Moving the Cursor Tool over the left or right border will change it to the Resize Tool 🔲 🔲 . The area inside the two green lines is where the change is happening. Note Bars to the left and right of it are not affected (remember the concept with the three Flex Markers). Pay attention to the waveform and how it changes, which gives you an indication of the actual result.

### ▶ **Moving Left ❹**

The screenshot on the top ❹ shows what happens when you *drag* the right border of the second Note Bar ❶ to the left:

- The Note Bar gets shorter (time compressed) while keeping its start position fixed (green line).
- The Note Bar to the right ❷ gets longer (time expanded) by the same amount while keeping its right border fixed (green line). Therefore, it starts earlier.

### ▶ **Moving Right ❺**

The screenshot on the bottom ❺ shows what happens when you *drag* the right border of the second Note Bar to the right:

- The Note Bar, which border you are dragging to the right ❶, gets longer (time expanded) while keeping its start position fixed (green line).
- The Note Bar to the right ❷ gets shorter (time compressed) by the same amount while keeping its right border fixed (green line). Therefore, it starts later.

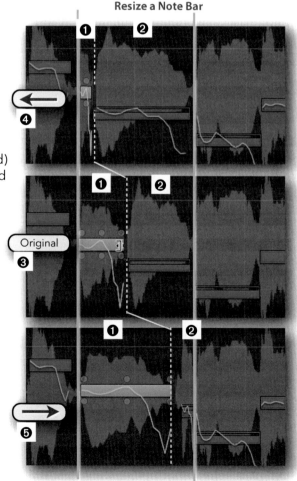

**Resize a Note Bar**

So what does that mean?

- 💡 You can quickly make time edits of single notes (Note Bars) "inside" your audio recording.
- 💡 Resizing the right border of a Note Bar lets you adjust the length of a note, make it longer or make it shorter by time compressing or time expanding it.
- 💡 Resizing the left border of a Note Bar lets you adjust the position (the start of the note). This also affects the note length because, this time, the right border stays fixed.
- 💡 Any resize action of a single Note Bar by dragging its border will also affect the adjacent Note Bar proportionally. But be careful, because that means, fixing a problem (adjusting the length or position of one note) could negatively affect the adjacent note (reposition it).

## Example 2 (resize)

But what if there is no adjacent Note Bar right next to the note you are resizing? For example, a pause or a noise that Logic didn't detect as a note (and therefore, no Note Bar).

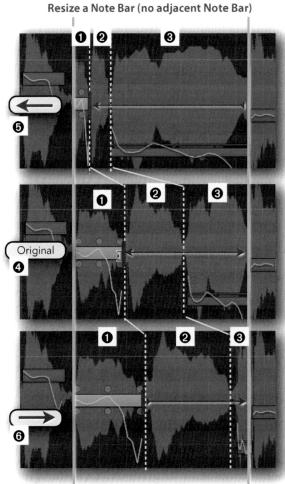

Resize a Note Bar (no adjacent Note Bar)

### ▶ Original ❹

Here is the same recording, (same waveform) that simulates that scenario. After the second Note Bar ❶ is a section without a Note Bar ❷ (lets pretend that this is noise that Logic couldn't detect as a note with a specific pitch). After that "pause" is the next Note Bar ❸.

### ▶ Moving Left ❺

Look closely at the screenshot to understand what happens when moving the right border of the second Note Bar ❶ to the left.

- The Note Bar gets shorter (time compressed ) as expected.
- The next Note Bar ❸ to the right (even if it is not directly adjacent) gets longer (time expanded) while keeping its right border in place (green line). The note now starts earlier.
- The area with no Note Bar ❷ in between gets squeezed (time compressed) and its start position moves to the left.

### ▶ Moving Right ❻

A similar effect happens when moving the right border of the second Note Bar to the right.

- The Note Bar ❶ gets longer (time expanded) as expected.
- The area with no Note Bar ❷ in between also gets longer (time expanded) and moves to the right.
- The next Note Bar ❸ to the right (even if it is not directly adjacent) gets squeezed (time compressed) while keeping its right border in place. The note now starts later.

## Example 3 (move)

In this example I will **move** a Note Bar instead of resizing its border. As you will see, you have to pay attention to the little details when altering the timing of Note Bars as to what exactly the outcome will be.

▶ **Moving a single Note Bar**

Moving a Note Bar means, you position the Cursor Tool over the Note Bar (it changes to a Hand Tool 🖐) and *drag* it left or right. However, dragging the Note Bar to the Left will NOT move the Note Bar. Instead, it will resize the left border with the same results we've just seen when resizing Note Bars.

- We drag the third Note Bar ❶.
- *Dragging* it to the left will move its start position to the left while keeping its end position in place (green line). The note gets time expanded ❷ and the Note Bar to the left gets time compressed ❸.
- *Dragging* the Note Bar to the right will move the start position to the right while keeping its right border in place (time compression) ❹. The Note Bar to the left gets time expanded ❺.

▶ **Moving multiple Note Bars**

The outcome is quite different when you have multiple adjacent Note Bars selected ❻.

- First of all, you can *drag* any of the selected notes.
- Only the last Note Bar gets stretched ❼ (time expanded) when *dragging* to the left or squeezed ❽ (time compressed) when *dragging* to the right. This is the same behavior as when "moving" a single Note Bar.
- The unselected Note Bar left of the first selected Note Bar gets stretched or squeezed accordingly ❾.
- The important thing is that any other selected Note Bar gets moved without being stretched or squeezed. Therefore, only their start position changes ❿.

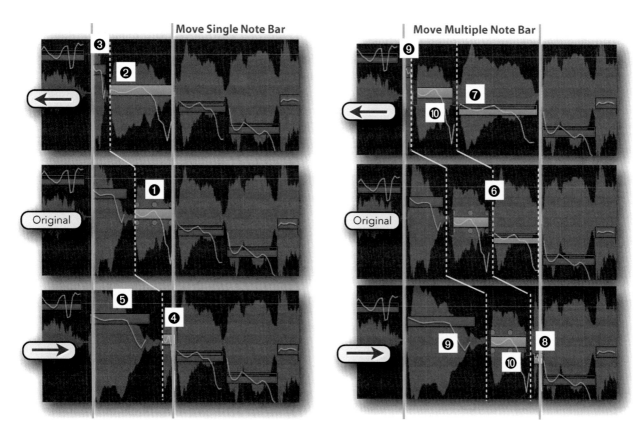

## Quantize Note Bars

Instead of moving Note Bars manually, you can use the Time Quantize command to move selected Note Bars to a specific Quantize Grid. This works like quantizing MIDI Events in the Piano Roll Editor.

The commands are available in the Local Inspector of the Audio Track Window. You have to make it visible from the Local Menu ❶ *View ➤ Show/Hide Local Inspector*

▶ **Time Quantize (Method 1)**

☑ Select the Quantize Grid from the Time Quantize Menu ❷

☑ Set the Quantize Strength with the slider ❸ between 0 (no quantization) to 100 (maximum quantization)

☑ Select the Note Bars you want to quantize

☑ *Click* the Quantize Button ❹ Q or use the Key Command (*Quantize Selected Events*) **Q**

Local Inspector

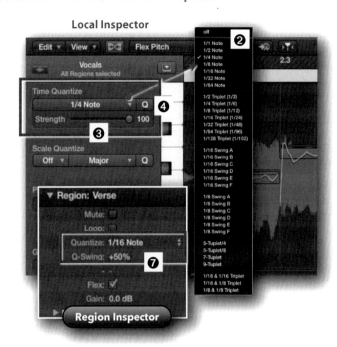

▶ **Time Quantize (Method 2)**

☑ Select the Note Bars you want to quantize first

☑ Whatever value you choose now as the Quantize Grid or the Quantize Strength will be applied directly to the selected Note Bars

▶ **Remove Time Quantize**

To remove any applied time quantization, just apply the Quantize Grid "Off" using method 1 or method 2.

When you apply a Quantize value to Note Bars that are not exactly in time ❺, then the Note Bars will move to that grid ❻. You also will see the underlying waveform adjusting on the timeline.

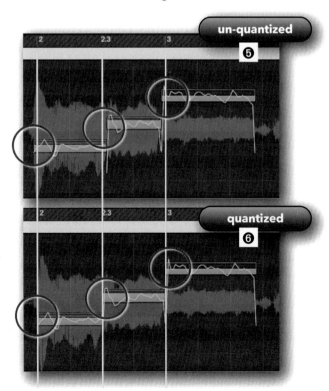

un-quantized
❺

quantized
❻

**Attention**

The Note Bars can be quantized with two different commands:

 **Local Inspector**: These are the Time Quantize controls ❷ in the Local Inspector of the Audio Track Editor.

**Region Inspector**: The Quantize controls ❼ in the Region Inspector of the Main Inspector can also be used to quantize the selected Note Bars.

# ➡ *Note Bars*

The Note Bars are created automatically based on the analysis of the Flex Pitch. However, this note detection might not be perfect all the time. Maybe there are two notes where Logic detected only one note or there was only one note when Logic thought there were two. In that case, there are a few editing commands that let you correct those mistakes.

**Split Note Bar**

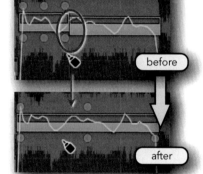
before

after

## 🌑 Split Note Bar in Two

> With the Scissors Tool you can *click* on a Note Bar to split it into two Note Bars at that time position. Now you can apply all those available edits to each one of the two new Note Bars separately.
>
> You can also use the Pencil Tool to *click* on an existing Note Bar to split it at that position.

## 🌑 Merge Two Note Bars

**Merge Note Bars**

before

after

> With the Glue Tool you can *click* on two selected Note Bars (that are adjacent with no gap in between) to merge them into one single Note.

## 🌑 Delete Note Bar

> With the Eraser Tool you can *click* on a Note Bar to delete it. Please note that you don't delete any audio portion, only the marker at that position that lets you perform edits on the audio waveform.

**Delete Note Bar**

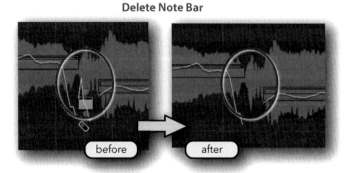
before     after

## 🌑 Create Note Bar

> With the Pencil Tool you can even click on a section of the waveform to create a new Note Bar. However, it seems that the analysis data is missing, because the editing procedures don't work quite as expected. So the practical use of this is questionable.

# Additional Flex Pitch Commands

The Local Edit Menu has two additional commands specific for Flex Pitch:

### ➡ *Analyze Audio For Flex Editing*

You can use the *Revert Pitch Curve* command from the Shortcut Menu to reset any edits you did on the Pitch Curve or set the various parameters back to their default value. However, if you want to reset the entire Audio Region to its original state after Flex Pitch analyzed it the first time, just select the Region(s) first and use this command.

### ➡ *Create MIDI Track from Flex Pitch Data*

This is an elegant "Audio to MIDI" transcription tool. For example, if you want to double the melody of an audio recording with a MIDI Instrument or print out the performance in music notation.

Select the Audio Region(s) on the Audio Track that you want to transcribe and apply the command.

- ☑ A new MIDI Track is created
- ☑ New MIDI Regions are created for each selected Audio Region
- ☑ A MIDI Event is created in the MIDI Region for each Note Bar in the Audio Region

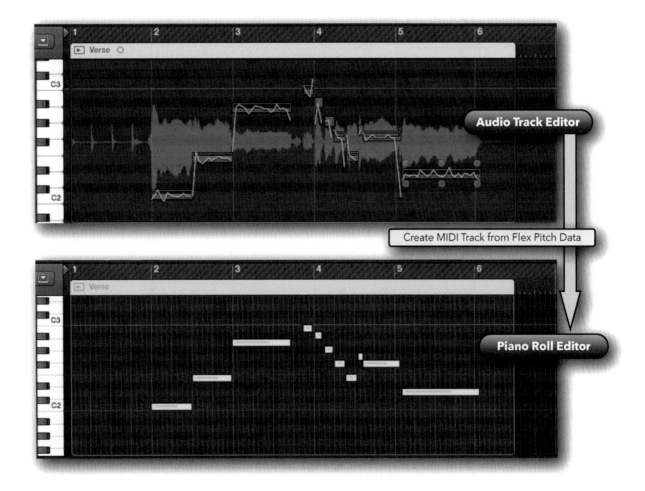

The Browsers Button  in the upper right corner of Logic's Main Window toggles the window pane on the right. This window pane has three tabs that let you switch between three Browser Windows. You use these Browser Windows to browse ("search for") specific files.

| **Project Browser** | **Media Browser** | **All Files Browser** |
|---|---|---|
|  |  |  |

The Project Browser (Project Audio Browser) lists all the audio files that you use in your Project, or have used but did not delete yet.

The Media Browser lets you search for all the audio and movie files on your drive, organized in special Smart Folders.

The All Files Browser lets you search for all the files on your drive that you can import into your Logic Project. In addition, it lets you "search inside" existing Logic Project Files to import specific elements of a Logic Project. For example, just import a specific Track or Tracks, or only components of a Track (Plugins, Regions, Routing, etc.), or import just specific Project Settings.

## ◉ Show/Hide Browser Window

To show a specific Browser is a two step process. First you open the window pane and then select which browser to display in that window pane, similar to the functionality of the Editors Pane.

▶ **Toggle the Window Pane**: Toggle the right window pane (Logic also calls this the Media Area) with the following commands:

- 🎱 *Click* the Browsers Button  in the Control Bar
- 🎱 Main Menu *View ➤ Show/Hide Browsers*
- 🎱 Key Command (*Show/Hide Media Area*) *F*

▶ **Select the Browser**: The window pane can display any of the three Browsers by selecting one of the three blue tabs on top of the window. When you open the window pane, it remembers which Browser was open when you closed it.
Only the All Files Browser has an unassigned Key Command (*Show/Hide File Browser*) that lets you toggle the window pane with the All Files Browser selected. The other two Browsers might need the extra click on the blue Browser tab.

The Project Browser (or *Project Audio Browser*), formerly known as the "*Audio Bin*", is the only Browser that can be displayed as a standalone window. This window even has its own name "Project Audio".

## Basics

I covered most of the Project Browser's functionality already in the *Recording Audio* chapter of my first Logic book. Here is a quick recap:

### 🎧 Audio File vs. Audio Regions

I hope you are absolutely clear about the difference between an Audio File and an Audio Region:

- An Audio File is ❶ stored on the hard drive.
- When using an Audio File in Logic (record, import), Logic creates an entry ❷ in the Project Browser that "points" to that Audio File ❶ on the hard drive.
- When you are using audio in Logic's Tracks Window, you are not using Audio Files. Instead, these are Audio Regions ❸, which are just a reference to a specific Audio File with the play instruction: "Play the Audio File ❶ from position a to position b".
- Editing Audio Regions means, editing the play instruction, not the actual Audio File. You can create multiple Regions referenced to the same Audio File, containing different play instructions.

### 🎧 Project Browser Concept

- Every Audio File that you import or record in your Project has an entry in the Project Browser ❹.
- These Audio Files in the Project Browser are linked to the actual Audio Files ❺ on your drive, most likely inside the Logic Project File or Project Folder.
- Below each Audio File entry ❺ in the Project Browser are the Audio Regions listed (the different "play instructions"). One Audio File has at least one Audio Region.
- Each Audio Region in the Tracks Window ❻ (placed on an Audio Track's Track Lane) has a corresponding Audio Region (a reference entry) in the Project Browser ❼ displaying the audio waveform. However, not every Audio Region in the Project Browser has to be used on a Track Lane ("unused Region").
- You can change (edit Audio Regions) that "play instruction" on the Track Lane, the Project Browser, the Audio Track Editor, or the Audio File Editor by resizing the Audio Region borders.
- You can create new Regions of an Audio File in the Project Bowser and drag them to the Track Lane. Creating new Audio Regions on the Track Lane (copy) will automatically create a new Audio Region entry in the Project Browser.
- Multiple copies ❽ of a single Audio Region can be placed on the Track Lane. They all refer to one Audio Region entry in the Project Browser. Changing one of those Audio Regions on the Track Lane, changes the other "clones" too, plus the Audio Region entry in the Project Browser.

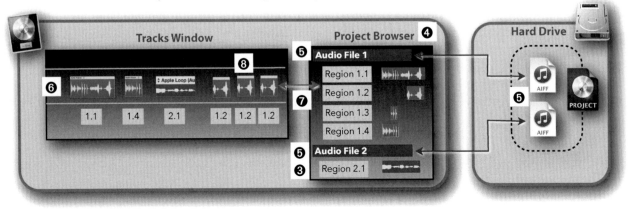

# Interface

### ➡ *Project Audio Browser vs. Project Audio Window*

The Project Browser (the window pane) and the Project Audio (standalone window) display the same content with the same user interface (with only minor differences).

Open the Project Audio Window with any of the following commands:

**Project Browser**

- 🎧 Main Menu *Window* ➤ *Open Project Audio*
- 🎧 Key Command (*Open Project Audio*) *cmd+8*
- 🎧 *Drag* the blue Project Tab out (tear-off)

### ➡ *Interface Elements*

Here are the different elements of the window:

### ⚫ Local Menus ❶

You have three Local menus, Audio File, Edit, and View. The Project Audio window has a fourth menu, the Option Menu, with just one command, "Strip Silence".

### ⚫ Audio File Path ❷

This area displays the file path of the selected Audio File. The Project Audio Window doesn't have that area. Instead, the Path is displayed in the additional *Location* column for each Audio File.

### ⚫ List ❸

The list area has four columns, plus a hidden one and the file path in the Project Audio Window.

- ▶ **Name**: This is the name of the Audio File or the Audio Region. *Click* on it to highlight the text so you can edit the name. Please note that changing the Audio File name will actually change the name of the file in the Finder.
- ▶ **Icons**: The clock symbol 🕐 indicates whether or not the audio file has tempo information embedded. The padlock symbol 🔒 is a clickable button. It prevents any changes to the Region when locked 🔒 .
- ▶ **Info/Waveform**: This section has two appearances. For an Audio File, it displays the file information. Sample Rate, Bit Depth, Channel information (symbols for mono, stereo, compressed, surround, etc.), and File Size. For an Audio Region it displays the waveform with tools to edit the Region right in this window.
- ▶ **bpm**: Logic embeds the Project's tempo in any newly recorded audio file, but only if the following checkbox is set: *Project Settings* ➤ *General* ➤ *Project Type* ➤ *use musical grid*. If there were programmed tempo changes during the recording, then there will be a hyphen listed (-). Importing any audio file that doesn't have tempo information will leave that field empty.
- ▶ **Location**: This column lists the file path for the Audio File (Project Audio Window only).

### ⚫ Control Bars ❹

- ▶ **Play Button** 🔊 : *Click* on the button to toggle "audition the selected Region". *Ctr+click* on the button to select the Channel Strip ❺ you play the audio through. The Prelisten Channel Strip is Audio Channel #256, which is automatically created for each Project in the Environment Window (without a Track assignment).
- ▶ **Cycle Button** 🔁 : Click on this button to toggle the Cycle Play for the played Region.
- ▶ **Volume Slider**: The slider controls the Volume Fader of the Prelisten Channel Strip (Audio Channel Strip #256). It has no effect if you have "Auto-select Channel Strip" selected from the Shortcut Menu.

## ➡ *Customize the Window*

The Local View Menu provides various commands on how to customize the Project Browser.

### ☠ Groups

This is a feature that you definitely want to use if you have tons of audio files and constantly need to scroll up and down half a mile. For example, you did a lot of takes during the session with the vocalist, the guitar player, or a sax player. Now instead of having one long list of audio files, you can create *Audio File Groups*. These are single line entries with a disclosure triangle that act like folders. You can now organize the audio files into those groups and use their disclosure triangle to show/hide the content.

Here is the procedure:

▶ **Create a Group**: When you use any of the following commands, a new line in the list will be created with the text entry box highlighted ❶. The Info field shows "Audio file group" ❷. Groups are always displayed on top of the list.

- ☠ Local Menu *View* ➤ *Create Group ... .*
- ☠ Key Command (*Create Group...* ) *ctr+G*
- ☠ *Ctr+click* on an Audio File in the list and select the command *Create Group ...* from the Shortcut Menu

▶ **Add Audio Files to Group**: There are two ways to do that:
- ☠ Select the Audio File(s) before creating a Group and all those files will be moved to the newly created Group.
- ☠ *Drag* a single or multiple selected Audio Files in the list over to a Group. A blue insertion line appears ❸.

▶ **Remove Audio Files to Group**: This action is a bit tricky. You have to drag the Audio File entry a little bit down to the left towards the disclosure triangle. The blue insertion line appears ❹ and the Group is selected ❺. Now move a tiny bit more to the left so the Group gets unselected and the beginning of the insertion line, the blue circle 🔵, moves a little to the left ❻. Release the mouse and the Audio File is removed from the list, back to the main list.

▶ **Delete Group**: To delete a Group, just select it and hit the *delete* key. This might sound scary, and the Dialog window with the message "Really delete the selected group?" ❼, also leaves you in the dark as to what happens to the Audio Files in that Group. The answer is, they just move back to the list.
You can also use the Local Menu *View* ➤ *Delete Selected Groups* or the unassigned Key Command for that action *Delete Selected Groups*.

There is one special command to create Groups automatically. The item from the Local Menu *View* ➤ *Group Files by* opens a submenu with three option. If you already have Groups assigned, then a Dialog Window ❽ gives you the option to leave those alone.

- **Location**: The path of each group becomes the Group name.
- **File Attributes ❾**: The Group name will be the File Info.
- **Selection in Tracks**: The Group name will be the various Track Names.

## 🌑 Viewing Options

There are a few other commands that let you adjust what is displayed and how it is displayed.

▶ **Show/Hide**

You can show or hide various elements in Project Browser.

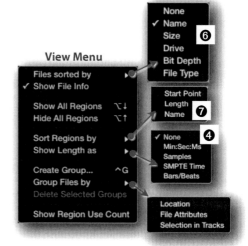

View Menu

- **File Attributes** *View ➤ Show File Info*: This determines if the File attributes are displayed in the File entry ❶.
- **Region Use Count** *View ➤ Show Region Use Count*: This displays a number ❷ next to the waveform of each Region entry to show how many times that Region is used on the Track Lanes.
- **Region Length** *View ➤ Show Length as*: This adds an additional column ❸ to the list displaying the length of each Region. Choose any unit from the popup menu ❹. "None" will hide the column.
- **Show/Hide Regions**: Each Audio File entry in the list acts as a folder with the Regions as their content. *Click* on the disclosure triangle ❺ next to an Audio File entry to show/hide its Regions.
- **Show/Hide <u>All</u> Regions**: You can also show/hide all Regions at once with the following commands.

    🌑 Menu Command *View ➤ Show/Hide All Regions*
    🌑 Key Command *opt+ArrowDown* or *opt+ArrowUp*
    🌑 *Opt+click* on the disclosure triangle acts as *Show All/Hide All Regions* in the list.

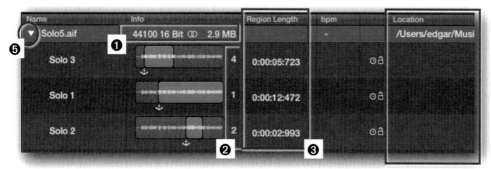

▶ **Sort Items**

You can choose how to sort the Files in the list and the Regions under each files.

- **Files ❻** *View ➤ Files sorted by* ➤: None (this lets you drag files up and down the list to create your own sort order), Name, Size, Drive, Bit Depth, File Type.
- **Region ❼** *View ➤ Sort Regions by* ➤: Name ❽, Length ❾, Start Point ❿

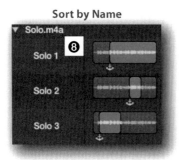

Sort by Name

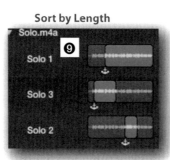

Sort by Length

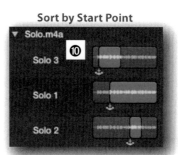

Sort by Start Point

▶ **Reorder-Resize**

*Drag* the header left or right to reorder the columns in the list and drag the divider line between the column 🔛 to resize their width.

# Managing Files and Regions

The Project Browser not only displays the Audio Files and Audio Regions in your Project, it is also the place where you "manage" those Audio Files and Audio Regions. I will cover that topic in the next chapter. Here is just a quick reference:

## ➡ Audio File Menu

**Add Audio File...** *ctr+F*: Opens an Open Dialog where you can audition and select any audio files from your drive to add to the Project Browser.

**Add Region** *ctr+R*: Create a new Region from the Audio File (or selected Region) to add to the Project Browser (not the Track Lane).

**Delete File(s)** *delete*: Moves the Audio File to the Trash (Undo possible).

**Optimize File(s)** *ctr+O*: Replaces the Audio File with a newly created Audio File that has all the unused section removed. The result is a shorter smaller Audio File.

**Backup File(s)** *ctr+B*: Creates a special copy of the Audio File with the extension "dup" that is used to undo destructive edits in the Audio File Editor with the "Revert to Backup" command (available in the Audio File Editor).

**Copy/Convert File(s)** *ctr+K* (also available from the Shortcut menu): Opens a Save Dialog with various options to save of copy of the Audio File to different formats.

**Move File(s) out of Project**: Moves the actual audio file on your drive from the Project File to any other Finder location, but keeps everything else how the audio file is used in the Project.

**Save Region(s) As...** (also available from the Shortcut menu): Creates a new Audio File from the currently selected Audio Region(s).

**Import Region Information**: Retrieves any stored Region information from the file.

**Export Region Information**: Writes the Region information to the audio file.

**Update File Information**: Looks up the File Attributes of the audio files to display in the Audio File entry of the Project Browser.

**Refresh Overview(s)**: Redraws the audio waveforms.

**Show File(s) in Finder** (also available from the Shortcut menu): Opens the Finder Window(s) to show the location of the selected Audio Files.

**Add to Tracks** (also available from the Shortcut menu): Adds the Audio Region to the selected Track at the current Playhead Position. If you selected multiple Files/Regions, then a Dialog Window provides the options on how to place those Audio Regions.

**Analyze Audio for Flex Editing**: Analyzes the file to detect transients that are required for Flex Editing (Overwrites manual transient markers).

Audio File Menu

Shortcut Menu

Add to Tracks

## ➡ Edit Menu

The Local Edit Menu provides the standard Undo, Edit, and Select commands. In addition to that you can enable the "Snap Edit to Zero Crossing", plus a command to disconnect or reconnect Split Stereo Files (doesn't seem to work).

The last line in the menu lets you edit the selected file in an external Sample Editor. This is the one you define in the *Preferences ➤ Audio ➤ Audio File Editor ➤ External Sample Editor*.

Pleas note that Logic's Main Edit Menu adapts to the local Edit Menu of the current Edit Window.

# File Attributes - Symbols

The Project Browser has a lot of little
symbols that indicate a specific status or format
of the Audio File or Audio Region. These symbols are
displayed either in the Info column ❶ or the Symbol
column ❷. Some of those symbols are also displayed on
the Audio Region in the Workspace ❸.

## 🔘 Info Column

The following symbols are displayed next to the Sample
Rate and Bit Depth ❶:

Uncompressed - mono: AIFF, WAV

Uncompressed - stereo: AIFF, WAV

Compressed - mono: mp3, m4a

Compressed - stereo: mp3, m4a

Apple Loop - mono

Apple Loop - stereo

Surround Sound format (multichannel)

Follow Tempo - mono: This symbol only appears
if any Region of that Audio File has Follow Tempo
enabled in the Region Inspector and the Tempo has
changed so it is changing the playback speed of the
Region.

Follow Tempo - stereo: This symbol is displayed
under the same conditions but with a stereo file.

## 🔘 Symbol Column

The following symbols are displayed in the Symbol
column of the Audio File ❹ or Audio Region ❺:

The Metronome Symbol indicates that this is an Apple Loop with
embedded transient markers that can follow the tempo. "One-shot" Apple
Loops still have the Apple Loop format symbol ⬚⬚ but not the Metronome
Symbol ⬚.

This indicates the Follow Tempo status (file is playing back at different
speeds) in addition to the symbol of the Tempo Information. It only displays
that one symbol regardless of the format of the actual file (mono, stereo,
surround).

Each Region has this symbol. It is the only clickable symbol and lets
you lock the Region so it cannot be resized.

Any file that is recorded in your current Project or a file that has Tempo
Information embedded (except Apple Loops) will display that Clock Symbol.
In addition, those Audio Files display the tempo value in the bpm column ❻.

The File is missing.

### Project Browser

| Name | | Info | | bpm |
|---|---|---|---|---|
| ▼ Uncompresse - mono.aif | ❷ | 44100 24 Bit ○ ❶ | 141.9 KB | 110.0 |
| Uncompresse - mono | | ○🔒 | | ❻ |
| ▼ Uncompressed - stereo.caf | | 44100 16 Bit ⦾ | 5.5 MB | - |
| Uncompressed - stereo | | 🔒 | | |
| ▼ Compressed - mono.m4a | | 44100 16 Bit ⟐ | 393.7 KB | - |
| Compressed - mono | | 🔒 | | |
| ▼ Compressed - stereo.m4a | | 44100 16 Bit ⦾ | 1.1 MB | - |
| Compressed - stereo | | 🔒 | | |
| ▼ AppleLoop - mono.caf | | 44100 16 Bit Ω | 250.3 KB | 80.0 |
| AppleLoop - mono | | 🔒 | | |
| ▼ AppleLoop - stereo.caf | | 44100 16 Bit ΩΩ | 68.7 KB | 90.0 |
| AppleLoop - stereo | | 🔒 | | |
| ▼ Surround.aif | | 44100 16 Bit ⊓ | 62.7 MB | - |
| Surround | | 🔒 | | |
| ▼ FollowTempo - mono.aif ❹ | ‹→› | 44100 24 Bit ‹→› | 518.7 KB | 120.0 |
| Follow Tempo ❺ | | ○🔒 | | |
| ▼ FollowTempo - stereo.aif | ‹→› | 44100 24 Bit ‹→› | 706.2 KB | 110.0 |
| FollowTempo - stereo | | ○🔒 | | |
| ▼ MissingFile#01.aif | ❗ | 44100 24 Bit ○ | 0.0 KB | 60.0 |
| MissingFile#01 | | ○🔒 | | |

### Workspace

The Media Browser is one of those cool features that Apple is coming up with at some point, implements it, but then forgets to tell us about it, or tell us how to use it. Maybe you came across the Media Browser in Logic Pro X or even in other apps, but chances are, you never used it. You might even ask yourself, why use it in the first place? Let's find out.

Media Browser: **a Command**
Media Browser: **a Window**

Before using the Media Browser, you have to understand the concept behind it. The big revelation is that  the "Media Browser" has two components:

It is a **Command** - it is a **Window**.

## Media Browser (#1) - the Command

There, in Logic's Main Menu *File ➤ Share ➤ Media Browser ...* ❶ is that mysterious "Media Browser" command. It is one of the commands that bounces your Project to a new audio file. You might understand the other destinations in that submenu where you can send your bounced mix to iTunes or SoundCloud, but what destination is Media Browser?

*File ➤ Share ➤ Media Browser ...*

Movie
Import ▸
Export ▸
Bounce ▸
Share ▸
  Song To iTunes...
  Ringtone to iTunes...
❶  Media Browser...
  SoundCloud...
  Export Song to Disk...

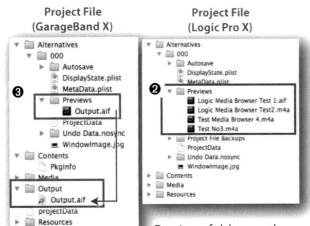

Project File
(GarageBand X)

Project File
(Logic Pro X)

The Media Browser destination is a special folder inside your Logic Project File. And with "inside" I mean, inside the Package File. Every Logic user should be familiar with the concept of a Package File because the Logic Project File is now a Package File that contains many files and folders inside that belong to that Project (Package File: *"A Folder disguised as a File"*).

One of those folders inside a Project File is the special "Previews" ❷ folder. When you bounce your mix using the *File ➤ Share ➤ Media Browser...* command, Logic will store that audio file in that Previews folder. That's the Media Browser destination. All these files inside the Previews folder are the so-called *"Preview Files"*. You can delete those files with the command *File ➤ Project Management ➤ Clean Up... ➤ Delete Media Browser Files*.

GarageBand X also has the same *Share ➤ Media Browser* command and it also saves the audio file of its mix to the Previews ❸ folder inside the GarageBand Project File (Logic and GarageBand Project Files have a similar file structure inside their Package File). The restriction in GarageBand is that you can have only one audio file in that Previews folder. Every new bounce will overwrite the previous one.  You cannot choose a name nor the file format for that Preview File. Logic, on the other hand, lets you name ❹ the Preview Files and offers two audio file formats, aiff and m4a, which you choose from the "*Quality*" popup menu.

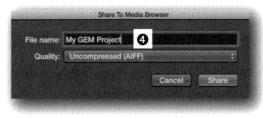

Share To Media Browser

File name: My GEM Project    ❹
Quality: Uncompressed (AIFF)
Cancel   Share

Now that we know that Logic creates these special Preview Files and stores them in the Previews folder ❷ when using the Media Browser command, the question is, why is it hidden in that place? Yes, you can open the Package File (*ctr+click* on the file and choose "Show Package Contents") and drill down to it, but that's too much work. The reason for the hidden location, you are not supposed to access the Preview Files, at least not manually. Guess what, there is a tool that can access those Preview Files and it has the same name as the command that creates those Preview Files - the "Media Browser".

# Media Browser (#2) - the Window

"Media Browser, the window" is the tool to access the Preview Files that were created with "Media Browser, the command" and hidden deep inside the Logic and GarageBand Project Files. The Media Browser window is available not only in Logic and GarageBand, but also in Final Cut Pro X and even other apps like Pages (v4) and Numbers. The whole Media Browser concept was originally a feature for Apple's iLife applications.

You open the Media Browser window in Logic and GarageBand with the same Browsers Button ![browsers button] in their Control Bar. In addition, in Logic you have to select the Media tab.

You can switch the Media Browser between different views by selecting the tab on top:
- **Audio**: In this view, only audio files are displayed
- **Movies**: In this view, only video files are displayed
- **Photos**: In this view, only image files are displayed (not available in Logic Pro X or GarageBand X)

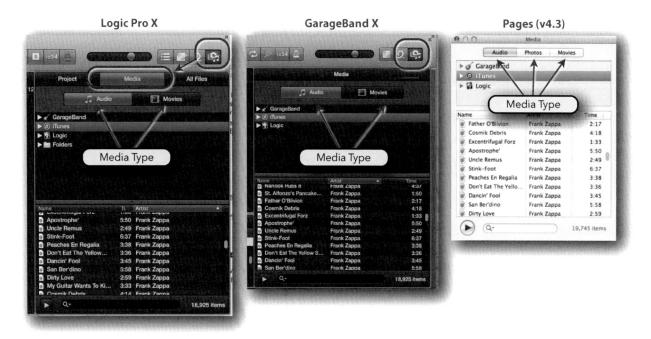

Let's have a closer look at that Media Browser window. Technically, it is a specialized Finder window. Instead of manually digging through Finder windows to search for media files on your drive (not only Preview Files) to use them in your Project, you can use the Media Browser to access relevant files much faster. You then can drag them from the Media Browser directly onto a Track in your Logic Project, everything from within Logic without switching to the Finder.

The Media Browser has four areas. They are like a search engine that work from top to bottom:

▶ **Media Type**: On top, you have the two big blue buttons. You choose to search for Audio files or Movie files.

▶ **Smart Folders**: The area below provides a list of items. These are Smart Folders, and based on what item you select, the relevant audio or video files (included in that Smart Folder) will then be displayed in the Results List below.

▶ **Media Files**: This area is a Results List, displaying all the media files from the selected Smart Folder above. You can scroll through the list and drag the files(s) directly onto the Track Lane.

▶ **Control Bar**: At the bottom of the window is the Play Button to audition the selected file. The file icon changes to a speaker icon ![speaker icon] The search field lets you enter text to search for the "Name", the embedded "Artist" or "Album" keyword in the files. The number next to it shows you how many items are in the Results List.

# The Media Browser Concept

 The Media Browser looks fairly simple so far. It just displays some audio or movie files and you drag them over to your Project. However, there is much more to it. Unfortunately, there is no detailed explanation about it in the official Logic User Guide.

The Media Browser concept was introduced with the suite of iLife applications (GarageBand, iMovie, iPhoto, iWeb, iDVD). The idea was to have a common browser window in those apps that displays specific types of media files (audio, movie, graphics) instead of navigating through individual Finder windows. This is the concept I explained at the beginning of this section. A procedure that is convenient when importing existing media files into one of those apps. This concept got adopted in the Pages and Numbers app and even pro apps like Logic Pro and Final Cut Pro. They all share this common Media Browsers Button that opens the Media Browser Window with a similar interface across all those apps.

### ➡ *App-related Media Files*

When you search in the Finder for media files, you are limited to how the audio files were organized, in which folders and subfolders. Therefore, you have to navigate through the folder structure to look for files (unless you use the OSX Spotlight search).

The advantage of the Media Browser is that it displays media files based on the following criteria:

**Content-creation App**

GarageBand, Logic, iMovie, and Final Cut Pro are so-called content-creation apps. They create Projects, i.e. a GarageBand Project or a Logic Project. When any of those icons are displayed in the Browser area, then you have media files related to those Projects on your drive and the Media Browser window displays them conveniently without you having to know where those files are stored. Please note, if you don't have Logic Projects or a Final Cut Pro Project on your drive, then the Media Browser won't display those items.

**Content-management App**

iTunes and iPhoto belong to the so-called content-management apps. They don't create new files (audio or graphics) they just manage them in their Library. The Media Browser will display all the files that are in those Libraries. However, the Media Browser lists only the relevant files. For example, when selecting iTunes in the Audio tab ❶, then it displays only the audio files in your iTunes Library and selecting iTunes in the Movies tab ❷, then it displays only the movie files in your iTunes Library. The same "smart" filtering happens with the iPhoto Library. When iPhoto ❸ is selected in the Movies tab, then you will see only the movies in your iPhoto Library and not the thousands of pictures you might have. Also, opening the disclosure triangle reveals the same structure you have in your iTunes or iPhoto Library. For example, you can search for audio files in a specific iTunes Playlist.

**Folder Content**

There is one item in the Browser's Movies tab that is not an app and that is the Movies ❹ item. It displays the content of the user's Movies folder that you can navigate through.

# Interface

### ➡ 1 - Media Type

Click on the Audio tab or Movies tab if you want to search for audio or movie files. The Media Browser will then only display those types of files.

### ➡ 2 - Smart Folders

The items in the upper section of the Media Browser displays special Smart Folders. When you open the Media Browser, it performs a search on your hard drive for specific audio and video files (that's why you might see a spinning beach ball the first time you select the Media Browser). It then displays the results in that area as special folders, Smart Folders. The folder icons hint at the origin of the found media files. If your hard drive doesn't have any relevant files, for example, from GarageBand or Final Cut Pro, then that item is not listed. Here is what we can find in the Audio tab.

- **iTunes**: Can display all the audio files in your iTunes Library. The iTunes folder contains subfolders for each of your Playlists in your iTunes Library. Selecting any of the subfolders, for example, a Playlist, will display only the audio files in the Results List that are part of that Playlist.

- **GarageBand**: Can display all the Preview Files that were bounced in GarageBand with the *Share ➤ Media Browser* command. These are the audio files in the "Previews" folder of each GarageBand Project that I mentioned before. Please note that the folder lists only GarageBand Projects that are stored in the following location *~/Music/GarageBand/*.

- **Logic**: Can display all the Preview Files that you have bounced in all your Logic Projects using the *File ➤ Share ➤ Media Browser...* command. Again, these are the files inside the "Previews" folder of a Logic Project. Remember that you can have multiple Previews folders inside a single Logic Project, one for each Alternative. Unlike the GarageBand folder, this "Logic" folder finds all Logic Projects regardless of where they are located on your drive.

- **Folders**: This item is an "Alias Container" that I explain in a moment.

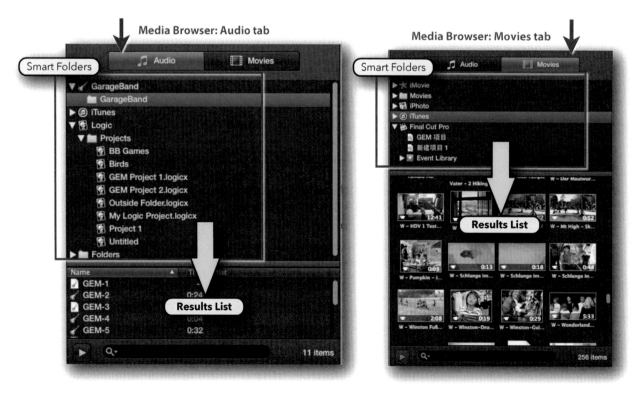

## ➡ 3 - Media Files (Results List)

Based on which item you selected in the Smart Folders section, you will see the enclosed media file in this Results list. However, there are a lot of "special behaviors" that you have to be aware of in order to make sense of what is displayed and how. Let me point out a few of those specialties:

The way the Media Browser displays the Logic and GarageBand Preview Files, for example, is not consistent, it is actually borderline confusing. Here is the difference:

### 🔵 GarageBand

First of all, you can select either the GarageBand item (the guitar icon) or the GarageBand folder (the folder icon). Both ❶ have the same effect on what is displayed in the Results List. The items listed in the Results List are the actual GarageBand Projects ❷ with their Project name. However, they can have two different icons. A white icon indicates a Project that doesn't contain a Preview File (you can't drag that item to your Project). An icon with just the guitar, on the other hand, is a Project that contains a Preview File. The Time column lists the duration of that audio file. You can drag it directly onto a Track in your Logic Project.

### 🔵 Logic

The Logic item can contain two folders ❸. Selecting the "Bounces" folder displays in the Results List all the audio files that are located in *~/Music/Logic/Bounces/*. This is the default folder when exporting your Logic Projects using the Bounce command. The second folder contains all the Logic Projects ❹ on your drive. Selecting a specific Logic Project will display its Preview Files ❺ in the Results List. If a Project doesn't have any Preview Files in its Previews folder, then the Results List is empty. If the Project has multiple Alternatives, then they can be revealed with the disclosure triangle. If you select the Logic item on top ❸, then the Results List displays all the Bounces, plus all the Preview Files.

### 🔵 iTunes

Selecting the iTunes item in the Browser Area is much easier.

**GarageBand Preview Files**

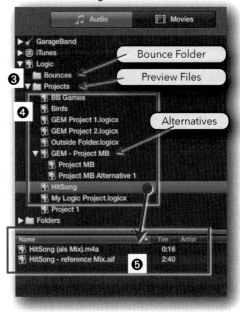

**Logic Preview Files**

**iTunes Selected**

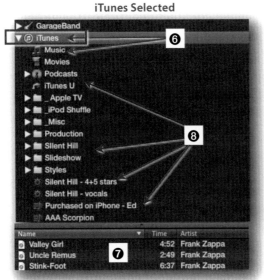

This has nothing to do with Preview Files.

Selecting the iTunes item or the Music item ❻ inside will display, in the Results List, all the audio files ❼ of your iTunes Library.

Selecting any other enclosed item, folder, or Playlist ❽, will display only the audio files for that selection.

### Folders

There is one special item in the Media Browser window. It is named "Folders" ❶, has a blue folder icon, and chances are it is not even listed in your Media Browser. The reason for that is, it is a dynamic "Alias Container" folder. Here is an example:

- Let's say you have a folder named "Special Loops" on your hard drive that contains audio files you often use in your Logic Projects.
- You can drag that folder from the Finder directly onto the Media Browser. The Media Browser then first creates that special Folders ❶ item which functions as a container, and puts an alias of the "Special Loops" folder ❷ inside.
- Now when you drag another folder (i.e. "SFX") onto the Media Browser, an alias of this SFX folder ❷ will be placed into that same Folders ❶ item, the "Alias Container".
- You can add more folders to it or remove them from the Folders item (by deleting the folder in the Media Browser).
- Selecting the "Folders" item will display all the media files contained in all Alias Folders in the Results List ❸. Selecting a specific Alias Folder, will only display its content in the Results List.
- Because these are true Alias Folders, you can move or add any files in the original folder in the Finder. The Media Browser then automatically updates the Results List respectively.

This Folders item is actually pretty useful if you have folders with often used files, for example, sound effects, signature sounds, stings, etc.

### ➡ *Preview Files*

There are three commands to preview an audio file:

- Select an item and *click* on the Play Button ▶ in the Control Bar at the bottom of the Media Browser window to toggle play and stop ⏸.
- Select an item and use the Key Command *space bar*. The Media Browser needs to have Key Focus (it has to be selected, indicated by the blue frame around it).
- *Double-click* on an item to play. You have to use the other commands to stop playback.

The file icon changes to a speaker icon 🔊 while playing.

# Import Media

## ➡ Import Movie

 To import Movie files from the Media Browser window, click on the Movies tab to switch to the Movies view first.

You can import one movie file per Logic Project to score music to it. There are multiple ways to import a Movie (more details about that in the chapter *Working to Picture*).

- *Drag* a movie file from the Media Browser onto your Project
- *Drag* a movie file directly from a Finder window onto your Project
- Use the Main Menu command *File ➤ Movie ➤ Open Movie* or the Key Command *opt+cmd+O* to open a movie file from an Open Dialog Window

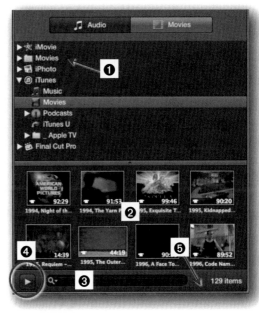
Media Browser - Movies

### 💀 Browse area

 The app icons represent all the apps that have movie files on your drive. If you don't have a specific app or it doesn't contain movie files, then it will not be displayed in the Browser area.

The Movies folder ❶ lets you navigate through the user's Movies folder to search for files.

### 💀 Results List

The Results List displays all the movie files ❷ based on what you selected in the Browser area, plus the search term in the search field ❸.

### 💀 Preview Movie

You can use the same preview commands:

- Select an item and click on the Play Button ▶ ❹ to toggle play and stop ⏸
- Select an item and use the Key Command *space bar*. The Media Browser needs to have Key Focus (it has to be selected, indicated by the blue frame ❺ around it).
- *Double-click* on an item to play it. You have to use the other commands to stop playback.
- When you start playing a movie file, the Results List area changes to display a Quicktime Window. Now you can use all those controls in the Quicktime window too. Volume, Pause, Playhead, Frame forward-backwards.

### 💀 Import Movie

 To import a movie, just drag the movie file from the Results List (or the QuickTime window) onto the Workspace of your Project and the movie file will be placed on the Movie Track.

## ➡ Import Audio

Importing any audio file from the Results List to your current Project is as simple as dragging it onto a Track Lane. Here are a few details to pay attention to:

The files in the list represent audio files and can only be dragged onto the Track Lane of an Audio Track.

▶ *Dragging* a file onto a MIDI Track or Drummer Track will change the Pointer Tool to a "do not enter" sign 🚫 ❶ and displays a warning message "Not an Audio Track".

▶ You can *drag* a file below the last Track Lane in your Workspace and Logic will create a new Audio Track first.

▶ When you *click-hold* the file, a "ghost icon" ❷ appears with the Pointer Tool displaying what type of audio file you are about to copy over (aiff, mp3, MPEG).

▶ When you continue to move it over to the Workspace, the following things will happen:

☑ The Pointer Tool gets a green plus ➕ sign ❸ to indicate that you are copying a file.

☑ A ghost region ❹ appears on the Track Lane to indicate the position of your Pointer Tool.

☑ A white crosshair ❺ helps you position the Region.

☑ A black Help Tag ❻ indicates the bar position of your Pointer Tool. You can only place it on the beginning of a bar.

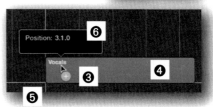

▶ Once you release the mouse, the audio file will be imported to your Project and an Audio Region will be placed on that Track Lane.

▶ The Track Name inherits the name of the audio file if it hasn't been manually named yet.

## ➡ Conclusion

Here are three screenshots that show the Media Browser in Logic, GarageBand, and Final Cut. Thanks to the Media Browser, you have quick access to all of your Logic Preview Files and Bounces from inside any of those applications. You don't have to switch to the Finder and you don't even have to know where the Projects are stored in case you want to use any of the Preview Files in those apps.

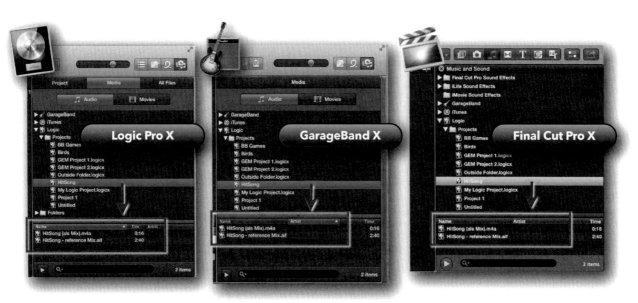

## All Files Browser

The All Files Browser represents an often underestimated or even unknown tool that is available to you in Logic. It provides some features and functionality that, once you know them, can become an important part of your Logic workflow.

> ### Search - Browse - Preview - Import

But wait a minute, didn't we already have that feature in the Media Browser? So what's the difference between the two?

### Media Browser

The Media Browser lets you search and browse only audio files and movie files on your drive(s). However, it provides a unique way with Smart Folder to present those available files without much digging around.

### All Files Browser

The All Files Browser lets you search and browse any supported files on your drive in a Finder-like window.

Its powerful feature is the ability to search for specific Tracks and Channel Strips in another Project and import them to your current Project.

### ➡ *Main Tasks*

You use the All Files Browser to search for specific items on your hard drive to perform the following tasks:

- ☑ Import supported files (MIDI, Audio, Loops, Movie, etc.) into your Project
- ☑ Import selected Tracks/Channel Strips and Project Settings from other Projects
- ☑ Open a Project

## Interface

The All Files Browser window has three areas:

▶ **Controls Area (top)**

This area lets you select various directories where you want to search for files. It lists the file path of the current folder. Its content is displayed in the View Area below.

▶ **View Area**

Please note that this main area performs a double duty. It can show the "File List View" or the "Track Import View".

▶ **Controls Area (bottom)**

The area at the bottom provides various buttons and controls. They can change depending on what is selected above.

## ➡ Controls Area (top)

The controls area on top of the Browser window provides mainly navigation control.

▸ **Directory Buttons ❶**: These three buttons lets you choose a specific directory on your computer. *Click* on a button to display its content in the List View Area below. To "drill" even more down in the folder structure, just *double-click* on a folder like in a Finder window.

- 🖥 *Computer*: *Click* on this button to show all the volumes connected to your computer (internal drives, external drives, network drives).

- 🏠 *Home*: *Click* on this button to show the content of your Home Directory.

- ⬛ *Project*: *Click* on this button to show the content of the folder your current Project is stored in.

▸ **Browse History ❷** ◀ ▶: These two buttons work the same as in a Finder window. *Click* on the Previous Button or Forward Button to step through the viewing history, the folder content you viewed previously or after.

▸ **Current Folder (path) ❸**: This section shows the folder path with the last folder being the one that is displayed in the List View below. You can *click* on a Folder to switch the view to that one.

▸ **File Info ❹**: Below the folder path is the file information of the currently selected file displayed.

▸ **View Button ❺** ☰ ⫼: These two buttons switch the File List between *List View* ❻ and *Column View* ❼. The Track Import View is always displayed in List View.

## ➡ View Area

The View Area displays the File List View per default. To switch to the Track Import View, you have to select a Logic Project in the list (even Logic 9 Projects). That switches the Control Area at the bottom to display the "*Import…*" Button ❽. This is the switch. By *clicking* it, Logic loads the Project, switches the View Area to the Track Import View and displays all its Tracks. Alternatively, you can use the menu command *File ➤ Import ➤ Logic Projects …* and select a Project in the Open Dialog to get to this window.

To switch back to the File List View, *click* on a folder ❾ or the Browse History Back Button In the Controls Area on top.

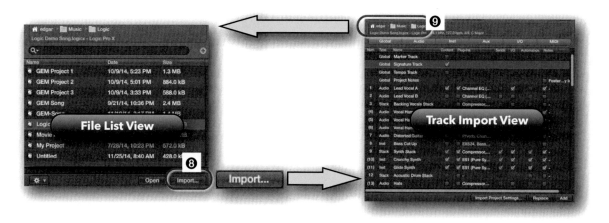

## ➡ Controls Area (bottom)

The Controls Area at the bottom changes its controls depending on which View is displayed and what file is selected:

### 💀 File List View

Here are the controls that are available when File List View is displayed.

- ▶ **Action Button** [⚙▾] : This button opens a popup menu with various commands. You can open the popup menu also by *ctr+clicking* on an item in the File List.
  - *Add selected Audio Files to Project Audio*: Please note that you can select and import multiple files (*sh+click*) at once.
  - *Convert ReCycle Files to Apple Loops*. This command is for Propellerhead's ReCycle files.
  - *New Folder*: This command lets you create a new folder in the currently displayed folder.
  - *Show in Finder*: This command opens a Finder Window displaying the selected file.
  - *Quick Look*: This command opens the Quick Look window of a selected Logic Project File.
- ▶ **Play Button** [◀] [◀] : *Click* the Play Button to audition the selected (media) file. It plays through Audio Channel 256 in your Project, the Prelisten "Channel Strip".
- ▶ **Volume Slider**: The slider controls the volume when auditioning a file. It is linked with the other volume sliders on the Loops Browser, Projects Browser, and Audio File Editor, which are all remote controls for the Volume Fader on the Audio Channel Strip 256.
- ▶ **Add**: Import an Audio File.
- ▶ **Open**: Import a Movie File, or open a Logic Project File.
- ▶ **Import**: Import any other file (i.e. MIDI File).
- ▶ **Import...**: This is the important button that, when a Logic Project File is selected, switches the View Area from File List View to Track Import View.

### 💀 Track Import View

The Controls Area only has three buttons when in Track Import View:
- ▶ **Add**: Add the selected Track(s) in the list to your Project below the selected Track.
- ▶ **Replace**: Replace the currently selected Track in your Project with the one in the Track Import View.
- ▶ **Import Project Settings...**: Opens the Import Project Settings Window.

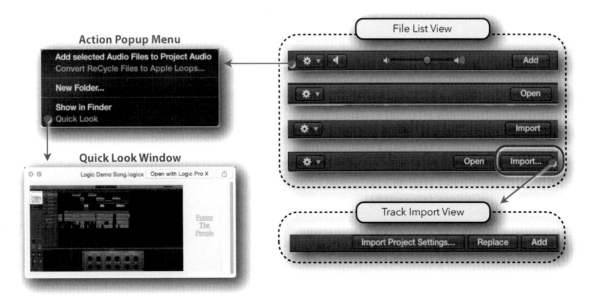

# File List View

The File List View is almost identical to a Finder Window. You can navigate through different folders on your connected hard drives. The File List displays all the files in the current folder and when you double-click on a folder, you open that folder to see what files are inside, and so on. However, there is one important difference. The File List View shows **only** files that are supported, which means, files that can be imported into your Logic Project, or a Logic Project itself that you can open.

## ➡ Browse

- **Directories**: Use the controls in the upper area ❶ to navigate through the directories ("directory" is the technical term for "folder").
- **Columns**: The list has three columns ❷: *Name*, *Creation Date*, and *Size*. If the item is a drive then the size displays "*Volume*" ❸ and if the item is a folder, then it displays "*Folder*" ❹. The *Path* ❺ column in the list displays a search result.
- **Sort**: *Click* on the Header to toggle the sort order between ascending [Size ▲] and descending [Size ▼].

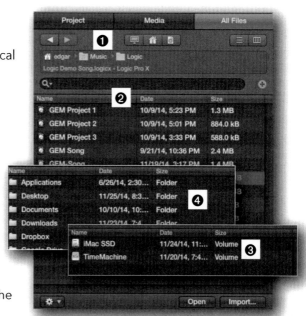

## ➡ Search

- **Search Conditions** [−][+]: Add a search condition with the Plus Button (up to ten) or remove a search condition by clicking on the Minus Button ❻. This lets you narrow down a search based on a wide variety of conditions ❼, the same way you perform searches in the Finder window.
- **Recent Searches**: The magnifying glass [Q▾] opens a popup window with your most recent search terms ❽.

## ➡ Audition

*Click* on the Speaker Button ❾ [🔊] to audition the selected file.

## ➡ Import

*Drag* a file(s) onto the Track's Track Lane or *click* the button ❿ in the lower right corner (*Add*, *Open*, *Import*) to add it at the Playhead Position of the selected Track.

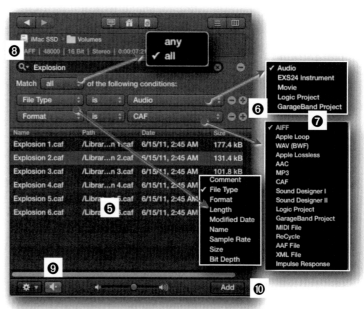

# Track Import View

The Track Import View, although a little bit hidden, is a very powerful feature that lets you view a list of all the used Tracks/Channel Strips in a Project (without opening it). You can cherrypick which Track and which components on its Channels Strip you want to import into your current Project:

- ☑ Individual Track
- ☑ Individual components on each Track
- ☑ Global Tracks
- ☑ Project Settings

When selecting a Logic Project in the File List View, an "**Import...**" button will be displayed in the lower Controls Area. When you *click* on it, the View Area switches from File List View to Track Import View and the Track information of that Project you've selected in the list will be loaded.

## ➡ *View*

**Filter Buttons ❶**: This is the first element on the window, the six Filter Buttons that let you choose which Track/Channel Strip Type you want to display, similar to the Channel Strip Type Filter Buttons in Logic's Mixer Window.

**Columns ❷**: You have a total of nine columns.

- **Number**: This column displays the Track Number. Number in parenthesis indicate that they belong to a Track Stack. Folder Tracks are indicated with a hyphen, for example, 5-1 (double-click to open the Folder Track).
- **Type**: Displays the Track Type.
- **Name**: Displays the Track Name or Channel Strip Name.
- **Content**: Select the checkbox to import the content (Regions) of that Track.
- **Plug-ins**: This field displays all the used Plugins on that Channel Strip in the order from top to bottom. Select the checkbox to import the Plugins with the Track.
- **Sends**: Select the checkbox to import all the Aux Sends on that Channel Strip, including the levels and the routing. It also imports any Aux Channel Strips that the Aux Send is routed to.
- **I/O**: Select the checkbox to import the input and output settings of the Channel Strip.
- **Automation**: Select the checkbox to import the Track Automation on that Track.
- **Notes**: Select the checkbox to import the Note Pad entries for that Track.

## ➡ *Customize View*

You can customize the view with the following commands. This will be stored with the Logic Preferences.

- *Click* drag the header to rearrange the order of the columns.
- *Ctr+click* on a header to display a Shortcut Menu ❸ where you can select which column to display.

## ➡ *Navigate/Select*

Here are a few rules on how to navigate and select individual elements:

- *Click* a checkbox to select that element (Content, Plug-in, Sends, etc.).
- A grayed-out checkbox indicates that this element is not available (no Regions, no Automation, etc.).
- Use the *ArrowUp* and *ArrowDown* key to step through the Tracks.
- Use the *ArrowRight* to select the checkboxes for the Track or *ArrowLeft* to deselect the checkboxes.
- Selecting a Track Stack will also select all its Subtracks and selecting any Subtrack will enable the Master Track and its Subtracks. However, you can *opt+click* on a Master Track or its Subtrack to select only that single Track.
- *Ctr+click* on a Track item to open a Shortcut Menu with the Quick Look command.

### 🔘 Preview Image (Quick Look)

Every time you save your Project, Logic saves a so-called "Preview Image". This is a screenshot of the Logic window (with the current key focus) stored in the Project File.

*/Alternatives/nnn/WindowImage.jpg*

This thumbnail image is displayed in "Quick Look". This is an OSX feature that lets you view or play a file without opening it in its application. In the Finder, you hit the space bar when a file is selected to open the Quick Look Window.

**Quick Look Window**

In the All Files Browser, you can open the Quick Look Window with the following commands:

- In the File List View, select a Logic Project file, *click* on the Action Button, and select "Quick Look" from the Action popup menu (or *ctr+click* on the file).
- In the Track Import View, *ctr+click* on a Track to open a Shortcut Menu with the Quick Look command.

#### Quick Look Window:

- **Zoom In**: The Preview Image has a pretty good resolution. When you resize the window, you can see a lot of details of your Logic's window.
- **Open Project**: *Click* this button ❶ to open that Logic Project.
- **Share Project**: *Click* on the standard Share Button ❷ ⬆ to open a popup menu with destinations where you can send that Project to.

## ➡ *Import*

▶ **Add**: *Click* the Add Button (Key Command *cmd +ArrowDown*) to add all the selected Tracks and their elements in the Track Import View to your current Project below the selected Track.

▶ **Replace**: Select a Track in your Project and *click* the Replace Button to replace it with the one Track selected in the Track Import View.

▶ **Import Project Settings...**: *Clicking* on the *Import Project Settings Button* will open the Import Settings Sheet that lets you select 15 individual Project Settings to import into your current Project. This will overwrite the current Settings. You can access this window with a separate Menu Command *File ➤ Project Settings ➤ Import Project Settings...* (Key Command *opt+cmd+I*) that lets you navigate to a Logic Project in an Open Dialog.

**Import Settings**

Your audio files are some of the most precious assets you have in your Project. One thing you want to make sure is that nothing bad happened to them. Besides some higher forces that sometimes can corrupt your files, there are plenty of actions that you can do on purpose or by accident that can negatively impact those assets. To avoid that, you always have to make sure that you know what commands affect your audio files, and in what way.

**Welcome to the world of Audio File Management in Logic**

## Project Management

# Basics

Before talking about Audio File Management we have to understand the Project Management, how the Projects manage their files, the Audio Files in particular.

### ➡ Logic Project File

The Logic Project File ❶ is the file Logic creates when you save your current Project that you have running in Logic on your computer.

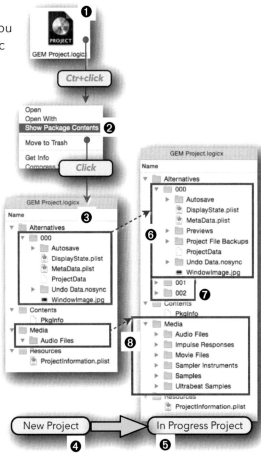

- The Project File is now a special file type, a *Package File* with the *.logicx* file extension.
- A Package File is a "folder disguised as a file", used for many purposes in OSX. You can open that special folder in the Finder by *ctr+clicking* on the file and selecting "Show Package Contents" ❷ from the Shortcut Menu.
- Logic stores all the related information of a Project inside that Package File ❸ as individual files organized in a specific folder hierarchy.
- The screenshot on the left ❹ shows that content of a Logic Project File saved from a newly created Project.
- The screenshot on the right ❺ shows the content of the same Logic Project File after I "worked" with it for a while.
- The original sub-folder "000" ❻, which represents the default Alternative, now has more files and folders added: The Autosave data, the Backup data and, the Preview folder with the "Media Browser" bounces.
- The additional folders "001" and "002" ❼ are the two additional Alternatives that I created.
- The content of the Media folder ❽ now has also grown quite a bit. This is the folder we are concentrating on in this chapter. These are the various media files, the so-called "Assets" of your Project.

## ➡ Project Assets: _Package or Folder_

We just saw a Project File storing all the Project-related Assets inside the Package File. However, this is only one option. Logic gives you two options now on how to organize those Asset Files. Whenever you save a new Project (or "Save As" a Project), the Save Dialog opens. Below the standard fields where you enter a file name, optional file tags, and the location for the file ❶, there are two radio buttons ❷ with the label "Package" and "Folder".

> ## Organize my Project as:

This is a very important decision, because it determines the structure of your Project File regarding how the Assets are organized with their Project. The default setting is "Package", and while this might work for you, you have to understand the implications for both options. Both have advantages and disadvantages and you cannot change that setting once you saved a Project with one or the other.

### 💀 Package

When you save the Project with the "Package" option, it creates the Project File as the Package File at the location you chose. In the example below, it is the Logic folder (inside the Music directory) ❸. When you open the Package File, you will see a Media folder ❹, and all the Assets that you store with your Project are stored in that location in individual subfolders.

- **Pro**: The advantage is that all the asset files are enclosed in one file. Moving that file around will make sure that all the media files stay with it. The special procedure required to open the Package File avoids the risk of accidentally deleting those files.

- **Con**: The disadvantage is that the file could get fairly big if you use a lot of large media files. Also, working on a film score requires a different workflow where you have multiple files (1m1, 1m2, 1m3, etc.). Storing (the same) media files with each Project File might not be practical.

### 💀 Folder

When you save the Project File with the "Folder" option, it creates a new folder ❺ at the location you chose, and it names that folder with the Project name you entered in the Save Dialog. The actual Project File is saved as a Package File ❻ (with the same name as the folder) inside that Project Folder. Now all the subfolders ❼ for the various asset files are also stored in that Project Folder next to the Project File. When you open the Package File ❽, you can still see all the Project-related files stored inside, however, there is no Media folder this time.

- **Pro**: The advantage is that you can work the way you were used to in Logic Pro 9, especially when working for film. You can save multiple Project Files to the same Project Folder that all share the same asset files. However, the new feature of working with Alternatives might provide a similar workflow.

- **Con**: The main disadvantage is just the "file safety". When moving Project Files around, make sure to move the actual Project Folder with the asset files.

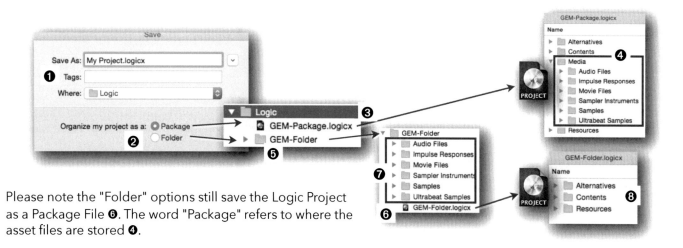

Please note the "Folder" options still save the Logic Project as a Package File ❻. The word "Package" refers to where the asset files are stored ❹.

## ➡ *Project Assets: <u>Copy or Reference</u>*

First, a a closer look at those asset files, where they are and where they come from. To answer this question, let's organize them into two groups:

☑ **Recorded Assets ❶**: These are mainly the audio files that you record in your Project. They are stored right in your Project, either inside the Project's Package Files or inside the Project Folder depending on the setting we just discussed. You can change that default location in the *Project Settings ➤ Recording ➤ Audio Recording Path*.

☑ **Imported Assets ❷**: These are all the assets that already exist on your drive ❸ (audio files, loops, samples, movie, etc.). You <u>import</u> them into your Project to use them. The procedure for importing, loading, or opening those files varies, but they all require the same decision:
Do you want to copy the files or reference ❹ the files?

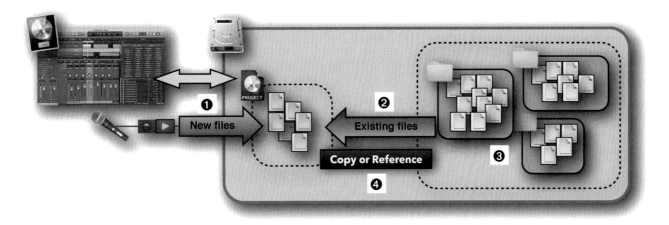

Here are the two methods on how to use the existing asset files in your Logic Project:

Assume you have a Logic Project and already recorded audio files ❺ in that Project. You have lots of other asset files ❻ stored on your drive and want to use some of them in your Project.

### 💡 Reference

With this method, Logic leaves the external files at their original location ❼ and only makes a note of their file path (where to find them) ❽. The files don't "belong" to the Logic Project and there is no indication on the file itself ❼ that it is used in the Logic Project xyz. If you delete or modify that file (without knowing that it is used by a Logic Project), then that could really mess up that Project.
Also, if you apply destructive audio file edits to that file (or delete it), it might have consequences for other Logic Projects that use that file (also as a reference).

### 💡 Copy

With this method, Logic copies ❾ the external files from their original location into your Project File. Now they are part of the Project File, independent from their original file. Editing or deleting the copied file only affects that Project. No worries that other "outside" files might change or get lost.

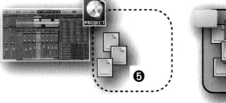

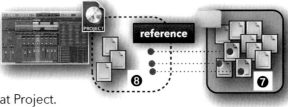
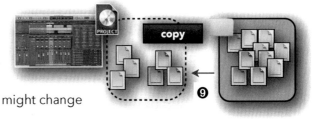

# Configuration

Here are the steps in Logic on how to setup those different methods of asset management:

### ➡ *Project or Folder*

As we've already discussed, the decision to organize the internal asset files in the Package File or in a Project Folder is made in the Save Dialog when you first save (or save as) your Project. You cannot change that later.

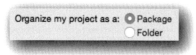

### ➡ *Copy (internal) or Reference (external)*

There are four windows in Logic where you can configure (or change) how to handle the Assets in your Logic Project. As I mentioned in the beginning of this chapter, those Project Assets are your precious material, so you have to know that these four windows exist, know about their different functionality, and know what effect they have regarding the location and relocation of asset files.

### 🐞 1 - Save Dialog

The Save Dialog lets you make the initial configuration whether you want to copy or reference asset files. You have not one but six checkboxes to set it for individual types of assets. Enable the checkbox to copy the asset file you import into your Project.

▸ **Audio Files**: If you enable this checkbox, then all audio files, including Audio Apple Loops will be copied to the Project Folder.

▸ **EXS Instruments and Samples**: If you enable this checkbox, then only EXS Instruments and Samples are copied that are not part of the Apple Sound Library (stored in the system directory). To include those files too, you have to enable the last checkbox at the bottom ("*Include Apple Sound Library Content*"). Although the Drummer Instrument is technically an EXS Instrument, its files will not be copied to your Project.

▸ **Alchemy audio data**: If you enable this checkbox, then only user-created Alchemy Samples are copied that are not part of the Apple Sound Library (stored in the system directory). To include those files too, you have to enable the last checkbox at the bottom ("*Include Apple Sound Library Content*").

▸ **Ultrabeat samples**: If you enable this checkbox, then only Ultrabeat Samples are copied that are not part of the Apple Sound Library (stored in the system directory). To include those files too, you have to enable the last checkbox at the bottom ("*Include Apple Sound Library Content*").

▸ **Space Designer impulse responses**: Impulse responses are audio files that function as the basis for convolution reverbs like Logic's Space Designer. And again, if you enable this checkbox, then only the Space Designer Impulse Responses files are copied that are not part of the Apple Sound Library (stored in the system directory). To include those files too, you have to enable the last checkbox at the bottom ("*Include Apple Sound Library Content*").

▸ **Movie file**: If you enable this checkbox, then the movie file you import into your Project will be copied to your Project File. If the file size of that movie file is in the range of a couple of gigabytes, then it might not be such a great idea to enable this checkbox.

▸ **Include Apple Sound Library Content**: If you enable this checkbox, then the three checkboxes for EXS, Ultrabeat, and Space Designer are enabled automatically and can't be disabled individually anymore until you disable this checkbox again. It actually makes sense not to include those files (only the custom files), because, even if you delete them by accident, you can re-download them from Apple again. Unless you want to archive your Projects with all included files.

Any MIDI data, including MIDI Apple Loops are always saved directly with the Project.

## 2 - Project Settings ➤ Assets ❶

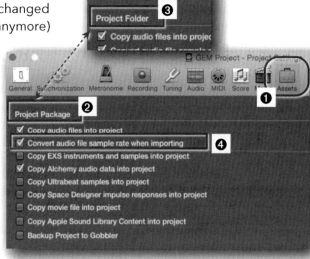

The configurations you made in the Save Dialog can be changed later at any time, if you decided to copy (or not to copy anymore) specific types of asset files when you import them to your Project.

Open the *Project Settings ➤ Assets*

- Any changes you make are in effect from the next time you save your Project.
- Any changes do not affect the files you have imported before. They keep their status (copied or referenced).
- The top of the page indicates if the current Project organizes Assets in the "Project Package" ❷ or the "Project Folder" ❸.
- This page has one additional checkbox that is not available during the initial configuration on the Save Dialog. It is "*Convert audio file Sample Rate when importing*" ❹. You might leave this checkbox enabled to avoid any pitch shifting when importing audio files with a different Sample Rate than the Project's Sample Rate.

## 3 - Consolidate Project ❺

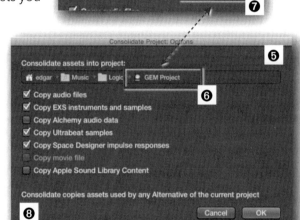

Although the Project Settings window in the previous step lets you change the copy/reference configuration for the asset files, it affects only future file imports and not the ones you already have in your Project. For example, you had a couple of audio files imported into your Project that are only referenced to their external location, but now want to keep them internally with your Project.

For that you need this third window, the *Consolidate Project* window that you open with the following commands:

- Menu Command *File ➤ Project Management ➤ Consolidate...*
- Key Command (*Consolidate Project*) **unassigned**

If you check a specific type of Asset file that is referenced and not copied to your Project yet, then this will copy those files into the Project.

- The top of the window displays the file path to the media folder of the current Project File.
- On the file path you can recognize if the current Project organizes its asset file in the "Project Package" (path ends with the project file ❻), or the "Project Folder" (path ends with the folder icon ❼).
- The Consolidation procedure also copies all the Asset Files that are used by any of the Alternatives in your Project ❽.
- Enabling the "Copy movie" option will pop up a Dialog Window ❾ reminding you that a movie file can drastically increase the size of your Project File.
- If you have Logic Notification enabled in OSX, then you will get a "*Consolidation completed*" message.

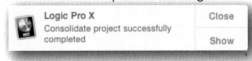

## 🌑 4 - Clean Up

Being in control of all the Asset Files in your Project means that you know exactly where they are because you

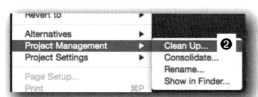

made a conscious decision which files to store "internally" with your Project (copy) and which ones to keep "externally" at their original location (referenced). However, being in control also means to know what to throw away, to decide what you might and might not need anymore. For this procedure, you need the fourth window, the *Clean Up*.

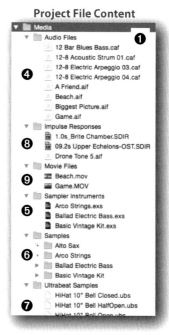

**Project File Content**

When you delete audio files in your Project, you get a Dialog Window with the option to remove them from your drive or to keep them. However, most of the Asset Files stay on your Project ❶, even if you don't use them anymore. For example:

- **Sound Content**: Loading different presets in the EXS24, Ultrabeat, and also the Sound Designer will not delete the files from the previously loaded preset that were copied to your Project File, and now, not used anymore. They are all left behind, increasing the size of your Project File. When you try different sounds on those instruments, keep in mind that their assets get only copied over when you save the Project.

- **Movie Files**: Although Logic can only open one Movie at a time, opening a new movie will not delete the previously loaded movie from your Project File (if you decided to copy movie files into your Project in the first place).

For this special "No (unused) File Left Behind" campaign, you use the fourth window, the *Clean Up Project* window that you open with the following commands:

🕹 Menu Command *File ➤ Project Management ➤ Clean Up...* ❷

🕹 Key Command (*Clean Up Project*) **unassigned**

The first Dialog Window lets you choose which types of files ❸ you want to remove (across all Alternatives in your Project).

- ☑️ **Unused Files** are all audio files ❹ in your Project Audio Browser that are not used in your Project (or an Alternative). This includes any EXS Instrument ❺, EXS Samples ❻, Ultrabeat Samples ❼, and Sound Designer Impulse Response Files ❽. Unfortunately, unused Movie Files ❾ are not included. You have to delete them manually in the Finder.

- ☑️ **Backups** are the files of the (up to 100) Backups of your Project that are created every time you save your Project.

- ☑️ **Media Browser Files** are the bounces that you create when using the *Share ➤ Media Browser...* command.

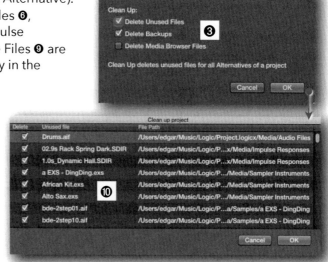

If you click OK, a second window pops up with a list of all the unused files ❿. You can individually select the files you want to delete. Select multiple files and click the checkbox to toggle the checkbox for all those files at once. Be careful, you cannot undo this step (unless you are up for some dumpster diving to get the files back out of the trash bin).

## ➡ *Project Management Summary*

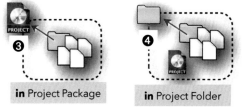

### 👹 Rename Project

You can rename your Project from within Logic. Please note that this is the name of the Project File, not the name of the current Alternative (which are the same when you start a new Project). *File ➤ Project Management ➤ Rename Project* ❶

### 👹 Organize Assets in your Project

This is the one-time setting in the Save Dialog ❷ that determines if you organize the internally stored Assets inside the Project Package ❸ or a parent Project Folder ❹.

### 👹 Store Assets in your Project

These four windows let you configure if you want to store the Project Assets internally ❺ (copy) with the Project or externally ❻ (reference) at their original location. Please note the difference between the *Imported Assets* and the newly *Recorded Assets*.

- **Imported Assets**: These are the files that already exist on your drive.
- **Recorded Assets**: These are the files that you newly record in your Project. If you chose in the *Project Settings ➤ Recording* ❼ to store them externally by defining a folder location outside the Project (*Set..*) ❽ then the Consolidate procedure can bring them back to the Project later.

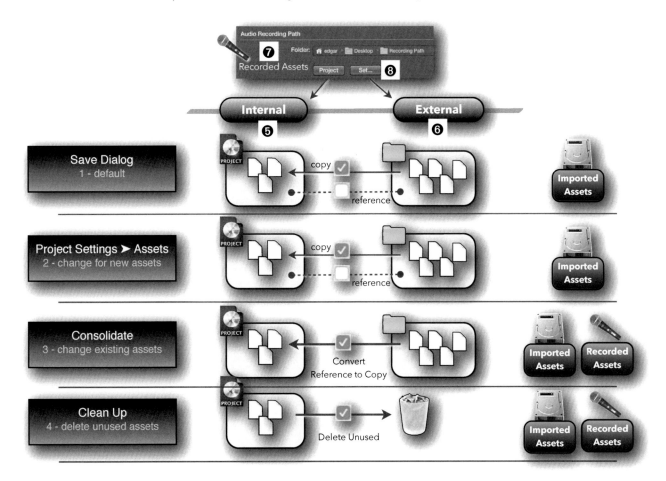

Besides these general Project Management procedures, you have individual Audio Management procedures that let you move individual audio files as I will discuss later in this chapter.

# Interleaved audio files vs. Split audio files

There is one specialty you have to be aware of when importing audio files. This is an exception to the settings that determine how to organize Assets (Copy or Reference).

To better understand that exception, we have to first discuss the important, and often misunderstood, concept behind Interleaved Files and Split Files.

➡ *Channels*

One of the main parameters of an audio file, besides Sample Rate and Bit Depth, are the "Channels", the questions about "How many Channels?". It has nothing to do with how many "input channels" (or Channel Strips) you have on your mixer. In this context, the channel information tells you if the audio file contains one or more independent audio signals, "one or more channels".

> **A single Channel represents a transmitted or a recorded Audio Signal, a single source**

There are three basic channel configurations for an audio file:

### One Channel (Mono)

If an audio file contains only one channel, then it is also referred to as "Mono". It carries the information of one single sound source. For example, the recording of one microphone, the output of an electric guitar, or the output of a mono mix of your song.

You cannot see from the "outside" how many channels are contained in an audio file when you look at it in a Finder Window. Open its Get Info Window ❶ (*cmd+I*) and in the "*More Info*" section is the file information listed, including the number of Audio Channels ❷. In this case "*Audio channels: 1*".

### Two Channels (Stereo)

If an audio file contains two channels, then it is referred to as "Stereo". For example, the recording of a stereo microphone, the stereo output of a synth, or the stereo output of your mixing board.

The Get Info Window will display "*Audio channels: 2*" ❸.

### Multi Channels (Surround)

If an audio file contains more than two channels, then it is referred to as "multi-channel", or "Surround". For example, the output bus of a surround mix.

The Get Info Window will display "*Audio channels: 6*" ❹ (or any other amount of channels).

Please note that you can edit Audio Regions referenced to Multi-Channel audio files, but the Audio File Editor only displays the left and right channel as a stereo waveform.

Please note that when importing a multi-channel audio file that is formatted as Surround, then Logic will import it as an interleaved Audio Region [▣]. If the audio file is not formatted, then Logic extracts the individual channels and creates separate mono Audio Regions [◯] for your Project.

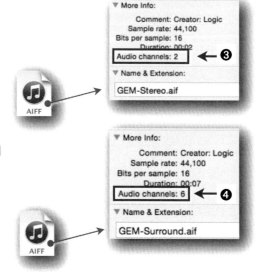

Once you import or record an audio file (in mono, stereo, or surround), then this channel information is listed on the audio file (in the Project Audio Browser ❶) and also on the Audio Regions (in the Tracks Window ❷ and the Audio Track Editor). Here are the symbols that I already showed in the *Browser* chapter:

▶ **Mono**:
- ▢ uncompressed (aiff, wav)
- ▣ compressed (mp3, m4a)
- ▣ Apple Loop

▶ **Stereo**:
- ◎ uncompressed
- ◫ compressed
- ◫◫ Apple Loop

▶ **Surround**:
- ▦ Surround Sound (multichannel)

Project Audio Browser

Tracks Window

## ➡ *Interleaved vs. Split*

### 💡 Interleaved

The term "interleaved" in regards to audio files just means that if you want to save more than one audio channels in a single file (for example, bounce the left channel and the right channel of your mixer output bus), then those channels have to be "combined" in that single audio file. In the case of a so-called "*Stereo Interleaved*" audio file, both audio channels (left and right) are stored in that one audio file.

**Interleaved:**
**An Audio File contains more than one channel**

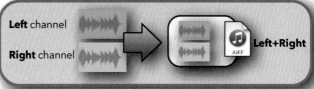
Stereo Interleaved File

### 💀 Split

Split audio files are mono, but they belong to a group of mono audio files, each one carrying the individual audio channels of a multi-channel audio signal. For example, you save (bounce) the left channel and right channel of your stereo output bus as individual single-channel audio files. One audio file contains the left channel of your mix and one audio file contains the right channel of your mix.

**Split:**
**An Audio File contains one channel of a multi-channel signal**

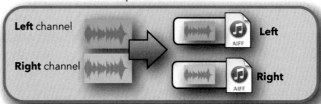
Split Stereo Files

*Attention*: Don't confuse "Stereo Interleaved" with "Joint Stereo". Joint Stereo is an encoding process for compressed audio files like mp3 to reduce the file size. The encoder analyzes the file to look for frequencies in each sample word that are present in the left and right channel. That data is then only stored once (joint) instead of twice (left and right channel), therefore, reducing the amount of bits to be saved.

## 🔘 Conditions

Here are the conditions for Logic to recognize a group of Split Audio Files:

☑ Every audio file belonging to a group of split files has to have the same file name with a letter at the end indicating what channel it contains.

☑ Stereo Split Files ❶ have the ending "L" for left channel and "R" for right channel.

☑ Surround Split Files ❷ (depending on the Surround Format) have the ending L, R, Ls, Rs, C, LFE (more details on that in the *Surround Sound* chapter).

☑ The file name and the channel indicator have to be separated by a dot or a hyphen.

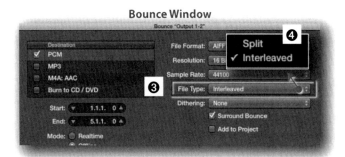

**2 Stereo Split Files**

StereoMix.L.aif
StereoMix.R.aif ❶

**6 Surround Split Files**

SurroundSplit-C.aif
SurroundSplit-L.aif
SurroundSplit-LFE.aif
SurroundSplit-Ls.aif
SurroundSplit-R.aif ❷
SurroundSplit-Rs.aif

## 🔘 Create Split or Interleave

Logic, as a default, creates interleaved files when bouncing a mix. However, the Bounce Window provides a File Type ❸ parameter where you can select from its popup menu ❹ if you want to bounce your mix as an *Interleaved* file or individual *Split* files.

The Convert Dialog (***Project Browser ➤ Audio File ➤ Copy/Convert File(s)...*** or ***Audio File Editor ➤ Audio File ➤ Save As...***) has an option (Stereo Conversion ❺) that also lets you create Split files.

In both cases, Logic automatically adds those channel indicators at the end of the file name you entered.

## 🔘 Import Split Mono Files

Logic recognizes groups of Split mono files based on those channel indicators of same-named audio files. The file import procedure for those files is a little bit different. Something you have to be aware of:

• You can select all split files (the two individual stereo split files or the six individual surround split files) to import them. Or, you can also just select one file of a group and Logic recognizes the other file(s) that belongs to that same group and automatically imports them all.

• However, Logic DOES NOT import the split mono files.

• Instead, Logic will convert those individual Split mono files to an Interleaved file (stereo or surround), saves that new file in the Audio File folder ❻ of the Project, and places that interleaved Audio File in the Project Audio Browser ❼. This is the new imported audio file.

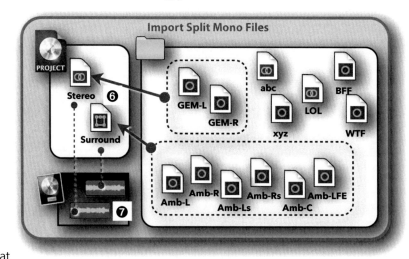

This is the import procedure for Split Mono Files:

> **Logic converts Split files to a new Interleaved file during import**

However, there are a few more little things you have to be aware of when dealing with split mono files.

### 🔘 Copy Assets Setting

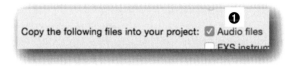

Having the checkbox "*copy audio files into Project*" ❶ enabled (as we discussed earlier), will copy ❷

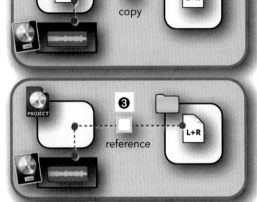

the imported files to the Project File. Having the checkbox disabled will only reference ❸ the imported files. However, because the import procedure for Split Mono Files is actually a "*create new, after converting*" procedure, the settings ❹ do not apply, it will always be a newly created interleaved file, converted from the split mono files you are importing.

To import a Split Mono File without having it converted, just change the channel indicators at the end of the file (.L or .R).

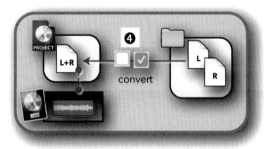

### 🔘 Bouncing to Split Mono Files

When you bounce to Split Mono Files, you have to pay attention to the checkbox "*Add to Project*" in the Bounce Window.

🔲 **Disabled ❺**: Logic creates the separate Split Mono Files in the folder you define in the Save Dialog. It automatically adds the channel indicators at the end of the file name, either .L and .R for a stereo bounce or the Surround channel indicators, depending on your Surround Format.

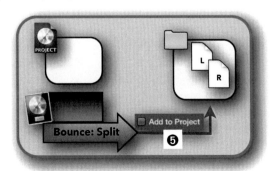

☑ **Enabled ❻**: When you bounce to Split Mono Files and have the "Add to Project" checkbox enabled, then again, Logic creates the new Split Mono Files in the Bounce folder. In addition, Logic creates an interleaved audio file of the bounce and places that into the Project's Audio File folder. That is the new file that ends up in the Project Audio Browser because of the "Add to Project" checkbox.

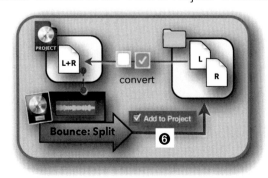

# Opening Backup Projects and Alternatives

There are different ways to open a Logic Project. Use the Open Dialog, double click on the Project File in the Finder or open it from the All Files Browser. All these commands open the "entire" Project including all its Alternatives.

However there are a few additional commands using "**Quick Look**".

## ➡ *Quick Look*

Quick Look is an OS X feature where you can view/audition any file in the Finder without opening the application that created (or can view) that file. For example, listen to an audio file, watch a video, or read any text document or spreadsheet directly in the Finder. Most files are supported with this mechanism, even Logic. Although you cannot play your Logic Project from the Finder, there are a few useful features that you should be aware of:

### 💀 Open Quick Look Window ❸

- 🎛 *Ctr+click* on the Project File ❶ to open the Shortcut Menu and select *Quick Look "name of the selected file"* ❷.

- 🎛 Select the file and press the *space* key. This is the default OSX Key Command for Quick Look.

The Quick Look Window has the following sections:

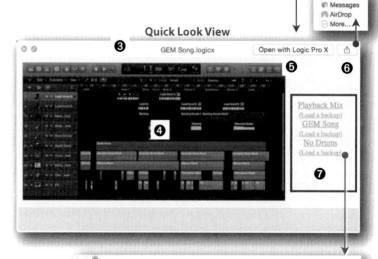

- ▶ **Preview ❹**: This is the Preview Image of your Project that Logic stores every time you save your Project.

- ▶ **Open Button ❺**: Use this button to open that Project File in Logic.

- ▶ **Share Button ❻**: This is the standard OSX Share Button that contains various destinations you can send the Project File to.

- ▶ **Load Options ❼**: This contains the additional open commands:

  - **Load Alternative**: Each Alternative in that Project is listed and, by *clicking* on it, will open the Project with that Alternative and not the one that was open when you saved the Project.

  - **Load a Backup**: After each name of the individual Alternative is the link "*(Load a backup)*". When you *click* on that, a new Window will open that lists all the Backups ❽ of that Alternative. In addition, this window also lets you choose a different Alternative from the popup menu ❾ on top.

In the previous section, we discussed the general settings for managing audio files on a Project level. Now, we will look at the commands that are available to the individual audio files themselves. They are located in two places:

▶ *Audio File Editor ➤ Local Menu ➤ Audio File*
▶ *Project Audio Browser ➤ Local Menu ➤ Audio File*

**Audio Files Editor:**
**Local Audio File Menu**

| | |
|---|---|
| Create Backup | ^B |
| Revert to Backup | ^⌥⌘B |
| Save A Copy As... | |
| Save Selection As... | ⌥⌘S |

**Project Audio Browser:**
**Local Audio File Menu**

| | |
|---|---|
| Add Audio File... | ^F |
| Add Region | ^R |
| Delete File(s) | ⌘⌫ |
| Optimize File(s)... | ^O |
| Backup File(s) | ^B |
| Copy/Convert File(s)... | ^K |
| Move File(s) out of project | |
| Save Region(s) As... | |
| Import Region Information | ^I |
| Export Region Information | ^E |
| Update File Information | |
| Refresh Overview(s) | |
| Show File(s) in Finder | ⇧⌘R |
| Add to Tracks | ⌘; |
| Analyze Audio for Flex Editing | |

There are quite a few commands, each one with their own details. As I mentioned at the beginning of this chapter, the audio files in your Project are very precious, and because those commands affect those audio files, you want to make sure they are affected in the right way.

# Record New Audio File

When recording new audio in your Project, you will see the Audio Region created right in front of your eyes on the Track Lane. But there is more than meets the eye.

Here is what happens behind the scene:

☑ At the beginning, the Project Audio Browser is just empty ❶.

☑ Once you record an audio signal on an Audio Track, a new Audio File ❷ is created and stored on your hard drive inside the Project File, Project Package, or Project Folder, depending on your settings.

☑ That new Audio File will be listed ❸ (has an entry) in the Project Browser.

☑ The Audio File entry displays the file information ❹: File Path, Sample Rate, Bit Depth, stereo/mono, etc.

☑ An Audio Region ❺ entry has been created below the Audio File entry.

☑ The listed Audio Region is placed as an Audio Region ❻ on the Track Lane in the Workspace at the position where you started the recording.

☑ Depending on the Input Selector of the Audio Channel Strip. The new Audio File will be a:

- ◯ Mono File
- ◎ Interleaved Stereo File
- ▦ Interleaved Surround File

Logic does not create split mono files during recording.

**Project Browser**

**Project Browser**

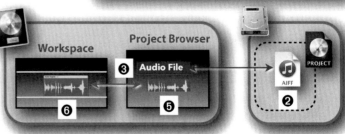

# Import Existing Audio File

This procedure lets you add an existing Audio File to your Project.

## ➡ *Add Audio File*

You can use the following commands:

- Menu Command *Project Browser ➤ Audio File ➤ Add Audio File...*
- Key Command (*Add Audio File*) *ctr+F*
- *Drag* an Audio File onto the Project Browser (from the Finder, the Media Browser, or the All Files Browser)
- There are other procedures that can also add an existing Audio File to your Project (Open Movie, Import Channel Strips, etc.)

Here is what happens:

- ☑ A new copy ❶ of the existing Audio File ❷ is placed to your Project File if "copy audio files to project" is enabled ❸.
- ☑ The Project Browser creates an entry ❹ for that Audio File. It displays the file path, where you can see if the file is located inside the Project (copy ❶) or somewhere on the hard drive (referenced).
- ☑ The Project Browser creates an Audio Region ❺ of that Audio File.
- ☑ No Audio Region is placed on your Workspace if you used an import command. *Dragging* an external Audio File onto the Workspace, on the other hand, will place the Audio Region, that is created in the Project Audio Browser, on the Workspace ❻.
- ☑ Please remember the special import rules for Split Mono Files we just discussed.

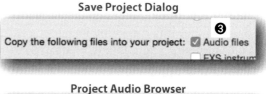

Save Project Dialog

Project Audio Browser

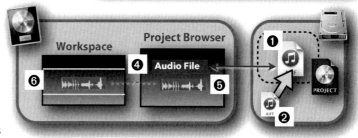

# Create New Audio File

The next group contains all the commands that let you create new audio files without recording an audio signal. First, a quick overview:

- **Save As**: The various commands let you save a copy of an existing audio file or section of an audio file to a new audio file.
- **Copy/Convert**: This command is similar to the "Save As" commands but can replace the existing audio file in your Project while keeping all the references in place.
- **Backup**: This command creates a special copy of an audio file that can be used to revert to after an ill-fated attempt of destructive edits of that audio file.
- **Bounce/Export**: These commands, spread all over various menus, let you create audio files based on different kinds of conditions and circumstance.

### ➡ *Save a Copy As...*

This command let's you save a copy of the current audio file. It's purpose is less for backing up and safety, but for those situations, when you want to use a specific audio file twice in your Project and want to apply different destructive audio edits to it.

The command is only available in the Audio File Editor:

- Local Menu *Audio File* ➤ *Save A Copy As...*
- The available Key Command with the same name is for saving Projects not audio files.

A Save Dialog provides the following settings:

- ▶ **Name and Location ❶**
- ▶ **Audio Format Settings ❷**: Sample Rate, Bit Depth, etc.
- ▶ **Add resulting files to Project Audio ❸**: Enable this checkbox to add the newly created Audio File back to your Project in the Project Browser.
- ▶ **Storage Info ❹**: Logic calculates the size of the new audio file, plus how much storage is available on the selected drive.

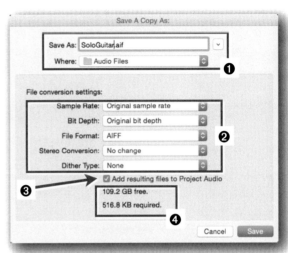

Here are two examples for the "Save As" command that shows how complex Audio File Management can get with all the various settings and commands:

### 🕱 Example #1:

- I selected the Audio File folder ❺ of the Project File as the location ❶. That means, the copied ❻ audio file will be located in the same folder as the original file ❼.
- I have the "Add resulting files to Project Audio" ❸ enabled. That means, the new audio file ❻ (the copy) is now listed in the Project Audio Browser ❽, linked to the audio file ❻ in the Audio File folder ❺ of the Project File.
- Although the "Add to Project Audio" ❸ option is considered an "import audio file" procedure, the file is already located inside the Project ❺, so nothing needs to be imported.
- Although a default Audio Region ❾ is automatically created in the Project Audio Browser, it is not placed on the Workspace ❿ yet.

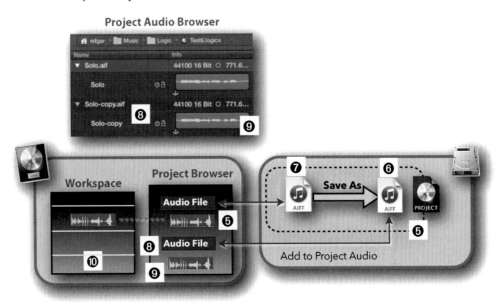

## 😀 Example #2

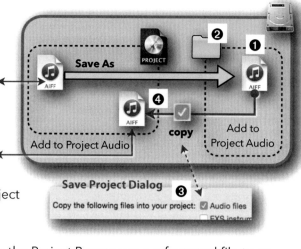

In this example, I save the copy of the Audio File to a folder somewhere on the hard drive, not inside the Audio File folder of the Project File.

- The new Audio File ❶ is now located in a folder ❷ somewhere on the drive.
- If I have "Add resulting files to Project Audio" enabled in the Save Dialog, then that is considered an "audio import". Unlike the previous example, now it has consequences because an import will happen. The outcome depends on the Project Settings checkbox for "copy files to Project" ❸ that we discussed earlier in the Project Management section.

- ☐ If copy is disabled, then the audio file is available in the Project Browser as a referenced file to an "outside" location ❷.

- ☑ If copy is enabled, then an additional copy ❹ of the audio file will be placed in the Project File and that is now available in the Project Browser.

## ➡ *Save Region / Selection As...*

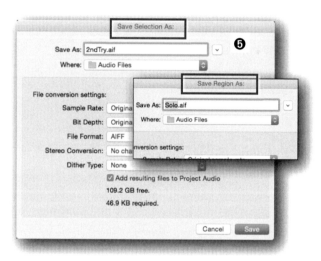

This command opens a Save Dialog ❺ with the same options. The only difference is that instead of saving a copy of the entire audio file, you are creating a new audio file from the current section.

There are two variations on how that section of the audio file is determined:

## 😀 Save Region As

This command saves the currently selected Region(s) as a new Audio File:

- 🔊 Local Menu *Audio File ➤ Save Region(s) As...* ❼
- 🔊 *Ctr+click* on a Region in the Project Audio Browser to open the Shortcut Menu *Save Region(s) As...* ❻

## 😀 Save Selection As

In the Audio File Editor, you can determine any section of the audio file by drawing a Selection Area on the Waveform Display ❽ and then use the following command:

- 🔊 Local Menu *Audio File ➤ Save Selection As...* ❾
- 🔊 Key Command (Save Selection As...) *opt+cmd+S*

### Project Audio Browser

Local Menu

Region ➤ Shortcut Menu

### Audio File Editor

## ➡ *Copy/Convert*

This is a very powerful command, a little bit of a swiss-army knife. Its name indicates that you can "copy" or "convert" an audio file. Although you can convert the file format of an audio file with the "Save As" command by selecting different parameters in the Save Dialog, this command has one extra feature, hidden in one obscure checkbox.

The command is only available in the Project Audio Browser:

**Project Audio Browser**

Local Menu          Region ➤ Shortcut Menu

- Local Menu *Audio File ➤ Copy/Convert File(s)...*
- *Ctr+click* on an Audio File in the Project Audio Browser to open the Shortcut Menu *Copy/Convert File(s)...*
- Key Command (*Copy/Convert File(s)...*) *ctr+K*

The command opens a Save Dialog with the same settings as the "Save As" command with the exception of that one checkbox "*Change file reference in Project Audio*" ❶.

### ☠ Change file reference in Project Audio ❶

This checkbox changes the command completely:

- ☐ **Disabled ❷**: Logic creates a copy ❸ of the original audio file based on the selected parameters and saves it to the chosen location. This is basically a "Save As" command with an optional conversion.

- ☑ **Enabled ❹**: The first part of the procedure is the same: Copy the audio file ❻ to the location with the selected conversion parameters. But here comes the important part. The reference in Logic to the original audio ❻ file is now replaced with the reference to the newly created audio file ❺. That means the original audio file ❻, listed in the Project Audio Browser ❼ is swapped with the newly created audio file ❺. All the Audio Regions ❽ for that audio file stay the same, because the length of the audio file did not change, only its format.

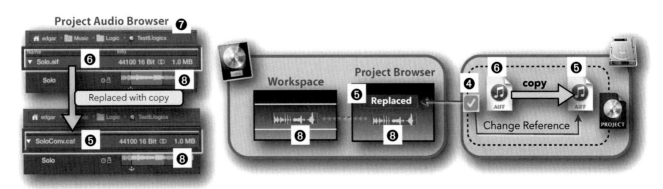

## *Parameters*

Although the available parameters in the Save Dialog are the same when you use the "Save As" command for an audio file, the Convert command let's you swap an "active" audio file that is used in your project, referencing all its Audio Regions. Logic just replaces all the references of the original audio file in your Project with the reference to the new converted audio file.

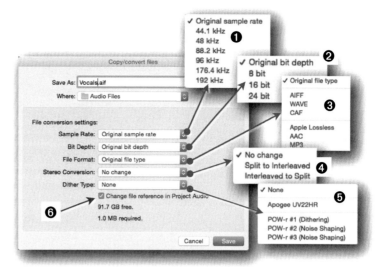

Here are the available parameters:

### ⚙ Sample Rate ❶

Select from six Sample Rates or choose "Original Sample Rate" to use the original Sample Rate of the audio file.

> ▶ Convert: Sample Rate Conversion is automatically performed by Logic (has to be checked in the Project Settings ❼) when you import audio files that have a different Sample Rate than the Project's Sample Rate. If that checkbox wasn't enabled during import, then you can fix that by converting the Sample Rate of specific audio files in your Project with this command. Please note that an audio file will playback faster or slower with different pitch if the audio file's Sample Rate doesn't' match the Project's Sample Rate.

### ⚙ Bit Depth ❷

Select from three Bit Depth settings (Resolution) or choose *"Original Sample Rate"* to keep the Sample Rate of the original audio file.

> ▶ Convert: When you down-sample (i.e. 24bit to16bit), make sure to use one of the Dither options below.

### ⚙ File Format ❸

Select an uncompressed audio file format (AIFF, Wave, CAF), a compressed audio file format (mp3, AAC, Apple Lossless), or keep the "Original file type".

> ▶ Convert: You can use this setting, for example, to convert an Apple Loop file 🎵 to a standard audio file 💿 (only as AIFF ❽). Please note that you would loose its Follow Tempo & Pitch capabilities.

### ⚙ Stereo Conversion ❹

LPX automatically converts all Split files to an interleaved file when importing them to your Project. So technically LPX doesn't support split files in your Logic Project anymore. Therefore, the "Split to Interleaved" command is obsolete, because there are no split files in a Logic Project to convert in the first place.

> ▶ Convert: Using the "Interleaved to Split" command will save the selected Stereo Interleaved file (not surround interleaved) in your Project as Split files to your drive. The enabled "Change reference" ❻ checkbox would re-import those files as an interleaved file again, so there is no point for that checkbox with this procedure.

### ⚙ Dither Type ❺

Dithering is a special procedure in digital audio that adds noise to the audio signal during the conversion process to make it sound better. This is a special kind of "good noise" that sounds better to the ear than the "digital" noise, which becomes audible in low level signals, caused by quantization errors. Dithering is used especially when downsampling a 24bit signal to a 16bit signal.

## ➡ *Backup*

Behind this Backup command is a simple, but extremely useful concept that I already discussed in the *Advanced Editing* chapter.

The Backup command is available in the Audio File Editor and the Project Audio Browser.

- Local Menu Command  ***Audio File Editor ➤ Audio File ➤ Create Backup*** ❶
- Local Menu Command  ***Project Browser ➤ Audio File ➤ Backup File(s)*** ❷
- Key Command (*Add Audio File*) ***ctr+B***

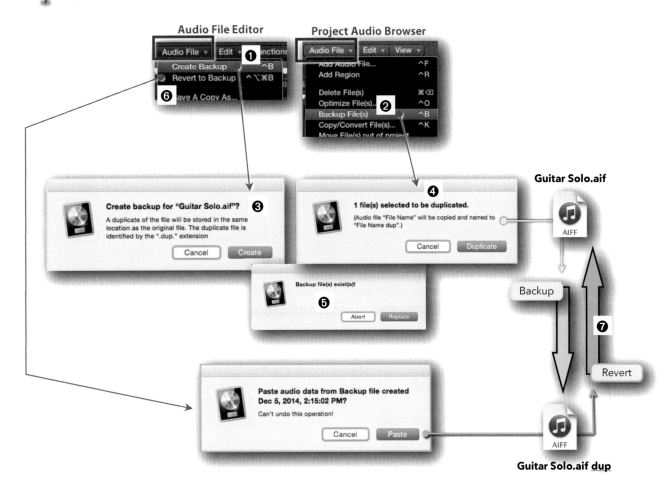

This is the basic concept:

- The Audio File Editor and the Project Audio Browser use a slightly different name for the same Backup command: "*Create Backup*" ❶ and "*Backup File(s)*" ❷.
- The technical difference is that the Audio File Editor creates one Backup file of the currently displayed audio file, but the Project Audio Window can create Backup Files of multiple selected audio files (in the Project Audio Browser) at the same time.
- Both commands prompt a different Dialog Window ❸ ❹ with the same outcome. They create a copy of the original audio file.
- If a backup file already exists, then an additional Dialog Window pops up ❺ with a "Backup file exist" warning.
- Only the Audio File Editor provides the Revert to Backup ❻ command to overwrite the existing audio file with the previously stored backup file ❼.

## 🖰 Backup Procedure

Technically, this special audio file Backup procedure is similar to the Convert command with the "Change file reference" options. However, instead of re-referencing to the saved file, the Backup feature lets you overwrite the existing audio file with the backed up audio file while maintaining all its references.

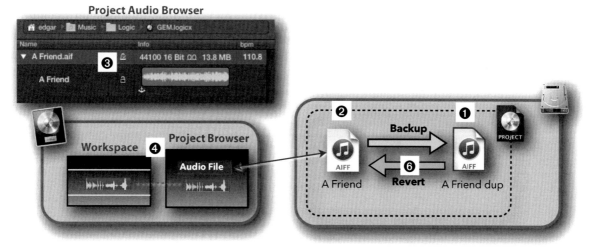

This is how it works:

- Whenever you are about to make some serious destructive edits to the audio file, use the Backup command.
- From the Audio File Editor, you make a backup of the currently display audio file and in the Project Audio Browser, you can select multiple audio files and create backup files for each selected one.
- Logic creates a copy ❶ of the selected audio file ❷ and adds the extension "dup" to the file name. It is stored in the same location as the original audio file.
- Nothing will change in the Project Browser ❸ or with the Audio Regions in the Workspace ❹. This is just a "save as" command for those files and doesn't affect the current audio files and its reference in the Project.
- Later, if you did some destructive edits to that file in the Audio File Editor (that you didn't like) and want to go back to the version when you saved the backup, you use only one command, the "*Revert to Backup*" command in the Audio File Editor ❺.

- Now, Logic automatically swaps out ❻ the current audio file ❷ (with all the not so great edits) with the version you saved with the *Backup* command earlier, the *dup* file ❶. No need to manually copy-paste, remembering where the original copy is, reestablishing the links to the Audio Region, etc. Everything is automatically taken care of with just that one command. A Dialog Window ❼ even tells you the time stamp of the backup file, plus the warning that you cannot undo that step!

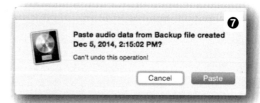

- Nothing has changed in the Project Audio Browser or the Workspace ❹. The whole procedure is completely transparent.
- Using the Backup command again on the same Audio File, will prompt a Dialog Window ❽ with a reminder that a Backup file for this audio file already exists. Click Replace to overwrite the existing "dup" file.

Unfortunately, those dup files cannot be deleted with the Clean Up command. They stay in the folder and you have to remove them manually if you want to save space.

## ➡ Bounce/Export

There is a wide variety of additional commands in Logic that can create audio files. They are for all different purposes and spread all over the place in different menus, some with their own Key Commands. The amount of available commands can be a bit overwhelming and the fact that some commands are listed multiple times in different menus under slightly different names doesn't help.

Here is an overview with screenshots of those menus where I marked the commands that can create new audio files. They are listed in the File Menu, the Edit Menu, and the Shortcut Menu when you *ctr+click* on a Region in the Workspace.

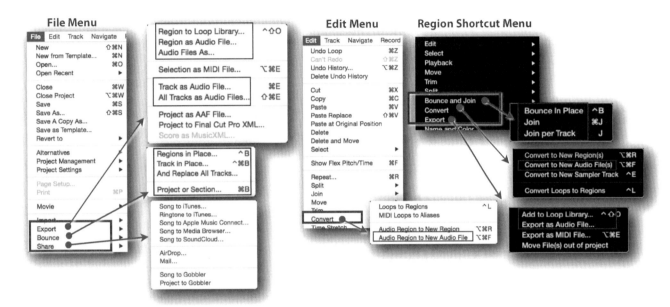

And here is another overview where I list only those audio-file-creating commands from those three menus. The commands that are identical, but with a different name are connected with a red line.

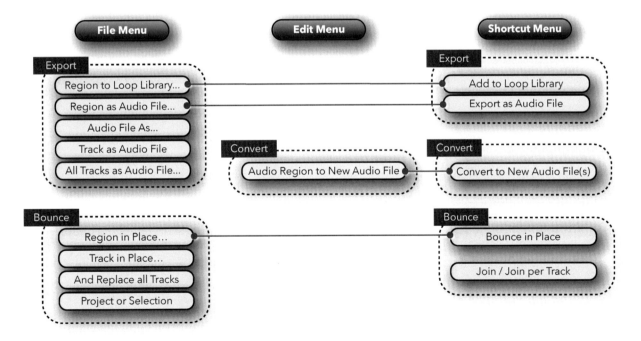

Next, I will go quickly over those commands with a focus on the file management.

## 🎯 Export

These are the commands that create new audio files based on the selection.

▶ *File Menu* ➤ *Export* ➤ ( **Audio File As...** )

Select one or multiple Regions in the Workspace. The command will copy their referenced audio file to the location you choose in the Export Dialog Window.

- ☑ **Setting**: No Format settings (audio file as is)
- ☑ **Project Audio Browser**: No import on Project Browser
- ☑ **Workspace**: No affect on the Workspace

▶ *File Menu* ➤ *Export* ➤ ( **Region to Loop Library...** ) **or** *Shortcut Menu* ➤ *Export* ➤ ( **Add to Loop Library** )

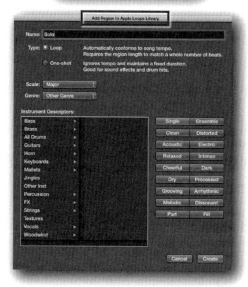

Select a single Region in the Workspace. The command will open a Dialog window that lets you configure the Apple Loop. There are no location settings because the file will be saved in the default user directory *~/Library/Audio/Apple Loops/ User Loops/ Single Files*

- ☑ **Setting**: No Format settings (auto converted to Apple Loops)
- ☑ **Project Audio Browser**: No import on Project Browser. You have to import the Loop from the Loop Browser if you want to use it in the current Project
- ☑ **Workspace**: No affect on the Workspace

▶ *File Menu* ➤ *Export* ➤ ( **Region as Audio File...** ) **or** *Shortcut Menu* ➤ *Export* ➤ ( **Export as Audio File** )

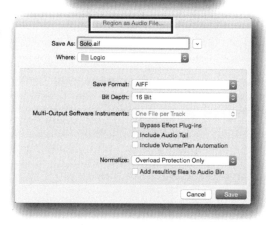

Select a single Region in the Workspace. The command will bounce the Region and export it based on the optional settings to the defined location. This new audio file can also be imported back to your Project.

- ☑ **Setting**: Format and Bit Depth, plus other settings can be applied to the new audio file
- ☑ **Project Audio Browser**: Checkbox available to add the audio file back to your Project
- ☑ **Workspace**: No affect on the Workspace

▶ *File Menu* ➤ *Export* ➤ ⬭Track as Audio File⬭

Select a single Track in the Tracks Window. The command will bounce that Track and export it based on the optional settings to the defined location. This new audio file can also be imported back to your Project.

- ☑ **Setting**: Format and Bit Depth, plus other settings can be applied to the new audio file
- ☑ **Project Audio Browser**: Checkbox available to add the audio file to your Project
- ☑ **Workspace**: No affect on the Workspace

▶ *File Menu* ➤ *Export* ➤ ⬭All Tracks as Audio File...⬭

The command will bounce all the Tracks in your Workspace and exports them based on the optional settings to the defined location. These new audio files with the additional "_bip" ending ("bounce in place") can also be imported back to your Project.

- ☑ **Setting**: Format and Bit Depth, plus other settings can be applied to the new audio files
- ☑ **Project Audio Browser**: Checkbox available to add the audio files to your Project
- ☑ **Workspace**: No affect on Workspace

## 💀 Convert

This is a similar command like the "Copy/Convert File(s)…" in the Project Browser that replaces an existing audio file. Here, only a specific Audio Region will be replaced, which is referenced to a newly created audio file.

▶ *Edit Menu* ➤ *Convert* ➤ ⬭Audio Region to New Audio File⬭ **or** *Shortcut Menu* ➤ *Convert* ➤ ⬭Copy to New Audio File(s)⬭

This will bounce the selected Region to a new audio file, stored in the defined location and imported back to the current Project. The new default Audio Region will be created in the Project Audio Browser and put on the Workspace to replaces the previous Region.

- ☑ **Setting**: Format and Bit Depth, plus other settings can be applied to the new audio file
- ☑ **Project Audio Browser**: New Audio File will be imported
- ☑ **Workspace**: The Audio Region of the new Audio File will replace the original Audio Region

# 🎱 Bounce

The Bounce commands are all "mix-downs" of a particular part of your Project.

▶ *File ➤ Bounce ➤*  **Project or Selection**

This is the main Bounce command that opens the Bounce Window with all the various bounce settings.

- ☑ **Setting**: Format and Bit Depth, plus other settings can be applied to the new audio file
- ☑ **Project Audio Browser**: Checkbox available to add the audio file to your Project
- ☑ **Workspace**: No affect on Workspace

▶ *File ➤ Bounce ➤* Region in Place... **or** *Shortcut Menu ➤ Bounce* Bounce in Place

This is a so-called "Bounce in Place" (bip). The selected Region will be bounced to a new audio file. That new audio file will be imported back to your Project and the default Audio Region of that new audio file will be placed at the same location on a newly created Audio Track. Please note that the Undo command doesn't delete the newly created audio file. It stays in your Project and has to be removed manually.

- ☑ **Setting**: The File Format cannot be changed, but a few settings regarding the bounce procedure can be
- ☑ **Project Audio Browser**: The new audio file is automatically imported back to your Project
- ☑ **Workspace**: A new Audio Region is placed on a newly created Audio Track

▶ *File ➤ Bounce ➤* Track in Place...

This is the same procedure as "Region in Place". This time all the Audio Regions on the selected Track are bounced to a single audio file (starting at the beginning of the Project), which is reimported and put on a new Audio Track.

- ☑ **Setting**: The File Format cannot be changed, but a few settings regarding the bounce procedure can be
- ☑ **Project Audio Browser**: The new audio file is automatically imported back to your Project
- ☑ **Workspace**: A new Audio Region is placed on a newly created Audio Track

▶ *File ➤ Bounce ➤* And Replace all Tracks

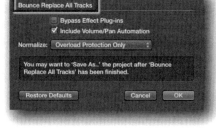

This command is a variation of the "Track in Place" command. This time, each Audio Track is bounced to a new audio file, and those audio files are placed back on their original Track, replacing the original Audio Regions with the new Audio Regions. It does not delete the previous audio files, they are still in the Project Browser.

This command can replace multiple small Regions on a Track with one single Audio Track, starting at the beginning of the Project.

- ☑ **Setting**: The File Format cannot be changed, but a few bounce settings can be
- ☑ **Project Audio Browser**: The new audio file is automatically imported back to your Project
- ☑ **Workspace**: All the Audio Regions in the Workspace are replaced with the new single Audio Regions and new Tracks are created for no-Audio Track bounces (MIDI Tracks, Drummer Track)

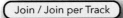 **Shortcut Menu ➤ Bounce ➤** Join / Join per Track

This command creates a new audio file based on the limitation that you cannot join non-contiguous audio files. This is technically a bounce-in-place procedure where Logic bounces the selected Audio Regions to a new file and puts it as a new Audio Region in that place.

- ☑ **Setting**: No settings available
- ☑ **Project Audio Browser**: The new Audio file is automatically imported back to your Project
- ☑ **Workspace**: The selected Audio Regions are replaced with a new continuous Audio Region based on the new audio file

## Change Existing Audio File

After this little detour into other audio file creation commands, let's go back to the Project Audio Browser and finish the last few commands related to Audio File and Project Management.

### ⚙ Optimize File

This command will not create a new audio file. Instead, it will change the original audio file destructively. This sounds scary, but it is actually a cool feature that is really practical in many situations when you try to "optimize files" to save storage space.

This is the concept:

- ▶ **Delete**: When you delete an audio file the entire recording is gone, deleted
- ▶ **Optimize**: When you optimize an audio file, you can delete specific (unwanted) sections of the audio file and keep only the wanted sections, and overwrite the "left overs" as a new smaller and shorter audio file

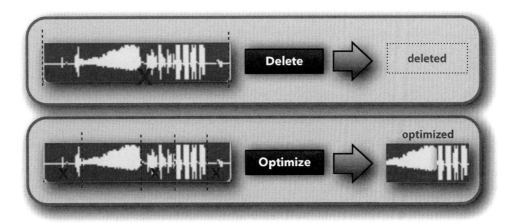

The Optimize command is available from:

- ⚙ Project Audio Browser: **Audio File ➤ Optimize File(s)...**
- ⚙ Key Command (*Optimize File(s)...*) **ctr+O**

Here is an example:

- I have an audio file (Vocals-Edit) ❶ from which I created two Regions ❷. Two sections that I use in my Project ❸.
- On the screenshot, I have a duplicate of the audio file (purple) ❹ on top to demonstrate the procedure. I marked five segments on that audio file (A - E) and you can see that I used segment B and D for the Audio Regions that I cut out from my audio file (blue).
- The Project Browser shows these two Audio Regions ❷, indicating with the blue color where along the original audio file those segments are.
- Now, when I apply the Optimize command to my audio file (Vocals-Edit) ❶, Logic will look at what segments (Audio Regions) of that audio file are used in the Project (in this case segment B and D), creates a new audio file with those two sections, and overwrites the original audio file. In addition, the Regions are re-referenced to the new overwritten audio file.
- As a result, nothing changed on the Workspace ❺. Logic only deleted the sections that were not used anyways. On the Project Audio Browser ❻, you can still see the name

of the original audio file, but its waveform has changed (section A, C, D, and E are deleted). The two Audio Regions are still showing the exact sections (B and D) ❼.

- You will also noticed that the file size has changed ❽, because you deleted sections of the original audio file. And this is the main purpose of the command, deleting sections of your recording that you (hopefully) don't need anymore in order to save space on your drive.
- When you apply the command, a Dialog Window ❾ pops up before executing the command. It lets you set additional "handles" before and after the section cuts, in case you need some space for crossfades. Set the slider ❿ between 0ms and 1,000ms (1 second).

You can actually use that command to delete (clean-up) unwanted sections in audio recordings. For example, you started a live recording and it took the band 5 minutes until they finally started their song. Now, just delete those 5 minutes from the audio file(s).

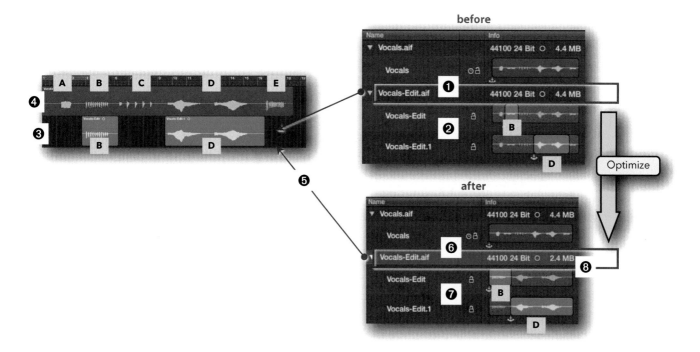

# Update Existing Audio File

The following two commands are writing to and reading from an audio file. However, that only affects the metadata in the audio file and doesn't alter any of the audio signal.

##  Export Region Information

Select an audio file in the Project Audio Browser and use any of the following commands:

- Local Menu *Audio File* ➤ *Export Region Information*
- Key Command (*Export Region Information*) *ctr+E*

Logic will add the information of all the Audio Regions ❶ for that audio file as metadata at the end of the actual audio file.

- A Dialog Window warns you that this will delete any existing Region Information contained in the audio file.
- Although it writes to the actual audio file ❸, it does not affect the audio data in the file.
- You can see that metadata when you open the audio file in a text editor and scroll all the way to the end ❹.
- Please note that this Region Information can only be added to uncompressed audio files (AIFF, WAV, CAF).

**Audio File (opened in text editor)**

**Project Audio Browser**

Export Region Information

##  Import Region Information

This is the same command in opposite direction. It imports any Region Information contained in an audio file, which means, those Audio Regions will be added to the Project Audio Browser for the selected audio file. A Dialog Window ❺ assures you that no existing Regions are overwritten.

The command is available as:

- Local Menu *Audio File* ➤ *Import Region Information*
- Key Command (*Import Region Information*) *ctr+I*

# Remove Existing Audio File

### 🔘 Move File(s) out of Project

This command is not really a complete remove like delete. It just moves the audio file to a different location that you define in the Dialog Window that pops up ❶. The reference in the Project Audio Browser will be updated.

Use any of those commands:

- 🔘 Project Audio Browser *Audio File* ➤ *Move File(s)*
- 🔘 *Ctr+click* on Region in Workspace: *Shortcut Menu* ➤ *Export* ➤ *Move File(s) out of project*
- 🔘 Key Command (*Move File(s) out of project*) *unassigned*

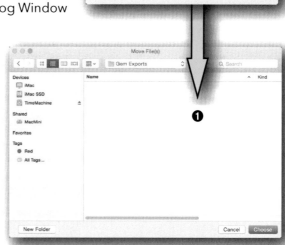

### 🔘 Delete File(s)

There are different delete commands. Be aware of when it removes the audio file only from the Project Audio Browser, and when it also deletes the actual audio file from the hard drive:

▶ **Delete Command #1**: When using any of the following commands, the selected audio files will be deleted from the Project Browser and the file will be moved to the Trash ❷. The Dialog Windows ❸ inform you about the action. The Undo command can bring the file back.

- 🔘 Project Audio Browser *Audio File* ➤ *Delete File(s)*
- 🔘 Key Command (*Delete File(s)*) *cmd+delete* (only works in the standalone Project Audio Window, not the Project Audio Browser)

▶ **Delete Command #2**: When using just the *delete* key to delete an audio file from the Project Audio Browser, then the audio file will only be deleted from the Project Audio Browser, but the audio file itself will not be moved to the Trash.

Use the command *File* ➤ *Project Management* ➤ *Clean up* to delete those orphan files from the Project File later.

▶ **Delete Region**: Deleting the last Audio Region in the Project Audio Browser will also remove its audio file. The audio file on the hard drive, however, is not deleted.

▶ **Delete right after recording**: If you hit the *delete* key right after recording a new file, then a Dialog Window pops up that gives you two options ❹:

- • **Delete** the Audio Region in the Workspace, plus the audio file from the Project Audio Browser and the hard drive.
- • **Keep** the audio file and the Audio Region in the Project Audio Browser and the hard drive, but remove the Audio Region on the Track Lane you just recorded on.

## Audio Settings

There are quite a few audio-related preferences and settings that let you fine-tune Logic. Don't think that, once you find the right configuration, you can forget about them. Depending on your Project (size, complexity) or the state of your Project (recording, editing, mixing), it might be necessary to change some of those settings during your production.

## Audio Preferences

 Remember to click the *Apply Changes* Button. Closing the Preferences Window will automatically apply the changes.

### ➡ *Core Audio*

Logic relies on the audio engine in OSX, which is called "Core Audio". Needless to say, if you use audio in your Project, then that checkbox has to be enabled.

Core Audio: ✔ Enabled

### 🌑 Disabled

One of the reasons you might turn it off (besides if you are using only external MIDI Instruments), is when you want to look at some MIDI Regions or other elements in a big Project that would require a couple of minutes to load. In that case, disable the checkbox and click the "Apply Changes" button. Now, every Project opens quickly because they don't load any of the Software Instruments or Audio FX Plugins.

Any Audio Plugin now has a red warning exclamation sign on the Plugin Button. Moving the cursor over the button pops up a black Help Tag with the name of the missing Plugin (also when Logic can't find a Plugin).

When you try to click on a Plugin button, you get a Dialog Window with a reminder that Core Audio is not available.

## ➡️ *Input Device / Output Device*

Besides enabling Core Audio, selecting the Audio Interface is the most important configuration step regarding audio in Logic. Any Audio Interface connected to your computer, and recognized by the Audio MIDI Setup utility, will be displayed in those two popup menus ❶.

## 💀 Audio MIDI Setup utility

Whenever you are configuring Audio Interfaces or have to troubleshoot interface issues, you have to have a closer look at the Audio MIDI Setup utility (*/Applications/Utilities/*). Beyond that, there are a few settings that are quite useful for Logic. Especially in OSX 10.10 Yosemite, there have been some minor changes.

**Audio MIDI Setup utility**

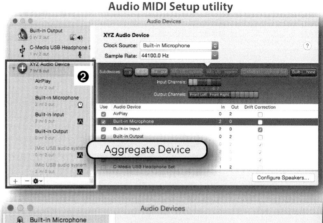

▸ **Aggregate Device ❷**: The OSX system and most audio apps like Logic only let you select one Audio Device. An Aggregate Device circumvents that limitation. Here, you can combine two or more hardware Audio Devices into one virtual Device. Choosing that Device in Logic makes all the inputs and outputs of all those "combined" Devices available.

▸ **Multi-Output Device ❸**: This is a new feature since OSX 10.8 Mountain Lion. It is similar to the Aggregate Device, but uses only the outputs of all the combined devices. This can be very useful in combination with the Airplay feature in OSX that lets you send audio over WiFi to an Apple TV or Airport Base Station. For example, you can set it up to send the output of Logic to your local Audio Device in your studio and simultaneously through Airplay to the recording booth or your living room.

## 💀 Exchanging Logic Projects

Here is one little detail to pay attention to when exchanging Logic Projects between different computers.

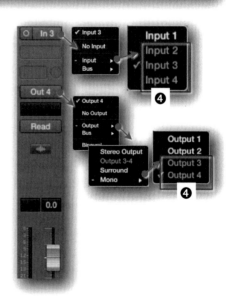

When you open a Logic Project on a computer that has less input and/or outputs available than the original Project, then those input/outputs will still be displayed in the popup menus, but they will be grayed out ❹.

Any Output Channel Strip that doesn't have a corresponding channel on the current Audio Device will be empty ❺. To listen to such a Project, you have to re-route the outputs of the affected Channel Strips.

## ➡ *I/O Buffer Size*

This setting might be the one that you have to change the most often, because the Buffer Size value is a trade-off between those two extremes:

   ▶ **Low (32)**: Low Latency (good) - High demand on CPU (bad)
   ▶ **High (1024)**: High Latency (bad) - Low demand on CPU (good)

## ☺ Latency

This is the delay between the input and output that doesn't matter during the mix, but can be a deal breaker during a recording:

- You hit the MIDI keyboard (input) and hear the sound (output) with a little lag
- You pluck your guitar (input) and hear the sound (output) with a little lag
- You sing into the microphone (input) and hear yourself in the headphones (output) with a little lag

One solution would be to use Hardware Monitoring on your Audio Interface (if available) or Logic's little helper, "Low Latency Mode" that I discuss a little bit later.

   ▶ **Resulting Latency**: The Resulting Latency is a combination of many factors, mainly the I/O Buffer Size and the quality of the Audio Interface. Also, choosing a higher Sample Rate will lower the Latency (with the negative impact of increased storage and higher CPU demand). Logic calculates the resulting Latency and displays it below the I/O Buffer Size setting.

**Attention**   Before you go into panic mode about a few milliseconds latency, do the real life math and remember how fast sound travels through the air. If a guitar player stands 1m ( about 3 feet) away from his speaker, he hears the sound with a 3ms delay. If he stands 2m away, then the "acoustic" latency will be 6ms.

## ☺ CPU Load

If the demand on the processor (CPU) is getting too high, then you hear clicks and in the worst case scenario, Logic will stop, and you will get a System Overload message. In my opinion, the worst case scenario is before you hear the click. That is when the CPU is starting to reach its limits and the sound already gets degraded before it is really audible with those clicks. That's why it is always a good idea to have the CPU Load Meter visible.

   ▶ **Load Meters**: They are displayed in the Custom Control Bar Display. *Double-click* on the Meter to open it as a Floating Window (now you can switch back to a different Control Bar Display if you like).

## ➡ *Recording Delay*

Most Audio Interfaces let Logic know through their driver what their latency is so Logic can automatically compensate for that during recording. If that doesn't happen, the Recording Delay parameter lets you manually set an offset between -5000 and +5000 Samples that is applied to the recorded signal. That means Logic is playing back the Audio Region with that offset.

## ➡ *24-Bit Recording*

A few notes about this checkbox:

☑ 24-Bit Recording
☑ Software Monitoring
☐ Input monitoring only for focused track, and record-enabled tracks
☐ Independent monitoring level for record-enabled channel strips

- This affects the Bit Depth for any audio files created during the audio recording in your Project. You still can import 16bit audio files and they can live next to each other in one Project.
- Disable the checkbox to record in 16bit.
- You still can choose a different Bit Depth during the Bounce procedure.
- 24bit requires more storage space, but you get better audio quality in return.
- 24bit is the standard for delivering audio files in film and television production.
- You can decide to stay in 16bit if you produce for Audio CD to avoid any conversion later, but using dithering to down-convert from 24bit to 16bit takes care of that.

## ➡ *Software Monitoring*

Software Monitoring is the mode in which you listen back to the signal you are recording through an Audio Interface:

- ▶ 🔊 **On**: The incoming signal ❶ is routed through Logic ❷, passing through all the Plugins on that Channel Strip. The pros, you can listen with the processed signal (compressed, reverb), the cons, you are dealing with the latency.

- ▶ 🔊 **Off**: The recorded signal ❸ is routed parallel directly to the Audio Interface' output ❹, avoiding any latency. However, you listen to the dry signal, unless you send just the reverb'ed portion of the signal you are recording back ❺ (which is ok with a few ms latency).

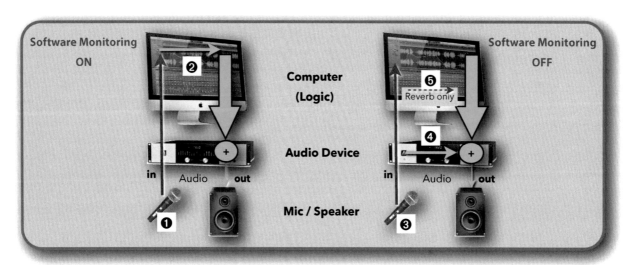

You don't have to go to the Preferences Window to toggle Software Monitoring on/off. These are the options:

- Software Monitoring has its own button ❻ that you can make visible on the Control Bar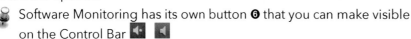
- Key Command (*Toggle Software Monitoring*) "***unassigned***"
- ***Preferences ➤ Audio ➤ Devices ➤ Software Monitoring***

## ➡ Input monitoring only for focused track, and record-enabled tracks

To understand the different modes and the functions of this preferences settings, you have to pay attention to the different states the Input Monitoring Button on the Track Header can have:

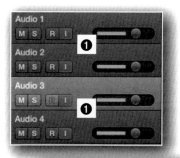

**☐ Input monitoring only for focused track, and record-enabled tracks**

This is the default behavior:

- **I Input Monitoring Off**: You won't hear the incoming signal (unless you record-enable the Track **R** )

- **I Input Monitoring On**: You will hear the incoming signal. You can even enable the Input Monitoring Button on multiple Tracks ❶ to listen to all those incoming signals

**☑ Input monitoring only for focused track, and record-enabled tracks**

When you enabled this preference, the behavior of the Input Monitoring Button will change the following way:

- Even if you have Input Monitoring enabled on multiple Tracks, only the selected Track ❷ (focused track) will have the Input Monitoring enabled **I**

- All other Tracks will have Input Monitoring disabled. Look at the Input Monitoring Buttons, they indicate that special off status ❸ **I**, which means "technically I'm enabled, but I was overwritten and disabled because my Track is not selected (or record enabled)".

- There is one exception: When you record-enable an unselected Track **R**, then it will turn monitoring on, displaying this button combination **R I** ❹.

## ➡ Independent monitoring level for record-enabled channel strips

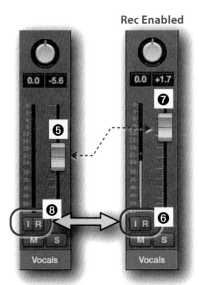

Rec Enabled

This setting is useful in the following situations: When working on your Project, you will start to mix when you are finished with the tracking, the recording of all the Tracks. However, recording and mixing often goes hand in hand very often. You already set the levels, maybe add some FX Plugins on the recorded Tracks while recording new Tracks.

It also happens often that you go back to a recorded Track and do some overdubs, or maybe even re-record a Track. In that situation you most likely change the Volume Fader. For example, you raise the volume during the recording of the vocals, so the singer can better hear himself. If you want to listen back in the right balance of the mix, you move the Fader down, or remember the position. Even worse, if you decide to do another take, you have to remember the Fader position you had before the recording, unless:

Enable this preference setting. Let's say the Fader is at -10dB ❺. When you record-enable **R** a Track ❻, it still stays at -10dB, but it now has its independent Volume level. You can adjust whatever level you need for the recording, i.e. +3dB ❼. Remember, this level does not affect the level you are recording! When finished recording and you disable the Record Enable

Button ❽ **R**, the Fader will go back to its non-RecEnabled position (-10dB ❺). Even better, if you record-enable the Track again, it remembered its +3dB position ❼.

## ➡ Processing Threads

Most modern computers have "multi-core" CPUs, which are multiple

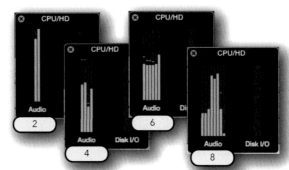

CPUs in one chip. You can look up how many cores your Mac has in the **Apple Menu ➤ About this Mac ➤ Overview ➤ Hardware** ❶. There is the "*Total Number of Cores*" listed. This is the number of "Physical Cores". However, most CPUs can run two threads on each core (doing two things at the same time). The number of "Virtual Cores" is, therefore, double as high.

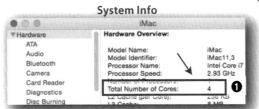

As a default, Logic has all the "Virtual Cores" (all Processing Threads) available to do its job. It is set to "Automatic"❷. However, you can limit the amount of cores you want to make available to Logic by choosing a number from the popup menu ❸.

The Load Meters represent each thread with an individual bar. There you can see how many threads you have available and how well Logic distributes the load across those available threads.

## ➡ Process Buffer Range

The I/O Buffer Size determines the size of the chunks an audio signal is chopped up when sent between the computer (Logic) and the Audio Device (and therefore, determining the latency). The Process Buffer Range, on the other hand, determines the size of the data chunks the "to be processed data stream" is chopped up, so it's the right size for the CPU to "chew on".

As with the Buffer size, the setting is a trade-off:

▶ **Small Buffer**: Faster audio processing (good) - more demanding on CPU (bad), leaving less resources or other tasks.

▶ **Large Buffer**: Less CPU demanding (good) - not fast enough (bad) for some demanding realtime processing tasks.

You can leave the default setting at "*Medium*"❹, or change it to *Small* (if you think your computer can handle it), or *Large* (if you are running Logic on an older CPU-challenged Mac). The type of potential error messages you will get from Logic, will tell you if there are problems with the setting for your current Logic Project.

## ➡ Rewire Behavior

I discuss the Rewire feature in the *Synchronization* chapter

## ➡ Maximum Scrub Speed / Scrub Response

I discuss these settings in the section about Scrubbing in a minute

The following Preference settings are in the General tab:

### ➡️ *Display audio engine overload message*

This is the Dialog window that pops up if Logic waves the flag because it can't handle all the processing tasks anymore. Always keep this checkbox enabled so you know "how Logic feels".

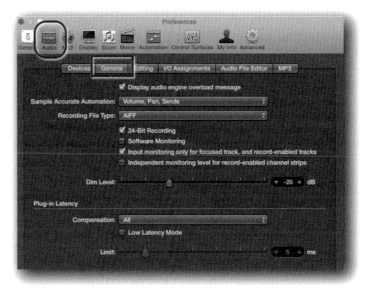

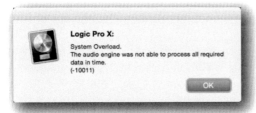

Once that Dialog pops up, make the necessary adjustment. For example, changing the buffer sizes, freeze some Tracks, or finally buy the new more powerful Mac that you always wanted.

### ➡️ *Sample Accurate Automation*

This setting determines the precision of the Automation Control Points. For automating levels, this might not be so critical, but automating any type of on/off switches should be as precise as possible. Although this is more CPU-intensive, you shouldn't go for anything less than precise.

If you are running into issues with CPU overloads, keep this setting in mind and see if you can tone it down, for example, if you don't have any critical automation on the Plugins.

### ➡️ *Recording File Type*

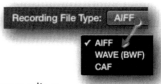

You can choose which audio file format Logic should use when recording audio in your Project. Most of the bounce procedures let you choose the audio file format separately

▶ **AIFF**: This is the default format. Keep its file limitation of 2GB in mind when recording live concerts with high Sample Rates. At 48kHz/24bit/stereo you need about 1GB/hour

▶ **WAVE (BWF)**: Broadcast Wave Format (BWF) is the professional version of this standard audio format used on PCs. It allows time stamping and has a limitation of 4GB per file

▶ **CAF**: The Core Audio Format (CAF) is a container file that can store different types of file formats plus metadata. Due to its 64bit architecture, you are limited to roughly about "hundreds of years" of recording time (which should be sufficient in most cases)

### ➡️ *Dim Level*

The Master Channel Strip has a unique Dim Button . When enabled, it lowers the output level of your mix, which is useful for lowering the volume during incoming phone calls (without changing any Fader position on your Mixer). The slider in the Preferences Window lets you set the amount of attenuation between 0dB and . -30dB

### ➡ Plug-in Latency

These three settings determine the configuration of the Plugin Compensation. I discuss that next in the *Low Latency* section.

### ➡ Crossfade for Merge and Take Comping

These sliders (now located in *Preferences ➤ Audio ➤ Editing*) set the default values for crossfades that are automatically created when using Quick Swipe Comping feature. I discuss that in the *Advanced Editing* chapter.

### ➡ I/O Assignments

The I/O Assignments Pane contains three sub-windows that are mainly for Surround settings (I cover that in the *Surround Sound* chapter). However, there are two settings that are important for Stereo Projects:

### 💀 Stereo Output ❶

This is actually a very important setting if you use a multi-channel Audio Interface. I discuss that next in the *Signal Flow* section.

### 💀 Bounce Extension ❷

These two entry fields let you enter the file extensions that are used when bouncing a stereo file to Split Stereo.

### ➡ Audio File Editor

I discuss those settings in the *Advanced Editing* chapter

### ➡ Mp3

The MP3 Pane lets you set the default parameters for bouncing your Project to MP3 files. Whatever you will configure in this Preferences Window ❸ will be the settings in the Bounce Window ❹ when selecting MP3 as the bounce option ❺.

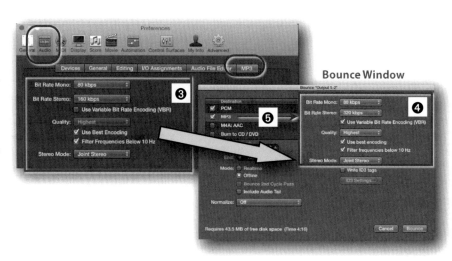

# Low Latency Mode

Latency is a very tricky subject with all DAWs. There are so many different types of Latencies and different settings affecting those different Latencies that it can be a bit confusing.

Here are the three types of Latencies that you can adjust in Logic:

- ▶ **I/O Latency**: This is the delay caused by the size of the buffer responsible for reading and writing the audio stream to and from your hard drive played through the Audio Interface. It is a latency that affects your entire system and is set with the *I/O Buffer Size*.

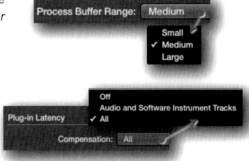

- ▶ **Processor Latency**: This is the delay caused by the size of the buffer the CPU uses to perform all the calculations necessary to process the audio signals. It is a latency that also affects the entire system and is set with the parameters: *Process Buffer Range*:

- ▶ **Plugin Latency**: This is a delay caused by an individual Plugin on a Channel Strip that needs the time to process the audio signal. Therefore, this is a latency that only affects individual Channel Strips with a specific latency-inducing Plugin. Channel Strips with different Plugins have different latencies caused by those Plugins, and therefore, creating a situation where the audio signals on different Channel Strips are out of sync.

➡️ *Plug-in Latency*

Let's have a closer look at the Plugin Latency and how Logic deals with it.

### 🌐 The Problem

We already discussed the global Latency issues of the I/O Buffer and Process Buffer. This is just a trade-off, where you have to find the middle ground between Latency and CPU requirements. The individual Latency introduced by Plugins is trickier, because it can be different for each Plugin, and therefore, different on each Channel Strip in your Project.

### 🌐 The Solution

To solve the problem of individual Plugin Latencies, Logic uses a procedure called "Plugin Latency Compensation". It looks at the loaded Plugins on the Channel Strips in your Project and delays audio streams or shifts them forward (earlier) to compensate for the different latencies, so all audio streams are in sync.

The popup menu for the Plug-in Latency Compensation has three options:

- ▶ **Off**: No Plugin Latency Compensation is applied.
- ▶ **Audio and Software Instrument Tracks**: Logic only compensates any Plugin Latency on the Audio Channel Strips and Software Instrument Channel Strips.
- ▶ **All**: Logic compensates any Plugin Latency on every Channel Strip.

To have the audio streams on all Channel Strips play in sync, it is recommended to select "All".

Logic uses two different procedures for the Plugin Latency Compensation based on what Channel Strip the Plugins are loaded:

## 🕹 Audio Track, Instrument Track

☑ Logic looks at each Audio Track and Software Instrument Track and calculates the combined latency introduced by all Plugins on each individual Channel Strip.

☑ When you play back your Project, then the Regions on those Tracks assigned to Channel Strips with Plugin Latency will start earlier by that calculated amount.

☑ Each Track is started earlier exactly by the amount Logic calculated for that specific Track based on its loaded Plugins.

☑ All the different delays on various Channel Strips are compensated and the audio signal on all Channel Strips is now in sync.

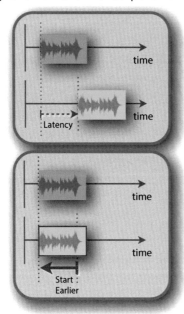

## 🕹 Aux Track, Output Track, others

If Plugins are loaded on any Channel Strip type other than Audio Channel Strips and Instrument Channel Strips, then the compensation procedure is different. Let's look at the Aux Chanel Strip:

☑ Logic looks at each Aux Channel Strip and calculates the combined latency introduced by all Plugins on that Channel Strip (i.e. 10ms).

☑ Now, Logic delays all other audio streams on other Channel Strips by that amount of 10ms to compensate for that delay, so all audio signals play in sync.

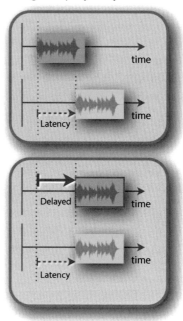

## 🕹 Playback pre-roll

This is a setting in the *Project Settings ➤ Audio* Window.

This checkbox should be enabled when you use Plugin Latency Compensation. It forces Logic to start a little bit earlier when you play back your Project. The value depends on the amount of delay compensation Logic applies to your Project.

This ensures that no signal is cut off at the beginning when playing back your Project.

**Project Settings ➤ Audio**

➡️ **Low Latency Mode**

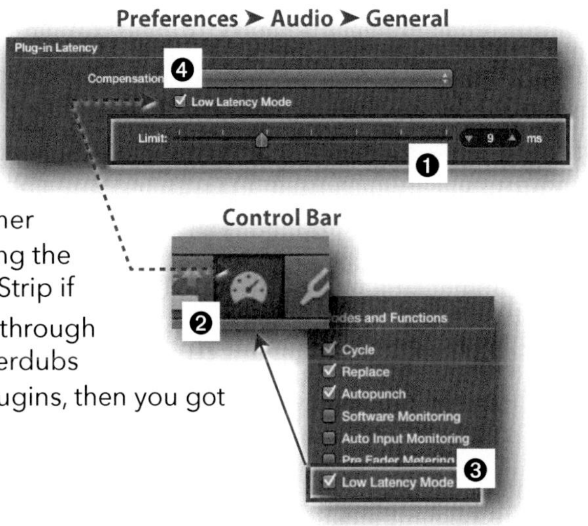

The Low Latency Mode is for those situations when you need to record on a Track that has a lot of (latency-inducing) Plugins loaded.

As we discussed earlier, this makes it impossible if the performer hears himself back with a slightly delayed signal. Usually, during the recording process, you won't use many Plugins on a Channel Strip if you record with Software Monitoring 🔊 enabled (monitoring through Logic with all effects). However, if you decided to do some overdubs during the mix, and already made "excessive" use of all the Plugins, then you got a problem. In that situation you can use Low Latency Mode.

Low Latency Mode requires two steps:

### Set the Latency Limit

In the *Preferences ➤ Audio ➤ General* Window, you can set a Latency Limit with a slider ❶ or the value field between 0ms to 30ms. This tells Logic the maximum amount of delay that you would accept during recording.

### Enable Low Latency Mode

Now when you enable Low Latency Mode on a Record-enabled Track, Logic looks at all the Plugins and Aux Sends that you use on that Channel Strip and turns them off, leaving only those Plugins enabled that wouldn't cause the Channel Strip to have a total Latency above the limit you set with the slider.

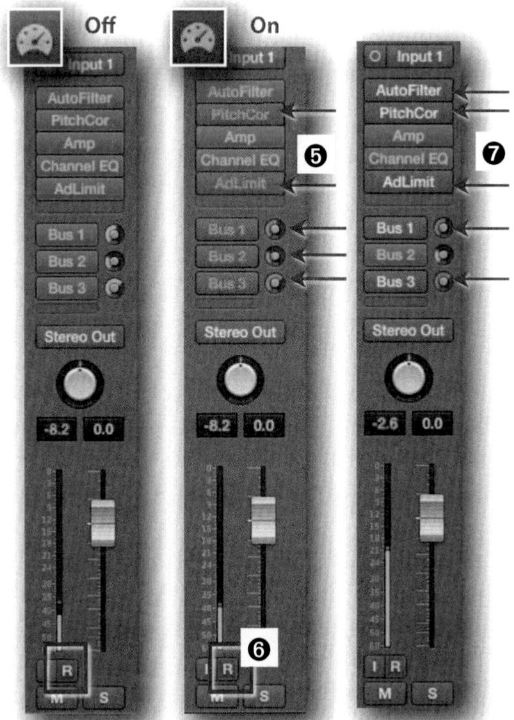

You can toggle the Low Latency Mode on/off with the following commands:

- Main Menu *Record ➤ Low Latency Mode*
- Key Command (*Toggle Low Latency Mode*) "**unassigned**"
- *Click* on the Low Latency Mode Button ❷ 🕐 in the Control Bar (the button is hidden by default and you have to make it visible in the Control Bar Configuration Window ❸).
- Checkbox ❹ in the *Preferences ➤ Audio ➤ General ➤ Low Latency Mode*

When enabled, Logic marks the Plugins and Aux Sends that are disabled on the Channel Strip orange ❺. You can adjust the Latency Limit Slider ❶ in the Preferences Window if you want to keep or remove more of the Plugins. The Channel Strip has to be record-enabled 🔴 ❻.

▸ **Practical Use**

Although the Low Latency Mode is a quick one-click solution for those situations, it is a little bit of a hit and miss. Having specific Plugins and Aux sends automatically turned off, might dramatically change the sound on that Channel Strip. Maybe some of those sound-changing Plugins are important for the performer when recording (compressor, reverb).

As an alternative, you can manually ❼ toggle specific Plugins and/or Aux Sends on that Channel Strip to find the best compromise between sound and latency.

# Scrubbing

"Scrubbing" is a special type of transport control used for editing when trying to narrow in on a position of a single Audio Region or a section in the Workspace of your Tracks Window.

Usually, you drag the Playhead along the Timeline to reposition it and then press play to play back that section. Now in Scrub Mode, the Playhead is "engaged", which means, the Playhead is in constant "manual" Play Mode, even when moved only a tiny bit. Logic always plays back when you move the Playhead. The speed and direction of your mouse movement controls the playback. By "wiggling" the Playhead back and forth around a specific area on the Workspace or Waveform Display, you are closing in on that spot. You might lower the volume of your speaker, because Scrubbing can create some really low frequencies.

I discuss the Scrubbing in the *Advanced Editing* chapter for Audio Files, here is how you scrub in the Workspace of the Tracks Window.

**Control Bar**

### Pause Mode = Scrub Mode

The functionality of the Playhead switches to Scrub Mode in the Tracks Window when you set Logic to Pause Mode.

- The Pause Button ❶ ![pause] is hidden from the Transport Controls by default. You have to make it visible on the Control Bar in the Control Bar Configuration Page ❷.

- You can also use the Key Command (*Pause*) "*Period key*" to switch to Pause Mode without the visible Pause Button, but the button gives you a nice visual feedback when you are in Pause Mode or not.

- *Click* on the Pause Button to switch to Pause Mode. The Play Button and the Pause Button light up ![play pause].

- You can click the Pause Button while your Project is in Stop Mode or while in Play Mode. In the latter case, the Project stops first and switches to Pause Mode.

- Now while in Pause Mode, *drag* the Playhead left or right to "scrub" along that area. All the Tracks are playing back accordingly.

- Logic only scrubs the Instrument Tracks in your Project by default. You can enable the Audio Tracks too in the *Preferences ➤ Audio ➤ Editing ➤ Scrubbing with audio in Tracks area* ❸.

**Preferences ➤ Audio ➤ Editing**

- Logic temporarily switches to Scrub Mode when you *drag* with the Scissors Tool ![scissors] or Solo Tool ![solo].

### Maximum Scrub Speed ❹

The speed of your mouse movements determines the playback speed in Scrub Mode. This setting in the *Preferences ➤ Audio ➤ Devices* lets you set the maximum playback speed in Scrub Mode to "Normal" (regular playback speed) or "Double" (double the regular playback speed).

### Scrub Response ❺

This setting in the *Preferences ➤ Audio ➤ Devices* determines how quickly the scrubbing (playback) responds to your mouse movement.

# Tuning

This is a Settings page that most Logic users most likely never use. It determines the tuning and the scale for the Software Instruments used in your Project. Please note that this is not stored with the Preferences, but with the Project Settings.

### 💀 Tuning ❶

Tuning refers to the reference pitch the Software Instruments are tuned to.

The standard tuning in western music use 440Hz for A above middle C. This is the default setting in Logic. You can set the reference pitch between -100cent (415.3Hz) … 0cent (440Hz) … +100cent (466.2Hz) in case you want to overdub some tracks of an orchestra or classical ensemble that often use different tuning than 440Hz.

### 💀 Scale ❷

The default setting is the *Equal Tempered* Scale used in western music. You can choose from a wide variety of alternate scales or create your own custom scale that all your Software Instruments will then be tuned to.

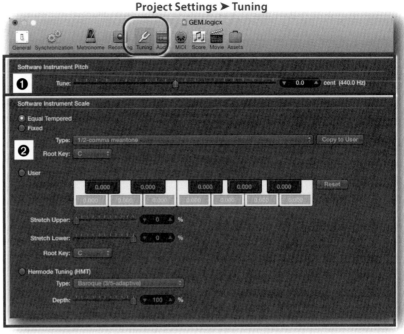

Project Settings ➤ Tuning

# Groove Template

Groove Template is a feature in Logic that lets you create custom Quantize Grids based on MIDI Events in a MIDI Region or the Transients in an Audio Region. If you recorded a bass player or a live drummer and you like the "feel" of that performance, you can define it as a Groove Template and use it to quantize other Regions in your Project to that Groove Template Grid.

### 💀 Create Groove Template

- ☑ Select one of more Regions that you like to use as the Groove Template reference. The Audio Region has to have Transients created (refer to the *Flex Time* chapter).

- ☑ Select "Make Groove Template" ❸ from the Quantize popup menu in the Region Inspector.

- ☑ The name of that Region will now appear at the end of the Quantize popup menu ❹ and can be used to quantize any Audio Region or MIDI Region.

Quantize Popup Menu

### *Be Aware:*

- Groove Templates are stored with the Project.
- If you delete the Region from your Project the Groove Template is based on, then the Groove Template is still visible in the popup menu, but has no quantize effect anymore.
- If you remove a Groove Temple from the list ❺, then Regions that were quantized with the Groove Template revert to no Quantize.

I already covered the Mixer Window and its relationship to the Environment in my first book "Logic Pro X - How it Works". In this chapter, I want to emphasize on those aspects with a closer look at the signal flow, things you have to know and have to be aware of when sending signals through Logic's Mixer.

# Basics

The most confusing part about the whole mixer and signal flow thing is the terminology. Too many similar terms that mean different things to different people. That's why it is crucial to know, for example, when you talk about "the input", what do you mean with that or what element you are referring to.

### ➡ *Components & Busses*

With analog mixing boards, everything was much easier and straight forward. A component was a piece of circuitry with an input and an output, and a bus was a wire that connected the output of one component to the input of another component. That's how you created a signal flow inside the mixer.

In a virtual mixer of a DAW, everything is digital. There are no wires where you send a signal from component A to component B. Now, chunks of data, consisting of 0s and 1s are sent to RAM Buffers located by their addresses. The good news is that you don't have to get a degree in computer science to use a virtual mixer in Logic. Its user interface (on the outside) is almost identical to a real mixer. Here is the basic signal flow:

The Channel Strips represent the Audio Components ❶ that process the audio signals, and the Busses represent the pipes that send (route) the audio signals between (Auxiliary Busses ❷) the Audio Components and also to (Output Busses ❸) and from (Input Busses ❹) the Audio Interface ❺.

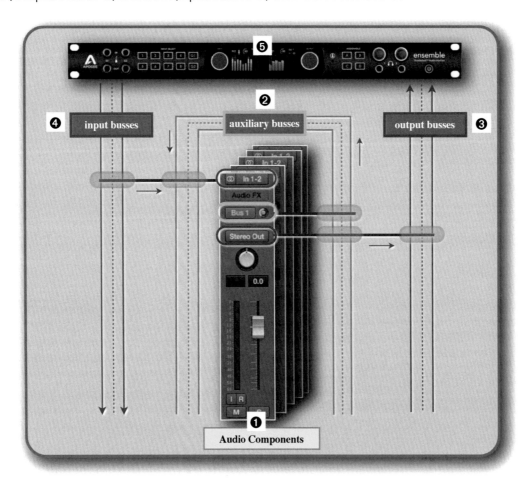

 **Component**

First, let's discuss the word "component", a very generic term used for different things. Here are just two:

▶ **Channel Strip Component**: The term "Channel Strip Component" is used in Logic for the individual elements on a Channel Strip that controls the audio signal flow on the Channel Strip (Pan, Sends, Inserts, etc.), or other interface elements (icons, color). You can show/hide individual Channel Strip Components ❶ to customize the look of your Mixer Window. The Input, Output, and Sends, for example, are different Channel Strip Components that affect the routing of the audio signal, the signal flow.

▶ **Audio Component**: I use the term "Audio Component" in the *Environment* chapter to describe the main building blocks in Logic, the ones that create your virtual studio. The Audio Components are all those elements "under the hood" that are responsible for processing audio signals in your virtual studio. Logic calls them "Channels". On the other hand, a Channel Strip ❷, is just an "Environment Object"❸ that you create in the Environment Window (or it is automatically created by Logic). Channel Strips are the "front end", the user interface, or remote control for the actual Audio Components ❹. Remember that you can create multiple Channel Strips, that "control" the same Audio Component (different Environment Objects assigned to the same Audio Component).

But there is not just one Channel Strip object, there are seven different types, the so-called "Channel Strip Types". A specific Channel Strip Type controls a specific type of Audio Component. For example, the ones that can record audio, others that can use Software Instruments as an input, etc. That means, the functionality of those different Channel Strip Types will also be slightly different.

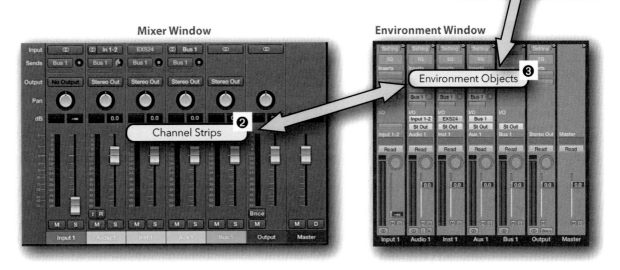

 **Bus**

The term "Bus" can be especially confusing in Logic. A Bus on a traditional mixer represents the wires where you can send a signal along. These are mainly the Input Busses ❺, the Output Busses ❻, and the Auxiliary Busses ❼, the different lanes (or pipes) that I showed on the previous page. However, as I already mentioned, your virtual mixing board in Logic doesn't run on wires. The concept in Logic is different:

An Audio Bus in Logic is also represented by an Audio Component. Three of the seven Channel Strip Types that are available in Logic are assigned to Audio Components that function as Busses.

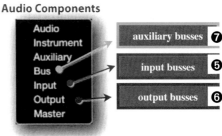

## ➡ *Routing*

Here is a summary of what you should know about Busses in Logic:

▸ Logic has seven different types of Audio Components (*Audio, Instrument, Auxiliary, Bus, Input, Output, Master*).

▸ Logic provides a total of 256 Audio Components for each *Audio, Instrument, Auxiliary,* and *Master,* and 64 Audio Components for *Bus*. The number of Audio Components for *Input* and *Output* depends on the number of input channels and output channels of the Audio Interface you use with Logic.

▸ Assigning an Audio Component to an Environment Object creates a Channel Strip. The type of Audio Component ❶ you are assigning it to determines what kind of Channel Strip Type ❷ it is.

▸ The three types of Busses in a traditional mixing console are represented in Logic as Audio Components:

- Input Busses: **Input Channel Strips ❸**
- Output Busses: **Output Channel Strips ❹**
- Auxiliary Busses: **Bus Channel Strips ❺**

▸ The following Channel Strip Components can route the signal on a Channel Strip to and from those "Busses"

- **Input Button ❻**: Audio signal is coming from the *Input Channel Strips* or the *Bus Channel Strips*
- **Output Button ❼**: Audio signal is going to the *Output Channel Strips* or the *Bus Channel Strips*
- **Aux Send button ❽**: Audio signal is only going to the *Bus Channel Strips*

▸ Routing basically means, connecting one Audio Component to another Audio Component.

▸ Each (invisible) Audio Component in Logic can be controlled by an (visible) Environment Object, the Channel Strip.

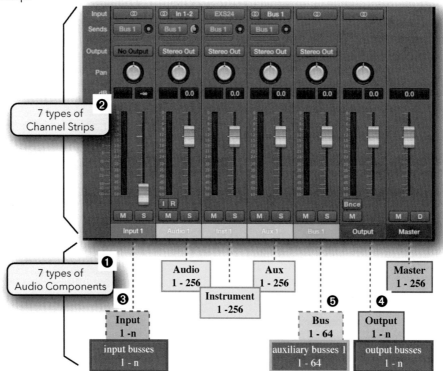

There is one more little detail about those three bus-impersonating Audio Components.

# ➡ *Unassigned Audio Components*

Whenever you route a signal in Logic to or from a Bus, think of that Bus as an Audio Component. However, that Audio Component doesn't have to have a Channel Strip assigned to it.

▸ **Output Bus**: Whenever you route the output of a Channel Strip to an Output Bus ❶ (Audio Component *Output* ❷), Logic automatically assigns that Audio Component to a Channel Strip (which makes it an Output Channel Strip ❸). All the audio signals that are sent to that Audio Component are summed together, and that summed signal can be processed on that Output Channel Strip before it reaches the output of the Audio Interface ❹ (or gets bounced to an audio file).

▸ **Input Bus**: Whenever you select an Input Bus ❺ on a Channel Strip, you route that input channel of the connected Audio Interface ❹ to that Channel Strip. That means, the source you connect to the Audio Interface (mic, guitar, etc.) reaches the input of that specific Channel Strip. However, that is not the whole story. Technically, the incoming signal from the Audio Interface is routed to its corresponding Audio Component "*Input*" ❻ and the Input Button on the Channel Strip actually selects that Audio Component. As an option, you can assign a Channel Strip object to that Audio Component (which makes it an Input Channel Strip ❼) and insert Audio FX Plugins if you want to record an audio signal with effects (i.e. Compressor). Please note that only the Inserts affect the Input Bus, not the Volume Fader or the Pan Knob on that Input Channel Strip.

▸ **Auxiliary Bus**: Whenever you select a Bus ❽ as the input of a Channel Strip (i.e. Aux Channel Strip), you route the sum of all signals that were sent to that Bus to the input of that Aux Channel Strip. Again, that is not the whole story. Technically, all the signals that are sent to that Bus, are sent to its corresponding Audio Component "*Bus*" ❾ and the Input Button on the Channel Strip actually selects that Audio Component. As an option, you can assign a Channel Strip object to that Audio Component (which makes it a Bus Channel Strip ❿) and insert Audio FX Plugins to process the summed signal before it reaches the input of the Aux Channel Strip.

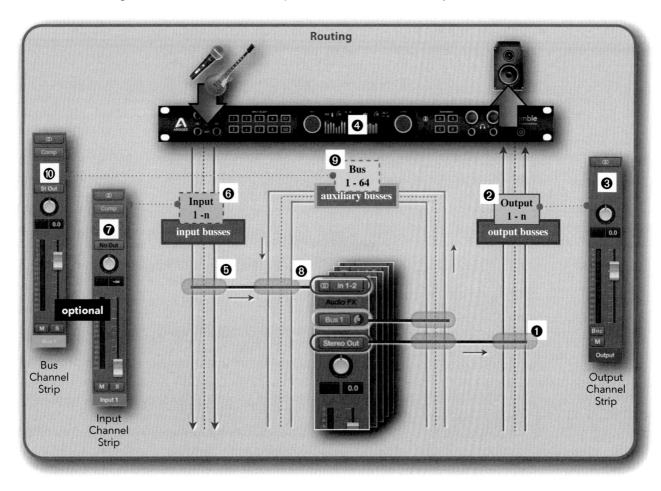

## ➡ Routing Option

Here are the available routing options for the seven different Channel Strip Types:

 **Input Channel Strip ❶**

- **Input**: <u>**Dedicated Input Channel (Hardware)**</u>
- **Send**: Auxiliary Busses
- **Output**: Auxiliary Busses, Output Busses

 **Audio Channel Strip ❷**

- **Input**: Input Busses, Auxiliary Busses
- **Send**: Auxiliary Busses
- **Output**: Auxiliary Busses, Output Busses

 **Instrument Channel Strip ❸**

- **Input**: Instrument Plugin
- **Send**: Auxiliary Busses
- **Output**: Auxiliary Busses, Output Busses

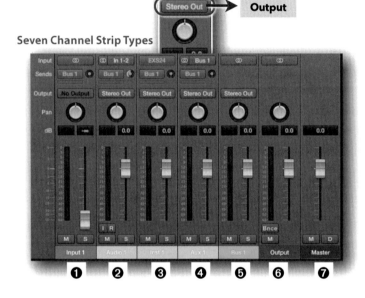

Seven Channel Strip Types

 **Aux Channel Strip ❹**

- **Input**: Input Busses, Auxiliary Busses, Instrument Outputs (Multi-Out), Rewire Bus
- **Send**: Auxiliary Busses
- **Output**: Auxiliary Busses, Output Busses

 **Bus Channel Strip ❺**

- **Input**: **Dedicated Auxiliary Bus**
- **Output**: Auxiliary Busses, Output Busses

 **Output Channel Strip ❻**

- **Input**: **Dedicated Output Bus**
- **Output**: <u>**Dedicated Output Channel (Hardware)**</u>

 **Master Channel Strip ❼**

- The Master Channel Strip has no routing capabilities. It functions as an additional control for the Audio Component *Output* (like a VCA). Its functionality changes quite a bit when mixing in surround. More on that in the *Surround Sound* chapter.

## ➡ *Additional Routing Option*

There are a few additional routing options affecting the signal flow besides the Input, Output, and Send that are hidden in some Plugins. Traditionally, the Inserts on an analog mixing console where the routing options that you had to do manually by plugging in patch chords in input and output jacks on a patch bay to send the audio signal to outboard gears and back to the Channel Strip. Most of the Inserts in Logic are hosted internally, but you still have the option with some Plugins to route audio signals in and out of the Channel Strip.

### 💀 External Instrument

*External Instrument* is a Software Instrument Plugin that you can load as an Instrument on an Instrument Channel Strip. It lets you use external Hardware MIDI Sound Modules, sending it the MIDI signal and receiving its audio signal back on the Input Busses ❶ (where the Module is connected to the Inputs of the Audio Interface).

**External Instrument Plugin**

### 💀 I/O Plugin

*I/O* is an Audio FX Plugin that you use to send the audio signal on the Channel Strip to an Output Bus ❷ (to the Audio Interface where you have an external FX Module hooked up), and then use an Input Bus ❸ to route the signal from the Audio Interface back to the Channel Strip.

**I/O FX Plugin**

### 💀 Side Chain

Some Audio FX Plugins (i.e. Compressor, Gate, Vocoder) have a Side Chain ❹ option. This is an audio input that you can use to control the Plugin. The Side Chain usually provides the Input Busses and Auxiliary Busses, plus the Audio Busses, which are basically the signals of the currently used Audio Channel Strips.

**Side Chain capable Plugins**

## ➡ *An Aux is not a Bus*

There is a potential confusion with some of the terms regarding Aux and Bus. Let's see if you can follow the following "logic":

- Via the "Aux Send" on a Channel Strip, you can route its signal to any of the 64 "*Busses*".
- These 64 *Busses* represent the 64 Audio Components "Bus".
- Remember, an Audio Component "Bus" doesn't need to be assigned to any Channel Strip, this is optional.
- These "Busses" are the so-called "Auxiliary Busses" on a standard mixing console.
- An Audio Component "Auxiliary" has to be assigned to a Channel Strip, which makes it an "Aux Channel Strip"
- Although you can route different types of signals into an Aux Channel Strip, it is mostly used to receive one of the 64 Auxiliary Busses (represented by the 64 Audio Components "Bus").
- When you create a new Aux Send on any Channel Strip and select "Bus n", then Logic automatically creates a new Aux Channel Strip and uses that Bus (the Audio Component "Bus n") as the Input for that Aux Channel Strip.
- So the Audio Component "Bus" (without any assigned Channel Strip) is the pipe and the Aux Channel Strip is the recipient of what is sent to that pipe.

# ➡ Logic Pro X - Signal Flow

Here is a simplified Signal Flow Diagram of the Logic mixer with the Busses and Audio Components:

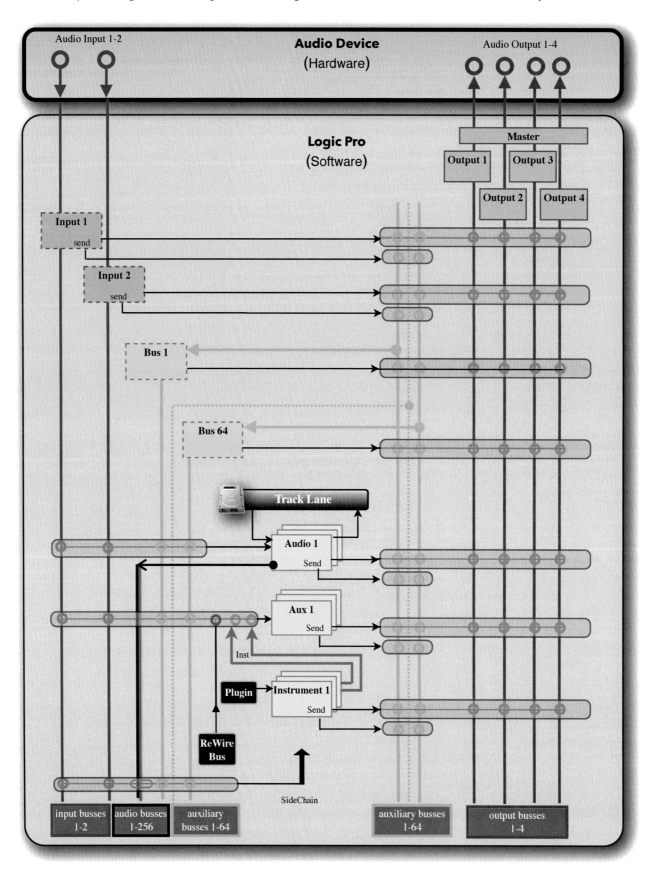

# Into the Channel Strip

In the previous section we looked at the signal flow in general without talking about the type of signal, and with type of signal I mean "how many channels" does a signal have. Yes, channels. Another term with so many different meanings. In this context, a channel means a discrete audio signal from a single source. For example, one microphone, or the signal from an electric guitar.

> **A single Channel represents a transmitted or a recorded Audio Signal, a single source**

An audio signal can have three different channel configurations:
- ▶ **One Channel**: This is what's called a mono signal
- ▶ **Two Channels**: This is what's called a stereo signal
- ▶ **Multiple Channels**: This is what's called a surround sound signal

The Channel Strips on traditional mixing consoles were "hard wired". Most of them were mono Channel Strips and some had one or two stereo Channel Strips. This determined what you could feed into a specific Channel Strip. Logic's Channel Strips are extremely flexible. They can adapt to whatever channel configuration you want it to be. Let's start with the Input.

There are different types of inputs you can feed into a Channel Strip. I sort them in the following three groups:

➡ *Instrument Plugin*

Only the Instrument Channel Strip has this option.

Instead of an Input Button, you have a Plugin Button ❶ on top of the Channel Strip that opens a popup menu ❷ with all the available Instrument Plugins. They function as the audio source for that Channel Strip (based on the MIDI signal it receives at its input).

🔘 **Channel Selection**

Each Plugin in the popup menu has a submenu ❸ with a selection of the available channel configurations. This determines how many channels you feed that Channel Strip. Different Plugins provide different options from mono, to stereo, and even 5.1 surround (I explain the special "*Multi Output*" a little bit later).

The Plugin Button itself doesn't indicate how many audio channels the Plugin is generating, but you can see it on the Volume Meter if you have one ❹, two ❺, or six ❻ LED bars.

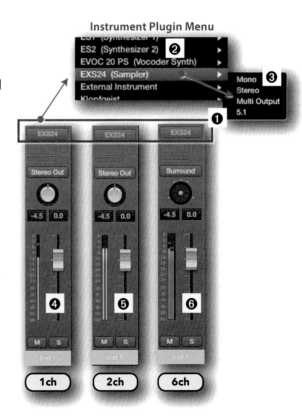

## ➡ *Input Busses*

The Audio Channel Strip ❶ and the Aux Channel Strip ❷ have the same type of Input Button:

### 🌑 Input Button

The Input Button consists of two buttons:

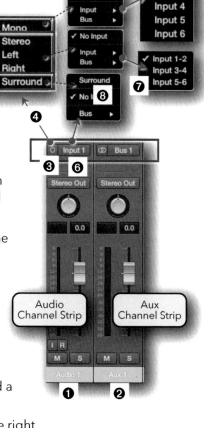

▸ **Channel Selection ❸**: The left button determines how many and also which channel you want to feed into the Channel Strip. You can click on the Button to toggle between Mono ⭕ and Stereo ⭕⭕, or *ctr+click* on the button to open the popup menu ❹ with more options:

- ⭕ *Mono*: This lets you select any of the Mono Busses ❺ from the button ❻ on the right to feed a mono signal into the Channel Strip

- ⭕⭕ *Stereo*: This lets you select any of the Stereo Busses ❼ from the button on the right to feed a stereo signal into the Channel Strip

- ⭕⭕ *Left*: This lets you select any of the Stereo Busses ❼ from the button on the right, but you feed only the left channel of the selected stereo pair as a mono signal into the Channel Strip

- ⭕⭕ *Right*: This lets you select any of the Stereo Busses ❼ from the button on the right, but you feed only the right channel of the selected stereo pair as a mono signal into the Channel Strip

- ⊞ *Surround*: This lets you select the surround input ❽ (six channels from the Audio Interface) or any of the Busses to feed a multi-channel surround signal into the Channel Strip

▸ **Bus Selection ❻**: The popup menu, that opens when you click on the right button changes depending on what Channel option you have selected on the button to the left ❸.

### 🌑 Audio Channel Strip only

The Audio Channel Strip does not only play what you feed it from the selected input busses ❻, it also plays back the Audio Region on the Track's Track Lane. Those Audio Regions also contain channels (one, two, or multiple) indicated by the Channel Symbol ❾. The Channel Selection you made with the left Input Button ❸ also determines which of those channels contained in the audio file will be fed into the Channel Strip. This is a quick way to play only one channel of a stereo file (Left ⭕⭕ or Right ⭕⭕) without splitting it first into two split mono files.

**Tracks Window**

These are the various Channel Symbols and their meanings:

- **Mono**: ⭕ uncompressed (aiff, wav), ⭕ compressed (mp3.m4a), ⭕ Apple Loop

- **Stereo**: ⭕⭕ uncompressed, ⭕⭕ compressed, ⭕⭕ Apple Loop

- **Surround**: ⊞ Surround Sound (multichannel)

### 💀 Aux Channel Strip only

The Aux Channel Strip is kind of a multi-purpose Channel Strip. The popup menu ❶ for the Input Button ❷ changes dynamically, depending on your current setup:

▶ **Bus**: This is the main use as a return for the Aux Sends (Bus 1-64).

▶ **Input**: If you select an Input Bus (the input channel of the currently used Audio Interface), then you can use it as a live audio input if you don't need to record it. For example, a sound module that plays along with your sequencer, the audio feed from an external video tape machine, an open mic from the recording room, or the live feed from a conference call.

▶ **Rewire ❶**: If you have a Rewire Slave running, then its audio returns will be displayed in the Input Menu ❸. I discuss that in the *Rewire* chapter.

▶ **Multi-Output Instrument Return**: If you have any Software Instrument Plugins loaded in your Project that are set to Multi-Output, then those Instruments will also be listed in the Input Menu ❹ with a submenu ❺ to select the individual outputs. I discuss the details in the Multi-Timbral section of the *Advanced MIDI* chapter.

### ➡ *Dedicated Audio Components*

The three Channel Strip Types (**Input Channel Strip, Output Channel Strip, Bus Channel Strip**), that represent one of three types of Busses we discussed earlier, have only one single Input Button that toggles between Mono and Stereo.

 **Mono** **Stereo**

### 💀 Input Channel Strip

Here is the important part. This button is not a simple mono/stereo switch. To better understand that, let's put all the pieces together we learned so far.

- The Channel Strip is actually an Environment Object "Input Channel Strip"
- This Environment Object is assigned to the Audio Component "Input"
- Each Input Channel of the currently selected Audio Interface is represented by an individual Audio Component (that Logic creates automatically when you select an Audio Interface)
- **Important**: Logic creates an Audio Component for each input channel (1, 2, 3, etc.), plus additional Audio Components for their stereo pairs (1-2, 3-4, etc.).
- When you create an Environment Object, you can assign it to a mono-channel Audio Component or a stereo-channel Audio Component.
- The different popup menus we saw earlier when selecting an Input ❻ for an Audio Channels Strip, show these different Audio Components, depending on if you selected mono ❼ or stereo ❽.
- When toggling the Input Button on an Input Channel Strip, you switch the assignment for that Channel Strip between the Mono and Stereo Component. For example, Input 1-2 <> Input 1, or Input 3-4 <> Input 3, etc.
- If you have the "Type and Number Label" ❾ displayed (Shortcut: *Channel Strip ➤ Channel Strip Component ➤*), then you can see which Audio Component the Channel Strip is assigned to.
- If you have the Environment Window open, you can see how this Input Button switches the assignment of the Audio Component for that Channel Strip.

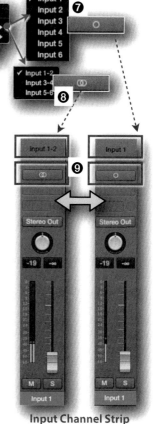

**Input Channel Strip**

## 🖥 Output Channel Strip

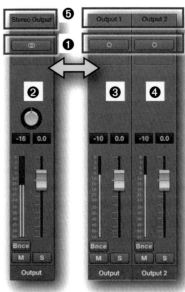

**Output Channel Strip**

First of all, let's be clear what the input of an Output Channel Strip means: It is the sum of all signals in your Project sent to this Output (for example, Output 1-2). That summed signal can be processed on that Channel Strip before it reaches the output channel of your assigned Audio Interface.

The Input Button ❶ on the Output Channel Strip behaves similar to the Input Channel Strip, with a little twist:

- Logic also creates Audio Components for each output channel (1, 2, 3, etc.) of the currently selected Audio Device, plus additional Audio Components for the stereo pairs (1-2, 3-4, etc.).
- The Input Button on the Output Channel Strip can be toggled between Mono [  O  ] and Stereo [  ∞  ].
- Again, the Channel Strip is just the Environment Object (Output Channel Strip) assigned to an Audio Component ("Output"), and toggling the Mono-Stereo Button switches the assignment of that Channel Strip between the mono-channel Audio Component and the stereo-channel Audio Component.
- *__Important__*: Switching the Input Button on an Output Channel Strip does not turn your output into a mono output! I will show a little later how to accomplish that.
- When switching a stereo Output Channel Strip to mono that is assigned to Audio Component "Output 1-2" ❷, then Logic creates a second Output Channel Strip and reassigns both Output Channel Strips to the separate "Output 1" ❸ and "Output 2" ❹. This does not change the output routing in your Project. You just control the output bus 1 and 2 now with two separate mono Channel Strips instead of a single Stereo Channel Strip (for example, apply different FX Plugins to the left and right channel).
- If you have the "Type and Number Label" ❺ displayed (Shortcut: *Channel Strip ➤ Channel Strip Component ➤*), then you can see which Audio Component the Channel Strip is assigned to.
- If you have the Environment Window open, you can see how this Input Button switches the assignment of the Audio Component for that Channel Strip. If switching the two mono channels back to stereo ❻, then one of the Environment Objects ❼ shows the message that this object can't be assigned to Audio Component "Output 2", because it is used in the stereo pair assignment.

**Environment**

## 🖥 Bus Channel Strip

A Bus Channel Strip is the (optional) Environment Object that is assigned to one of the 64 internal Audio Components "Bus". It also has the Stereo-Mono Input Button ❽, however, it functions differently:

- When you send a stereo signal to Bus 1 (Auxiliary Busses 1), it will be sent to the Audio Component "Bus 1". That signal then can be used as an input signal on any Audio Channel Strip or Aux Channel Strip.
- Technically, you don't need to create a Channel Strip for that Audio Component "Bus 1". The Bus Channel Strips are redundant in a basic Aux Send setup.
- If you created a Bus Channel Strip, then its controls (including the Input Button) are affecting the summed signal on that bus.
- For example, when you send a stereo signal to "Bus 1" and select mono [  O  ] ❾ on "Bus Channel Strip 1", then that signal on Bus 1 will be mixed down to a mono signal and is available now as a mono signal when you select it as an input on an Audio Channel Strip or Aux Channel Strip.

**Bus Channel Strip**

# Inside The Channel Strip

The signal flow on a Channel Strip is not only determined by the Input selection. In addition to selecting Mono ◯ ◯◯ ◯◯ (one channel ) or Stereo ◯◯ (two channels) from the Input Button, that determines how many channels you are feeding the Channel Strip, there are other components that can affect the amount of channels while "traveling through the Channel Strip".

Here is an example with three Channel Strips routed to a Stereo Output. I demonstrate these examples with a surround sound signals later in the *Surround* chapter.

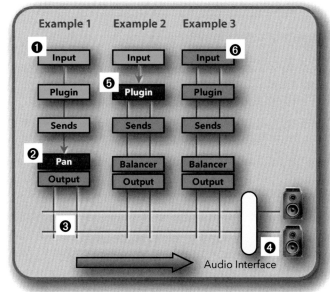

- ▶ **Example 1**: The input signal ❶ is mono (one audio channel). It passes through the Audio FX Plugins (still mono) and any Aux Send is sent as a single audio channel. The Pan Knob ❷ now lets you "place" the single channel between the two output channels ❸, which goes to the two speakers connected to the output jacks of the Audio Interface ❹ (or bounced to an audio file).

- ▶ **Example 2**: The input again is mono, but you are feeding it to a Stereo Plugin ❺. That Stereo Plugin creates a stereo signal (two channels) out of the single channel, for example, using a stereo reverb or a stereo delay, etc. From now on, the signal inside the Channel Strip is stereo, which means Aux Sends are also stereo (stereo bus) and the Pan Knob now functions as a Stereo Balancer.

- ▶ **Example 3**: In this example, you are feeding a stereo signal (two channels) to the input ❻. The entire Channel Strip stays stereo, with stereo Aux Sends and the Stereo Balancer at the end of the Channel Strip.

## 💀 Plugins

Any Audio FX Plugin that you select from the Audio FX Plugin popup menu has a submenu ❺ that determines the input-output routing of the Plugin. That means, how many audio channels are you sending in and how many audio channels coming out of the Plugin. An option with only one word configures the Plugin with the same input and output channel configuration (I explain the surround options in the *Surround Sound* chapter).

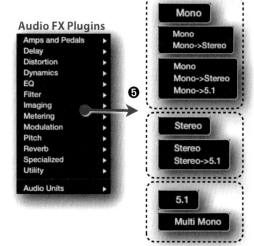

- • Mono, Stereo, 5.1, Multi Mono

Any option with the "->" sign describes how the input channels are converted to the output channels:

- • Mono->Stereo, Mono->5.1, Stereo->5.1

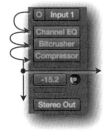

Please note that when you load multiple Audio FX Plugins, then the signal flow runs from top to bottom (daisy chained). The Input of the channel Strip feeds the input of the first Plugin, the output of the first Plugin feeds the input the second Plugin, and so on. The channel configuration of the output of the last Plugin determines how many channels are sent to the Auxiliary Busses via the Aux Send. Any Plugin in the chain can change the channel configuration based on their submenus ❺.

## Aux Sends

*Clicking* on the Aux Send Button ❶ opens the popup menu with all the 64 Auxiliary Busses ❷, represented by the Audio Component "*Bus 1*" ... "*Bus 64*". The name in parenthesis ❸ are the names of the Aux Channel Strip(s) that use that Bus as an input (Audio Channel Strips that use that Bus as an input are not displayed), or the custom names entered in the *Mix ➤ I/O Labels ...* window.

▶ **No Channel Information**: The popup menu has no indication how many channels a specific Bus carries. The Bus (or let's say the Audio Component "Bus") automatically adjusts to whatever signal you are sending to it from the Channel Strip. As we have just learned, that is determined by the output of the last Audio FX Plugin on that Channel Strip (or the Pan Knob, if you selected the "Post Pan" ❹ option).

▶ **Yes Channel Information**: One way to find out how many channels a specific Bus has, is to look at the Aux Channel Strip that uses that Bus as an input. The Input Button ❺ of the Aux Channel Strip (as we discussed earlier) displays the corresponding Channel Symbol ( ), or look at the Volume Meter ❻ that also gives you a hint.

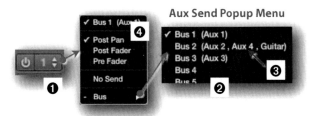

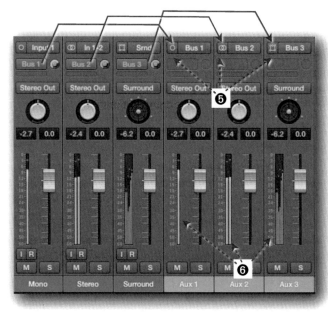

**Aux Send Popup Menu**

## Out of the Channel Strip

Now let's look at the final destination of the signal flow, what is coming out of the Channel Strip. Please note that there are a few more components than just the Output Button that determine the Output of the Channel Strip.

▶ **Output Button**: Where do you route the audio channels on the individual Channel Strips to.

▶ **I/O Assignments ❼**: A little, often overlooked, setting that has a word to say about where the output signal ends up.

▶ **Pan Control ❽**: A control in different shapes and forms that distributes the channels of the Channel Strip to the Output Busses.

▶ **Pan Law ❾**: Another easy to be overlooked setting that affects the Pan Control.

▶ **Bounce ❿**: As part of the Output considerations, the Bounce Window also has a few settings that lets you store the output channels as individual mono signals (split mono files) or combined signals (interleaved stereo or surround files).

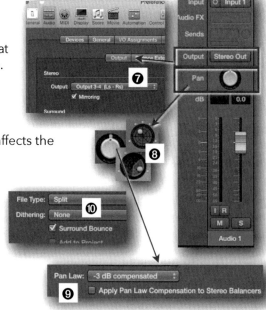

## ➡ *Output Button*

The Output Button ❶ on each Channel Strip selects the Output Bus (represented by the Audio Component "Output"). That means, you decide where the signal at the end of the Channel Strip will flow to.

A few things to know about the Outputs:

- As we discussed in the Input Section, the number of available Outputs depends on the currently selected Audio Interface (*Preferences ➤ Audio ➤ Devices ➤ Output Device*). Logic automatically creates Audio Components for each output channel of that Audio Interface.
- Same as with the input channels, Logic creates separate Audio Components for the individual (mono) output channels (Output 1, Output 2, etc.) and also creates Audio Components for the stereo pairs (Output 1-2, Output 3-4, etc.).
- For each new Project, Logic automatically creates the Output Channel Strip object "Output" ❷ assigned to the Audio Component "Output 1-2". This is the default output selected for new Channel Strips.
- The Output Button popup menu ❸ displays three formats you can choose from:

  ▶ **Stereo Output**: All the stereo pairs for the current Audio Interface are listed. In parenthesis are the User names ❹ that you can setup in the I/O Labels Window ❹ (*Mix ➤ I/O Labels...*).

  ▶ **Surround**: Selecting this option will change the Pan Control to Surround Control using output busses for the surround format that you configured in the *Preferences ➤ Audio ➤ I/O Assignments*. More details about that in the *Surround Sound* chapter.

  ▶ **Mono**: This last option opens a submenu ❺ with all the mono outputs of the current Audio Interface. Selecting any of the mono outputs will remove the Pan Control from the Channel Strip. The output signal from the Channel Strip will be sent directly to a single output channel.

**I/O Labels Window**

## ☺ Scroll to follow the Signal Flow

The Output Button (and the Aux Send Button) has a hidden functionality.

**Inspector Channel Strips**

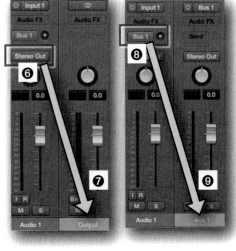

  ▶ **Output Button**: *Double-click* on the Output Button and the Mixer scrolls to the right to display the now selected Output Channel Strip. This is useful when you have a lot of Tracks and the Output Channel Strip is placed all the way on the right end of the Mixer Window.

  ▶ **Aux Button**: Same technique for the Aux Channel Strips. *Click* the Aux Send Button of any Channel Strip and the Mixer Window scrolls to (and selects) the Aux Channel Strip that uses that Bus as its input.

**Inspector Channel Strip**: There is a similar functionality with the two Inspector Channel Strips in the Main Inspector. *Click* the Output Button ❻ on the left Channel Strip to display that Output Channel Strip ❼ on the right, or *click* on an Aux Send Button ❽ to display that Aux Channel Strip ❾ on the right.

## ➡ I/O Assignments

There is a setting buried deep in the Preferences window (*Preferences ➤ Audio ➤ I/O Assignments ➤ Output*) that affects where the signal flows through the Output.

Preferences ➤ Audio ➤ I/O Assignments ➤ Output

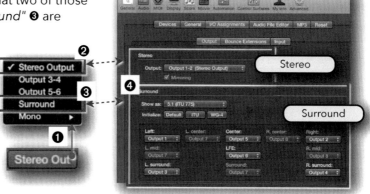

- When you open the popup menu for the Output options by clicking the Output Button ❶ on a Channel Strip, you have to be aware that two of those options, "*Stereo Output*" ❷ and "*Surround*" ❸ are only *variables*. They don't show what actual output channel you are sending the signal to.

- These two variables have to be configured ❹ in the I/O Assignments Preferences window (*Preferences ➤ Audio ➤ I/O Assignments ➤ Output*), which can also be accessed directly from the Main Menu *Mix ➤ I/O Assignments...*

- The default settings works in most Logic setups and that's why you might never need to visit that page. However, there are some interesting options that could be useful in some situations.

## 💀 Stereo Output Configuration

Here is how you configure the Stereo Output. I show the Surround configuration in the *Surround Sound* chapter.

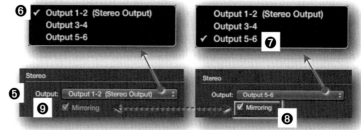

- The Output ❺ parameter determines which output channel of your current Audio Interface is used when "Stereo Output" ❷ is selected from the Output Button ❶ of a Channel Strip. The popup menu displays all the available stereo output pairs.

- If you choose "Output 1-2" ❻, then the signal on a Channel Strip is routed to output channel 1-2 of your Audio Interface when you select "Stereo Output" ❷ on its Output Button.

- If you choose "Output 5-6" ❼, then the signal on a Channel Strip is routed to output channel 5-6 of your Audio Interface when you select "Stereo Output" ❷ on its Output Button.

- **Mirroring**: If you choose any output channel other than "Output 1-2", then the Mirroring checkbox will be available (it is grayed out ❾ when Output 1-2 is selected). When you select the Mirroring checkbox, then the output signal of the Channel Strip is also sent to Output 1-2 (mirrored ❽), in addition to the selected output ❼ (i.e. Output 5-6). This lets you feed the output of your mixer to a second destination (recording booth, feed for a video conference, headphones amp, etc.).

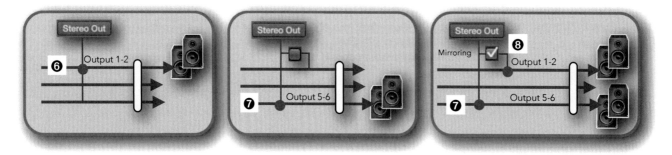

## ➡ Pan Control

The Pan Control lets you control how to assign the output signal of a Channel Strip to the selected output busses. The Pan Control can have different appearances and functions:

- ▸ ❶ **None:** If you select a mono output channel from the Output Button, then the Pan Knob will disappear from the Channel Strip because there is no need for it. The signal will be routed directly to one specific output channel.

- ▸ ❷ **Pan Knob**: If the signal on the Channel Strip is mono, but the output routing is stereo, then the Pan Knob functions as a panorama control. It sets how much of the mono signal is sent to the left or right output channel and by doing so positioning the mono signal on the stereo field.

- ▸ ❸ **Balance Knob**: If the signal on the Channel Strip is stereo and it is routed to a stereo output, then the Pan Knob functions as a balance control, called a "Stereo Balancer" (it still looks the same). Moving the knob to the left lowers the level of the right channel and vice versa. Use the *Direction Mixer* ❻ Plugin for more pan options of a stereo signal. It lets you move the stereo signal as it is more to the left or right, flip the channels, or change the "spread" to make it more mono (in phase) or more stereo (out of phase). Please note that the Output Channel Strip has a Balance Knob too, and you can also use the Direction Mixer on the Output Channel Strip.

- ▸ ❹ **Binaural Panner**: If the Output is set to stereo, then you can select *Binaural* ❼ as an additional option in the Output popup menu, which changes the Pan Knob to the Binaural Panner. *Double -click* on the Panner to open a separate floating window with all the controls ❽. This can be used for special headphone mixes. However, you can use the *Binaural Post-Processing* ❾ Plugin (*Audio FX Plugins ➤ Imaging ➤*) to process the pan effects for speaker playback.

- ▸ ❺ **Surround Panner**: If the output is set to Surround, then the Pan Knob changes to the Surround Panner or Surround Balancer. More on that in the *Surround* chapter.

## ➡ Pan Law

Pan Law is a setting that affects how the Pan Knob on a Channel Strip works. If you are recording your song and set your levels and pan position so they just sound the way you like, then you might not need to bother with that setting. However, if your work requires accurate level settings, for example, when importing or exporting stems, then you should read the next pages where I explain how Pan Law works.

## 🔘 Pan Knob Concept

Let's start with a simplified diagram that demonstrates how a Pan Knob works. This should also clarify why a Pan Knob functions as a Stereo Balancer when using it on a stereo Channel Strip. I will cover all those audio production topics in my next book in the Graphically Enhanced Manuals (GEM) series:

*"Recording Techniques 2.0 - The New Handbook"*

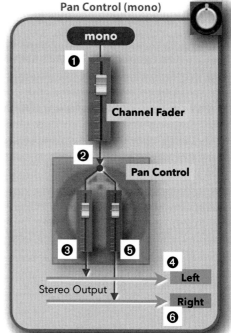

▶ **Mono (Panorama)**: This is what happens when you feed a single channel (mono signal ❶) into the Pan Control.

- The signal will first be split into two signals ❷.
- The left signal runs through a volume fader ❸ before it is added to the left bus ❹ of the Stereo Output.
- The right signal runs through its own volume fader ❺ and is added to the right bus ❻ of the Stereo Output.
- Turning the Pan Knob to the left will lower the right volume fader ❺. The more you turn to the left, the more the right fader is turned down, all the way to -∞dB (mute). At this moment, you will hear the signal on the Stereo Output only coming out of the left speaker ❹.
- Turning the Pan Knob to the right will lower the left volume fader ❸. The more you turn to the right, the more the left Fader is turned down, all the way to -∞dB. At this moment you will hear the signal on the Stereo Output only coming out of the right speaker ❻.

▶ **Stereo (Stereo Balancer)**: This is what happens when you feed two channels (stereo signal ❼) into the Pan Control.

- You still have the two faders inside the Pan Control.
- The only difference is that the incoming signal doesn't have to be split up, because you are already feeding the Pan Control two signals.
- The left channel of the Channel Strip is feeding the left volume fader ❽ inside the Pan Control and the right channel of the Channel Strip is feeding the right volume fader ❾ inside the Pan Control.
- Turning the Pan Knob to the left will lower the right volume fader ❾. The more you turn to the left, the more the right fader is turned down, all the way to -∞dB. At this moment, you will hear the signal on the Stereo Output only coming out of the left speaker.
- Turning the Pan Knob to the right will lower the left volume fader ❽. The more you turn to the right, the more the left Fader is turned down, all the way to -∞dB. At this moment, you will hear the signal on the Stereo Output only coming out of the right speaker.

*Attention*: Turning the Pan Knob on a stereo signal will not affect the stereo image (although it sounds like you are shifting the stereo signal to the left or right). You are only affecting one channel at a time (one fader inside the Pan Control), depending upon which side you are turning the knob. If you want to shift the stereo signal to the left or right while keeping its stereo balance (relative volume of left-right channel), then you have to add the Audio FX Plugin *"Direction Mixer"* onto the Channel Strip.

## 💀 Pan Law options

There are three options you can choose for the Pan Law from the Pan Law popup menu ❶ in the *Project Settings ➤ Audio.*

In the following diagram, I show the two volume fader positions inside the Pan Control when the knob is turned all the way to the left ❷, at the center ❸, and all the way to the right ❹.

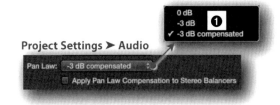

Project Settings ➤ Audio

▶ **0dB ❺**: This is the behavior I just described. Turning the Pan Knob to one side will just lower the level on the opposite channel. However, this has a potential problem:

Remember that the first step in the Pan Control is to split the single channel into two channels. If that mono signal had a level of 0dB, then having two of those signals with 0dB would double the overall level. Think about one drummer playing versus two drummers playing, it becomes twice as loud. In technical terms, twice as loud means +6dB (only if the two signals are in-phase). Now think about it. If you have a mono signal and you move the Pan Knob between extreme left 🔘 to extreme right 🔘, then not only would the signal move from left to right, it would also change its level. On the extreme left and on the extreme right position, only one channel is playing. However, the more you move the Pan Knob to the center, the louder the signal gets, because, in the center position the signal is playing through the left and right channel, therefore, sounding twice as loud.

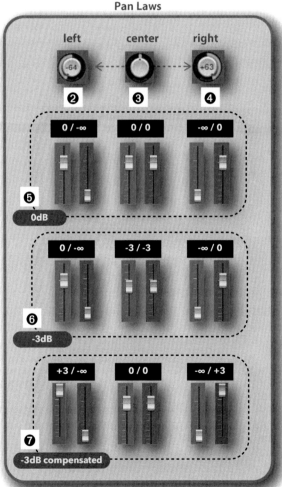

Pan Laws

▶ **-3dB ❻**: This Pan Law option changes the behavior of the Pan Control to eliminate that problem:

- Both faders are lowered by -3dB when the Pan Knob is at the center position (total of -6dB).

- Moving the Pan Knob to the left will gradually move the right fader to -∞dB, which means you loose a -3dB signal.

- However, at the same time while moving the Pan Knob to the left, the left fader will gradually move up by 3dB (to the 0dB position) to compensate for the loss of the right signal.

- The same thing happens when you move the Pan Knob to the right. The left fader will move down to -∞dB, while the right fader moves up to 0dB.

- The result of all of this is that when panning between left-center-right, the level of signal stays the same.

▶ **-3dB compensated ❼**: While the -3dB Pan Law maintains the same level when panning, it has the negative "side effect" that it lowers the signal by 3dB when the Pan Knob is at the center position. The "-3dB compensated" Pan Law takes care of that.

- In the center position, the two faders stay at 0dB, meaning that the mono signal is passing through with its original level.

- Moving the Pan Knob to the left will again gradually move the right fader to -∞dB and raise the left fader by +3dB to maintain the same overall level.

- Moving the Pan Knob to the right will gradually move the left fader to -∞dB and raise the right fader by +3dB to maintain the same overall level.

## Pan Law - Stereo

Once you understand the functionality of the Pan Control when using it on a mono Channel Strip vs. on a stereo Channel Strip and then wrap your head around the Pan Law concepts, then you should have no problem understanding the effect of the final checkbox "Apply Pan Law Compensation to Stereo Balancers".

- First of all, "Stereo Balancer" is another word for "Pan Knob used on a stereo Channel Strip".

- Now we know that the Pan Knob functions the same regarding its two internal faders. The only difference is that in mono, you feed the same signal to the those faders, while in stereo, you feed the individual left and right stereo signal to those left and right faders.

- Because the Pan Law only determines what the faders are doing in response to the Pan Knob position, it doesn't matter if the signal going through those two faders is a dual mono signal, or a true stereo signal.

- The effect of the checkbox is the following:

  - ☐ The Pan Law setting only affects the Pan Knob of mono Channel Strips. Stereo Channel Strips use the default "0dB" settings.

  - ☑ The Pan Law setting you choose from the popup menu is applied to Pan Knobs on mono Channel Strips and Stereo Channel Strips.

*Attention:* If you need to maintain accurate levels of your signals (stereo or mono) when passing through the Pan Control, then you should set the Pan Law to "0dB". Please note that it is set to "-3dB compensated" by default for a new Project.


# Mixing to Mono

Sometimes you need to make a mono mix of your Project for some reason. This is not as easy as pushing a mono button. Everything in Logic seems to be automatically in stereo. Here is a tip how to switch between mono and stereo mixing..

As I pointed out in this chapter, changing the Input Button on an Output Channel Strip from Stereo ▭ to Mono ▭ doesn't let you mix your Project to mono. You just have two separate Channel Strips. Here is how you can mix your Project to a mono file:

- ☑ Insert the Audio FX Plugin "*Gain*" ❶ into the Output Channel Strip.

- ☑ Enable the Mono Button ❷ in the Gain Plugin Window. This sums the stereo signal on the Output Channel Strip into a dual mono signal. This little button lets you toggle your mix between stereo and mono to check for phase cancelation issues.

- ☑ Now bounce ❸ the Project with the File Type set to "Split" ❹ in the Bounce Window. This will bounce the Stereo Output to two split mono files (.L and .R).

- ☑ Because you merged the Stereo Output busses to mono, both audio files will be identical and you can use either one as the mono mix of your Project (just delete the extension ".L" or ".R" of the fine name).

Plugins ➤ Utility ➤ Gain

Bounce Window

Output Channel Strip

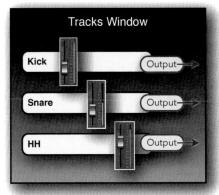

Tracks Window

"Grouping" is a common technique when mixing a Project. It is the procedure of combining multiple Channel Strips and "treat" that group as one.

For example, you have three Channel Strips for the individual Tracks of a drum recording (Kick, Snare, HH). You have set the balance on the three Channel Strips, but want to raise the level of the entire drum set. Instead of raising each Volume Fader individually by the same amount, you use the grouping technique.

There are different ways to group Channel Strips, each with their own advantages and disadvantages:

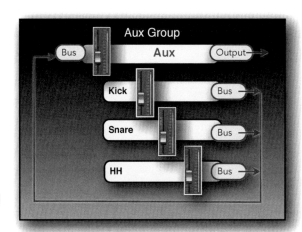

###  Aux Groups

This technique is also known as a Summing Group or Audio Group. In our example, you send the output of all three Channel Strips not to the output, but to a bus and use that bus as the input of an Aux Channel Strip. You still can control each individual Track with its own Channel Strip while controlling the "sum of all" Channel Strips (their summed audio signal) with the Aux Channel Strip.

The *Summing Stack* version of Logic's Track Stacks uses this technique.

###  VCA Groups

VCA stands for "Voltage Controlled Amplifier". It describes the type of Faders where the position of the Fader determines a specific voltage level. That voltage level controls an amplifier the signal on the Channel Strip runs through. Changing the Fader position, changes the control voltages that is sent to the amplifier on that Channel Strip, which changes the signal level running through that Channel Strip. The Fader of the Master Channel Strip just adds an additional voltage signal that offsets the VCA level on the individual Faders.

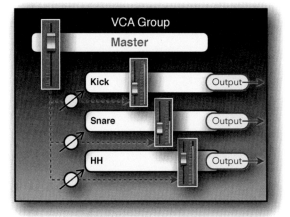

The *Folder Stack* version of Logic's Track Stacks and the VCA Faders use that technique.

###  Channel Strip Groups

This technique "links" a wide variety of controls and elements on all Channel Strips that you assign to the same group. This is the most powerful grouping techniques because it goes beyond Faders and signal flow, as we will see in a moment.

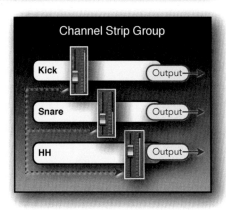

### Ad-hoc Group

This technique is a variation of the Channel Strip Group. It lets you link Channel Strip controls of selected Channel Strip together just by temporarily (ad-hoc) selecting Channel Strips without assigning them first to a Group.

# Aux Groups

Aux Groups (also referred to as Summing Groups or Audio Groups) are a common mixing technique. It has one major advantage over all the other grouping techniques, "Group Processing".

Here is the basic concept:

▸ **Aux Group**: You have a group of Channel Strips ❶ that you want to control as an Aux Group. For example, six Channel Strips with the individual Tracks of a drum recording (Kick, Snare, HH, etc.).

▸ **Summing Bus**: On all those Channel Strips (they don't have to be adjacent), you change the output routing. Instead of sending the output to the Stereo Output, you send them to the same Bus (in this example, "Bus 1"❷).

▸ **Aux Return**: You create an Aux Channel Strip ❸ with that same "Summing" Bus as its input ❺ ("Bus 1"). Logic automatically creates that Aux Channel Strip when you choose a Bus on any Channel Strip (Aux Send or Output).

▸ **Stereo Output**: The output of the Aux Channel Strip ❹ is routed as a default to the Output Channel Strip ❺.

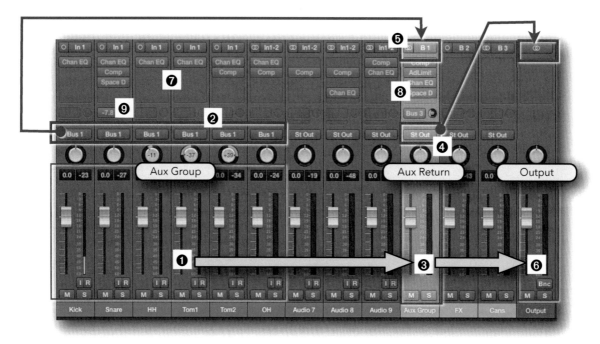

## A few things to consider:

• This grouping technique allows you to adjust the level ❶ and effects ❼ on the Channel Strips in that group individually to get the balance and the individual sounds right.

• Use the Volume Fader ❸ on the Aux Return to adjust the overall level of the entire group (the whole drum set) or conveniently fade the group in or out with one single fader.

• The main advantage of an Aux Group is that you can apply effects (and Aux sends) ❽ to the Aux Return, which affects the entire group, the summed signal. For example, compress the summed signal, apply EQ or FX Plugins, or use the Aux Sends.

• Using Aux Sends ❾ on the individual Channel Strips of the Aux Group is problematic. For example, fading out (or lowering) the Volume Fader of the Aux Return will lower the volume of the summed signal, but the level of the Aux Send on the individual Channel Strips is not affected, and therefore, could change the balance between wet/dry. For example you would fade out the Aux Return ❸, but the Channel Strip for the Snare ❾ still sends its signal to the Reverb.

• Logic's Summing Stack is an easy way to create an Aux Group. It has the additional advantage that the Volume Fader of the Aux Return (the Main Track of the Summing Stack) also controls the Aux Sends of the individual Tracks in the Group.

# VCA Groups

This is one of the big new features introduced in LPX v10.1. But before using this VCA feature, it requires a basic understanding of the concept of VCA Faders (used in high-end mixing consoles) in order to decide when and how to use it in your mix.

### ● VCA Concept

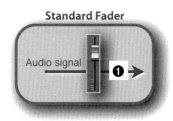

Here is a little background information to get the terminology right:

- ▶ **Standard Fader**: A standard Fader on an analog mixing console functions like a resistor. The audio signal runs through the Fader ❶ and by moving the Fader up or down, you affect how much of the audio signal goes through, and therefore, determining the audio level.

- ▶ **VCA Fader**: A VCA Fader (similar to a synthesizer component "VCA") uses a circuitry, a so-called VCA ❷ (Voltage Controlled Amplifier/Attenuator). The VCA component determines how much of the audio signal (the level) goes through, that means how much to amplify or attenuate the signal passing through that VCA. Here is the important part: The Fader ❸ itself is not part of the signal chain, it only sends out a control signal ❹ (DC, Direct Current), that sets the amount of amplification or attenuation for the VCA. A Fader is controlling a VCA, hence the name "VCA Fader". Moving the Fader ❸, will change the value of the control signal ❹ it is sending to the VCA ❷, resulting in a change of the audio signal level that runs through the VCA. Although the Faders in the Logic Mixer are based on computer code (processing data), you can think of those Faders as VCA Faders.

**VCA Fader**

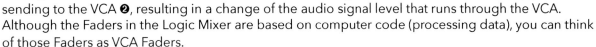

- ▶ **VCA Master Fader** (VCA Channel Strip): So the Fader on each Channel Strip is technically a VCA Fader that sends its control signal to the VCA component on that Channel Strip to set the audio level (the volume). Now in addition to those VCA Faders, there are so-called *VCA Master Faders*. These are Channel Strips that contain only a VCA Fader ❺ that sends out a control signal ❻. There is no audio signal running through those Channel Strips (VCA Channel Strips). Be careful with the terminology, because these "VCA Master Faders" are also called just "VCA Faders".

**VCA Master Fader**

- ▶ **VCA Group**:  Now here is the important part. The VCA component on each Channel Strip (the element in the audio signal flow that sets the audio level) can receive two control signals. One control signal is coming from its own Fader ❼ on the same Channel Strip, and a second control signal ❽ can come from a VCA Master Fader ❾. The actual result (how much the VCA on a Channel Strip changes the signal level) is the sum of both control signals. All the Channel Strips that receive their additional control signal from the same VCA Master Channel "belong

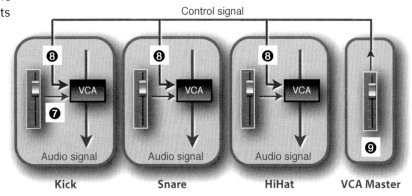

to that VCA Group". You can have multiple VCA Master Faders in your Mixer controlling different groups of Channel Strips, but each Chanel Strip can only be controlled by one Master VCA Fader ❽ (in addition to its own VCA Fader ❼).

## 🔵 VCA Usage

There are a few things you have keep in mind when using VCA Master Faders:

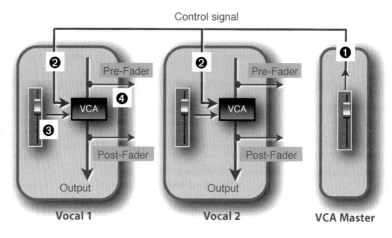

Control signal

Vocal 1    Vocal 2    VCA Master

- ▶ Technically, the Master VCA Fader sends a level offset ❶ to all Channel Strips ❷ it is controlling.
- ▶ Lowering the VCA Master Fader by 10dB will lower the signal level on all its Channel Strips in that VCA Group by 10dB.
- ▶ Moving the VCA Master Fader will not move the Fader on the Channel Strips that are controlled by that VCA Master Fader. The control signal goes directly to the VCA component and doesn't control the Fader on that Channel Strip.
- ▶ You can still move the Fader on each Channel Strip ❸ independently. It is just one of the two control signals that (combined with its own Channel Fader) determines the VCA level.
- ▶ Any Aux behavior on a Channel Strip doesn't change regardless of being assigned or not assigned to a VCA Master Fader. Pre-Fader Sends ❹ are located before the VCA, and therefore, are not affected by the level change coming from the VCA Master Fader ❷ or the Channel Strip Fader ❸.
- ▶ Any Automation on the individual Channel Strip is not affected by the VCA Master Fader, it just acts as an offset to the automation. You can even automate the VCA Master Channel itself if you want.

## ➡ *VCA Implementation in Logic*

### 🔵 VCA Slot

First, the Channel Strip in Logic has a Channel Strip Component, "VCA", which is hidden by default. When enabled, it adds an additional VCA Slot ❺ (a little black window, similar to the Group Slot) below the Pan Knob. Output ❻, Bus, and VCA Channel Strips don't have that Slot.

The VCA Slot has three functions:

- ▶ **Button**: *Click* on it to open the VCA Menu to manage the VCA Group assignment for the current Channel Strip
- ▶ **Display**: The VCA Slot shows the name of the assigned VCA Master Fader for that Channel Strip
- ▶ **Assign VCA Group**: *Opt+click* on a slot to assign the same VCA Group that was last added to a Channel Strip.

You can make the VCA Slot visible on all Channel Strips with the following commands:

- 🔘 *Ctr+click* on the Channel Strip background to open its *Shortcut Menu ➤ Channel Strip Components ➤ VCA*
- 🔘 *Ctr+click* on the Channel Strip background to open its *Shortcut Menu ➤ Configure Channel Strip Components* and select VCA ❼ from the window
- 🔘 Use the Key Command (*Show/Hide VCA*) *unassigned*
- 🔘 Creating the first VCA Fader automatically adds the VCA Slot to the Channel Strip

**Configure Channel Strip Components Window**

## 🌐 VCA Menu

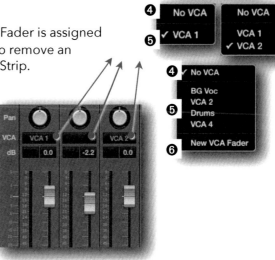

When you *long-click* on a VCA Slot, it opens the VCA Menu with all the commands to manage the VCA Group assignment for that Channel Strip.

The VCA Menu displays three sections:

▶ ❹ Top **No VCA**: This item is selected if no VCA Master Fader is assigned to that Channel Strip. It also functions as a command to remove an assigned VCA Master Fader from the current Channel Strip.

▶ ❺ MidIdle "**available VCA Faders**": This section lists all the currently available VCA Master Faders. If no VCA Master Fader has been created yet, then the section is not displayed. Select a VCA Master Fader from the menu to assign it to the current Channel Strip. The currently assigned VCA Fader has a checkmark.

▶ ❻ Bottom **New VCA Fader**: This command is only displayed if the current Channel Strip doesn't have a VCA Master Fader assigned to it. It creates a new VCA Master Fader and assigns it to the current Channel Strip.

## 🌐 VCA Master Fader

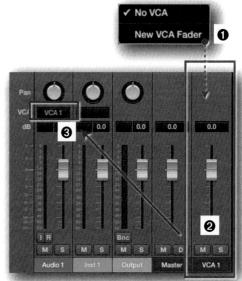

You can create a VCA Master Fader with the following commands:

🎚 **VCA Menu**: Using the "New VCA Fader" ❶ command from the VCA Menu creates a new VCA Master Fader Channel Strip ❷ and assigns it to the Channel Strip ❸ from where you selected the command.

🎚 **Key Command**: Using the Key Command (*Create New VCA Fader*) *unassigned*, creates a new VCA Master Fader without assigning it to any Channel Strip. However, it will now show up in the VCA Menu so you can assign it to any Channel Strip.

🎚 **Options Menu**: The Mixer's Options Menu includes the new command "*Create New VCA Fader*", which changes to "*Create New VCA Fader for Selected Channel Strips*" when you have one or more Channel Strips selected.

🎚 **Environment**: You can also create a VCA Master Fader in the Environment from its local menu *New* ➤ *Channel Strip* ➤ *VCA*

## 🌐 Using VCA Master Faders in Logic

Here are the various procedures, plus a few things you have to be aware of:

• A newly created VCA Master Fader is placed in the Mixer Window next to the Master Channel Strip ❷

• New VCA Master Faders are named VCA 1, VCA 2, etc.

• *Double-click* the Channel Strip Name of the VCA Master Fader to enter a new name for the VCA Fader. This will update the name in the VCA Menu and in the VCA Slot ❸ on each Channel that is assigned to that VCA Fader ("belongs to that VCA Group").

• Changing the color of the VCA Channel Strip will change the font in the VCA Slot accordingly.

## ➡ VCA Faders under the Hood

With the information so far, you can already start using the VCA Faders in your Project. However, there is more to the VCA implantation in Logic that meets the eye. Here is a more in-depth look at that topic:

The VCA Faders are not something completely new in Logic, they are more the extension of a feature that was already there. To better understand what I mean by that, we have to dig a little bit deeper. Once you read through the following pages, you will see why that background information might be necessary to avoid potential confusion. Keep in mind that VCA Faders are an advanced mixing and routing technique, and especially with a large scale mix, things can get pretty complicated, pretty fast.

### 💀 A Peek into the Environment

In the Environment chapter, we will learn about Channel Strip Types. Here is a quick rundown:

- Logic represents a virtual studio that is made up of **Objects**, the building blocks of that studio.
- The Objects are created and managed in the Environment where you create your virtual studio.
- There are different types of those Objects. One **Object Type** is called a **Channel Strip**.
- Logic differentiates between seven different **Channel Strip Types**.
- In the Logic Environment Window, those Channel Strip Objects look like old Logic 9 style Channel Strips. The more cooler looking Channel Strips in the Mixer Window are basically just aliases of those objects.
- The **Audio Channel Strip** or the **Instrument Channel Strip** are two of those Channel Strip Types. Another one is the "**Master Channel Strip**" ❶, that Logic creates automatically in each Project.
- The **Object Inspector** in the Environment displays the Channel Strip Type in the "Channel" Parameters, in this case, "Master" ❷.
- *Click* on the "Channel" Parameter to open the popup menu ❸ with a list of all seven Channel Strip Types.

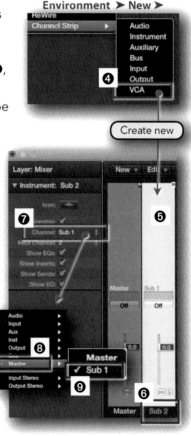

### 💀 Confusing Terminology

- The popup menu under the Local Menu *New* ➤ *Channel Strip* ➤ also lists the seven Channel Strip Types to create those new objects. However, the type "**Master**" is listed here as "**VCA**" ❹.
- Selecting VCA from this menu, creates a new Channel Strip Object. Let's assume it is a "**VCA Channel Strip**" ❺ and let's assume that it is just another name for Master Channel Strip.
- However, the new object that gets created is named "**Sub 2**" ❻, the second object in that category. But wait, it gets even better.
- The new Channel Strip Object (that we created with the "VCA" command ❹) and that is named "Sub 2" ❻, is listed in the Object Inspector ❼ under the "Channel" Parameter popup menu in the "Master" ❽ section as "**Sub 1**"❾ in its Submenu. Makes sense?
- Whenever you create a Folder Stack in your Project, Logic automatically creates such a "Sub n" Channel Strip Objects which is technically Master Channel Strips type.
- Whenever you create a VCA Fader in your Project, Logic automatically creates that same "Sub n" type of Channel Strips, which is again a Master Channel Strips type, however, it names them "**VCA 1**".

### 🎱 Type and Number Label

"*Type and Number Label*" is a term you should be aware of. Let's look at a Channel Strip Object, which has two Labels:

- ☑️ **Type**: These seven Labels describe the type of Channel Strip: Audio, Input, Aux, Inst, Output, Bus, Master/VCA.

- ☑️ **Number**: Logic has a limited number of each of those Channel Strip Types (mostly 256). The Number Label is the sequential number, added to the Type Label. For example, "Audio 1" ... "Audio 256", or "Aux 1" ... "Aux 256".

This Type and Number Label is displayed in various places:

- 🎚️ The Track Inspector in Logic's Main Window displays it as the "Channel" Parameter ❶

- 🎚️ It can be displayed in the Mixer Window at the top of each Channel Strip ❷. This component is hidden by default and can be made visible, for example, with the Local Mixer Menu *View ➤ Configure Channel Strip Components* ❸

- 🎚️ It is also displayed in the Environment Window's Object Inspector.

### 🎱 Channel Strip Type "Master"

With that Type and Number Label in mind, lets look at the Channel Strip Type "Master" through the history of Logic:

▶ **Master Channel Strip**

Logic automatically creates a Master Channel Strip ❹ in every Logic Project. This was the default behavior way before Logic Pro X. This Master Channel Strip is technically a VCA Master Fader. That terminology, however, was never used.

▶ **Stack Master Channel Strip**

In Logic Pro X, the Folder Stacks were introduced. The Main Track of a Folder Stack (a so-called Stack Master Channel Strip) is technically also a VCA Master Fader. But again, that terminology was not used. However, the Channel Strip Type "Master" was extended. Those Stack Master Channel Strips now also belonged to the Channel Strip Type "Master". Instead of numbering the object thru as "Master 1", "Master 2", Master 3", etc, Logic names only the first object "Master" (the original Master Channel Strip). When you create a new Folder Stack, Logic creates a new object assigned to that Channel Strip Type Master. The Type and Number

**Mixer Window**

Label, however, is "Sub 2" (2, because it is the second object of that type). The Channel Strip Name is "Sub 1", because it is the Main Track of the first Folder Stack. This is were the numbering offset comes from.

▶ **VCA Channel Strip**

With the introduction of VCA Faders in LPX v10.1, the compromise and weird naming convention got even worse. Because the Channel Strip Type "Master" was in its functionality a VCA Channel Strip all along, there was no problem that the new VCA Channel Strip now also belongs to that Channel Strip Type "Master". When you create your first VCA Channel Strip, Logic again creates an object assigned to the Channel Strip Type "Master". Again, the Type and Number Label will be "Sub 1" ❺ and the Channel Strip Name will be "VCA 1 ❻. No number offset this time ❼.

**Mixer Display Filter Buttons**

Mixer Display Filter Buttons

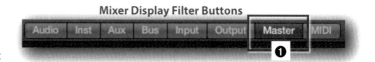

Here is something you have to look out for about the functionality of the Mixer Display Filter Buttons:

- Using the Mixer Display Filter Button "Master" ❶ to hide the Master Channel Strip will also hide all the VCA Channel Strips.
- Although the Stack Master Channel Strips (of a Folder Stack) also belong to the Channel Strip Type "Master", they are not affected by that Master Filter Button und will not be hidden. Those Channel Strips cannot be hidden from the Mixer at all.

 **Mixer Location**

The VCA Channel Strips are placed on the far right of the Mixer Window next to the Master Channel Strip. However, when you assign a VCA Fader to a Track (to edit automation), it will move to the left, following the order of its Track Number.

➡ *All Together Now*

The most important aspect to understand about all three kinds ❷ of Master Channel Strips, is that they are based on the VCA Fader ❸ concept. They just send a control signal ❹ and carry no audio signal. But keep in mind that they are slightly different in their behavior, as we've just discussed.

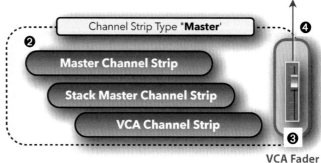

When you use all three kinds of the Channel Strip Type "Master" in your Project (Master Channel Strip, Stack Master Channel Strip, VCA Channel Strip), then you can create some complex routing and grouping configurations, and you really have to pay attention to avoid any confusion or surprises.

Here are two examples of using Folder Stacks and VCA Faders at the same time:

- Any Stack Master Channel Strip ❺ will also be listed in the VCA Slot ❻ and the VCA Menu ❼ with the other VCA Channel Strips. This lets you assign that Master Track ❺ to a Channel Strip ❽ that doesn't "belong" to that Folder Stack.
- The other way around, you could re-assign the Channel Strip of a Subtrack (belonging to a Folder Stack) to a VCA Master Fader so its Volume is controlled "outside" the Folder Stack.

**Folder Stacks and VCA Faders**

Here is another example of a Mixer layout that uses all three kinds of Channel Strip Types "Master". You have to keep an eye on which Channel Strips are carrying audio signals (blue), and which one are only sending control signals (red).

▶ **Master Channel Strip ❶**: The Master Channel Strip functions as a VCA Master Fader .
  - This is a default configuration that you cannot change. Therefore, there is no VCA Slot on the Output Channel Strip ❷ to assign it to a different VCA Fader.
  - In a Stereo Project, the Master Channel Strip controls only the Output Channel Strip 1-2.
  - In a Surround Project, the Master Channel Strip controls all the Output Channels that are used in the current Surround Format.
  - Setting any Output Channel to Solo Safe Mode 🅂 (*ctr+click* on Solo Button) will disable the incoming control signal from the Master Channel Strip.

▶ **Stack Master Channel Strip ❸**: The Master Track of a Folder Stack functions as a VCA Master Fader.
  - The default name is "Sub 2", "Sub 3", etc., depending on how many Folder Stacks you already have in your Project.
  - It will be displayed in the VCA Slot ❹ like the other VCA Master Faders.
  - Once you rename the "Sub n", then there is no indication in the VCA Slot Menu which of the VCA Faders is a Folder Stack or a "regular" VCA Fader.
  - You can identify a Folder Stack VCA in the Mixer by the Track Stack disclosure triangle ❺.
  - Because the Folder Stack VCA is assigned to a Track ❻, it has a Track Number, and therefore, will be placed on the Mixer in that order and not at the right end of the Mixer.

▶ **VCA Channel Strip ❼**: The VCA Channel Strip functions as a VCA Master Fader.
  - The default name is "VCA 1", "VCA 2", etc., depending on how many VCA Faders you already have in your Project.
  - It will be displayed in the VCA Slot ❽ like any other VCA Master Fader.
  - The VCA Channel Strip is not assigned to a Track by default. Therefore, it is placed on the right side of the Mixer, next to the Master Channel Strip.
  - Once a VCA Channel Strip is assigned to a Track ❾, it will move to the left, to a position according to its Track Number ❿.

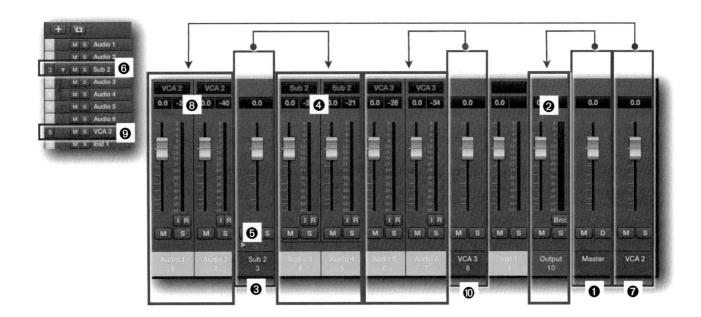

# Channel Strip Groups

## ➡ Concept

Here is an overview on how Channel Strip Grouping is implemented in Logic:

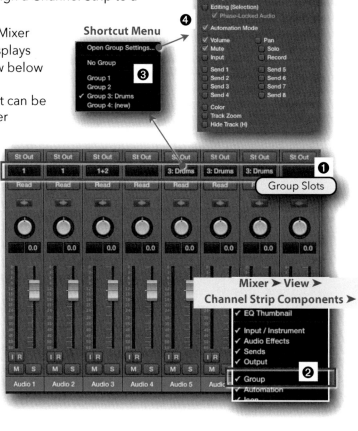

Groups Window

Shortcut Menu

- ▶ **Groups**: You can have a total of 32 Groups available in a Project. They are created one at a time when you assign a Channel Strip to a new Group.
- ▶ **Group Slot**: Each Channel Strip in the Mixer Window (even MIDI Channel Strips) displays the "Group Slot"❶, a black little window below the Output Button. This Channel Strip Component is displayed by default, but can be hidden ❷ if you don't use Groups (Mixer Window: Local Menu *View ➤ Channel Strip Components ➤*).
- ▶ **Group Assignment**: You assign a Channel Strip to a Group in the Shortcut Menu ❸ that opens when you *click* on the Group Slot.
- ▶ **Groups Menu**: This menu lets you do three things:
  - Assign the Channel Strip to any of the 32 available Groups (even to multiple Groups)
  - Remove a Channel Strip from a Group assignment
  - Open the Groups Window
- ▶ **Groups Window**: The Groups Window ❹ lets you manage and configure the individual Groups.

## 🌑 Group Slot Appearance

The numbers in the Group Slot can have the following appearance:

- ▶ **Single Number ❺:** The number of an assigned Group will be displayed in the Group Slot as a yellow number.
- ▶ **Multiple Numbers ❻**: If you have a Channel Strip assigned to multiple Groups, then the first three Group numbers are displayed (with a plus sign). If you have a Channel Strip assigned to more than three Groups, then three dots ❼ will indicate that.

- ▶ **Number and Name ❽**: If you named a Group, then the Group number and the Group name will be displayed in the Group Slot. With multiple assigned Groups, only numbers will be displayed.
- ▶ **Dimmed Display ❾**: If a Group is disabled, then the display will be dimmed. A group number is not dimmed when the Channel Strip is assigned to multiple (active) Groups.

## ➡ Group "Membership"

Here are the various commands on how to assign a Channel Strip to a Group or multiple Groups:

### 👤 Add/Remove Channel Strips to Groups

▶ **Add** to Group: *Click* on the Group Slot of a Channel Strip, which opens the Groups Menu.

- *No Group assigned*: If you haven't assigned any Groups yet, then the Groups Menu displays only the command "*Group 1: (new)* " ❶. Select it to create "Group 1" and assign it to that Channel Strip.

- *One Group assigned*: If you have "Group 1" created by assigning it to a Channel Strip, then the Groups Menu has changed the next time you open it. Now it lists "Group 1" (the existing one) and "Group 2: (new)" ❷. The "new" in parentheses indicates that "Group 2" is the next to be unassigned Group number. If you assign it, then the Groups Menu changes again, and so on. The last item in the Groups Menu is always the next, unassigned Group number with the added "(new)" ❸ up to "Group 32".

- *Multiple Groups assigned*: If you have named a Group, then that name ❹ will be placed next to the number.

▶ **Add to the same Group**: *Opt+click* on the Group Slot to add that Channel Strip to the same Group that has been assigned to the previous Channel Strip.

▶ **Add to multiple Channel Strips**: *Sh+drag* across multiple Channel Strip to create an "ad-hoc" Group (multiple Channel Strips are selected). Selecting any Group in the Group Slot of one Channel Strip will assign that same Group to all the selected Channel Strips.

▶ **Assign Multiple Groups**: *Click* the Group Slot to open the Groups Menu and *sh+click* on a Group to add that Group assignment to the existing Group assignment of the current Channel Strip.

▶ **Remove Group**: *Click* the Group Slot and select "No Group" from the Groups Menu.

### 👤 Toggle Groups (Group Clutch)

You can temporarily disable Groups if you want to make changes on a specific Channel Strip without affecting all the other Channel Strips that belong to the same Group. You can toggle specific Groups or all Groups on ❺ and off ❻ at once. A disabled Group is indicated by a gray number in the Group Slot.

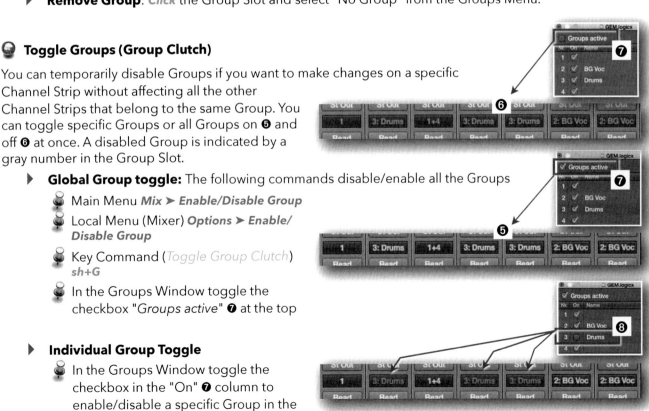

▶ **Global Group toggle:** The following commands disable/enable all the Groups

- 🎚 Main Menu *Mix ➤ Enable/Disable Group*
- 🎚 Local Menu (Mixer) *Options ➤ Enable/ Disable Group*
- 🎚 Key Command (*Toggle Group Clutch*) *sh+G*
- 🎚 In the Groups Window toggle the checkbox "*Groups active*" ❼ at the top

▶ **Individual Group Toggle**
- 🎚 In the Groups Window toggle the checkbox in the "On" ❼ column to enable/disable a specific Group in the list.

## ➡ *Groups Window*

The Groups Window can be displayed in two areas. Please pay attention to the interface details:

- ▶ **Floating Window**: You can resize the height of the window to display all 32 Groups.
- ▶ **Group Inspector**: The Groups Window can also be displayed in Logic's Main Inspector between the Region Inspector and Track Inspector.
  - The Groups Window automatically appears in the Main Inspector once you assigned a Channel Strip to the first Group. It cannot be removed from the Inspector, even if you un-assign all the Groups.
  - The window height cannot be adjusted and it only displays 4 Groups at a time.
  - You can hide the Inspector with the disclosure triangle (*or double-click* on its Header) so only its header is visible.
  - When you *drag* the header to tear the Group Inspector off as a Floating Window, it will be removed temporarily from the Main Inspector. However, when you close the Floating Window, it will move back to the Main Inspector.

These are the various commands to open the Groups Window:

- Main Menu *Mix > Show Groups*
- Key Command (*Open Group Settings*) *sh+opt+G*, only opens the window
- Key Command (*Show/Hide Groups Window*) *unassigned*, toggles the window
- *Click* the Group slot of a Channel Strip, and then choose "*Open Group Settings…*" from the Groups Menu (or *click+hold* and release the mouse)
- *Double-click* the header area (or *click* the disclosure triangle) of the Group inspector, to toggle the Inspector view
- *Drag* the header from the Group Inspector to tear off a separate floating window

### ☻ Windows areas

The Groups Window has three areas:

- ▶ **Group Clutch ❶**: On top of the window is the Group Clutch checkbox. This enables/disables all the Groups at once and has the same effect as the *Enable/Disable Groups* command (*sh+G*).
- ▶ **Groups List ❷**: This area lists all the currently assigned Groups. The Floating Window lets you resize the height of the Groups Window so you can see more Groups in the List, or you have to scroll.
  Selecting a Group from the list will display its settings in the Settings Area ❹ underneath:
  - **Nr**: This is the sequential number of each Group.
  - **On**: This checkbox lets you enable/disable a specific Group if you don't want to use the global "Group Clutch" command (*sh+G*).
  - **Name**: This field lets you name the Group. *Double-click* on it to enter/edit the name.
  - **Hide**: Enable the checkbox to hide all Tracks belonging to that group. It toggles the Hide Button [H] [H] on the Track Header. The checkbox displays a hyphen if those buttons of grouped Tracks are in different states. *Click* on it to switch all to *Hide* or *Unhide*.
- ▶ **Settings Area ❸**: This area, which can be hidden with the disclosure triangle, displays all the controls for the Group that is currently selected ❺ in the Group List above.

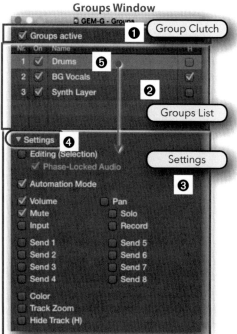

Groups Window

### 💀 Group Settings

Let me repeat again: The Settings Area displays the configuration of the selected Group above. Every Group can be individually configured based on what you use it for. You might use a group to control only the Volume Faders of all the Background Vocal Tracks. Maybe another group to use the show/hide track button on the entire rhythm section. You can even use only the Group editing feature to conveniently edit together all the eight Tracks of a drum recording.

You have to play around with those options to explore them and see how you can customize specific groups for your own needs. Remember, this is not just a feature to group Volume Faders together, its capabilities go way beyond that.

- ▶ **Editing (Selection)**: This is an often overlooked, but a very powerful feature. It lets you edit the Regions of all the grouped Tracks together. This is especially useful for multitrack recording, when you record, for example, a drum set with multiple microphones. Now you can do all the edits (select, trim, cut, move, etc.) on one Region and all the other Regions on the Tracks in that same Group will follow accordingly.

  - Flex Time: Enabling Flex and even performing Flex Time edits (moving Flex Markers) will work as Groups.
  - QuickSwipe: The Edit group works on the Comp Region but not the Region Selection inside.

- ▶ **Phase-Locked Audio**: Defines whether an edit group is phase-locked or independent when quantizing audio. This is necessary on multitrack audio recording where acoustic signals bleed into different microphones (different tracks). Phase-locked guarantees that any time related edits will be adjusted with sample accuracy on all Tracks. This is necessary to avoid phase shifting, which could negatively impact the sound.

  - The green Q Button ▣ (Q-Reference) will appear on the Track's Track Header. I will discuss Q-Reference in the next section.
  - All Audio Regions on a grouped Track must have the same start and end position to use phase-locked audio Quantization.
  - Phase-locked must be enabled to Flex-edit grouped Tracks.

- ▶ **Automation Mode**: When selected, then changing the Automation Mode or the Enable Automation Button ▣ Track of one Track changes the automation mode of all Tracks that belong to that same Group.
  A few things to be aware of:

  - The checkbox only affects the status of the Automation Mode Buttons of the grouped Channel Strip.
  - Automation itself is always recorded on all automation-enabled Tracks, either when you move a control directly or when the control is moved by a group.
  - The Automation writes the values of the individual controls (position of the individual Channel Strip) not the value of the control you are moving (maintaining its offset).
  - Deselecting the group or removing a Group will keep the automation Control Points.

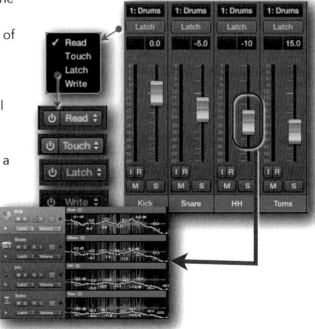

▸ **Volume, Pan**: Volume and Pan controls function as relative changes when grouped together. You can move, for example, the Fader of any Channel Strip, and the Faders of all the Channel Strips belonging to the same Group will move relatively by the same amount.

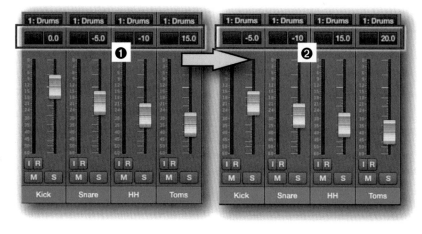

In this example, I lowered the volume on one Fader ❶ by 5dB, which lowered the Volume on all Faders ❷ by 5dB. Remember that the Faders don't move linear due to the exponential dB-Scale. You can also type a numeric value for the volume level in the entry box above the Fader. This is just an alternate way to move the Fader, which moves all the other Faders accordingly.

▸ **Sends (1-8)**: These eight checkboxes ❸ only affect the Aux Send knobs ❺ of a specific Aux Send Slot, the level you send on that Aux Slot.

Please note that Channel Strips can have different Busses selected on a specific Aux slot.

Toggling the Aux Button does not affect the Group, even if you see the level on the knob go down.

To assign a specific Bus to an Aux Slot to all Channel Strips in a Group at once, you have to use the Ad-Hoc Grouping feature (explained in a minute).

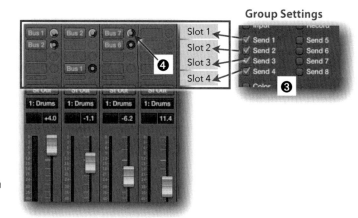

▸ **Solo** [S] [S]: If enabled, the Solo Button toggles all the grouped Channel Strips together
  - *Opt+click* to solo only a single Channel Strip.
  - Channel Strips that are in Solo-safe Mode [S] (*ctr+click*) are excluded from being solo'ed.

▸ **Mute** [M] [M]: If enabled, the Mute Button toggles all the grouped Channel Strips together.

▸ **Record Enable** [R] [R]: If enabled, the Record Enable Button toggles all the grouped Channel Strips together. If multiple Channel Strips have the same audio input selected, then only one Channel Strip can be the record-enabled Channels Strip. A Dialog Window ❺ will warn you about this situation.

▸ **Input** [I] [I] : If enabled, the Input Monitor Button toggles all the grouped Channel Strips together between Input Monitoring on/off.

▸ **Color**: If enabled, it assigns the same Track Color to all Channel Strips when selected from the Color Pallet.

▸ **Track Zoom**: When selected, zooming a Region in the Workspace zooms the Regions of all Tracks in that Group.

▸ **Hide Track (H)** [H] [H]: When selected, all Tracks in that Group are set to either *Hide* or *Don't Hide* by toggling the Button on the Track Header. You can also use the H checkbox ❻ in the Group List to toggle all Hide buttons for a Group. Using the hide feature is very convenient to hide specific Tracks. You can even create Groups only for that hide purpose. Use the global Hide Button [H] on the Menu Bar of the Tracks Menu to toggle all Tracks Hide/Unhide.

## ➡ *Q-Reference*

Here is a closer look at the Q-Reference feature with its special Q Button [Q] that appears when you enable "Phase-Locked Audio" in the Group Settings.

Q-Reference is a special Quantize parameter, so let's start with some Quantize basics first. The Quantize feature relies on two elements. It needs to know **what** to move and **where** to move "it". The "where to move it" part, that determines how far the quantize command moves "it" from its original time position, is configured with the various Quantize Parameters (discussed in great details in my first Logic book). The "it" part, meaning what is moved, depends on the type of Region. For MIDI Region, it is easy. There are discrete MIDI Events, and that is what the Quantize command will move based on those parameters. However, Audio Regions are different. There are no discrete events, only one continuous waveform. Therefore, Logic has to create "virtual events" first before it can quantize an Audio Region. These virtual events are the Transient Markers that Logic places at sudden amplitude peaks in the waveform. These Transient Markers, that I already discussed in the *Flex* chapter, function now as the reference points for the Quantize command, called the "Q-Reference". When you apply a Quantize command to an Audio Region, Logic moves sections of the audio waveform to quantize it. For these procedures, Quantize relies on those Q-References".

If you look at the Track Inspector of an Audio Track, you can see the Q-Reference parameter ❶. It is checked, but also grayed out, so you cannot disable it. The reason for that "hands off" settings is what I just explained. As a default, Logic creates the Transient Markers for the MIDI Region on that Track which it uses as Q-Reference. That's Logic's way of saying "please don't turn it off, I need those".

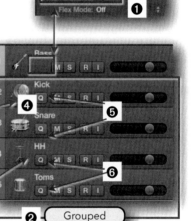

### Back to Group Editing:

When you assign Tracks to a Group ❷ and enable the Editing, plus the Phase-Locked option, the following things will happen:

- That Q-Reference parameter in the Track Inspector becomes active ❸ (not grayed out anymore).
- A new button appears on the Track Header for that grouped Track. It is the Q-Reference Button [Q] ❹.
- The Q Button ❹ and the Q-Reference Parameter ❸ are the same, you can toggle either one.

### What does that mean:

As I mentioned, the reason why the Q-Reference couldn't be disabled was because the Quantize command needs it, so why can you disable it now? Great question. The Q-Reference, those Transients, were only used by the Quantize command to decide how to move the sections of an audio waveform (based on the quantize Parameters). Logic doesn't care where those references are coming from. If you quantize one Audio Region, then the Q-Reference from that Audio Region is the only reference. However, when you quantize a group of Audio Regions (A, B, C, D), lined up on different Tracks, then you can tell the Quantize command, "use only the transients from Region A", or maybe from Region A and Region B, as the Q-Reference when you quantize all the Regions in that Group (A, B, C, D).

### Conclusion:

- When you have a multitrack recording, for example, four microphones on a drum set (Kick, Snare, HH, Toms), and group those Tracks with Editing and Phase-Locked enabled in the Group Settings, then you have the four Q Buttons enabled.
- You can leave the Q Button enabled for the Kick and Snare ❺, but disable it for the HH and Toms ❻. The Q-Reference checkboxes are now disabled ❼ in their Track Inspector.
- Logic quantizes the four Tracks (Kick, Snare, HH, Tom) based on the Transients of the Kick and Snare Track. Remember that you can edit those transients in the Audio File Editor to optimize the results.

# Ad-hoc Groups

The Ad-hoc Group is a simple, but still powerful little grouping feature that requires no configuration whatsoever. Here is how it works:

Let's assume you have a couple of Channel Strips in the Mixer Window that you want to apply some changes to. For example, lower the volume by 10dB, add an Aux Send, or load an FX Plugin on all those Channel Strips.

### ☑ Make a Selection

First, select the Channel Strips that you want to apply the changes to ❶:

 *Sh+click* on individual Channel Strips to add (or remove them) to the Group. Be careful to click on the background of the Channel Strip and not on any of the controls.

 *Drag* across contiguous Channel Strips (lasso around) to select them all.

### ☑ Make the Changes

Now, whatever changes you make on one Channel Strip, will apply the same changes to all the selected Channel Strips. For example:

- Mover the Volume Fader ❷
- Move the Pan Knob ❸
- Select Mute ❹
- Select an Automation Mode ❺
- Select a Channel Strip Group ❻
- Select an Aux Send ❼
- Load Plugins ❽

When done, don't forget to de-select the Ad-hoc Group by clicking on an unselected Channel Strip.

It's that simple. By the way, this technique also works in the Tracks Window, for example, to select any Button on the Track Headers of all selected Tracks.

# Freeze

The Freeze feature in Logic is like a simplified, one-click bounce-in-place command.

### ▶ Problem

When you work on your Project, you record Track after Track, edit the Tracks, apply Flex edits, add Software Instruments, then add more Software Instruments, then add FX Plugins, and even more FX Plugins, etc. However, at some point, your Project might stop unexpectedly and you will get one of those nasty Dialog Messages warning you about a "System Overload". That means, all those Plugins and all those Tracks in your Project require more CPU power than your computer can provide. You have two options, either you head to the Apple Store and by yourself a more powerful Mac, or you can use Logic's Freeze feature.

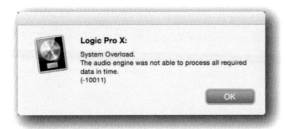

Logic Pro X:

System Overload.
The audio engine was not able to process all required data in time.
(-10011)

OK

### ▶ Solution

Playing back a Track with a CPU-intensive Instrument Plugin like *Sculpture*, plus CPU-intensive Audio FX Plugins like the *Adaptive Limiter* or the *Amp Designer* Plugin means that your computer has to perform all those calculations in real time. That's why you might reach a point where your computer can't process all those calculations in real time anymore. If you would bounce a "CPU demanding" Track to an audio file and then, instead of playing the original Track, you play back an Audio Track with that single Audio Region, then the computer wouldn't have to do all those real-time calculations anymore. The Track would still sound the same. That is basically what the Freeze feature does with a very simple and easy to use interface.

### ▶ How does it work?

This is what happens when "freezing" a Track:

☑ Logic will bounce the Track to an audio file.

☑ No new Track is created. You stay on the same Track. Instead of the current Regions on the Track Lane (which are still visible), Logic now plays back the bounced audio file in the background.

☑ You can determine if you want to include all the FX Plugins during the bounce, in addition to the Software Instrument Plugin.

☑ You still can use all the other controls on a frozen Track: Volume, Pan, Automation, Aux Sends, Output Routing.

☑ All the frozen Plugins are disabled (saving CPU) and the Regions are locked so you can't edit them while in frozen mode.

☑ If you need to make changes on the Plugin or have to make Region edits, then you just unfreeze the Track, make the edits, and freeze the Track again with the click of a button.

### ▶ Advantages

• Freeze Tracks to use more Plugins than your computer could handle in real-time.

• If you want to play back a big Project on a less powerful computer, freeze Tracks with CPU intensive Software Instrument Plugins and FX Plugins and save the Project.

• If you want to play back a Project on a different computer that doesn't have specific (third-party) Plugins installed, then freeze the Tracks with those Plugins that are not available on the other computer.

### ▶ Limitation:

• Freeze only works on Audio Tracks, Software Instrument Tracks, and the Drummer Track.

• Freeze doesn't work with the I/O Plugin or the External Instrument Plugin.

• Freeze doesn't work with External MIDI Instruments.

## ➡️ *How to use Freeze*

The Freeze feature involves four easy steps:

- ☑️ Step 1 - Select Freeze Mode
- ☑️ Step 2 - Show Freeze Button
- ☑️ Step 3 - Enable Freeze + Start Play
- ☑️ Step 4 - Disable Freeze

### 🔵 1 - Freeze Mode

Before you use the Freeze feature, you have to select which of the two Freeze Modes you want to use. The Audio Tracks and Software Instrument Tracks display the Freeze Mode Parameter ❶ in the Track Inspector. *Click* on it to select from the popup menu ❷.

The two Freeze Modes lets you choose which elements in a Track you want to Freeze. The Regions on the Track Lane are always frozen in either mode.

Tracks Window

### ▶ Source Only ❄️

This mode is useful when you want to freeze a CPU-heavy Instrument Plugin but still want to have access to all the FX Plugins. Another usage is Flex Time. Using a lot of Flex edits on a Track can also be demanding on your CPU resources. That's why the Freeze Mode automatically switches to *"Source Only"* mode when you enable Flex Mode.

- Audio Track: Freezes only the Regions
- Instrument Track (Drummer Track): Freezes all the Regions and the Software Instrument Plugin

### ▶ Pre Fader ❄️

This mode is useful when you have a lot of CPU-intensive Plugins on a Track.

- Audio Track: Freezes the Regions and the Audio FX Plugins
- Instrument Track (Drummer Track): Freezes the Region, the Software Instrument Plugin, the Audio FX Plugin, and the MIDI FX Plugins

### 🔵 2 - Show Freeze Button

Once you selected the proper Freeze Mode, you have to make the Freeze Button ❸ visible first in order to start the Freeze process. It is part of the Track Header Components that is hidden by default. You can enable it in the Track Header Configuration Window ❹ or select it from the Track's Shortcut Menu ❺. Here are the different commands:

- Main Menu *Track ➤ Configure Track Header...*
- Key Command (*Configure Track Header*) *opt+T*
- *Ctr+click* Track Header to open the Shortcut Menu *Configure Track Header...*
- *Ctr+click* Track Header to open the Shortcut Menu *Track Header Components ➤ Show Freeze* ❺

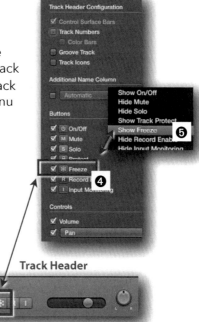

Track Header Configuration

Track Header

Once made visible, the Freeze Button ❄️ is displayed on the Track Header ❸ of all Tracks next to the Record Enable Button.

## 3 - Enable Freeze + Play

Once you have selected the Freeze Mode and the Freeze Button is visible on the Track Header ❶, you are ready to freeze the Track(s). This involves two steps:

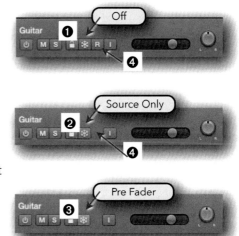

☑️ *Click* on the Freeze Button on the Track(s) you want to freeze. This enables Freeze Mode. The button turns either blue ❷ 🔷 (*Source Only* mode is selected) or green ❸ 🔷 (*Pre Fader* mode is selected).

Please note that the Record Enable Button ❹ [R] will disappear to indicate that you cannot record on a frozen Track.

☑️ Start the playback with any of the navigation commands (i.e., hit the Play Button ▶️) to start the freeze process.

This is what happens next:

- Logic performs an offline bounce (you won't hear any audio during the bounce).
- It starts to play from the beginning of the Project to the end (regardless where the Playhead was positioned).
- A Progress Window ❺ is displayed during the bounce.
- A single uncompressed 32 -bit aiff audio file is created for each freeze-enabled Track, starting at the beginning of the Project to the last event on that Track (not necessarily the end of the Project).
- The bounced audio files are stored inside the Project's Media file in the folder "*Freeze Files.nosync*" ❻.
- You can copy those files (not move!) to use them outside the Project if you like.

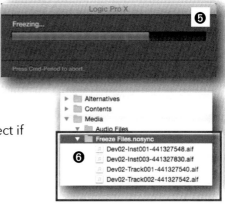

## 4- Unfreeze

Once you have frozen a Track, you cannot make changes on those elements anymore.

- Trying to make changes to frozen Regions will pop up a Dialog Window ❼ reminding you of the frozen state and gives you the option to unfreeze that Track.
- Moving the mouse over a Plugin Slot will change the Cursor Tool to a white snowflake ❽, indicating that the Audio FX Plugin or the Software Instrument Plugin is frozen. The MIDI FX Plugins don't change to a snowflake, they just don't respond to any clicks.

*Click* on any active Freeze Button (blue 🔷, or green 🔷) on a Track Header to unfreeze that Track. The buttons turn inactive 🔷 and the corresponding (frozen) audio file inside the Project File will be deleted right away.

# Strip Silence

Strip Silence is a tool for audio files that works like a Noise Gate. However, unlike a Noise Gate that is placed in the audio signal flow and works "online", Strip Silence is an "offline" procedure, that lets you adjust visually, which part of the waveform is "silenced". The remaining sections of the waveform are trimmed into individual Audio Regions.

> **Strip Silence = a Visual Noise Gate**

➡️ *Why do I need Strip Silence?*

### 💀 The Situation

- ☑️ You record a guitar section. The guitar player plays pauses throughout his part.
- ☑️ You record background vocals. They double only a few phrases throughout the chorus.
- ☑️ You record a horn section. They play only a couple of riffs.
- ☑️ You record a whole band with multitrack recordings. Not every instrument is playing all the time.

### 💀 The Result

If you are not constantly punching in and out (and risking to miss a part), you will record a lot of (unused) silence in between the parts the performers are actually playing. The problem is that it is not real silence. Even when the performer doesn't play or sing, there is often some acoustic "bleed" from other instruments that are playing at the same time, or the sound coming out of the headphones that had to be cranked up for one of those half-deaf musicians.

### 💀 The Problem

Here are only a few of the potential problems:

- ☑️ Even with a low level audio signal, Logic treats it as an audio signal that it processes based on the Plugins and Sends you have enabled on that Track. Multiply that with all the Tracks that process "silence" at any time and you might end up burning a lot of unnecessary CPU cycles.
- ☑️ Any unwanted crosstalk from other microphones is added to your mix and can negatively impact the sound of your mix. Any heavy compression will pull those unwanted signals even higher when the singer, for example, pauses.
- ☑️ Electric Guitars can produce noise and hum sounds that can be disturbing when they constantly appear between notes.
- ☑️ Sometimes, you decide in the mix that you want to drop a bar or a phrase, for example, from the guitar solo. If you automate the Guitar Track and mute that phrase, then you don't want to have it still play through the microphones of the vocalist (if they were recorded together).

The Strip Silence feature displays the waveform of an Audio Region where you adjust various parameters that determine which part of the waveform you want to **keep** and which one you want to **cut** - strip silence.

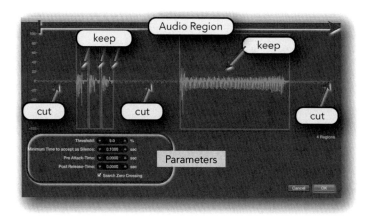

## ➡ *How do I use Strip Silence?*

Here are the four steps on how to use the Strip Silence function:

 **1 - Select the Audio Region**

You apply the Strip Silence function to an Audio Region **❶**, one at a time. So first, you select a Region, either in the Tracks Window, the Audio Editor, or the Project Audio Browser/Window.

 **2 - Choose the Command**

Now choose the Strip Silence command, which is available in multiple places:

- *Ctr+click* on an Audio Region in the Tracks Window: *Shortcut Menu ➤ Split ➤ Strip Silence...* **❷**
- *Ctr+click* on an Audio File in the Project Audio Browser: *Shortcut Menu ➤ Split ➤ Strip Silence...* **❸**
- Project Audio Window (not the Project Audio Browser) *Options ➤ Strip Silence...* **❹**
- Key Command (*Strip Silence...*) *ctr+X*

Shortcut Menu: Audio File
(Project Audio Browser)

Shortcut Menu: Audio Region
(Workspace or Audio Track Editor)

Project Audio Window ➤ Options ➤

 **3 - Make the Adjustments**

Once you selected the Strip Silence command, the Strip Silence Window **❺** will open. It displays the audio waveform of the Region and provides the parameters to determine which section you want to keep and which one to cut (silence).

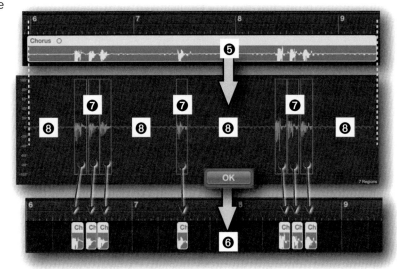

 **4 - OK**

Once you *click* "OK" **❻**, the original Audio Region is cut into several Audio Regions based on the section that was marked as "keep" (blue box **❼**), leaving out the sections that were marked to "cut" (outside the blue box **❽**).

 **Optional**

After the Strip Silence operation, you can add the following commands:

- Apply Fade-ins and Fade-outs to the Regions in the Workspace to smoothen the edges if necessary.
- Use the "Optimize File" command in the *Project Audio Browser ➤ Audio File ➤ Optimize File(s)*. It lets you remove the silent sections from the actual audio file to save storage space (I discussed that in the *Advanced Editing* chapter).
- Pack the Regions into Folder Regions if you want to properly loop a group of smaller Regions with spaces in between.

## ➡ *Strip Silence Parameters*

You have five parameters ❶ available in the Strip Silence Window that let you adjust the sections. These parameters are similar to the ones you find on a Gate Plugin:

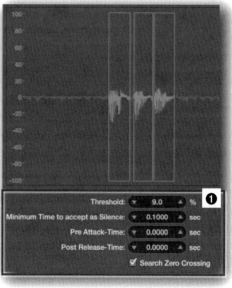

- ▸ **Threshold**: The Threshold value sets the amplitude of the audio signal in percentage % (default is 4%). If the audio signal is above that threshold level, then it is marked as the beginning of an Audio Region until the audio signal falls below that threshold level, which is marked as the end of the Audio Region (one blue box indicates one Region). When the audio signal rises again above that Threshold level, then it will be marked as the beginning of a new Audio Region until the audio signal falls below that Threshold again (the second blue box), etc.

- ▸ **Minimum Time to accept as Silence**: This is like the 'Hold Time" on a Gate Plugin. It determines how much time must have passed since the signal went above the Threshold level (Region start) before it can be marked as a Region end (default 0.1s). This avoids a situation where you could end up with too many chopped little Regions.

- ▸ **Pre Attack-Time**: This parameter lets you place the start of the Region by a specific value (offset) prior to the detected position. This is useful when you have audio signals with a slow attack that might get cut off at the beginning.

- ▸ **Post Release Time**: This parameter lets you place the end of the Region by a specific value (offset) later than the detected position. This is useful when you have audio signals with a ring-out (release) that might get cut off when it falls below the Threshold.

- ▸ **Search Zero Crossing**: This parameter ensures that the beginning and end of a Region is always at a zero crossing, when the amplitude of the audio signal crosses the zero line to avoid any clicks.

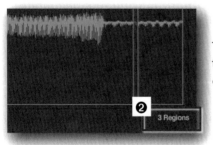

The Strip Silence Window displays the number Regions ❷ that are created based on the current settings.

**Project Audio Browser**

Regions created by Strip Silence

## ➡ *Project Audio Browser*

All the new Regions that are created by the Strip Silence command are, of course, listed in the Project Audio Browser ❸.

If you use the Strip Silence command in the Project Audio Browser instead of the Tracks Window, then you'll get a Dialog Window ❹ if that Audio Region is used in your Workspace. You have two options:

- ☑ **Don't Replace**: The newly created Regions are only placed in the Project Audio Browser and the Regions in the Workspace stay untouched.

- ☑ **Replace**: All instances of this Region used in the Workspace are replaced by the newly created (chopped) Regions.

# Drum Replacement / Doubling

This is another powerful, but yet easy to use feature in Logic.

▶ **What you Have**

If you recorded a Drum Set with individual microphones for Kick, Snare, HH, Toms, etc., then you end up with individual Audio Tracks in your Project containing the Audio Regions for those recordings.

▶ **What you Want**

Sometimes, you won't get the perfect sound for the Kick drum or the Snare for whatever reasons, or during the mix, you realize that a drum sound should have sounded differently. You wish you could re-record it with different drums.

▶ **What Logic can Do**

Logic has a feature that lets you do exactly that. You can replace individually recorded live drums in your Project with any sampled drum sounds or add a sampled drum sound to the recorded one if it just needs a little more bottom end or more high end to cut through the mix.

▶ **How Logic Does it**

This is the simple procedure:

- ☑ Logic analyzes the Audio Region(s) ❶ and creates Transient Markers ❷ at the sudden amplitude peaks (most likely the drum hits).
- ☑ Logic creates a new Software Instrument Track ❸ with the EXS24 Plugin and loads a Preset with drum samples.
- ☑ The Library Window opens where you can select different drum Presets.
- ☑ Logic creates a MIDI Region ❹ on the new Software Instrument Track that contains individual notes at the position of every detected Transient. Those notes, that include velocity information based on the level of the amplitude peak, are mapped to the drum sample in the EXS Instrument.
- ☑ A Dialog Window with various parameters lets you fine tune the configuration before committing to it.

➡ *How to use Drum Replacement*

Here are the steps on how to replace or double your drum tracks:

🥁 **1 - Select Drum Track**

First, you select an Audio Track with Audio Region(s) ❶ of an individually mic'ed drum sound (a mixed drum

track might work, but is much more work because you have to manually isolate specific drum sounds).

🥁 **2 - Select the command**

You can select the command from two places:

- 🥁 Main Menu *Track ➤ Replace or Double Drum Track...*
- 🥁 Key Command (*Replace or Double Drum Track...*) *ctr+D*

Logic now creates the following elements:

- ☑ Creates new Instrument Track ❸ below the Audio Track ❺
- ☑ Loads the EXS24 onto that Track with the Patch "*Acoustic Kick C3 1*" loaded
- ☑ Opens the Library window to let you choose other drum samples
- ☑ Creates a new MIDI Region ❹ with MIDI notes at each Transient Marker
- ☑ Opens the Drum Replacement/ Doubling Window

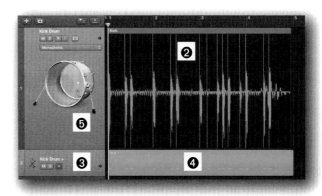

**3 - Configuration**

You adjust the basic configuration in the Replacement Window ❶:

▸ **Instrument**: Select any of the four Instruments from the popup menu ❷. The is the Instrument you want to replace or double. Therefore, by selecting an Instrument, Logic makes the appropriate changes and chooses the loaded EXS24 Instrument and the note that is placed in the MIDI Region to trigger that note:

- Kick: Trigger Note "C1" (Auto), EXS Instrument *Factory ➤ Drums & Percussion ➤ Single Drums ➤ Kicks ➤ Acoustic Kicks ➤ Acoustic Kick C1 1*

- Snare: Trigger Note "D1" (Auto), EXS Instrument *Factory ➤ Drums & Percussion ➤ Single Drums ➤ Snares ➤ Acoustic Snares ➤ Acoustic Snare D1 1*

- Tom: Trigger Note "A1" (Auto), EXS Instrument *Factory ➤ Drums & Percussion ➤ Single Drums ➤ Toms ➤ Acoustic Toms ➤ Acoustic 13" TomsA1 1*

- other: Trigger Note "C3 (60) H BONGO", no EXS Instrument is loaded. The previously loaded Instrument stays and you can select the EXS Instrument in the Library with the sound that you want to replace.

▸ **Mode**: You can choose between two modes with only one slight difference:

- Replacement: The Regions on the Audio Track will be muted

- Doubling: The Regions on the Audio Track will not be muted

▸ **Relative Threshold**: By setting the threshold between -40dB and 0dB, you adjust the sensitivity for Logic when detecting the Transients. When you move the slider you will see the effect on the Audio Region (more or less Transients) and the MIDI Region (more or less note)

▸ **Prelisten**: This plays back the Audio Track and the new Instrument Track in Solo Mode. Enable Cycle Mode for the length of the Region.

▸ **Trigger Note**: Selecting Kick, Snare, or Tom from the Instrument popup menu will set the Trigger Note to "Auto" ❸. However, you can choose any of the 128 MIDI notes from that popup menu ❹ to change the MIDI notes in the newly created Region to that note (in case you use a custom Drum Patch with a specific drum mapping).

▸ **Timing Offset**: You can set a timing offset between -30ms to +10ms to have the MIDI Notes placed earlier or later than its corresponding transient. This setting is only necessary to compensate possible latencies or improper truncated drum samples.

▸ **Set average attack time**: Set the average offset of all the Audio Regions on the original Audio Track.

 **4 - Execute**

Click OK to confirm the settings. Of course you can manually edit the new MIDI Regions or replace the EXS Instruments ❺ or the Instrument Plugin all together, maybe with Ultrabeat or your favorite third-party Drum Sampler.

# Speed up - Slow down

There is one little audio feature tucked away in the Region Inspector that lets you speed up the beginning of an Audio Region or slow down the ending of an Audio Region. It uses the Fade In/Out parameters in the Region Inspector.

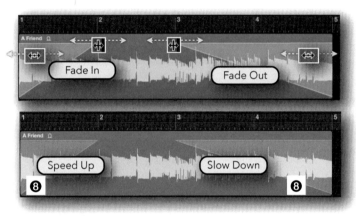

Region Inspector

- ▶ **❶ Fade In / Speed up**: Select from the popup menu to switch between Fade in and Speed Up.
- ▶ **❷ Length**: This is the length of the Fade in or Speed up in Ticks.
- ▶ **❸ Curve**: This determines the shape of the curve between -99 (logarithmic) … 0 (linear) … +99 (exponential).
- ▶ **❹ Fade Out / Slow Down**: Select from the popup menu to switch between Fade Out and Slow Down.
- ▶ **❺ Length**: This is the length of the Fade Out or Slow Down in Ticks.
- ▶ **❻ Type**: Select from the popup menu if the Fade Out is a standard Fade Out or a crossfade into the next consecutive Audio Region (its Fade In parameters are redundant in that case).
- ▶ **❼ Curve**: This determines the shape of the curve between -99 (logarithmic) … 0 (linear) … +99 (exponential).

*Drag* the length of the Fade area with the Fade Tool 🔲 and change the Curve with the Fade Curve Tool 🔲

## Speed up / Slow Down

When you choose the Speed Up or Slow Down option, the shaded Fade area will be displayed in red ❽. You can also apply different curves ❾ to the Speed UP and Slow Down

## Varispeed

The Speed Up and Slow Down feature is technically a Region-based Varispeed. This is independent from the Project-based Varispeed that you can enable in the Control Bar Display (needs to be made visible in the Control Bar Configurations Window).

Control Bar Display

- ▶ **Speed Only**: This changes the speed of your Project without affecting the pitch.
- ▶ **Varispeed (Speed and Pitch)**: This changes the speed and the pitch to emulate a classic tape varispeed.
- ▶ **Varispeed and MIDI**: This changes the speed and pitch, and in addition, includes the MIDI Instruments by transposing them in semitone steps (except drum Tracks).

## Plug-in Manager

The Previous Audio Units Manager in LPX 10.0.7 has been replaced with the new Plug-In Manager ❶ in LPX 10.1. You can open it in two ways:

- Main Menu *Logic Pro X* ➤ *Preferences* ➤ *Plug-In Manager...*
- Key Command (*Plug-in Manager...*) *unassigned*

# Interface

Before getting into it, let's look at the interface first to understand the structure and the underlying rules of the Plug-in Manager in order to avoid any potential confusion down the road:

- ▶ **Header ❷**: The "*Restore Factory*" button lets you reset the structure to the default setting and the Search Field on the right lets you search the Plugin List for a Plugin by name, manufacturer, or Plugin type.

- ▶ **Sidebar ❸**: As we will see in a moment, this is the most important element in understanding how the Plugin Manager works.

- ▶ **Plugin List ❹**: This area lists the Plugins depending on what item is selected in the Sidebar.

- ▶ **Control Bar ❺**: The bottom of the window has two buttons "*Disable Failed Audio Units*" and "*Reset & Rescan Section*" that are the same from the previous Audio Units Manager in LPX 10.0.7. The "*Done*" Button closes the window, initializes the Plugins and applies the new structure to the Plugin Menus.

**Plug-in Manager**

# Plugin Menu

The next step is to understand how the Plugins are displayed in the various Plugin Menus, that open when you click on a Plugin Button in Logic. These Plugin Menus have an underlying structure that the Plugin Manager feed into.

Here are the rules:

▶ Logic has three types of Plugin Menus:
  - ❶ **Instrument Plugin Menu**
  - ❷ **Audio FX Plugin Menu**
  - ❸ **MIDI FX Plugin Menu**

▶ Although each of the three Plugin Menus only displays the Plugins for that type, the menus all follow the same structure. Plugins are grouped into five specific sections (divided by lines). The potentially confusing part is that not every Plugin Menu displays all sections, so you have to know what section you are looking at.

- ❹ **Currently loaded Plugin**: The first section is displayed in every menu. It is only a single line item that displays the name of the currently loaded Plugin in that slot. If no Plugin is loaded, then it lists "*No Plug-in*".

- ❺ **Top Level Plugins**: This section lists individual Plugins. Please note that these are not folders. The triangles on the right open a submenu with the output options for each Plugin. The Audio FX Plugin Menu ❷ does not display that section by default.

- ❻ **Categories**: This section lists folders, the so-called *Categories*. The triangle opens the submenu with the Plugins inside that Category folder, or another subfolder. The MIDI FX Plugin Menu does not display that section by default ❸.

- ❼ **Drum Machine Designer**: This item is only displayed in the Instrument Plugin Menu. It loads the Drum Machine Designer, which is technically not even a Plugin as I explain later.

- ❽ **Plugin Type Categories**: This section lists all the available Plugins grouped by Plugin Types. The submenus further group the Plugins by Manufacturers.

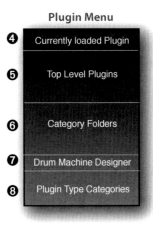

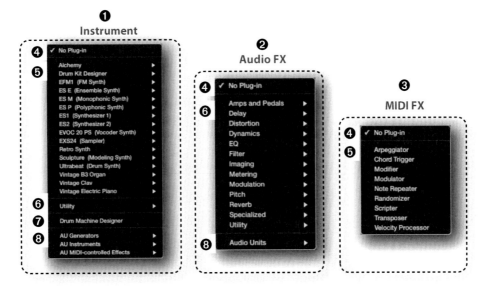

# Plugin Manager

Now with the proper understanding of the structure of the Plugin Menu, we can better understand the functionality of the Plugin Manager.

## Sidebar

The Sidebar of the Plugin-Manager has four sections:

- ▶ **❶ Show All**: This is a read-only item. Selecting this item will display all the available Plugins on your computer in the Plugin List ❿ to the right.

- ▶ **❷ Top Level**: Selecting this item will show all the Plugins in the Plugin List to the right that are listed in the "Top Level Plugin" ❺ Section of the Plugin Menu. You can customize this content by dragging Plugins from the Plugin List ❿ on the right onto this item ❷ to add them to the Top Level Plugin Section.

- ▶ **❸ Category**: This section represents the "Category Folders" ❻ section in the Plugin Menu. Each item in this section of the Sidebar is a folder that is listed in the Plugin Menu's Category Folder" section ❻. You can customize the content of each folder by dragging Plugins from the Plugin List ❿ on the right onto an individual folder item ❸ to add them to an individual Category Folder ❺. You can also customize the Category Folders themselves by creating new Folders (and subfolder) or deleting Folders from that section ❸.

- ▶ **❾ Manufacturer**: This section again is read-only. It displays the Manufacturers of all the Plugins that you have installed on your computer. Selecting an item (the name of a Manufacturer) will display their Plugins in the List ❿ to the right. All those Plugins in this section ❾ (which are all Plugins on your computer) are displayed at the bottom of the Plugin Menu in the "Plugin Type Category" ❽ section. However, they are grouped by Plugin Type first, and then with subfolders organized by manufacturers.

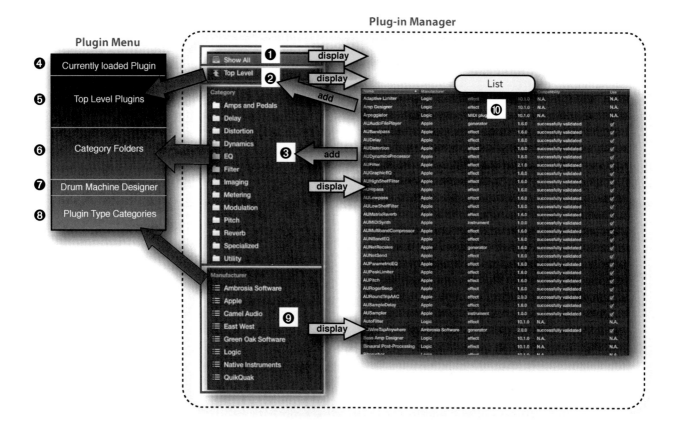

## ➡ *Organize Procedure*

This is the important part to understand about the Plugin Manager. You have complete control over these two sections in the Plugin Menu. Please note that a Plugin can be displayed in one or the other section, but not both. Placing a Plugin in one section will automatically remove it from the other section if it was there:

> ▸ **❶ Top Level section**
> ▸ **❷ Category section**

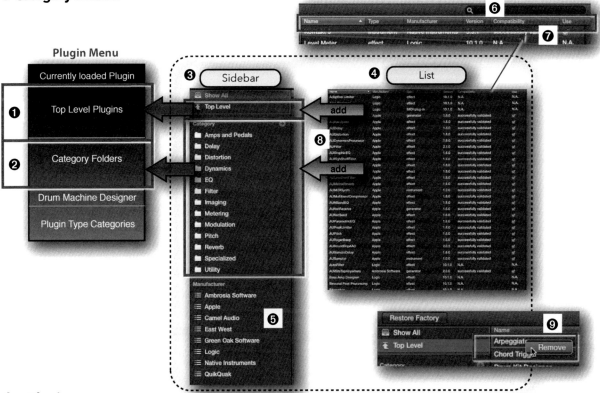

### 💀 Display Plugin

The procedure can't be easier:

> ▸ **Find the Plugin**: *Click* on any item in the Sidebar ❸ (which are like folders) to display their Plugins in the Plugins List ❹ on the right. Use the manufacturer items ❺ at the bottom of the Sidebar, or use the *Show All*, to display all Plugins. Optionally, enter a search term in the Search Field ❻ to find that specific Plugin in the currently displayed list.

> ▸ **Display the Plugins**: The Plugins are displayed in the List ❹ showing their properties in six columns ❼. You can resize and rearrange the columns by *dragging* the column header left or right, and also sort the list by *clicking* on a specific column. *Click* again to toggle between ascending and descending sort order.

> ▸ List Columns: **Name**, **Type** (generator, instrument, effect, MIDI plug-in, MIDI-controlled effect) **Manufacturer** (Apple, Logic, third-party manufacturer) **Version**, **Compatibility** ("Successfully validated", "crashed validation), **Use** (checkbox).

### 💀 Add/Remove Plugin

Please note that the following procedures just add or remove Plugins from specific locations in the Plugin Menu. The actual installed Plugins are not affected.

> ▸ **Add the Plugin**: *Drag* ❽ one or multiple selected Plugins from the List ❷ onto the Top Level item and/or any Category folder to add the Plugin(s) to that section of the Plugin Menu.

> ▸ **Remove the Plugin**: To remove a Plugin from the Top Level section or any of the Category Folders, *click* on that item in the Sidebar to display its content in the List ❷ and hit delete, or *ctr+click* on the item and *click* "*Remove*" ❾ from the Shortcut Menu.

**Organize Category Section**

The Category Section in the Plugin Manager displays folders that let you group the Plugins in various categories. The Plugin Manager lets you freely manage that section, adding, renaming, and deleting those folders.

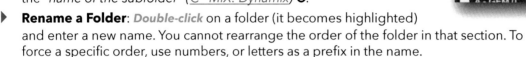

▶ **Create a Folder**: *Click* the Plus Button ⊕ on top of the Category section ❶. This will add a new folder to the Sidebar. Its name "Untitled" is highlighted, so you can enter your custom name for that folder.

▶ **Create a Subfolder**: Although the Sidebar displays only one folder level, you still can create nested subfolders ❷ that are then displayed as additional subfolders in the Plugin Menu ❸. The procedure is the same as creating a new folder by clicking the Plus Button ⊕ first. The trick is in the naming. Type the "*name of the parent folder*" (C - MIX), followed by a "*colon*" (C - MIX:), then a "*space*" (C - MIX: ), followed by the "*name of the subfolder*" (C - MIX: Dynamix) ❸.

▶ **Rename a Folder**: *Double-click* on a folder (it becomes highlighted) and enter a new name. You cannot rearrange the order of the folder in that section. To force a specific order, use numbers, or letters as a prefix in the name.

▶ **Delete a Folder**: Select a name and hit the *delete* key or *ctr+click* on a folder an select "Remove" ❹ from the Shortcut Menu. This action removes the Plugins assigned to that folder from the Plugin Menu.

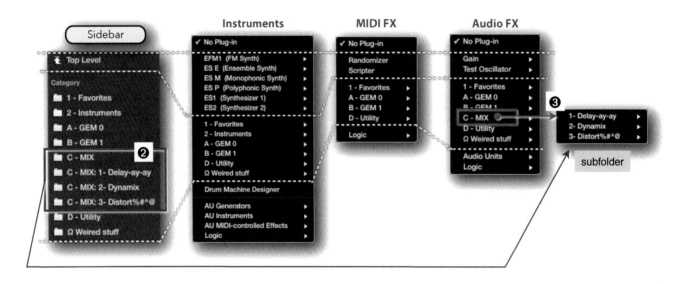

*Attention*

A Category Folder is only displayed in the Category section of the Plugin Menu if it contains a Plugin for that Plugin Type. For example, the Instrument Plugin Menu ❺ doesn't show the "C - Mix" Category folder that I created in the Plugin Manager, because it doesn't contain any Instrument Plugins.

Use the "Restore Factory" ❻ button at the top of the Plugin Manager to reset everything to the default settings. A Dialog Window warns you that this action resets all your settings, which can't be undone!

## External MIDI Instrument

When you use Logic to compose music with MIDI Synths, Samplers, and Drum Machines, you can do that completely inside Logic, "in the box". Logic itself comes with a wide variety of Instrument Plugins that will cover most of your sound requirements. You can install additional AU Plugins from third-party vendors to add to your arsenal of those internal Software Instruments. However, there are still composers out there, who own old (and new) Hardware Instruments and want to use those "external" Instruments with Logic.

### 🔘 "Internal" Instruments

When you work exclusively "in the box", you need only a MIDI Keyboard connected directly to your computer (maybe via a MIDI Interface if the keyboard doesn't have a USB port). This MIDI Keyboard generates the MIDI notes you play and record in Logic.

All the sound sources are inside Logic in the form of Software Instrument Plugins. You use an Audio Interface (or the built-in audio device) to connect to your speakers to monitor your mix - and that's it.

### 🔘 "External" Instruments

In order to use external Instruments that generate their sound outside of Logic, you need some additional setup and configurations.

There are two kinds of connections required:

▶ **MIDI Out**: You have to send the MIDI signal from Logic to the External Instruments, most likely through a MIDI Interface.

▶ **Audio In**: The sound the External Instruments are producing, based on the MIDI data you send them, needs to be sent back into Logic (via an Audio Interface), so you can mix those signals together with the other audio signals in your Project.

Of course, you can use External Instruments along with Internal Instruments in your Project, plus audio recordings. In this section of the chapter, we'll look how to setup and configure Logic to use those **"External MIDI Instruments"**.

# Some Basics

To better understand the setup for External MIDI Instruments, you need a little background information about MIDI routing in Logic. I will get into that in great detail in the Environment chapter. Here are the basics:

## 🌑 MIDI Routing

▸ **AMS**: Every external MIDI Device that you want to use with Logic has to be present in the Audio MIDI Setup ❶ (AMS) utility (located in */Applications/Utilities/*). Think of it as the "OSX bouncer" for everything MIDI, the gatekeeper. If a MIDI Device doesn't have the proper driver installed or something is wrong with the cabling, then it won't show up in the Audio MIDI Setup app, and it won't be available in Logic.

▸ **MIDI Devices**: The external MIDI Keyboard ❷ you use to play the various MIDI Instruments (and record MIDI) in Logic has to be present in the AMS. If you want to use any External MIDI Instrument ❸ as an external sound source, then that MIDI Instrument has to be present in the AMS too. A Device can also be represented by a special MIDI Interface that an External Instrument is connected to via MIDI cables.

▸ **MIDI In**: Any recognized MIDI Device in the AMS will be listed in the Environment Window in the Physical Input Object ❹. This Environment Object is cabled to another Environment Object, the Sequencer Input, and this connection makes any incoming MIDI signal ❷ available on any selected Track in the Tracks Window ❺ to be recorded as MIDI Regions on the Track's Track Lane.

▸ **MIDI Out**: However, MIDI signals have to be sent into the other direction, out of Logic, to the External MIDI Instrument ❸ if you want to use it with Logic. For that, Logic uses special Environment Objects, so-called MIDI Instrument Objects ❻ (the exception is the External Instrument Plugin).

▸ **MIDI Objects**: Logic automatically creates a MIDI Object in the Environment when needed for an External MIDI Instrument (or you can create it manually). This object can be assigned to any Track.

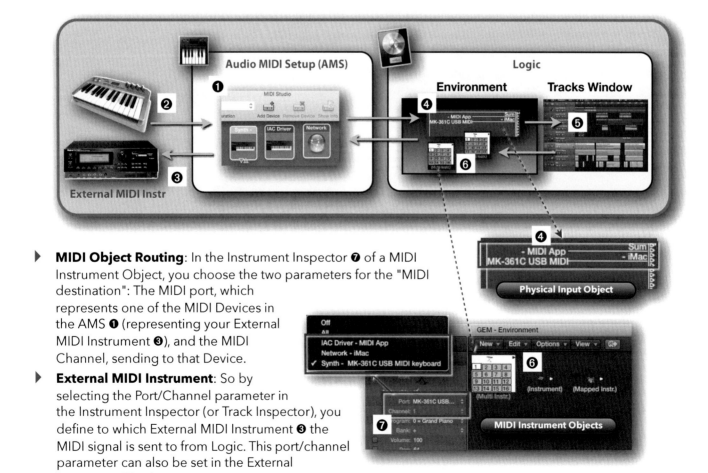

▸ **MIDI Object Routing**: In the Instrument Inspector ❼ of a MIDI Instrument Object, you choose the two parameters for the "MIDI destination": The MIDI port, which represents one of the MIDI Devices in the AMS ❶ (representing your External MIDI Instrument ❸), and the MIDI Channel, sending to that Device.

▸ **External MIDI Instrument**: So by selecting the Port/Channel parameter in the Instrument Inspector (or Track Inspector), you define to which External MIDI Instrument ❸ the MIDI signal is sent to from Logic. This port/channel parameter can also be set in the External Instrument Plugin.

# Configuration

The configuration of the External MIDI Instrument can be a little bit confusing if you don't pay attention to a few details. Let's start with the New Tracks Dialog:

### 🎹 New Tracks Dialog

New Tracks are created in the "*New Tracks Dialog*", and that's where you have to start to pay attention. This window can have two appearances that you toggle with a checkbox in the *Preferences ➤ Display ➤ General* ❶. A bigger window ❷ with nice icons and a smaller window ❸ without the eye candy. It's a personal preference. Unfortunately, the icons are not the only difference. The interface varies, especially for setting up MIDI Tracks.

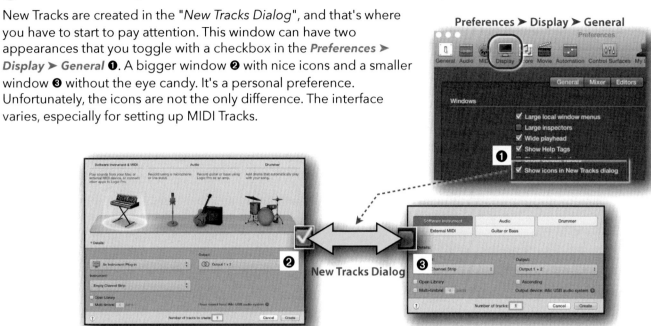

There are three types of MIDI Tracks, or two, depending on how you look at it. Here is a quick overview with screenshots of their different settings in both windows for their individual configuration:

> 1 - **Software Instrument Track** ❹: This creates a MIDI Track assigned to a Software Instrument Channel Strip.

> 2 - **Software Instrument Track (with External Instrument Plugin)** ❺: This creates a MIDI Track, also assigned to a Software Instrument Channel Strip, but with the special "*External Instrument*" Plugin already loaded.

> 3 - **External MIDI Instrument Track** ❻: This Track creates a MIDI Channel Strip, that is technically not a real (audio) Channel Strip. The Track is actually assigned to a MIDI Instrument Object in the Environment that doesn't carry any audio signal.

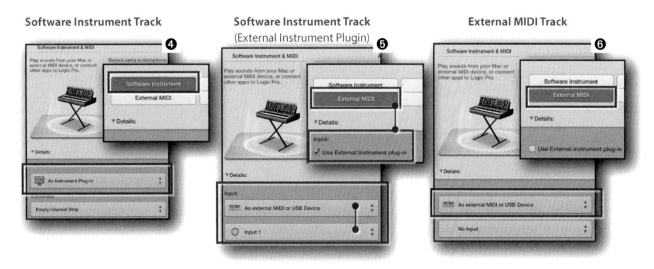

# ➡ 1 - Software Instrument Track

This selection in the New Tracks Dialog creates a MIDI Track that is assigned to one of the 256 Software Instrument Channel Strips.

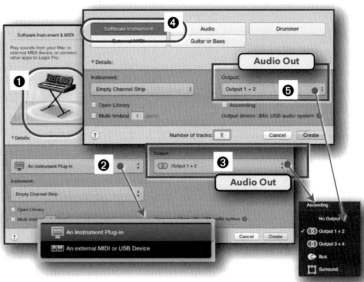

## 🎧 New Tracks Dialog

- ▶ **"With Icons" window**: In this window, you select the keyboard icon ❶ and then select "*An Instrument Plug-In*" ❷ in the Details section below. The Output ❸ button lets you pre-select the output bus for the Channel Strip.

- ▶ **"Without Icons" window**: In this window, you just select the "Software Instrument "❹ button, plus select the output bus ❺ for the Channel Strip.

- ▶ You can also use the Menu Command *Track ➤ New Software Instrument Track* or Key Command *opt+cmd+S* to create a new Software Instrument Track. It applies the settings that you chose previously in the New Tracks Dialog.

## 🎧 Routing

Please review the detailed discussion in my first book about Logic's main concept about Track vs. Channel. This is important to understand the context of setting up the External MIDI Instrument.

- **Track**: In the diagram, the gray box represents the Track ❻ in the Tracks Window. This is the element that stores the MIDI data as MIDI Regions ❼ on its Track Lane.

- **Channel Strip**: In the diagram, the light box inside represents the object that is assigned to that Track, in this case, an Instrument Channel Strip ❽. That object (which is an Environment Object), is displayed as a real Channel Strip ❾ in the Mixer Window.

- **Assignment**: By creating a new Track in the New Tracks Dialog, Logic creates a new Track and assigns an object (Channel Strip) to that Track based on the settings you make in that window.

- **Reassign**: At any time, you can assign any other object to that Track, without affecting the data on that Track (i.e. the MIDI Regions). *Ctr+click* on the Track Header to open the Shortcut Menu and navigate through the "Reassign Track" ❿ submenus. This separation between a Track (the component that stores the MIDI data) and the Channel Strip (the component that plays the MIDI data) is important to understand when switching between internal and external Instruments for the same MIDI data. For example, you recorded some MIDI Regions on Track assigned to a Software Instrument Plugin, but now, want it to be played by an external Hardware Synth.

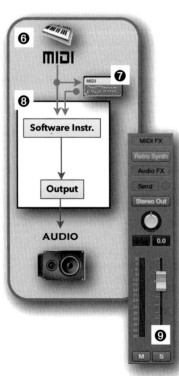

**Tracks Window**

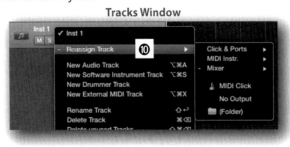

## ➡ *2 - Software Instrument Track (with External Instrument Plugin)*

This selection in the New Tracks Dialog creates a MIDI Track that is also assigned to a Software Instrument Channel Strip. The main difference, however, is that it preselects a special Software Instrument Plugin on that Channel Strip that is actually not an Instrument Plugin (a sound source), more like a "Routing Plugin" for MIDI signals and audio signals.

### 🌐 Concept

▶ The Instrument Plugin "*External Instrument*", is listed together with the other Instrument Plugins in the Plugin Menu ❶ (in the Utility Folder). It is loaded on the Instrument slot ❷ of the Instrument Channel Strip.

▶ When you open the Plugin Window, it has two sections:
  - **MIDI Out ❸**: One popup menu, the MIDI Destination, lists all the available MIDI Devices in the AMS, and the other popup menu lets you select the MIDI Channel (the MIDI data is sent to).
  - **Audio In ❸**: The Input popup menu lists all the input channels of your current Audio Interface. Select the input that you connected the audio out of your External MIDI Instrument ❺. You can even adjust the Input Volume with the slider or the numeric value field.

Here is a comparison of the Instrument Channel Strip with the two types of Instruments:

▶ **Internal Instrument (Sound Source)**: The Plugin ❻ represents the actual sound source. It receives the MIDI input from the Track ❼ and generates the sound that then runs through the Channel Strip as an audio signal.

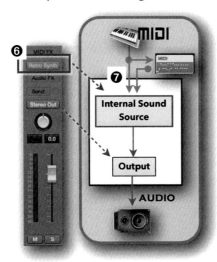

▶ **External Instrument (Sound Source)**: The Plugin ❾ routes the incoming MIDI signal via the selected MIDI port to an external MIDI Instrument ❽, the external sound source. Its audio signal is routed back ❿ to the Plugin and runs through Channel Strip as an audio signal.

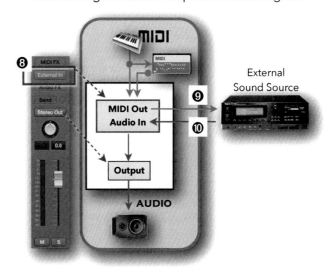

## ⚙ New Tracks Dialog

Here is how you configure the New Tracks Dialog for a new Track using the External Instrument Plugin:

▶ **"With Icons" window**: In this window, you have to make five selections:

- 1 - Select the keyboard icon ❶
- 2 - Select "*An external MIDI or USB Device*" ❷ in the Details section below.
- 3 - **MIDI Out**: This menu lets you select the output port and channel ❸ where you want to send the MIDI signal to, representing your External MIDI Instrument.
- 4 - **Audio In**: This menu lets you select the audio input channel ❹ of your current Audio Interface where you connected your External MIDI Instrument, to send its audio signal back.
- 5 - **Audio Out**: This lets you set the output channel ❺ for that Channel Strip.

▶ **"Without Icons" window**: In this window, you make the following selections:

- 1 - Select the "External MIDI" ❻ button
- 2 - Enable the checkbox "*Use External Instrument plug-in*" ❼.
- 3 - **MIDI Out**: Same button as in the other window. Select the MIDI port and channel ❽ where your External MIDI Instrument is connected to.
- 4 - **Audio In**: Same button as in the other window. Select the audio input channel ❾ of your Audio Interface, where you connected your External MIDI Instrument to.
- 5 - **Audio Out**: Same button as in the other window. Select the output channel ❿ for that Channel Strip.

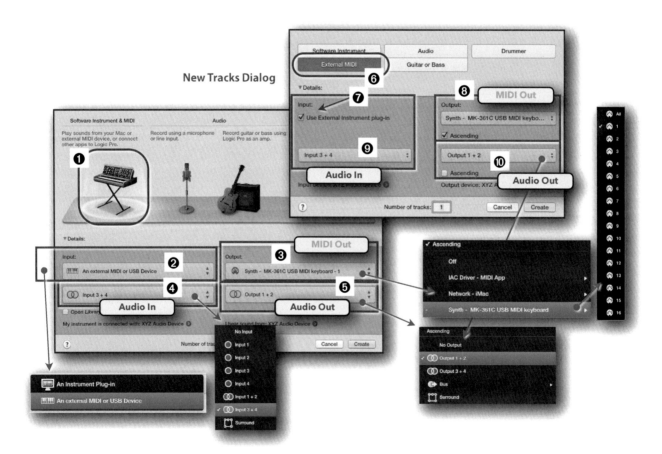

New Tracks Dialog

Please note that the Menu Command *Track ➤ External MIDI Track* DOES NOT create this type of MIDI Track (it creates the one I describe in the next section). You still can choose the Menu Command *Track ➤ New Software Instrument Track*, select the "*External Instrument*" Plugin manually and configure it in the Plugin window.

## ➡ 3 - External MIDI Instrument Track

This is the third option to create a MIDI Track (and the second option on how to configure an External MIDI Instrument).

### 🕱 Concept

Instead of using the External Instrument Plugin on an Instrument Channel Strip, with this method, you use a total different approach:

▶ **Instrument Objects**: You create a new Environment Object, a so-called MIDI Instrument Object.

▶ **Types of MIDI Instrument Objects**: Logic has three different types of those MIDI Instrument Objects:

- Single Channel Instrument ❶: Used for single-channel MIDI sound modules.
- Multitimbral Instrument ❷: Used for multi-timbral MIDI sound modules.
- Mapped Instrument ❸: Used for MIDI Drum Machines.

▶ **MIDI to External Device**: The Instrument Object functions as a "MIDI-out Router" ❹. You assign the Object to a MIDI Track and all the MIDI signals on that Track that are sent to that Object ❺ (from the Track Input or from the Track Lane) will be sent to the external MIDI destination ❻ that you choose for that Object in the Object Inspector ❼ (in the Environment), which is the same as the Track Inspector (in Logic's Main Window).

▶ **External Destination**: TheTrack Inspector has two parameters that let you select the external MIDI Destination ❻:

- **Port**: This popup menu ❽ lists all the external MIDI Devices (recognized by the AMS).
- **Channel**: Select over which MIDI Channel you want to send the MIDI signal to the external MIDI Device.

▶ **Audio Return**: Unlike with the External Instrument Plugin that had a return path for the audio signal (coming from the External MIDI Instrument), the MIDI Object is a "one way street". You have to route the audio signal back to the mixer separately by creating an Aux Channel Strip ❾ and choose the input channel of your Audio Interface (the external MIDI Instrument is connected to) on that Aux Channel Strip. Alternatively, you can us an Input Channel Strip, but that would require that you set it up in the Environment Window.

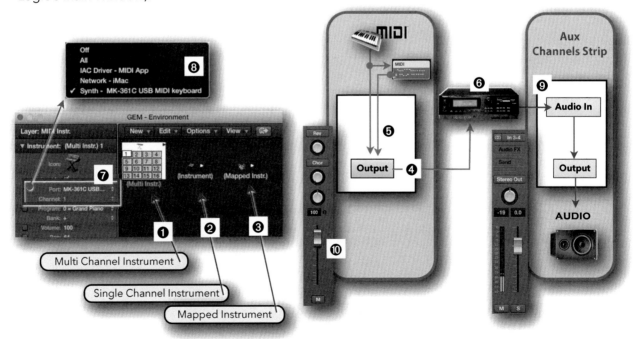

A MIDI object can be displayed as a special MIDI Channel Strip ❿ in the Mixer window, although, it does not carry any audio signal like all the other Channel Strips.

## 🎹 New Tracks Dialog

Here is how you configure the New Tracks Dialog to create a new Track assigned to a MIDI Instrument Object:

▶ **"With Icons" window**: In this window, you have to make four selections:
- 1 - Select the keyboard icon ❶
- 2 - Select "*An external MIDI or USB Device*" ❷ in the Details section below.
- 3 - **MIDI Out**: This menu lets you select the output port and channel ❸ where you want to send the MIDI signal to, your External MIDI Instrument.
- 4 - **Audio In**: Make sure that "*No Input*" ❹ is selected. In that case, the new Track will be an Instrument Object. If you select any input, then the new Track will be assigned to an Instrument Channel Strip with the "External Instrument" Plugin selected.

▶ **"Without Icons" window**: In this window, you make the following three selections:
- 1 - Select the "External MIDI" ❺ button
- 2 - Make sure to have this checkbox "Use External Instrument plug-in" disabled ❻. In this window, the checkbox is the switch to determine if the new Track is assigned to a MIDI Object (off), or to an Instrument Channel Strip with the "External Instrument" Plugin selected (on).
- 3 - **MIDI Out**: Same button as in the other window. Select the MIDI port and channel ❼ where your External MIDI Instrument is connected to.

New Tracks Dialog

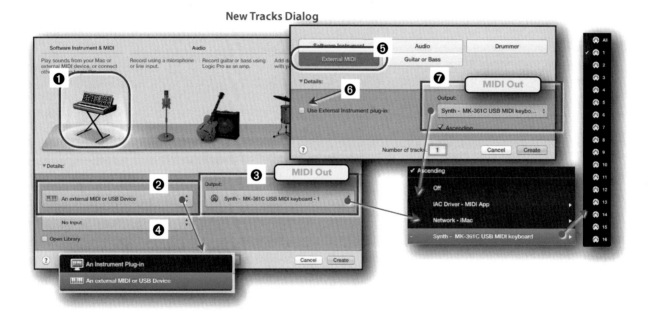

A few more things to consider:

▶ You can also use the Menu Command *Track ➤ New External MIDI Track* or the Key Command *opt+cmd+X* to create this type of MIDI Track.

▶ To create an Aux Channel Strip as the audio return from the external Hardware Instrument, choose the Local Menu Command ❽ in the Mixer *Options ➤ Create New Auxiliary Channel Strip* or Key Command *ctr+N*

Mixer Window ➤ Options

▶ The MIDI Object that is automatically created in the Environment is a Multi-timbral MIDI Instrument in the *MIDI Instr.* Layer named "*GM Device*" ❾.

▶ Deleting a MIDI Track will not delete its MIDI Object in the Environment.

## 💀 Advanced Settings

Using the MIDI Object to connect an External MIDI Instrument to Logic provides much more flexibility to your configuration than using the method with External Instrument Plugin.

Here are a few considerations:

- You can create individual MIDI Objects based on the type of external MIDI Instrument you have ❶. For example, single-channel, multi-timbral, or Mapped Instruments.
- Your External MIDI Instrument can be a computer by itself, running another version of Logic as a slave ❷, that you send the MIDI data via the MIDI Objects.
- You can quickly change the destination Device (port) in the Track Inspector, including its MIDI parameters ❸.
- You can also select the MIDI Device and their channels directly in the Library Window ❹.
- You can control the MIDI parameter on the special MIDI Channel Strip ❺ along with the other Channel Strips in your Mixer.
- The Volume and Parameter controls on the Tracks Header can control the MIDI Volume and Pan on the MIDI Devices ❻.
- Use the "*IAC*" Device (Inter-Application Communication) in the Audio MIDI Setup utility to route MIDI to other apps on your Machine or on your network, using the "*Network*" Device.

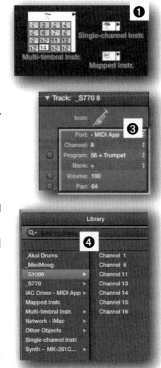

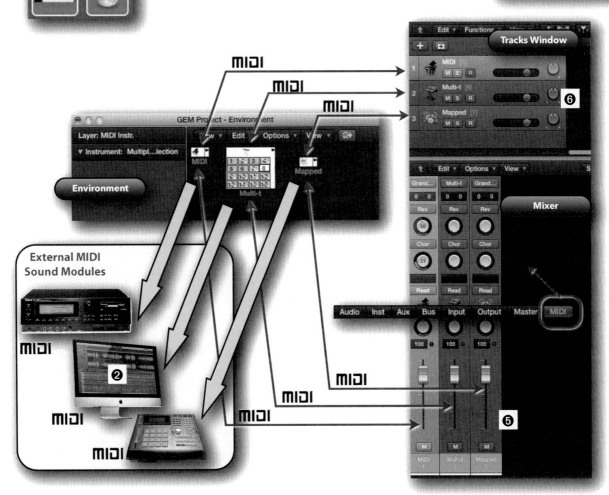

# Which Configuration

I hope you have a better understanding now about the two types of MIDI Instruments you can use in your Logic Project. All the Software Instrument Plugins that you load inside Logic are the "Internal MIDI Instruments", and all the MIDI sound sources that create their sound "outside" of Logic are the "External MIDI Instruments". To use any of those External MIDI Instrument, you have two options on how to connect them to Logic, using an External Instrument Plugin on an Instrument Channel Strip, or use a MIDI Instrument Object with an additional Aux Channel Strip for the audio return.

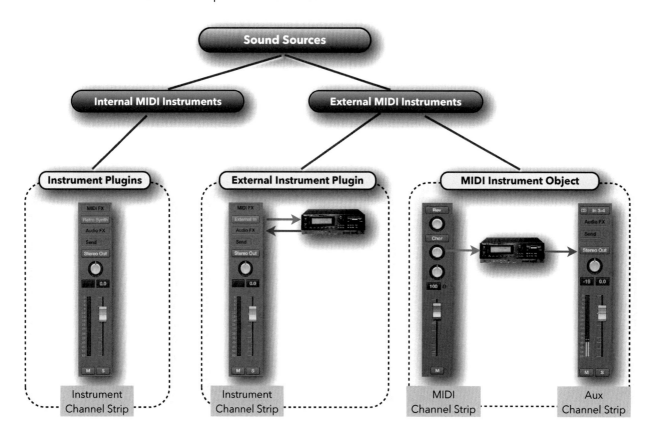

## ➡ *External MIDI Instrument Configuration - Which one to choose?*

As you have seen, these two options are quite different in their configuration and both have advantages and disadvantages. It depends on what type of external MIDI Instrument you have, how you will use it, plus a few other considerations:

### 💿 External Instrument Plugin

- Pro: Easy to setup. Only one Channel Strip for the sending and receiving signal. You only work with the familiar Instrument Channel Strip and don't have to deal with those MIDI Instrument Objects in the Environment.

- Cons: This method is limited and doesn't allow for more advanced configurations. You can't use Mapped Instruments for Drum Machines.

### 💿 MIDI Instrument Object

- Pro: The configuration is more flexible, especially if you create those objects manually in the Environment. You can use special Mapped Instruments for Drum Machines. More on all those features in the *Environment* chapter.

- Cons: You have to deal with two Channel Strips per Instruments. Advanced operations require more knowledge about the inner works of the Environment.

Using MIDI in your Logic Project can be as easy as connecting your MIDI Keyboard to your Computer, launch Logic, create a Software Instrument Track with a synth plugin loaded, and voilà, you play that synth. Record what you play as MIDI Regions, and Logic will play it back. However, life isn't always that easy, especially when it comes to MIDI and MIDI in Logic. There are many hidden obstacles that can make your production life miserable, because MIDI doesn't work or doesn't work the way you expect it to work.

Recording audio, while having its own challenges, is actually easier compared to MIDI. Once you get your audio signal inside Logic, you have succeeded. Press record and watch the level. That's pretty much it (from an extremely simplified point of view). MIDI, on the other hand, is not just one continuous stream of digitized audio samples. A MIDI signal is a non-continuous flow of chunks of data, each chunk containing different types of data, different messages, depending on what you send from your MIDI controller.

Troubleshooting MIDI and making sure that the MIDI signal flows as smoothly as possible, requires a little knowledge of the MIDI signal itself. Its data structure and specific rules are written down in the MIDI specifications. Although it is not rocket-science, reading and trying to understand those MIDI specs can be quite challenging for most.

The bad news is that there is at least some basic understanding of MIDI required to use MIDI in your Project. The good news, I have already spent a few pages on my "Logic Pro X - How it Works" book to introduce the basic concepts of Logic.. If you want to learn a little bit more, I can highly recommend the very entertaining video tutorial by Peter Schwartz, "MIDI Demystified" (available at MacProVideo.com).

## Signal Flow & Content Filter

There are two elements you have to watch out for when dealing with MIDI:

▶ **Flow**: Where does the MIDI signal go to. Does it leave source A, (the MIDI Keyboard), does it arrive at its destination (Logic), does it play the right sound source (Plugin).

▶ **Content**: Even if the MIDI signal flows successfully from A to B and arrives at its destination, there is still the important question about the content, did the right stuff (MIDI messages) arrive? Just because you received the Amazon package from UPS, doesn't mean that the package contains exactly what they are supposed to ship to you in the right size.

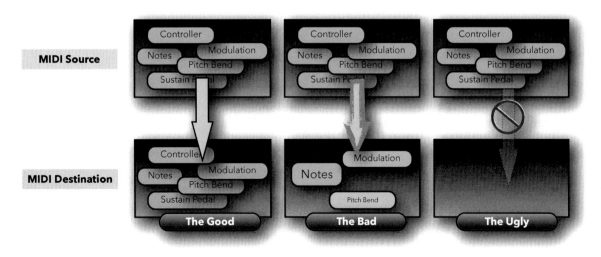

I will break down the MIDI signal flow discussion into four steps, four elements you have to be aware of when dealing with MIDI.

▶ **1 - MIDI Signal Flow**: This is the fist step of following the signal from source to destination through the different components along the way.

▶ **2 - MIDI Filter**: These are the components along the signal flow that can remove parts of the signal, specific MIDI messages.

▶ **3 - MIDI Channels**: MIDI Channels are an integral part of the MIDI Message, like individual lanes you can send the message along the way.

▶ **4 - MIDI Parameters**: These are the components that do not filter, but alter the existing MIDI Messages.

## ➡ *1 - MIDI Signal Flow*

Here is the very basic MIDI Signal Flow, getting MIDI into Logic:

### 🌐 MIDI In - MIDI Out

- The External MIDI Keyboard ❶ is connected to your computer, where OSX lists that MIDI Device in the Audio MIDI Setup utility ❷ if it recognizes it (proper cable, proper driver).

- The "first point of entry" in Logic is the Environment. Every new Logic Project contains the Physical Input Object ❸, which lists all the (enabled) MIDI Devices from the Audio MIDI Setup.

- As a default, that Physical Input Object is connected (cabled ❹) to the default Sequencer Input Object ❺. It is the representation of the Tracks Window ❻ (formerly known as the Sequencer).

- Any Track in the Tracks Window that is selected or Record Enabled will receive the MIDI input signal

❶ to play its Software Instrument Plugin (or External MIDI Instrument) and record the MIDI signal as MIDI Regions on the Track's Track Lane.

- To send MIDI out of Logic is only necessary when you want to use an External MIDI Instrument as a sound source, as we have just discussed in the previous section. An exception is the Control Surfaces that I cover in a later chapter.

- The external MIDI Device ❼ that you want to send the signal to is selected on an individual MIDI Track in its Track Inspector ❽ (or the External Instrument Plugin). The available MIDI Devices are the ones listed in the Audio MIDI Setup ❷.

- The MIDI routing to the "outside" is usually done through a MIDI Instrument Object ❾ In the Environment.

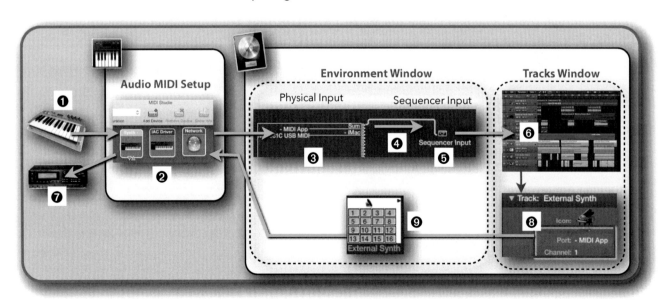

## ☻ Check the Flow

In case the MIDI signal from your MIDI Keyboard does not "arrive" at its destination on your MIDI Track in Logic, you have to find out where the flow got interrupted. As we have just seen, the signal goes through various components, so you have to check at those stages.

### ☑ Check OSX Input

Your first checkpoint (besides checking the MIDI or USB cable ❶) is the Audio MIDI Setup. If the MIDI Device doesn't show up, then you might have a driver issue. Check compatibility between your device driver and the current OSX version you are using. If the Device icon is visible, but grayed out, that means, it was recognized before but has a problem now.

If the Device is visible and you want to make sure AMS receives a signal, click on the "Test Setup"❷ icon in the Control Bar. Now, when AMS receives a MIDI signal, it makes a noise and flashes the screen. The "Rescan MIDI" icon next to it, tells OSX to search again for MIDI Devices.

### ☑ Check Logic Input

The Clicks & Ports Layer in the Environment Window has by default two objects placed between the Physical Input Object and the Sequencer Input Object. The Keyboard Object ❸ displays any incoming note with a black dot on the keys, and the Monitor Object ❹ lists every incoming MIDI Event similar to the Event List. This is the place to check if (and what) the MIDI signal is reaching Logic and if it is passed along to the Tracks Window.

### ☑ Check Tracks Window Input

You can see directly in the Tracks Window if you get incoming MIDI signals or not. The Control Bar Display lights up two LEDs ❺ next to the Time Signature. The upper LED indicates incoming and the lower LED indicates outgoing MIDI Events. If you switch to the Custom Display Mode, then you can have the MIDI Activity ❻ fields display the actual MIDI Message.

### ☑ Check MIDI Keyboard

You can use Logic's internal Musical Typing ❼ Window (*cmd+K*) to play the currently selected Track and see if you have an issue with the signal coming from the outside ❶.

### ☑ Check Overall MIDI Flow

You can use any third-party utility app, like the free "MIDI Monitor" ❽, to troubleshoot any kind of MIDI signal flow issues on your computer.

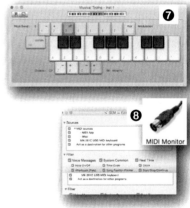

Here is the overview where along the signal flow you can check for vital signs:

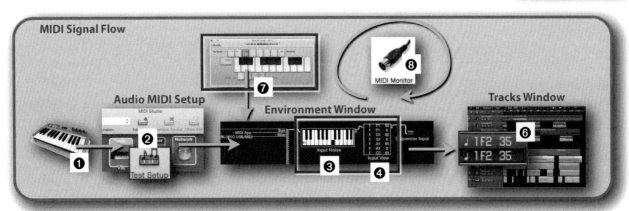

## ➡ 2 - MIDI Filter

While in the first step we want to make sure not to lose our MIDI signal, in this step, we want to eliminate part of the MIDI signal on purpose.

### 🎱 Input Filter

This is a simple and easy procedure.

In the **Project Settings ➤ MIDI ➤ Input Filter**, you can find seven checkboxes for seven types of MIDI Messages. Just click on the one that you want to eliminate. The messages are filtered out ❶ right before they reach the selected Track ❷. You can still see all the incoming messages in the MIDI Activity Display ❸.

There are two approaches:

Project Settings ➤ MIDI ➤ Input Filter

- **No Filters**: As a default, all checkboxes are off. You can leave it that way and don't bother with that page at all. Nothing gets filtered out.
- **Selected Filter**: If you don't know what System Exclusive data is, or your MIDI Keyboard doesn't have Polyphonic Aftertouch, then chances are, you never need those types of MIDI data. I would recommend, filtering all data types that you don't use. This has the advantage that you don't record redundant data (i.e. Aftertouch), or send data by accident that could mess up your Project (i.e. Program Change). Just keep this window in mind in case you need to record Program Change data or any of the other ones you filtered out, and pulling your hair out, why Logic doesn't record that.

### 🎱 Controller Assignment

This is not an official MIDI filter, but nevertheless a filter that eliminates specific MIDI Events. It is one of the lesser known facts in Logic, one you should definitely be aware of.

Logic has a window called Controller Assignments. It belongs to the topic of Control Surfaces that I cover in a separate chapter later in the book. This is the window where you map external hardware controllers to specific parameters in Logic. An external controller can be anything that sends MIDI Messages, including your standard MIDI Keyboard that you use to play and record your MIDI Instruments in Logic.

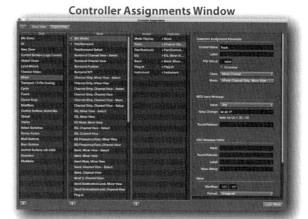

Controller Assignments Window

For example, if you assign the MIDI message "Note On C3" (by pressing the note C3 on your MIDI keyboard) to a specific parameter in this window, then that MIDI Message is filtered out, and is not available for recording in your Track. Imagine you did that assignment by accident (by pressing some buttons). Now when you record your MIDI Tracks, every note is recorded in your MIDI Region except the notes C3. That would be a nice task for troubleshooting if you don't know about it.

The notes are filtered out ❹ before they reach the Physical Input Object ❺ and are, therefore, not even visible in the Environment anymore when you use a Monitor Object ❻.

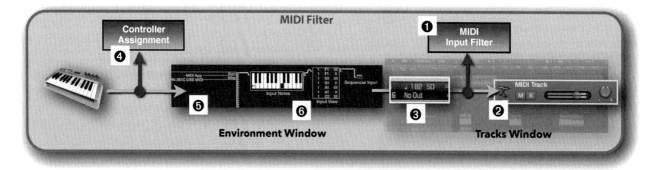

## ➡ *3 - MIDI Channels*

In this third step about the MIDI Signal Flow we talk about the important "MIDI Channel". Let's review a few basics about MIDI:

### 💀 Terminology

▶ **MIDI Signal**: A MIDI signal is actually a series of individual MIDI Messages. When you play on your MIDI keyboard, it generates those MIDI Messages that are sent out through its MIDI output port.

▶ **MIDI Message**: There are two types of MIDI Messages: System Messages and Channel Messages.

▶ **Channel Message**: There are 7 types of Channel Messages and whatever data they carry (Note, Pitch Bend, Controller) they all include a Channel information, a so-called *MIDI Channel*.

▶ **MIDI Channel**: Each Channel Message has to be set to a specific MIDI Channel between 1 and 16.

### 💀 MIDI Components

▶ **Generate MIDI Message**: A MIDI Controller (your MIDI Keyboard), generates the MIDI Message and can send it to a Sequencer to record (store) those MIDI Messages, or send it to a Sound Module to "play" those MIDI Messages.

▶ **Store MIDI Message**: A Sequencer (that's how DAWs were called in the olden days) can store (record) MIDI Messages that they receive from a MIDI Controller. They can also send those stored MIDI Messages to a Sound Module when playing back the Sequencer.

▶ **Receive MIDI Message**: A Sound Module receives MIDI Messages directly from the MIDI Controller (live), or from the Sequencer (playback). Either way, it is the component that produces sound (audio signal) from the incoming MIDI Messages (MIDI signal).

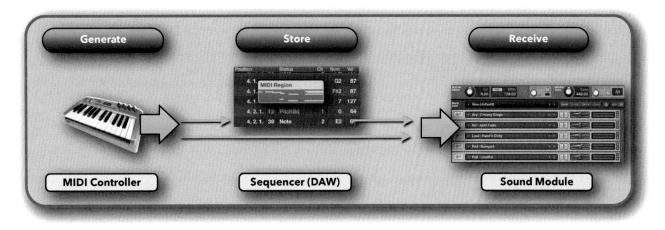

### 💀 Sound Module

You have to differentiate between two different types of Sound Modules, which is important regarding the MIDI Channels:

▶ **Mono-Timbral**: This is a device with one sound generator, either monophonic (can play only one voice) or polyphonic (can play multiple voices).

▶ **Multi-Timbral**: This is a device that contains multiple sound generators (mostly polyphonic). Each sound generator can use a different Sound Preset, known as Patch (Bass, Synth, String).

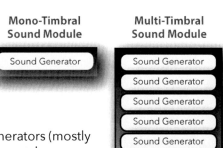

### Channel Mode

The MIDI Channel is that additional information that is sent and stored with each MIDI Channel Message. But the MIDI Channel plays another role on the receiving part, the Sound Module:

Each Sound Module has to be set to a specific Channel Mode, which determines how the Sound Module reacts to MIDI Channels contained in the incoming MIDI Messages. The MIDI Specs defines the various Channel Modes (Omni, Poly, Mono) for different purposes, but I demonstrate only the most common scenarios:

▶ **Mono-Timbral - Any**: All of Logic's Instrument Plugins are Mono-Timbral. One Sound Module (the Plugin) equals one sound generator. In that case, the Sound Module doesn't really care what MIDI Channel is contained in the MIDI Message, it just plays the sound based on the incoming message.

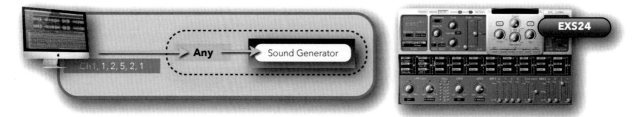

▶ **Mono-Timbral - Match**: In the days before you had countless plugins, you used Hardware Synthesizers that were daisy-chained from the source through the various synths (MIDI out ➤ MIDI in ➤ MIDI thru ➤ MIDI in ➤ MIDI thru …). The MIDI signal runs through the cable, containing all the MIDI messages, but each Sound Module plays only those MIDI Events that match its own MIDI channel.

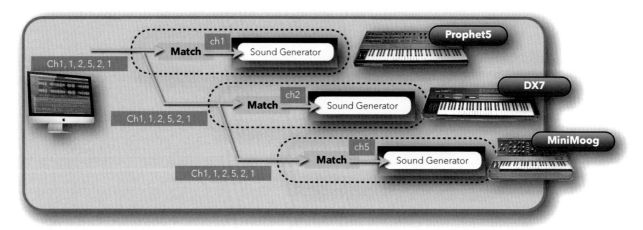

▶ **Multi-Timbral - Match**: Each sound generator unit inside a Multi-timbral Sound Module can be set to a specific MIDI Channel and only plays incoming MIDI Messages that match that MIDI Channel. Many popular Instrument Plugins are multi-timbral (Kontakt, Play, Omnisphere, etc.). This requires special attention in Logic regarding the routing of the MIDI Channels, but also the audio output channels.

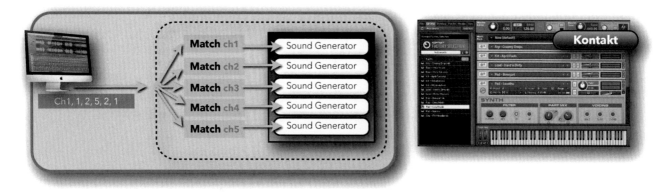

## 🎚️ MIDI Channel Matching

After that little detour into the MIDI basics, let's see what happens in Logic with those MIDI Channels. Let me say upfront that you have to keep a close eye on those MIDI Channels, or you might lose control over MIDI Messages and have a hard time figuring out who is playing what, and where, and why not.

Here are the five checkpoints for the MIDI Channel:

▶ ❶ - **MIDI Controller**: As I mentioned earlier, every MIDI controller that generates MIDI data assigns each message (MIDI Event) a specific MIDI Channel. The default is most likely MIDI Channel 1, but some controllers can set it to any MIDI Channel.

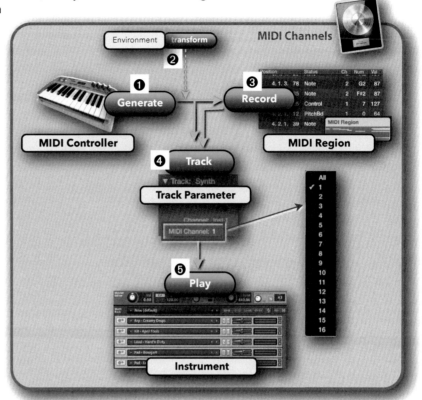

▶ ❷ - **Environment**: I list this step just to let you know that you can intercept the MIDI Message already in the Environment before it reaches the Tracks Window. Here, you can mess with every part of the MIDI Message including the MIDI Channel, i.e. the "Channelize" function in the Sequencer Object or the Transformer Object. More on that in the Environment chapter.

▶ ❸ - **MIDI Region**: When you record an incoming MIDI signal on a Track, it stores the MIDI signal as individual MIDI Events. Each MIDI Event is stored with its own MIDI Channel, the one sent from the MIDI Controller (assume that it passed the Environment "unharmed"). You can see those MIDI Channels in the Event List under the Channel column where you can easily change them.

▶ ❹ - **Track Parameter**: This is the most important part. The Track Inspector displays all the Track Parameters, which are playback parameters for the object (Instrument) assigned to the current Track. One of the Track Parameters is the MIDI Channel. That means, regardless of what MIDI Channel the incoming MIDI Events are set to, this parameter can overwrite it when the signal passes through this component, and that's why this is such an important setting. There are two types of settings:

- **All**: Selecting "All" in the MIDI Channel popup menu lets all MIDI Messages pass through with their original MIDI Channel.
- **Ch1 ... 16**: Selecting any MIDI Channel from the popup menu will change the MIDI Channel of any incoming MIDI Message to that specific MIDI Channel number.

▶ ❺ - **Instrument**: The Instrument is the last step of the MIDI Channel chain, the component that receives the MIDI signal to play through a sound generator. It is important what type of Instrument it is.

- Mono-Timbral: If the Instrument is a Mono-timbral Instrument, acting as one Sound Source, then it might play back on **ANY** MIDI Channel. This is how all the Logic Instrument Plugins behave, and that's why you don't have to pay too much attention to MIDI Channels in a basic setup.
- Multi-Timbral: If the Instrument is a Multi-timbral Instrument with multiple Sound Sources that can each load different Sound Presets (Patches), then it might require that the incoming MIDI signals **MATCH** a specific MIDI Channel the individual Sound Sources are set to.

I discuss the topic of Multi-timbral instruments and how to configure them in Logic in a moment.

## 🎛 Track Inspector

There is one potential confusion I want to point out about the Track Inspector in regards to the MIDI Channel parameter. The Track Inspector displays the parameters of the object that is assigned to the current Track. Different types of objects have different parameters available, and that's why the Track Inspector looks different for the different types of objects. Let's have a closer look at the MIDI Channel Parameter for those different types of objects.

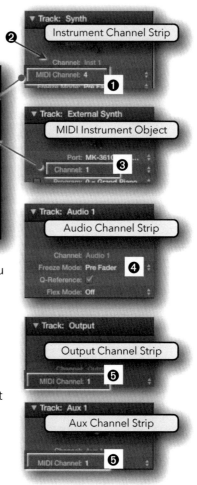

- **Instrument Channel Strip**: The parameter is labeled "MIDI Channel" ❶, so no confusion. However, pay attention to the parameter above. It is named "Channel"❷. This refers to the "Channel Strip Type and Number" of the current object and has nothing to do with MIDI Channels.

- **MIDI Instrument Object**: The Track Inspector for a MIDI Instrument Object has a parameter named "Channel". ❸ This is where you have to pay attention, because it has nothing to do with the "Channel" parameter we have seen on a Channel Strip Object. Here, it refers to the MIDI Channel of that MIDI Object.

- **Audio Channel Strip**: The Track Inspector for the Audio Channel Strip doesn't have a MIDI Channel parameter ❹. There is no receiving component for that parameter.

- **Other Channel Strip Objects**: All the other Channel Strip Objects still list the "MIDI Channel" ❺ parameter without a real functionality (with the exception of the Aux Track when used for the multi-outputs of a Software Instrument Track).

## ➡ 4 - MIDI Parameters

The last step of "*keeping an eye on the MIDI data along the Signal Flow*" are the various MIDI Parameters. The MIDI Channel was just one of them. There are multiple stages along the MIDI signal flow where you can alter the individual MIDI Parameters.

The different parameters for a MIDI Event can represent real values or offset values:

- ▶ **Real Value** (stored): These are any parameter values that you generate (playing with your MIDI controller) and record on a MIDI Region. Once stored in the MIDI Region, you can view those "real" values and change them in the various MIDI Editors. For example, change the position, the pitch, or any other parameter.

- ▶ **Playback Offset Value** (on-the-fly): The Region Inspector and the Track Inspector provide parameters that let you apply an offset to the real parameter values of the stored MIDI Events. For example, transpose the notes, apply a velocity offset. While the Region Parameter applies those offsets per Region, the Track Inspector applies its offsets to all the MIDI Regions on that Track, in addition to the offset the Region Inspector had applied. As you can see, you need to keep an eye on both Inspectors to make sure they are set to the parameter values you want (in case you set some offsets previously and forgot about them).

- ▶ **Playback Offset Value** (stored): While all those on-the-fly parameter offsets are not visible when you look at the MIDI Event in the MIDI Editor ("I see the note D4, then why is it playing F3?"), the Quantize Parameter is the exception. It actually moves the position of a MIDI Event visually in the MIDI Editor. Changing the quantize value will move it to a different position, and turning Quantize off will move it to its original value.

**Functions ➤ MIDI Region Parameters ➤**

| | |
|---|---|
| Apply Quantization Permanently | ^Q |
| Apply All Parameters Permanently | ^N |
| Apply All except Channel | ❻ |
| Apply All except Channel and Delay | |

You can convert offset values to "real" values ❻ with commands in the Tracks Window's Local Menu *Functions ➤ MIDI Region Parameters ➤*

Here is a diagram that shows the big picture regarding the MIDI Flow and the different stages where the MIDI Parameters can be changed:

▶ ❶ **MIDI Controller**: You generate the original MIDI data on your MIDI controller.

▶ ❷ **MIDI Transformer**: In the Environment window, you can place a MIDI Transformer Object in the MIDI signal flow to change any MIDI Parameters before the MIDI signal arrives at the Track input or any other object it is cabled to.

▶ ❸ **Region Thru Parameter**: The Region Inspector displays the special "*MIDI Thru*" Parameters when no MIDI Region is selected in the Workspace. These are the Parameters that are copied over to any newly created MIDI Region (recorded or "penciled in") as their default Region Parameter.

▶ ❹ **MIDI Editor**: The various MIDI Editors let you change the original parameter values for each MIDI Event.

▶ ❺ **Region Parameter**: The Region Inspector lets you apply offset values to specific Parameters for the currently selected MIDI Region(s). Make sure the "MIDI Thru" Parameters are not set to any offset value you don't want to have applied to any new MIDI Region.

▶ ❻ **Track Parameter**: The Track Inspector lets you set specific offset values to Parameters that apply to all MIDI Events that are sent to the selected MIDI Instrument.

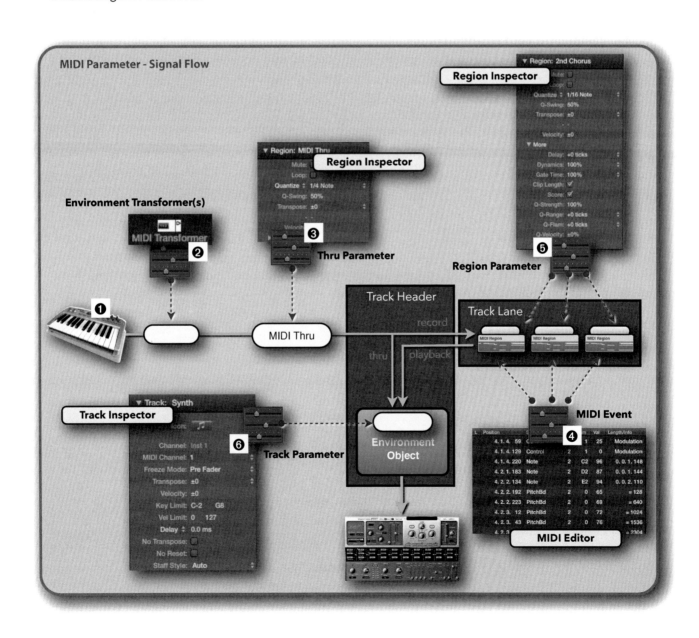

# Reset Messages

When playing back your MIDI Project, MIDI Events get sent in all directions based on the Signal Flow we just discussed. Those MIDI Events can be Notes, but also, all sorts of Controllers, Sustain Pedal, Modulation Wheel data, Pitch Bend data, etc. At any time when you stop the playback, the MIDI Instruments stay in that last state. For example, the last event was a Sustain Pedal on-message, a Pitch Bend up-value, or other controller messages you fabricated with some Environment Objects. Now when you move the Playhead to a different position and start the playback again, the MIDI Instruments would continue to play with the new MIDI signal coming in. That could mean that the next few notes play while the Sustain Pedal is still on (it didn't receive an off-message), or they play with the Pitch Bend value up (it didn't receive a Pitch Bend 0 message), and so on. In that case, you need a command to send it the "neutral", the default values to the MIDI Instrument, a so-called **Reset Message**.

Other circumstances are when you want to send specific default values, or send a "panic" message (reset everything) when you are dealing with stuck notes or any other sudden weirdness.

The main questions about the Reset Command are:

> ## What will be sent - To Whom will it be sent - When will it be sent

### ➡ Full Reset - All Notes off

There is one special Reset Message, the *Full Reset* that you can trigger with the following command:

 *Double-click* on the MIDI Activity field in the Control Bar Display (has to be set to the Custom Display Mode to be visible).

This is what happens:

- Logic sends out a MIDI Note-off message for each 128 notes on all 16 MIDI Channels to all MIDI Instruments in your Project
- The Messages are sent to Software Instruments and MIDI Instrument Objects
- The lower MIDI Activity field displays the MIDI Message while they are sent out (very fast)
- If you *double-click+hold* on the upper filed, then it displays "Full Reset…"

### ➡ Reset Software Instruments

Logic automatically sends a reset message to its Software Instruments when you start playback. This ensures that any controller and pitch bend is set to its neutral position and any still ringing note is turned off.

You have three separate checkboxes in the *Preferences ➤ MIDI ➤ Reset Messages* to send individual reset messages for Software Instruments. It seems that Software Instruments react differently to Logic's reset messages, so the results can be a bit inconsistent.

Preferences ➤ MIDI ➤ Reset Messages

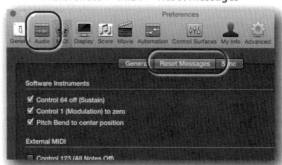

➡️ *Reset MIDI Outputs*

🙂 **Send To Whom?**

The following Reset commands are only sent to the output of MIDI Instrument Objects ❶ in your Project. These are used for external MIDI Instruments, or when using a Multi Instr. Object cabled into an Instrument Channel Strip with a Multi-timbral Plugin (which I will explain a little bit later in this chapter).

**Preferences ➤ Audio ➤ Reset Messages**

🙂 **Send what?**

Which type of MIDI Messages are sent out is set with individual checkboxes in the *Preferences ➤ MIDI ➤ Reset Messages* ❷

The available checkboxes are for various controllers, the Pitch Bend, plus the Instrument Settings.

▶ **Instrument Settings**:

The last checkbox "*Send used instrument settings on reset*" is for those three settings ❸ available in the Track Inspector if a Track is assigned to a MIDI Instrument Object ❶. You can set the Program Number, Volume, and Pan value and have it sent out with the Reset command (checkbox must be enabled in the Track Inspector ❸). This was useful for older external MIDI hardware, to send them default setting values.

Those Instrument Settings can also be sent to Instruments that have these settings enabled when you load your Project *Project Settings ➤ MIDI ➤ General* ❹

**Project Settings ➤ MIDI ➤ General**

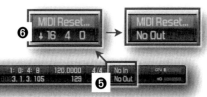

🙂 **Send When?**

The Reset Message can be sent with the following actions/commands:

- 🔈 Hit the 0 key while in Stop Mode.
- 🔈 *Double+click* on the Stop Button 🔳 in the Control Bar.
- 🔈 *Click* on the MIDI Activity field ❺ in the Control Bar Display (has to be set to the Custom Display Mode to be visible). The upper value will display "MIDI Reset…" ❻ and the lower field displays the values that are sent out to any External MIDI Instruments (if available). The values are passing by quickly, don't blink if you want to see them.
- 🔈 The Reset Messages are also sent out when you close your Project.

▶ You can exclude individual Tracks from receiving the Reset messages by selecting the "*No Reset*" ❼ checkbox in the Track Inspector.

## ➡ *Chase*

The Chase feature is kind of a special Reset
Command that takes care of the following problem:

When you play back a Region somewhere in the
middle, then it could sound differently as when you
play it from the beginning:

▶  ❶: When you have a long drone note at the beginning of a Region, but
you start later in the Region, then the
Project would sound without that drone
note, because there is no Note-on
Message.

▶  ❷: When you have a Region with a Sustain-
on at the beginning, but start it in the
middle, then it would play that section
without the sustain.

▶  ❸: When you play a Region that has Mod
Wheel data and you start in between where
there are no Control Points, then that note would sound without vibrato.

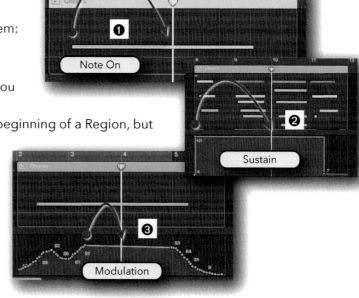

### 🌑 Chase "backwards"

When Chase is enabled, Logic is looking back on each MIDI
Track all the way to the beginning (across multiple Regions)
for any MIDI Events on that Track and "updates" those
Events. It starts notes that are "ongoing" ❶ and sets any
controller value to the previous value ❷ ❸.

The Chase feature can be enabled for separate MIDI
Messages with their individual checkboxes ❹. They are
pretty much self explanatory, except maybe the following:

Project Settings ➤ MIDI ➤ Chase

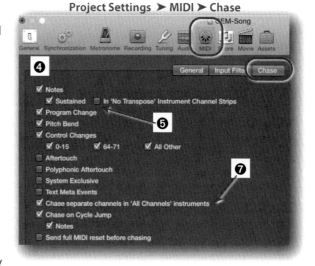

▶  **Notes: In 'No Transpose' Instrument Channel Strips
❺**
The Track Inspector for Instruments has a checkbox
labeled "No Transpose" ❻. This lets you mark Drum
Tracks or other Tracks that you want to exclude from any
global Transpose commands. You can use those marks to also exclude them from the "Note Chase". For
example, if you have a long note that you played for a Cymbal Crash, you don't want it to be triggered in
between. This is also useful to mark Tracks that trigger SFX.

▶  **Chase Separate channels in "All Channels" instruments ❼**
If you use a Multi Instr. MIDI Object ❽, then the Chase will be separately
on all its 16 sub-channels.

▶  **About Key Switches**
Using Key Switches is always a problem when
starting somewhere in between. The Note
Chase only works when starting on an
ongoing note. So the trick is to extend Key
Switching Notes from one Key Switch note to
the next one ❾ (use the legato command), so
the correct Key Switch note is always been
sent regardless of where you start.

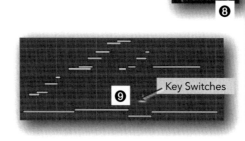

# Basics

There is a lot of confusion about Multi-timbral Instruments, especially how to use them in Logic and how to set them up. In order to understand how to do it and why to do it a specific way, we have to get some basic understanding about the terminology and the concepts behind Multi-timbral Instruments. Let's start with the following three terms: **Multi-Timbral**, **Multi-Voice**, **Multi-Output**.

## ➡ *Multi-Timbral*

I already touched this topic in the previous section about MIDI Channels and sure enough, when talking about Multi-timbral Instruments, you have to talk about MIDI Channels. To understand the term "Multi-Timbral", replace the word "Timbral" with "Sound Generator".

### 💀 Mono-Timbral

Mono-Timbral

A Mono-timbral Sound Module (this can be a hardware device or a software device in the form of a plugin) contains one sound generator. For example, you send a MIDI signal (the notes c-d-e) to that sound generator and it plays those MIDI notes based on the preset you loaded into that sound generator. This can be a string sound, a piano sound, etc. The important part is that you can only load one sound preset at a time: "One Sound Generator" = "Mono Timbral".

MIDI Signal

All of the early MIDI Synthesizers where all Mono-Timbral. Most of the Software Instrument Plugins nowadays are also mono-timbral, including all of Logic's Software Instruments.

> ## Mono-Timbral = One Sound Generator

### 💀 Multi-Timbral

Multi-Timbral

A Multi-timbral Sound Module contains multiple sound generators in one device or Plugin. For example, you select a string sound in Sound Generator #1 and a piano sound in Sound Generator #2. Now when you play the notes c-d-e, you will hear them played by the string and piano sound at the same time. Of course, you can send different MIDI notes to each sound generator in a Sound Module. That's where the MIDI Channels come in. Each sound generator inside a Multi-timbral Sound Module can be set to an individual MIDI Channel (between #1 and #16), for example, sound generator #1 to MIDI Ch#1 and sound generator #2 to MIDI Ch#2. Now when you want to send MIDI Notes to sound generator #2, just send them on MIDI Channel #2 and they will be played only by sound generator #2.

MIDI Signal
MIDI Signal
MIDI Signal
MIDI Signal
MIDI Signal

The early Hardware Sampler Instruments like the AKAI S1000 and Roland S770 were multi-timbral and most of the "flagship" Software Instruments like *Kontakt*, EastWest *Player*, or Spectrasonics' *Omnisphere* are multi-timbral too.

> ## Multi-Timbral = Many Sound Generators

## ➡ *Multi-Voice*

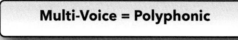

EXS24

The term "Multi-Voice" describes the "polyphony". Great, explaining one technical term with another technical term.

- A monophonic sound generator can produce only "one"-"sound" ("mono" "phone"). The term sound means, in this context, one note or any kind of noise. You can play only one note at a time on a monophonic synth, no chords.
- A polyphonic sound generator can produce "many" - "sounds" ("poly" - "phone"). On a polyphonic synth, you can play multiple notes at the same time, for example, chords.
- The number of "voices" determines how many "notes" you can play simultaneously.
- A "Multi-Voice" Sound Module is, therefore, just another term for "polyphonic" Sound Module.
- On the EXS24, you can set the amount of voices you need (up to 64) ❶, and also change it to monophonic ❷ to let it play only one voice at a time. This is useful for sounds with portamento glide effects.

> **Multi-Voice = Polyphonic**

## ➡ *Multi-Output*

The term Multi-Output refers to the audio output of the Sound Module.

Except for some old Hardware Synthesizers that had only a mono audio output, most of the synthesizers have a stereo audio output. Sampler Instruments or Workstations that are multi-timbral (now we know what that means) can even have multiple stereo outputs. This allows you to route specific sound generators to separate audio outputs.

### 🌑 Software Instruments

Software Instrument Plugins don't have physical audio output jacks, they have virtual output jacks. If you step through the Instrument Plugin Menu ❸ in Logic, you will notice that the different Logic Instruments have different output options ❹.

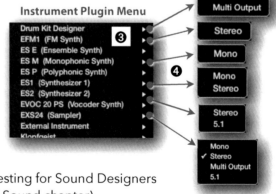

- ▶ **Mono / Stereo**: Some have only one option, either Mono (ES M) or Stereo (EFM1), others offer both options (ES1).

- ▶ **5.1**: The ES2 even offers a "5.1" option, which means, it has true Surround Sound Patches, which might be interesting for Sound Designers working in surround (more on that later in the Surround Sound chapter).

- ▶ **Multi Output**: If you look at the Drum Kit Designer and the EXS24, you will see the "Multi Output" option. Especially Multi-timbral Plugins like Kontakt or Play provide a wide range of different Multi Outputs routings ❺. Multiple Mono outputs, multiple Stereo Outputs, or a mix of both. This lets you route specific sound generators, individual modules inside the Plugin, to specific outputs. We will see in a moment how we get these Multi Outputs onto our Logic Mixer.

Play: Output Options

Stereo
5.1
Multi Output (9xStereo)
Multi Output (1x5.1, 8xStereo)    ❺

# MIDI Input

There are two ways on how to setup Multi-timbral Instruments in Logic. Assign multiple Tracks to the same Instrument Channel Strip or create a Multi Instr. MIDI Object in the Environment.

### ➡ Multiple Tracks - Single Instrument Channel Strips

To understand this setup, again, you have to be clear about the relationship between a Track and a Channel Strip Object.

- A Track ❶ on the Tracks Window is just a container that stores time-based information (Regions) on its Track Lane.
- A Track has to be assigned to an Environment Object (usually a Channel Strip Object ❷) to play back that data (the Regions) through a Channel Strip.
- A Track can be re-assigned at any time to a different Channel Strip ❸. This doesn't change the data contained on that Track (Region). It only plays that data through a different Channel Strip.
- Each Track in your Project is usually assigned to a different Channel Strip ❹. Different Tracks containing different Regions are played by different Instrument Plugins on those different Channel Strips.
- However, multiple Tracks can also be assigned to the same Channel Strip ❺. That means, the data on all those Tracks (all their Regions) are played through the same Channel Strip, the same Instrument Plugin.
- Each Track can be set to a specific MIDI Channel ❻ in their Track Inspector. The MIDI Regions on a Track are then sending their MIDI data on those specific MIDI Channels to the Plugin on the assigned Channel Strip.
- A Multi-timbral Instrument Plugin that is loaded on that Channel Strip receives data from the MIDI Regions of all Tracks it is assigned to. Now, the Instrument Plugin can route the incoming MIDI signals to its individual modules ❼ (that are set to individual MIDI Channels #1, #2, #3, #4) based on the MIDI Channels embedded in the MIDI signal coming from specific Tracks. For example, Track 1 (sending on Ch1) plays Module #1 (set to Ch1), Track 2 (sending on Ch2) plays Module #2 (set to Ch2), etc.

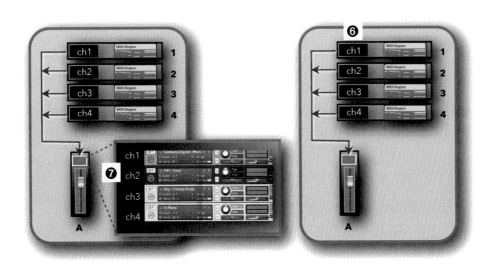

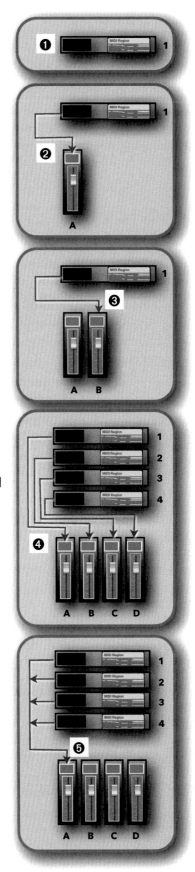

### 🌑 MIDI Channel

I already discussed in an earlier section about the MIDI Channel, the importance of the MIDI Channel Parameter in the Track Inspector.

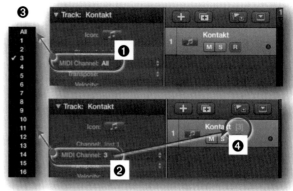

- **All**: Selecting "All" ❶ in the MIDI Channel popup menu lets all MIDI Messages (from the MIDI input or from the MIDI Region on that Track) pass through unaltered with their original MIDI Channels.

- **Ch1 ... 16**: Selecting any MIDI Channel ❷ from the popup menu ❸ will change the MIDI Channel of any incoming MIDI Message to that specific MIDI Channel number. Please note that the MIDI Channel number is now also displayed next to the Track Name in brackets ❹.

That means, in order to send the MIDI signal on a specific Track to a specific "receiving" Channel of the Multi-timbral Sound Module, you choose the corresponding MIDI Channel in the Track Inspector. All the MIDI signals are "channeled" to the Sound Source on that specific MIDI Channel.

### 🌑 Create New Track

You can create those additional Tracks for Multi-timbral Instruments in different ways:

▶ **Automatic**: When you select the Software Instrument ❺ option in the New Tracks Dialog (*opt+cmd+N*), a checkbox ❻ will appear in the Details section below with the label "*Multi-timbral parts*" and an entry field to enter any number between 1 and 16. This is what happens:

- Logic creates as many Tracks ❼ as the number you entered (in this case, 4).
- Logic creates one new Instrument Channel Strip ❽ and assigns all those Tracks to that same Instrument Channel Strip.
- Each Track is assigned to a different MIDI Channel Number, starting with MIDI Channel 1.
- You can see the new Tracks in the Track List with their individually assigned MIDI Channel Number ❾ in brackets, which represent the destination channels of the Multi-timbral Plugin ❿ that is loaded to the Instrument Channel Strip ❽ that all those Tracks are assigned to.

▶ **Manual**: You can create additional Tracks, assigned to that same Instrument Channel Strip, with the command *Track ➤ Others ➤ New Track With Next MIDI Channel* (*ctr+return*) - only if the current Track is not set to MIDI Channel "All"! This creates a new Track assigned to the same Channel Strip as the currently selected Track and sets the new Track to the next higher MIDI Channel Strip in the Track Inspector. In this case, it would be MIDI Channel 5.

Track ➤ Others ➤

| | |
|---|---|
| New Track With Duplicate Settings | ⌘D |
| New Track With Next MIDI Channel | ⌃↵ |
| New Track With Same MIDI Channel | ⌃⇧↵ |

New Track For Overlapped Regions

**New Tracks Dialog**

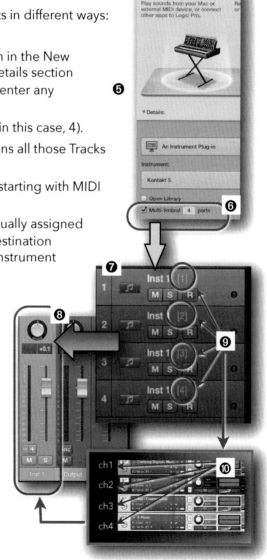

➡ *Multi-Instrument MIDI Object*

This is a more advanced option to configure Multi-timbral Instruments in Logic that requires some knowledge about the Environment Window. You can read the *Environment* chapter first if you are new to this or want to freshen up your knowledge about the Environment.

These are the first three steps:

▶ Create a Multi-Instrument MIDI Object ❶. There are two ways to do that:
  - Open the Environment Window, go to the Mixer Layer, and select from the Local Menu *New ➤ Multi-Instrument.*
  - Open the New Tracks Dialog and create an External MIDI Instrument (I explained all the details at the beginning of this chapter). This will automatically create a Multi Instrument MIDI Object in the Environment.

▶ Create an Instrument Channel Strip ❷:

▶ Cable the MIDI Object to the Instrument Channel Strip ❸:

The Multi Instrument MIDI Object doesn't act as an External MIDI Instrument (not routed to an external MIDI port ❾, OFF). Instead, the MIDI Object is now a "front end" for the Instrument Channel Strip ❷ that you have it cabled into.

- Use the "Reassign Track" ❹ command in the Track's Shortcut Menu (*ctr+click* on the Track Header) and select a MIDI channel ❺ from the last submenu when drilling down to the various submenus (representing the location in the Environment).

- If you select Channel 1 ❺, then any MIDI Signal on that Track ❻ (from the input or from the MIDI Regions), gets sent to the Channel 1 submodule of the Multi Instrument MIDI Object ❶, which sends its data via the cable ❸ to the MIDI Ch1 of the Software Instrument Plugin ❼ loaded on that Instrument Channel Strip ❷.

- The Track Name ❽ has the MIDI Module Number displayed next to the name, plus the MIDI Channel in brackets.

- The Track Inspector ❾ displays the "*Channel Parameter*" and the "*Port*" (which is off, because you use it as an internal object and don't route it to the outside via a MIDI port).

- Please note that you cannot change the *Channel* Parameter ❾ in the Object Inspector to choose a different MIDI Channel in the Environment. Instead, you click on one of the numbers in the object to select a different submodule. In the Track Inspector, you can select a different MIDI Channel (= submodule) from the popup menu.

- Use the same command *Track ➤ Others ➤ New Track With Next MIDI Channel* (*ctr+return*) to create a new Track assigned to the next MIDI Channel (submodule) on that Multi-Instrument MIDI Object ❶.

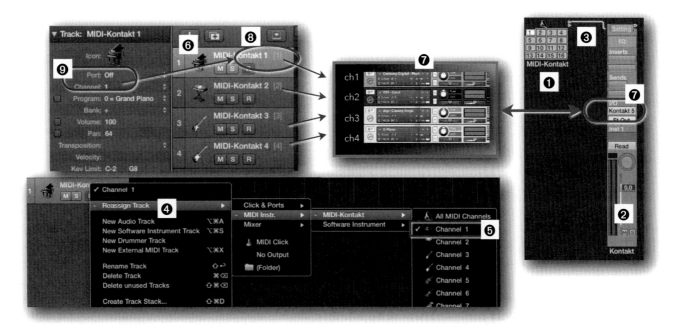

# Layer vs. Multi-Player Recording

When you play/record MIDI in Logic and have more than one sources (MIDI Controllers) or more than one destination (MIDI Tracks), then you have to be aware of the two modes available in Logic. This applies to Multi-timbral Instruments, but also to regular Instrument Tracks.

## Layer Recording

This is the default MIDI play/record mode in Logic:

> **Sending**: All MIDI Controllers (cabled to the Sequencer Input Object in the Environment) will send their MIDI signal to the Tracks Window ❶.

> **Receiving**: You route all those incoming MIDI signals in the Tracks Window to a specific Track by selecting that Track ❷. In addition, all the Tracks that have their Record Enable Button 🅁 activated ❸ will also receive the MIDI input. You will hear a so-called "layered" or "stacked" sound, playing all the sound modules on those enabled Tracks together at the same time.

> **Play**: The sending MIDI Channel from the Controller is overwritten with the MIDI Channel ❹ set in the Track Inspector on each individual Track enabling you to play Modules on different MIDI Channels ❺ with one sending device.

> **Record**: During the recording, you will see only the red MIDI Region created on the selected Track ❷, but when you stop, Alias Regions ❻ are created on all other Record-enabled Tracks.

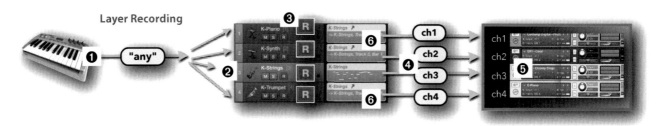

## Multi-Player Recording

Multi-Player Mode is activated with the checkbox ❼ "*Auto demix by channel if multitrack recording*" in the *Project Settings ➤ Recording ➤ MIDI*, which results in a different behavior:

> **Matching MIDI Channel**: If you set the MIDI Channel of the sending MIDI Controller ❽ to the same MIDI Channel a record-enabled Track is set to in its Track Inspector, then that MIDI signal is routed only to that Module ❾.

> **Non-matching MIDI Channel**: If none of the record-enabled Tracks match the MIDI Channel of an incoming MIDI signal, then it will be routed to the currently selected Track ❿, regardless of its MIDI Channel.

**Project Settings ➤ Recording ➤ MIDI**

> **Play/Record**: The MIDI Controllers play and record only to the specific Tracks, enabling you to have multiple players play and record different Instrument Tracks in Logic at the same time.

# Mixer Window

Depending on which method you use to configure Multi-timbral Instruments in Logic, it will have an effect on the Mixer Window too. Here is what you have to look out for:

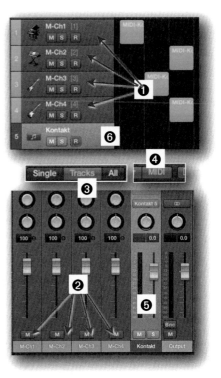

## 😀 Multi Instrument MIDI Object

This is what you see in the Mixer when you use a Multi Instrument MIDI Object:

- Each Track ❶, assigned to a Multi Instrument MIDI Object, will show up as an individual MIDI Channel Strips ❷ in the Mixer Window (Tracks Button ❸ is selected in the Mixer Window).
- Each submodule of a Multi Instrument Object has its own Channel Strip. In our example, four Tracks are assigned to four submodules of a Multi Instrument Object. Four Channel Strip are shown.
- The controls on those MIDI Channel Strips are all MIDI Controllers (no audio is passing through those Channel Strips). If you don't need those Channel Strips, then disable their view by disabling the MIDI Filter Button ❹ in the Mixer Window.
- The Instrument Channel Strip with the Software Plugin loaded is displayed as a separate Channel Strip ❺. It contains all the audio signal controls.

This setup provides a separation between MIDI and Audio: You use individual Tracks ❶ for recording the MIDI Regions on their Tracks and one separate Track ❻ assigned to the Instrument Channel Strip ❺ loaded with the actual Multi-timbral Instrument Plugin.

## 😀 Multiple Tracks - Single Instrument Channel Strips

This is what you see in the Mixer Window when using multiple Tracks with a single Instrument Channel Strip:

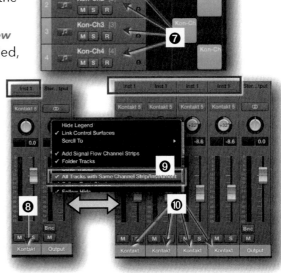

- Each Track ❼ is assigned to the same Instrument Channel Strip ❽ (just sending on different MIDI Channels) and that's why you see only one single Instrument Channel Strip in the Mixer Window.
- However, there is a setting in the Local Mixer Window *View* ➤ *All Tracks with Same Channel Strip/Instrument* ❾. If enabled, it will display a Channel Strip ❿ for each Track ❼ that is assigned to that Channel Strip.
- In our example, you will see four Channel Strips, but they are all duplicates. Changing the Fader or Knob on one Channel Strip will move the other controls too. If you display the "Type and Number Label" on top of the Channel Strip, then you see that they represent the same component (Inst 1).
- Selecting one Channel Strip will still select the corresponding Track and you can actually name those Channel Strips differently, even if they are representing the same component.

With this setup, you record on the Track that is assigned to the actual Instrument Plugin (not a separate MIDI Object). And by the way, it is easier to configure than the Multi-Instrument MIDI Objects.

## ➡ *Audio Output Routing*

Now let's have a look at the audio output of a Multi-timbral Instrument.

**Audio Output Jacks**

❶

It is great to have multiple independent sound generators in one sound module, to send independent MIDI signals to each one. You can have it play the piano part, the string part, and the drums all in one module or Plugin. However, at some point, you also might want to have separate audio outputs for each sound generator inside that sound module that enables you to set different volumes, EQs, Aux Sends, and all sorts of audio treatments for the string sound, the piano sound, and the drums you have playing in that one module.

In case of hardware sound modules, they provide multiple output jacks ❶ on the back to connect them to individual Channel Strips on your mixer. But how does that work with Plugins?

Loading a Plugin onto an Instrument Channel Strip restricts that plugin to the Output of that one Channel Strip and that output is usually just a stereo output ❷. So, when using a Multi-timbral Plugin like Kontakt or Omnisphere that can load multiple Patches, all those Patches ❷ are routed to that same stereo output bus ❸.

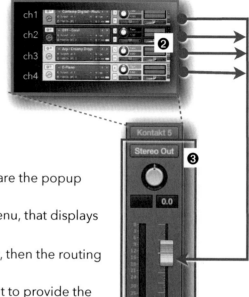

### 🔘 The Logic Solution

Here is how Logic solves that problem:

- A Plugin can provide different output routing options. These are the popup menus ❹ that I showed earlier.
- Each Plugin has a submenu when selecting it in the Plugin Menu, that displays the available output options.
- If the Plugin has the option "Multi Output" ❺ and you select it, then the routing capabilities in the Mixer will change.
- Note 1: A Plugin doesn't have to be a Multi-timbral Instrument to provide the "Multi Output" option. In Logic, the EXS24, Drum Kit Designer, and Ultrabeat, all provide the Multi Output option.
- Note 2: You can switch between the output options once a Plugin is loaded. That means, you can start with a stereo output and later when you decide to route the Patches to separate outputs, you can select that option in the submenu. All the current settings stay the same and you don't have to reload/ recreate everything.

### 🔘 Add/Remove Aux Button

If you load an Instrument Plugin with the Multi Output ❺ option, then the Instrument Channel Strip will display two additional buttons ❻ above the Mute Button. These Buttons create special Aux Channel Strips that are used to route the Multi Outputs to.

**Instrument Plugin Menu**

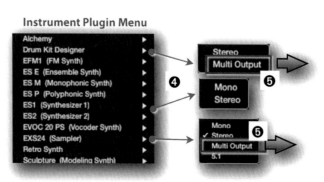

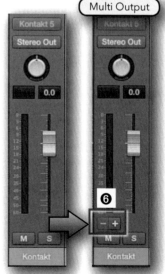

## 🎧 Multi Output Aux Channel Strips

Here is how these special Multi Output Aux Channel Strips work:

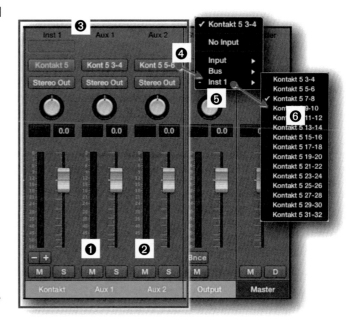

- *Click* the Plus button on the Instrument Channel Strip that has the Multi Output Plugin loaded and a new Aux Channel Strip is automatically created and placed next to the Instrument Channel Strip ❶.
- *Click* again to add another Aux Channel Strip next to it ❷, and so on.
- *Click* the Minus Button to remove the Aux Channel Strip furthest on the right. You can't rearrange the order of those Aux Channel Strips.
- There are no divider lines ❸ between the Instrument Channel Strip and its Aux Channel Strip. They appear as one big Channel Strip.
- A new Aux Channel Strip will automatically have its input selected. It will be the individual outputs in the order ❻ they are provided by the Plugin.
- You can change the input selection by *clicking* on the Input button ❹ of the Aux Channel Strip and select an output.

- The Input Selection popup menu changes dynamically. When you load a Multi Output Plugin in your Project, it automatically adds the item "Inst 1" ❺, with the submenu displaying its individual output options ❻.
- Unfortunately, all available multi output Plugins are only listed as "Inst 1", "Inst 2", etc. ❼ and you have to select their submenu first to see which Plugin it is. However, if you have multiple Multi Output Plugins loaded (for example, two EXS24), then there is no way to tell which one is which.

## 🎧 Special Aux Channel Strips with Extra Powers

These Aux Channel Strips created by the Multi Output Instrument Channel Strips are special with a hidden secret:

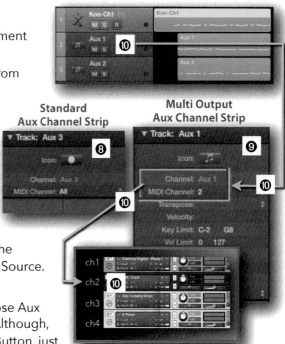

Standard Aux Channel Strip

Multi Output Aux Channel Strip

- If you create a Track for a standard Aux Channel Strip from the Mixer's Local Menu *Options ➤ Create Tracks for Selected Channel Strips* (*ctr+T*), then the Track Inspector ❽ for that Track lists only the Icon, the Channel, and the MIDI Channel.
- However, if you create a Track for one of those Multi Output Aux Channel Strips, then you'll have the full parameter set ❾ as a Track assigned to an Instrument Channel Strip.
- The MIDI output ❿ of such an Aux Track is routed to the Plugin of its parent Instrument Channel Strip, and the *"MIDI Channel"* Parameter determines to which Sound Source.

**Big Secret** — You can use this as an option to record on those Aux Tracks, routed to a Multi-timbral Instrument. Although, the Aux Track doesn't have a Record Enable Button, just select that Aux Track and hit record - it works.

MIDI Transform is a separate window in Logic that lets you apply some serious "brain surgery" to the selected MIDI Events (and also Logic's proprietary Meta Events and Fader Events). It lets you transform selected MIDI Events based on computer-based if-then conditions.

The MIDI Transform window is similar to the Transformer Object in the Environment with the main difference that the Transformer Object applies operations online placed in the MIDI signal flow while the MIDI Transform Window lets you apply MIDI operations offline to any MIDI Events in any selected MIDI Regions.

# Concept

You open the Transform Window with the following commands:

- Main Menu Command *Window ➤ Open MIDI Transform*
- Key Command (*Open Transform*) *cmd+9*
- Key Command (*Show/Hide Transform*) *unassigned*. This command toggles the window
- Various MIDI Editors Local Menu *Functions ➤ MIDI Transform*

➡ *Window Elements*

The Transform Window has the following sections:

▶ **Condition Area ❶**: The parameters in this section let you set the condition which MIDI Events to select.

▶ **Operation Area ❷**: The parameters in this section let you define what operation is applied to the selected MIDI Events.

▶ **Map Area ❸**: The Graph provides a visual representation of the before-after operation for specific parameters using the maps feature.

▶ **Commands ❹**: You have three types of commands available to execute the operation.

▶ **Operation Modes ❺**: Four Operation Modes define how the operation is executed.

▶ **Transform Set Presets ❻**: All the Parameters in the Transform Window can be stored as Presets and recalled from the Presets popup menu.

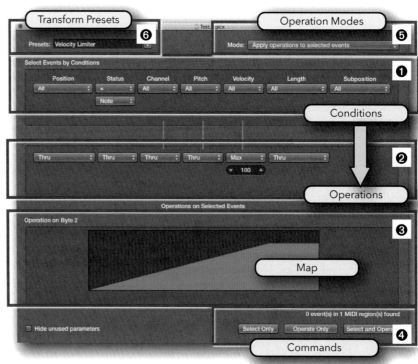

## ➡️ *Transform Set Presets*

The settings of all the Transform Parameters in the Transform Window, a Transform Set, can be stored as a Preset.

### 🔘 Factory Presets

You don't have to learn how to setup a transform operation yourself, just use any of the 17 factory presets ❶ by selecting them from the Presets popup menu ❷. The Logic User Guide explains the functionality of each Preset:

http://help.apple.com/logicpro/mac/10/#lgcp215831be

### 🔘 Custom Presets

If you configure your own Transform Sets, then you can save them as your own Presets that are then displayed in the Presets popup menu below the factory Presets ❸.

The process of creating and renaming is a bit unusual:

☑️ Select the "*Create Initialized User Set*" ❹ from the Presets menu, which opens a Dialog Window ❺.

☑️ **Create New Set**: Select "*Create*" in the Dialog Window to create a new "initialized" Parameter Set with the name "New Parameter Set".

☑️ **Duplicate Existing Set**: *Click* on "*Rename*" to create a Duplicate Set of the current Transform Set with the name "New Parameter Set".

☑️ **Rename Set**: To rename any of your custom Presets, *click* on the name in the Presets popup field ❷ and enter a new name. When you hit enter, the same Dialog Window ❺ pops up (it displays the name you just entered). Now *click* on the Rename button to rename the existing Preset. If you click on the Create button. It creates a duplicate with the name you entered.

The Presets popup menu is also available directly as a submenu when you access the MIDI Transform command in the MIDI Editor's Local Menu *Functions ➤ MIDI Transform ➤*

### 🔘 Import Presets

Transform Set Presets are part of the Logic *Project Settings*, which means, your Custom Presets will be stored with your current Project. You can import Transform Set Presets from other Projects with the Import Project Settings command

*File ➤ Project Settings ➤ Import Project Settings...* and enable the "Transform Sets" checkbox ❻.

*A few things to be are of:*

- You can only import all Custom Presets from a Project, not individual ones
- Importing the Project Sets from another Project will overwrite any existing Custom Transport Sets in your current Project
- There is no command to delete a specific Custom Preset once you created it and it is listed in the Preset Menu ❸

## ➡ **Operation Concept**

Here is a quick overview of the concept of the Transform Window:

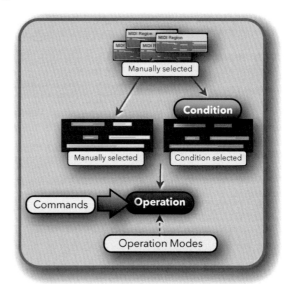

- ☑ You select the MIDI Regions that should be "operated on".
- ☑ In those Regions, you can select MIDI Events manually.
- ☑ Alternatively, you can let the Transform Window select Events in those Regions, based on the Condition Parameters you determine.
- ☑ You can use one of three Operation Commands that perform an operation (based on the Operation Parameters you determine) to the manually selected Events or the selected Events based on the Conditions.
- ☑ In addition to the Operation Parameters, you have to select one of four Operation Modes, that determine the details on how the operation is executed.

## ➡ **Operation Modes**

Before using the Transform command, you have to select a Mode that determines how the command is applied. There are four Modes available in the Mode popup menu:

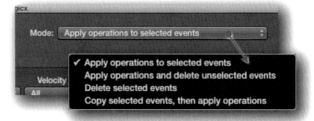

- ▸ **Apply operations to selected events**: The operation is applied to all selected Events (manually selected or selected by the Condition).
- ▸ **Apply operations and delete unselected event**: The selected Events will be transformed, and in addition, all the unselected Events will be deleted. You can use this command as a filter that deletes all the MIDI Events that don't meet the Condition (all Operation Parameter set to "thru").
- ▸ **Delete selected events**: This mode deletes all the selected MIDI Events regardless of the Operation Parameter.
- ▸ **Copy selected events, then apply operations**: This mode copies the selected Events to the Clipboard first before applying the operation, in case you want to paste the original Events at some other place.

## ➡ **Operation Commands**

At the bottom of the Transform Window are the three buttons that let you apply the operation. The info line above displays how many Regions you have selected and how many "transform-able" Events in those Regions are found.

- ▸ **Select Only**: This command will not change any MIDI Event (no Transform Operation applied). It will only select all the Regions and Events that meet the parameters set in the Condition Area.
- ▸ **Operate Only**: This command will apply the operation only to the manually selected Events without using the Condition Parameters.
- ▸ **Select and Operate**: This command will select all the Events based on the parameters in the Condition Area and applies the operation to those Events based on the parameters in the Operation Area.

# ➡ *Detailed View*

Here is a diagram with a more detailed view about the Transform window:

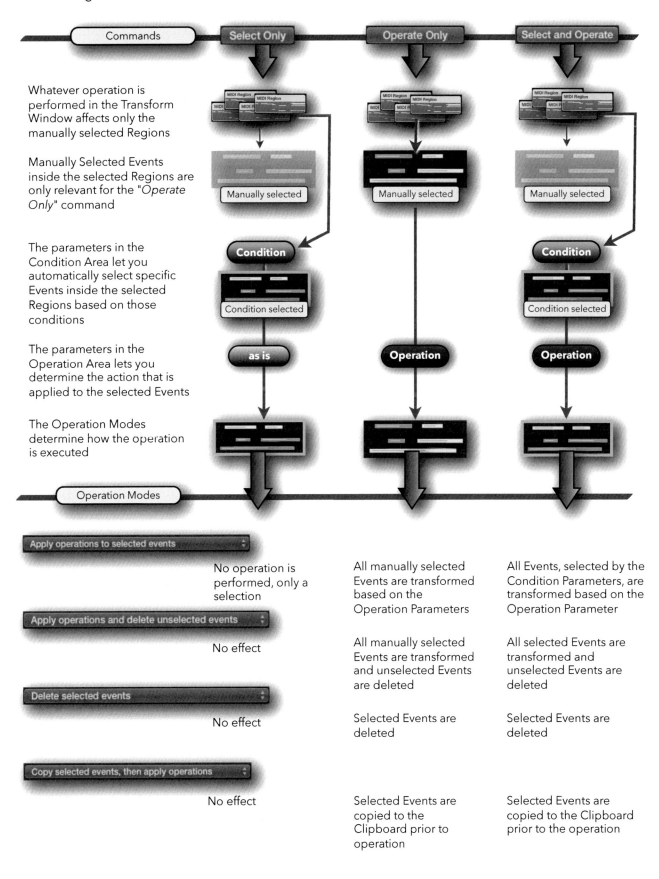

# Selection Condition

The purpose of the Condition Parameters is to select all the Events in the currently selected Region in your Project that meets the condition based on those parameters.

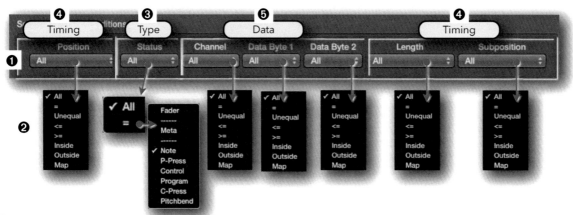

This is how it works:

▶ **Seven Parameters ❶**: You have a total of seven parameters that you can set a condition for. Events are only selected if they meet all the conditions of all seven parameters.

▶ **Conditions Popup Menu ❷**: Each parameter has a popup menu that lets you select the condition that has to be met. Any parameter set to "All" means, no conditions (not restrictions) for those parameters.

▶ **Status ❸**: The Status Parameter is the most important parameter, because it can restrict the selection to a specific type of Event. These are the standard MIDI Events (Note, Pitch Bend, Controls, etc.) but also Logic's Fader Event (for Track Automation) and Meta Events ("all purpose" Events).

▶ **Timing Parameter ❹**: Three of the parameters let you set a condition based on the timing of an Event. That is the Position (start time), the Length, and the Subposition inside a bar. The last one lets you select, for example, all the Events on the second beat of each bar.

▶ **Data Parameter ❺**: Three of the parameters represent the content of the actual MIDI Message. This is the MIDI Channel, the first Data Byte (Note Value, Controller Number, or Pitchbend value), and the second Data Byte (Note Velocity, Controller Value, or Pitchbend value).

▶ **Value Conditions**: Timing and Data parameters have the same popup menu with 8 options for the Value Conditions.

- *All ❻*: No condition, which means, any value meets the condition.

- *Single Value ❼*: Selecting any of these four item conditions (Equal, Unequal, Smaller/Equal, Larger/Equal) will display a single value field below to specify the condition.

- *Value Range ❽*: Inside and Outside are conditions that let you set a range between two values. Therefore, two value fields will be displayed.

- *Map ❾*: This is a special, more scientific approach to set a condition. Here is the explanation from the Logic User Guide: *Two numerical parameters are specified, and the incoming value is first converted by the map, to create a mapped value. The mapped value is then compared with the two parameters to see if it falls inside them. Incoming events with a mapped value that falls within the range will fulfill the condition—all other events will not fulfill the condition.*
*Any questions?*

# Operation Parameters

The Operation Parameters define what parameters on each of the selected Events are changed (transformed) when you use the operation command.

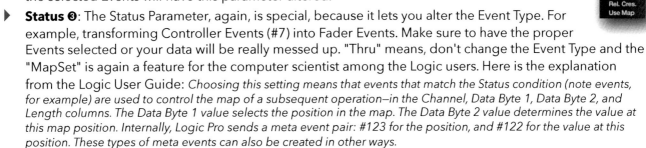

▶ **Six Parameters ❶**: You have the same Parameters available as in the Conditions Area, without the Subposition.

▶ **Operation Popup Menu ❷**: Each parameter has a popup menu that lets you select how to alter that parameter of an Event. Setting a parameter to "Thru" means, none of the selected Events will have this parameter altered.

▶ **Status ❸**: The Status Parameter, again, is special, because it lets you alter the Event Type. For example, transforming Controller Events (#7) into Fader Events. Make sure to have the proper Events selected or your data will be really messed up. "Thru" means, don't change the Event Type and the "MapSet" is again a feature for the computer scientist among the Logic users. Here is the explanation from the Logic User Guide: *Choosing this setting means that events that match the Status condition (note events, for example) are used to control the map of a subsequent operation—in the Channel, Data Byte 1, Data Byte 2, and Length columns. The Data Byte 1 value selects the position in the map. The Data Byte 2 value determines the value at this map position. Internally, Logic Pro sends a meta event pair: #123 for the position, and #122 for the value at this position. These types of meta events can also be created in other ways.*

▶ **Operations**: All Parameters (except Status) have the same operations listed in their menu. There will be one or two value fields displayed to enter the value for that operation.

- *Thru*: No changes.
- *Fix*: Set the parameter to one fixed value.
- *Add*: Adds the numeric value to the parameter. For example, increase the velocity, transpose notes, shift the position of an Event, or lengthen notes.
- *Sub*: Subtract a numeric value from any parameter.
- *Min*: Set all parameter values that are below this value to this number. For example, increase notes with low velocity without affecting velocity values above that threshold.
- *Max*: This is the reverse operation. It reduces parameter values above that threshold to the set value.
- *Flip*: The entered value becomes the pivot point where every value is reversed around the pivot point by the same distant. For example, with a pivot point set to 80, a value of 90 (10 above) becomes 70 (10 below) and a value of 82 (2 above) becomes 78 (2 below). Use it to experiment with melodies or note positions.
- *Mul*: The parameter value is multiplied by the value you enter in the field (4 decimal places). Used to transform Regions to half speed. (Half Speed Preset).
- *Div*: The parameter value is divided by the value you enter in the field (4 decimal places). Used to transform a Region to double speed. (Double Speed Preset).
- *Scale*: This is a combination of *Mul* and *Add*. The top value multiplies the parameter value, and the bottom value is then added to the result or subtracted if you enter a negative value.

- *Range*: This is a combination of the *Min* and *Max* operation. Values outside the range are replaced by the values of the range limits.
- *Random*: Random values are generated within the set limits.
- *+-Rand.*: A random value between zero and the set value (positive or negative) is added.
- *Reverse*: The parameter value is reversed within its value range (no value fields available).
- *Quantize*: The parameter value is quantized to a multiple of the set value.
- *Qua & Min*: A combination of the *Quantize* and *Min* operation.
- *Expon.*: The parameter value is scaled exponentially within the values 0 and 127. The set value determines the shape of the curve. Positive values result in the exponential, and negative values result in a logarithmic curve.
- *Crescendo*: This creates a smooth increase or decrease between the two set values. The Selection Condition for the Position has to be set to "Inside" for this to work.
- *Rel.Cres*: Same effect as the Crescendo operation, but this time, the previous values of the parameters are taken into account, preserving the relative feel of the original Events.
- *Use Map*: The values, determined by the map, will be used for this operation.

## ➡ *Universal Map*

Here is how the Map in the Transform Window works:

▶ The Transform Window contains only one map. Any parameter that uses the Map function uses that one map.

▶ The Map Area is only visible if the map feature is selected in one of the Parameters (Selection Condition or Operation).

▶ The Map displays an input-output mapping ❶. The x-axis represents the input (before) with 128 bars. The y-axis represents the output (after), the height of each bar is (0-127).

▶ You can define the map in different ways:
- Enter the input-output pair numerically with the two value fields ❷
- *Draw* with the mouse across the map area
- *Click* on the "Initialize" ❸ button to create a linear curve
- *Click* on the two buttons ❹ to "Invert" or "Reverse" the mapping
- *Click* the "Smooth" ❺ button (repeatedly) to smooth out the curve

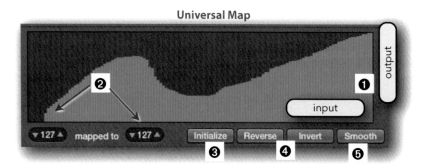

Universal Map

## ➡ *Exchange parameter*

You can reroute the value of each of the three Event parameters (Channel, Data Byte 1, and Data Byte 2) to the value of a different parameter from this group by *clicking* (toggle through) on the dot ❻ of the blue line between those parameters.

This exchange happens before the applied operation.

## ➡ *Hide unused Parameters*

*Click* on the checkbox ❼ in the lower left corner to hide any Parameter that is not used in the current Transform Set. This makes it easier to see what will happen, especially when looking through different Presets.

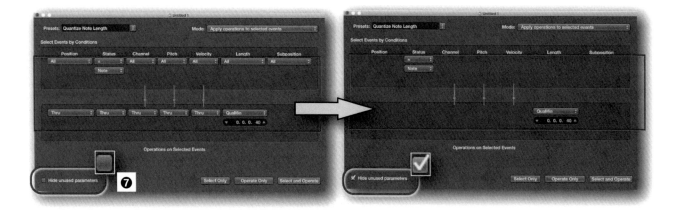

The Step Editor is one of Logic's MIDI Editors, which means, it lets you display and edit the content of MIDI Regions (the individual MIDI Events) in its own special way. So let's find out what's so special about this one.

> Although the name "Step Editor" is new in Logic Pro X, the editor itself is not. It is pretty much the same editor from previous Logic versions, formerly known as the "**Hyper Editor**".

## Basics

### ☻ Do I need the Step Editor?

To answer this question, you have to explore it first to find out what it can do, and especially, what it can do that the other MIDI Editors cannot do. After all, the Step Editor is pretty easy to use, and it is definitely worth the time to invest to see if there are some functions and procedures that you can incorporate into your workflow regardless what type of music you are producing with Logic.

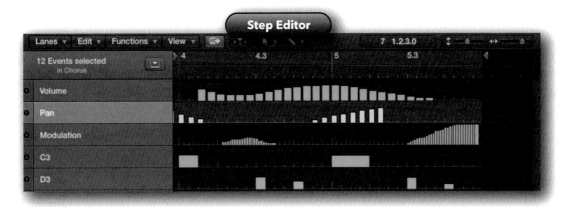

### ➡ *Open the Step Editor*

In the typical Logic fashion, there is not one, not two, but many different ways you can open the Step Editor:

- Open in the Editor Pane on the bottom of the Main Window:
    - Key Command (*Show/Hide Step Editor*) **unassigned**
    - Main Menu *View* ➤ *Show/Hide Editor* (and *click* the Step Editor Tab, if not selected)
    - Key Command (*Hide/Show Editor*) *E* (and *click* the Step Editor Tab, if not selected)
    - In the Control Bar, *click* the Editor Button 🎛 (and *click* the Step Editor Tab, if not selected)
    - *Double-click* on a MIDI Region in the Tracks Window. This has to be configured in the *Preferences* ➤ *General* ➤ *Editing* ➤ *Double-clicking a MIDI Region Opens* ➤ *Step Editor*
    - *Double-click* on the upper Divider Line to close the Window Pane or *drag* it all the way down

- Open as a separate Window (you can open this window multiple times):
    - Main Menu *Window* ➤ *Open Step Editor*
    - Key Command (*Open Step Editor*) **unassigned**
    - *Drag* the blue Step Editor Tab in the Step Editor Window to tear it off as a separate window

## ➡ *Concept*

Because the Step Editor has some unique ways to display MIDI data, it also has some unique terminology we have to learn first. So let me start with laying out the concept of the Step Editor with those new terms.

- ▶ **MIDI Region ❶**: Like any other MIDI Editor, you select a MIDI Region in the Tracks Window first. That is the content that is displayed and can be edited in the Step Editor (only one Region at a time).
- ▶ **MIDI Events ❷**: The individual MIDI Events inside the selected MIDI Region is the data that is displayed in the Step Editor. That can be MIDI Notes, Continuous Controller, Pitch Bend, etc., but also Logic's internal MIDI-like Events (Fader and Meta).
- ▶ **Steps ❸**: Each individual MIDI Event is displayed in the Step Editor as a green vertical beam, the so-called Steps.
- ▶ **Ruler ❹**: Like the Piano Roll Editor, the Step Editor is linked to a Ruler on to, referencing the timeline from left to right. Therefore, the placement of the Steps ❸ on the horizontal axis indicates the time position of each Step (the MIDI Event), and the height of the beam indicates their value.
- ▶ **Lanes ❺**: Instead of displaying the MIDI Events in one single Display Area like the Piano Roll, the Step Editor can filter the MIDI Events by MIDI Event types and display them in their own Display Area, on so-called "Lanes". You can create as many Lanes as you want, each Lane displaying only one MIDI Event Type (see below for the exception to that rule).
- ▶ **Lane Inspector ❻**: The Lane Inspector, located in Logic's Main Inspector, displays all the Parameters of the currently selected Lane, where you configure what MIDI Event is displayed on that Lane, and also how it is displayed.
- ▶ **Lane Sets ❼**: All the Lanes that you see in the Step Editor are saved as a Lane Set. You can create different Lane Sets with different Lanes (amount of Lanes and the displayed MIDI Events) displaying different aspects (different data) of the same selected MIDI Region ❶.
- ▶ **Lane Set Menu ❽**: The Lane Set Menu is a button, also located on the Main Inspector, that lets you manage the different Lane Sets ❼.

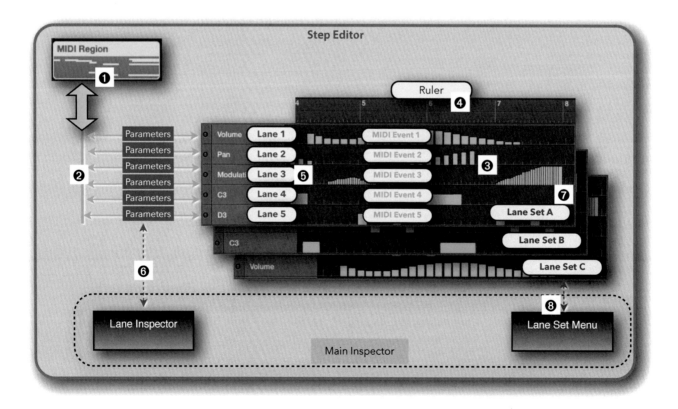

# ⇒ *Interface*

The Interface elements are similar to other MIDI Editors:

## 💀 Main Inspector

Whenever you select the Step Editor, the Main Inspector on the left will show the two Step Editor specific areas.

▸ **Lane Set Menu ❶**: This is a single Button that opens the menu with all the commands related to Lane Sets. Most of the commands are also available in the Local Lane Menu ❸.

▸ **Lane Inspector ❷**: This Inspector displays all the Parameters for the currently selected Lane.

## 💀 Menu Bar

The Step Editor's Menu Bar ❹ contains the usual elements:

▸ **Local Menus**: The Lanes Menu ❸ contains all the Step Editor related commands while the Editor, Functions, and View Menu contain the same commands as the other MIDI Editors. The Link Modes are listed in the View Menu, they don't have separate Buttons 🔗 🔗 🔗.

▸ **MIDI Out** 🔊: *Click* to toggle the MIDI Out Mode (MIDI Note audition). When turned on, any MIDI Event you click on, will play that MIDI note.

▸ **Catch Playhead** 🔲: Toggle the Catch Mode. You can also enable "Scroll in Play" from the View Menu.

▸ **Tool Menus ❺** ▸ ▾ ✏ ▾ : The *Command Tool Menu* is set to the Pencil Tool ✏ by

default, which you might use the most for creating and editing Steps. Remember that you can enable the third *Control Tool Menu* in the *Preferences ➤ General ➤ Editing ➤ Right Mouse Button open Tools Menu.*

▸ **Info Display** `115  1.3.4.0` : This field displays the value and time position of your current cursor position on a Lane.

▸ **Zoom Slider** 🔲🔲 : These are the standard horizontal and vertical Zoom Sliders. All the other Zoom commands work too, for example, *cmd+ArrowKeys*.

## 💀 Ruler

The Ruler indicates the Beginning ▷ and End ◁ Marker ❻ of the currently displayed Region ❼. On the left, you have the Global Tracks 🔲 ❽.

## 💀 Display Area

The Display Area shows the Lanes with three sections:

▸ **HiHat Mode**: *Click* the dot to create HiHat Groups.

▸ **Lane Header**: The Header contains only the name of the Lane. *Click* to select or *drag* a Lane to rearrange. You can resize it ❾ horizontally.

▸ **Lanes**: The Lanes display the Steps.

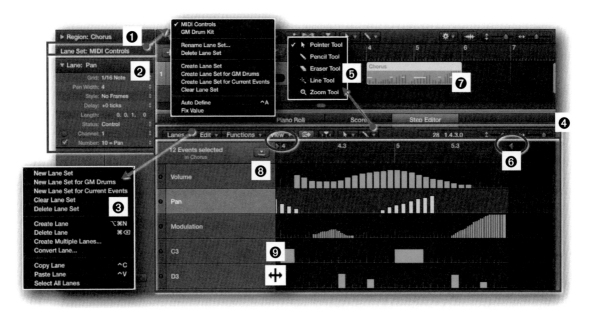

# Lane Sets

So the Step Editor is structured in three layers. The <u>Steps</u> (the MIDI Events) are displayed on <u>Lanes</u>, and a group of Lanes is stored as a <u>Lane Set</u>. Let's start with the top hierarchy, the Lane Sets.

Lane Set Menu

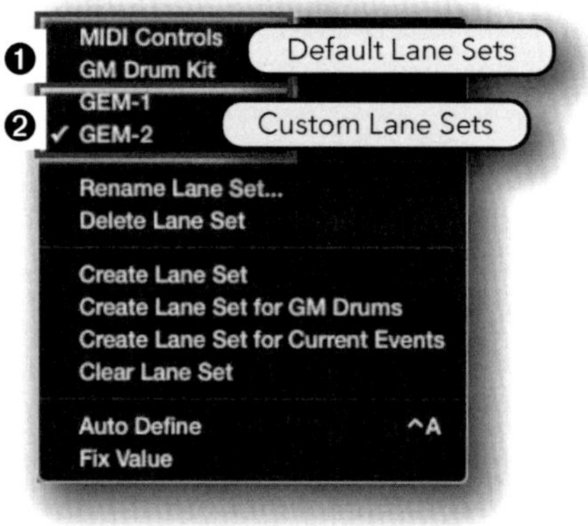

### Select Lane Set

Choose a Lane Set from the Main Inspector *Lane Set Menu ➤ New Lane Set* . The first two Lane Sets are the Default Lane Sets ❶ and any custom Lane Set ❷ you created will be listed below.

### Default Lane Sets

A new Project already has two default Lane Sets created:

▶ **MIDI Controls ❸**: This Lane Set has individual Lanes for the most common controller types. For example, Volume, Pan, Modulation, etc. This is the Lane Set that is used when you open the Step Editor the first time.

▶ **GM Drum Kit ❹**: This Lane Set has Lanes that match the note names of the General MIDI (GM) drum map. This lets you use the Step Editor like a pattern-based drum machine, where each beat is manually entered on a grid.

Lane Set: MIDI Controls    Lane Set: GM Drum Kit

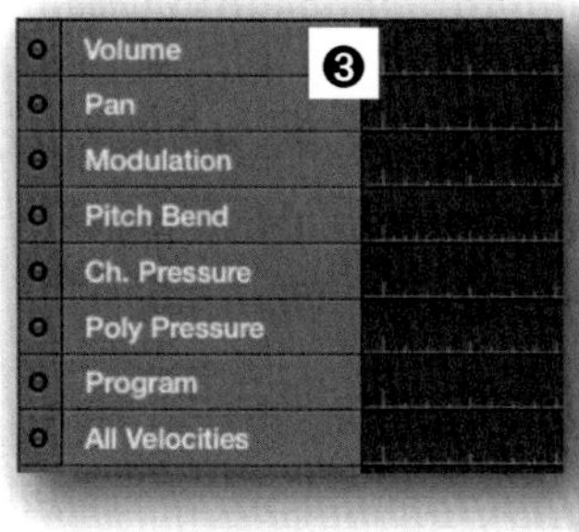

### Create a Lane

There are three commands to create a specific Lane Set:

▶ **New Lane Set**: Use any of the following commands to create a new Lane Set that contains only one Lane for the Volume Controller (CC#7):

- Local Menu *Lanes ➤ New Lane Set*
- Main Inspector *Lane Set Menu ➤ Create Lane Set*
- Key Command (*Create Lane Set*) *unassigned*

▶ **Lane Set from Current Events**: This creates a new Lane Set with individual Lanes for each Event Type that is selected in any of the other MIDI Editors:

- Local Menu *Lanes ➤ New Lane Set for Current Events*
- Main Inspector *Lane Set Menu ➤ Create Lane Set for Current Events*
- Key Command (*Create Lane Set from Current Events*) *unassigned*

▶ **Lane Set for GM Drums**: This creates a new Lane Set with individual Lanes for the notes defined in the GM (General MIDI) Drums specifications, including drum names and HiHat Modes.

- Local Menu *Lanes ➤ New Lane Set for GM Drums*
- Main Inspector *Lane Set Menu ➤ Create Lane Set for GM Drums*
- Key Command (*Create Lane Set for GM Drums*) *unassigned*

### Rename Lane Sets

Select the Lane Set and choose the command from the Main Inspector *Lane Set Menu ➤ Rename Lane Set...*

### 🔊 Clear Lane Sets

This command resets the Lane Set to the same as when you use the Create Lane Set command, which creates only one Lane for the Volume Controller:

🔊 Local Menu *Lanes* ➤ *Clear Lane Set*

🔊 Main Inspector *Lane Set Menu* ➤ *Clear Lane Set*

🔊 Key Command (*Clear Lane Set*) *unassigned*

### 🔊 Delete Lane Sets

Select the Lane Set you want to delete and choose any the following commands. This doesn't affect any MIDI data:

🔊 Local Menu *Lanes* ➤ *Delete Lane Set*

🔊 Main Inspector *Lane Set Menu* ➤ *Delete Lane Set*

🔊 Key Command (*Delete Lane Set*) *unassigned*

## Lanes

Now let's step down to the next level, the Lanes inside a Lane Set. The commands related to the Lanes are listed in the Local Menu "*Lanes*"❶:

### 🔊 Select Lanes

These are the commands to select Lanes:

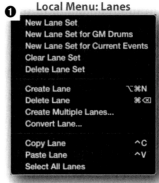

❶ **Local Menu: Lanes**

New Lane Set
New Lane Set for GM Drums
New Lane Set for Current Events
Clear Lane Set
Delete Lane Set

Create Lane             ⌥⌘N
Delete Lane             ⌘⌫
Create Multiple Lanes...
Convert Lane...

Copy Lane               ^C
Paste Lane              ^V
Select All Lanes

▶ **Single Lane**: *Click* the Lane Header

▶ **Multiple Lanes**: *Cmd+click* on one Lane after another

▶ **All Lanes**: Choose the command Local Menu *Lanes* ➤ *Select All Lanes* or use the Key Command (*Select All Lanes*) *unassigned*

### 🔊 Create Lanes

▶ **Create Lane**: This is actually a "duplicate" command. Select a Lane and then choose any of the following commands, which creates a new Lane below the currently selected Lane with the same Lane Parameters. After you duplicate the Lane, you can adjust the Lane Parameters for the Event Type you need:

🔊 Local Menu *Lanes* ➤ *Create Lane*

🔊 Key Command (*Create Lane*) *opt+cmd+N*

▶ **Auto Define Lanes**: This command lets you create a New Lane for a specific type of Event:

☑ Enable from the Main Inspector *Lane Set Menu* ➤ *Auto Define* or use the Key Command (*Toggle Auto Define*) *ctr+A*

☑ Go to the Event List Editor. Now, on any Event you click in the Event List, the Step Editor will create a new Lane for that Event Type.

☑ Disable Audio Define.

▶ **Create Multiple Lanes**: You can create multiple Lanes, each one for each Event Type in a specific MIDI Region.

☑ Select the MIDI Region

☑ Choose the command Local Menu *Lanes* ➤ *Create Multiple Lanes...* or use the Key Command (*Create Multiple Lanes...*) *unassigned*

❷

Create Lanes for selected or all events of current region?

Cancel     Selected     All

☑ A Dialog Window ❷ lets you choose to create Lanes for all Events or only the selected Events in the current Region.

### ⚇ Copy/Paster Lanes

You can copy one or multiple Lanes in the same Lane Set or between different Lane Sets:

- ☑ *Click* on a Lane Header to select one Lane, or *cmd+click* on multiple Lane Headers to select multiple Lanes
- ☑ Use the command from the Local Menu *Lanes ➤ Copy Lane* or use the Key Command (*Copy Lane*) *ctr+C*
- ☑ Select a different Lane Set (optional) and use the command from the Local Menu *Lanes ➤ Paste Lane* or use the Key Command (*Paste Lane*) *ctr+V*

### ⚇ Convert Lane

You can convert the Lane Parameters of an existing Lane, even the Event Type, without changing the actual values of the Steps. For example, converting Modulation data into Volume data. The following commands open a window that displays the current Parameters on the left ❶ (grayed out) and the Parameter you want it to be changed to ❷ on the right.

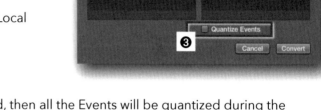

Convert Lane Parameter

- ⚇ Select a Lane and use the command from the Local Menu *Lanes ➤ Convert Lane...*
- ⚇ Key Command (*Convert Lane...*) *unassigned*
- ⚇ *Double+click* the Lane Header

▶ **Quantize Events ❸**: If this checkbox is enabled, then all the Events will be quantized during the conversion based on the Grid value. You can use this procedure to quantize Events on a Lane (if you don't change any other parameters in that window).

### ⚇ Rearrange Lanes

Drag a Lane up or down to rearrange the order. You can drag only one Lane at a time.

### ⚇ Delete Lanes

Select one or multiple Lanes and use the command from the Local Menu *Lanes ➤ Delete Lane* or use the Key Command (*Delete Lane*) *cmd+delete*.

## Lane Inspector

The Lane Inspector displays all the nine Lane Parameters for the currently selected Lane. This determines what type of MIDI Event is displayed on that Lane, how the Steps are displayed plus a few other settings.

Same as with the Region Inspector where you can select multiple Regions to apply the same parameters to all the selected Regions, the Lane Inspector also lets you select multiple Lanes to apply the parameters to all of them.

- • *Click* the Lane Header to select a Lane
- • *Cmd+click* to select multiple Lanes to apply the Lane Parameter changes to all the selected Lanes

### ⚇ Name

The name of the Lane is displayed on the Lane Header ❹ and also on the Header of the Lane Inspector ❺. *Double-click* on the Header to edit the name.

## Grid

The Grid Parameter is important when creating or editing MIDI Events (Steps). It is a mixture between quantize and snap feature. Whatever Step you are creating on a Lane, or moving horizontally (on the timeline), is restricted to that Grid.

Changing the Grid does not affect any existing Events on the Lane (with the exception of the "Quantize checkbox in the Convert Lane Window).

When working on drum grooves, you can create multiple Lanes for the same MIDI Event, for example, the note D1 for the Snare. Then, use a 1/4 Grid for the regular snare groove and a separate Lane with 1/32 Grid to create rolls and fills.

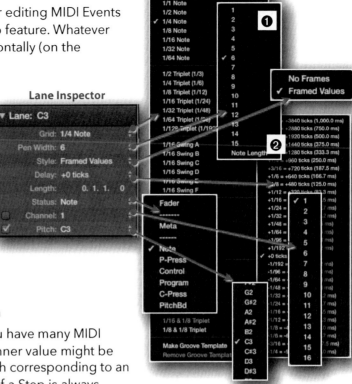

## Pen Width

The Pen Width determines the width of the beam

- ▶ **1 - 15 ❶**: This is just a visual setting. If you have many MIDI Events (continuous controller), then a thinner value might be more suitable. The value of 15 is the width corresponding to an 8th note on the Lane. The time position of a Step is always referenced to the left border of the beam regardless if its width.

- ▶ **Note Length ❷**: If the Event Type is a MIDI Note (Status: *Note*), then the popup menu lists the extra value "*Note Length*". This is the only setting that relates the bar width to the duration of a MIDI Event. It only makes sense for MIDI Notes (Status: *Note*), because other MIDI Events, for example, Volume, Pan, Pitch Bend, etc., are single time-address Events without a duration. Technically, MIDI Notes are also single time-address Events (one for Note-on and one for Note-off), but they are treated as one Note Event with a duration value.

Pen Width

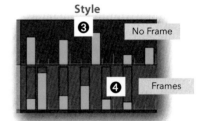

## Style

This parameter has two values:

**No Frame ❸**: The value of each MIDI Event is displayed as a beam

**Framed Values ❹**: The value of each MIDI Event is displayed with a frame around the beam

Style

## Delay

This parameter lets you apply a timing offset for all the Events on that Lane.

You can enter any Tick value or select a specific value from the popup menu, which displays ticks and their corresponding musical value.

Move your mouse over the delay value and a Help Tag displays the Ticks and its corresponding time in milliseconds (ms) ❺.

## Length

This parameter lets you set the length of newly added Note Events.

### Status

The Status Parameter ❶ determines the Event Type that is displayed on the selected Lane. It opens the same popup menu ❷ as in the Event List with all the different MIDI Event Types and Logic's own MIDI-like Events (Fader, Meta). The selection you make here determines what is displayed as the last Parameter in the Lane Inspector, which defines the detail about the Event Type, the so-called "First Data Byte"❸.

### First Data Byte

This is the last parameter in the Lane Inspector and is called the "First Data Byte" ❸. Because the content of the "First Data Byte" of a MIDI Message is different for different Event Types, the name of the Parameter and the available values change depending on the selected Status Parameter ❶. For example, for Notes, it displays the *Pitch* of the Note Event, and for Controllers, it displays the Controller *Number*. The checkbox ❹, however, is very important:

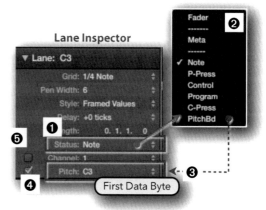

- ☑ Only that specific MIDI Note (Status: Notes) or Controller Number (Status: Control) will be displayed in the selected Lane.

- ☐ The "First Data Byte" (this parameter) is ignored and the Lane displays, for example, all MIDI Notes or all Controller Numbers (Volume, Pan, Modulation, Sustain, etc.) depending on what is selected as the Status Parameter. ❶

### Channel

The Channel Parameter lets you select a specific MIDI Channel (1-16). The function depends on the status of the checkbox next to it ❺:

- ☑ Only MIDI Events that match the selected MIDI Channel will be displayed in the selected Lane.

- ☐ The MIDI Channels of the Event is ignored. All the Events are displayed regardless of their individual MIDI Channel.

## Create & Edit Steps (MIDI Events)

Although you can record your MIDI Events (online) or create them in any of the other MIDI Editors (offline), the Step Editor has some advantages over the other MIDI Editors regarding the creation and the editing of MIDI Events. Here are the available techniques and commands:

### Select Steps

Be careful when selecting Steps. Here, it is not just clicking on it. When you click on a Step, you actually edit its value, the height of the beam.

These are the commands on how to select Septs:

- ▶ **Single Step**: *Sh+click* on a single Step to select/de-select one or multiple Steps
- ▶ **Multiple Steps**: *Sh+drag* over adjacent Steps to select them all (lasso around)
- ▶ **All Steps/per Lane**: *Click* the Lane Header to select all Steps in that Lane
- ▶ **All Step/all Lanes**: *Cmd+click* on multiple Lane Headers to select all the Events in all those Lanes

### 👤 Add Steps

When creating new Steps, keep an eye on the Info Display ❶ in the Menu Bar. It shows the time position and the value of the new Event when you click at the current cursor position.

> ▶ **Add single Step**: *Click* with the Pencil Tool 🖊 on the Lane at the time position you want to create the new Event. The *Command-Tool Menu* is set to the Pencil Tool by default, so you can *cmd+click* right away without changing Tools. Creating a new Event on the Lane outside the MIDI Region (to the right of the *End of Region Marker* ◀) will extend the length of the currently selected MIDI Region (and reposition the *End of Region Marker*).

> ▶ **Add Multiple Steps (Draw)**: *Drag* with the Pencil Tool 🖊 on the Lane at the time position you want to create a new Event to draw the curve.

### 👤 Edit Step Values

There are multiple functions on how to edit Steps on a Lane.

> ▶ **Edit single Step**: *Dragging* the beam up or down with the Pointer Tool 🖱 or the Pencil 🖊 will change its height, and therefore, its value. The black Help Tag displays the current value while dragging.

> ▶ **Edit multiple Steps (contiguous)**: *Drag* across contiguous Steps with the Pointer Tool 🖱. The Value of each individual Step will follow the cursor position and the black Help Tag displays the position and value of the current Event.

> ▶ **Edit multiple Steps - relative**: *Sh+click* on the beams to select the Steps you want to change. Then, *drag* any of the selected beams up or down. All selected Steps will move with it while keeping their relative position. Be careful and drag only straight up or down. Moving to the side will overwrite the neighboring Step you moved the mouse over by accident.

> ▶ **Draw linear Curve**: *Click-hold* with the Line Tool 📏 at an Event and draw across left or right to an end point ❷. A thin line shows the resulting linear curve that the value of the Events will adjust to. Release the mouse to apply those values ❸.

> ▶ **Fix Value**: Select a beam and then activate "Fix Value" from the Lane Set Menu. This will mark the value of the selected Events as the Preset Value. Now, every newly created MIDI Event will have the Preset Value. Drawing a linear curve with the Line Tool 📏 will use that Preset Value as the starting value of the linear curve.

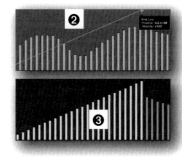

### 👤 Move Steps

Moving Steps along the timeline is restricted to the currently selected Grid value for that Lane.

> ▶ **Single Step**: *Sh+drag* a Step left or right along the Lane.

> ▶ **Multiple Steps**: *Sh+click* on the beams to select the Steps you want to change (even on different Lanes). Then, *sh+drag* any of the selected beams left or right.

> ▶ **Nudge Steps**: Use any of the Nudge Commands to move the time position of any selected Step(s) along the Lane. This is not restricted to the current Grid in the Lane Inspector.

> ▶ **Move between Lanes**: You can also move Steps between Lanes. This will convert the Step(s) to the Event of the new Lane.

> ▶ **Lock Position**: You can SMPTE-lock any Step so it can't be moved to a new position (until you "Unlock" it again). Select the Step(s) and choose from Local Menu *Functions ➤ Lock SMPTE Position* (*cmd +PageDown*). There is no visual indication in the Step Editor if a Step is locked or not. You have to open the Event List or the Event Float for that ❹ 🔒.

Event List

### 🔘 Copy Steps

The Copy commands are the same as the Move commands, just use *sh+opt+drag*

### 🔘 HiHat Groups

HiHat Groups let you imitate a real-life behavior, where an instrument (not only HiHats) can't play two specific notes (sounds) at the same time. For example, an open HiHat and closed HiHat, or a rim shot and a side stick on a Snare.

- The Lanes must be adjacent to be linked as a HiHat Group.
- You can create multiple HiHat Groups in one Lane Set.
- Adding an Event to a Lane of a HiHat Group will delete any Event on other grouped Lanes on that position.

This is the simple procedure:

- ☑️ *Click* the blue dot ❶ to the left of the Lane
- ☑️ *Click* the blue dot on the adjacent Lane to add this Lane to the HiHat Group. A dotted line will link both Lanes together
- ☑️ *Click* on any blue dot that is part of a HiHat Group to remove it from that group

### 🔘 Delete Steps

- ▶ **Single Step**: *Click* on a single Step with the Eraser Tool 🖊 or select it and press *delete*
- ▶ **Multiple Steps (non-contiguous)**: *Click* on single Steps with the Pointer Tool 🖱 to select them and press *delete*
- ▶ **Multiple Steps (contiguous)**: *Drag* across contiguous Steps with the Eraser Tool 🖊
- ▶ **Similar Steps**: Use the Key Command (*Select Similar Regions/Events*) *sh+S* or (*Select Equal Regions/Events*) *sh+E*, then press Delete

### ➡ *Conclusion*

I hope you get some ideas on how to incorporate the Step Editor into your workflow.

Although it is mostly used to edit drum patterns, you can also use it as an extended MIDI Draw Display. Remember that the Piano Roll can only display one MIDI Event Type in the MIDI Draw area. The Step Editor is kind of a multi-lane MIDI Draw Display. If you line up a standalone Piano Roll Editor ❷ and a standalone Step Editor ❸, then you can view multiple Controllers ❹ next to the actual MIDI Notes ❺ of the same selected MIDI Region. It is not perfect and requires that you adjust the Zoom Levels and Link Modes (save as Screensets), but it is a workaround until Logic (hopefully) adds the feature that lets you view multiple MIDI Draw Lanes in the Piano Roll, similar to the Automation Lanes in the Tracks Window.

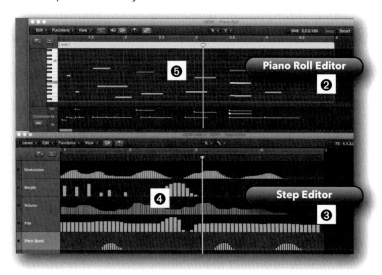

# History

### ➡ *Good Old Days*

In the "good old days" of audio production, after everything was recorded nicely on your tape machine, you would proceed to the next step and mix your tracks. That means, you would apply all kinds of leveling and processing to make your song sound the way you wanted. The leveling and processing could mean fixed settings (one fixed EQ, one fixed fader position, etc.), or you could apply the settings dynamically (i.e. changing the volume fader for the vocals or other instruments during the song to change the balance of your mix to emphasize those specific instruments during specific parts of your song.

Prior to any automation system, the sound engineer had to remember what fader to move, and when, and how much, and "perform" that in real time while playing back the tape. Sometimes, the assistant and even the band members had to give a helping hand to press a button or move a control during a very complex mix. That mix was performed "live" and if one person was "off", the whole mix had to be performed again.

In addition, if you decided early on in the mix that a track would require some dynamic changes (i.e. turn on a big reverb send on one snare hit), you would have to perform that switch every time from now on during the mix process while you continue working on other elements of your mix.

Then finally in the early 90, the first automated mixing consoles came to the rescue. First, they provided only the option to automate the Volume Fader, sometimes in the form of motorized Faders.

When you performed a movement, that movement was recorded and a motor inside the Fader moved it accordingly when you played back that section. Moving Faders were something a sound engineer could use to impress the producer or band, especially on big consoles.

These systems were pretty complex because the mixing board had to be synced to the tape machine via timecode, and the data that was generated by the controls were either recorded on that tape or on a separate storage in the mixing console. First, only the Volume Fader could be automated, but with the introduction of digital mixing consoles, virtually every control could be automated.

### ➡ *Now*

Nowadays, in the world of Digital Audio Workstations (DAW), the tape machine is replaced by a sequencer (your hard drive) that records your music and your automation data. Everything is in perfect sync, without the need for synchronizers. Everything is integrated - you work "in the box".

In addition, you can edit the automation data manually like your other MIDI or audio data. The interface and functionality is so simple nowadays that you don't have to wait with the automation until you finished recording your Project. Automation is now a creative process that you can use while you are developing your song. Although way simpler (and much more powerful) than automated mixing consoles, you have to learn the concepts and workflows of automation to use them creatively in your Project. So, let's get into it.

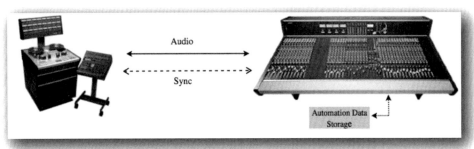

# Automation in Logic

Now let's see how Automation is implemented in Logic. First of all, Automation is not just one feature in Logic that can be explained on a few pages. Instead, it is a set of features and different types of Automation, and the topic can get very deep as you can see by the length of this chapter.

If you are new to this, then you have to learn a set of new terms and what they mean. Even if you are familiar with automation, you might have to "re-learn" some of the terminology, because Logic might use them differently.

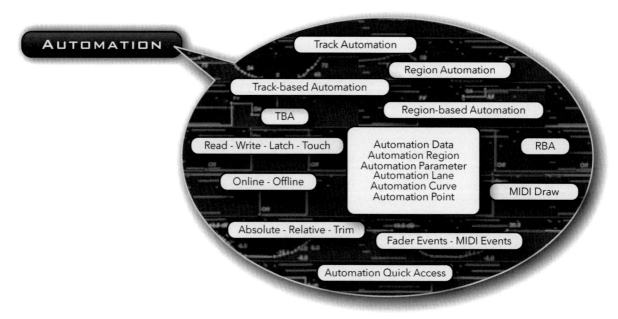

I decided to split the Automation topic into two chapters.

▶ **Automation**: In this chapter, I'll go over all the elements of the most common type of Automation, Track Automation.

- ☑ Track Automation
- ☑ Automation Modes
- ☑ Online vs. Offline
- ☑ Automation Editing

After learning the user interface and the functionality of Track Automation, you will have all the required tools to fully automate your mix without the need to know about the advanced features. However, once you are familiar with basic Track Automation, you can proceed to the next level to learn the more advanced automation techniques.

▶ **Automation (Advanced)**: In the second chapter, I explain all the new features introduces in LPX v10.1. In addition, I will provide the big picture to show how all these elements are implemented in Logic. Remember, like so often in Logic, it can get pretty complex, pretty fast. You have to understand how the features and functionalities work in order to avoid any potential confusion.

- ☑ Region Automation
- ☑ MIDI Draw
- ☑ Absolute vs. Relative vs. Trim
- ☑ Convert Automation

# Math Background

Here is a quick look at the basic concept of Automation with a little bit of a math background.

## Scenario ❶

### ▶ Real Life

You set the Fader for the vocal track on your mixing board to 0dB. You start to play the Project and throughout the 3 minutes of the song, you leave the Fader at that position without changes.

### ▶ Math Representation

You might remember from your math class that you could draw that as a graph. The x-axis represents the duration of the song (playing for 3 minutes) and the y-axis represents the position of the Fader (the value of the volume parameter).

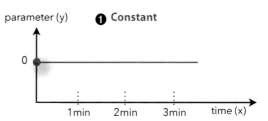

The Result: The parameter value (the Fader) stays constant

## Scenario ❷

### ▶ Real Life

In real life, you probably find that the singer moved a little bit too close to the microphone during the song at 1 min, and you have to gradually lower the Volume Fader to -10dB when reaching the 2 minute mark. At that point, the singer seemed to realize that and moved away from the mic, but this time a bit too far. You compensate that by raising the Volume Fader back up, all the way to +3dB by the time the song reaches the 3 minute mark.

### ▶ Math Representation

The mathematical function is a visual representation of the movement I just did with the Fader. The parameter value starts at 0 and stays at that value up to the 1 minute mark. Now the value decreases gradually to -10 and when the graph reaches the 2 minute mark on the time axis, it gradually increases to +3 when it reaches the 3 minute mark on the time axis.

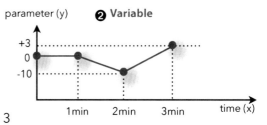

The Result: The parameter value (the Fader) varies over time

Now let's lets' get started with the Track Automation. Remember, I will ignore the elements that are not necessary for the basic functionality of the Track Automation (Region Automation, MIDI Draw, Trim, Relative, Absolute) to keep it simple and concentrate on the basic operation.

## Concept

Track Automation, also referred to as "Track-based Automation" or "TBA", is the most common type of Automation. It is similar to the concept of automated mixing consoles.

This is the basic concept:

▸ **Graph**: The Track Automation can be displayed as a graph ❶ that shows how the value of a specific Parameter changes over time.

▸ **Parameter**: Virtually every control ❷ on a Channel Strip, Plugin,or Smart Controls (Fader, Knob, Button, etc) can be automated. That also means, each Parameter has its own graph.

▸ **Track**: A graph is displayed along the entire Track, from the beginning ❶ of the Project to the end ❸, independent of any Regions on that Track.

▸ **Source**:  You create Track Automation either offline (by drawing the graph) or online (by  recording your "performance"). Performing means, you move your Onscreen Controls in Logic ❷ and record that movement (which is displayed as the graph ❶). You can also move Logic's onscreen controls remotely by using an external hardware, (called a Control Surface ❹) and even with a MIDI Controller ❺. All these devices require a proper configuration in Logic's Controller Assignments Window ❻ (which I will discuss in a separate chapter).

▸ **Advantage**: One of the main advantages of using Track Automation in Logic is its accuracy, which provides up to 10-bit values and a sample-based time resolution.

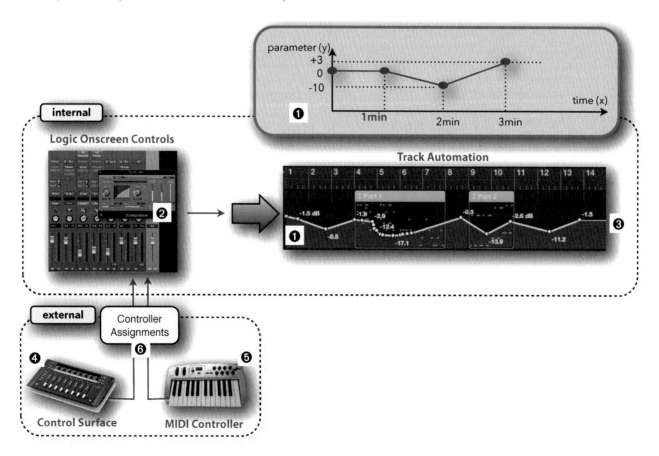

# Terminology

The graph describes the "behavior" of a specific parameter (i.e. the Volume Fader), its movement over time (the length of the song). Instead of doing the movements manually every time you play back your song, you describe (record, store) the movement first with a graph and every time you play back your song, Logic performs that movement automatically.

Let me first introduce the terminology for Automation in Logic:

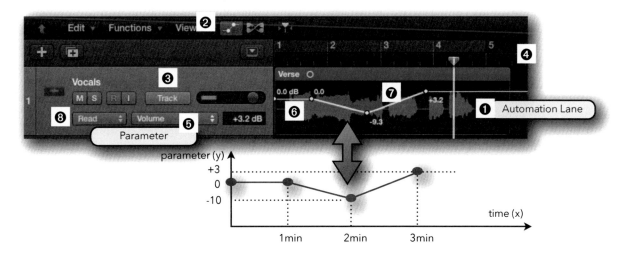

### ❶ Automation Lane (Graph Area)

The area that displays the graph (Automation Curve) is called the Automation Lane or Automation Track. You have to enable the *Show/Hide Automation Button* ❷ in the Menu Bar of the Tracks Window and enable the *Track Automation Button* ❸ on the individual Track Header to display the Automation Lane on a specific Track. The Track Lane for that Track then changes to a mini Track Lane with the active Region Header and leaves the rest of the space to display the Automation Lane.

### ❹ Timeline (x)

The time axis of the graph is already there in Logic. It is the Timeline of your current Project represented by the Ruler on top of the Workspace.

### ❺ Automation Parameter (y)

The Volume is only one possible Parameter on a Track that you can automate. Virtually any Parameter on a Track can be automated. That includes the main components on a Channel Strip (Volume, Pan, Sends, Mute, etc.), any parameter of any loaded Plugin (Instrument Plugin, Audio FX Plugin, and MIDI FX Plugin), and also any Onscreen Control of the Smart Controls. The Automation Parameter

Button ❺ on the Track Header opens a popup menu with all the available Parameters. Select an item to show its Automation Curve.

### ❻ Control Points

The red dots on the math graph represent the values of the parameter at a specific time. In math class, these were called the "coordinates", but Logic calls them "Control Points" or "Automation Points" (other applications use the terms "Nodes" or 'Keyframes'). These Automation Control Points define the Automation Curve.

### ❼ Automation Curve

Logic connects the Automation Control Points along the Automation Lane, resulting in the Automation Curve that always starts at the beginning of your Project, all the way to the end. This line represents the change of the Parameter value over time: Staying constant, going up, or going down.

### ❽ Automation Mode

There are four different Automation Modes, *Read*, *Latch*, *Touch*, and *Write* (if you don't count "*OFF*"), that describe a specific Automation behavior, plus two variations *Trim* and *Relative*.

# Create Automation Data: Online - Offline

The graph determines how the Parameter value changes throughout the song, so the next question would be: "How do you create that graph, the so-called Automation Curve?"

There are two methods of creating or editing an Automation Curve, online and offline:

**Offline**: Draw the Automation Curve manually with the Mouse

**Online**: Move the Controllers in real time during playback

## Create New Automation Curves

▶ **Offline**

This is the same method as creating MIDI Events. You use your Mouse Pointer and click on the Automation Lane to create Control Points. Logic automatically connects those Control Points to display the resulting Automation Curve.

▶ **Online**

This is like a live recording where you "perform" the automation. You select a specific Automation Mode (Write, Touch, Latch) for the Tracks you want to create Automation for and start playing back your Project. Any Parameter you change (by moving an Onscreen Control or with an external controller) will be "recorded" as new Control Points with the Automation Curve forming in front of your eyes.

## Edit Existing Automation Curves

▶ **Offline**

You just edit the Control Points or the lines between the Control Points with various Cursor Tools. This is like editing any other MIDI Events, because Control Points represent individual Events, the so-called Fader Events.

▶ **Online**

The same Automation Modes (Write, Touch, Latch) that are used to write automation data are used to "overwrite" any existing Automation Curve as the Playhead moves along. This is similar to the Replace Mode when you record audio or MIDI data over existing data.

# Show me the Automation

Technically, you can use Automation in Logic in online mode without the need of seeing the actual graph. This is like working on a mixing console that doesn't provide a user interface. You perform your mix and record the Fader movements. The mixer then plays back those movements and you would only "see" that when you have moving faders. If necessary, you just overwrite the movements like you would when overdubbing on a Track.

However, if you want to see the Automation Curve or want to edit the Automation Curve offline, you first have to make the Automation visible.

 **Show/Hide Automation Button (Automation View)**

This is a global button on the Tracks Window's Menu Bar that toggles the visibility of the automation data and the various automation controls. Please note that showing Automation the first time will automatically enable Track Automation on all Tracks and sets the Automation to Read Mode.

▶ This button is a global button that toggles the view of all Tracks.

▶ You can either show [icon] ❶ or hide [icon] ❷ the Automation on all Tracks. You can also toggle the Automation View with:

    🎛 Main Menu *Mix ➤ Show/Hide Automation*

    🎛 Key Command (*Show/Hide Track Automation*) *A*

▶ Hiding the Automation doesn't affect the actual automation data, you just won't see it.

▶ The button is automatically disabled [icon] when the Show/Hide Flex Button next to it is enabled [icon].

▶ When Automation is shown, the following things will change. Make sure the Tracks are zoomed in vertically high enough and resized wide enough to display all those components:

    ☑ The Track height increases ❸ to accommodate the additional controls on the Track Header.

    ☑ The Track Lane splits into a dual-lane. The mini Track Header ❹ on top displays the Region Header of any existing Region, and the area underneath (still showing the visible Region Content, slightly dimmed) is now the Automation Lane ❺ displaying the Automation Curve.

    ☑ The Track Header displays five additional elements (only if the Track Header is tall enough):

      • The Automation Button [Track] ❻ (This button also toggles between Track Automation and Region Automation).

      • The Subtracks Disclosure Triangle ❼.

      • The Automation Mode Button ❽.

      • The Automation Parameter Button ❾.

      • The Automation Value/Trim Field ❿. This element is only displayed if the Track Header is wide enough.

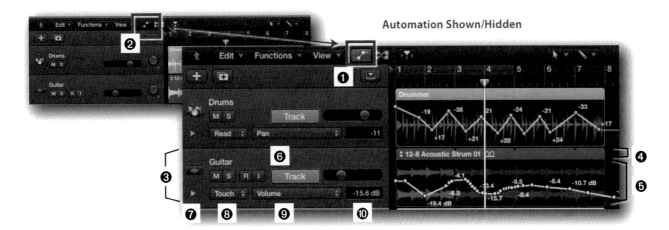

Automation Shown/Hidden

**Enable Automation Button (Automation on/off)**

The Enable Automation Button is displayed on each Track when the Show Automation Button is enable .

▶ The Enable Automation Button is a "multi-purpose" button with Click Zones that appear when you move the Mouse Pointer over it.
- **Left ❶**: *Click* on the left to toggle its Power Button. This turns the Automation on ❷ or off ❸ for that Track
- **Right ❹**: *Click* on the right to toggle between Track Automation and Region Automation (discussed in the next chapter)

▶ You can *click-hold* on the button and then *drag* vertically across multiple Track Headers to turn them all on or off (or switch between Track Automation and Region Automation)

▶ Disabling the Automation on a Track just bypasses the Track Automation data, it does not delete it.

▶ Disabling the Automation will dim ❺ the Automation Curve on the Automation Lane (gray, no color).

**Enable Automation Button on/off**

## ➡ *Channel Strip*

The Automation can also be toggled on the Channel Strip of the corresponding Track. However, the functionality is slightly different:

▶ The Automation Mode Button displays its current mode in individual colors ❺ if the Automation is enabled.

▶ The Automation Mode Button displays its current mode without color ❻ if the Automation is disabled.

▶ You can toggle the Automation on/off on the Channel Strip with the Power Button [⏻] ❼ that appears (as a Click Zone) when you move the Pointer Tool over the button.

▶ That means that the Power Button of the Automation Mode on the Channel Strip corresponds to the Power Button of the Enable Automation Button on the Track Header ❶.

▶ There is a special color for the Read Button ❽ (green font on gray background). This indicates that Automation is enabled on that Track, but there is no Track Automation data created yet.

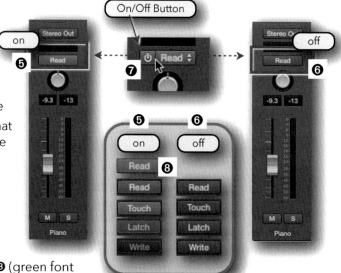

# Automation Parameter Menu

Below the Track Automation Button on the Track Header is the Automation Parameter Button ❶. It opens the Automation Parameter Menu that lets you select which Automation Parameter to display in the Automation Lane ❷. The name of the currently selected Automation Parameter is displayed on the button. You can also access the menu from the Shortcut Menu when you *ctr+click* on the Automation Lane.

The popup menu is highly dynamic. The displayed menu items depend on how the Channel Strip/Track is configured.

▶ **Smart Controls** ❸ (if available): This first item opens a submenu with all the Onscreen Controls of the Track's Smart Controls ❹ (only visible if Smart Controls are configured). These Parameters are extremely powerful because one control can be mapped to multiple Parameters across all the loaded Plugins on the Channel Strip. See my manual "Logic Pro X - How it Works" for details about the Smart Controls.

▶ **Main** ❺: This item opens a submenu with all the main Parameters of the Channel Strip (Volume, Pan, Solo, Mute, Sends, Plugin Bypass, etc.). Please note that you can automate the Power Button of each Audio FX Plugin (it is called Insert #n Bypass).

▶ **MIDI FX Plugins** (if available) ❻: Next are all the MIDI FX Plugins listed (with their slot numbers) that are loaded on that Channel Strip with a submenu listing all their Parameters that can be automated.

▶ **Instrument Plugin** (if available) ❼: Next is the Instrument Plugin listed (if one is loaded onto that Track). It is always assigned to the slot number #1 of the Audio FX Plugins.

▶ **Audio FX Plugins** (if available) ❽: Next are all the Audio FX Plugins listed (with their slot numbers) that are loaded on that Channel Strip with a submenu listing all their Parameters that can be automated.

▶ **Display off** ❾: This option, when selected, displays no Automation Curve for any of the Automation Parameters on the Automation Lane. Choose this option when you want to use MIDI Draw on the Track Lane.

▶ **Parameters with Automation Data** ❿: The next sections in the menu list all the Automation Parameters that have automation data programmed. The currently displayed Automation Parameter has a check mark and is also listed on top of the menu.

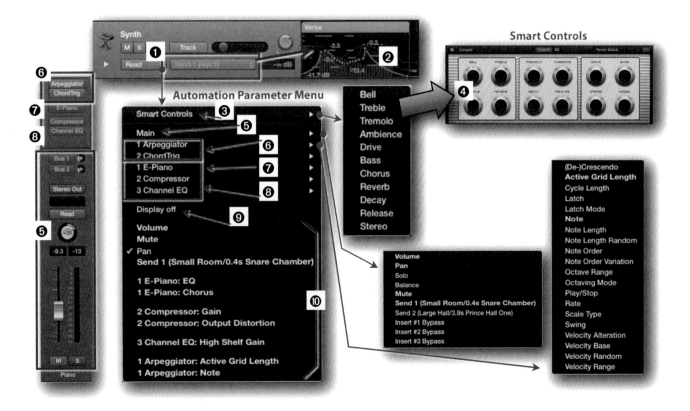

# Automation Lane(s)

When the Show/Hide Automation Button ❶ is enabled ![icon] in the Tracks Window's Menu Bar, then all the Region's Track Lanes split into two lanes. That means, the Automation Lane is actually part of a double lane with an upper section ❷ and a lower section ❸. You have to be very careful where to click. Each of those sections have their own Click Zones that change the Mouse Pointer to a specific Tool and resulting actions.

## 💀 Track Lane (Region Header) ❷

The upper section of the Track Lane is now the mini Track Lane.

- ▶ The mini Track Lane still displays the Region Header of any Region and is not affected when switching between Automation enabled [Track] ❹ and Automation disabled [Track] ❺.

- ▶ Any click action you usually perform on the "full-size" Track Lane still works on that mini lane (i.e. select, move, resize, loop, etc.). If you want to edit a Region with the Mouse Pointer while the Automation Lane is visible, you have to point precisely at the Region Header.

- ▶ *Ctr+click* anywhere on the mini Track Lane to display the standard Shortcut Menu for the Track Lane.

- ▶ The mini Track Lane still displays the grid lines ❻ where there is no Region so you have the vertical time reference to the Ruler.

## 💀 Automation Lane (Automation Track) ❸

The lower section of a Track Lane, below the mini Track Lane, is now the Automation Lane (Logic calls it Automation Track).

- ▶ It is important to understand that this is "Track-based" Automation, which means, the Automation Curve "belongs" to the entire Track (its assigned Channel Strip to be specific) and not individual Regions. It is a continuous graph along the Track's Timeline from the beginning to the end of your Project.

- ▶ Any mouse action on the Automation Lane (click, drag, etc.) does not affect any Region. The dimmed Region Content (Waveform, MIDI Events) on the Automation Lane is just visible for better orientation. The Automation Lane has its own set of click actions that I will discuss in a moment.

- ▶ Different Automation Parameters display the Control Points and the Automation Curve in a specific color.

- ▶ The Track Automation Button ❹ toggles the Automation on/off for all Automation Parameters on a Track. However, you can disable individual Automation Parameters with their own Power Button that is revealed as a Click Zone when you move the Pointer Tool over the Button.

- ▶ *Ctr+click* on the Automation Lane to display a Shortcut Menu with automation-specific commands.

## ➡ *Main Track*

The previous screenshot showed three Tracks, each displaying the split Track Lane with a single Automation Lane ❶ for each Track.

- 🔘 The Automation Lane displays the Automation Curve ❷ of the Automation Parameter that is currently selected from the Automation Parameter Menu ❸. This is the active curve that can be edited.
- 🔘 Other Automation Curves for the Track (not currently selected) are also visible, but slightly dimmed ❹. This is useful to see if there is any other automation data present.
- 🔘 If you want to edit (or better view) the Automation Curve of a different Automation Parameter, you have to select it in the Automation Parameter Menu ❸ to change the Automation Lane display.

However, Logic can display multiple Automation Lanes for a single Track to display multiple Automation Curves at once along the Timeline. Logic calls these additional Automation Lanes "Subtracks" and you can show/hide them with the Subtracks Disclosure Triangle ❺ that becomes visible on the Track Header when you enable the Show/Hide Automation Button 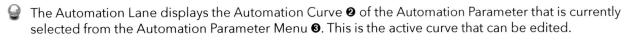 on the Tracks Window's Menu Bar.

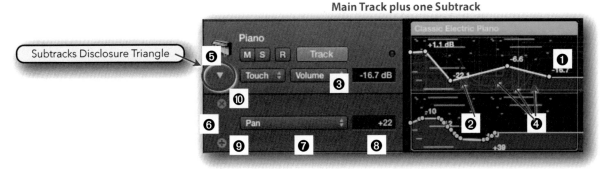

## ➡ *Subtracks* ❻

Each Subtrack has its own Subtrack Header that extends into its Automation Lane. Please note that only the Main Track displays the mini Track Lane.

- **Automation Parameter Button ❼**: This button opens the same popup menu as on the Main Track Header. You choose which Automation Parameter to display on that Subtrack.
- **The Automation Value/Trim Field ❽**: This field displays the Parameter value at the current Playhead Position. *Drag* it up or down to raise or lower the entire Automation Curve (0.1dB increments) to quickly apply an offset to it, or just *click* on it to select all Control Points.
- ⊕ **Button ❾**: *Click* that + icon to add another Subtrack below. The button only appears when you move the Mouse over the Subtrack Header. *Opt+click* on the Subtracks Disclosure Triangle to open one Subtrack for each Automation Parameter that has existing automation data.
- ☒ **Button ❿**: *Click* that x icon to remove that Subtrack (it does not remove any Automation data!). The button only appears when you move the Mouse over the Subtrack Header.
- **Reorder**: *Drag* a Subtrack Header up or down to reorder the Subtracks. Toggling the disclosure triangle will maintain the selected Subtracks.

Here are a few examples of what you will see on the Automation Lane:

Automation is hidden. The Show/Hide Automation Button is disabled ❶.

Automation is visible ❷, but Track Automation is disabled ❸ on that Track. The taller Track Header displays the additional controls (Track Automation and popup menus, etc).

Track Automation is enabled ❹ (Automation Lane visible), but no Automation is created yet (no Automation Curve). A dimmed straight line ❺ indicates the current value of the control, in this case the Volume Fader. The number value is also displayed at the beginning of the line.

The Automation Curve has only one Control Point ❻ at the beginning of the Project, creating a straight line. You still can move the Volume Fader, which updates the straight Automation Curve.

Busy Automation Curve (Volume) on the Automation Lane with many Control Points ❼.

Same Automation Curve (Volume) active, but only visible as a dimmed ❽ curve because a different Automation Parameter (Pan ❾) is selected.

Volume is again selected as the current Automation Parameter with the Volume Automation Curve visible. Other Automation Curves are also active and can be (barely) seen as dimmed curves ❿.

Now let's learn how to generate automation data. At the beginning of this chapter, I already introduced the two different ways as to how to create/edit automation data:

▶ **Offline**: Drawing automation data with your mouse.

▶ **Online**: Moving controllers in real time and record that movement as automation data.

Let's start with the Online Automation.

## Automation Mode

The key element when performing online automation are the different Automation Modes.

> **Automation Modes are like Record Modes for Automation Data**

**Recording MIDI data**: Recording a MIDI keyboard requires the following main steps:

- ☑ Select a <u>Record Mode</u>
- ☑ Enable the Track
- ☑ Play the song and record the performance of the keyboard player as MIDI data

**Recording Automation data**: The steps are similar:

- ☑ Select an <u>Automation Mode</u> on the Track you want to generate Automation data
- ☑ Play back your Song (this can be either in Play Mode or Record Mode)
- ☑ Move the Controllers you want to record as automation data

Each Track can be set individually to different Automation Modes. These modes determine how the Track behaves regarding automation data. Logic displays the active Automation Modes on the Channel Strip in different colors when Automation is enabled and in gray when Automation is disabled. The Track Header displays the current Automation always as a gray button regardless of the Automation status.

🔘 **Automation Disabled** [⏻ Trk]: **Ignore current Automation data**

Any existing automation data is ignored (Automation Mode Buttons on the Channel Strip have no color).

▶

🔘 **Automation Enabled** [⏻ Trk]: **Play back current Automation data**

Any existing automation data is played back.

▶ Read

(if Read Mode is enabled, but there is no automation data yet, then you will see this button [ Read ] )

🔘 **Automation Enabled** [⏻ Trk]: **Record new Automation data**

Any controller movement will be recorded as new automation data based on three different behaviors (overwriting any existing Automation data).

▶

(I'll discuss these special Modes in the next chapter  )

The Automation Mode can be set individually for each Track on the Track Header or the Channel Strip.

## ➡ *Track Header*

The controls are only visible if the Show Automation Button  in the Tracks Window's Menu Bar is enabled. Remember, this button only controls the visibility of Automation in the Tracks Window. That means that Automation could be enabled with various Automation Modes on different Tracks, you just wouldn't see it.

- ☑ If the Track Automation Button is disabled `Track` ❶, then any existing automation data on that Track will be ignored (bypassed). The Automation Mode Button displays the currently selected (but inactive) Automation Mode ❷.

- ☑ If the Track Automation Button is enabled `Track` ❸, then the Automation Mode depends on which of the Automation Modes is selected from the Automation Mode Menu ❹.

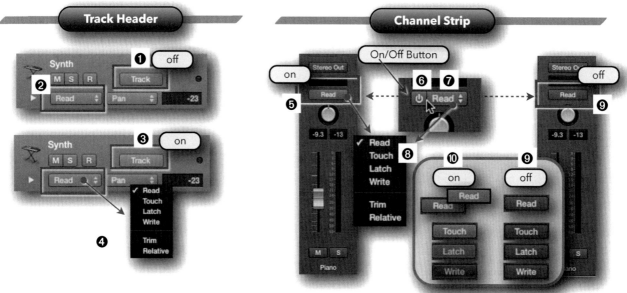

## ➡ *Channel Strip*

Two things to be aware of:

- The visibility of the Automation Mode Button on the Channel Strip, located above the Pan Knob ❺, can be toggled on/off by *ctrl+clicking* on the Channel Strip to choose *Channel Strip Components* ➤ *Automation* or select it from the *Configure Channel Strip Components* ➤, or select the same commands from the local View Menu.

- The Automation Mode Button reveals two Click Zones when moving the Mouse Pointer over it. On the left is the Power Button 🔘 ❻ and *clicking* on the right ❼ will open the same Automation Mode Menu ❽ as in the Track Header.

- ☑ If the Power Button is disabled 🔘 ❾, then any existing automation data on that Track will be ignored (bypassed). The button displays the currently selected Automation Mode, but it has no color.

- ☑ If the Power Button is enabled 🔘 ❿, then the Automation Mode depends on which of the modes is selected from the Automation Mode Menu. The buttons are colored to indicate the active mode.

There are a wide variety of Key Commands that let you switch to a specific Automation Mode for the selected Track or all Tracks.

**Key Commands for switching Automation Modes**

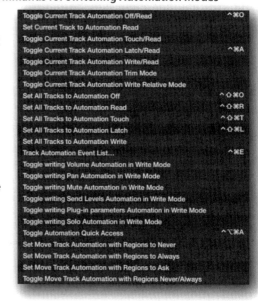

These are the behaviors for the four main Automation Modes (I will explain Trim and Relative Mode in the following chapter):

Any Parameter with automation data on that Track will follow its Automation Curve when the Project is played back (in Play Mode or Record Mode). It has priority over any manual controller changes. You can change the Parameter value (i.e. Volume Fader) while your Project is not playing, but as soon as you start playing back your Project again, the Parameter value will follow the Automation Curve.

Any Parameter with automation data on that Track will follow its Automation Curve when the Project is played back. At the moment you touch a controller (on the screen with your mouse or an assigned external controller), then data will be written as automation data. Any existing automation data will be overwritten at the current Playhead Position. When you release the mouse, the value of the current fader position (i.e. -20dB) changes back to the value of the existing automation data for that Parameter. How fast it ramps up or down to the existing value can be set in the Preferences Window *Preferences ➤ Automation ➤ Ramp Time* ❶.

### A few More Things

▸ The Preferences Window lets you select what kind of Parameter is written as automation data ❸: Volume, Pan, Mute, Send, Plug-in, and/or Solo. You can also toggle the checkboxes with individual Key Commands.

▸ When you write new automation data, then the Automation Parameter Button switches automatically to the Parameter of the Controller you are currently moving. This way, you can see the Automation Curve for that Parameter you are currently writing for.

▸ There are two Key Commands *Write Automation to End* and *Write Automation to Right Locator* that overwrite any existing automation data with the current value when in Write Mode while playing your song.

▸ Although you can set the Automation Mode individually for each Track, the Group Settings Window ❹ lets you check "Automation Mode" so it switches together for all Channel Strips that belong to that specific Channel Strip Group. Keep in mind that the actual Automation Curve on a Channel Strip will only control that Channel Strip not the Channel Strips in that same group.

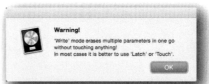

The behavior in Latch Mode is the same as in Touch mode until you release the controller. Now, instead of going back to any existing value, the current value will be written after you release the controller until you stop playback.

This is the most dangerous mode that needs special attention. Any existing automation data of any Parameter will be overwritten with the current Parameter value while playing back (without touching a control). Of course, any controller movement you perform will be recorded as new automation data. A Dialog Window warns about the "risks"

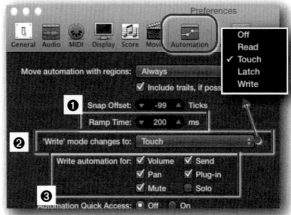

The Preferences Settings "Write mode changes to" popup menu ❷ lets you choose to which Automation Mode Logic will switch after you stop your pass recording in "Write Mode".

**Automation Preferences**

**Group Settings Window**

# Step-by-step Procedure

Here are the required steps when you want to create automation data using the Online procedure:

## ☑ 1) Show Automation

Enable the Show/Hide Automation Button 🔀 in the Tracks Window's Menu Bar. Remember, this is not necessary for the Automation functionality. You could read/write Automation by using the controls on the Channel Strips that are not affected by the Show/Hide Automation Button, but having the controls visible on the Track Header and seeing the Automation Curve provides a better visual feedback.

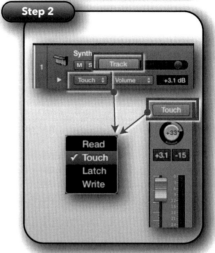

## ☑ 2) Select Automation Mode

Select the Automation Mode on the Track you want to write automation data. You can do this in the Track Header or on the Channel Strip:

- Track Header: Enable the Track Automation Button Track and select, for example, the Touch Mode from the Automation Mode Button.
- Channel Strip: Select the Touch Mode from the Automation Mode Button. It turns yellow to indicate that it is active Touch .

## ☑ 3) Start Playback

Start your Song at the position where you want to write the new automation data.

## ☑ 4) Move your Controller

Please note that it is not necessary to select the Automation Parameter first. At the moment you move an Onscreen Control (i.e. Volume Fader or Pan Knob), the Automation Parameter Button automatically switches to that Parameter and displays its Automation Curve in the Automation Lane. This has the following advantages:

- You don't have to pre-select an Automation Parameter.
- You can write multiple parameters in one pass.
- If you have an external controller, then you can write multiple controllers at the same time (i.e. moving the Volume Fader and Pan Knob at the same time).
- Any control you touch (on the Channel Strip, on an open Plugin Window, or the Smart Controls) will be written.
- The Track Lane always displays the Automation Curve of the current Automation Parameter you are writing, so you can see any existing automation data for that parameter.

## ☑ 5) Stop Playback

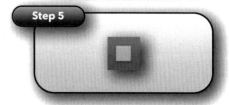

After you stop the playback, remember to switch the Track to Read Mode to avoid any accidental overwrite or repeat from Step 3) to record more Automation.

Here are two examples of how the Automation Lane should look after you've written your automation data:

### 💀 Continuous Controller (Fader, Knob)

Whenever you moved the controller, Logic creates Automation Control Points with that controller value. When you don't move the controller, then you would just see a horizontal line.

### 💀 Switch

When you automate a switch (i.e Mute Button), then you would see only two values for the Control Points, maximum (button enabled: muted) and minimum (button disabled: un-muted).

## Tips

Using Online Automation is a very quick and straightforward way to write automation data. After you understand the procedures, you have to play around with it to get comfortable with it. The functionality is very flexible with the different commands and modes so you can develop your own procedures to fit your personal workflows. Here are some tips:

- ☑ You can enable multiple Tracks at the same time to write automation for multiple Tracks in a single pass. This is important to balance two or more Tracks against each other.
- ☑ Using a Key Command, you can switch all Tracks at once between Read and Touch so you don't have to switch individual Tracks. It's like live mixing, whatever controller you want to change, it is "hot" and ready to be written.
- ☑ You can use the Undo command to quickly undo the last pass (or multiple passes) if you didn't like it.
- ☑ To overwrite a small or long section of automation data (re-write), make sure to choose the suitable mode (Touch, Latch, Write).
- ☑ Even if the Automation Curves are not visible, the Controls (Fader, Knobs, and Buttons) are moving, following their automation data to provide a visual feedback of what is happening. Even the little thumbnail picture of the Channel EQ on top of the Channel Strip will update the frequency curve if you have it automated.
- ☑ For more precise editing of automation data, use the Offline procedure, which I explain in the next section.

I cover the advanced Automation Modes (Trim, Relative, Region Automation) in the next chapter.

While the Online procedure is a very intuitive way to automate your mix (it just "records what you mix"), sometimes, the Offline procedure could be a better solution. After all, it is like editing MIDI Events, a procedure most users are already familiar with, unlike dealing with various Automation Modes. However, Logic provides so many tools and procedures for Offline automation that it could be a little bit overwhelming. I will introduce all those options one at a time, so at the end, you can choose the tools that suit your workflow best.

## Step-by-Step Procedure

Here are the required steps for creating automation data using the Offline procedure:

☑ **1) Show Automation**

The Show/Hide Automation Button ⟋ has to be enabled ❶ in order to see all the automation related controls in the Tracks Window.

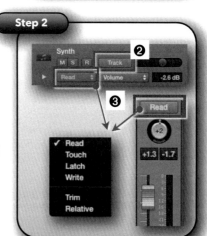

☑ **2) Enable Track Automation**

The Track Automation Button 〔 Track 〕 has to be enabled ❷ if no Control Points have been created yet. After that, it can be on or off. If off, the Automation Curve is still visible and can be edited, just in gray color. However, if you want Logic to perform the existing Automation, then you have to enable it and the Automation Mode has to be set to "Read" 〔 Read 〕 ❸.

☑ **3) Select Automation Parameter**

Select the Automation Parameter that you want to create/edit (i.e. Volume) by *clicking* on the Track Header's Automation Parameter Button ❹ and select it from the menu ❺.

☑ **4) Create/Edit Automation Curve**

The Automation Lane displays the Automation Curve ❻ for the selected Automation Parameter. This is the area where the offline procedure takes place, creating/editing the Automation Curve (automation data) with various Cursor Tools ❼.

# A few little Details

Before introducing all the procedures for Offline Automation, let me point out a few important details:

➡ **Cursor Tools**

Use the Key Command (*Show Tool Menu*) *T* to display the Tool Menu and quickly select a different Tool. Of all the available Cursor Tools in Logic, the following six Tools are used for Offline Automation:

 Pointer Tool

Pencil Tool

Eraser Tool

 Automation Select Tool

Automation Curve Tool

Marquee Tool

➡ **Automation Curve**

Remember, the Automation Curve for a specific Automation Parameter can have three stages:

### ⚫ No Control Point (default)

When there are no Control Points on the Automation Lane (no automation data has been created yet or they have been deleted), then a thin horizontal line indicates the current value of the selected Automation Parameter. In that case, changing the Volume Slider will move the line up or down accordingly.

### ⚫ Single Control Point

The first Control Point will always be placed at the beginning of the Project at (i.e., bar 1) with the current value of the Controller (in this case, the Volume Slider at -5dB).

Because you only have one Control Point defined at that moment, you can still move the Automation Curve by moving the Onscreen Control of that Parameter (i.e. Volume Slider).

### ⚫ More than one Control Point

Once there are more than one Control Points created, then you could still move the actual controller of the Parameter (i.e. Volume Slider), but as soon as you start the playback, the controller follows the movement of the Automation Curve (moved by invisible hands). From now on, the Automation Curve is in control (unless you bypass the automation data by turning the Track Automation Button off `Track` .

▶ **Disable individual Automation Curve**
Similar to the Track Automation Button that reveals a Power Button when you move over it with the mouse, the Automation Parameter Button also provides such a Power Button that lets you individually disable the Automation Curve for that Parameter. The Automation Curve turns gray to indicate that.

➡ *Control Points and Automation Curve*

There are a lot of details that can be easily overlooked when working with the Automation Curve. Some are very subtle, but they are important to know in order to understand what happens or what is displayed when working with various tools on the Automation Curve.

### Nothing is selected

If nothing is selected, then the Control Points and the resulting Automation Curve have a specific color, based on the Automation Parameter it represents.

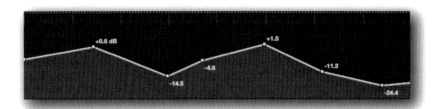

### One Control Point selected

If one Control Point on the Automation Curve is selected, then you will see the following changes:
- The selected Control Point turns white ❶.
- The line of the Automation Curve to the previous and to the next Control Point also turns white ❷.
- A thin, dark-shaded area ❸ appears around the Control Point. This is hard to see and will be covered when there is a Region in that position.
- A vertical alignment guide ❹ will appear at the position while you click on. This alignment guide runs vertically across the entire Workspace. Its position will be displayed in the Control Bar Display ❺ and on a black Help Tag ❾ that pops up, as long as you press down the mouse button. This is helpful when moving Control Points along the Timeline to align to other objects.

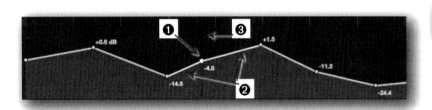
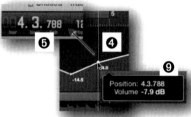

### Control Point as Hinges

Look at the following diagram that demonstrates the moving behavior: When you move a single Control Point (red) ❻, all the other Control Points (black) stay fixed. The segments of the Automation Curve (red) that are connected to the selected Control Point ❻ move with it when you move the Control Point, but only on that side. The other ends (to the left ❼ and to the right ❽) stay fixed. Think of those Control Points as hinges that hold that line segment in place. This way, you can move the Control Point ❻ and the Automation Curve updates accordingly. You can even move/ copy a Control Point beyond the adjacent Control Point. I explain that behavior a little bit later.

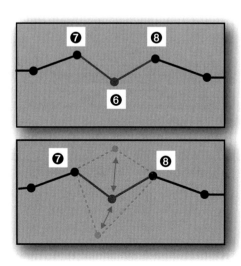

## ⚫ Two Control Points selected

If more than one Control Point is selected, then you will see the following changes:

- All the selected Control Points turn white ❶.
- The line of the Automation Curve from the previous Control Point of the first selected Control Point all the way to the following Control Point of the last selected Control Point also turns white ❷.
- The dark-shaded area ❸ spans now from the first to the last selected Control Point. Again, this is hard to see and will be covered when there is a Region in that position.
- A vertical alignment guide will appear again at the position you click on ❹ (either on a Control Point or on the line). This alignment guide runs vertically across the entire Workspace, but here is a big difference. The Control Bar Display ❺ does not display the position of this alignment guide (your click position). Instead, it displays the position of the left border of the shaded area (which is the position of the first selected Control Point).

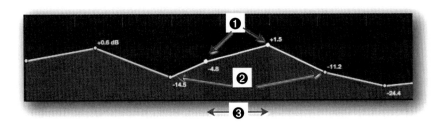
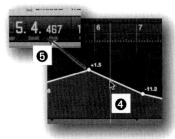
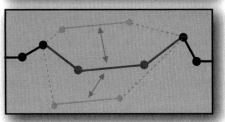

### Control Point as Hinges

Now let's look at the following diagram:

The two selected Control Points ❻ move together, keeping the shape of the line segment in between ❼ intact. The two Control Points, the one before ❽ and the one after ❾ the selection, act as hinges again. Also, you can move/copy an entire section of selected Control Points left or right beyond the adjacent (unselected) Control Point. More on that behavior a little bit later.

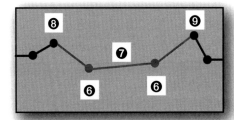

## ⚫ Multiple Control Points Selected

The same concept applies when you have more than two Control Points selected ❿. The entire line segment between the first and last selected Control Point moves as one unit (indicated by the shaded area) and the previous and next Control Points act as hinges.

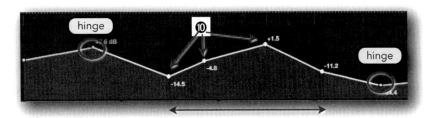

## ➡ *Interpolation*

Here is one little detail I want to mention regarding the Automation Curve and the concept of interpolation.

The screenshot on the right shows two Automation Curves.

▶ **Online Automation**

> The first curve is created with Online Automation by moving the Volume Fader down to create a Fade Out. Logic created multiple Control Points while you moved the Fader to reflect the changing parameter values for the Volume.

▶ **Offline Automation**

> The second curve also represents a Fade Out, but this time, I used Offline Automation by manually creating only two Control Points, one at the beginning and one at the end of the fade. Logic interpolates the missing Control Points along the line and creates "invisible" Control Points that are sent to the Parameter when playing back that section. In this case, a gradually decreasing value of the Volume Parameter.

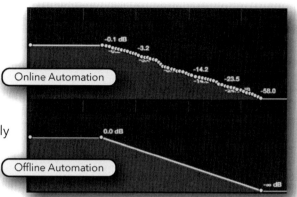

Check the section about the Event List in the next chapter for more details about the interpolation data.

## ➡ *Sample Accurate Automation*

There is one hidden Automation setting in the Preferences that is very important.

*Preferences ➤ Audio ➤ General ➤ Sample Accurate Automation*

This setting seems to be a left over from the times when our computer didn't have the CPU power of today's machines. The Logic User Guide mentions that using Sample Accurate Automation is more demanding on the CPU and by turning it off, or using it only on some components, lets you better balance your processing power needs in your Project.

Two things:

- First of all, turning Sample Accurate Automation off could dramatically shift the timing of Control Points. For example, automating an on/off switch (Mute) exactly on a downbeat can open or close the button too early or too late to a point where you can actually hear the "mistake".

- In addition, computers nowadays are so powerful that you shouldn't encounter any negative side effects when using Sample Accurate Automation on all components.

That means, choose the third option from the menu, "**Volume, Pan, Sends, Plug-In Parameters**".

# Mouse Commands

Now let's go over the various commands of adding and editing Control Points that ultimately make up the shape of the Automation Curve using your Mouse Pointer. Please note that these commands are also possible when the Automation is disabled on a Track [ Track ].

## ➡ Select Control Point(s)

Here are the mouse commands that let you select Control Points:

- *Click* on a Control Point with the Pointer Tool ▲ or Automation Select Tool ⬂ to select it. Remember, this will also select the part of the curve to the previous and next Control Point.
- *Click* on the Automation Curve with the Automation Select Tool ⬂ to select the Control Point before and after the clicked position.
- *Sh+click* on Control Points or the Automation Curve with the Pointer Tool ▲ or the Automation Select Tool ⬂ to add multiple Control Points (even if they are not adjacent). The same command will deselect Control Points from a group if they were selected before.
- *Drag* a selection around Control Points ("lasso around") with the Pointer Tool ▲ or Automation Select Tool ⬂ to select all the Control Points inside that area.
- *Sh+drag* to add or remove a selection from a selected group.
- *Opt+click* on a Control Point of the Automation Curve with the Pointer Tool ▲ or Automation Select Tool ⬂. This will select all Control Points to the right of the click position.
- *Click* on a Region Header with the Automation Select Tool ⬂ or Automation Curve Tool ⬂ to select all the Control Points between the left and right border of that Region.
- *Click* on the Automation Value/Trim Field to select the entire Automation Curve. *Click* again to deselect all (*Long-click* if there is only one Control Point).

- *Click* on the Automation Lane (the background) with the Pointer Tool ▲ or Automation Select Tool ⬂ to deselect any selection.

## ➡ Add Control Points

Please pay attention to what Cursor Tool you use and what state the Automation Curve has.

**Add** the first Control Point:
- *Click* anywhere on the Automation Lane with the Pointer Tool ▲. The value will be the current Onscreen Control position regardless where you click.

**Add** Control Points to an existing Automation Curve:
- *Double-click* anywhere in the Automation Lane with the Pointer Tool ▲.
- *Click* anywhere in the Automation Lane with the Pencil Tool ✏.
- *Click* on the Automation Curve with the Pointer Tool ▲ or Pencil Tool ✏.
- *Drag* with the Pencil Tool ✏ to draw a line. The slower you drag, the more Control Points are created along your movement.

**Add** Control Points with the Marquee Tool ⊞:
- *Drag* a Marquee Selection on a single Automation Lane and then *click* on it (with the Pointer Tool) to create two Control Points (1 Tick apart) at the left and two at the right border of the Marquee Selection.

## ➡ **Delete Control Points**

These are the various mouse commands to delete Control Points:

- *Double-click* on a single Control Point with the Pointer Tool 🔺
- *Drag* across Control Points with the Eraser Tool ◤ (make sure no Region is selected)
- Select one or multiple Control Points and hit the *delete* key

## ➡ **Move Control Points**

You can move a single Control Point or a selection of multiple Control Points (even if they are not adjacent) just by *dragging* them up/down/left/right. Please pay attention to the following details:

- Moving a Control Point left or right over existing Control Points will delete those Control Points.

- Holding the *shift* key after (!) you move the Control Point will restrict the movement to that direction (horizontal or vertical), unless you move to an extreme position, which will "unlock" that restriction.

- Holding down the *control* key after (!) you move the Control Point will restrict it to a vertical movement with a finer 0.1dB resolution.

- To move a selection, you can drag any of the selected Control Points, the line between the Control Points, or the area (above or below the line) between the first and last selected Control Point (the shaded area I described before).

- **Marquee Selection**: Create a Marquee Selection with the Marquee Tool ⊞ first and then move the selection of all Control Points inside (plus additional Control Points at the left and right border of the Marquee Selection) by *dragging* the Marquee Selection (with the Pointer Tool). Existing Control Points at the destination will be deleted.

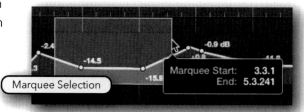

- **Trim Field**: Drag the Automation Value/Trim Field up or down to move the entire Automation Curve up or down by 0.1dB increments. This is a quick way to apply a value offset to the Automation Curve. Of course, this doesn't work with switches that have only two positions (i.e. mute, un-mute).

- **Control Bar Display**: Please note that the LCD in the Control Bar displays different positions. It is the position of the Control Point when moving a single Control Point or the position of the first selected Control Point when moving a group of selected Control Points.

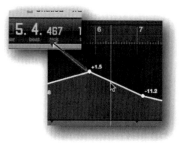

## ➡ **Copy** *Control Points*

As usual, the copy commands are the same as the move commands, just with the additional option key pressed down.

- Hold down the *option* key after (!) you've clicked the Control Point and *drag* it left or right to copy the Control Point (or a group of selected Control Points) to that new position while keeping its value.

- Create a Marquee Selection with the Marquee Tool ⊞ first and copy all Control Points inside hat selection (plus additional Control Points at the left and right border of the Marquee Selection) by *opt +dragging* the Marquee Selection (with the Pointer Tool). Existing Control Points at the destination will be deleted.

## ➡️ *Bend the Automation Curve*

Logic automatically applies a straight line between two different Control Points, resulting in a linear increase or decrease of the value. However, you can also bend the curve between two Control Points to apply an exponential value change. For this you have to use the Automation Curve Tool.

Please note that by holding down the *shift+control* key, the Pointer Tool 🔺 (while over the Automation Lane) switches to the Automation Curve Tool 🔺 so you don't have to manually switch to that tool.

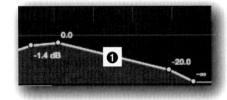

Here is an example of a Volume curve with a straight line ❶ going down from 0dB to -20dB to demonstrate the functionality of the Automation Curve Tool:

- When you *click* with the Automation Curve Tool 🔺 on or above the Automation Curve, then the Control Point before that click position will be selected.

- The segment of the Automation Curve between the selected Control Point to the following Control Point will be bent using the Automation Curve Tool. That's the segment over which you move the Automation Curve Tool around.

- **Up/down**: *Dragging* the Automation Curve Tool up ❷ or down ❸ will gradually change the linear shape of that segment to an exponential shape.

- **Left/right**: *Dragging* the Automation Curve Tool left ❹ or right ❺ will gradually change the linear shape of that segment to an S-shape.

- **Reset**: *Click* on the segment to reset it to the straight line ❻.

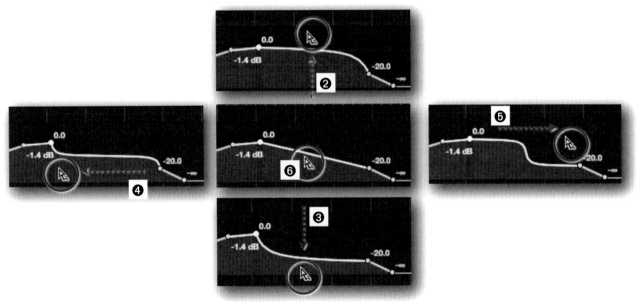

## ☠️ Multiple Bends

You can also select multiple Control Points first and then drag with the Automation Curve Tool to apply a curve to all the selected segments at once. *Click* on the selected Automation Curve to reset all the curves back to straight lines again.

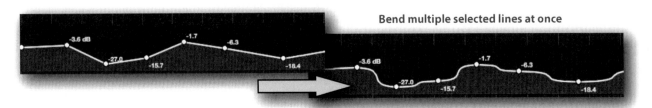

Bend multiple selected lines at once

# Key Commands / Menu Commands

Instead of using the Mouse Commands to create/edit the Automation Curve, you can use any of the Key Commands or Menu Commands to speed up your automation workflow. Before I introduce those commands, I want to point out an important issue when using automation. You have to be aware of that in order to better understand why these commands might be necessary.

The following example demonstrates a Guitar Track that has three Regions. These three Regions represent three parts of your song, the Verse, the Bridge, and the Chorus ❶. Let's assume you want to lower the volume during the Bridge part by creating an Automation Curve.

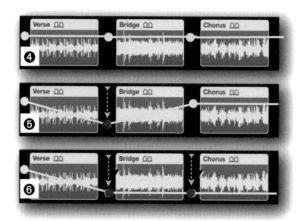

### 😵 Approach 1

❷ You create a new Control Point before the Bridge that you can use to set the volume level for the Bridge.

❸ When you lower that Control Point, however, you get two unwanted "side effects": First of all, the Verse now gets gradually lowered to the Control Point you just moved, and the lower level for the Bridge stays at that level, which means, the Chorus also plays at that lower level.

### 😵 Approach 2

❹ Now, in addition to the Control Point before the Bridge, you also create another Control Point after the Bridge.

❺ Lowering the Control Point before the Bridge now guarantees that the Chorus stays at its original level, but the Verse still decreases its level and the Bridge increases instead of staying at the lower level.

❻ When you lower both Control Points (before and after the Bridge), it keeps the lower level now constant for the Bridge, but again, the level stays there for the Chorus, similar to the example ❸.

### 😵 Approach 3

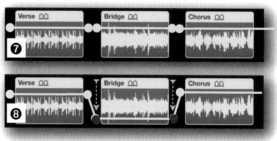

❼ This is the trick that provides the proper solution. You have to create two (!) Control Points before and two (!) Control Points after the Bridge. These Control Point pairs can be right next to each other (1 Tick apart).

❽ Lowering the Control Points of each pair that are on the "inside" of the Bridge (or lowering the line between those two Control Points), now only lowers the level for the Bridge. As you can see, the other Control Points of the pair next to them guarantee that the Automation Curve before and after the Bridge is not affected. Remember the diagram with the two fixed Control Points that act as hinges, these are those hinges.

## Conclusion

Every time you want to change the Automation Curve, make sure to create those pairs of Control Points on either side of your edit to ensure that the part of the Automation Curve before and after the edit is not affected. The commands in Logic labeled as "2 Automation Points" create those pairs of Control Points.

**Two questions**

When using a command to create a Control Point, you have to ask yourself two questions: How many Control Points are created and where?

##  How Many?

All the commands that are labeled "Create 2 Automation Points ...", refer to that pair of Control Points that are created just 1 Tick apart. They look as one Control Point and you have to zoom in all the way to see both of them.

**Create 2 Automation Points at Region Border**

## Where?

Besides knowing **what** a command is creating (one or two Control Points), the second question is **where** does it create those Control Points. Think about it; by using a mouse command, you can create a Control Point anywhere you click. However, sometimes you need a Control Point exactly at the border of a Region or the current Playhead position. Although you can click there, it would not be very accurate, especially if you are not zoomed in all the way. In that case, you use a command that creates a Control Point exactly at that "pre-defined" position.

The names of the available commands are pretty long, and before I explain them, I want to group them by their location to get a better overview.

Think of three "pre-defined" locations where Logic can create Control Points:

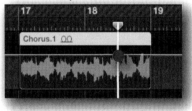

@ Playhead Position

▶ **Playhead Position**

This is a very versatile command because you have a wide variety of commands that let you place the Playhead to specific locations (Cycle Locators, Marker, Snap Position, etc.). You can use that to place the Playhead there first and then use the Automation command to place a Control Point exactly at that position.

▶ **Region Borders**

@ Region Border

Placing Control Points exactly at Region borders is very important as we have just seen. Regions often represent special sections of your recordings on a Track and this allows you to apply automation only to the boundaries of a Region without affecting the other Regions.

▶ **Marquee Selection Borders**

@ Marquee Selection Border

There are no specific Menu Commands for creating Control Points at the border of a Marquee Selection, but I wanted to include the option in this category because the borders of a Marquee Selection also represent a "pre-defined" location. Instead of a command, you just *click* on the Marquee Selection (with the Pointer Tool) in the Automation Lane to create two Control Points on the left and right border of the Marquee Selection.

➡ *Create at Playhead Position*

There are two types of commands that let you create Control Points at the current Playhead Position. Each one can create one or two Control Points at that position.

### 💀 Only Volume, Pan, and Sends

The first command is practical for quickly creating Control Points for the most important Parameters: Volume, Pan, and Sends. A procedure often called "Snapshot Automation".

- ☑ The command creates one or two Control Points (available as two individual commands) with the current value of the Volume, Pan, and Aux Sends (if available) at the current Playhead Position.
- ☑ The Control Points will only be created on the currently selected Tracks in the Tracks Window.
- ☑ Channel Strips that are not assigned to a Track in the Tracks Window (i.e. Aux Channel Strip) have to be assigned to a Track first to be included in that command.
- ☑ The Automation Parameters don't have to be visible in the Tracks Window. They are created in the background.
- ☑ The Show/Hide Automation Button 🔀 and the Track Automation Button ⬛Track don't even have to be enabled for this command. They will be automatically enabled when you apply the command.
- ☑ The command is available from the Main Menu and as assignable Key Command.
  - 🎚 Main Menu *Mix ➤ Create Automation ➤ Create 1 Automation Point each for Volume, Pan, Sends*
  - 🎚 Main Menu *Mix ➤ Create Automation ➤ Create 2 Automation Points each for Volume, Pan, Sends*
  - 🎚 Key Command (*Create 1 Automation Point each for Volume, Pan, Sends*) *unassigned*
  - 🎚 Key Command (*Create 2 Automation Points each for Volume, Pan, Sends*) *unassigned*

### 💀 All Visible Parameters

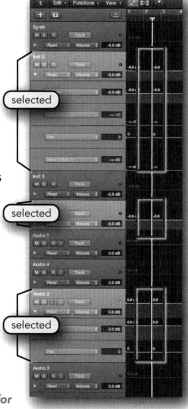

The second command for creating Control Points at the Playhead Position will include all visible Automation Parameters.

- ☑ The command creates one or two Control Points (available as two individual commands) with the value of the visible Parameters at the current Playhead Position.
- ☑ Make additional Automation Parameters on a Track visible by using the Automation Subtracks.
- ☑ The Control Points will only be created on the currently selected Tracks in the Tracks Window.
- ☑ Channel Strips that are not assigned to a Track in the Tracks Window (i.e. Aux Channel Strip) have to be assigned to a Track first to be included in that command.
- ☑ The Show/Hide Automation Button 🔀 and the Track Automation Button ⬛Track have to be enabled to have the Automation Parameter visible. Otherwise, the commands will be grayed out.
- ☑ The command is available from the Main Menu and as assignable Key Command.
  - 🎚 Main Menu *Mix ➤ Create Automation ➤ Create 1 Automation Point for Visible Parameter*
  - 🎚 Main Menu *Mix ➤ Create Automation ➤ Create 2 Automation Points for Visible Parameter*
  - 🎚 Key Command (*Create 1 Automation Point each for Visible Parameter*) *unassigned*
  - 🎚 Key Command (*Create 2 Automation Points each for Visible Parameter*) *unassigned*

## ➡ *Create at Region Border*

There are two commands available that let you create Control Points at the Region borders for the currently selected Automation Parameter on the Track Header (not the Subtracks!). Each command can create one or two Control Points at the position. Please pay attention to the detailed conditions.

### 🪐 At every selected Region Border

This is the easiest of the two commands.

- ☑ The command creates one or two Control Points (available as two individual commands) at the Region borders of any selected Region on any Track. It is only available as Key Commands.
    - 🎚 Key Command (*Create 1 Automation Point at Every Region Borders*) **ctr+cmd+1**
    - 🎚 Key Command (*Create 2 Automation Points at Every Region Borders*) **ctr+cmd+2**
- ☑ The Show/Hide Automation Button 🔲 doesn't have to be enabled for this command. It will be automatically enabled when you apply the command.

### 🪐 At the first and last selected Region Border

Pay attention to the details as to what that means:

- ☑ The Control Points will only be created on the currently selected Regions, even on multiple Tracks with the following conditions:
    - If one Region is selected, then the Control Point will be at the left and right border.
    - If a series of Regions are selected, then the Control Points are placed at the left border of the first, and right border of the last Region.
    - If there is an unselected Region between a group of selected Region(s), then each group is treated individually with the Control Point at the left border of the first and right border at the last Region.
- ☑ The command creates one or two Control Points (available as two individual commands) at the border.
    - 🎚 Main Menu *Mix ➤ Create Automation ➤ Create 1 Automation Point at Region Borders*
    - 🎚 Main Menu *Mix ➤ Create Automation ➤ Create 2 Automation Points at Region Borders*
    - 🎚 Key Command (*Create 1 Automation Point at Region Borders*) **sh+ctr+cmd+1**
    - 🎚 Key Command (*Create 2 Automation Points at Region Borders*) **sh+ctr+cmd+2**
- ☑ The Show/Hide Automation Button 🔲 doesn't have to be enabled for this command. It will be automatically enabled when you apply the command.

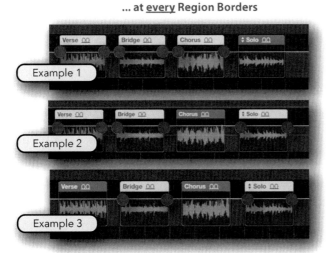

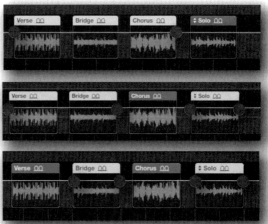

⇒ **Delete Automation**

The Menu Command *Mix ➤ Delete Automation ➤*
contains a submenu with various delete commands.
They are also available as Key Commands.

*Attention*: The commands (with the exception of "Delete
All Automation") will also apply to any Region
Automation

Main Menu: Mix ➤ Delete Automation ➤

| | |
|---|---|
| Delete Visible Automation on Selected Track | ^⌘⌫ |
| Delete All Automation on Selected Track | ^⇧⌘⌫ |
| Delete Orphaned Automation on Selected Track | ^⇧⌫ |
| Delete Redundant Automation Points | ^⌫ |
| Delete All Automation | |

- **Delete Visible Automation on Selected Track**: This applies only to the Automation Curve of the currently selected Track, the Main Track, not any visible Automation Subtracks. You can select multiple Tracks in the Tracks Window to apply that command to all the selected Tracks at once.

- **Delete All Automation on Selected Track**: This will delete all the automation data of one or multiple selected Tracks.

- **Delete Orphaned Automation on Selected Track**: When copying automation data from a Track that includes specific Automation Parameters (i.e. Send 1 or a parameter from a Distortion Plugin) to a Track that doesn't have those Automation Parameters, then those Automation Parameters are "unassigned" or "orphan" maybe because the destination Track doesn't have the Distortion Plugin. These data, labeled "unused", will be deleted with this command.

- **Delete Redundant Automation Points**: Any Control Point that can be deleted without affecting the shape of the Automation Curve is a "redundant" Control Point. For example, with three adjacent Control Points with a -15dB value that create a straight horizontal line, you can delete the second Control Point and the line is still the same.

- **Delete All Automation**: This deletes all Track Automation data in your current Project.

## Numeric Editing

Besides using the graphical interface of an Automation Curve
to create/edit Offline Automation, you can also use a numerical
interface. This is the same interface you use to edit MIDI events
numerically, called the "Automation Even List".

There is a little more background necessary that I will explain in
a separate section a little later.

**Automation Event List**

**Tracks Window**

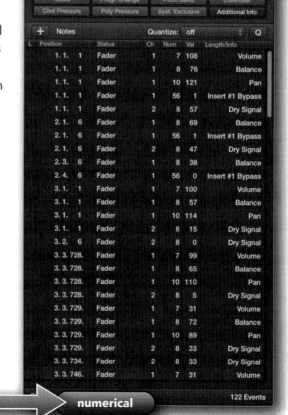

11 - Automation

## Additional Offline Operations

Next are a few additional offline commands that are useful when working with automation data that you should incorporate into your workflow.

## Move Track Automation with Regions

Think about the following situation: You have an eight bar guitar solo in your song for which you spent a lot of time to create elaborate automation, i.e. riding the volume fader, panning left-right for some ping-pong effects, automated some of the Reverb sends, plus, you automated the Mute Button to cut out a few notes. Later you decide that you want to repeat that guitar solo also at the end of the song. You can easily copy the Audio Region of the guitar solo, but now, you have to re-recreate all those automation steps. Unless you have a feature called "Move Automation with Regions" (or "Region Automation" which I explain in the next chapter).

We already learned at the beginning of this chapter that Track Automation is independent of any Region on the Track Lane. However, Logic is "aware" of any active Automation Parameter between the left and right border of a Region on the Track Lane. An Automation Preference called "*Move Track Automation with Regions*" determines what happens when you move or copy such a Region with "underlying Track Automation". You can choose from three different options ❶:

▶ **Never**: Moving any Region does not affect the existing automation data.

▶ **Always**: Moving a Region will always move the underlying Track Automation with it.

▶ **Ask**: Logic will open a Dialog Window ❷ that lets you choose to copy or not to copy automation data with the Region.

   ☑ **Include trails, if possible ❸**: This option will copy automation data that occurs after the Region, which might be important for the Region, i.e. a fade out for the delay effect that happens after the last note recorded on that Region.

You can set the Preference in various locations:

 ❹ *Preferences ➤ Automation*

 ❺ Main Menu *Mix ➤ Move Track Automation with Regions ➤*

 ❻ Shortcut Menu when *ctr+clicking* on the Automation Lane

 ❼ Key Commands. They are *unassigned*

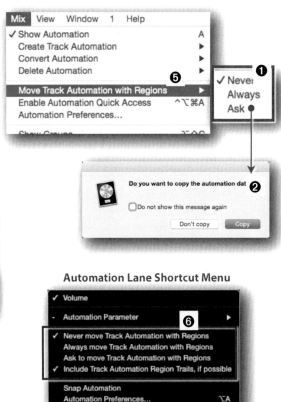

Preferences ➤ Automation

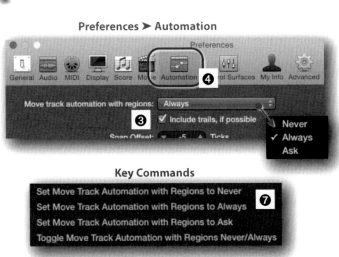

**Key Commands**

**Automation Lane Shortcut Menu**

Here is an example that demonstrates the outcome of the preference setting:

### ➡ Don't move Automation with Region

I copied the Region ❶ on the left and as you can see, the automation data is not affected. This could be problematic. For example, if the original Region had a fade out at the end, then you wouldn't hear the copied Region ❷ because the Fader is still down ❸.

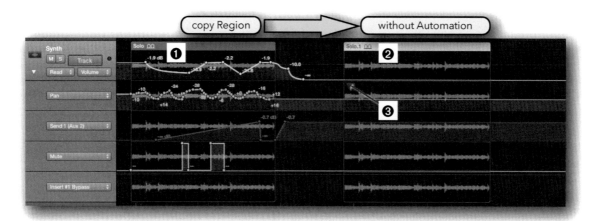

### ➡ Move Automation with Region

This screenshot shows the copied Region with automation data ❹. You can also see the effect of the "Include trails, if possible" option. The additional automation data after the right border of the original Region is also added at the end of the copied Region ❺.

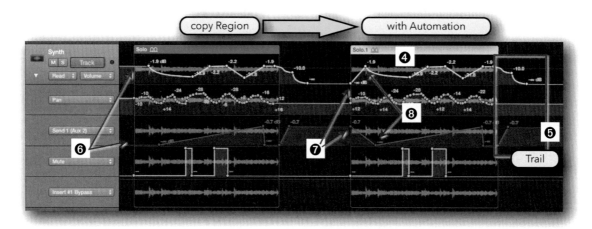

**Potential Problem**: If you look closely at the automation data, then you would realize that the copied Region would NOT sound exactly like the original Region. Although you copied the automation with the Region, the data got screwed up. Look at the value of the Volume and Send data at the left border of the original Region ❻. There is no Control Point. Now look at the left border of the copied Region ❼. Logic added a Control Point repeating the value of the previous Control at that position. From that value (which is the value of the Control Point prior to that position), a line will connect to the first copied Control Point ❽ of the original Region. To avoid this, it is always a good idea to use the command "Create Automation at Region Border" first to guarantee the integrity of the automation inside the boundaries of a Region. This also applies to any Cut and Insert operation you perform with your Regions.

Also, please note that deleting a Region will also delete the automation data at that position when you have "Move Automation with Region" option selected.

# Copy/Move Automation Curves

This is a special operation that lets you copy the Automation Curve from one Automation Parameter to another on the same Channel Strip.

**Examples:**

- You have automated the control for Aux Send 1, and now, added another Reverb to the Channel Strip that you want to replicate with the same curve.
- You programmed the Mute Button on your Channel Strip and now want to mute the pre-fader Aux Sends the same way.
- You programmed the Volume Fader and want to replicate the same movement on the Cutoff filter of the Software Instrument Plugin on that Channel Strip.

Here is the procedure:

☑ From the Automation Parameter Menu ❶ select the Automation Parameter that you want to copy ❷. The Automation Curve for this Parameter is displayed in the Automation Lane ❸.

☑ Now go to the Automation Parameter Menu again and *opt+click* on the Automation Parameter Button and select the destination Parameter ❹ you want the current Automation Curve copy/move to.

☑ A Dialog Window ❺ pops up giving you two options:

 ▶ **Convert**: This is a move command. It will move the current Automation Curve to the Automation Parameter you selected from the menu.

 ▶ **Copy and Convert**: This is a copy command. It will copy the current Automation Curve to the Automation Parameter you selected.

**Tracks Window**

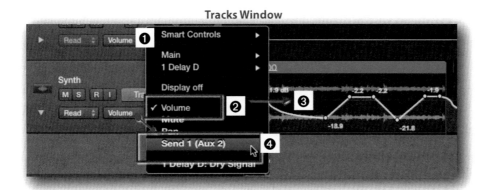

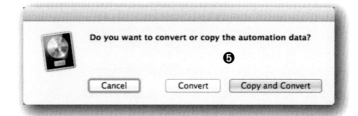

The command is called "convert" because the value of each Control Point for a specific Automation Parameter has a specific ID (a Channel number and Fader number). Moving or copying an Automation Curve of a specific Automation Parameter just "converts" the Channel number and Fader number of all those Control Points while keeping their values.

More on that in the section about the Automation Event List.

# Copy Control Points between Tracks

While the previous command lets you convert an entire Automation Curve to a different Automation Parameter on the same Channel Strip, the following command lets you copy-paste an entire Automation Curve (or a section of it) of an Automation Parameter from one Track to another Track.

### 👤 This is the procedure:

- ☑ Select the Automation Parameter ❶ on the Track that you want to copy. This can be the Main Track or any Automation Subtrack.
  - *Click* on the Automation Value/Trim Field ❷ to select the entire Automation Curve, or
  - *Sh+drag* around a section of the Automation Curve if you want to copy only a portion of it, or
  - *Sh+drag* around multiple sections that don't have to be adjacent. In the screenshot below, you can see two sections of the Automation Curve selected ❸, ❺, and one section in between that is not selected ❹.
- ☑ Use any of the copy commands, i.e. *cmd+C* or *Edit ➤ Copy* to copy the selected Control Points to the clipboard.
- ☑ Now, select the Track you want to copy the Automation Curve to ❻ (second screenshot). You don't have to select a specific Automation Parameter.
- ☑ This is important: Place the Playhead ❼ at the position you want to copy the Automation Curve to. This will be the paste position of the first Control Point of the Automation Curve that you copied.
- ☑ Use any of the paste commands, i.e. *cmd+V* or *Edit ➤ Paste* to execute the paste command. The Automation Parameter automatically switches to the type of Automation Parameter you just copied so you can see the result on the Automation Lane right away.

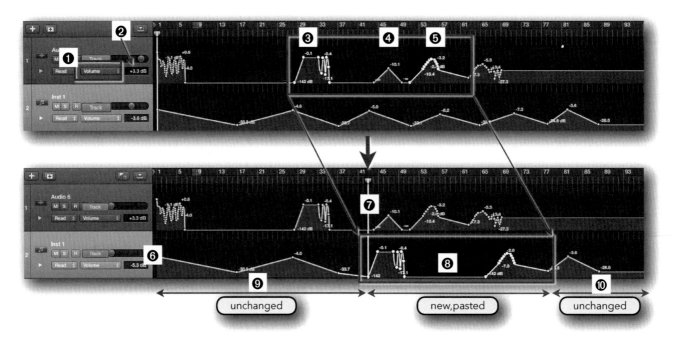

You can see on the second screenshot the result after the paste command. The original segment ❸-❹-❺ is now copied, starting at the Playhead Position ❼ (the Playhead will actually move to the last copied Control Point after the paste command), overwriting any existing Control Points. However, the Control Points of the middle part ❹ of the copied section were not selected and therefore, are not copied ❽. The Automation Curve before ❾ and after ❿ the pasted curve stay unchanged.

Please keep in mind that you can copy paste only one Automation Curve at a time.

## Copy Automation with a Marquee Selection

There is another copy procedure and that involves the Marquee Tool ⊕. This lets you copy a section of one or multiple Automation Curves defined by a Marquee Selection.

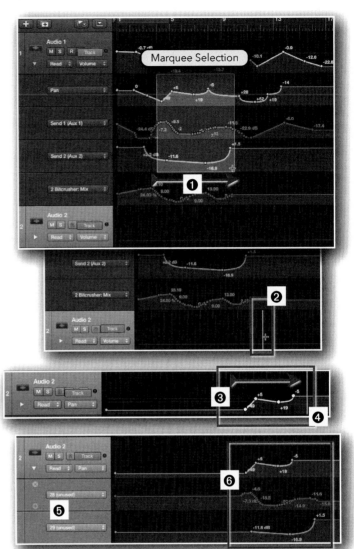

☑ **Step 1 - Select Source:** *Draw* a Marquee Selection ❶ with the Marquee Tool ⊕ on one or across multiple (visible and adjacent) Automation Lanes that include all the Control Points you want to copy.

☑ **Step 2 - Copy Selection:** Hit the copy command, i.e. *cmd+C*.

☑ **Step 3 - Define Destination:** *Click* with the Marquee Tool ⊕ on the position of the Automation Lane (on the same Track or a different Track) you want to paste the Control Points to. Clicking with the Marquee Tool (instead of dragging) creates a single Marquee Line ❷ (not a selection or range), representing a single address.

☑ **Step 4 - Paste to Destination:** Hit the paste command, i.e. *cmd+V*. Logic now copies the content of the clipboard to that position.

- Imaging that Logic lines up the left border ❸ of the copied Marquee Selection (currently on the clipboard) at the Marquee Line ❷ and copies every Control Point of all Automation Parameters from the Marquee Selection to that Track.

- The Marquee Line automatically moves ❹ to where the right border of the copied Marquee Selection would end.

- Please note that the Automation Parameters don't have to be visible in separate Automation Lanes for this procedure.

- Once you make all current Automation Parameter visible on their Subtracks ❺, then you can see all the copied Control Points ❻.

## Copy Automation in the Event List

In addition to all the graphical copy procedures, you can also use the Automation Event List to copy-paste the individual Control Points between Tracks numerically. I discuss that in the next chapter.

**Automation Event List**

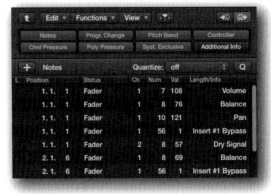

# Snap Automation

Snap Automation is another important feature you have to keep in mind when creating/editing Control Points.

I mentioned earlier that Control Points are similar to MIDI Events. And like MIDI Events, you can apply a Snap value (an underlying grid) that the Control Points follow when you create them or move them around. Actually, Control Points follow the same Snap value ❶ that you selected for the MIDI Events in the Snap Menu ❷. You just have the option to enable or disable the Snap behavior for Control Points with the "Snap Automation" option.

You can toggle Snap Automation with the following commands:

- *Snap Menu ➤ Snap Automation* ❸
- *Ctr+click* on the Automation Lane *Shortcut Menu ➤ Snap Automation* ❹
- Key Command (*Snap Automation*) *unassigned*

**Tracks Window**

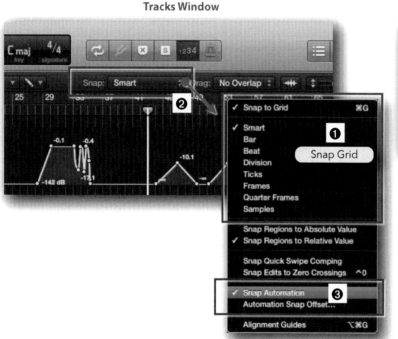

**Automation Lane: Shortcut Menu**

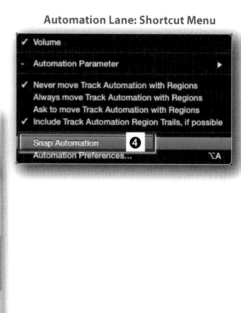

## ➡ *Snap Offset*

The *Preferences ➤ Automation* Window lets you set a Snap Offset between -99 and +99 Ticks (the default is -5 Ticks). Whenever you move a Control Point while Snap Automation is enabled, Logic moves the Control Point by that amount off the actual snap grid.

This is useful when compensating for any latency or to make sure that a mute button is on/off in time.

**Preferences ➤ Automation**

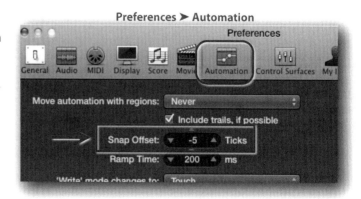

## Absolute - Relative - Trim

Let's start the advanced chapter for Automation with "Trim - Relative - Absolute", the new features that were introduced in LPX v10.1. They are the cause for some confusion for different reasons. Some users have to learn this new concept of using Automation and other users have to "re-learn" it, because they are familiar with the concept but maybe with different terminology and implementation.

Because this is the advanced section, let's dive a little bit deeper and look at the architecture first and then see what labels/terms Logic is using for that.

## Absolute Values - Offset Values

The following is in my opinion the missing link  that is necessary when trying to understand what these new Automation Modes do.

### ➡ *Standard Operation (Absolute Values)*

Think about the standard operation of the Onscreen Controls on the Mixer, for example, the Volume Fader, the Pan Knob, and the Aux Send Knobs.

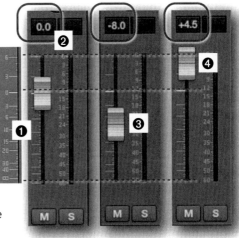

**Volume Fader**

- When you move those controls, they send a specific value to the Parameter they represent (Volume, Pan, Aux Send).
- A scale ❶, a numerical display ❷ or a temporarily visible Help Tag indicates the value that represents the current position of the control.
- Let's call that the Absolute Value, the current position of the controller indicating the current value that is sent to the Parameter.
- When you enable Automation for any of the three Automation Modes (Touch, Latch, Write) and you touch the control, then that Absolute Value will be written as automation data in the form of an Automation Control Point on the Automation Lane.

  - If the Volume Fader is at -8dB ❸ and you touch it, you create that Absolute Value of -8dB. If the Fader is positioned at +4.5dB ❹ and you touch it, you generate that Absolute Value of +4.5dB.
  - If the Pan Knob is positioned at +25 ❺ and you touch it, you write the Absolute Value of 25 as automation data.
  - If the Aux Send Knob is positioned at -17.8dB ❻ and you touch it, you write the Absolute Value of -17.6dB as automation data.

- When you move an Onscreen Control while Automation is enabled with any of the three Automation Modes, then those Absolute Values (that correspond to the position of the control) will be written as automation data.

**Pan Knob** ❺

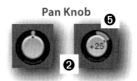

**Aux Send Knob** ❷

❻

## ➡ *Offset Operation (Offset Values)*

**Automation Modes**

The Standard Operation I just described is nothing special. This is how a Fader or a Knob works in Logic. When writing automation data in any of the three Automation Modes (Touch, Latch, Write ❶), they will generate Absolute Values based on the Standard Operation of those controls.

However, when adding the Trim or Relative option ❷ to an Automation Mode, then that Standard Operation of a controller changes. Let's call this an "Offset Operation". That is the first thing you have to realize when you select the Trim or Relative option.

**Pitch Wheel**

### 😊 Offset Operation vs. Pitch Wheel Operation

The Offset Operation changes the mechanics of the controller. It is similar to the functionality of a Pitch Wheel ❸ on a MIDI Controller, which has the following characteristics.

- ☑ The controller is centered at a neutral position (no value, no changes)
- ☑ Moving the controller in one direction out of its neutral position creates positive Offset Values, moving the controller to the other direction, creates negative Offset Values.
- ☑ The controller always snaps back to its neutral position when you take your hands off it.

### 😊 Three Controllers Only

Only three types of controllers in Logic can change to that Offset Operation when selecting Trim or Relative to generate Offset Values. All the other Onscreen Controls on the Channel Strip and any Plugin will only function in Standard Operation creating Absolute Values. Let's have a closer look:

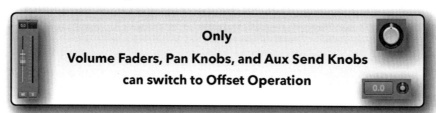

**Only Volume Faders, Pan Knobs, and Aux Send Knobs can switch to Offset Operation**

▶ **Fader**
- The Fader Knob is positioned at the center with an offset value of 0dB (no value change)
- There are three scale markers ❹ that represent the following Offset Values: Center (0dB), Top (+24dB), and Bottom (-24dB)
- The yellow line indicates the current value (the Absolute Value) of the Volume Parameter
- The Fader snaps back to its center position (0dB) when you release it

▶ **Aux Send Knob**
- The Knob is positioned at the center ❺ with a value of 0dB (Offset Value 0)
- You can turn the knob all the way to the right to generate an Offset Value of +24dB, or all the way to the left to generate an Offset Value of -24dB.
- The Knob snaps back to its center position (0) when you release it.

▶ **Pan Knob**
- The Knob position ❻ represent the same values as in Standard Operation. Center (0), right (Offset Value +63), left (Offset Value -64)
- The only difference to Standard Operation is that the Pan Knob snaps back to its center position when you release it.

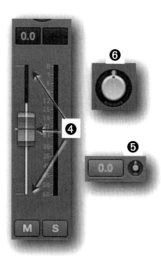

## ➡ *Write Absolute Values or Write Offset Values*

Let's have another look at the Automation Mode Menu and see what the Standard Operation and Offset Operation have to do with Automation Modes:

**Automation Modes**

### 🔘 **Read Automation ❶**

In Read Mode, all the Onscreen Controls are in Standard Operation. The position of the control (i.e.,Volume Fader) represents the absolute value that is sent to the Parameter (i.e., Volume).

### 🔘 **Write Automation (absolute values) ❷**

When selecting any of the three write modes (Touch, Latch, Write), then all the Onscreen Controls in Logic (Channel Strips, Smart Controls, Plugins) operate in Standard Operation ❹ and generate Absolute Values ❺. This is the standard operation of Track Automation that I described in the previous chapter.

**Automation Modes without Trim or Relative**

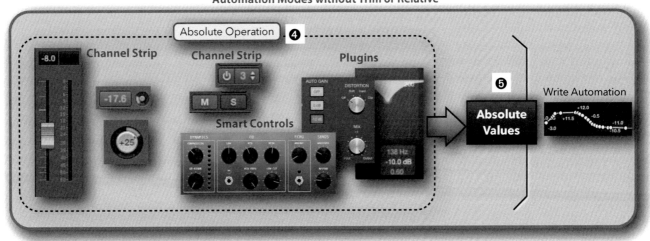

### 🔘 **Write Automation (offset values) ❸**

If you also select "Trim" or "Relative" ❸ from the menu in addition to Touch, Latch, or Write ❷, then the Volume Faders, the Pan Knobs, and the Aux Send Knobs change to Offset Operation ❻. Writing automation with those controls now will generate Offset Values ❼. Any other Onscreen Control still works in Standard Operation ❽ and generates Absolute Values ❾. The Trim or Relative setting has no affect on those controls.

**Automation Modes with Trim or Relative**

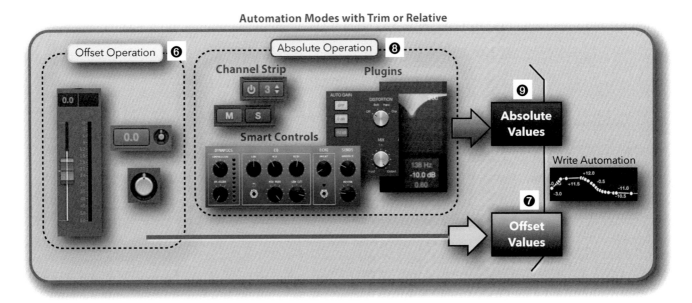

## ➡ *Generating both Values*

The purpose of generating Offset Values is to "adjust" an existing Automation Curve that was created with Absolute Values. If you have an existing Automation Curve and you overwrite it, then you just overwrite it with new Absolute Values, the new Fader movements.

For example, if you've created complex automation for a vocal track and only want to lower the volume at a specific section, but keeping the "shape of the curve", you would have to recreate the same Fader movements, just a little bit lower. That could be quite challenging. Instead, you just add Offset Values to the existing Absolute Values. You could do that in offline mode by selecting the Automation Curve and drag it down. However, switching the Fader to Offset Operation to generate Offset Values lets do the "adjustment" also online, performing it live. You move the fader up from its neutral position to raise the existing Automation Curve as it is or move the fader down from its neutral position lower it. Here is the concept:

### ☻ Standard Operation ➤ Absolute Values

Whatever position you move the Fader Knob in Standard Operation, that is the Absolute Value that it generates and is written as automation data. In this example, the Fader starts at the -10dB position, moves up to 4dB, and so on, and at the end moves all the way down to the bottom.

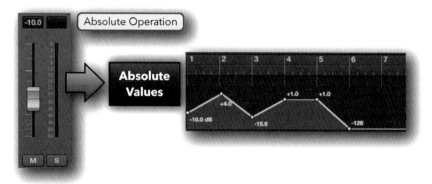

### ☻ Offset Operation ➤ Offset Values

Any movement with the Fader in Offset Operation always starts at the 0dB position (the neutral position) and ends at the 0dB position. In between, you move the Fader up to create a positive Offset Values, or move the Fader down to create negative Offset Values.

### ☻ Combine both values

Logic now combines both Automation Curves by adding the Offset Values to the Absolute Values.

The first screenshot shows both Automation Curves overlaid and the second screenshot shows the resulting Automation Curve, the final values that are sent to the Volume Parameter.

- Bar 1, 2: The offset is 0dB, therefore, the absolute values don't change
- Bar 3: The Offset Value goes down to -5dB. This flattens the rise of the Absolute Value a bit and reaches only -4db, instead of +1dB
- Bar 4: The Absolute Values stays at 1dB, but the Offset Values increase from -5 to +5, creating a rise from -4 to+ 6
- Bar 5, 6: The Offset Values stay at +5, so the movement of the Absolute Values stay the same, just 5dB higher
- Bar 7: The Offset Value goes back to 0, its neutral position.

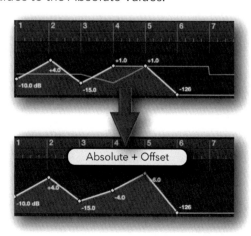

# ➡ *How to combine Absolute Values and Offset Values*

Here is a diagram that demonstrates how the Offset Values are applied:

## 💀 Online

▶ **No Trim, no Relative**: When selecting Touch, Latch, or Write ❶, the Fader works in Absolute Operation ❷, writing Absolute Values to the Automation Curve ❸.

▶ **Trim**: When you add Trim ❹ in the Automation Mode Menu, the Fader works in Offset Operation ❺, writing Offset Values. These Offset Values ❻ are also written to the Absolute Curve ❸. They trim (effectively change) the existing curve by adding the Offset Values to the existing Absolute Values.

▶ **Relative**: When you add Relative ❼ from the Automation Mode Menu, the Fader also works in Offset Operation ❺, writing Offset Values. But here is the big difference. These Offset Values are written to a separate Automation Curve, the "Relative (±)" Curve ❽. Both Automation Curves are combined during playback in real-time ❾.

## 💀 Offline

To edit automation offline by drawing the Automation Curve with the Cursor Tools, you first select the Automation Parameter from the Automation Parameter Menu to display its Automation Curve.

Here is the difference to watch out for:

The three types of Automation Parameters that can generate Offset Values (Volume, Pan, Aux Send) now have a submenu with two items ❿.

▶ **"Absolute"**: Selecting this item will display the Absolute Automation Curve ❸ for that Parameter.

▶ **"Relative (±)"**: Selecting this item will display the Relative Automation Curve ❽ for that Parameter.

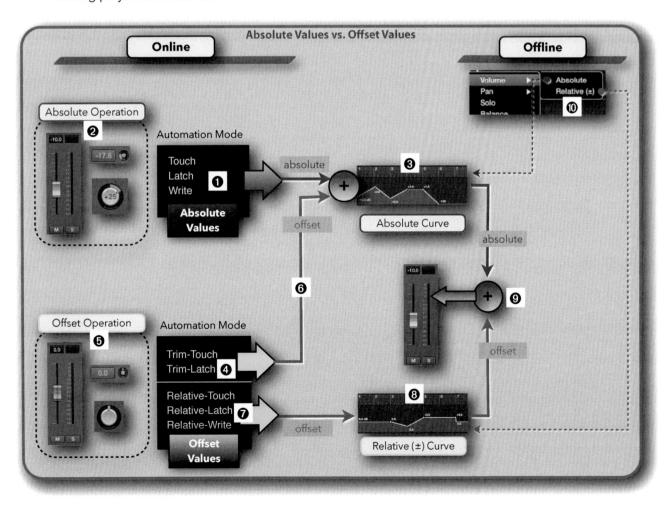

# Trim or Relative

Now let's look how all that is implemented in Logic.

## ➡ *Automation Modes*

When you want to write automation with your Onscreen Controls (or use an external Control Surface that acts as a remote control for those Onscreen Controls), you have to choose an Automation Mode first.

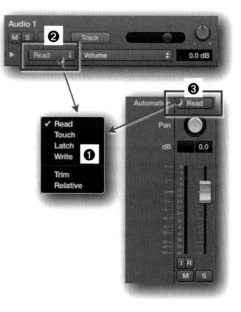

### 💀 Automation Mode Menu ❶

Click on the Automation Mode Button on the Track Header ❷ or the Channel Strip ❸ to open the menu with the available Automation Modes.

- ▶ **Read**: The Read Mode is for playing back automation data only.
- ▶ **Touch, Latch, Write**: These are the next three Automation Modes for writing automation data. As we have just discussed, they write <u>Absolute Values</u>.
- ▶ **Trim, Relative**: The next two items, Trim and Relative, are not additional Automation Modes, they are options that you can add to Touch, Latch, or Write Mode. Selecting Trim or Relative will change the behavior of Touch, Latch, and Write, so they generate <u>Offset Values</u> instead of Absolute Values.

### 💀 How many different Automation Modes?

This is the procedure for selecting an Automation Mode to write automation data (Online Automation):

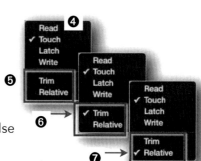

- Select one of the three Automation Modes ❹ (Touch/Latch/Write) from the menu.
- With this Automation Mode, Absolute Values are created, if nothing else is selected ❺.
- Adding either *Trim* ❻ or *Relative* ❼, changes the Automation Mode to generate Offset Values.
- Be careful, the menu lets you make selections that don't make any sense, for example Read+Trim.
- The Automation Buttons ❽ have the added T- or R- on the label to indicate if Trim or Relative is selected.
- You have a total of eight different Automation Modes for writing automation data ❾ (this is not a real menu, just a mock-up).

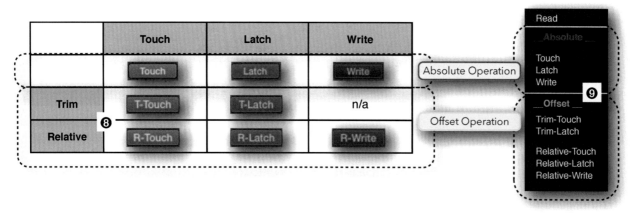

| | Touch | Latch | Write |
|---|---|---|---|
| | Touch | Latch | Write |
| **Trim** | T-Touch | T-Latch | n/a |
| **Relative** | R-Touch | R-Latch | R-Write |

➡️ *Trim Mode*

Here are the various operations when Trim is selected. Remember, the Onscreen Controls change to Offset Operation and generate Offset Values that are applied (added) directly to the existing Absolute Automation Curve.

Here is an example with the Trim-Touch Mode.

The first thing that will change when choosing selecting Trim are the three types of controls on the Channel Strips that change from Absolute Operation to Offset Operation:

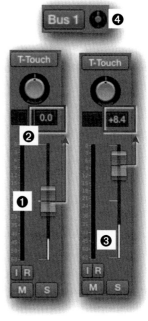

▸ **Volume Fader**: The Fader knob turns transparent and is centered in the middle ❶ (the neutral position). The scale lines will also change with one in the center (0dB), one on top (+24dB), and one at the bottom (-24dB). The display field above ❷ indicates in dB how much you've moved the fader away from its center position (the Offset Value). The yellow line ❸ along the Fader indicates the actual value of the Automation Curve at the current Playhead Position. If you play your Project, this yellow line will follow the existing Automation Curve accordingly.

▸ **Pan Knob**: The Pan Knob is also centered. This could be the least obvious change, because the knob might be centered on that Channel Strip anyway.

▸ **Aux Sends**: The Aux Send Knobs now behave more like a Pan Knob. They are centered (0dB, no change) ❹. You can turn a knob all the way to the right (+24db), or all the way to the left (-24dB).

🌑 **Fader Action in Stop Mode** 🔲

In Stop Mode, there are two scenarios for "Trim-Touch" Automation. Here is an example with an Automation Curve for the Volume parameter ❺:

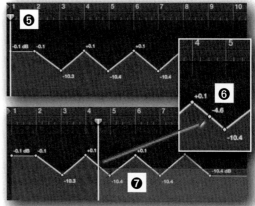

▸ *Click*: When you click on the Fader, a new Control Point ❻ is created on that Automation Curve at the current Playhead Position. Please note that when you *click-hold* the Fader, a red line ❼ appears on the Automation Lane with a shaded area, indicating the Fader Position. When you clicked the Fader, it was in the 0dB position (the neutral position with no Offset Value applied), therefore, the red line crosses the Automation Curve and the Playhead.

▸ *Click-drag*: When you click-drag the Fader, a Control Point is again created on the Automation Curve at the current Playhead Position, and in addition, a second Control Point is created at the same Position (1 Tick apart) with the parameter value of the Fader position when you release the mouse. For example, if you dragged the Fader down by -10dB ❽, then this second Control Point is -10dB lower than the first clicked Control Point. But here is the important part: The entire Automation Curve ❾, starting from the Playhead Position, is lowered by the amount you changed the Fader (in this example 10dB lower). The -10dB Offset Value is applied to that section of the Automation Curve.

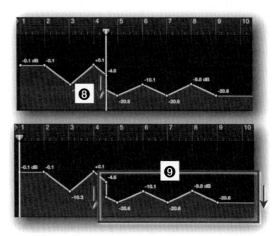

### 🌀 Fader Action in Play Mode ▶

When using Trim-Touch Mode while you're playing back your Project, the outcome will be the following:

I use the same example with the Automation Curve for the Volume parameter. This time, I play from bar 1 and at bar 4, I lower the Fader by 10dB, hold it there and release it at bar 7.

- The Fader movement is indicated in real time by the movement of the red line ❶.
- The yellow line on the Fader moves up or down to follow the existing Automation Curve accordingly ❷
- When you release the Fader (or stop the playback when in Trim-Latch Mode), that red Automation Curve that you just performed with the Fader is applied as an offset to the existing (yellow) Automation Curve between bar 4 and 7, they will be merged. I just trimmed that section of the existing Automation Curve ❸ with the Offset Values of my Fader movement. Although you hear the combined value in

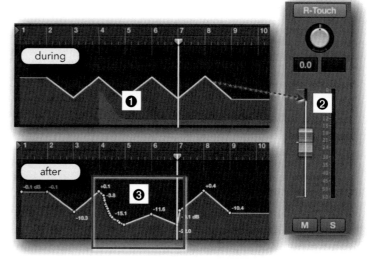

real time, the "redraw" of the Automation Curve happens when you stop the playback.

Please note that without the Trim behavior, the resulting Automation Curve would look like the red line, the absolute volume parameter. Instead, the values of the red Automation Curve are applied as an offset to the existing Automation Curve to trim it, maintaining its original shape (depending upon your new Fader movement).

### 🌀 Write Absolute First

Before writing Trim Automation, make sure that there is something to trim in the first place. Technically you could write Trim Automation for a Parameter that doesn't have an Automation Curve, but practically, it makes not much sense.

### 🌀 ~~Trim Write~~

It is possible to select Write Automation and Trim in the Automation Mode Menu ❹, however, this combination does not exist.

- The Fader ❺ (Pan and Aux Send) do not switch to Offset Operation
- The Automation Mode Button on the Channel Strip keeps the Write Button ❻ Write , indicating that you are still in Write Mode (without the Trim option)

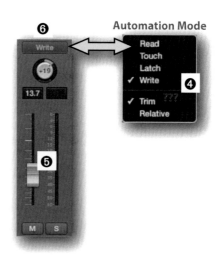

## ➡ *Relative Mode*

When selecting Relative from the Automation Mode Menu, the three controller types (Fader, Pan, Aux Sends) will again change to Offset Operation generating Offset Values. However, as I have shown previously on the diagram, the outcome is different:

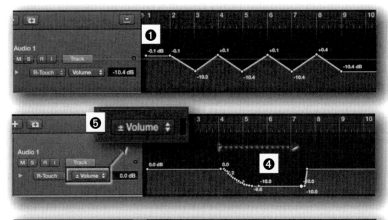

In this example (Touch-Relative), I use the same Track with the same Automation Curve for the Volume Parameter ❶.

- Again, I lower the Fader by 10dB at bar 4 ❷ and release the Fader at bar 7 ❸. While I'm doing the movement, the original Automation Curve disappears and my current Fader movement is written on the Automation Lane as a new yellow Automation Curve ❹.

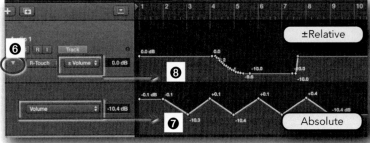

- If you look at the Automation Parameter Button ❺, you can see that it has changed from "Volume" to "±Volume". What you are looking at is the new Automation Curve, the "Relative Automation Curve" for the Volume Parameter. These new values will be added as an offset to the parameter value of the Absolute Automation Curve ❶ in real time when you play back the Project.

- Logic automatically switches to that second Automation Curve ("±Volume", "±Pan", "±Send") when you write Automation in Relative Mode.

- When you open another Automation Lane (clicking on the Subtracks Disclosure Triangle ❻ next to the Automation Mode Button), then you can see both Automation Curves for that same Volume parameter, Absolute Curve (Volume) ❼ and Relative Curve (±Volume) ❽.

### 💀 Overwrite Relative Automation Curve

Because the Offset Values that are generated in Relative Mode are written to a separate Automation Curve ❽, you can overwrite that Relative Automation Curve (or section of it) the same way you overwrite the Absolute Automation Curve. You can choose their different behaviors by using Touch-Relative, Latch-Relative, and even Write -Relative. Trim the Relative Automation Curve, that's where it gets really interesting.

### 💀 Disable Relative Automation Curve

The Automation Button has a Power Button ❾ 🔘 that is displayed (as part of a Click Zone) when you move the mouse over the button. This lets you bypass the Automation Curve of individual Parameters.

You can use this also on Relative Automation Curves to temporarily bypass the offset applied to the Absolute Automation Curve.

# Offline: Absolute - Relative

Trim and Relative are two options for the Automation Mode when you want to write automation online. However, does this also effect the way you create/edit automation offline?

### 🔘 Automation Parameter Menu

To edit automation data offline, you click on the Automation Parameter Button ❶ to select the Automation Parameter from the menu ❷. This makes the Automation Curve visible on the Track Lane. Of course, you can use the Subtrack Disclosure Triangle to make multiple Automation Lanes (Subtracks) visible to view and edit them at the same time. All these Automation Lanes display the "Absolute Automation Curve" of their Parameter.

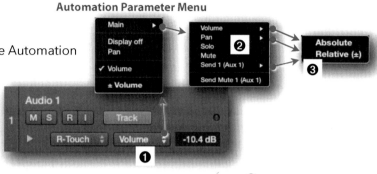

- We discussed the three types of Parameters (Volume, Pan, Aux Send) that change their functionality when using Trim or Relative Mode. They also have a specialty when it comes to Offline Automation.
- Those Parameters are listed in the Main submenu ❷ of the Automation Parameter Menu, but unlike any other Parameter, they also contain their own submenu with two items ❸: "Absolute" and "Relative (±)".

  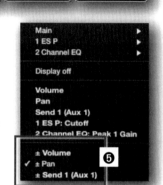

  ▶ **Absolute**: Select "Absolute" to display on the current Automation Lane the Automation Curve that was written with the basic Automation Modes (Touch, Latch, Write), or were overwritten with Trim Mode.

  ▶ **Relative (±)**: Select "Relative (±)" to display the Automation Curve, containing the Offset Values, written with any of the Relative Automation Modes (Relative-Touch, Relative-Latch, Relative-Write).

- Same as with the absolute Automation Curve, if you haven't written any Relative Automation yet, then the Automation Curve will be empty (inactive line) and you can manually create a Relative Automation Curve manually by drawing the Control Points.
- The subtle change in font type for "Absolute" and "Relative (±)" ❹ indicates if there is automation written for that Automation Curve. Bold font mean automation exists.

- The Automation Parameter Menu lists all the Parameters that have an Automation Curve at the bottom of the menu (in bold ). The Parameters for the Relative Automation Curves are grouped at the very bottom of the menu ❺.

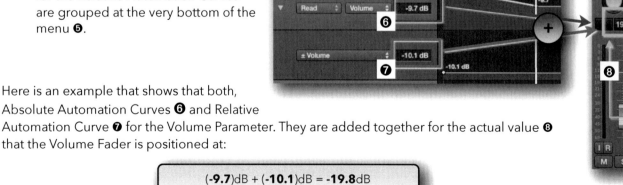

Here is an example that shows that both, Absolute Automation Curves ❻ and Relative Automation Curve ❼ for the Volume Parameter. They are added together for the actual value ❽ that the Volume Fader is positioned at:

$$(\textbf{-9.7})\text{dB} + (\textbf{-10.1})\text{dB} = \textbf{-19.8}\text{dB}$$
absolute · offset · result

# Basics

"Region Automation" is a new feature introduced in LPX v10.1. It lets you store the automation data in existing MIDI Regions (or Audio Region, and even Drummer Regions) so you can move the automation data with the Region. But, wait a minute, can't we do that already with Track Automation?

### ☺ "Move Track Automation with Regions"

I discussed this feature in the previous chapter about Track Automation.

> *Remember the following situation: You have an eight bar guitar solo in your song for which you spent a lot of time to create elaborate automation, i.e. riding the volume fader, panning left-right for some ping-pong effects, automated some of the Reverb sends, plus, you automated the Mute Button to cut out a few notes. Later you decide that you want to repeat that guitar solo also at the end of the song.*

With Track Automation, you enable "Move Track Automation with Regions" ❶ and all the Control Points of the Automation Curve between the left and right border of that Region are moving with the Region, wherever you copy or move the Region (even to a different Track).

Although this is a very simple and easy procedure, it has the potential of altering the mix depending on how the Regions and the Control Points are positioned on the Track. Please refer to the previous chapter about Track Automation where I demonstrate that situation.

### ☺ Enclose with Region Automation

Instead of temporarily "attaching" the Control Points to the Region with this "Move Track Automation with Regions" command, the Region Automation feature lets you store the Automation Control Points directly in the individual Region. Now, wherever you move that Region, the Control Points will move with it, and therefore, guarantee the integrity of your Automation.

Region Automation can not only be used on MIDI Regions ❷, it lets you store Automation Control Points in existing Audio Regions ❸ and Drummer Regions ❹ as well (even Folder Regions and Take Folder Regions).

**Track Automation vs. Region Automation**

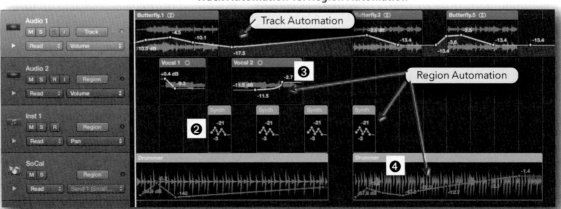

## ➡ The Big Picture

Before showing you how to use Region Automation, lets's look under the hood to better understand how Logic is doing that. Region Automation is not a new term, it was used in previous Logic versions,. However, all the ever changing terms and implementations in the past are really confusing. So let me start with a diagram that shows the big picture about Automation in Logic.

**Events** and **Storage** in this overview are the two most important aspects when talking about Logic's Automation in general. Virtually everything related to Automation has to do with these two "elements".

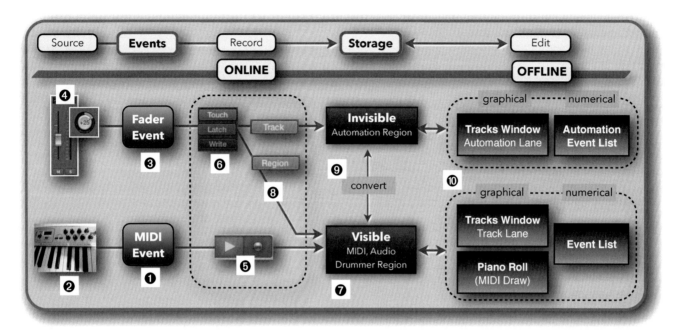

### 🂠 Events

The Event type describes the type of data that is recorded, stored, or edited in Logic (I ignore Logic's Meta Events for this discussion).

▸ MIDI Events ❶: These are the individual MIDI messages generated by a MIDI Controller ❷

▸ Fader Events ❸: These Events are generated in Logic internally when you move an Onscreen Control ❹ (Fader, Knob, Button)

#### Record Events (online):

One of their important distinction is how you record those Event Types:

• Record Mode: MIDI Events are recorded with the standard  Record Mode ❺

• Automation Mode: Fader Events can only be recorded using any of the available Automation Modes ❻

### 🂠 Storage

All the various Events can be stored in two types of "containers":

▸ Invisible Regions ❾: Fader Events created by Track Automation are stored in hidden Automation Regions. Instead of having those Regions placed on the Track Lane, Logic shows the content of those Automation Regions, the Fader Events, as Control Points and Automation Curves on the Track Lanes.

▸ Visible Regions ❼: These are the three types of Regions that you use in Logic's Workspace on the Track Lanes to build your Project: MIDI Regions, Audio Regions, and Drummer Regions. Now with the Region Automation ❽, Logic can also store Fader Events in those Regions (plus Folder Regions and Take Folder Regions).

#### Editing (offline)

Both storage options, Visible Regions and Invisible Regions provide multiple options how to display and edit those Events offline ❿.

# Region Automation - Online

## ➡ Concept

Here is the diagram again to show the basic concept of Region Automation in Logic:

### Track Automation vs. Region Automation

The implementation is very simple and easy to understand when you follow these logical steps:

- Both, Track Automation and Region Automation, let you record the movement of any Onscreen Control ❶ on a Channel Strip, Plugin, or Smart Control (Fader, Knobs, Buttons, etc.).
- You can move the controls with your mouse or via an external Control Surface.
- The Onscreen Controls generate Fader Events ❷.
- You can record those Fader Events only with the Automation Modes ❸ (Touch, Latch, Write, plus Trim and Relative).
- The Enable Automation Button on each Track Header lets you choose between "Track Automation" ❹ and "Region Automation" ❺, which determines where the Fader Events are stored.
- Track Automation stores the Fader Events in invisible Automation Regions, which will be displayed as the Automation Curves ❻ on the Automation Lane of a Track.

- Region Automation stores the Fader Events in a standard MIDI Region ❼ on the Track Lane together with all the other MIDI Events ❽ that might have been recorded to that MIDI Region. Fader Events can also be recorded to Audio, Drummer, Folder, and Take Folder Regions.
- Region Automation cannot create a Region itself. A Region (MIDI, Audio, or Drummer Region) has to be present on the Track Lane at the position where you want to record Region Automation!
- The Fader Events recorded in a Region can also be displayed as an Automation Curve, but this time, only between the left and right border of those Regions ❾.
- The Fader Events recorded on a Region can also be displayed in other MIDI Editors together with the other content (i.e., MIDI Events) of that Region.

**Region** Enabling Region Automation on a Track does two things:

- ☑ Lets you write automation data (Fader Events) to an existing Region on the Track Lane
- ☑ Lets you display the automation data (that is stored in a Region) directly on the Region that is placed on the Track Lane

## ➡ *Online Recording Procedure*

Here is how to record Region Automation online:

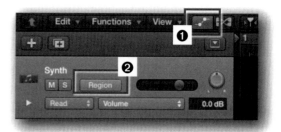

▶ **Show Automation**: First, you have to enable the Show/Hide Automation Button ❶ ![icon] on the Menu Bar to make all the elements on the Track visible that are needed for Automation.

▶ **Switch to Region Automation**: Track Automation is selected (and enabled) by default when you first show the Automation. *Click* on the Automation Button ❷ to toggle between Track Automation `Track` and Region Automation `Region`.

**Power Button**

- *Please note*: This button only toggles the visibility of the interface elements of either Track Automation or Region Automation. Switching to Region Automation does not disable the data for Track Automation and vice versa.

▶ **Disable Automation**: You toggle Automation on/off with the Power Button ❸ that appears as a Click Zone on the left side of the button when you move the Pointer Tool over it.

- *Please note*: This button toggles the Automation on/off for both, Track Automation data and Region Automation data. You can also toggle individual Automation Parameters on/off with the Power Button on the Automation Parameter Button ❹ (only available if there is automation data for that Parameter).

▶ **Record Region Automation**: Select an Automation Mode like Touch, Latch, or Write (with the optional Trim or Relative) on a Track. Now moving any Onscreen Controls (Fader, Knob, Button, etc) will still generate Fader Events, but now they will be stored (written to) the Region on that Track Lane and visible on the Region right away ❺.

- *Please note*: Region Automation data is only written if the Playhead moves across a Region on that Track. Movements will not be recorded if you are outside any Region boundaries.

▶ **Edit Region Automation**: The recorded Fader Events are displayed as Control Points (and their resulting Automation Curve) directly on the Region ❺. You can edit the Control Points (and add new ones) with the same editing techniques that you use for editing the Automation Curves of Track Automation.

- *Please note*: Because Region Automation is stored as Fader Events in Regions, you can edit those Events also in other MIDI Editors.

▶ **Pay attention**: There are a few things you have to watch out for when using Region Automation:

- The Channel Strip has no indication if Region or Track Automation is selected on its assigned Track. It only shows the Automation Mode Button ❻. Check the Track Header ❼ for the currently selected Automation before writing automation.
- Automation has to be visible ![icon]. When you hide the Automation ![icon], then data will be written as Track Automation even if you have Region Automation selected before hiding the Automation elements.
- If there are no Regions on the Track Lane, then selecting an Automation Mode (Touch, Latch, Write) will switch to Track Automation.

# Region Automation - Offline

Pretty much the same techniques you are using for editing Track Automation are also available to edit Region Automation. However, there are a few small details you have to pay a "little" attention to, and there are a few "not so little" details that you have pay "a lot of" attention to, especially when using Track Automation and Region Automation together.

## ➡ *Track Lane*

First, let's recap how the Workspace and the Regions change their appearance depending on the three conditions:

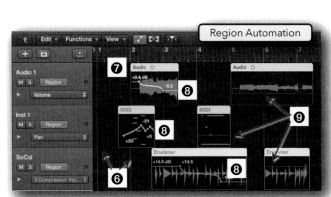

### 💀 **No Automation**

Hide Automation ⬚

- The Track Lanes display the vertical divider lines ❶ that extend from the Ruler. They are covered when a Region is placed on the Track Lane at that position.
- The Regions on the Track Lanes have two visual sections: Region Header Area ❷ with the name and optional symbols plus the Region Content Area ❸ displaying the audio waveform, MIDI Events or the Drummer Events. You can *click* anywhere on the Region to move it and *ctr+click* on it to open the Region Shortcut Menu.

### 💀 **Track Automation**

Show Automation ⬚, Track Automation ⬚ Track

- The Track Lanes are split.
- Region Header Area ❹: The area along the Region Header still shows the divider lines. You have to *click* on that section of the Region to move it and *ctr+click* on it to open the Region Shortcut Menu.
- Region Content Area ❺: This section along the Region Content functions as the Automation Lane, which displays the Automation Curve from the beginning to the end of the Project. This is where you edit the Automation Curve. The Region Content is still visible but dimmed.

### 💀 **Region Automation**

Show Automation ⬚, Region Automation ⬚ Region

- The Track Lane again acts as a single Track Lane displaying the divider lines ❻. However, the Regions are still split.
- Region Header Area: ❼ You can only *click* on that section of the Region to move it and *ctr +click* on it to open the Region Shortcut Menu.
- Region Content Area ❽: The content (waveform, MIDI Events) is still dimmed because the area is used to display the Automation Curve of the currently selected Automation Parameter. A Region without any automation data for the currently selected Automation Parameter displays a default line ❾. This indicates an important value as we will see in a moment.

### 🎧 One more Appearance

There is one more type of appearance:

Even if Show Automation is enabled ![icon] and either Track Automation `Track` or Region Automation `Region` is selected, you still can select "Display Off" ❶ from the Automation Parameter Menu. Now the Track Lane is displayed the same way as when Hide Automation is selected ![icon].

---

### ➡ *Automation Parameter*

Next up, the Automation Parameter. Its function is (almost) the same in Track Automation and in the Region Automation. But before discussing the Automation Parameter, let's put it into the context of the two important elements, Fader Events and Storage.

**Onscreen Control ➤➤ Fader Event ➤➤ Automation Parameter**

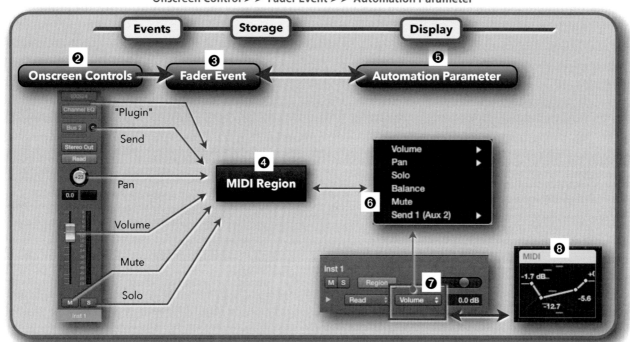

☑ The Onscreen Controls ❷ that you move on the Channel Strip (Plugin, and Smart Controls) are recorded as Fader Events ❸ to the Region that functions as the storage container, for example, a MIDI Region ❹.

☑ To display individual Fader Events that are stored (recorded) in that Region, you select an Automation Parameter ❺ from the Automation Parameter Menu ❻ by *clicking* on the Automation Parameter Button ❼.

☑ The values for the selected Automation Parameter ❼ are displayed on the Region ❽ as Control Points

☑ This is the same concept as in Track Automation: Each Automation Parameter ❼ represents an individual type of Fader Event ❸ that represents an individual Onscreen Control ❷.

> **Each <u>Automation Parameter</u> represents an individual type of <u>Fader Event</u>**
> **that represents an individual <u>Onscreen Control</u>**

## Automation Parameter Button

Here is a closer look at the Automation Parameter.

- *Click* on the Automation Parameter Button ❶ to open the menu ❷ and select the Automation Parameter that you want to display on the Regions.
- This selection affects all the Regions on that specific Track, which means, all the Regions on that Track display the same Automation Parameter. With MIDI Draw, you can choose an individual Parameter for each Region (which I'll explain later).
- Each Automation Parameter can be bypassed individually with the Power Button ❸ 🔘 that appears as a Click Zone on the left side of the button when you move the Pointer Tool over it.
- The Automation Parameter Menu is basically the same in Track Automation and Region Automation. This shows, that any Parameter (Channel Strip, Plugins, Smart Controls) that you can write as Track Automation can also be written as Region Automation.
- *Here is the specialty*: The Automation Parameter Menu on a Software Instrument Track ❹ and Drummer Track ❺ has an additional section, the MIDI Control Submenus (CC#) ❻.

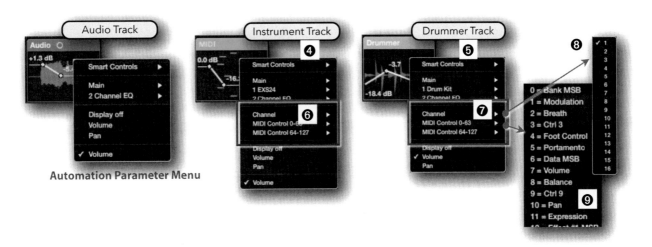

Automation Parameter Menu

## Continuous Controller (CC)

To better understand that submenu, you have to know about "Continuous Controller" (also referred to as "Control Change"). Here is a quick summary:

There is a special type of MIDI message called a "Continuous Controller" (CC). This MIDI message contains three informations:

☑ **Channel** (1-16): Like most of the MIDI messages, it is assigned a specific MIDI Channel Number.

☑ **Controller Number** (0-127): This number defines the type of controller. Many of the numbers are pre-assigned to specific functions, for example 1=Modulation, 7=Volume, 11=Expression.

☑ **Value** (0-127): This number defines the value for the controller set in the message.

Now back to the Automation Parameter Menu. Instead of selecting a Fader Event from the Automation Parameter Menu to be displayed on the Regions, you can select that special "MIDI Control" Event ❼, one of the 128 Continuous Controllers to be displayed directly on the Region (without opening a MIDI Editor).

- ▶ **Channel ❽**: The first submenu lets you select the MIDI Channel (1-16).
- ▶ **MIDI Control ❾**: The list of the 128 Controller are split into two submenus, 0-63 and 64-127 so you don't have to scroll down half a mile.

## 🎧 MIDI Control Submenus

This is the point where the discussion about Automation is starting to get complicated when you try to understand why the Continuous Controllers are listed in the Automation Parameter Menu. That's why we look again at the two elements **Events** and **Storage**.

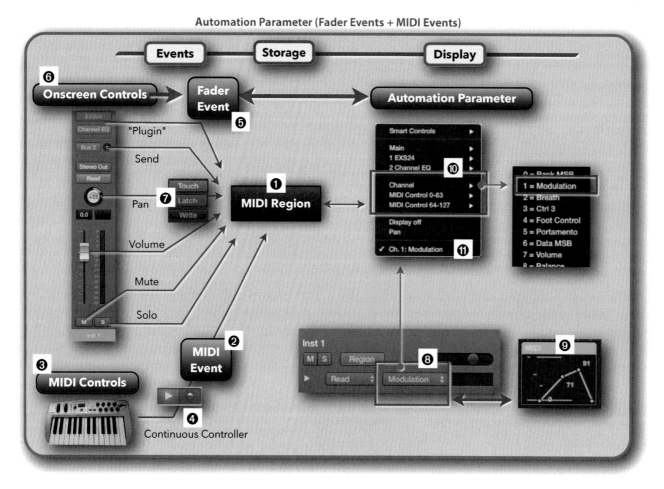

The MIDI Regions ❶ are mainly for the storage of MIDI Events ❷, recorded from a MIDI Controller ❸ using the standard Record Mode ❹.

☑️ Using Region Automation 🔲Region, you can also record Fader Events ❺ (representing specific Onscreen Controls ❻), by using the Automation Mode ❼ and store them also in the same MIDI Region ❶ that you used to record MIDI Events ❸ to.

☑️ Here is the important part:

• Usually, in Region Automation, the Automation Parameter Button ❽ lets you select a specific Automation Parameter (representing a specific Fader Event ❺) to display its Control Points directly on the Region ❾.

• On a Software Instrument Track, you now have also the option to display one type of MIDI Events directly on the Region, the Continuous Controller (CC). You select any of those 128 controllers from those additional submenus "MIDI Control" ❿.

• Any Continuous Controller data stored in the Region ❶ will be displayed in the Automation Parameter Menu ⓫. They are easy to spot, because they are listed with a Channel Number, for example, "Ch. 1".

***And here is the short summary of that extended explanation***: Region Automation 🔲Region has the option on Software Instrument Tracks to display and edit Continuous Controller data directly on the Region on the Track Lane of the Workspace. That's it. But wait for the MIDI Draw section later in this chapter, where it gets really "interesting".

## ➡ *Automation Subtracks*

Now let's look at the Subtracks in Region Automation. They basically work the same as in Track Automation.

▶ **Open Subtracks**: *Click* the Subtrack Disclosure Triangle ❶ to toggle the visibility of the Automation Subtracks. The Region gets extended ❷ across the Subtracks, displaying the content (MIDI Events, Waveform) on all Subtracks, but the Region Header ❸ is only visible on the Main Track.

▶ **Add/Remove Subtracks**: Move the mouse over the Track Header of a Subtrack to display the two buttons on the left side. *Click* the ⊕ Button ❺ to add another Subtrack and *click* the ⊠ Button ❻ to remove that Subtrack.

▶ **Select**: *Click* on the Automation Parameter Button ❻ to select from the menu ❼ the Automation Parameter that will be displayed on all Regions of that Subtrack.

▶ **Bypass**: Move the mouse cursor over the Automation Parameter Button to reveal the Power Button ❸ ⏻ that appears as a Click Zone on the left side of the button. It lets you bypass individual Automation Parameters, including the CC Controls.

The Automation Parameter Button itself has no indication if it is on or off. However, the Automation Curve turns gray ❽ when the Automation Parameter is bypassed and the Event List will display a dot in the L-Column ❾ next to those bypassed Event.

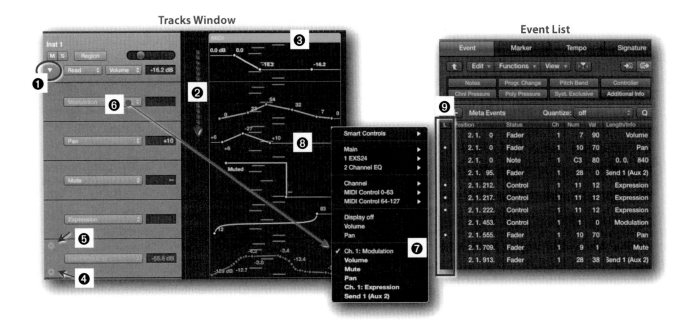

Tracks Window
Event List

*Please note*: Region Automation on a MIDI Region provides the following advantages:

- You can quickly disable specific Continuous Controller. For example, bypass the Modulation, a function that is not possible in the MIDI Editor.
- With the Subtracks, you can conveniently display multiple Continuous Controller on multiple lanes to view them together for better editing. This is also not possible with the single-lane MIDI Draw feature in a MIDI Editor.
- Be careful, turning off Region Automation 🔲 Region on a Track will also disable all the MIDI controllers (i.e Modulation) on all Regions on that Track.

➡ **The Automation Value/Trim Field**

Another element of the Automation is the field next to the Automation Parameter Button (on the Main Track and all Subtracks), the *Automation Value/Trim Field* ❶ (it is hidden when the Track Header is not wide enough).

This field has multiple functions that you have to be aware of:

▶ **No Automation**: With no automation data present, the field shows the current value ❹ of the selected Automation Parameter, which is also indicated by the gray line ❺ in the Automation Track. *Opt+click* on the Value/Trim Field sets the parameter to its minimum value. *Opt+click* on the Onscreen Control ❻ set it to its unity level.

▶ **Value Display** (Fader Events) ❷: With automation data, the field will display the value of the selected Automation Parameter at the current Playhead Position.

▶ **Value Display** (Continuous Controller) ❸: If you select a Continuous Controller as the Automation Parameter, then the field stays black, no value display.

▶ **Move Over**: When you move the cursor over the field, it will display the word "Trim" with a blue arrow above and below.

▶ **Display Off**: The field is also black when the Automation Parameter is set to "Display off" [Display off ⇕]. *Clicking* on the field now will set the Automation Parameter to "Volume".

▶ **Select All Control Points**: *Click* on the field to toggle all Control Points on all Regions on that Track to be selected or deselected.

▶ **Delete Control Points**: Having all Control Points selected provides an easy way to delete all Control Points of a specific Automation Parameters (hit the *delete* key). This works for Track Automation, but unfortunately, not for Region Automation, even if the Control Points are selected on the Regions . However, the Control Points are also selected in the Event List, so you can use the delete command there.

▶ **Trim Control Points**: *Drag* the field up or down to raise or lower the entire Automation Curve (0.1dB increments) to quickly apply an offset to it. This is applied to all Control Points for that Automation Parameter on all Regions on that Track.

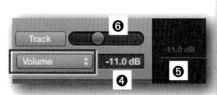

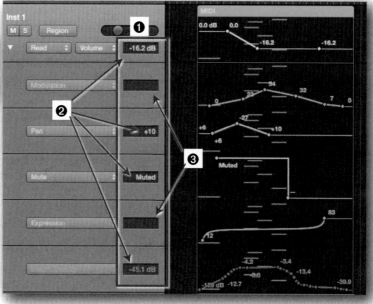

## ⇒ *Create new Control Point*

As I mentioned before, creating and editing of Control Points is pretty much the same in Track Automation and Region Automation. Here are just a few things that need some attention with Region Automation.

### 🔵 Online

▶ A Region without any automation data (no Control Points) for the currently selected Automation Parameter shows a thin horizontal line ❶ that indicates the current value of the that Parameter. This is the position of the corresponding Onscreen Control. For example, the Fader is at 0dB position.

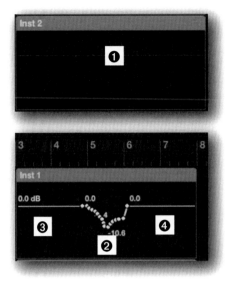

▶ When you record new automation online on that Region, using the Automation Modes, then three things will happen:

- Control Points are created on the Region in real-time ❷ representing the moving position of the Onscreen Controller.

- A single Control Point ❸ is created at the left border of the Region. Please note that you cannot see a Control Point there but when you click on that position (beginning of the line), then that Control Point will be deleted. You can also verify the existence of that Control Point when looking at the Event List.

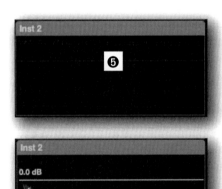

- The Automation is drawn as a flat line to the end of the Region ❹ (in case there are no further Control Points)

### 🔵 Offline

▶ When you have the same "empty" Region ❺, and you *click* with the Pointer Tool 🔲 anywhere on the Region (not the header), then you create a single Control Point at the beginning of the Region ❻ with the value of the current Onscreen Control. The thin gray line turned into a colored line representing the current Automation Curve. Again, you can't see the Control Point, but its there.

▶ When you click with the Pencil Tool 🔲 on the Region, then the following will happen:

- A single Control Point will be created exactly at the click position ❼.

- The corresponding Onscreen Control (fader, knob, etc.) will change its position to reflect that value. In this example, -9.4dB.

- No Control Point will be created at the beginning of the Region ❽.

- The Automation is drawn as a flat line to the end of the Region ❾.

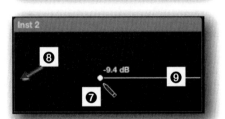

▶ When you use the Value/Trim Field to drag the values up or down, then that missing Control Point at the beginning of the Region will be added with the same Parameter value ❿.

- Please note that when displaying Continuous Controller on the Region, this "adding first Control Point" action will not happen. However, everybody with some MIDI experience knows that this is not a good idea, so better draw the Control Point at the beginning of the Region manually.

## ➡️ *Looped Region Automation*

If you have Region Automation data in a Region and loop that Region, then the automation data will also be looped. You can see the Automation Curve grayed out ❶ on the looped Region and changing the Automation Curve on the original Region will update the looped Region accordingly.

## ➡️ *Relative Automation Curve*

The additional Automation Modes "Trim" and "Relative" do also work for recording Region Automation. You can also display the additional "Relative±" Parameter for Volume, Pan and Sends by selecting them on the Automation Parameter Button ❷, and see the Fader Events in the Event List. A Relative Automation Curve is shown in the Track Lane of the Absolute Automation Curve as a thin line ❹ if it is not displayed on its own Subtrack.

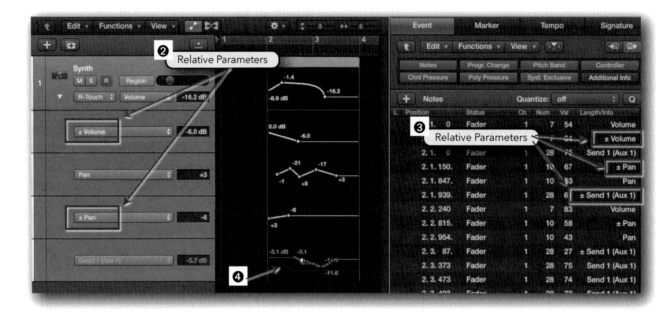

## ➡️ *Deleting Automation*

The various commands for deleting existing automation data (Main Menu *Mix* ➤ *Delete Automation* ❺) apply only to Fader Events, not MIDI Events (Continuous Controller). However the commands affect automation data in both Track Automation and Region Automation.

To delete All Region Automation, use the Key Command (*Delete All Region Automation*) or *ctr+click* on a Region and select the command from the Shortcut Menu *Automation* ➤ *Delete All Region Data* ❻.

# Getting Along: Region Automation and Track Automation

## 🌑 Track Automation vs. Region Automation

Here are a few considerations when using both Automation types:

- Switching between Track and Region just switches the user interface. Any recorded data with Track Automation or Region Automation is still active.
- Turning off the Power Button will bypass both, Track Automation and Region Automation data.
- Turning off the "Show Automation" button only *hides* the Automation controls. Any Track Automation or Region Automation is still active.
- Writing Automation with the Onscreen Controls on the Channel Strip while Automation is hidden 🔘 in the Tracks Window defaults to the Track Automation, even if Region Automation was selected before.

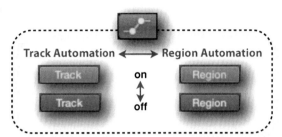

## ➡️ *Project Settings*

## 🌑 Conflicts

When using Track Automation and Region Automation on the same Track, there is the chance that you create conflicting data. For that situation, there are two settings in the *Project Settings ➤ General* ❶.

▶ **Region automation takes priority over track automation**: If you have recorded automation data for a parameter in a Region (i.e Volume), but also have automation data for the same parameter already recorded on the Track Automation, then you will get conflicting data. Both data is sent to the Volume Parameter, trying to follow the Control Points from the Region and from the Track. In this case, select the checkbox ❷ and then any Track Automation data for that parameter is suspended between the left and right border of the Region containing that same parameter.

▶ **Use preset parameter value for regions without region automation (if no track automation is present)** ❸: If you don't have any recorded Track Automation data for a parameter, only Region Automation data, then that could cause problems. Unlike Track Automation, that always defines a parameter value from the beginning to the end of the song (even with only one Control Point), Region Automation defines the parameter values only inside the Region.

In this example ❹, only the Region in the middle has Region Automation data ❺. When you stop playing at bar 5, then the Fader Value would be -12dB, but when you stop at bar 4, then the value would be 0dB. Skipping to the first or the third Region would continue to play with the last Fader value depending on where you have stopped before (bar 4 or bar 5). However, when this checkbox is enabled, then every Region that has no automation data, plays back at its default value. This would be the position you moved the Fader manually before starting the playback. You can see that value as a thin line ❻ without any Control Points.

# Introduction

➡ *Terminology*

The confusion about Automation is often based on the use of different terminology, or even worse, the same terminology but a different understanding what a term means. On top of that, there might be different opinions on what is considered Automation and what is just plain MIDI recording. Logic adds to this confusion by often changing how it uses specific terms and also changing the meaning behind those terms.

As you know by now, Logic doesn't have one single button that turns "Automation" on or off, and one way how that Automation works. Instead, there are different types of Automations, different functionalities, and different terminology. So the topic of Automation is already complex, but when you change the wording, the meaning, and the functionality, then things are getting even more complex.

Look at the screenshots below from different versions of Logic over the years:

- The term "**Track Automation**" ❶ is pretty consistent. Sometimes you will also find the terms "**Track-based Automation**" ❷, "**TBA**" or "**TA**".
- The old term "**Hyper Draw**" ❸, which was renamed to "**MIDI Draw**" ❹ in LPX, was previously considered the same as **Region Automation** ("**Region-based Automation**" ❺, "**RBA**", "**RA**", "**Region Data**" ❻).
- In LPX v10.1, things have changed yet again, and now Logic makes a clear distinction for the functionality of "Region Automation" Region ❼ (which I just discussed on the previous pages) and "MIDI Draw" ❹ (which I will discuss on the following pages).

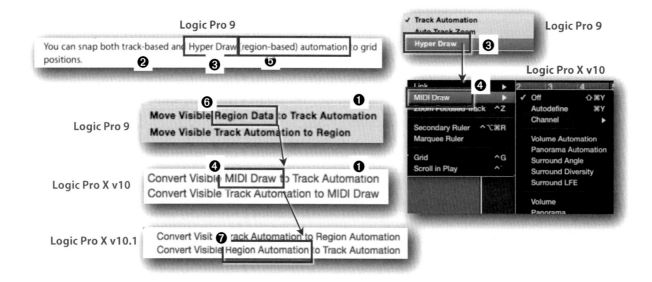

To avoid getting trapped in that tangled web of different terms, I introduced the diagram at the beginning of the chapter so you understand the underlying functionality (follow the arrows), know the meaning of all the elements involved, and therefore, the meaning of the terms that are attached to those elements or functions.

As long as you stay on top of the **Events** (Fader Events vs. MIDI Events) and the **Storage** (MIDI Region vs. Automation Region), you can easily get through all the confusion and better understand Logic's implementation of Automation. This is especially important when we now look at the MIDI Draw feature.

The two terms, "Track-based Automation and "Region-Based Automation", that are often used to describe a specific type of Automation refer to the **Storage** location, the place the automation data is written to. Let's review what we discussed with Logic's Automation so far, using those two terms:

## 💀 Track-based Automation

Track-based Automation data is stored in the hidden Automation Region. There is only one Automation Region for each Track and its data is displayed along the entire Track ❶ as a single Automation Curve regardless of its Regions, hence the name "Track-based". This is the main type of Automation similar to automated mixing consoles.

The automation data, recorded in the Automation Region as Fader Events ❷, can only come from one source, the Onscreen Controls ❸. One of its main advantages is the accuracy, which provides up to 10-bit values and a sample-based time resolution:

> ▶ **Onscreen Controls ❸**: You can stay "in the box" and use your mouse to perform the movement of any of the Onscreen Controls in Logic ❸ (fader, knobs, buttons). You can also use a MIDI Controller ❹ with the MIDI protocol or a dedicated Control Surface ❺ using one of the other protocols (Mackie, Eucon, etc.) to remotely move the Onscreen Controls. All these devices require a proper configuration in Logic's Controller Assignments Window ❻ (which I will discuss in a separate chapter).

Track Automation ❼ also provides the graphical interface to view the Track-based Automation data.

## 💀 Region-based Automation

Region-based Automation data is stored in standard MIDI Regions ❽ (and even Audio, Drummer, Folder, and Take Folder Regions).

The automation data, recorded in those Regions, can come from two sources:

> ▶ **Onscreen Controls ❸**: They generate Fader Events ❷ that are stored in the Region ❽.

> ▶ **MIDI Controller ❹**: They generate MIDI Events ❾, mainly "Continuous Controller", that are stored in the Region ❽.

Region-based Automation can be displayed graphically in two ways:

> ☑ **Region Automation ❿**: Show the Automation Curve directly on the Region in the Workplace.

> ☑ **MIDI Draw ⑪**: Show the Automation Curve directly on the Region in the Workspace or in the MIDI Draw Area of the MIDI Editor

And this is often the cause of confusion:

> Region-based Automation can be displayed with **Region Automation** or **MIDI Draw**

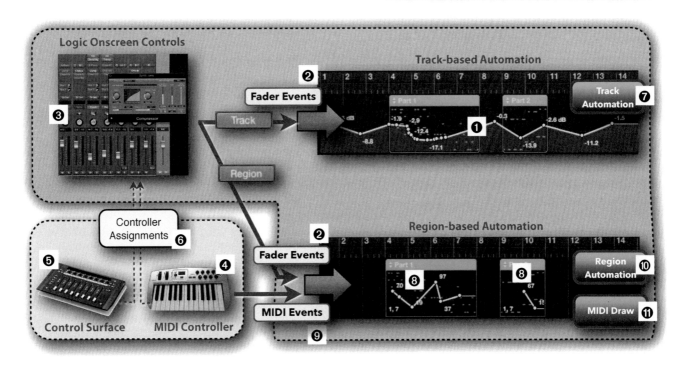

So if "MIDI Draw" is an additional feature to display the "Region-based Automation" (automation data stored in a Region), let's add it to our earlier diagram to show how it fits into the big picture of Logic Automation.

**Track Automation vs. Region Automation vs. MIDI Draw**

## Track Automation `Track`

The term "Track Automation" describes two aspects: How to record automation and how to display that automation data graphically:

▸ **Record Online**: Record Fader Events ❶ via Automation Modes ❷ to the Automation Regions ❸.

▸ **Graphical Interface** (**Offline**): Display Fader Events ❶ (that are stored in the Automation Region ❸) in the Tracks Window ❹ as Control Points along the Automation Lane.

## Region Automation `Region`

The term " Region Automation" also describes two aspects: How to record automation and how to display that automation data graphically:

▸ **Record Online**: Record Fader Events ❶ via Automation Modes ❷ to MIDI Regions ❺ (or Audio, Drummer, Folder, or Take Folder Regions).

▸ **Graphical Interface (Offline)**: Display Fader Events ❶ (that are stored in the MIDI Region ❺) on the Tracks Window ❻ as Control Points directly on the Region. It also can display one type of MIDI Events, the "Continuous Controllers".

## MIDI Draw

The term "MIDI Draw" describes only one aspects: How to display Events (Fader Events and MIDI Events) graphically:

▸ ~~**Record Online**~~: MIDI Draw is only an offline feature for displaying and editing Events. There is no such thing as "*record in MIDI Draw*". The recording part would be just standard MIDI recording, where you record MIDI Events ❼ via Record Mode ❽ to MIDI Regions ❺, but that has nothing to do with MIDI Draw itself.

▸ **Graphical Interface (Offline)**: Display the content of a MIDI Region ❺ (Fader Events ❶ and MIDI Events ❼), in two locations: The MIDI Draw Area ❾ in the MIDI Editor (Piano Roll and Score Editor) and in the Tracks Window ❿, directly on the Region. The last one looks similar to Region Automation ❻, and that can be the cause for confusion.

# Background Information

MIDI Draw, as the name implies, has something to do with MIDI. So, in order to better explain the MIDI Draw feature and how it differs from Region Automation and Track Automation, I want to discuss a few MIDI-related topics first before showing how to use MIDI Draw.

Let's gather some "awareness" by going through the following nine steps and review those important topics:

### Step 1: MIDI Signal Flow

What components are involved when recording a MIDI signal in Logic? A quick review.

### Step 2: MIDI Automation?

Is there such a thing as "MDI Automation"? It sure looks like.

### Step 3: What is Automation?

What is the definition of Automation anyway? Let's break it down.

### Step 4: Types of Event

MIDI Events, Fader Events, and Meta Events. What are they, where are they coming from, what's the difference?

### Step 5: Event Types ➤➤ Parameter

Parameters on the various popup menus represent Events, but which Parameter belongs to which Event Type?

### Step 6: Fader Events vs. MIDI Events

Fader Events and MIDI Events share a similar data structure, but there is a fundamental difference in how they are used when automating Parameters.

### Step 7: Input - Output

Channel Strips have virtual inputs and output for their controls. That's were they send and receive the automation data via Fader Events. Special attention is needed for Instrument Channel Strips, which have an additional input, a MIDI Input.

### Step 8: Volume and Pan Parameter

There is a little checkbox in the Project Settings that messes up the clear distinction between MIDI Events and Fader Events. This might be a more important topic for longtime Logic users than beginners.

### Step 9: Mono-timbral vs. Multi-timbral Instruments

Two types of Instrument Plugins. One of them desperately needs the proper setting of the aforementioned checkbox.

Now let's go on this little "awareness" detour before continuing with the MIDI Draw topic.

## ➡ *Step 1: MIDI Signal Flow*

Here is a quick review of the MIDI Signal Flow in Logic, the basic concept when "playing" MIDI Instrument in your Project:

- 🔘 **MIDI Controller ❶**: This is the source, usually your external MIDI Keyboard, that generates the MIDI data.
- 🔘 **MIDI Messages ❷**: When you play on your MIDI keyboard, it generates MIDI Messages, in this case MIDI Notes ❸ that it sends out through its MIDI or USB port. However, in addition to MIDI Notes, you can create other types of MIDI Message. For example, you have one or two wheels ❹ that generate Modulation and Pitch Wheel data. Your keyboard might even have knobs and faders ❺ that let you send so-called "Continuous Controller" data that let you control various parameters on your sound module (i.e. cutoff frequency, resonance, volume, etc.)
- 🔘 **MIDI Track ❻**: If you have your MIDI Keyboard connected to Logic, you can select a MIDI Track and all those MIDI messages from your keyboard are directed to that Track. In order to hear what you play on your external MIDI Keyboard, you need to load a MIDI Sound Module onto that Track first.
- 🔘 **MIDI Sound Module ❼**: In Logic, the MIDI Sound Module is the Software Instrument Plugin ❽ that you load on the MIDI Track (therefore, the term Software Instrument Tracks).
- 🔘 **MIDI Region ❾**: Any MIDI message that "arrives" at that MIDI Track can be recorded as MIDI Events in MIDI Regions.
- 🔘 **MIDI Editor ❿**: Various MIDI Editors can "open" those Regions and let you edit (or create new) MIDI Events.

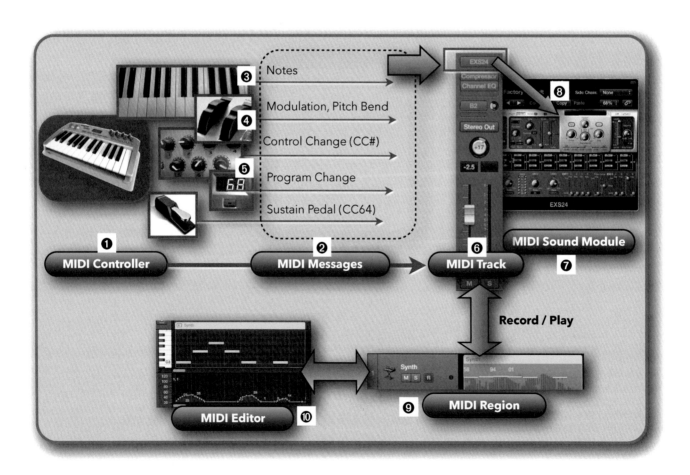

## ➡ *Step 2: MIDI Automation?*

Here is an example of a single MIDI
Region ❶ and five different views of the
Piano Roll Editor displaying the content
of that MIDI Region (its MIDI Events)
with MIDI Draw enabled.

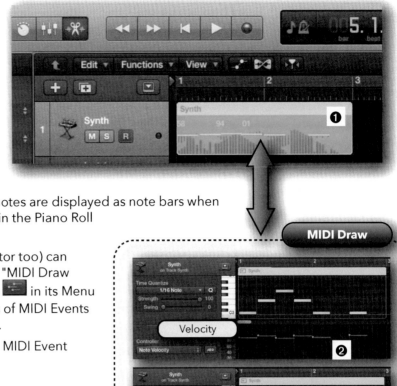

The main content of a MIDI Region are
the MIDI Notes, or Note Events. These
are the notes that you recorded while
playing on your MIDI Keyboard. Those notes are displayed as note bars when
viewing the content of the MIDI Region in the Piano Roll
Editor.

The Piano Roll Editor (and the Score Editor too) can
display an additional area, the so-called "MIDI Draw
Area" by toggling the MIDI Draw Button 🔲 in its Menu
Bar. This area can display different types of MIDI Events
that might be stored in the MIDI Region.

The five screenshots show the following MIDI Event
types for that Region:

> ❷ Velocity
>
> ❸ Continuous Controller #1 (Modulation)
>
> ❹ Pitch Bend
>
> ❺ Program Change
>
> ❻ Continuous Controller #74 (Brightness)

The Velocity data ❷ is special, because it is part of the
MIDI Note Event itself. They just describe how hard you
hit the individual key on the MIDI Keyboard. But look at
all the other data. What happens when you play back
that Region?

▸ The CC#1 Events ❸ <u>automatically</u> change the
Modulation Parameter on the Sound Module.

▸ The Pitch Bend Events ❹ <u>automatically</u> change the
pitch on the Sound Module.

▸ The Program Change Events ❺ <u>automatically</u>
change the Patch on the Sound Module.

▸ The CC#64 Events ❼ <u>automatically</u> change the
Cutoff Frequency on the Sound Module.

I think you realized already:

**This looks like automation data**

These are not Fader Events that we've seen with Track
Automation or Region Automation that correspond to specific Onscreen Controls on your Channel Strip.
These are MID Events stored in a MIDI Regions displayed by the MIDI Draw feature in the Piano Roll Editor.
Maybe this also belongs to Region Automation, but why does it use the MIDI Draw feature or is it yet another
thing, maybe "MIDI Automation"?

Let's hold on to those questions and continue with the next step.

## ➡ *Step 3: What is Automation?*

In this chapter, we covered Track Automation, Region Automation, and just came across a possible new one, "MIDI Automation". Maybe we should look at the term "Automation" itself and see what defines Automation.

### 🔵 Parameter

When you "automate something" in your mix, then that "something" is a specific parameter. For example, you automate the Volume Parameter on a Channel Strip by recording your movement of the Channel Strip Fader. Or you automate the Aux Send Parameter on a Channel Strip by recording your movement of the Aux Send Knob. So the first thing in Automation is to determine the Parameter that you want to automate. You do that just by moving its corresponding Onscreen Control.

### 🔵 Event (Value@Time)

Every change of the position for a specific Parameter is recorded as a single Event. That Event contains three informations:

- ☑ The **Parameter** that describes what Onscreen Control the data belongs to (i.e., Volume)
- ☑ The **Time** that describes when a Parameter changed its value (i.e., bar 2, beat 1)
- ☑ The **Value** that describes the new value at that time (i.e., -10dB)

> Automation Events determine:
>
> What **Parameter** with what **Value** at what **Time**

### 🔵 How to display Events?

So, recorded Automation is basically a sequence of Events, each one containing those three informations (Parameter, Time, Value) stored in a Region.

As we know from MIDI Editors, you can display Events in different ways. The same is true for automation data.

- **Numerical User Interface**: The Event List can displays all the Events that are stored in a Region in the form of a list, numerically. The different columns display the information for Parameter/Value/Time.

- **Graphical User Interface**: The graphical user interface in the form of an x/y-graph can display a single Parameter by placing its Events as coordinates (so-called Automation Control Points) on an x/y axis and connect those points to show a continuous line, the so-called Automation Curve.

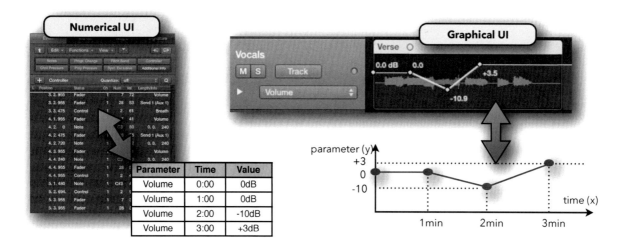

| Parameter | Time | Value |
|-----------|------|-------|
| Volume | 0:00 | 0dB |
| Volume | 1:00 | 0dB |
| Volume | 2:00 | -10dB |
| Volume | 3:00 | +3dB |

## ➡ *Step 4: Types of Events*

Logic stores all the different Parameters that you automate as different Events. When you talk about a specific Parameter, you have to know its corresponding Event when you want to identify it in the Event List or choose it from a popup menu. Let's have a closer look at those Events in Logic. This will get a little technical, but once you understand those underlying structures, many things regarding Automation will make more sense.

### 💀 MIDI Message

Here is a quick review about the structure of MIDI Event:

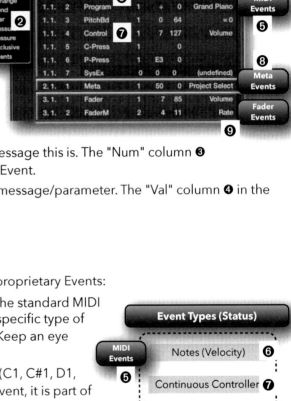

- ▶ There are two types of MIDI Messages:
  - **Channel Messages**: These are messages that include a MIDI Channel information.
  - **System Messages**: These are general messages for timing and other system-related tasks.
- ▶ A Channel Message carries up to three chunks of data, so-called bytes.
  - **Status Byte**: This carries the information about what type of message it is. The "Status" column ❶ in the Event List displays this Status for each Event. The popup menu next to the Plus button lists 8 Statuses ❷ (Event Types) that you can create manually.
  - **Data Byte 1**: This further specifies what type of message this is. The "Num" column ❸ in the Event List displays this information for each Event.
  - **Data Byte 2**: This carries the actual value for that message/parameter. The "Val" column ❹ in the Event List displays the value for each Event.

### 💀 Standard vs. Proprietary Events

In addition to the standard MIDI Events, Logic uses its own proprietary Events:

- ☑ **MIDI Events ❺**: MIDI Events in Logic are based on the standard MIDI Messages. Each type of Event (Status) represents a specific type of message (Note, Pitch Bend, Program Change, etc). Keep an eye on the following two Event Types:
  - **Note ❻**: This message carries the actual note (C1, C#1, D1, etc). The Velocity of a Note is not a separate Event, it is part of the Note Event (the second Data Byte).
  - **Continuous Controller** (Control Change) ❼: This is a special type of Event that uses its first Data Byte to define 128 individual Controllers. The second Data Byte then defines the value for that specific controller.
- ☑ **Meta Events ❽**: These are messages that are defined by Logic and only used inside of Logic for various purposes. They follow the same data structure as standard MIDI Events, and therefore, can use the same MIDI Editors for display and editing.
- ☑ **Fader Events ❾**: These are also Logic-proprietary Events that follow the data structure of standard MIDI Events. Each Onscreen Control on a Channel Strip is assigned its own Fader Event. I will show that in more detail a little bit later.

Here is a look at two popup menus, the Automation Parameter Menu and the MIDI Draw Menu. Both show a list of Parameters where you choose which one to display in a graphically way. These menus show MIDI Events and Fader Events and you have to know which is which in order to display and edit the right Parameter.

## Automation Parameter Menu

You open the Automation Parameter Menu ❶ by clicking on the Automation Parameter Button ❷ on the Track Header.

I covered that menu already, and if you remember, it is highly dynamic. It shows different items depending on the Track Type (Audio, Instrument, etc.), and also depending on if you have Track Automation or Region Automation selected.

The screenshot shows an example where I indicate which Parameter is a Fader Event and which one is a MIDI Event.

  ▸ **What you see**: The Automation Parameter Menu shows mainly Fader Events and only the Instrument Track, when set to Region Automation, displays the submenus for MIDI Events (Continuous Controller) ❸.

## MIDI Draw Menu

You can open the MIDI Draw Menu from three locations:

  ◦ Piano Roll Editor (or Score Editor) ❹: MIDI Draw Inspector
  ◦ Piano Roll Editor (or Score Editor) ❺: Local View Menu
  ◦ Tracks Window ❻: Local View Menu

The MIDI Draw Menu is always the same (with one exception that I explain in a minute).

  ▸ **Fader Events ❼**: The section on top lists the Fader Events
  ▸ **Continuous Controller ❽**: The middle section lists nine of the most used Continuous Controller. The "Other…" item opens another menu ❾ with a list of all 128 Continuous Controllers to choose from.
  ▸ **MIDI Events ❿**: The next section lists four more MIDI Events: The Note Velocity, Pitch Bend, Channel Pressure, and Program Change.
  ▸ **Smart Controls**: The bottom section displays Smart Controls Parameters ⓫, if the Track, the MIDI Region is placed on, has any Smart Controls assignment configured (most of them do).

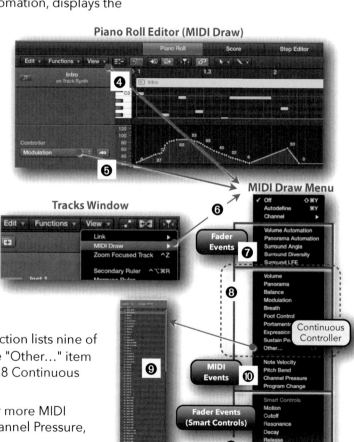

Automation Parameter Menu

Piano Roll Editor (MIDI Draw)

Tracks Window

MIDI Draw Menu

## ➡ *Step 6: Fader Events vs MIDI Events*

Now we know that when you choose a Parameter from one of those popup menus (Automation Parameter Menu, MIDI Draw Menu), we have to know what type of Event that Parameter is based on, a Fader Event or a MIDI Event. There is a fundamental difference between those two types of Events.

Let's look at two things:

- ☑ **Source ❶**: Where do Events come from during the recording,
- ☑ **Destination ❷**: Where do Events go to when you play them back from their storage ❸, the Regions.

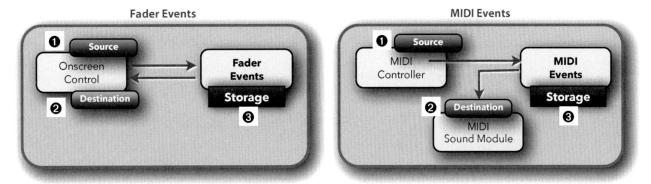

### 🎧 Fader Events

With Fader Events, the source and the destinations are the same.

- ▶ **Source = Destination**: You move an Onscreen Control ❹ on the Channel Strip, Plugin, or Smart Control, for example, the Volume Fader (you also can move it remotely via and external Control Surface). This is the source ❺ that generates the Fader Event, for example, the Fader Event "Volume". It will be stored ❻ in the Automation Region (when using Track Automation) or MIDI Region (when using Region Automation). When you play back that Fader Event "Volume" from the Region, then the destination ❼ will be the Volume Fader again, the same source that generated the Fader Event in the first place.

- ▶ **Position ➤ Value**: With Fader Events, not only is there a direct connection between a specific Onscreen Control and its corresponding Fader Event, a specific position of the Onscreen Control (knob at 11 o' clock position) also corresponds to the same specific value of the corresponding Fader Event.

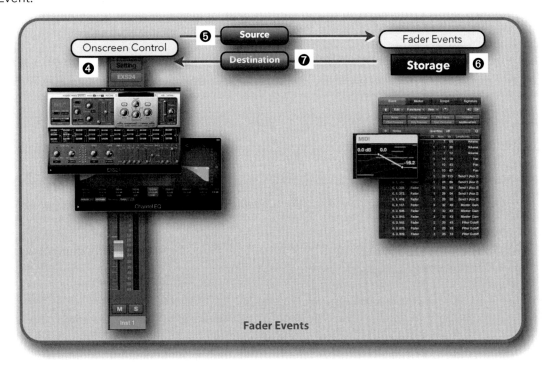

## 🌑 MIDI Events

MIDI Events are completely different from Fader Event, because the source and the destination are not the same.

▶ **Source ❶**:

The source of a MIDI Event is a MIDI Controller ❷ that sends out MIDI messages so Logic can store them as MIDI Events in MIDI Regions ❸.

▶ **Destination ❹**

Who is receiving, "playing" the MIDI Events? It has to be a MIDI Track:

- When you play back the MIDI Region on that Track, then those MIDI Events are sent to the Software Instrument Channel Strip ❺ the Track is assigned to (or to an external sound module using the External MIDI Channel Strip).
- The Software Instrument Plugin ❻ that is loaded on that Channel Strip acts as the MIDI Sound Module that receives the MIDI Events and "plays" them.
- The destination ❹ for the stored MIDI Events has nothing to do with the source ❶ of the MIDI Events.
- You can change the destination at any time by loading a different Software Instrument Plugin ❻ on the Channel Strip.

▶ **Position ➤ Value**:

Unlike with Fader Events where the position of an Onscreen Control always relates to a specific value for the Fader Event, with MIDI Events, a specific value does not guarantee the same result when played back.

- When the MIDI Events are MIDI Notes, then the sound module knows to play a note with a specific pitch based on the information embedded in the MIDI Event.
- However, MIDI Events of the type "Continuous Controller (CC#)" are different. The way a sound module reacts or "interprets" the "Continuous Controller" Events depends on the Patch ❼ that is loaded on the Plugin and how that Patch is programmed ❽. For example, If you send a Continuous Controller CC#1 (Modulation) with the maximum value of 127 to a sound module, then you don't know how much modulation effect you will get, if any at all (if that controller is not used in that Patch). It is up to the sound module how the MIDI Parameters are programmed. Therefore, the same value of a MIDI Event ❸ can have different outcomes depending on how different the sound patches are programmed.

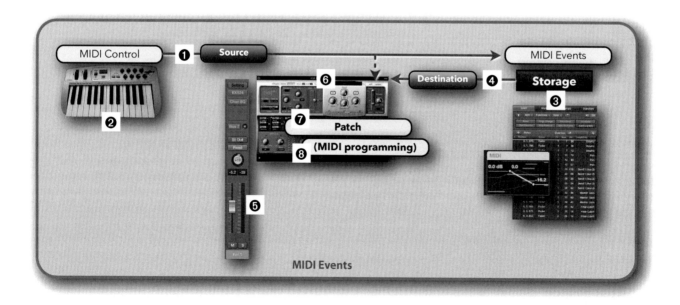

# ➡ *Step 7: Input - Output*

In this step, we look at another very important aspect, the input and output of a Channel Strip in regards to the Fader Events and MIDI Events.

Virtually every Onscreen Control on a Channel Strip, including its Plugins, and the Smart Controls has a corresponding Fader Event to automate virtually every Onscreen Control.

▶ **Output**: Moving an Onscreen Control ❶ on a Channel Strip (or remotely ❷ moving it via a Control Surface) will generate the corresponding Fader Event ❸ at the output of the Channel Strip, which can be recorded as automation data in a Region ❹ on the Track the Channel Strip is assigned to. You can even connect a cable in the Environment from the Channel Strip object and route its output to another object (more on that in the Environment chapter)

▶ **Input (Fader Event)**: When you play back the automation data from the Region ❹, then those Fader Events ❸ are routed to the input of the Channel Strip ❺ of that Track to move the Onscreen Controls accordingly.

So far, this is the default behavior for all Channel Strips. However, an Instrument Channel Strip has an additional input:

▶ **Input (MIDI Event)**: Software Instrument Channel Strips use an additional input, a MIDI Input ❻. The Software Instrument Plugin on an Instrument Channel Strip functions as a MIDI Sound Module, and like any other Sound Module, it must have a MIDI Input. Technically it has two MIDI ins:

  ☑ **From Input**: Selecting a Track in the Tracks Window routes the MIDI signal from your external MIDI Controller directly to the Software Instrument Plugin on that Track

  ☑ **From Regions**: Playing back a MIDI Region on that Track will route those MIDI Events to the Software Instrument Plugin on that Track.

  The Instrument Plugin also has its Onscreen Controls ❼ that generate Fader Events and can receive those Fader Events ❽ to automate those controls independent from the MIDI Module.

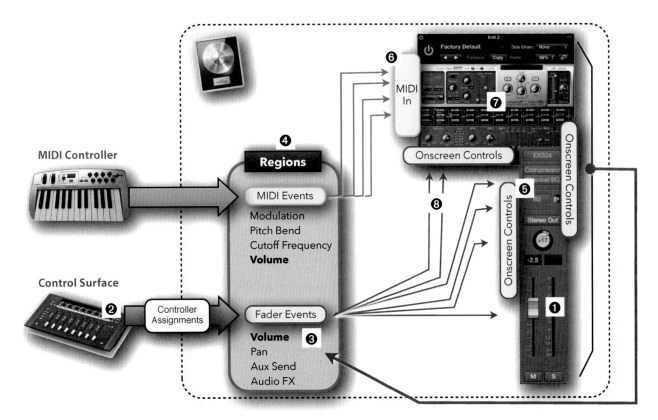

## ➡ *Step 8: Volume and Pan Parameter*

In this step I discuss an issue that causes a lot of confusion in regards to Automation, the controls for Volume and Pan. One of the reasons is that LPX v10.0.7 changed the behavior of these two controls and many long-time Logic users had to relearn that new concept.

Let me try to explain what is going on here:

### 🌑 Fader Events

- A Channel Strip has a Volume Fader ❶ and a Pan Knob ❷. Therefore, there are two corresponding Fader Events for those two Onscreen Controls ❸: Fader Event "Volume" and Fader Event "Pan".
- Using the Onscreen Controls to write automation for these two Parameters will record ❹ those Fader Events to the Automation Region (when using Track Automation) or to the MIDI Region (when using Region Automation).

### 🌑 MIDI Events

- The MIDI Event type "Continuous Controller" also defines the Parameter "Volume" ❺ and "Pan" ❻. Volume is Continuous Controller number 7 (CC#7) and Pan is Continuous Controller number 10 (CC#10)
- These are MIDI Events, sent from a MIDI Controller. ❼ Therefore, they are routed to the MIDI Input of the Software Instrument Plugin and control the Volume and Pan of the MIDI Sound Module (if it is programmed in the current Patch).

Here is a signal flow diagram that demonstrates the new behavior:

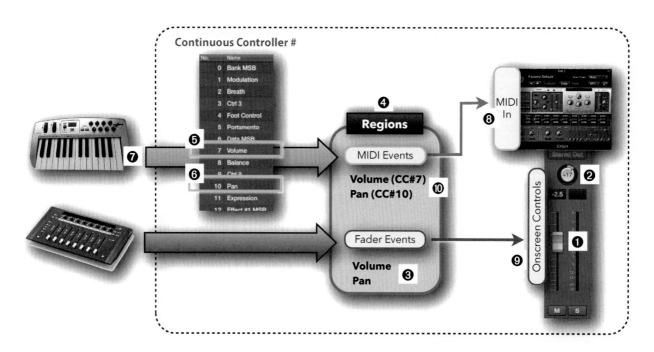

Although it is always hard to relearn old habits, this new default behavior is much better, because it is logical, makes sense, and it is easy to understand. Fader Events ❸ control the Onscreen Controls ❾ and MIDI Events ❿ control the Sound Module ❽, the Software Instrument Plugin.

Logic now provides a checkbox in the Project Settings that lets you revert to the old behavior. However, there are a few small "consequences" you have to be aware of in order to avoid any further confusion.

## Control Change 7/10 controls Volume/Pan of channel strip objects

Here is the checkbox in the *Project Settings* ➤ *MIDI* ➤ *General* ➤ *Miscellaneous* that was introduced in Logic Pro X v10.0.7 It is labeled "*Control Change 7/10 controls Volume/Pan of channel strip objects*"❶. "Control Change 7/10" refers to "Continuous Controller CC#7 (Volume) and CC#10 (Pan)".

This is the basic functionality:

**unchecked (default)**: This is now the default behavior when creating a new Logic Project:

MIDI Event CC#7 (Volume) and CC#10 (Pan) ❷ are sent to the MIDI Sound Module ❸, the Software Instrument Plugin on that Channel Strip. They will not control the Volume Fader and Pan Knob on the Channel Strip ❹.

This is a huge improvement for anybody who uses multi-timbral instruments, which I will demonstrate on the next pages.

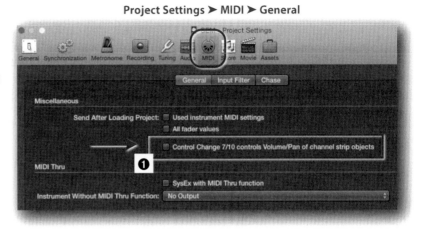

**Project Settings ➤ MIDI ➤ General**

**checked**: This was the default behavior in earlier Logic versions. MIDI Event CC#7 (Volume) and CC#10 (Pan) ❷ will control the Volume Fader and the Pan Knob on the Channel Strip ❹ and are not sent to the Software Instrument Plugin ❸ on that Channel Strip.

Any Fader Events ❺ for the Volume and Pan on the Channel Strip are still sent ❻ to those controls regardless of the checkbox

Here is a diagram that shows where the Volume and Pan data is directed to, based on the setting of the checkbox. You can see the potential conflict ❼ when the checkbox is enabled. Both, the MIDI Events ❷ and Fader Events ❺ can send (possibly conflicting) data to Volume and Pan on the Channel Strip ❹.

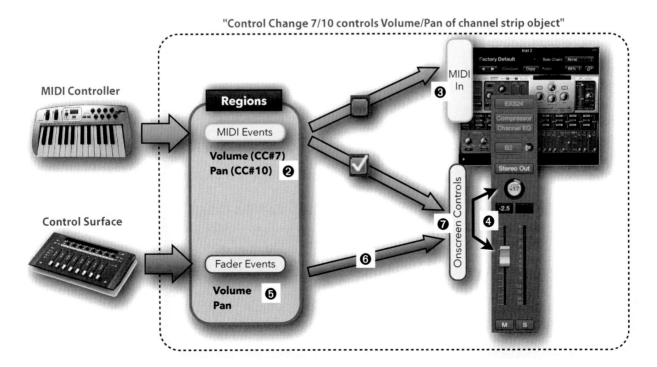

There are a few "side effects" you have to be aware of when using this checkbox:

▶ **MIDI Draw Menu**

This is the menu I mentioned earlier that can be accessed from three locations (Tracks Window, MIDI Editors):

**MIDI Draw Menu**

■**unchecked (default)**: The menu displays two items, "Volume Automation" and "Panorama Automation" ❶. These are just different terms for "Fader Event - Volume" and "Fader Event - Pan". This enables you to select the Fader Events for Volume and Pan in addition to the MIDI Events for Volume and Pan ❷ to display and edit them on the Region.

☑**checked**: The two Fader Events "Volume Automation" and "Panorama Automation" are not available because the MIDI Events CC#7 and CC#10 are directed to the Onscreen Controls, and therefore, acting as Fader Events already.

▶ **Region Automation**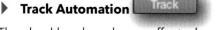

In Region Automation, you can record both, Fader Events and MIDI Events for Volume and Pan.

■**unchecked (default)**: The MIDI Events ❸ control the Volume and Pan on the Software Instrument Plugin via MIDI and the Fader Events ❹ control the Volume Fader and Pan Knob on the Channel Strip. They both can "live together" without creating any conflict. If it makes sense, that is another question.

☑**checked**: Now the MIDI Events are directed to the Onscreen Controls, acting as Fader Events. If you have already Fader Events for Volume and Pan, then you get conflicting data because both Events send their values to the same Onscreen Control.

**Event List**

**Automation Parameter Menu**

▶ **Track Automation** `Track`

The checkbox has also an affect when using Track Automation, however, this is not as easy to grasp. Here are a few things:

■**unchecked (default)**: The Automation Region is "reserved" for Fader Events. Track Automation only records Fader Events. Technically, you can write a MIDI Event (CC#7 or CC#10) when viewing the Track Automation data in the Automation Event List (*ctr+cmd+E*), but when you toggle the checkbox, then the MIDI Events (Control) will be changed to Fader Events (Status column now reads "Fader")

☑**checked**: The following behavior is a little strange. When you enable the checkbox, then any Fader7 and Fader 10 changes to Control7 and Control 10 when you have the Automation Event List open. Although the Automation Region is reserved for storing Fader Events, this seems to be an exception so the "checkbox" behavior stays true: CC#7 and CC#10 act as Fader Events. So technically, at the end, nothing has changed regarding what is controlled (CC#7 controls Volume Fader) and if you don't have the Automation Event List open, you wouldn't notice any difference.

## ➡ *Step 9: Mono-timbral vs. Multi-timbral Instruments*

All of Logic's Software Instrument Plugins are mono-timbral. That means, you can load only one Patch at a time. Multi-timbral Instruments, on the other hand, can load multiple Patches, each one set to an individual MIDI Channel so they can be played at the same time.

With Mono-timbral instruments, it wouldn't mater if you control the volume on the Sound Module itself using MIDI Events CC#7, or controlling the Volume Fader on the Channel Strip the Plugin is loaded by using the Fader Event. You are controlling a single Patch

A problem occurs when using multi-timbral instruments like Kontakt or Play that can have more than one Instruments loaded on that one Plugin. The Volume Fader on the Channel Strip controls the output of the Plugin, and therefore, like a Master Fader, affects the volume of all Patches/Instruments loaded on that multi-timbral Software Instrument.

### Software Instrument Plugin: Kontakt (Multi-timbral)

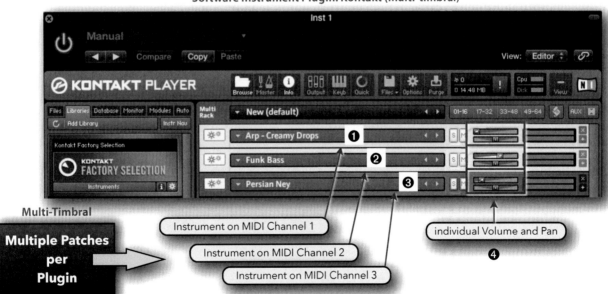

In the following example, I use the Kontakt Plugin on an Instrument Channel Strip. It has three Instruments loaded "Arp" ❶, "Funk Bass" ❷, and "Persian Ney" ❸. Each Instrument is set to its own MIDI Channel, Ch1, Ch2, and Ch3, and each Instrument has its own Volume and Pan control ❹ that can be controlled via MIDI Event CC#7 and CC#10.

Here are the two different scenarios depending on the checkbox setting "*Control Change 7/10 controls Volume/Pan of channel strip objects*" when sending CC#7 and CC#10 on different MIDI channels:

## ☑ checked

MIDI Event CC#7 (Volume) and CC#10 (Pan) will control the Volume Fader and Pan Knob on the Channel Strip ❶ regardless what MIDI Channel ❷ these controllers are set to. That means you can't control the individual Volume and Pan on each Instrument ❸ inside the Kontakt Plugin.

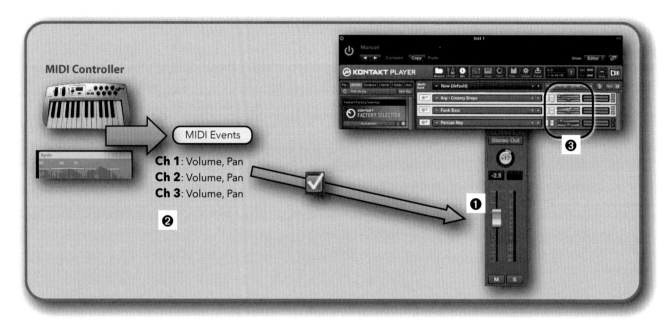

## ☐ unchecked

MIDI Event CC#7 (Volume) and CC#10 (Pan) will not control the Volume Fader and Pan Knob on the Channel Strip ❹. They are directed to the Kontakt Plugin. Now, sending CC#7 and CC#10 on individual MIDI Channel 1, 2, or 3 ❺ lets you control the Volume and Pan on those individual Instruments ❻ that are assigned to that specific MIDI Channel. You still can use the Fader Events ❼ to control the Volume Fader and Pan Knob of the Channel Strip ❹ to control the overall Volume and Pan of the Kontakt Plugin.

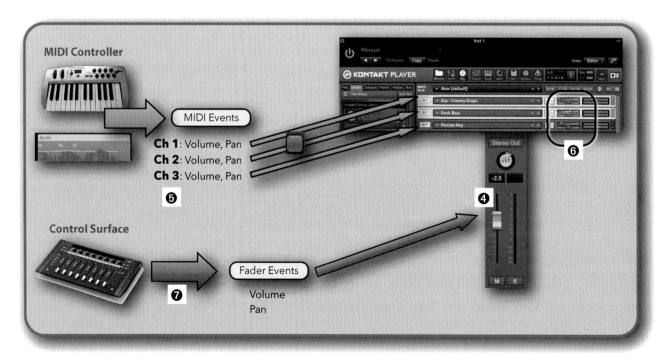

# Display MIDI Draw

After all the previous informations about Parameters, Fader Events, and MIDI Events we should be well prepared to understand the somewhat strange ways how MIDI Draw is implemented and figure out what MIDI Draw is. Be careful, it has a "split personality". MIDI Draw is two things, a MIDI Editing Tool and an Automation editing Tool.

> ## MIDI Draw = MIDI Editing Tool & Automation Editing Tool

Here again is the diagram with the big picture about Automation in Logic.

**Track Automation vs. Region Automation vs. MIDI Draw**

### ➡ What is MIDI Draw?

Here is a quick summary of what MIDI Draw is:

- MIDI Draw is a display feature ❶
- It can display the content ❷ of a MIDI Region, Audio Region, or Drummer Region
- The content are Parameters, which can be MIDI Events ❸ or Fader Events ❹
- You can display one Parameter at a time as an Automation Curve with Control Points representing individual Events ❺
- The Automation Curve can be edited with the same Automation Tools as with Track Automation and Region Automation
- MIDI Draw can be displayed in the Piano Roll Editor and Score Editor in their separate MIDI Draw Area ❻
- MIDI Draw can also be displayed directly on the Regions ❼ in the Workspace, which is almost identical to display/edit Region Automation

> ## MIDI Draw displays the Region Content (MIDI Events and Fader Events)
> ## as an Automation Curve

## ➡ MIDI Editor

The MIDI Draw feature is available in the Piano Roll Editor and the Score Editor. I demonstrate it for the Piano Roll Editor but their functionality is pretty much the same in both editors.

### ⊙ Interface

When MIDI Draw is enabled, it opens a second area below the Matrix with the MIDI Notes. Both areas are linked to the same Ruler, so you can use them as two parallel lanes to display and edit two MIDI Events. The upper Note Display Area ❶ uses a Matrix view to display the horizontal Note Bars and the lower MIDI Draw Area ❷ functions as an x/y graph that display Events as Control Points connected together to form an Automation Curve ❸. The only exception is when selecting the Parameter "Note Velocity". In that case the MIDI Draw Area displays horizontal lines ❺ that correspond to the horizontal note bars above, showing the velocity (and duration) of those note bars.

For example, have the MIDI notes displayed in the upper area and the ModWheel data in the lower area. Actually, the upper area always displays the notes, and only the MIDI Draw Area lets you choose what Parameter (Type of Event) to display.

### ⊙ Display the MIDI Draw Area

To "enable MIDI Draw" means to make the MIDI Draw Area visible. You can do that in different ways:

- *Click* on the MIDI Draw Button 🔲 ❺ in the Menu Bar to toggle MIDI Draw on/off
- Choose any Parameter from the MIDI Draw Menu that you can access via the Local Menu *View ➤ MIDI Draw ➤* ❻. It automatically displays the MIDI Draw Area.
- Key Command (*MIDI Draw: Autodefine*) *cmd+Y* lets to step through the available Parameters for the currently selected Region, which also displays the MIDI Draw Area if it was hidden.
- Key Command (*MIDI Draw: Disable*) *sh +cmd+Y* hides the MIDI Draw Area. This command is also available from the MIDI Draw Menu "Off".

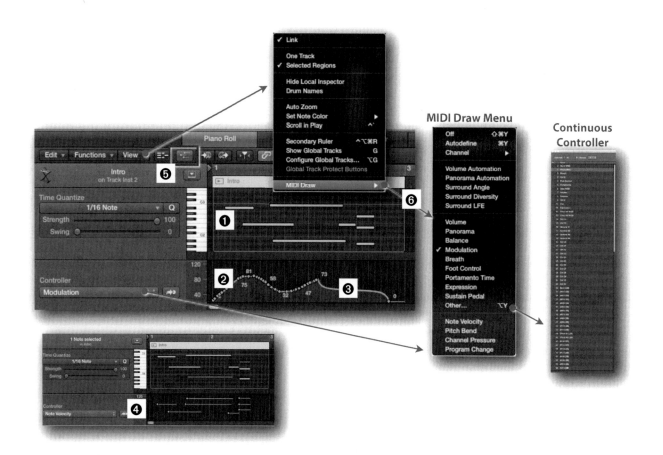

## 💀 Select Parameter

This is the part where it gets interesting. What Parameters can be displayed in the MIDI Draw Area and how do you select them? First, let's go over the various commands:

**What is a Parameter**: As we discussed earlier, the MIDI Draw Menu lists Parameters, so-called MIDI Draw Parameters. They are similar to the Automation Parameter in the Automation Parameter Menu and represent either MIDI Events or Fader Events. There are three ways how you can select a Parameter to be displayed in the MIDI Draw Area:

**Piano Roll Editor (MIDI Draw)**

- ☑️ **Select Parameter from Menu**: Open the MIDI Draw Menu ❶ from the Local Menu ❷ *View ➤ MIDI Draw ➤* or by *clicking* on the Controller Button ❸ in the Local Inspector (you can toggle it from the Local Menu *View ➤ Show/Hide Local Inspector*)

- ☑️ **Select Next Available Parameter**: Although Logic explains that command as "Set the MIDI Draw parameters automatically", what it does is select the <u>next available</u> Parameter every time you use that command. Even the name for the command "Autodefine" is strange. Why not just "Next Available Parameter". There are three ways how to step through the available Parameters.

  - 💧 Local Menu *View ➤ MIDI Draw ➤ Autodefine* ❹
  - 💧 Key Command (MIDI Draw: *Autodefine*) *cmd+Y*
  - 💧 "Next Setting Button" 🔘 ❺: This is a also a strange label for that button. The button just selects the next available Parameter to be displayed in the MIDI Draw Area just like the Autodefine command (there is no "assigning settings"?)

- ☑️ **Select Specific Parameter**: Most of the commands from the MIDI Draw Menu are available as Key Commands ❻ so you can switch to a specific Parameter (i.e. Modulation, Breath, etc.) just by hitting a key combination.

## 💀 MIDI Draw Menu

Hear are a few things you have to pay attention to in the MIDI Draw Menu:

- If the selected MIDI Region is on an External MIDI Track, then the 5 Parameters that represent Fader Events are grayed out ❼. They don't exist on that Channel Strip

- Please remember that the two Parameters ❽ "Volume Automation and "Panorama Automation" are only displayed when you have the checkbox "*Control Change 7/10 controls Volume/Pan of channel strip objects*" disabled in the *Project Settings ➤ MIDI ➤ General* . If the checkbox is enabled, then those two Parameters are not displayed ❾.

## 🦆 Edit Automation in the MIDI Editor

This is an important aspect of the MIDI Draw feature. Earlier, we tried to define what Automation is and see if MIDI Draw can also be considered Automation. As we will see, that is the gray area.

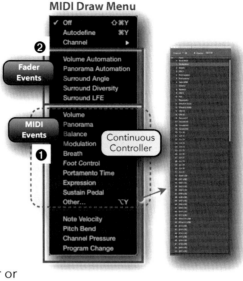

**MIDI Draw Menu**

Think about it:

- The MIDI Editors are for editing MIDI Regions.
- The Piano Roll, for example, displays the content of a MIDI Region as MIDI Notes (in the upper area) and any other MIDI Events in the lower MIDI Draw Area.
- However, the MIDI Draw Area should also be able to display Fader Events because they follow the same data structure as a MIDI Event.

This is how it works:

▸ **Display MIDI Events**: All the eligible MIDI Events are listed as Parameters in the Menu ❶.

▸ **Display "listed" Fader Events**: The MIDI Draw Menu also lists five Parameters ❷ that are based on Fader Events, including the Fader Event "Volume" and the Fader Event "Pan" and if you used Region Automation to record the Onscreen Controls for the Volume Fader or the Pan Knob, then those Events can be displayed in the MIDI Draw Area. Be careful when using (editing) Volume or Pan Parameter to make sure if they control the Chanel Strip (Volume Automation) ❸ or the MIDI In of the Software Instrument Plugin (Volume) ❹.

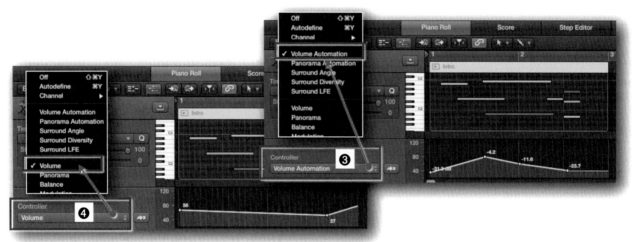

▸ **Display "unlisted" Fader Events**:
But how about other Fader Events that are not listed in the MIDI Draw Menu? For example, when you use Region Automation to automate the Aux Sends or any Onscreen Control on a Plugin or Smart Controls. You still can display those Fader Events, however, you have to use the "step through" feature with the "Autodefine" command (*cmd+Y*), or *click* on the "Next Settings" Button 🔲 ❺ to step through the available

Parameter in that Region. The name of the Fader Event is displayed in the Controller Button ❻. Ready to edit Region Automation in the MIDI Editor.

## ➡ Tracks Window

The MIDI Draw feature is also available in the Tracks Window. Here, the lines are getting really blurry when we want to figure out if MIDI Draw is considered an Automation feature or not.

The difference is that the Events are displayed directly on the Region, the way we saw it with Region Automation.

There are three different setups how to use MIDI Draw in the Tracks Window. Judge for yourself if you think that is a little bit too much to remember.

##  Setup 1

With this setup, you hide Automation, so all the Automation elements on the Track Headers are not displayed. You could consider this the default MIDI Draw setup, because all you have to do is select a Region(s) and choose the Parameter from the MIDI Draw Menu that is located at the Local Menu *View ➤ MIDI Draw ➤*.

- ☑ **Hide Automation**
- ☑ **Select a Region(s)**
- ☑ **MIDI Draw Menu**: *Make Selection*

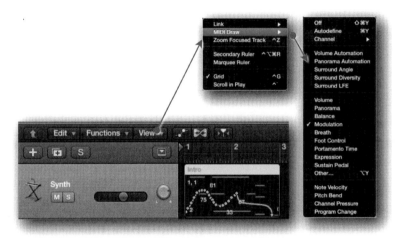

##  Setup 2

This is a variation of the first setup. Maybe once you look at it, you want to forget it right away because it doesn't add any functionality. It just lets you display MIDI Draw with more steps. The effect is that when you are in Track Automation and set the Automation Parameter to "Display off", you basically fall back to display MIDI Draw.

- ☑ **Show Automation**
- ☑ **Track Automation**
- ☑ **Automation Parameter** Display off
- ☑ **Select a Region(s)**
- ☑ **MIDI Draw Menu**: *Make Selection*

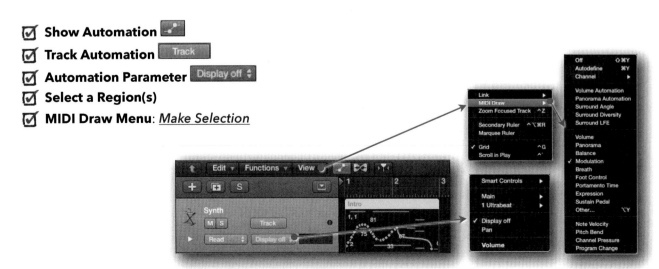

This is a hybrid situation that actually shows the best what the difference is when displaying a Region in Region Automation and MIDI Draw. The short answer: There is none!

When you show Region Automation, then you can select in the Automation Parameter Menu which Parameter to display on the Region.

- ☑ **Show Automation**
- ☑ **Region Automation** Region
- ☑ **Select a Region**
- ☑ **Parameter**: _Make Selection_

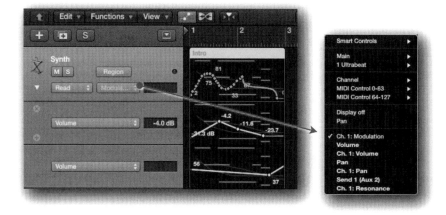

There are a few minor differences between Region Automation and MIDI Draw:

- Making a selection from the MIDI Draw Menu only affect the Main Track. Region Automation lets you display multiple Subtracks to displaying different Parameters on different Automation Lanes.
- Selecting a Parameter in Region Automation switches all Regions on that Track to that Parameter. MIDI Draw, on the other hand, can display a different Parameter for each Region on a Track.

- The Automation Parameter indicates if the Parameter is an Absolute or a Relative Automation Curve, for example "Volume Absolute" and Volume Relative±". The MIDI Draw Menu doesn't provide that distinction and would display "Volume Automation" in both cases.

---

**Region Automation = MIDI Draw**

(regarding most display and offline editing)

---

So when you think about it, this setup proves that for the display and editing part, the Region Automation and MIDI Draw feature in the Tracks Window are pretty much the same.

Remember one restriction: The only MIDI Events that Region Automation can display are Continuous Controller.

### Editing MIDI Draw

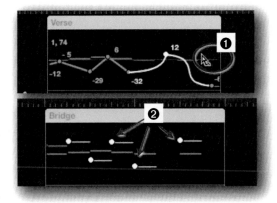

Using MIDI Draw, you can edit MIDI Events and Fader Events inside a Region on the Track Lane the same way as you would edit Region Automation. After all, MIDI Events (except MIDI Notes) are also represented by Control Points that form an Automation Curve.

Most of the edit commands and various Cursor Tools ❶ also work in that area on the Track Lane so you don't have to open the Piano Roll Editor for quick edits. You could even display the Velocity data (although not really considered automation data) to drag the Velocity bars ❷ up or down to make some quick velocity changes for specific notes. If you look at it, the Velocity is also displayed as single Control Point (representing the MIDI Note) with an extending line that represents the duration of that note.

### Number Indicator

The MIDI Draw Area displays one or two numbers at the left border.

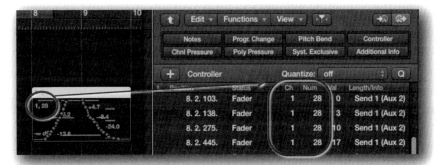

- **MIDI Events**: The first number indicates the MIDI Channel and the second number the Controller Number (i.e. #1=Modulation, #2=Breath, #4=Foot Controller, etc.). The Length/Info column in the Event List displays the name of the control.

- **Fader Events**: The first number indicates the Slot Number of the Onscreen Control (Ch column) and the second number the specific Controller (Volume, Mute, Send 1, etc.). The Length/Info column in the Event List displays the name of the control.

### Parameter Display Memory

The Region remembers its last selected Parameter in MIDI Draw. When you switch to Track Automation and then back to MIDI Draw, any Region will display the last selected MIDI Draw Parameter.

### High Enough

Very important. You have to drag the Track Header high enough to display MIDI Draw Parameter.

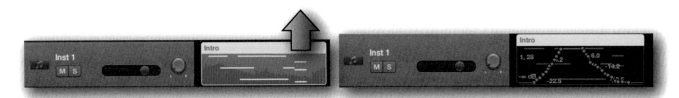

## ⚫ MIDI Draw Menu and Region Type

Depending on the type of the selected Region, the MIDI Draw Menu might not have all the Parameters available. It might display them grayed out. Please note that the MIDI Draw Menu also shows at the bottom of the menu any Smart Controls that are assigned on the current Track.

▶ **No Region ❶**: If no Region is selected, then all the Parameters in the menu are grayed out

▶ **MIDI Region (Instrument Plugin) ❷**: A MIDI Region located on a MIDI Track that is assigned to a Instrument Channel Strip will have all Parameters available

▶ **MIDI Region (External MIDI Track) ❸**: A MIDI Region located on a MIDI Track that is assigned to an External MIDI Channel Strip will have the Parameters that are based on Fader Events disabled. The Channel Strip for an External MIDI Track is not a real Channel Strip. Its controls are MIDI controls. Therefore, when you record Track Automation using one of the Automation Modes (Write, Touch, Latch), the recorded data is Controller Events and not Fader Events.

▶ **Audio Region ❹**: Audio Regions will have all the Parameters related to MIDI Events grayed out, because this Channel Strip doesn't have any MIDI Sound Modules that can receive MIDI Events..

▶ **Drummer Region ❺**: You can't use MIDI Draw with Drummer Regions. All the Parameters are grayed out.

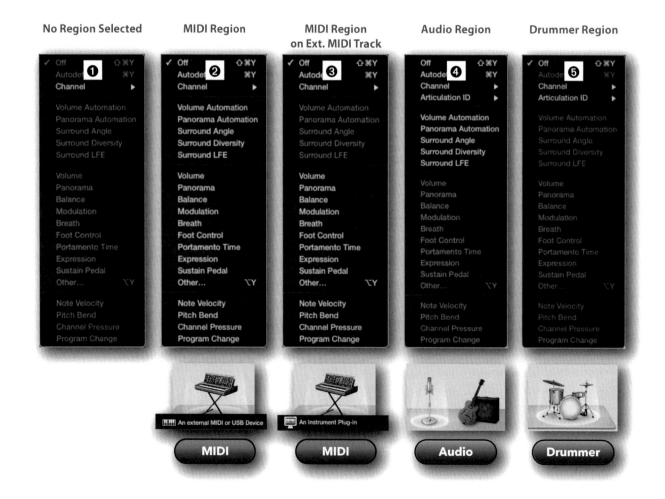

Most of the Offline Automation is done with a graphical user interface in the form of the Automation Curve. That's what I covered so far. As we know by now, the Automation Curve itself is made up of Control Points and these are the individual Events that can be edited numerically like any other MIDI Events.

**Geek Alert** Be warned. What I discuss in this section is a real advanced topic, and chances are, you may never need it when using automation in your Project. Nevertheless, the information is useful to get a better understanding on how automation is implemented in Logic.

## Event List vs. Automation Event List (AEL)

Editing Control Points numerically is done in the Event List Editor, the same window that is used for editing MIDI Events. Although the Logic User Guide uses the term "Automation Event List" for numerically editing automation data, this is the same Event List window interface, just displaying automation data (on a special Display Level) instead of MIDI data.

### Accessing the Automation Event List

You can display Fader Events that are stored in Regions (recorded with Region Automation) directly in the Event List and the Event Float just by *clicking* on them. This is the same procedure as for MIDI Events.

However, to view Fader Events that are recorded with Track Automation ❶, you have to use a special window, the "*Automation Events List*" (AEL), which opens as a separate window ❷.

☑ Select a Track that has Track Automation.

☑ Use the Key Command (*Automation Event List*) **ctr+cmd+E** to open the Automation Event List to view the Fader Events recorded with Track Automation on that Track.

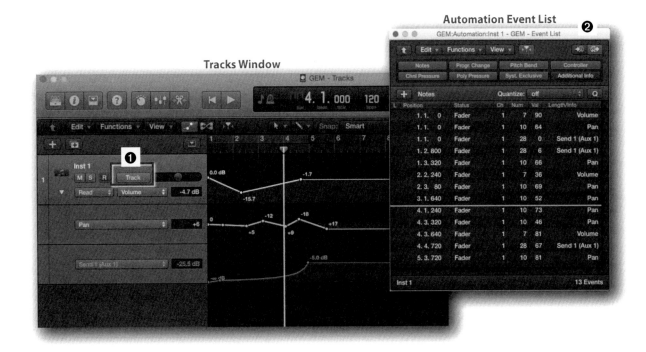

# Data Type (Fader)

Now that we can see the actual automation data in the Event List, let's have a closer look at the type of data.

Although the automation data in the Event List looks similar to MIDI data (MIDI Events), they are not MIDI Events. Logic uses its own proprietary type of data for a wide variety of tasks. The data structure for that special data is similar to MIDI Events, and that is the reason why it can also be displayed in the Event List without the need for a separate editor. Think of this proprietary data as an extension to the MIDI protocol.

## ➡ MIDI Events

If you look at the List Editor when it displays MIDI Events, then you can see in the Status column ❶ the different types of MIDI Events (this information is contained in the Status Byte of a MIDI message). The blue buttons ❷ on top of the Event List represent the seven of the eight available Statuses. The buttons function as show/hide buttons. Click on a button to hide that type of MIDI Event (the button turns from blue to gray) in the Event List.

## ➡ Meta Events

Some of Logic's "MIDI Event-like" data is called Meta Events. Whenever you are using data that is based on those Meta Events, the Event List will display "Meta" ❸ for that event in the Status column. The Info column ❹ displays what type of Meta Event it is. For example, various Score Symbols, commands for Recall Screensets, Goto Marker, etc. *Click* on the Number value to open a popup menu with a list of all the defined Meta Events.

There is no Show/Hide Button on top for Meta Events. They are always displayed, even if all the buttons are disabled ❺. A little tip on the side: The Name ❻ next to the Plus icon is actually a button that opens a popup menu. Here you select the type of Event you can create manually with that Plus button. As you can see, you can also create Meta Events ❼ manually in the Event List.

## 💀 Display Level

Meta Events are displayed together with the other MIDI Events in the Event List ❽. However, you have to pay attention to the Window Title ❾ of the Event List (only visible when you display the Event List as a separate window). I explain all the details in my first book "Logic Pro X - How it Works" how to decipher what the names, hyphens, and colons mean, plus the important concept about Display Levels. Here, "Super Hit:Chorus" means that the Event List displays the data of the Display Level 2 (the Region "Chorus"), below the Display Level 1, which is the root level, your Project "Super Hit".

# ➡ *Fader Events*

In addition to the Meta Events, Logic uses another proprietary Event type, the Fader Event. These Events are used for the Track Automation and Region Automation.
Each Control Point represents a single Fader Event.

- There are actually two types of Fader Events used for Automation. The **Fader ❶** Event and the **FaderM ❷** Event. The last one is used for the MIDI FX Plugins.

- The seven Show/Hide Buttons ❸ on top of the Event List have no effect, they only relate to MIDI Events.

- The "Additional Info" Button ❹, however, is important. If enabled (blue), it will show all the "invisible" Control Points", the interpolated (calculated) values between two visible Control Points in the Automation Lane.

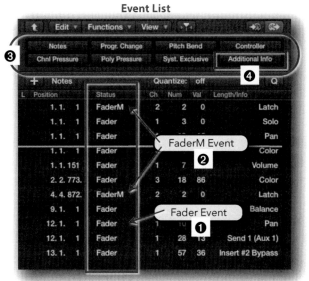

Event List

## 🔘 Invisible Control Points

I mentioned the term "interpolation" earlier. This is the important concept about the difference between the Control Points and the actual Automation Curve.

- The Control Points are the coordinates, the actual automation data that defines the value of a specific Automation Parameter. In example below, you can see the two Fader Events, the first one ❺ (at bar 1) with the value of 90 and the second ❻ one (at bar 2) with the value 0.

- Logic draws a line between these two Control Points to create the resulting Automation Curve ❼.

- When you play back between bar 1 and 2, the Fader value doesn't jump from value 90 to value 0, instead, it gradually moves. Logic interpolates the additional data along the Automation Curve for that Parameter with gradually decreasing values.

- The Event List can show/hide all those invisible Control Points by clicking on the "Additional Info" Button ❽. In this example, when you scroll down ❾ in the Event List, you can see that Logic created about 300 additional Control Points between bar 1 and bar 2.

- Please note that the Event List still lists only "2 Events"❿ in the Status Bar, the visible Control Points.

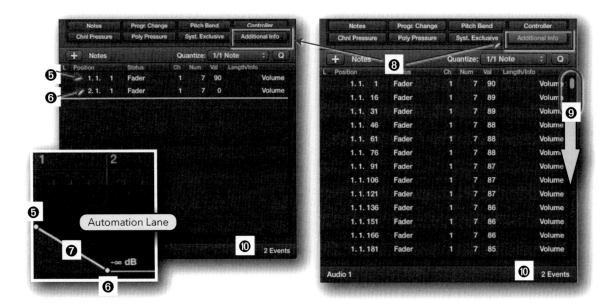

# Fader Events

## ➡ *Data Structure*

Here is the data format of a Fader Event the way it is displayed in the Event List: Each Event has seven fields, the seven columns. The additional field, Articulation ID, can be displayed, but has no function for the Fader Events:

**Event List**

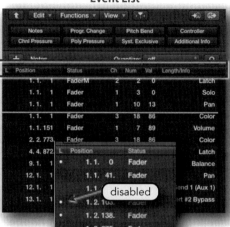

- 🌑 The Status is the important field that tells you what type of Event it is.
  - ▸ **Status**: Fader is the type of data used for all automation data with the exception of the MIDI FX Plugins. They use the FaderM data type.

- 🌑 Where is the Control Point located?
  - ▸ **Position**: This is the position of the Control Point that can be displayed as Musical Time (bars/beats) or Absolute Time (SMPTE). Use the local View Menu command "Event Position and Length as Time" to toggle the display mode.
  - ▸ **L**: You can SMPTE Lock each individual Control Point the same way as MIDI Events. A padlock 🔒 is displayed for locked Control Points. See explanation below. The column can also display a dot if that Parameter is disabled with Power Button ⏻ on the Automation Parameter Button.

- 🌑 What Automation Parameter does the Control Point represent?
  - ▸ **Channel**: The specific Automation Parameter a Control Point belongs to is determined by two values, the "Channel" and the "Number". The Channel value specifies the component the Parameter belongs to and the Number value specifies the exact Parameter on that component.
    - Ch 1: All the main parameters of a Channel Strip (Fader, Pan, Send, etc.) have Ch1.
    - Ch 2-16: These numbers indicate the slot number 1-15 for the used Audio FX Plugins. Please note that an Instrument Channel Strip uses slot 1 for the Instrument Plugin and slot 2-15 for its Audio FX Plugins.
  - ▸ **Number**: Each number represents a specific Parameter on the current Channel Strip.
  - ▸ **Info**: This field lists the actual name of the Parameter (the corresponding Onscreen Control).

- 🌑 What is the value of the Control Point (Automation Parameter)?
  - ▸ **Value**: This is the value of the Control Point. You can slide the number up/down or enter a new value numerically. However, some Parameters use values higher than 127. The higher number (used for Smart Controls Parameter) will be displayed but you cannot edit them.

**Fader Events Assignment**

| Type | Channel | Number | Info | Remarks |
|------|---------|--------|------|---------|
| Fader | 1 | 3 | Solo | |
| | 1 | 7 | Volume | |
| | 1 | 8 | Balance | |
| | 1 | 9 | Mute | |
| | 1 | 10 | Pan | |
| | 1 | 15, 25, 26, 27 | Surround | only available when Surround is selected |
| | 1 | 28 - 35 | Aux Send 1 - 8 | |
| | 1 | 56 - 71 | Bypass Inset #1- #15 | |
| | 1 | 256... / 352... | Smart Controls | 256 and up for knobs, 352 and up for switches |
| | 2 ... 16 | 0 - 127 | Plugin Parameter for Slot 1 ... 15 | Each Plugin has its own Parameter-to-Number assignment |
| FaderM | 2 ... 9 | 0-127 | Plugin Parameter for Slot 1 ... 8 | Each Plugin has its own Parameter-to-Number assignment |

## ➡ *Edit Fader Events*

The editing of Fader Events is similar to MIDI Events. You can *double-click* on it and enter a numeric value or *drag* a value up/down. You can also *drag* a selection of multiple Events at the same time or use the copy/ paste functionality. These are the three main edits you can perform:

- Change the position of a Control Point
- Change the value of a Control Point
- Convert a Control Point to a different Parameter. For example, you can move a Control Point from Aux Send 1 to Aux Send 3.

Please note that changes to the "visible" Control Points will also apply to the "hidden" Control Points of the interpolated automation data accordingly.

## 😎 Value Jumps

Here is the procedure how to create sudden value jumps. Let's say you want to suddenly lower the Volume Fader at bar 3 from 0dB to -10dB:

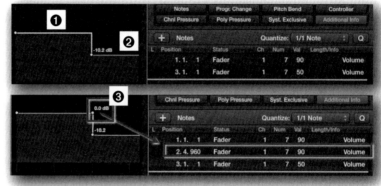

☑ Select the Control Point at bar 1 and use the copy-paste commands.

☑ A new Control Point will be created with the Position field selected. Just type in 3.

☑ The new Control Point is now placed at bar 3 with the same value 90 (=0dB).

☑ Double click that Value and enter 50 (= -10dB).

You can see the two Control Points in the Automation Lane without the expected interpolation line. The first value stays steady ❶ and jumps down at the second Control Point ❷.

However, when you select the Automation Curve, Logic "cleans up" after you and adds the required Control Point ❸ 1 Tick before the next Control Points. This ensures the straight line between two Control Points.

## ➡ *SMPTE Lock*

The command "Lock SMPTE Position" ❹ in the local Functions Menu of the Event List lets you toggle that status for individual Fader Events.

Please note that in Logic the Fader Events, like any other MIDI Events, are locked to the Musical Time grid of bars/ beats. This is all good when you work on a song-based Project. But what if you have a Track in your Project (i.e. dialog) that is SMPTE-Locked and therefore, independent from any Tempo changes you apply during the production? If you use automation on that Track, then you also might want to SMPTE-Lock the automation data (the Fader Events in the Event List) before you make any tempo changes in your Project.

Select one or multiple Control Points and choose the command:

**Event List**

 Event List Local Menu *Functions* ➤ *Lock SMPTE Position*

 Key Command (*Lock SMPTE Position*) *cmd+PageUp*

 The Toolbar in Logic's Main Window also provides a Lock/Unlock SMPTE Button

A Control Point that is SMPTE locked displays the padlock icon 🔒 in the first "L" column ❺.

# Automation Window (A Parallel Universe)

If you think messing around with Control Points in the Event List is an advanced feature, let's take it up a notch and look at the next example.

☑ Create a new Project with one Audio Track and create with the Track Automation one Control Point ❶ for the Volume Fader.

☑ The default Link Mode for the Tracks Window is "Off". Set it to "Same Level" ❷.

☑ While the Audio Track is selected, open the Automation Event List with the Key Command *ctr+cmd+E* ❸.

☑ When you *click* on that one Control Point ❶ in the Automation Lane of the Tracks Window, then the Automation Event List also selects that Fader Event, the one Fader Event ❹ representing that one Control Point on the Audio Track.

☑ Now click on the "Display Level Up Button" [icon] ❺ in the Automation Event List.

☑ This changes the Display Level of the Event List Window ❻ and also (!) the Tracks Window ❼. But at what strange place did we end up now?

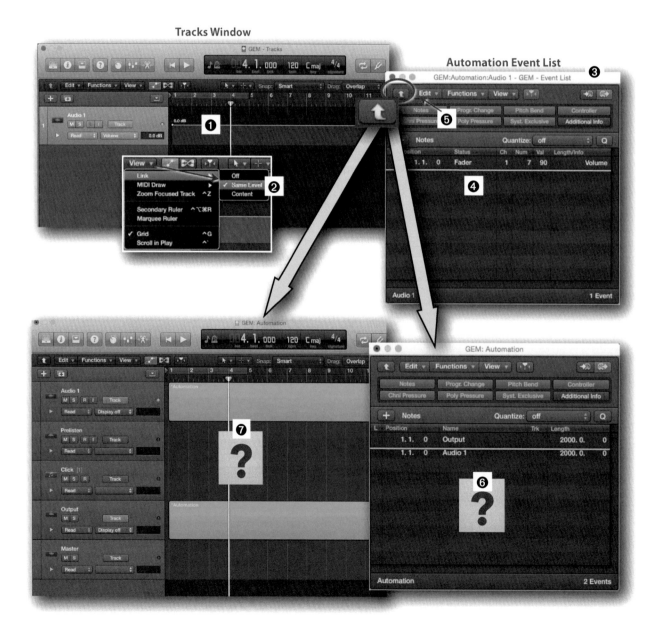

**Tracks Window**

**Automation Event List**

428                    12 - Automation (advanced)

## ➡ *Review: Display Level - Link Mode*

The two concepts, **Display Level** and **Link Mode**, are very important elements of the Logic architecture. I explain them in great detail in my first Logic book "Logic Pro X - How it Works". I recommend to review those 11 pages in the Basics chapter to understand the next steps I'm about to explain.

### ◉ Display Level

Similar to a hard drive where you save your files (your data) in folders and subfolders, Logic also organizes its data (the music you record in your Project) in a similar folders-subfolders structure. By using the Finder in OSX, you can look at the top level of your hard drive (the root directory, Display Level 0). If that level has any folders, you can open them to display the folder content. This would be "Display Level 1". If that one contains more folders, then you can open them, stepping down to "Display Level 2", and so on.

Here is an example how that concept looks like in Logic:

▶ In Logic, "Display Level 0" is your Tracks Window ❶ displaying the Tracks with all the Regions on it.

▶ Even the Event List can display "Display Level 0" ❷, showing all the Regions on a vertical timeline as a list.

▶ Pay attention to the Window Title. It displays the name of your Project, representing Display Level 0. In this example "GEM Song" ❸.

▶ The Piano Roll window shows Display Level 1, the content of the Region "Chorus"❹, its MIDI Events.

▶ When the Event List (as a standalone window) shows Display Level 1 ❺, it indicates that in the Window Title. Now it reads "GEM Song:Chorus" ❻. It uses the colon as a divider similar to the forward slash in OSX when describing the path name to a specific file or folder. In this example, it means, the window displays the content of the "Chorus" Region (Level 1), which itself is part of the "GEM Song" (Level 0).

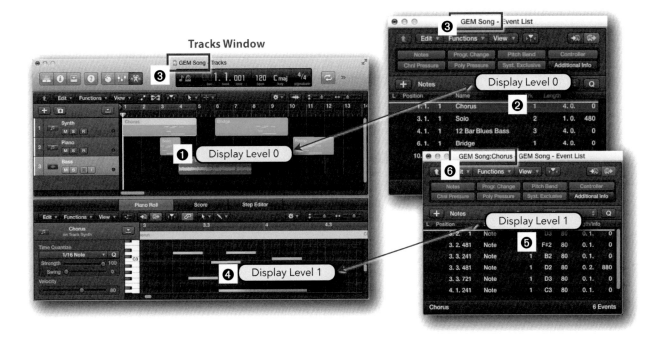

If you use Logic's advanced feature "Folder Regions", then you can create an even deeper Level structure.

For example, "GEM Song:SectionA:Verse" ❼ could mean: The current window displays the Region "Verse" (Level 2), which is part of the Folder Region "SectionA" (Level 1) as part of the "GEM Song" (Level 0).

## Link Mode

The Link Mode in Logic is a handy feature that can change the Display Level of a window automatically depending on what Display Level is selected in a different window.

- **Off**: The window's Display Level is not controlled by any other window.
- **Same Level**: The window is switched to the same Display Level as the currently selected window.
- **Content**: This window displays the content of the currently selected window, if possible. This means one level further down.

**Link Modes**

## ➡️ *Automation Data*

Now let's look again at the automation data while paying attention to those Display Levels and Link Modes to figure out what is going on. Always keep an eye on the Window Title. For that you have to open the Event List as a separate window (Key Command *cmd+7*) because the Event List displayed as a window pane in Logic's Main Window doesn't have its own Window Title. Make sure its Link Mode is set to "Content".

## Example 1:

Assume that we do a similar example as before:

☑ We create a new Project, create a new Audio Track, record two Regions on it (Verse and Verse 2), and create one Automation Control Point for the Volume Fader.

☑ *Click* on the Control Point to select it. The Event List switches its view to display that automation data.

When we look at the Window Title, it reads "**GEM Song:Automation:Audio 1**"❶. Based on what we have just discussed, this would mean:

The window displays the content of the Region "Audio 1" (Level 2), which is located in the Folder Region "Automation" (Level 1), which is located on the top level of your Project "GEM Song" (Level 0).

However, we didn't create a Folder Region named "Automation" in our Song and also no Region "Audio 1" in such a Folder Region.

Let's do one more step:

☑ *Click* on the "Display Level Up" Button 🔼 ❷. This switches the window to display the content of the Automation Region "GEM Song:Automation" (Display Level 1) as you can see in the Window Title ❸. The content are two Regions named "*Automation Output 1-2" and "*Automation Audio 1"❹.

☑ *Click* on the Display Level Up" Button 🔼 ❺ again. This switches the window to display the

content of the top level "GEM Song" (Display Level 0) as you can see in the Window Title ❻. The content are the two Regions names "Verse" and "Verse 1"❼ we created earlier.

## 🎧 Example 2

To find out more about the mysterious Automation Folder Region, let's do the same procedure with a little variation:

We set the Link Mode (in the local View Menu) of the Tracks Window from "Off" (its default) to "Same Level"❶. You can also use a separate Main Window for that (Key Command *cmd+1*).

Now, let's repeat the same steps from Example 1, but keep an eye on what is happening in the Tracks Window.

☑ The Tracks Window displays the top level, your Project (Level 0), indicated by the Window Title "GEM" ❷. When we select the Control Point ❸, the Event List switches its view to display the selected Control Point on that special Display Level 2 ("GEM:Automation:Audio 1") ❹.

☑ When you *click* the Display Level Up Button ❺ in the Automation Event List, the window changes to Display Level 1 ("GEM:Automation"❻). But now, the Tracks Window also changes to that same Display Level ❼. Remember, we set the Link Mode for the Tracks Window to "Same Level"❶. The Window Title of the Tracks Window now reads "GEM:Automation", which means that it displays the content of the Folder Region "Automation". This is the content ❽ of that mysterious Folder Region that Logic seems to create automatically to store the data for the Track Automation.

☑ *Click* on the Display Level Up Button 🔼 on the Tracks Window ❾. It moves up, back to the top level again ❷, displaying your Project with all its Regions.

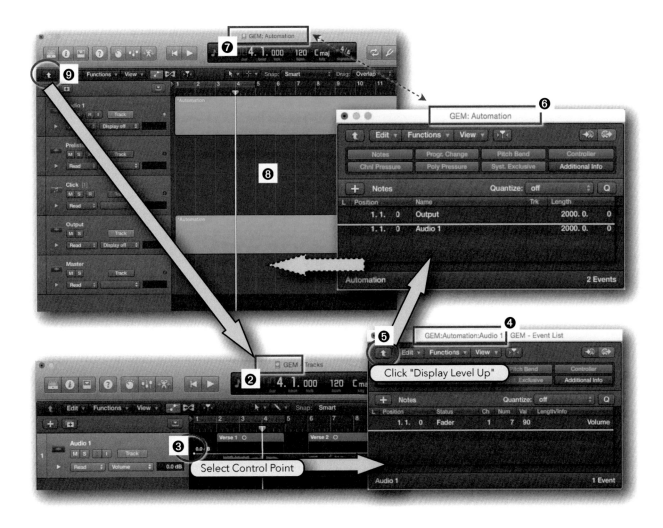

## ➡ *Automation Arrange Page*

As we have seen in the previous examples, to access that special Automation view in the Tracks Window (once called the "Automation Arrange Page") is kind of tricky. In addition, it seems that this page is a hidden Folder Region. Maybe all that is a hint from Logic not to use it or mess with it in the first place. Here is a summary of what you see and what you can do with it (at your own risk).

### 🔘 What You See

Here is an overview of what you see in the Automation Arrange Page:

- The window displays all the current Environment Objects in your Projects as Tracks. This is similar to the "All" view in the Mixer Window.
- The automation data for a Track (if available) is displayed as one single Region named "*Automation".
- The Regions start at the beginning of your Project and end at bar 2000 (!), regardless where your End-of-Project Marker is set to and were the Control Points are located.
- Remember, you are looking at the content of the invisible Automation Folder Region on Display Level 1. Using the Display Level Up Button will change the view to Level 0, to show the default view of the Tracks Window again with all your Regions.

**Tracks Window: "Automation Arrange Page"**

### 🔘 What You Can Do

You can use most of the elements on the window to do what you would do on the default Tracks Window:

- All the controls on the Track Header are working as usual.
- You can display the Event List Pane and edit the Control Points on that level. For example, copy, change, move, convert, etc.
- Even the Piano Roll Editor can be used when displaying the MIDI Draw Area for Control Events.
- When you show the Automation, then the Track Lane splits as usual to the mini Track Lane (which represents the Automation Region and the Automation Lane (where you can edit the Automation Curve).
- You can resize the Region and even split them, but if you try to do any "forbidden" action, you will get one of those interesting Dialog Windows.

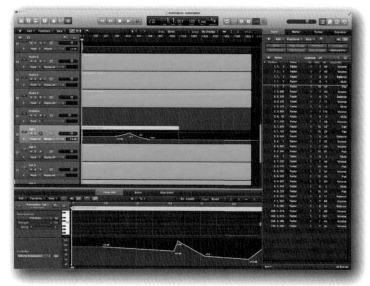

## Basics

There are four commands for converting Automation. Although this seems to be an easy task to just convert Region Automation to Track Automation and vice versa, you have to be very careful  when using any of those commands.

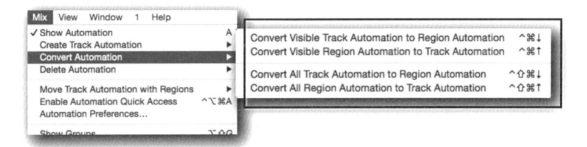

I will demonstrate these commands on two examples in this section to point out just a few of the "consequences" these commands can have. You should use them only if you have a clear understanding of Track Automation and Region Automation. Often times, there will only be sections of automation data moved, leaving you with the situation where you have both, Track Automation data and Region Automation data on a Track. That is something you should try to avoid, unless you know how to manage such a situation.

### Convert Region Automation to Track Automation

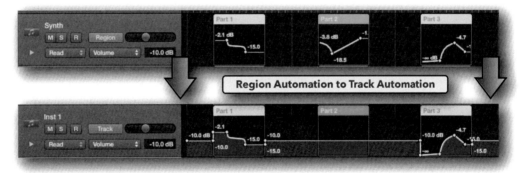

### Convert Track Automation to Region Automation

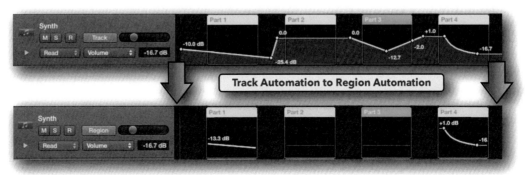

## ➡ Convert Automation: Procedure

The "Convert Automation" command is technically a "Move Automation" command. You can move Events in two directions. However, there are two important things you have to to be aware of:

▸ Track Automation (stored in the "invisible" Automation Regions) contains only Fader Events. Therefore, only Fader Events are moved from Track Automation to Region Automation.

▸ Because the invisible Automation Regions only "allow" Fader Events to be stored, any MIDI Events (Continuous Controller) are not moved from Region Automation to Track Automation.

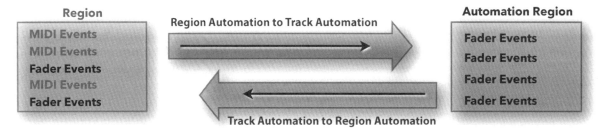

The commands for converting Automation are pretty long, but they would be even longer if you include all the additional conditions you have to be aware of. You have to pay special attention to what Tracks and Regions are selected.

 **Region Automation to Track Automation**

- **❶ All** the Fader Events of all the selected Regions are moved from the MIDI Regions to the Automation Region on their Tracks.

- **❷** Only the currently **visible** Fader Events of all the selected Regions are moved to the Automation Region on their Tracks.

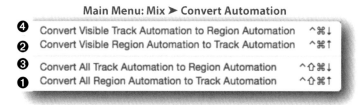

 **Track Automation to Region Automation**

- **❸ All** the Fader Events in the Automation Region of the currently selected Track that occur on the Timeline between the left and right border of any selected Region will be moved to those Regions.

- **❹** Only the currently **visible** Fader Events on the selected Main Track (located in the Automation Region) that occur on the Timeline between the left and right border of any selected Region will be moved to those Regions.

## ➡ "Display Off" vs MIDI Draw "Off"

As you've seen, it is very important to make sure what is selected and what is visible before you apply any of these commands. Especially be clear on the function of those two "off" settings:

- **Display off** (in the Automation Parameter Menu ❺) switches the display on the Automation Lane. Instead of Track Automation Parameter, it can now display the Region Automation on the Regions.

- **OFF** (MIDI Draw Menu ❻) switches the Automation Parameter Button to "Display off".

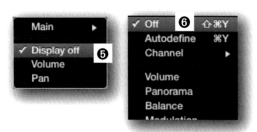

# Region Automation ➤ ➤ Track Automation

There are a few details you have to pay attention to when "converting" (moving) Region Automation to Track Automation:

### 🎱 Before

- The first screenshot ❶ shows three MIDI Regions, all of them containing Volume Automation
- The first and third Region ❷ are selected. That means that the convert command applies only to the visible MIDI Parameter of those two Regions.
- Here is the important part. You have to pay attention to the position of the Onscreen Control, in this case, the Volume Fader ❸. It is set to -10dB. This might not seem to be important, but it is, as wee will see in the next step.

### 🎱 After

- The second screenshot ❹ shows the result after I applied the "Convert Visible Region Automation to Track Automation" command.
- The Automation button switched from Region ⟨ Region ⟩ to Track ⟨ Track ⟩ ❺.
- That Track now has a single continuous Automation Curve ❻, the Track Automation.
- The two Automation Curves from the first and third Region are copied exactly to this new Automation Curve ❼.
- The Automation Curve of the second Region hasn't been copied. There are no Control Points in that section on the new Automation Curve ❽.
- And here is the important part again: What happens to the sections outside the areas where the Automation Curves have been copied? A horizontal line has been established by adding additional Control Points at the beginning of the Project ❾ and at the left and right border ❿ of the selected Regions (the one with the copied Automation Curve). The value of those Control Points is the value of the Onscreen Control ❸ by the time you performed the command, in this example -10dB.

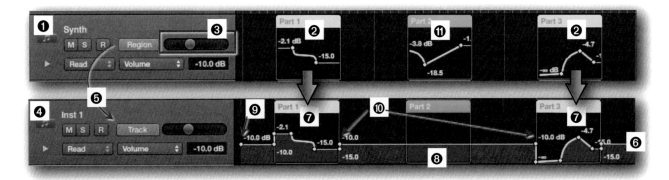

### 🎱 Aftermath

The Region Automation (Control Points for the Fader Event "Volume") of the second Region stayed in that Region ⑪. It is not visible on the second screenshot ❹, because the Track shows Track Automation ❺ and not Region Automation. That means, both Track Automation and Region Automation will send Fader Events to the same Parameter (Volume).

**Project Settings ➤ General**

To avoid any potential conflicts, enable the checkbox "*Region automation takes priority over track automation*" in the ***Project Settings ➤ General***.

# Track Automation ➤ ➤ Region Automation

Also, watch out when "converting" automation from Track Automation to Region Automation:

- The first screenshot ❶ shows a Track with four Regions. It is set to Region Automation and it shows that there are no Control Points stored inside the Regions. You can only see the gray default line ❷ that indicates the current value of the Automation Parameter, the position of the corresponding Onscreen Control, Volume Control in this case.

- The second screenshot ❸ shows the Track Automation on that Track, the Automation Curve for the selected Automation Parameter "Volume".

- The third screenshot ❹ shows the result after I selected the first, second, and third Region, and choose the command "Convert visible Track Automation to Region Automation. The Track switches to Region Automation, but look at what happens at the individual Regions:

  - Region 1 ❺: There were no visible Control Points at the position of that Region, but a decreasing line, which indicates "invisible" interpolated Control Points. They were copied to the Region and that is what you see now as Region Automation. The Track Automation only kept two Control Points, at the beginning and end of the Region as you can see in the fourth screenshot ❾ that shows the "left overs" of the Track Automation after Control Points were copied to Region Automation.

  - Region 2 ❻: There were also no visible Control Point over that Region, but because the line was horizontal, that means, no value change, and therefore, no Control Points. As a result, no Control Points are copied to the Region. The Track Automation stayed the same in that area ❾.

  - Region 3 ❼: This Region was not selected, and therefore, no Automation was moved to the Region.

  - Region 4 ❽: There are two visible Control Points that fall between the left and right border of this Region. They are copied to the Region Automation, including the exponential shape of the Automation Curve. An additional Control Point is created at the beginning of that Region. As you can see in the screenshot 4 that shows that Track Automation ❾, the two Control Points, plus the shape, were removed from Track Automation, but again, two new Control Points were added at the beginning and end of the Region. The linear shape between those Control Points can cause a problem, because they represent invisible Control Points which are different than the Control Points from the Region Automation with the exponential shape. Again, have the "Region Priority" settings enabled in the Project Settings to prevent any conflicting data.

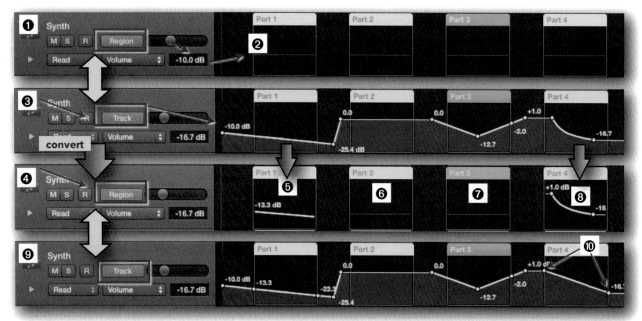

This was just a simple example that demonstrates the potential pitfalls when moving automation data between Track Automation and Region Automation. So you better keep an eye on it when you use those commands.

# External MIDI Instrument

And finally, a look at a "specialty". Remember that you can write Track or Region Automation data from the Mixer Window using the Automation Modes (Touch, Latch, Write) on the Channel Strip if you don't need to see the Automation Curve or need to edit the automation data offline on the Track Lane.

If you look at the Mixer window with all the different Channel Strips, there is, in addition to the seven main Channel Strip types (Audio, Instrument, Aux, Bus, Input, Output, Master), the External MIDI Channel Strip. This type of Channel Strip (created when choosing "External MIDI" ❶ for a new Track) looks similar to the other ones but has different controls available. Be careful when using any Automation on that:

**New Tracks Window**

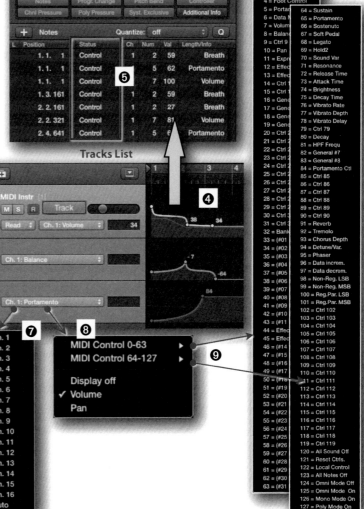

- ▸ There is no audio signal running through that Channel Strip.
- ▸ All the controls on that Channel Strip are MIDI controls ❷. You can have up to 5 freely assignable controls on a Channel Strip ❸ (click on its button and select from the menu).
- ▸ The Track Automation ❹ creates Control Events ❺ instead of Fader Events, which are stored as Control Events (exception to the rule) in the Automation Region. You can see in the Automation Event List ❻ that these are Control Events.
- ▸ The Automation Parameter Button is a double button (in addition to the Power Button on the far left. *Clicking* on the left opens the MIDI Channel Menu ❼. *Clicking* on the right opens the Automation Parameter Menu ❽.
- ▸ The Automation Parameter Menu is also different. It lists the 128 Control Change types divided into two menus ❾ (0-63, 64-127).

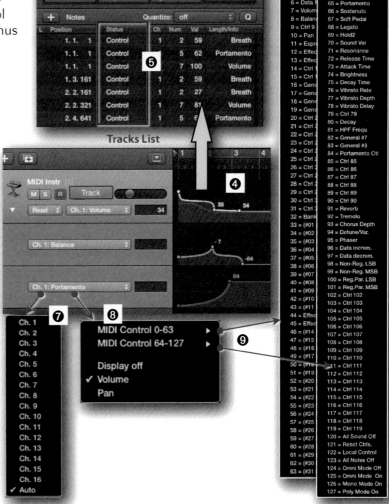

You can use external hardware controllers instead of your mouse to move faders and knobs or push buttons on your Logic interface. Online Automation doesn't care (doesn't know), if you move a controller with the mouse or if the onscreen controller is moved remotely by an external hardware controller.

## Control Surfaces

Logic calls those external hardware controllers "Control Surfaces" and I cover that topic in a separate chapter later in my book. In this section I want to explain the feature "Automation Quick Access". This solves a big problem: "You don't have the money to buy one of those expensive Control Surfaces".

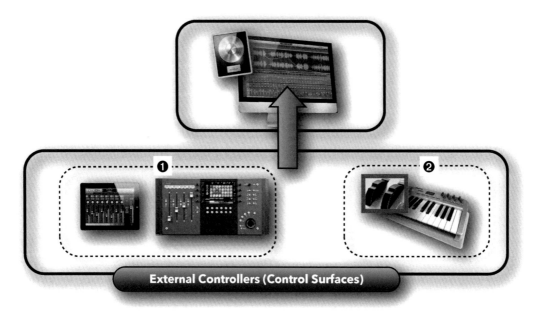

External Controllers (Control Surfaces)

There are two types of devices that you can use as external controllers:

### 🔵 Dedicated Hardware Controllers ❶

Depending on the model and price tag, those devices have usually multiple controllers (faders, knobs, buttons) that can be assigned to Onscreen Controls like faders, knobs, and buttons in Logic. The external controllers (sometimes in a group of 8) often simulate Channel Strips and are assigned to a group of Channel Strips in Logic. This has the advantage that you can use multiple controls on the device at the same time to control, for example, multiple faders and knobs simultaneously, which is not possible when you only use your mouse.

### 🔵 Standard MIDI Keyboard ❷

A MIDI controller like your MIDI Keyboard might have only the usual Modulation Wheel or maybe a single Fader. If you could assign that Modulation Wheel to a Fader, then you can still only control one parameter at a time, but at least you would have a finer control than by moving the mouse up and down.

With "Automation Quick Access", Logic provides a feature that makes that single external controller extremely powerful and flexible with the least amount of configuration necessary when controlling different Parameters.

# Automation Quick Access

The concept of Automation Quick Access is as simple as powerful.

☑️ **Step 1 - Assign**: You assign a single external hardware controller (i.e. the Modulation Wheel on your MIDI Keyboard) as your main controller with the click of a "Learn" button.

☑️ **Step 2 - On/Off**: Now you toggle the feature on/off. Whenever you want to use that assigned external controller to control one of Logic's Onscreen Controls, just enable Automation Quick Access. If you want to use the external controller for its regular function again (i.e. sending MIDI Modulation data), disable Automation Quick Access.

☑️ **Step 3 - Select Parameter**: To choose which of Logic's onscreen controls to control with the hardware controller, simply select it from the Automation Parameter Menu of the selected Track Header. The hardware controller controls whatever the currently selected Automation Parameter is.

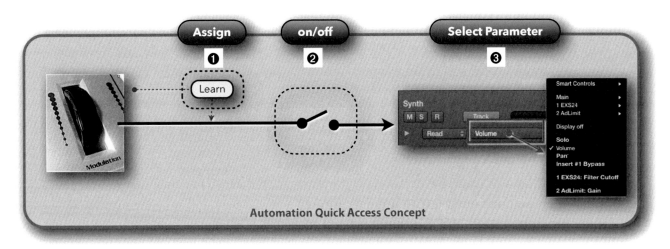

**Automation Quick Access Concept**

**Preferences ➤ Automation**

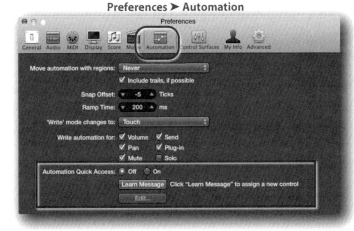

## ➡️ *Step 1- Assign External Controller*

Before you can use Automation Quick Access, you have to "tell" Logic which external MIDI controller you want to use. You do that one-time configuration (unless you want to use a different MIDI controller at some point) on the Automation page of the Preferences window.

You can access that window with any of the following commands:

 Main Menu *Logic Pro X ➤ Preferences ➤ Automation...*

 Main Menu *Mix ➤ Automation Preferences...*

 On the Automation Lane *Shortcut Menu ➤ Automation Preferences...*

Key Command (*Open Automation Preferences*) **opt+A**

Here is the detailed configuration procedure:

- ☑ *Click* the "On" button ❶ to enable Automation Quick Access (turned off by default).

- ☑ *Click* the "Learn Message" button ❷ (the button changes to the "Done" button). This puts Logic in a temporary "Listening Mode". Whatever MIDI signal is coming in next (the MIDI message you are about to send from your external MIDI controller) that will be flagged as the Automation Quick Access MIDI Message.

- ☑ A Dialog Window will pop up if this is the first time you are setting up Automation Quick Access. *Click* the Assign Button ❸.

- ☑ Now move the external MIDI Controller ❹ to send a MIDI signal. Logic records that Input Message, which functions as the "ID" for the External MIDI Controller. For example, If you moved a Mod Wheel on your MIDI Keyboard that is set to MIDI Channel 1, then Logic will record "Control Change 1 (=Modulation) on MIDI Channel 1 on that specific port". That means, whenever Logic receives a MIDI Message with CC#1 on ch1 from that MIDI port, it will re-direct that message (values) internally to be used to control the current Automation Parameter. A few things to keep in mind:

  - As long as Logic is in this "Listening Mode" it "flags" any incoming MIDI Message until you go to the next step.

  - You can have multiple MIDI Keyboards set to the same MIDI channel and Logic would still

identify the right controller based on the MIDI input port.

- As long as Automation Quick Access is enabled, the Mod Wheel data will not reach the Sequencer Input and can, therefore, not be recorded as MIDI data on a Region!

- ☑ Remember that when you clicked the "Learn Message" button it changed to the "Done" button. Whenever you see this button, Logic is in "Listening Mode". *Click* on the Done Button to exit the "Listening Mode" and keep the last MIDI message as the External MIDI Controller ID. The button changes back to its original state "Learn Message" ❷.

- ☑ There is an additional button labeled "Edit..." ❻. *Click* on it to open the Controller Assignments Window. This is a scary looking page for configuring Control Surfaces (here you can assign the Controller manually). *Click* on the "Easy View" ❼ button to hide all the advanced elements. You can see the "Input message" ❽, which is the MIDI Message that your MIDI Controller sent and the Channel Strip Parameter ❽. It is automatically set to "Selected Track" ❾, which means, the external controller is not assigned to a specific Channel Strip, instead, it controls whatever Channel Strip is currently selected.

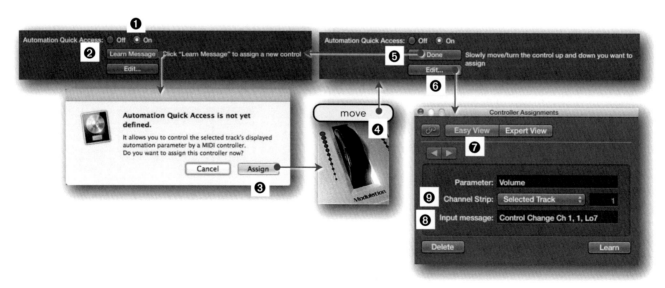

You have to do the setup procedure only once if you want to keep that assignment.

Please note that this configuration is stored in a separate preference file:

*~/Library/Preferences/com.apple.logic.pro.cs*

## ➡ Step 2 - Enable/Disable Automation Quick Access

Once you assigned an external MIDI Controller, you can toggle the Automation Quick Access mode on and off with any of the following commands:

- Main Menu *Mix ➤ Enable/Disable Automation Quick Access*
- Key Command (*Toggle Automation Quick Access*) *ctr+opt+cmd+A*

If you haven't setup the controller yet, then the Dialog Window will popup that lets you start the assignment by clicking the "Assign" button.

It is a good idea to turn Automation Quick Access on only when you need it. As I mentioned before, whatever controller you have assigned, that controller cannot be recorded onto a MIDI Track. For example, if you need the Mod Wheel to record your Synth solo.

## ➡ Step 3: Select the Automation Parameter

Once the external MIDI Controller is configured (Step 1) and Automation Quick Access is enabled (Step 2), you can use it to control any Automation Parameter. It is the one displayed in the Automation Parameter Button of the selected Track. To control a different Parameter, just select it from that popup menu.

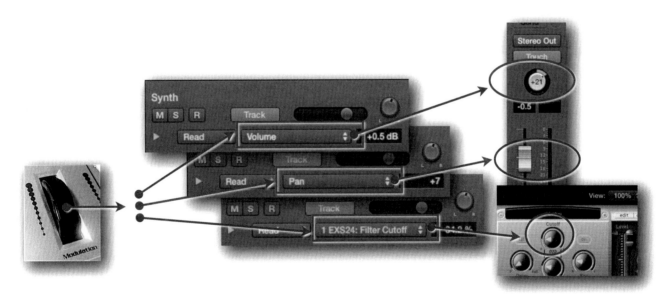

This is a very elegant solution. If you write your Online Automation one at a time, you can use the Automation Quick Access to use your external MIDI controller to perform any movement.

The other advantage is that you don't have to have the Onscreen Control visible to use Online Automation. For example, when you want to control a Parameter on a Plugin with your mouse, you have to open the Plugin Window first. With the Automation Quick Access, you just choose the Parameter from the Automation Parameter Menu on the Track Header and record the automation with your external MIDI Controller (i.e. the Cutoff Frequency of your Instrument Plugin).

# Conclusion

This concludes my manual *"Logic Pro X - The Details"*.

If you find my visual approach of explaining features and concepts helpful, please recommend my books to others or maybe write a review on Amazon or the iBooks Store. This will help me to continue this series.
To check out other books in my "Graphically Enhanced Manuals" series, go to my website at:
www.DingDingMusic.com/Manuals

To contact me directly, email me at: GEM@DingDingMusic.com

More information about my day job as a composer and links to my social network sites are on my website:
www.DingDingMusic.com

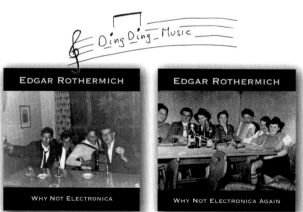

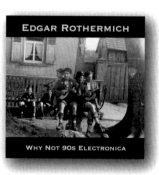

Listen to my music on SoundCloud

Thanks for your interest and your support,

*Edgar Rothermich*

Made in the USA
Lexington, KY
30 September 2017